ROUTLEDGE HANDBOOK OF PEACEBUILDING

This new Routledge Handbook offers a comprehensive, state-of-the-art overview of the meanings and uses of the term 'peacebuilding', and presents cutting-edge debates on the practices conducted in the name of peacebuilding.

The term 'peacebuilding' has had remarkable staying power. Other terms, such as 'conflict resolution' have waned in popularity, while the acceptance and use of the term 'peacebuilding' has grown to the extent that it is the hegemonic and over-arching term for many forms of mediation, reconciliation and strategies to induce peace. Despite this, however, it is rarely defined and often used to mean different things to different audiences.

Routledge Handbook of Peacebuilding aims to be a one-stop comprehensive resource on the literature and practices of contemporary peacebuilding. The book is organised into six sections:

- Part I: Reading peacebuilding
- Part II: Approaches and cross-cutting themes
- Part III: Disciplinary approaches to peacebuilding
- Part IV: Violence and security
- Part V: Everyday living and peacebuilding
- Part VI: The infrastructure of peacebuilding

This new Handbook will be essential reading for students of peacebuilding, mediation and post-conflict reconstruction, and of great interest to students of statebuilding, intervention, civil wars, conflict resolution, war and conflict studies and international relations in general.

Roger Mac Ginty is Professor of Peace and Conflict Studies at the Humanitarian and Conflict Response Institute and the Department of Politics at the University of Manchester. He edits the journal *Peacebuilding* and his latest book was *International Peacebuilding and Local Resistance: Hybrid forms of peace.*

ROUTLEDGE HANDBOOK OF PEACEBUILDING

Edited by Roger Mac Ginty

Routledge
Taylor & Francis Group

LONDON AND NEW YORK

First published 2013
by Routledge
2 Park Square, Milton Park, Abingdon, Oxfordshire OX14 4RN

Simultaneously published in the USA and Canada
by Routledge
711 Third Avenue, New York, NY 10017

First issued in paperback 2015

Routledge is an imprint of the Taylor & Francis Group, an informa business

British Library Cataloguing in Publication Data
A catalogue record for this book is available from the British Library

Library of Congress Cataloging in Publication Data
Routledge handbook of peacebuilding / edited by Roger Mac Ginty.
p. cm.
ISBN 978-0-415-69019-5 (hardback) –
ISBN 978-0-203-06817-5 (e-book) 1. Interpersonal relations.
2. Peace. 3. Conflict management. I. Mac Ginty, Roger, 1970–
HM1111.R68 2013
303.6´6–dc23
2012030935

ISBN 13: 978-1-138-92270-9 (pbk)
ISBN 13: 978-0-415-69019-5 (hbk)

Typeset in Bembo
by HWA Text and Data Management, London

Dedicated to John Darby, 1940–2012
Mentor, Scholar, Wit, and Peacebuilder.

CONTENTS

Contributors	x
Tribute	xvii
Abbreviations	xviii
Introduction	1
Roger Mac Ginty	

PART I
Reading peacebuilding   **9**

1 The problem-solving and critical paradigms	11
Michael Pugh	
2 The evolution of peacebuilding	25
Stephen Ryan	
3 The limits of peacebuilding theory	36
Gerald M. Steinberg	

PART II
Approaches and cross-cutting themes   **55**

4 Gender and peacebuilding	57
Maria O'Reilly	
5 Religion and peacebuilding	69
Mohammed Abu-Nimer	

 6 Reconciliation   81
    Emma Hutchison and Roland Bleiker

 7 The politics of memory and peacebuilding   91
    Marc Howard Ross

PART III
Disciplinary approaches to peacebuilding   **103**

 8 International relations theory and peacebuilding   105
    Dominik Zaum

 9 Social psychology and peacebuilding   117
    Shelley McKeown

10 Anthropology and peacebuilding   132
    M. Anne Brown

11 Economists and peacebuilding   147
    Jurgen Brauer and Raul Caruso

12 Sociology and peacebuilding   159
    John Brewer

13 History and peacebuilding   171
    Anthony Oberschall

14 Quantitative approaches   183
    Patrick M. Regan

PART IV
Violence and security   **195**

15 Securitization and peacebuilding   197
    Necla Tschirgi

16 Security sector reform   211
    Mark Sedra

17 Disarmament, demobilization and reintegration   225
    Alpaslan Özerdem

18 Zones of peace   237
    Landon E. Hancock

19 Peacebuilding, law and human rights   249
    Christine Bell

PART V
Everyday living and peacebuilding   **261**

20 Employment and household welfare   263
    Patrícia Justino and Ricardo Santos

21 Organic versus strategic approaches to peacebuilding   276
    Sherrill Stroschein

22 Education and learning   287
    Patricia A. Maulden

23 Youth   296
    Siobhan McEvoy-Levy

PART VI
The infrastructure of peacebuilding   **309**

24 The international architecture of peacebuilding   311
    Edward Newman

25 The political economy of peacebuilding and international aid   325
    Susan L. Woodward

26 Statebuilding   336
    Susanna Campbell and Jenny H. Peterson

27 Civil society   347
    Thania Paffenholz

28 Indigenous peacebuilding   360
    Anthony Wanis-St. John

29 Urban planning and policy   375
    Scott A. Bollens

    Conclusion   387
    Roger Mac Ginty

    Index   391

CONTRIBUTORS

Mohammed Abu-Nimer is Full Professor at American University's School of International Service in International Peace and Conflict. He is director of the Center for Peacebuilding and Development and the co-editor of the *Journal of Peacebuilding and Development*. He has published many books and articles on peacebuilding in Islam, interfaith dialogue and conflict resolution. He has edited the book *Peacebuilding By, Between and Beyond Muslims and Evangelical Christians* (Lexington, 2009). abunimer@american.edu

Christine Bell is Professor of Constitutional Law, University of Edinburgh. Her research interests lie in the interface between constitutional and international law, gender and conflict, and legal theory, with a particular interest in peace processes and their agreements. She has participated in a number of peace negotiations. She has authored two books: *On the Law of Peace: Peace Agreements and the Lex Pacificatoria* (Oxford University Press, 2008) and *Peace Agreements and Human Rights* (Oxford University Press, 2000). Christine.bell@ed.ac.uk

Roland Bleiker is Professor of International Relations at the University of Queensland. His most recent books are *Divided Korea: Toward a culture of reconciliation* (University of Minnesota Press, 2005/2008) and *Aesthetics and World Politics* (Palgrave, 2009), and as co-editor, *Mediating Across Difference: Pacific and Asian approaches to security and conflict* (University of Hawaii Press, 2010). Bleiker is currently working on a collaborative project that examines how images – and the emotions they generate – shape responses to humanitarian crises. bleiker@uq.au.edu

Scott A. Bollens is Professor of Urban Planning and Warmington Endowed Professor of Peace and International Cooperation, University of California, Irvine. He studies the roles of urban policy and city building amidst nationalistic ethnic conflict and political transitions. Over the past 17 years, Professor Bollens has interviewed over 240 urban professionals, political leaders, and community representatives in Jerusalem, Belfast, Johannesburg, Nicosia (Cyprus), Sarajevo and Mostar (Bosnia), Barcelona and Basque cities (Spain), and Beirut. His most recent book is *City and Soul in Divided Societies* (Routledge, 2012) which integrates first-hand reportage, academic analysis, and personal narrative. bollens@uci.edu

Jurgen Brauer is Professor of Economics at the Hull College of Business, Augusta State University and Visiting Professor of Economics at Chulalongkorn University, Bangkok. He co-edits *The Economics of Peace and Security Journal* and is co-author of *Peace Economics: A macroeconomic primer for violence-afflicted states* (USIP Press, 2012). jbrauer@aug.edu

John Brewer is Sixth Century Professor of Sociology at the University of Aberdeen. He is a former President of the British Sociological Association. He is a member of the UN Roster of Global Experts, a Member of the Royal Irish Academy, a Fellow of the Royal Society of Edinburgh, an Academician in the Academy of Social Science and a Fellow of the Royal Society of Arts. He is author or co-author of sixteen books and over 100 peer reviewed papers. During the last decade his work has focused primarily on mapping the sociology of peace processes. j.brewer@abdn.ac.uk

M. Anne Brown is a Senior Research Fellow at the School of Political Science and International Studies, the University of Queensland. She is also a founding member of PaCSIA, a peace and conflict research and practice NGO. Research and applied interests focus on political community across division, peacebuilding and state formation in hybrid states, social dialogue processes, and changing forms of citizenship. She is the author of *Human Rights and the Borders of Suffering: the Promotion of Human Rights in International Politics* (Manchester University Press, 2002) and editor of *Security and Development in the Pacific Islands: Social Resilience in Emerging States* (Lynne Rienner, 2007). anne.brown@uq.edu.au

Susanna Campbell is a Research Fellow at the Centre on Conflict, Development, and Peacebuilding at the Graduate Institute of International and Development Studies, Geneva. Since 1996, she has been commissioned by over a dozen organizations – think tanks, governments, international organizations, and international non-governmental organizations – to study the capacity of international actors to prevent violent conflict and build peaceful states. She has published widely, including with the Council on Foreign Relations Press, *Journal of International Peacekeeping*, *Journal of Peacebuilding and Development*, and Zed Books. She received her PhD in 2012 from Tufts University, Massachusetts. Susanna.campbell@tufts.edu

Raul Caruso is Professor of Economics at the Istituto di Politica Economica, Università Cattolica del Sacro Cuore, Milan, Italy, and editor of *Peace Economics, Peace Science, and Public Policy*. Raul.caruso@unicatt.it

Landon E. Hancock is an Associate Professor at Kent State University's Center for Applied Conflict Management and Department of Political Science. His work focuses on ethnic conflict and peacemaking. He has published articles in several journals including *Ethnopolitics* (2011), *Peace & Change* (2011), *Peace and Conflict Studies* (2011), *Conflict Resolution Quarterly* (2011), *Irish Political Studies* (2011), *Journal of Peace Education*

(2010), and *International Studies Review* (2008). With Chris Mitchell he edited *Local Peacebuilding and National Peace* (2012) and *Zones of Peace* (2007). He continues to work on issues related to identity conflict, peace processes, post-conflict reconstruction and transitional justice. lhancoc2@kent.edu

Emma Hutchison is a Postdoctoral Research Fellow in the School of Political Science and International Studies at the University of Queensland. Before this, Emma was the 2010 Australian EUI Postdoctoral Fellow at the European University Institute, Florence, Italy. Her current key research projects question the role of trauma and emotions in world politics, as well as the role that images play in shaping global responses to humanitarian crises. Her research has appeared in edited books as well as scholarly journals, such as the *Review of International Studies*, *International Relations*, *Global Society* and the *European Journal of Social Theory*. e.hutchison@uq.au.edu

Patrícia Justino is a Research Fellow at the Institute of Development Studies, Brighton. She is the Head of the Conflict, Violence and Development cluster at IDS, director of MICROCON (www.microconflict.eu) and co-founder and co-director of the Households in Conflict Network (www.hicn.org). p.justino@ids.ac.uk

Roger Mac Ginty is Professor of Peace and Conflict Studies at the Humanitarian and Conflict Response Institute and the Department of Politics at the University of Manchester. He edits the journal *Peacebuilding* and his latest book was *International Peacebuilding and Local Resistance: Hybrid forms of peace* (Palgrave, 2011). roger.macginty@manchester.ac.uk

Patricia A. Maulden is Assistant Professor of Conflict Resolution and Director of the Dialogue and Difference Project with the School for Conflict Analysis and Resolution at George Mason University, Washington DC. Her research interests include generational and gendered dynamics of conflict and peace, social militarization and demilitarization processes, and peacebuilding practices. She designs and implements experiential learning programs that bridge peacebuilding theory and practice from the student as well as the host community perspective. She is currently investigating the post-conflict paradox of engaging war while creating peace, and exploring peacebuilding over time, more specifically the trajectories of post-conflict knowledge. pmaulden@gmu.edu

Siobhan McEvoy-Levy is Associate Professor of Political Science and Peace and Conflict Studies at Butler University in Indianapolis, Indiana. McEvoy-Levy's work focuses on youth and armed conflict, peace processes and post-conflict peacebuilding. She has published many articles and book chapters on these topics and is also the editor of and a contributor to *Troublemakers or Peacemakers? Youth and Post-Accord Peacebuilding* (2006), co-author with Borer and Darby of *Violence, Youth and Truth* (2006), and author of *American Exceptionalism and US Foreign Policy* (2001). smcevoy@butler.edu

Shelley McKeown is a lecturer in psychology at the University of Hertfordshire. In 2012 she completed her PhD research at the University of Ulster under the guidance of Professor Ed Cairns and Professor Maurice Stringer. Her research interests lie within the area of understanding and improving intergroup relations. She currently has a number of published articles focusing on micro-ecological behaviour, intergroup contact, shared space and peacemaking youth programmes in Northern Ireland.

Edward Newman is a Senior Lecturer in the Department of Political Science and International Studies at the University of Birmingham, UK. Before joining the University of Birmingham he was Director of Studies on Conflict and Security in the Peace and Governance Programme of the United Nations University. He teaches and researches on security studies, including critical approaches and 'human security'; intrastate armed conflict, civil war and political violence; and peacebuilding and reconstruction in conflict-prone and post-conflict societies. He is also the Editor-in-Chief of the Routledge journal *Civil Wars*. e.newman.1@bham.ac.uk

Anthony Oberschall is emeritus Professor of Sociology at the University of North Carolina at Chapel Hill. He has authored books and articles on collective action, social movements, ethnic conflict, political violence and terrorism, as well as on conflict management. His latest book is *Conflict and Peace Building in Divided Societies* (2007). He was an expert witness at the International Criminal Tribunal for the Former Yugoslavia. He is finishing a book titled *The Truth Deficit in America* which deals with falsehood, deceit, and misinformation in politics and the marketplace of ideas on public policy and problem-solving. tonob@email.unc.edu

Maria O'Reilly is a PhD candidate at the Department of War Studies, King's College London. Her main area of interest is the question of women's agency in post-conflict settings, which she explores by drawing on perspectives from peace and conflict studies, feminist theory and memory studies. Her current research examines the relationship between trauma, memory and women's activism around transitional justice issues in post-war Bosnia-Herzegovina. maria.o'reilly@kcl.ac.uk

Alpaslan Özerdem is Professor and Director of the Centre for Peace and Reconciliation Studies, Coventry University, UK. Specializing in the politics of disaster response, reintegration of former combatants and post-conflict state building, he is co-author of *Disaster Management and Civil Society: Earthquake Relief in Japan, Turkey and India* (I.B. Tauris, 2006), author of *Post-war Recovery: Disarmament, Demobilisation and Reintegration* (I.B. Tauris, 2008) and co-editor of *Participatory Research Methodologies in Development and Post Disaster/Conflict Reconstruction* (Ashgate, 2010), is co-author of *Managing Emergencies and Crises* (Jones & Bartlett, 2011) and co-editor of *Child Soldiers: From Recruitment to Reintegration* (Palgrave Macmillan, 2011). a.ozerdem@coventry.ac.uk

Thania Paffenholz is Senior Researcher at the Centre for Conflict, Peacebuilding and Development at the Graduate Institute of International and Development Studies, Geneva. She previously was Director of the Centre for Peacebuilding (KOFF) at Swisspeace in Bern. Her focus is on peacebuilding theory and practice; development-peace nexus; evaluation in peacebuilding. She also works as an advisor to international and national governmental and non-governmental organizations. Her book publications include *Civil Society and Peacebuilding: A critical assessment* (2010); *Aid for Peace: A guide* *for planning and evaluation for conflict zones* (2007); and *Peacebuilding: A field guide* (2000). thania.paffenholz@graduateinstitute.ch

Jenny H. Peterson is a Lecturer in Humanitarian and Conflict Response at the Humanitarian and Conflict Response Institute at the University of Manchester. An early career scholar, she has published in *Disasters* and *International Studies Quarterly*. Her first monograph is *Building a Peace Economy: Liberal Peacebuilding and the Development Security Industry* (2012).

Michael Pugh is Professor of Peace and Conflict Studies, University of Bradford, and Leverhulme Emeritus Fellow. He has been editor of the journal *International Peacekeeping* and the Cass Peacekeeping book series for the twenty years since their foundation. He edited *Regeneration of War-torn Societies* (2000), and co-authored with Neil Cooper and Jonathan Goodhand *War Economies in a Regional Context* (2004). He led the ESRC-funded Transformation of War Economies team and is co-editor of *Whose Peace? Critical Perspectives on the Political Economy of Peacebuilding* (2008). m.pugh@bradford.ac.uk

Patrick M. Regan is a Professor in the Joan Kroc Institute for International Peace Studies and the Department of Political Science, University of Notre Dame. His interests are in violent conflict and its resolution, particularly in the context of civil war. His publications include *Organizing Societies for War: The Process and Consequences of Societal Militarization* (1994), *Civil Wars and Foreign Powers: Interventions and Intrastate Conflict* (2000) and, *Sixteen Million One: Understanding Civil Wars* (2009). He has also authored or co-authored articles in the *Journal of Politics*, *Journal of Conflict Resolution*, *Political Research Quarterly*, *International Interactions*, and the *Journal of Peace Research*.

Marc Howard Ross is William R. Kenan, Jr. Emeritus Professor of Political Science at Bryn Mawr College. He has researched in Canada, East Africa, France, Northern Ireland, the Middle East, Spain, and South Africa. His current work focuses on the role that cultural performance and memory play in the escalation and de-escalation of ethnic conflict. He has written or edited eight books including *Cultural Contestation in Ethnic Conflict* (2007), *Culture and Belonging in Divided Societies: Contestation and Symbolic Landscapes* (2009), *The Culture of Conflict* and *The Management of Conflict* (1993), and over 75 journal articles and book chapters. mross@brynmawr.edu

Stephen Ryan is a Senior Lecturer in Peace and Conflict Studies at the University of Ulster's International Conflict Research Institute (INCORE). His latest book is *The Transformation of Violent Intercommunal Conflict* (2007) and he has written over thirty articles and book chapters on ethnic conflict, the United Nations and conflict resolution. His main research interests are the dynamics and transformation of intercommunal conflict. He is the University of Ulster Coordinator for an international Marie Curie training site on sustainable peacebuilding and is the Course Director of the MSc in Applied Peace and Conflict Studies. S. Ryan@ulster.ac.uk

Ricardo Santos is a PhD candidate in development economics at the Institute of Development Studies, Brighton.

Mark Sedra is an Adjunct Lecturer in the Department of Political Science at the University of Waterloo, Canada and the President of the Security Governance Group. His research focuses on the topic of post-conflict state-building with an emphasis on security issues. He has conducted research on a number of countries and regions, including Northern Ireland, the Middle East, and the Balkans; however, the bulk of his research in recent years has centered on Afghanistan. msedra@uwaterloo.ca

Gerald M. Steinberg is Professor of Politics and founder of the Program on Conflict Management and Negotiation, Bar Ilan University, Israel. His research focuses on diplomacy, military strategy and arms control, and human rights as a form of soft power. He has worked with international organizations such as NATO, UN University, OSCE, and SIPRI; and is president of NGO Monitor, a Jerusalem-based research organization. Academic publications include articles entitled *The centrality of confidence building measures: Lessons from the Middle East*, *Postcolonial theory and the ideology of peace studies*, and *The politics of NGOs, human rights and the Arab–Israel conflict*. Steing@mail.biu.ac.il

Sherrill Stroschein is a Senior Lecturer in Politics and director of the program in Democracy and Comparative Politics at University College London. She was previously an Academy Scholar at the Harvard Academy for International and Area Studies and an Assistant Professor at Ohio University. She is a member of the Executive Board of the Association for the Study of Nationalities. Her publications examine the politics of ethnicity in democracies with mixed ethnic or religious populations, most recently her book *Ethnic Struggle, Coexistence, and Democratization in Eastern Europe* (Cambridge University Press, 2012). s.stroschein@ucl.ac.uk

Necla Tschirgi is Professor of Practice, Human Security and Peacebuilding at the Joan B. Kroc School of Peace Studies at the University of San Diego. In the last fifteen years, she has increasingly specialized in conflict prevention and peacebuilding – focusing on the nexus between security and development. She has been an in-house consultant/Senior Policy Advisor with the Peacebuilding Support Office at the United Nations Secretariat in New York, the Vice President of the International Peace Academy, and helped establish and lead the Peacebuilding and Reconstruction Program at the International Development Research Centre (IDRC) in Ottawa. neclatschirgi@sandiego.edu

Anthony Wanis-St. John is Assistant Professor at American University in Washington, DC. His research and teaching focus on international negotiation and conflict resolution, with a special emphasis on peace processes. Dr. Wanis-St. John is an advisor to the Academy of International Conflict Management and Peacebuilding at the United States Institute of Peace. He is the author of *Back Channel Negotiations: Secrecy In Middle East Peacemaking* (Syracuse University Press, 2011). He was guest editor of the journal *International Negotiation* vol. 13, no. 1 (2008) 'Peace processes, civil society and secret negotiations' and has published in *Journal of Peace Research*, *Negotiation Journal*, *International Peacekeeping* and the *Harvard Negotiation Law Review*. wanis@american.edu

Susan L. Woodward is Professor of Political Science at the Graduate Center of the City University of New York. Her current research focuses on transitions from war to peace, the concept of state failure, and post-war state-building. She was a senior fellow at the Centre for Defence Studies, King's College, London, 1999–2000 and at The Brookings Institution, 1990–1999, and a professor of political science at Yale University, 1982–1989, Williams College, 1978–1982, and Northwestern University, 1972–1977. Her writings include *Balkan Tragedy: Chaos and Dissolution after the Cold War* (1995), and *Socialist Unemployment: The Political Economy of Yugoslavia, 1945–1990* (1995). swoodward@gc.cuny.edu

Dominik Zaum is Reader in International Relations at the University of Reading, and a Senior Research Fellow in Conflict and Fragility at the UK's Department for International Development. He has published widely on state- and peacebuilding issues. His recent books include *The Sovereignty Paradox: The Norms and Politics of International Statebuilding* (2007), *The United Nations Security Council and War: The Evolution of Thought and Practice since 1945* (2008, with Vaughan Lowe, Adam Roberts, and Jennifer Welsh), *Corruption and Peacebuilding: Selling the Peace?* (2011, with Christine Cheng), and *Power after Peace: The Political Economy of State-Building* (2012, with Mats Berdal). d.zaum@rdg.ac.uk

A TRIBUTE TO
JOHN DARBY

John and I worked together in a variety of peace processes for more than twenty years. It took us to Prague, Cyprus, Sri Lanka, Singapore, Nepal, and Northern Ireland.

I sat in a lot of meetings with John. The rooms typically held people from different sides of nasty conflicts. John would start each meeting with a similar presentation that I came to greatly appreciate. In our debriefings in the evenings or end of sessions he would return to the same ideas. More or less this is what he would tell people when he spoke his first words.

> I am not here to give you solutions or answers. I am a visitor here. This is your place, your home, not mine. You know your challenges. You are the ones who will make decisions.

> I come from a place that has had a lot of division and violence. I know what it feels like to have people from outside come to help. We had a lot people who came in during the long years of our troubles. The most helpful were those who shared what they knew but did not presume to know better than us.

> So I am here to share things we have learned from comparisons of different peace processes. Each place and process is unique. And each has some parallel challenges. Comparison may help. That will of course be up to you.

> We appreciate the courage it takes to meet and talk with people from outside. We promise to hold that courage with the respect it deserves.

John embodied humility. For the learned academic and seasoned practitioner he had grown to be, he was amazingly without the appendage of a large ego that seems to come with these genres of persons and professions. I can never remember him taking the low road of competition or one-upmanship. It was truly a rare gift and trait.

John Paul Lederach, University of Notre Dame

ABBREVIATIONS

ABM	Anti-Ballistic Missile
ANC	African National Congress
CDD	Community-Driven Development
CDU	Christian Democratic Union
CEOSS	Coptic Evangelical Organization for Social Services
COIN	Counter-insurgency
CPIA	Country Policy and Institutional Assessment
CRC	Community Relations Council
DAC	Development Assistance Committee
DDR	Disarmament, Demobilization and Reintegration
DFID	Department for International Development
DOENI	Department of the Environment Northern Ireland
DPKO	Department of Peacekeeping Operations
DRC	Democratic Republic of Congo
ECHO	European Commission Humanitarian Aid and Civil Protection
ECP	Escola de Cultura de Pau
EDSA	Epifanio de los Santos Avenue
ETA	Euskadi Ta Askatasuna
EU	European Union
FARC	Revolutionary Armed Forces of Colombia
FID	Forum for Intercultural Dialogue
FMLN	Farabundo Martí National Liberation Front
FSSCA	Fund for Self-Sufficiency in Central America
GAM	Gerakan Aceh Merdeka
GNP	Gross National Product
GPI	Global Peace Index
GWOT	Global War on Terror
HDI	Human Development Index
HFZ	Harm Free Zone

HIPC	Highly Indebted Poor Countries
IATI	International Aid Transparency Initiative
ICC	International Criminal Court
ICTY	International Criminal Tribunal for the Former Yugoslavia
IDDRS	Integrated Disarmament, Demobilization and Reintegration Standards
IDP	Internally Displaced Person
IEP	Institute for Economics and Peace
IFI	International Financial Institution
IFOR	Implementation Force
IMF	International Monetary Fund
IO	International Organization
IPE	International Political Economy
IPTF	International Police Task Force
IR	International Relations
IRA	Irish Republican Army
ISAF	International Security Assistance Force
JAM	Joint Assessment Mission
KFOR	Kosovo Force
KLA	Kosovo Liberation Army
LTTE	Liberation Tigers of Tamil Eelam
LZP	Local Zone of Peace
MNLF	Moro National Liberation Front
NATO	North Atlantic Treaty Organization
NGO	Non-Governmental Organization
NILT	Northern Ireland Life and Times
OECD	Organization for Economic Cooperation and Development
OEF	Operation Enduring Freedom
OSCE	Organization for Security and Cooperation in Europe
P2P	People-to-People
PCIA	Peace and Conflict Impact Assessment
PER	Project on Ethnic Relations
PICAR	Program on International Conflict Analysis and Resolution
PON	Project on Negotiation
PRIO	Peace Research Institute Oslo
PRSP	Poverty Reduction Strategy Paper
QUANGO	Quasi-Autonomous Non-Governmental Organization
R&D	Research and Development
RMDSz	Democratic Union of Romanians in Hungary
RPA	Rwanda Patriotic Army
SALT	Strategic Arms Limitation Talks
SALW	Small Arms and Light Weapons
SFOR	Stabilization Force
SIT	Social Identity Theory
SLIG	Suffolk-Lenadoon Interface Group
SPLA	Sudan People's Liberation Army
SRRP	Stewartstown Road Regeneration Project

SSR	Security Sector Reform
UDMR	Democratic Union of Romanians in Hungary
UN	United Nations
UNAMA	United Nations Missions in Afghanistan
UNAMI	United Nations Assistance Mission in Iraq
UNAMSIL	United Nations Mission in Sierra Leone
UNDP	United Nations Development Programme
UNESCO	United Nations Educational, Scientific and Cultural Organization
UNICEF	United Nations Children's Emergency Fund
UNMIBH	United Nations Civilian Office in Bosnia Herzegovina
UNMIK	United Nations Interim Mission in Kosovo
UNPROFOR	United Nations Protection Force
URI	United Religious Initiative
USAID	United States Agency for International Development
WACI	West Africa Coast Initiative
ZOP	Zone of Peace
ZOPFAN	Zone of Peace, Freedom and Neutrality
ZOPIF	Zones of Peace International Foundation

INTRODUCTION

Roger Mac Ginty

In the mid-1980s, when the editor was at secondary school in Northern Ireland, the government introduced a peacebuilding scheme in which Catholic and Protestant schoolchildren could meet each other in a supervised environment. Catholic and Protestant children were, and largely still are, taught in separate schools in Northern Ireland. Indeed, both communities tend to live apart, residing in different areas of towns and cities, socialising in different venues, and following different sports or teams. Against a backdrop of continuing violence, much of it nakedly sectarian, the British government developed an 'education for mutual understanding' initiative whereby Catholic and Protestant school kids would at least learn about 'the other side', their religion and culture. The scheme made perfect sense, on paper. It rationalised that conflict could be lessened if new generations grew up able to respect each other and understand why the other side acted in the way it did. The initiative was straight out of the conflict transformation paradigm: education, self-learning and mutual understanding would be the key to a bright new future in which today's children grew up to be tomorrow's reconciled citizens.

So on a Friday afternoon, a group of teenagers from the other school in the town trooped into our school hall. We were all pleased to be spared normal lessons but were wondering what was going to unfold. The Catholic kids sat on one side of the hall, and the Protestant kids on the other. Both groups eyed each other. A teacher from the other school addressed the hall. He explained the thinking behind the scheme and how Northern Ireland's future lay with us, the kids. He then told us to make friends with the kids on the other side of the room and sat down. It was a toe-curling, tumbleweed moment. No one was going to stand up, march across the room and introduce themselves to the other side with everyone looking on. Then teenage bravado kicked in and one of the kids from my school murmured, mockingly, the name of a Protestant woman who had been murdered in the locality the week before. A slow murmur of sectarian abuse started, and ended with kids from both sides shouting at each other, until the teachers intervened and stopped the event. Both groups of kids trooped out separately and the event was not repeated during my school career.

The story illustrates the gulf that is often present between peacebuilding theory and practice. Great hope and optimism do not always lead to the desired result. Peace cannot be 'made' to happen. Often it is a by-product or happy accident of other processes that are not directly related to peacebuilding. For example, a shared economic endeavour

1

may lead to the lessening of barriers between individuals and communities as they work together, possibly leading to social or cultural interactions. Yet there are many conscious attempts to 'build' peace, particularly in the aftermath of civil wars. Peacebuilding has become a fixture in the policy and academic worlds. Significant amounts of money are devoted to it, and an infrastructure of organisations (governmental and non-governmental) has developed along with a peacebuilding vernacular of key phrases. There is a material culture as well, with careers, grants, donors, and NGOs all bound up in the peacebuilding world.

This Handbook unpacks the meanings and practices associated with 'peacebuilding'. It is not a 'how to' guide. Instructional manuals are best left to mechanical and electronic devices that operate without the vagaries of human emotion such as ethnicised incitement, or feelings of hurt, loss and envy. Instead, it is a state-of-the-art summary of debates on peacebuilding, and the ethical and practical challenges that peacebuilding faces. It draws on the expertise of a varied group of authors, many of whom have practical experience in conflict and post-conflict settings. The book does not attempt to push a particular line of argument or endorse a particular approach to peacebuilding. Instead, the book provides a forum for a critical appraisal of peacebuilding: what works and what doesn't? Are there lessons that can be transferred – with care and local adaptation – between locations? Is peacebuilding associated with particular ideologies or worldviews? What are the new trends in peacebuilding? These questions, and others, are the focus of the book.

Despite thousands of conferences and workshops that aim to discover or disseminate 'best practice', there is no single-transferable gold standard of peacebuilding practice out there. Different techniques work in different circumstances at different times. Introduced at the wrong time, some peacebuilding initiatives may be ineffective, or even do harm. Luck plays a large role, as do the thousands of other factors that might work alongside peacebuilding such as economic development or imposed security changes.

Reading peacebuilding

The Handbook places significant emphasis on how we 'read' peacebuilding. As a reader – a student, a practitioner, a policy maker – our approach to reading is informed by a particular set of assumptions and worldviews. Many of these are subconscious, deeply patterned into how we interpret and process information. Indeed, it patterns what we read: often we read material that we think we will like. So it is important to reflect on how we – the readers – approach this text. Do we come to the term 'peacebuilding' with a particular conflict in mind? Do we believe that some conflict outcomes are better than others? Do we generally favour particular methodological or disciplinary approaches? Are we disposed towards qualitative or quantitative methodologies? Do we believe gender to be important or unimportant in peacebuilding?

This emphasis on how we 'read' peacebuilding means that we have to look beyond the practices of peacebuilding or the world of initiatives, projects and programmes. We need to look at the ideas and structures that shape these practices. Although peacebuilders may see themselves as a 'neutral' party attempting to mediate between conflicting groups, they operate in and through a political and ideological milieu. Much of this ideological patterning is subtle, so embedded in the structure of practices and language that it is difficult to notice. The most significant ideologies that shape contemporary peacebuilding are related to a liberal optimism that believes that human societies can be perfected, and a trust in institutional fixes. In many cases these 'liberal peace' interventions are well intentioned, but they carry along with them immense cultural baggage (Mac Ginty and Richmond 2009). The vast majority of peacebuilding initiatives occur in the global south but are designed, directed and funded from the global north. This is hugely significant. It means that for many people, peacebuilding is something that is 'done' to them. It is imposed as part of a wider set of power relations in which actors from the global north, and elites in their own country, hold many of the top cards.

The Handbook begins with a chapter by Michael Pugh that outlines the two dominant approaches to peacebuilding and the study of peacebuilding (Cox 1981). The first is the problem-solving approach which adopts a functionalist 'we can fix it' approach to the problems of conflict. It accepts that conflict is part of the human experience and attempts to find ways to minimise the impact of conflict on life. It seeks to develop systems and institutions that will mitigate the impact of conflict and help divided communities cooperate.

The second approach is the critical paradigm that seeks to go further than the problem-solving approach. It maintains that the problem-solving approach is merely engaged in superficial short-term fixes that fail to ask wider questions about power relations in society. According to the critics, it is not enough to provide venues for Israeli and Palestinian kids to come together unless wider structural inequalities of apartheid are addressed. For the critics, many of the peacebuilding activities undertaken by international organisations, states and INGOs are akin to rearranging the deckchairs on the Titanic. Supporters of the problem-solving approach counter that they must play with the cards that are dealt to them rather than wish for a handful of aces. They cannot change the meta-picture overnight and instead are forced to engage in piecemeal activities that will at least alleviate suffering or give people an opportunity to make a change.

There is no doubt that the problem-solving paradigm is dominant both in terms of peacebuilding practices and in the study of peacebuilding. Generally speaking, most peacebuilding scholarship from the United States can be placed in the problem-solving paradigm (see, for example, Crocker, Hampson and Aall 2005). Of course, there are many exceptions to this (for example Nordstrom 2004; Johansen 2004), but much of the output from US universities and think-tanks is policy-oriented and interested in offering 'solutions' to the problems faced by international organisations and INGOs. This literature tends to be apolitical in the sense that it avoids major questions of where does power lie. Most of the critical literature comes from Europe, the United Kingdom and colleagues in the global south (see, for example, Richmond 2005; Roberts 2011; Chandler 2010). This literature questions the underlying bases of conflict and dominant approaches to peacebuilding. In particular, it has developed a critique of the 'liberal peace' or the dominant form of peace-support intervention favoured by leading states, international organisations and international financial institutions.

Policy makers in foreign ministries and international organisations tend to be interested in (and commission) work from the problem-solving paradigm. Again there are exceptions to the rule, but generally governments and international organisations are interested in policy-relevant information that will suit pressing needs. The problem-solving camp, generally, is not in the business of challenging accepted norms. The result, according to the critics, is 'epistemic closure' or like-minded academics and policy-makers talking to each other and a continuation of policy regardless of whether it works or not. They charge that there is a cosy political economy of backscratching going on between academics and consultants who give non-threatening advice and policymakers who do not want to see the boat rocked.

This problem of epistemic closure bedevils the study of peacebuilding. Critical scholars tend to talk to critical scholars, attend each other's conferences, and read each other's works. Problem-solving scholars likewise tend to read problem-solving works and dismiss critical scholarship as being out of touch. According to the problem-solvers, the critics are too theoretical and are bound up in arcane conceptual discussions while there are real and pressing needs that can be addressed. The Handbook seeks to mitigate this problem by including both problem-solving and critical scholars. The editor will leave it to the reader to play the delicate game of working out which authors are 'critical' and which as 'problem-solving'!

To assist in 'reading' peacebuilding, the Handbook contains a series of chapters from different disciplinary perspectives. Sociology, economics, social anthropology, social psychology, history and international relations have all approached the study and practice of peacebuilding from different perspectives. The authors of these chapters were tasked with the question: what has your discipline ever done for peacebuilding? The chapters are written from the perspective of an advocate of a particular approach. What should become clear is that no single discipline has a monopoly of wisdom over approaches to peacebuilding. A hybrid approach is recommended whereby scholars and policymakers pick the best ideas and insights from each discipline. The 'Disciplinary approaches to peacebuilding' part of the Handbook includes a chapter by Patrick M. Regan on quantitative methodologies. Again there is something of a trans-Atlantic divide in scholarship, with scholars from North America being more open to quantitative methodologies while European scholars tend to prefer conceptual and case study approaches (for a wonderful contribution to this debate see Cramer 2002). Regan's chapter sets out, in a very patient way, the case for quantitative methodologies.

People and institutions

Institutions are a necessary feature of life. If well organised, they can bring certainty, security and an orderly means for the distribution of public goods such as education or healthcare. They can replace arbitrary decision-making processes with transparent and fair means. They also offer efficiency, making it easy and cost-effective for governments and others to administer. But, of course, institutions can also be impersonal, culturally inappropriate and inefficient. This balance between the needs and desires of people(s) and institutions lies at the heart of much of contemporary peacebuilding. This issue runs through the Handbook.

A major pillar of much contemporary peacebuilding has been statebuilding, or the rebuilding of state institutions after war (Call and Wyeth 2008). Such institutions are often necessary, and international actors in particular place significant emphasis on them. By creating institutions similar to the ones in their own countries, international peacebuilders create an interface with which they can more easily interact. So rather than finding and speaking to the 'head man' in the village who assumed his position because of his family, international peacebuilders often create a layer of bureaucracy that they can easily identify with: mayors, councillors and officials. International peacebuilding actors have invested heavily in a 'good governance' agenda over the past two decades, encouraging and compelling post-conflict governments to adopt administrative and financial practices that are transparent and efficient. The logic behind this is clear: bad governance in the form of discriminatory practices or corruption is a major factor behind the onset and continuation of violent conflict. By addressing bad governance, perceptions of corruption and discrimination will lessen and conflict should be minimised (Collier 2007).

But critics point out that the 'good governance' agenda, and the institutions that it introduces, often ushers in forms of governance that are inflexible and culturally inappropriate. The new institutions, they contend, are often identikit Western formats that prove to be poor exports (Mac Ginty 2011). Indeed, some critics charge that the good governance agenda amounts to a form of neo-colonialism in which western methodologies of governance are patterned over local methodologies. When allied with the failure to overhaul the power inequalities in the post-conflict society, particularly income and ownership inequality, good governance becomes part of a top-down process that stamps out local opinion. In truth, such a perspective underestimates the ability of local actors – national elites and communities – to slow, subvert, exploit and avoid international interventions. This is not to deny that international peacebuilding actors often have immense power: they usually control peacebuilding budgets and the design of projects. Yet, local actors also have significant agency with the result that western ideas and projects often become 'hybridised' as they come into contact with local communities.

Caution is required in any attempt to romanticise the 'local' or 'indigenous', and peacebuilding approaches that are 'bottom-up' (Mac Ginty 2008). Many of these have the very real advantage of being authentic and in tune with local cultural mores. But, in certain circumstances, they can also perpetuate patriarchy, the dominance of one group over another, and forms of governance that are non-transparent. Any judgement of peacebuilding interventions needs a cool-headed assessment of whether it works or not. Both top-down and bottom-up approaches require sensitivity and a humility that recognises that no single approach is likely to have all the answers.

What seems necessary is that institutions, and the international agendas that often support these institutions, are not privileged ahead of the needs and desires of people. This is more easily said than achieved, particularly as popular opinion in deeply divided societies is often highly partisan. Communities might be only too willing to believe a narrative in which 'the other side' benefits from institutions while 'our own side' does not.

A crucial issue involves security institutions (the focus of a number of chapters in the Handbook). It is difficult to imagine how communities can constructively engage with one another if they do not feel secure enough to do so. Over the past two decades, huge energies have been invested in security sector reform and in the demobilisation of former combatants in post-peace accord societies (Özerdem 2008). This has involved the reorganisation of judiciaries and police forces, and the disarming of non-state armed actors so that the state becomes the only legitimate armed actor. Liberty versus Order debates are common in most societies, but the issues tend to be more acute in societies emerging from violent conflict. People must feel secure enough in order to put the conflict behind them and get on with life. Yet, how much security is enough? And who should provide it? And should security be privileged over liberty? Contemporary Afghanistan provides a good example of how this can go wrong. In order to secure areas against the Taliban, the United States Central Intelligence Agency has flooded areas with arms. This might provide 'security' against the Taliban, but it stores up problems for the future.

Many post-conflict statebuilding interventions have followed the 'institutionalisation before liberalisation' path (Paris 2004). That is, they have prioritised the building and strengthening of institutions over the extension of rights. For the reasons mentioned above, the focus on institutions is understandable. But this brings problems too. In Rwanda, for example, the post-genocide government has become entrenched (largely as a result of external peace-support assistance) and is showing signs of refusing to loosen the grips of power.

The drive towards the institutionalisation of peacebuilding is strong. Pecebuilding, in the formal sense of initiatives and programmes is promoted and funded through institutions: states, the United Nations and its agencies, the European Union, the African Union, the World Bank, INGOs and NGOs. There is an increasingly professionalised cadre of peacebuilding personnel who use a specialised vernacular and adopt common working practices and codes of conduct. There are moves to standardise the analysis and evaluation tools that peacebuilders use. While such technocracy and bureaucratic standardisation offers advantages, it also brings with it the danger that creativity, alternatives and localised initiatives are excluded.

While institutions, large and small, do have a crucial role to play in peacebuilding, ultimately it is people who experience peace and conflict in their homes, workplaces, schools and everyday lives. There is a danger that the professionalisation of peacebuilding gives too much authority to 'experts' and 'peacebuilding professionals'. It is often individuals, families and communities who have to do the 'heavy lifting' of peacebuilding by learning to live with their neighbour from another religious group or learning to work alongside someone who shares very different political views. This everyday tolerance and diplomacy is hugely overlooked in the peacebuilding literature. It often occurs at the micro-level of the village, street or neighbourhood. It rarely involves the symbolism of a peace treaty signing ceremony. Instead it is comprised of daily small steps: tolerating the co-worker from the other group, a judicious silence when a wrong word could start an argument, a shared economic endeavour. None of this is to romanticise the local or suggest that individuals and communities always make the correct choices. It is, instead, to encourage us to pay attention to this micro-level and to put into its proper perspective the elite level bargaining between senior politicians and international organisations.

Organisation of the book

The Handbook is designed to be accessible and comprehensive. The chapters are short and free of extraneous uses of Latin and references to dead French philosophers. As with any book of this nature, there are omissions. Conceivably, the book could have had 130 chapters instead of 30, but a line had to be drawn somewhere. The book also has a bias to the global north in that most of the contributors (and the editor) are based at universities in that region. One issue that the academy urgently needs to address is how we can cooperate with scholars from the global south. The email addresses of all the contributors are listed by their biographies so feel free to get into correspondence with the authors.

The chapters are clustered together into six parts. Part I 'Reading peacebuilding' is intended to help place peacebuilding in context. It begins with a chapter by Michael Pugh that outlines the critical and problem-solving approaches to peacebuilding. This is followed by a chapter by Stephen Ryan on the historical evolution of peacebuilding. What becomes clear from this chapter is that the concept has been changing and that there have been important recent changes to how major international organisations approach peacebuilding. Chapter 3, on the limits of peacebuilding theory, challenges the optimism and faith that underpin many peacebuilding approaches. The chapter serves as a useful antidote to many of the dominant perspectives on peacebuilding that are blithely uncritical of the concept.

The chapters in Part II examine a number of the approaches and cross-cutting themes that inform peacebuilding policy and practice. All of the issues covered in these chapters play an important role in the building of peace, or placing obstacles in the path of peacebuilding. What is interesting about a number of these issues is the extent to which they attain prominent roles or are somehow sidelined. It is clear, for example, that peace and conflict are gendered, yet often the issue of gender is regarded as somehow marginal to the 'real' issues.

Part III focuses on what the social sciences have to say about peacebuilding. Each of the disciplines approaches the subject differently and deploys different methodological approaches to unpack peacebuilding. A side-by-side reading of the chapters allows us to think about how the different disciplines can complement each other. It is not enough for us to simply say 'multidisciplinary approaches are best' and move on. We need to take time to learn what the different disciplines can say in relation to peacebuilding and how this might help in concert with other disciplines. Part III tries to go beyond the blithe statement that 'multidisciplinary studies are good'.

Violence and security is the focus of Part IV, while Part V examines everyday living and peacebuilding. Here the focus is on the lived experience of peace in terms of the individual and the community. While peacebuilding is often discussed in terms of societies and institutions, it is often experienced in terms of households, the education of children, and community sentiment. This bottom-up experiential element of peacebuilding is one of the least studied, yet crucially important, aspects of the subject. The last part, Part VI, examines the infrastructure of peacebuilding or the various institutions that engage in peacebuilding. The chapters in this part view peacebuilding from different levels: the international institutions such as the UN and World Bank, national governments in terms of statebuilding, non-governmental organisations through civil society, cities through urban planning, and local communities through indigenous approaches to peacebuilding.

Sadly, one of the original contributors to the book, Professor Ed Cairns, a social psychologist at the University of Ulster, was tragically killed in a road accident before he could finish his chapter. He was a gentleman and a scholar, and did much to illustrate how social psychology can contribute to peace.

The book is dedicated to one of the founders of the study of peacebuilding: Professor John Darby of the Kroc Institute at the University of Notre Dame. John was my first employer, a wonderful mentor, and a collaborator on many projects on peace processes (Darby and Mac Ginty 2000; 2008). He combined razor sharp analysis and the wit of a genius. He was particularly interested in the comparative study of peace processes and was much involved in behind-the-scenes advice to governments and groups trying to find their way out of violent conflict. He was a true inspiration to a generation of scholars who followed in his wake. He will be missed.

References

Call, C. and V. Wyeth (2008) *Building States to Build Peace*, Boulder, CO: Lynne Rienner.

Chandler, D. (2010) *International Statebuilding: The rise of post-liberal governance*, London: Routledge.

Collier, P. (2007) *The Bottom Billion: Why the poorest countries are failing and what can be done about it.* Oxford: Oxford University Press.

Cox, R.W. (1981) 'Social Forces, States and World Orders: Beyond international relations theory', *Millennium: Journal of International Studies*, 10(2): 126–55.

Cramer, C. (2002) 'Homo Economicus Goes to War: Methodological individualism, rational choice and the political economy of war', *World Development*, 30(11): 1845–64.

Crocker, C.A., F.O. Hampson, and P. Aall (2005) (eds) *Grasping the Nettle: Analyzing cases of intractable conflict*, Washington DC: United States Institute of Peace Process.

Darby, J. and R. Mac Ginty (eds) (2000) *The Management of Peace Processes*, Basingstoke: Macmillan.

Darby, J. and R. Mac Ginty (eds) (2008) *Contemporary Peacemaking: Conflict, peace processes and post-war reconstruction*, 2nd edn, Basingstoke: Palgrave.

Johansen, R.C. (2004) 'Revising peacebuilding tools ravished by terrorism, unilateralism and weapons of mass destruction', *International Journal of Peace Studies*, 9(2): 31–55.

Mac Ginty, R. (2008) 'Indigenous peacemaking versus the liberal peace', *Cooperation and Conflict*, 43(2): 139–63.

Mac Ginty, R. (2011) *International Peacebuilding and Local Resistance: Hybrid forms of peace*, Basingstoke: Palgrave.

Mac Ginty, R. and O. Richmond (eds) (2009) *The Liberal Peace and Post-war Reconstruction: Myth or reality?* London: Routledge.

Nordstrom, C. (2004) *Shadows of War: Violence, power, and international profiteering in the twenty-first century*, Berkeley: University of California Press.

Özerdem, A. (2008) *Post-war Recovery: Disarmament, demobilization and reintegration*, London: IB Tauris.

Paris, R. (2004) *At War's End: Building peace after civil conflict*, Cambridge: Cambridge University Press.

Richmond, O.P. (2005) *The Transformation of Peace*, Basingstoke: Palgrave.

Roberts, D. (2011) *Liberal Peacemaking and Global Governance: Beyond the metropolis*, London: Routledge.

PART I

Reading peacebuilding

1

THE PROBLEM-SOLVING AND CRITICAL PARADIGMS

Michael Pugh

Introduction

The literature on peacebuilding is rich and extensive, a sign that the issue has entered the mainstream of debates on global security. In addition to in-house and think-tank briefing papers for practitioners and policymakers, academic studies have offered major insights into the practices of peacebuilding. When I first began identifying the issue in the early 1990s there were hardly any scholarly articles, let alone books, on the subject. Now my shelves are groaning with the weight of books and reports on peacebuilding. There are many ways of cutting this literature cake: case studies; thematic issues such as democratization, security sector reform and conflict resolution; and policy prescriptions. This study offers another categorization. It suggests that two broad categories of thinking about peacebuilding can be applied: problem-solving and paradigm (or foundational) critique. It is probably true to say that practitioners and policy makers are almost exclusively concerned with problem-solving, that is to say, how to make the existing systems of peacebuilding work more effectively. Academics on the other hand are more divided, and individuals often engage in thinking about both system effectiveness and the foundations on which the system is based. Foundational critique usually means questioning the assumptions that lie behind the practice of peacebuilding and the framework of ideas and implementations that make up the paradigm within which people think and act. In other words a foundational critique attempts to go beyond the limits of analysis established by hegemonic orthodoxies.

The purpose of this study is twofold. First, it demonstrates significant variation at the problem-solving level within the dominant peacebuilding paradigm, here identified as a 'subparadigm' of art of government and political economy known as neoliberalism. Second it contends that while a new focus on local ownership, ingenuity and sovereignty in war-torn societies may be replacing the concept of shared sovereignty between local and foreign peacebuilders given currency by Stephen Krasner (2005: 69–83), those in the peacebuilding industry, whether scholars, editors, policy advisers, decision makers or practitioners, neglect the import of limits on peacebuilding analysis. This contribution

11

begins by considering the significance of foundational critique as distinguished from problem-solving. The middle section examines two discourses of problem-solving represented by the UN Secretary-General's report on Peacebuilding of 2009, and a United Nations Development Programme (UNDP) commissioned report of 2008 on post-conflict economic recovery. The final section indicates the contours that mark off problem-solving from foundational critique.

The significance of critique

In a seminal essay on world order, Robert Cox (1999: 3–28) identified approaches to interpreting and coping with international relations that posited a binary and partly adversarial conceptualization of problem-solving and paradigm shifting. Perhaps a heuristic device, the classification nevertheless drew attention to a predominant mode of thinking and policy making associated with internationalism that lies in reinforcing conceptual frameworks. In the sphere of peacebuilding, refining ideas of intervention and rendering them more efficient represents a quest for perfection within defined limits. Indeed scholarly livelihoods depend in large measure on improving the status quo at the behest of political authorities – as advisers, contractors and subcontractors of research projects. Cox regarded this approach as problem-solving, which certainly allowed for critique of concepts and ways of doing things, but within a particular ideological framework. His alternative stipulated foundational critique with the promise of revolutionary emancipation. Depending on the nature of the critique, and Ken Booth (1997: 111) among others engaged in open, personal confession in this vein, it could lead to an emancipatory quest: emancipation from both orthodox knowledge framing and from the authority that comes from unchallenged power that often poses as 'common sense' or coping with 'the real world'. Critique, then, required interrogation of authority, including the authority of hegemonic theories, for as Cox (1981: 128) contended, theory was always constructed for a purpose and in someone's interests. A former UK cabinet minister, Tony Benn (1998: col. 685), neatly supplied a trope of interrogation in a parliamentary debate on the EU: 'what power do you have; where did you get it; in whose interests do you exercise it; to whom are you accountable; and, how can we get rid of you?'

The critical approach was only partly adversarial because it required an appreciation of immanence. That is to say, it required critics to assert a degree of autonomy that would enable them to seek free spaces, contradictions and resistances *within* existing orthodoxies and trends that might identify and facilitate emancipatory goals. For new worlds always contain residues of the old. Not that it is a simple matter to detect immanence in trends of hegemony and subservience – for example whether authorities trying to protect elite and corporate interests by controlling access to the internet will overcome resistance to this form of biopower. Historically, one can identify 'revolutions' associated with ideologies, technological innovation and cataclysmic events (such as the First World War). Innovation in communications since the advent of computer technology forged development in a host of spheres, including in thinking about, teaching and implementing ideas of peace and peacebuilding. Movements also affect thought and behaviour subtly over decades. For example, theories of political economy which, as Michel Foucault (2010: 131 ff) explains, include neoliberal economics from the 1930s in Freiberg, and which took root in post-Second World War West Germany, did not transform into a US variety and global status for another fifty years. Its defining problematic was how to model the exercise of political power on principles of the free market, projecting them on to the art of government and demanding state activity to protect and promote capital.[1] As this survey will show, the current institutional framework of peacekeeping and peacebuilding has been deeply affected by this particular move, sustained by the dispersal of business models into public service. Obviously not all shifts can be considered emancipatory when the political dynamics result in substituting one form of unquestioned authority by another. Nor, obviously, is it to imply that the upholders of liberalization themselves conform to its values, adhere to international law or practise meaningful democracy at home. That is why scholars in their exercise of autonomy properly engage in permanent critique.

At this point it is useful to consider the relationship between problem-solving and foundational critique. The argument here, evidenced by two examples of peacebuilding discourse, is that a disaggregation of problem-solving helps distinguish immanent emancipatory analysis from debates that reproduce and buttress a particular framework. Far from abandoning the relevance of foundational critique, such distinctions can help indicate where contours might be drawn between an imagined, constructed and perhaps reified problem-solving framework, with its internal varieties, and the contemplation of alternatives. One can begin by problematizing the notion of limits and contours. Where does framing begin and end, what intellectual and conceptual territory do paradigms cover, and can competing ideologies such as Marxism, Keynesian welfarism and Friedmanite neoliberalism co-exist? Given multiple interpretations of historical development, and the constant invention, destruction and reinvention of ideologies, how can the contours of a paradigm be firmly inscribed, if at all, or are they penetrable, pliable and transitory?

Three counterpoints can be made. First, the contours of any framework can be scripted as competitive, overlapping and coexisting in tension: represented as dotted lines through uncertain territory. This allows for coincidence of interest in emancipation and the detection of immanence, as well as limitations, that can strengthen rather than weaken core concepts in foundational critique. Second, capitalist cultures of political economy, a main concern here, may be fragmented, particularist and diverse, but they have a common root and purpose in using the state and international organizations to facilitate capital accumulation. Put bluntly, 'transnational corporations can do whatever they please' through corruption and denial of political control, as the US political system among others amply testifies (Mészáros, 2005: 374). Third, a framework may exhibit subaltern or dependent status as a subparadigm, one that incorporates agents and epistemic communities in a specific goal but which also conforms to a broader overarching conceptualization of how things should work. Thus an epistemic community of aid and relief institutions has constructed a concept of 'build back better' or 'reconstruction plus' to respond to wars and disasters. As evident in Haiti it has been actively promoted by the World Bank, UK government and international NGOs including Oxfam, World Vision and ActionAid. It represents a western view of poverty and underdevelopment in which, as Niomi Turley (2012: chapter 5) writes, 'disasters do not simply "interrupt" development, but provide a new platform from which to create an "improved" society based on liberal social, economic and political principles, at the expense of traditional subsistence means of living or local efforts to recuperate'. In other words, it fits into the overarching neoliberal ideology that merges security and development; 'romanticizes the local' as victims or illiberal; builds hollow institutions; designs economic life to reproduce assertive capitalism; equates peace with statebuilding; and assumes that interveners have privileged knowledge about peace issues. The paradigm is mobilized with a package of transformation policies – an assemblage construed by academics as the 'liberal peace' (Richmond 2005; Duffield 2007).

Two problem-solving modes in peacebuilding debates

The analysis now turns to the two examples of problem-solving in peacebuilding, a framework deeply affected by the overarching neoliberalism of corporate governance and development. They have been chosen because they can also be said to represent extremes within the conceptualization of liberal peacebuilding. The first appeared in 2009 as a report under the imprimatur of the UN Secretary-General, Ban-ki Moon (UNSG 2009). The second appeared in 2008 commissioned by the UN Development Programme (UNDP).[2] They are taken in reverse chronological order because the UN report bears the hallmark of orthodoxy, reinforced by corporate governance, in contrast to the earlier UNDP-sponsored report, which had a more emancipatory and intersubjective approach. The latter arose from collaboration between the UNDP's Bureau for Crisis Prevention and Recovery and a team of independent academic researchers. It carried the disclaimer that it did not represent the views of the UNDP or its member states. For ease of reference, however, they will be referred to here as the Secretary-General's Report and the UNDP Report respectively.

The Secretary-General's Report on peacebuilding

The Secretary-General's Report certainly presented some rethinking about peacebuilding. Perhaps this indicated that academic critiques from the late 1990s had filtered into debates, for there were echoes of work by academic critics of the liberal peace, of liberal imperialism in peacebuilding and of the neglect of local agency.[3] The Report announced the critical need for building local capacities and national ownership to provide motivation and accord legitimacy to peacebuilding processes. It affirmed that international assistance should mobilize existing capacities and not undermine them (§V: 49). It recognized that '[l]ocal and traditional authorities as well as civil society actors, including marginalized groups, have a role to play in bringing multiple voices to the table for early priority-setting and to broaden the sense of ownership around a common vision for the country's future', including women 'as victims of conflict and drivers of recovery' (§III: 12). The Report noted the legacy of war economies, because '[f]ailure to restore State authority, particularly in remote border areas, may create new sources of threat or permit wartime practices of smuggling or illegal trade in natural resources to persist or even expand, undermining State revenue' (§II: 8). Protecting livelihoods and generating employment were also mentioned. But all these were passing nods in the direction of an emancipatory repositioning. The thrust of the Report concerned interventionist efficiency.

Acknowledging a crisis in peacebuilding, the authors noted that it took several years for interested external agencies to align their strategies and provide sufficient resources to implement a common strategic vision. The host authorities, the UN and its international partners could have 'a much greater and earlier collective impact if we agree on an early strategy with defined and sequenced priorities, and align action and resources behind that strategy' (§I: 6). This necessitated preset institutional reconfiguration and central planning. It represents the first of four discernible contradictions in the liberal paradigm.

First, national ownership is incompatible with the centralizing, institutionalist approach that comprised two-thirds of the Report – the 'Agenda for Action' (§V). The Agenda undertook to: create coherence through 'integrated missions'; enhance UN leadership through the Resident Co-ordinator with leadership teams 'that can be rapidly supplemented by additional pre-identified expertise'; and to build 'strategic partnerships' with others such as NATO, the EU and the World Bank. Solidifying UN bureaucracy and institutionalization – from the Peacebuilding Commission to the expert planning teams at UN headquarters – reinforces integrated, centralized and unaccountable bases of finance, firepower, knowledge and industry well beyond the reach of those most affected. For inhabitants it offered a peace owned nationally (or at least by a compliant government), but determined with self-replicating certitude and increasing clout by others. The structure would be protected by:

> the development of mutual accountability measures whereby my senior representative is both empowered and held accountable for his or her performance by the system and at the same time he or she can hold each part of the system accountable for implementing agreed roles and activities, consistent with their mandates, based on the integrated strategic framework.
>
> (§V: 36–7)

Accountability to the populations affected was completely absent.

To escape a self-referencing accountability system requires, first, a greater openness on the part of UN managers and field workers to critique. This would encompass accountability through their roles in mediating the impacts of top-down policies on the everyday life of the affected populations, not just engaging in financial transparency for the US Treasury (Gasyuk 2012). Second, it would mean a shift in cultural politics away from the kind of organized hypocrisy expressed by former High Representative in Bosnia and Herzegovina, Paddy Ashdown (2007: 83), when he admitted bringing pain to the poor, which politicians in the United Kingdom 'would reject without a second thought'. Third, it would mean diluting or ending immunities, such as that anticipated by the pioneering Human Rights Advisory Panel in Kosovo, established to investigate human rights violations attributed to a UN field mission, but which was emasculated by the UN Interim Administration Mission in Kosovo (UNMIK) to protect its own immunities regime (Momirov 2012).[4]

In sum, in this Report the concept of local ownership was more rhetorical than real. Discussion of local ownership was in fact squeezed between sections on enhancing UN capacities and generating wider international support. By definition, local autonomy is meaningless without resistance to the power of external actors, particularly their financial power. As Albin Kurti (2011), Kosovar intellectual and MP put it in an address highly critical of peacebuilding in general: 'while national capitalism imposed imperialism and colonialism; multinational capitalism brought international protectorates'. Peacebuilding, said Kurti, meant that the 'uncivilized' struggling for self-determination and justice in sites 'labelled fragile or failed' required good governance brought by the 'civilized'.

A second contradiction derives from the Report's eulogy of the World Bank. It had its own special section and was mentioned several times as 'a critical strategic partner' (§VII: 91). Indeed the Bank, under its US director, has considerable prominence in practice. It secured a special relationship with the UN department of Peacekeeping Operations as part of Jean-Marie Guéhenno's peacekeeping reforms, has representation on the Peacebuilding Commission, convenes donor conferences, sets agendas for financial strategies, uses Trust Funds to exert leverage where it has no direct role and, backed by IMF conditionalities, prioritizes statebuilding so that neoliberal political economies can be institutionalized. Donors and the UNDP tend to work within the culture of conditionality established by the International Financial Institutions (Woodward 2012). The Report proposed a special mechanism to improve strategic coordination between UN headquarters and the Bank because it: 'has a critical mass of expertise in the provision of public sector management support at the national level. In some critical areas for immediate post-conflict action, such as public finance and basic monetary and fiscal policy, the World Bank and the International Monetary Fund, respectively, are the main source of international knowledge, expertise and capacity' (§V: 56).

Such a sweeping endorsement of 1980s–90s neoliberalism implicates the UN in the enterprise of fusing peace with capital accumulation. Certainly, the World Bank has supported welfare and health reforms in the third world, and its Fragile and Conflict Affected Countries Programme is widely considered as an 'ally in peacebuilding' (International Peace Institute 2010: 5). But it has been one of the institutions with responsibility, alongside the International Monetary Fund, the World Trade Organization and donor agencies, for structural adjustment policies and the 1999 Washington consensus, primarily instituted to open spaces for capital accumulation. Further, the Report presented needs assessments conducted by the UNDP, World Bank and EU Commission as a methodology rather than an ideological tool. Needs assessments provided the basis for discussion with national actors, 'leading in time to the development of a national framework for peace consolidation and recovery' (§§V: 41–44). The concept strongly resembles the Poverty Reduction Strategies (PRSPs) of yesteryear, whereby the World Bank set national budget limits and privileged such ideas as micro-finance, privatization and state support to small and medium-sized enterprises. As Pablo Leal (2007: 541) contends, the mantra of participation served not to facilitate the agency of the poor and reduce their subjugation by the state and its international backers, but to create 'a populist justification for the removal of the state from the economy and its substitution by the market'. Peacebuilding, it seems, can only occur within limits determined, above all, by ideological conditionalities and budgetary constraints.

Third, the Report made no clear distinction between peacebuilding and statebuilding. The post-conflict government needed to build core state capacities for basic public services, security, rule of law and safeguarding human rights, because '[v]isible peace dividends that are attributable to the national authorities, including early employment generation and supporting returnees, are also critical to build the confidence in the government and the peace process' (§III: 18). Peace dividends attributable to the state reinforce the elitist notion that lodges legitimacy in authorities favoured by the 'international community', rather than in the customary social contracts and grounded legitimacy of socially meaningful institutions. Critics make a much clearer, and necessary, distinction between peacebuilding and statebuilding. Not only do some communities regard their allotted state as largely meaningless, as in sites as far apart as Bougainville, Haiti and Bosnia and Herzegovina, but the attempt to build one has often been a cause of conflict, as in Kosovo. Nor did the Secretary-General's Report say anything about horizontal and vertical inequalities as a cause of conflict – in contrast to the UNDP-commissioned report which stated that '[w]ar results *from* as well as *in* socioeconomic and political imbalances' (UNDP 2008: xix and 17–22, original emphasis).[5]

Fourth, the Secretary-General's Report observed the need to 'address root causes' of conflict, as if these could be self-evident or agreed upon. Since root causes can be attributed to events or persons no longer relevant and to motive forces beyond, as well as within, the sites of conflict, the quest is ideologically loaded. A constant refrain in the liberal narrative of intervention is that if only war-torn societies had been blessed with democracy, good governance, civil society, open markets and human rights, in short more like western societies, then conflict would have been less likely. This bears no close examination, since liberal development entails the pursuit of capital accumulation, class war and intolerance of illiberalism to the point of wreaking havoc on non-liberal forms. And since these forces are not necessarily compatible with democracy, including at the level of granting immunities to the purveyors of such moves, the root cause discourse can be exposed as exclusive. There would be no space for instance to include Austro-German geopolitical interests as an abiding factor in the Balkan conflicts since the retreat of the Ottoman Empire.

Therefore in spite of the crisis in liberal peacebuilding the framing of the debate in this Report can best be considered as an effort to perpetuate a hierarchical view of peacebuilding through increased efficiency. The UN's institutional answer to crisis required interventions and therapeutic treatment to protect subalterns from the (unacknowledged) consequences of contradictions in the system of global governance. An integrated, expertly-managed, partner-laden and unaccountable mechanism designed to uphold a statist, hierarchical and feral capitalist order, is unlikely to address them. Discourses postulating the merger of peace and development of a particular kind, as well as the absorption of peacekeeping into peacebuilding (Hirschmann 2012; de Carvalho and Ettang 2011: 3–12), have encapsulated moves to consolidate powerful interests. Even the prose style betrayed neoliberal corporate thinking – 'growing the pool of potential candidates', 'delivery of tasks', 'how to bring peacebuilding upstream' and 'a go-to source of knowledge'. The Report's response to 'global resource constraints' and 'the most vulnerable bear[ing] the brunt of economic downturn' was to ensure greater efficiency and focus in the use of resources (§VII: 87). Such language has cloaked economic austerity to address the depression triggered by international financial centres since 2007. Since the Report's publication, however, even the leading lights of the International Monetary Fund, World Bank, World Trade Organization and other international institutions have expressed alarm at the consequences of their own neoliberal prescriptions, warning against the social and economic dangers of 'aggressive austerity' (Elliott 2012: 26). Nevertheless, short of the abolition or root and branch reform of these institutions, the sponsorship of global capital accumulation will continue to result in the exploitation of nature and labour, exacerbating environmental depletion and economic injustices. Only a radical structural transformation of the global socio-economic and political order could effectively deal with this.

The UNDP Crisis Prevention and Recovery Report

Whereas the Secretary-General's Report reflected problem-solving to maintain bureaucratic and corporate interests, the UNDP Report offered striking evidence of purposeful, emancipatory revisionism. The latter's discourse featured such slogans as 'nurturing indigenous drivers' and 'enabling local ingenuity' to foster liberation from top-down peacebuilding. The Secretary-General's Report seems not to have been unduly influenced by the research and recommendations of the UNDP team. In general, also, the latter took a more nuanced approach to context, and disaggregated data on conflict countries to indicate, for example, that peace agreements increasingly referred to employment and the well-being of inhabitants. The UNDP Report's emancipatory elements can be categorized into two groups: the autonomy of inhabitants; and human security through economic well-being.

First, the Report made a presumption about autonomy and sovereignty, moving beyond participation and firmly rejecting the inscription of survivors as lacking economic capacity apart from skills in crime and corruption. It claimed that '[i]ndigenous drivers provide the most viable platform on which to base post-war recovery efforts and international support. Policies that harness and build on social processes and interactions on the ground, and on local capacities, are more likely to be successful and self-sustaining' (UNDP 2008: xvii). The researchers recognized that informal economies were not simply a threat to the states but contributed to survival. Populations could be credited with energy and resilience: '[p]eople who live in post-conflict settings do not, in general, wait passively for external agents to finance and direct their activities. Rather, they take charge of their lives with determination and show hard work and ingenuity in resuming or developing new activities' (UNDP: xix). Inhabitants were therefore competent to establish priorities for recovery.

Second, although preoccupied with issues of economic growth, the Report did not assume that growth alone would suffice to establish recovery. Rather, the authors privileged the enrichment of human capital through distributive policies and support for well-being, in health and education for example (ibid: 61). Growth also needed to be responsive to inequalities with benefits of increased productivity leading to equitable distribution – a radical enough proposal for wealthy economies at peace where workers have not shared in the proceeds of increased productivity. This Report highlighted income generation, rapid employment expansion, and welfare provision as keys to peacebuilding. For example, employment could be expanded through investment in labour-intensive infrastructure projects, as in Sierra Leone, where the UN mission (UNAMSIL) employed former soldiers to build roads. However, like the Secretary-General's Report the UNDP researchers adopted a statist approach – seeing peace dividends as critical to rebuilding a social contract between citizens and the state – though low government revenues would restrict public investment. Neoliberal structural adjustment in the 1980s and 1990s had squeezed public investment (and arguably siphoned it off to repay loans). The necessary capital would likely have to be privately sourced though the results of privatization had been mixed partly because the process was often corrupt (ibid: 121) (rather than acknowledging that it depleted public goods). Moreover, from a critical perspective the blurring of statebuilding and peacebuilding noted earlier has become a key problem highlighted by Oliver Richmond (2011: 46–50) among others, since for many societies states do not necessarily hold the key to social contracts.

In support of trends that had the power of immanence, the UNDP Report provided evidence that overseas development assistance for infrastructure, including World Bank loans, was recovering after reaching a low point in 2002. The Bank had moved to streamline donations, establish post-conflict progress indicators and in 2004 create a Trust Fund of US$25 million for stressed countries (a tiny fraction of the amount paid in bonuses to UK bankers that year) (UNDP: 92).[6] In addition, the Report showed a tentative correlation between strong growth and social inclusiveness, as evidenced from Mozambique where agriculture, the main source of income, had received investment. However, the Report drew shaky inferences from GDP statistics about weak and strong post-conflict growth. For example, the 10.5 per cent average annual growth in the 12 post-conflict years in Bosnia and Herzegovina was presented as 'strong', a figure artificially inflated by the inclusion of new sectors such as services. GDP statistics say little about the quality of growth. The UNDP's Human Development Index (HDI) provides some validation, indicating for example, that Rwanda (a supposedly inclusive, strong growth state), had the fastest improvement in the HDI ratings of post-conflict countries and an index of purchasing power parity per head moving from 100 at the end of the war to about 160 by 2007 (comparable to the level when the conflict began in 1994). But the authors do not appear to have attended to data on unemployment, or Gini coefficients of inequality (whereby 100 per cent means one person has all the income and 0 per cent means everyone has the same income). In Rwanda for example concentration of capital in the *akazu* (cronies of the Tutsi elite) meant that the Gini coefficient reached 51 per cent by 2006 (Davies 2008: 217; UNDP: 117). Unemployment data are admittedly unreliable, but known to persist at high levels (20 per cent and above) long after conflict ends. The national statistics agency of Bosnia and Herzegovina recorded the registered unemployment rate at 43.5 per cent of the working age population in November 2011 (though stripping out people in 'illegal' employment brings that down to 27.3 per cent), even though the IMF estimated GDP growth at 1.7 per cent in 2011 compared with 0.7 per cent the year before (at: www. bhas.ba/saopstenja/2012/NEZ_2011M11_001_01_BH.pdf). The poverty rate was falling but still over 18 per cent of the population were living below the poverty level twelve years after the war.

Nevertheless, the UNDP-commissioned team presented solutions to the peacebuilding crisis through emancipatory concepts and recommendations. It attempted to avoid treating hosts as referent objects. And the Report itself imparts evidence of a significant shift in problem-solving in debates about peacebuilding. The Secretary-General's Report undoubtedly exhibited a contrast to it. But does this mean that the UNDP's outer contours impinge on foundational critique, rendering the latter insecure? For several reasons, however, it reinforces the argument for critique of the peacebuilding subparadigm. It framed the debate in a construct that conforms normatively to the liberal peace paradigm.

It referred to 'normal' development – as if 'normal' can be taken for granted or presages convergence with an ideal. Absence of normality was conceived as lack of basic security and low economic confidence; weak fiscal capacity and reduction of government revenue; weak mechanisms for preventing illegal activity; high criminality; mass movement of people; and macroeconomic challenges such as debt, inflation and budget deficits (UNDP: 41). A year or two later much of this could be considered normal for capitalism. By contrast, José Antonio Ocampo and colleagues have proposed not only fiscal and price stability, but also policies of state loss-leading infrastructure building, technological innovation and employment policies (2008: 1–47). In this regard also, the Report did not recognize that the western liberal peacebuilding monopoly was being broken by Chinese, Latin American and Islamic approaches to post-conflict recovery (Mac Ginty 2008: 690–708).

The Report also subscribed to the misleading signifier: building back *differently and better* (UNDP: 5, original emphasis). Obviously, war economies embody developmental dynamics (though the Report stressed deterioration), and they have legacies that preclude a return to the *status quo ante* (Cramer 2006). In fact the Report called for reform rather than restoration, requiring a 'rigorous analysis of pre-war flaws and distortions' (UNDP: 65). But it strongly implied that those in charge of assistance would do the analysis and decide the content behind the adjective 'better'. As Toby Dodge (2012) explains, the post-war plan for Iraq was to turn it into a model neoliberal state. It failed dramatically. Nevertheless, the UNDP Report asserted that foreign direct investment was crucial, when the evidence for this is thin since rather than driving indigenous development it is a route to foreign capital accumulation through tax breaks and profit repatriation, and often has more to do with resource extraction than local development. Another pivotal, almost crusading, task in peacebuilding has been transformation through the creation of favourable business environments, empowering local entrepreneurs with enterprise zones, subsidies for small and medium-sized enterprises, and micro-credit initiatives. This last generates little employment and often results in merely recycling poverty (Bateman 2010). Yet stable countries with supposedly sublime business environments – pretenders to financial thrones such as Iceland, and barons of enterprise such as Ireland and Latvia – were either princes of the casino crisis or early and serious victims.

Another recommendation sought to avoid unaccountable international governance in the form of parallel, externally staffed bureaucracies performing government functions, 'pairing the highly skilled expatriate with an indigene inside the government bureaucracy' (UNDP 2008: 161). But this also risks unaccountable decision-making of the kind that led to the resignation of one of the few female Kosovar ministers in Kosovo's interim government. In Palestine, as Mandy Turner explains (2009: 562–77), the International Task Force on Palestinian Reform, whose members included the United States, the EU, the World Bank and the IMF, operate a 'sophisticated web of control', obliging the Palestinian Authority to submit to auditing controls on a daily basis, and introducing punitive austerity for a population with poverty rates in 2008 of 79.4 per cent in Gaza and 45.7 per cent in the West Bank.

Evidently, the UNDP and donors vary over what needs to be done in peacebuilding, but the culture of restructuring for capital is all-pervasive. 'Build back better' amounts to structural adjustment that replaces social contracts with fiscal contracts and produces or reinforces a class of non-insured (Duffield 2008: 145–65). Neoliberal policies also oblige post-conflict countries to open their economies and undermine domestic production vulnerable to foreign imports. Both the Secretary-General's and UNDP reports kept silent about the global trade regime that benefits countries with strong comparative advantages.

Conclusion: Contours of peacebuilding and emancipation

Peacebuilding has come to mean revising the structures that led to conflict, and inevitably that means diminution of sovereignty. Externals cannot do this without echoing, if not replicating, colonization processes, whether through hit-and-run imperialism, or denial and working through so-called 'local empowerment' (Chandler 2006). Diverse alterities are denied in peacebuilding situations revealing a fatal contradiction in liberalism: tolerance limited to principles that are exclusionary. In common with colonial power, international actors and agencies in peacebuilding disavow their impositions with discourses of good governance, law and order, stakeholding, participation, local ownership, empowerment, and trouncing spoilers.

The contours of peacebuilding are drawn by frames of reference that in discourse, agenda setting and 'norm entrepreneurship' privilege efficient performance, and reflect the concerns, including economic concerns, of major interests in intervention. The problem-solving reports discussed here still remain fairly representative of the peacebuilding framework, though in its emancipatory disposition the UNDP Report and some earlier examples on globalization belong at one extreme (Malhotra 2003). The 'build back better' approach still dominates the peacebuilding industry, though taking increased account of customs and traditions. Under the auspices of the Department of Peacekeeping Operations (DPKO) and the Department of Field Support, further reform proposals in 2009 aimed to strengthen partnerships with other international organizations to improve centralized efficiency through a 'New Partnership Agenda' (Department of Peacekeeping Operations and Department of Field Support 2009). However, the alliance between the Peacebuilding Commission, the DPKO and the World Bank places uniformed peacekeepers and civilian peacebuilders in the position of guarding and working within a political construction of economic progress that has had ruinous consequences for social and economic equality. The close relationship is consecrated in the 'Principles and Guidelines' for peacekeeping (or 'Capstone Doctrine' of January 2008 – see Figure 1.1).

Neoliberal policies may have softened at the edges but no hegemonic international institution in the global economy diverts from the dogma that '[c]ountries must reaffirm that none will resort to growth-destroying protectionism and demonstrate that trade restrictions introduced in response to the economic crisis will be rolled back' (Elliott 2012: 26). Not only does this liberal dictatorship deny the history of protectionism that explains growth and camouflage the interests of transnational capital served by accumulation through free trade, it also assumes a causal relationship between free trade and peace, a fallacy exposed by the collapse of Yugoslavia, and by the force and structural violence required to establish 'open economies' that local authorities then have to manage (Klein 2007; Chang 2002). As Robert Cox (1992), among others, notes, '[c]onsequently, just as in one-party, authoritarian regimes, politics is about depoliticizing people, by removing the economic determinants of everyday conditions from political control'.

Foundational critique is more important than ever, and this examination suggests that the subparadigm of peacebuilding depends on the overarching paradigm of neoliberalism.

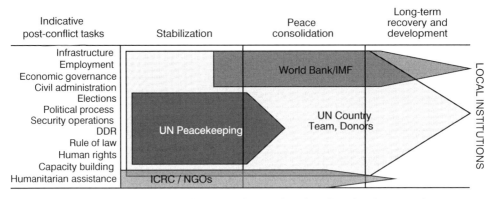

Figure 1.1 The core business of multi-dimensional United Nations Peacekeeping operations

Transformation of liberal peacebuilding is unlikely to suffice without addressing its linkages to the instability of capitalism. This requires an imagination beyond the neoliberal paradigm to which peacebuilding has been subservient. It involves interrogation of the way in which peacebuilding exacerbates the subaltern status of war-torn societies. It would encompass a commensurately greater focus on the need for far-reaching change in the international economic and political structures and institutions that try to determine what might be termed 'the limits of potential' for life, to foster economic empowerment, redistribution and welfare rather than protection of capital. The international disciplinary mechanisms could pay more attention to the larcenists at the top than to the arsonists at the bottom. Rights agendas could be open to the inclusion of socio-economic rights through, for example, democracy in the workplace and protection of public, socially-owned and community property from dispossession by private accumulation. Above all, political communities should be able to set their own economic priorities including protection of economic activities from the deleterious effects of global integration. For Cox, a necessary correlative shift would encompass a world order, 'in which different traditions of civilization could co-exist, each based on different intersubjectivity defining a distinct set of values and a distinct path towards development' (Cox 1993: 265).

However, it is worth noting that critiques, while commonly agreed on the necessity to question power, diverge on the role of the state. Patently, states can give expression to identity, as suggested by the quest for statehood by Albanian Kosovars and Palestinians. As experienced by Cubans, it might be a polity best able to provide security and welfare to societies, however basic, enabling defence against predatory interests, including corporate power. Some regard the contemporary role of the capitalist state as the handmaiden of an economic system that exploits much of the world's population without democratic control. Thus David Harvey (2003: 29) highlights the importance of '[r]eformulating state power along more interventionist and redistributive lines, curbing the speculative power of finance capitalism, and decentralizing or democratically controlling the overwhelming power of oligopolies and monopolies'. This may be only a partial, temporary or contested step, since étatism as an end rather than process can lead to concentration and abuse of power in the hands of political and administrative elites. It is certainly true, historically, that states are here today and gone tomorrow, perhaps best considered a passing (in)convenience.

Nevertheless, the contours of foundational critique are marked by resistance to power and exploitation. Foundational critiques acknowledge, therefore, the intruder's inability to create stable identities or institutions with organic roots. As Richmond (2011: 214) comments, 'local agency, resistance, and liberation open up the politics of peacebuilding more fully, and require an engagement with agonistic mediation of difference'. Subaltern agency involves coping in a variety of ways that derail intentions, however much the intentions are portrayed as enlightened. Consequently, international policy makers and bureaucrats might be relegated to servants of peace rather than of national interest, neo-imperial liberal superiority, so-called free markets and placatory discourses of rights that privilege the rights of capital over the labour it exploits.

Notes

1 Guided by Röpke, Rüstow, Hayek and von Mises.
2 The project was managed by the late Karen Ballentine.
3 See, for example, Neil Cooper, 'On the Crisis in the Liberal Peace', *Conflict, Security Development*, Vol. 7, No.4, 2007, pp.605–16; Oliver P. Richmond, 'Emancipatory Forms of Human Security and Liberal Peacebuilding', *International Journal*, Vol. 62, No.3, 2007, pp.458–77; and Beate Jahn, 'The Tragedy of Liberal Diplomacy: Democratization, Intervention and Statebuilding II', *Journal of Intervention and Statebuilding*, Vol.1, No.2, 2007, pp. 211–29.
4 When in 2008 the Privatization Agency of Kosovo replaced the EU-run Kosovo Trust Agency for privatising state and social assets, the new director accompanied by Kosovo police encountered nothing but the fragments of destroyed records. 'PAK Official Work Report, 2008–09', Prishtina, 2009.
5 On inequalities see Frances Stewart and Valpy FitzGerald (eds) (2001), *War and Underdevelopment*, 2 vols, Oxford: Oxford University Press.
6 £4 billion was paid in bonuses in the UK finance and insurance sector in the financial year 2004–05. George Eaton, 'Bank bonuses make a mockery of the Tories' rhetoric', *The New Statesman*, 20 July 2011 (at: www.newstatesman.com/blogs/the-staggers/2011/07/unacceptable-bonuses-block). Last accessed 19 June 2012.

References

Ashdown, P. (2007) *Swords and Ploughshares: Bringing Peace to the 21st Century,* London: Wiedenfeld & Nicholson.
Bateman, M. (2010) *Why Doesn't Microfinance Work?: The Destructive Rise of Local Neoliberalism,* London: Zed.
Benn, T. (1998) Hansard, House of Commons, 16 November, 319, col. 685.
Booth, K. (1997) 'Security and Self: Confessions of a Fallen Realist', in K. Krause and M.C. Williams, *Critical Security Studies: Concepts and Cases*, London: UCL Press: 82–120.
de Carvalho, G. and D. Ettang (2011) 'Contextualising the Peacekeeping and Peacebuilding Nexus', *Conflict Trends*, 3: 3–12.
Cox, R. (1981) 'Social Forces, States and World Orders: Beyond International Relations Theory', *Millennium*, 10(2): 126–55.
Cox, R. (1992) 'Globalization, Multilateralism, and Democracy', John Holmes memorial lecture to the Academic Council on the United Nations System (ACUNS), 1992 (at: www.acuns.org/membersubm/johnholmes/globalizat). Last accessed 19 June 2012.
Cox, R. (1993) 'Structural Issues of Global Governance: Issues for Europe', in S. Gill (ed.), *Gramsci, Historical Materialism and International Relations*, Cambridge: Cambridge University Press, pp. 259–89.
Cox, R. (1999) 'Civil Society at the Turn of the Millennium: Prospects for an Alternative World Order', *Review of International Studies*, 25(1): 3–28.
Chandler, D. (2006) *Empire in Denial The Politics of Statebuilding*, London: Pluto.

Chang, H.J. (2002) *Kicking Away the Ladder: Development Strategy in Historical Perspective*, London: Anthem.

Cramer, C. (2006) *Civil War is not a Stupid Thing: Accounting for Violence in Developing Countries*, London: Hurst.

Davies, R. (2008) 'Rwandese Diasporas and the Reconstruction of a Fragile Peace', in M. Pugh, N. Cooper and M. Turner (eds), *Whose Peace? Critical Perspectives on the Political Economy of Peacebuilding*, Basingstoke: Palgrave Macmillan: 208–23.

Department of Peacekeeping Operations and Department of Field Support (2009) 'A New Partnership Agenda: Charting a New Horizon for UN Peacekeeping', UN New York, July.

Dodge, T. (2012) 'Enemy images, coercive socio-engineering and civil war in Iraq', *International Peacekeeping*, 19(3): 208–23.

Duffield, M. (2007) *Development, Security and Unending War*, London: Polity.

Duffield, M. (2008) 'Global Civil War: The Non-Insured, International Containment and Post-Interventionary Society', *Journal of Refugee Studies* 21(2) 145–65.

Elliott, L. (2012) 'IMF warns of risk posed by global austerity plans', *The Guardian*, 20 January. p. 26.

Foucault, M. (2010) *The Birth of Biopolitics. Lectures at the Collège de France, 1978–1979*, Basingstoke: Palgrave Macmillan.

Gasyuk, A. (2012) 'UN is to be put on a starvation diet', *Russia Today*, 24 January (available at: http://rt.com/politics/press/rossijskaya-gazeta/un-us-budget-organization/en). Last accessed 19 June 2012.

Harvey, D. (2003) *The New Imperialism*, Oxford: Oxford University Press.

Hirschmann, G. (2012) 'Peacebuilding in UN Peacekeeping Exit Strategies: Organized Hypocrisy and Institutional Reform', *International Peacekeeping*, 19(2): 170–185.

International Peace Institute (2010) *From New York to the Field: A Dialogue on Peace Operations*, report of a conference of UN member states and SRSGs, on 19 June 2009, New York: International Peace Institute.

Klein, N. (2007) *The Shock Doctrine*, London: Penguin.

Krasner, S. (2005) 'The Case for Shared Sovereignty', *Journal of Democracy* 16(1): 69–83.

Kurti, A. (2011) 'International Protectorate', TedxVienna (available at: http://www.youtube.com/watch?v=TYci38HqlDU) at 3min, 40secs, c. November. Last accessed 3 June 2012.

Leal, P.A. (2007) 'Participation: the ascendancy of a buzzword in the neo-liberal era', *Development in Practice*, 17(4–5): 539–48.

Mac Ginty, R. (2008) 'Indigenous Peacemaking versus the Liberal Peace', *Cooperation and Conflict*, 43(2): 690–708.

Malhotra, K. (2003) *Making Global Trade Work for People*, London: Earthscan.

Mészáros, I. (2005) *The Power of Ideology*, London: Zed Books, rev.edn.

Momirov, A. (2012) 'Local Impact of "UN Accountability" Under International Law: The Rise and Fall of UNMIK's Human Rights Advisory Panel', *International Peacekeeping*, 19 (1): 3–18.

Ocampo, J.A., S. Spiegel and J.E. Stiglitz (2008) 'Introduction', in J.A. Ocampo and J.E. Stiglitz (eds), *Capital Market Liberalization and Development*, Oxford: Oxford University Press, pp. 1–47.

Richmond, O.P. (2005) *The Transformation of Peace*, Basingstoke: Palgrave Macmillan.

Richmond, O.P. (2011) *A Post-Liberal Peace*, London: Routledge.

Turley, N. (2012) 'British INGOs in Post-Tsunami Tamil Nadu: Mediating a Liberal Peace?', unpublished PhD thesis, University of Bradford.

Turner, M. (2009) 'The power of "shock and awe": The Palestinian Authority and the road to reform', *International Peacekeeping* 16(4): 562–77.

UNDP (2008) *Post-Conflict Economic Recovery: Enabling Local Ingenuity*, Bureau for Crisis Prevention and Recovery, New York.

UNSG (2009) 'Report of the Secretary-General on peacebuilding in the immediate aftermath of conflict', General Assembly 63rd session, 11 June, UN doc., A/63/881–S/2009/304.

Woodward, S. (2012) 'The IFIs and post-conflict political economy', in D. Zaum and M. Berdal (eds), *Power after Peace*, Oxford: Oxford University Press.

2

THE EVOLUTION OF PEACEBUILDING

Stephen Ryan

Start with what they know, build with what they have.

(Lao Tzu, date unknown)

There is a story of a Spanish soldier, who just before he died was asked if he would forgive all of his enemies. He replied that he did not have to, because he had killed them all. However, such final one-sided victories are rare, especially in cases of large-scale intergroup conflict. Whereas it might have been possible in earlier eras to eliminate whole groups of people, such as the Trojans, Carthaginians or Melians, this does not seem to be an acceptable or achievable goal in the modern era – even the worst genocides of the past hundred years did not succeed in totally eradicating their intended targets. Every instance of large-scale intergroup violence therefore leaves in its wake the problems associated with creating better relations in the post-violence era. Sometimes this will be in the context of military defeat of one side, as was the case with the southern states in the US Civil War or the German defeat in 1945. More recent cases would include Afghanistan, Iraq or Sri Lanka. Sometimes the ending of violent conflict is the result of a negotiated peace agreement between the parties, as was the case in Bosnia, Northern Ireland or South Africa.

The contexts may vary, but the historical evidence suggests that it is never easy to address the post-violence stage of intergroup conflict in a manner that promotes healthy and positive relations. For the experience of violence leaves behind problems that can be resistant to short-term 'solutions'. This might be especially true of situations where one side has been decisively beaten and where a 'culture of defeat' can emerge, accompanied by complex psychological and cultural responses that might include new myths about the past, a need to blame their defeat on subversive elements, and the refusal to accept the demands of the victors for moral and spiritual surrender (Schivelbusch 2001).

The emergence of the concept of peacebuilding

The phenomenon of what we now call peacebuilding is therefore not new. As Cutillo (2006: 1) notes, 'external assistance for post-war rebuilding had clear antecedents in the reconstruction of Western Europe and Japan after World War II'. The concept of peacebuilding, however, only entered into the mainstream in 1992, when it appeared in the United Nations (UN) document *An Agenda for Peace*. Since then it has become one of the most discussed concepts in the fields of international politics, peace and conflict research and development studies and as a result has become the subject of a substantial literature.

Galtung (1976) is credited with inventing the concept of peacebuilding. He regarded it as one component of a tripartite conflict resolution strategy that also included peacekeeping and peacemaking and believed that it should be an 'associative approach' that aims to build better infrastructures of peace. One would be hard pressed to recognize Galtung's approach in *An Agenda for Peace*. In part this is because of Galtung's abstract language. His use of terms like equity, entropy and symbiosis contrast starkly with the more mundane language of the 1992 UN document. Furthermore, Galtung's recognition that we need to find multiple peacebuilding 'interaction channels' that are non-state does not find enough of a resonance at the UN, which is particularly state-centric.

Galtung's work acted as a catalyst for other studies including contributions by Harbottle (1980) and Fisher (1993). However, peacebuilding remained a neglected idea until the start of the 1990s when a number of factors made it more germane. As a progressive and sanguine idea one might be surprised to find it being so quickly embraced in the study of international politics, which has not always been receptive to hopeful thinking. However, after the end of the Cold War it appeared well matched to what might be called an optimistic turn in world society that was based on a number of developments. The first was the changing nature of armed conflict, and in particular the decline of wars between sovereign states and the rise of what came to be called 'ethnic conflicts'. Inter-state conflicts are often settled by each party withdrawing back to an internationally recognized frontier (maybe with some territorial readjustment) after which the parties can lead relatively separate lives. In the case of conflicts within states, however, different cultural groups still have to live together in a single jurisdiction when the armed conflict stops, and this seems to demand peace strategies that, in Galtung's terminology, are associative rather than dissociative (Galtung 1969).

The end of the Cold War unfroze some of these protracted intra-state conflicts that had been linked to superpower rivalries and this allowed for greater international involvement in emerging peace processes in these locations including Namibia, Cambodia, El Salvador, and Northern Ireland. The first of these missions set in motion so-called second generation peace operations that attempted to 'implement a comprehensive settlement' (Goulding 1993). Sustained peacebuilding work by the UN as a separate named activity really started here, though a lot of what the UN was doing before this through its specialized agencies might be considered peacebuilding by another name. At the same time as demand for more peace operations increased, the end of the superpower confrontation reduced the likelihood that the Security Council would be paralyzed by a veto and so allowed the UN to take more decisive actions. This seemed like a particularly neat development, where the demand for more international involvement was matched by the ability of the UN to supply the resources needed.

Furthermore, the way the Cold War ended, through non-violent revolutions that overthrew repressive regimes, seemed to confirm the impression that world society was experiencing an unstoppable wave of democratization. This produced an infectious mood of 'democratic optimism' (Mayall 2000). Given the prevalence of such views in the early 1990s it was not hard to believe that positive interventions in conflict situations to promote greater freedom were working with the tide of history and this might have further encouraged a more crusading form of liberal interventionism.

Alongside such developments, there was also a growth in the idea that human rights protection was more important than respect for state sovereignty. Sisk (2001: 2) has noted how this created 'new opportunities for innovation in peace process design'. It also led to an increase in multilateral humanitarian intervention (Chandler 2002; Hoffmann 1996; Ramsbotham and Woodhouse 1996; Wheeler 2000). This raised the inevitable question: what should be done to build a better society after the intervention had taken place? It was a question taken up by the 2001 *Responsibility to Protect* report that was subsequently adopted by the UN. Chapter 5 of this document addresses the 'responsibility to rebuild'. This focuses on security, justice and reconciliation, and development issues, but is sensitive to the distortions caused by external interventions and is anxious to promote the idea of achieving local ownership.

It is also important to realize that these developments occurred as the liberal peace hypothesis emerged as one of the most influential doctrines of the post-Cold War era. Indeed, by the end of the twentieth century it is not unreasonable to think of it as the dominant peace theory. As such it was inevitable that it would impact on thinking about peacebuilding. This is despite the fact that in its original version this hypothesis was restricted to the narrow claim that democratic states do not go to war against each other (Doyle 1983). However it did not stay confined to this realm and policymakers, in particular, began to apply it to intra-state as well as inter-state conflict despite the absence of clear empirical data to support this move. President George W. Bush, for example, could justify US interventions by referring to the 'transformative power of liberty' (Appiah 2004: 6). The problem was that such statements ignored academic studies that warned about the dangers inherent in an overly simplistic approach to the link between democracy and peace (see, for example, Snyder 2000), and it was an underestimation of the importance of peacebuilding that contributed to the problems that Washington ran into in Iraq and Afghanistan.

The evolution of peacebuilding at the UN

Re-reading *An Agenda for Peace* (Boutros-Ghali 1992) one is struck by how little it has to say about peacebuilding. Just five paragraphs are devoted to the concept, which is defined earlier in the document as 'action to identify and support structures which will tend to strengthen and solidify peace in order to avoid a relapse into conflict'(par. 21). A whole paragraph is devoted to de-mining. The final paragraph addresses the need for action to enhance 'support for the transformation of deficient national structures and capabilities, and for the strengthening of new democratic institutions' (par. 59). It identifies two main peacebuilding scenarios. The first is 'civil strife', where a number of strategies are mentioned, including:

> disarming the previously warring parties and the restoration of order, the custody and possible destruction of weapons, repatriating refugees, advisory and training support for security personnel, monitoring elections, advancing efforts to protect human rights, reforming or strengthening governmental institutions and promoting formal and informal processes of political participation.
>
> (par. 55)

The other situation is international conflicts between states. Here the report identifies a number of possibilities, including 'concrete cooperative projects which link two or more countries in a mutually beneficial undertaking' and 'joint programmes through which barriers between nations are brought down by means of freer travel, cultural exchanges and mutually beneficial youth and educational projects' (par. 56). This idea of inter-state peacebuilding has not been given the attention it might deserve, probably because of the infrequent occurrence of conventional wars since 1992.

There are several criticisms that can be directed at the *Agenda*'s approach to peacebuilding. Firstly it conceptualizes it as 'post-conflict' and this is problematic for two reasons. The first is that no society is 'post-conflict', since conflict is ubiquitous – maybe post-violence would be a better term, though a violence-free society is also hard to imagine. The second problem is that by seeming to restrict the idea of peacebuilding to the final stage in the cycle of violent conflict it promotes a limited view of what peacebuilding could be. Even at the time it was published Roberts (1993) thought the document over estimated the ability of the UN to organize complex peace operations and underestimated the difficulties with funding and Security Council approval that were likely to arise. Rupesinghe (1998) argued that it was too narrow because it underestimated the role that NGOs can play in peace processes. There was no awareness of the dangers posed when trying to change political and economic structures in deeply divided societies: that democratization and development could produce conflicts as well as resolve them.

Yet *An Agenda for Peace* acted as a catalyst. This is evident from the large number of important studies that emerged within the next decade (see, for example, Doyle and Sambanis 2000; Kumar 1997; Lederach 1997; Maynard 1999; Pugh 2000; Reychler and Paffenholz 2001). An examination of the topic of articles published in the *Journal of Peace Research* is also instructive here. Between 1982 and 1991 no articles had the term peacebuilding in their titles, though it is discussed in one article by Galtung (1985). In this ten-year period there is just one other article that deals with what might be thought of as 'peacebuilding' matters – youth and conflict in Israel/Palestine (Spielmann 1986). However, between 1992 and 2001 the volume of articles on peacebuilding topics starts to increase, though not as quickly as one might have imagined. During this time there were four articles with peacebuilding in their title, all of them in 2001 with the first in the January edition (Pugh and Cobble 2001). There were also about a dozen other articles on peacebuilding themes including democratization and elections, power-sharing, peace education, community relations, forgiveness and reconciliation, youth attitudes and civil society. From 2002 to 2011 there is an acceleration of output. Although there were only three articles that included peacebuilding or 'building peace' in their titles, the number that dealt with peacebuilding topics was over thirty (including transitional justice, community relations, conflict identities, reconciliation, forgiveness, peace and development, refugees, truth recovery and democratization).

Three years after *An Agenda for Peace*, and on the fiftieth anniversary of the founding of the UN, the Secretary-General issued a *Supplement to an Agenda for Peace* (Boutros-Ghali 1995) that offered more information about the UN's vision of peacebuilding (it devoted ten paragraphs to this topic). It can be viewed as part of a process whereby 'the concept was progressively expanded' through the UN (Ramsbotham 2000: 173). The *Supplement* recognizes the validity of the post-conflict approach, but now proposes that it 'can be as valuable in preventing conflict as in healing the wounds after conflict has occurred' (par. 47). In most other respects the approach to peacebuilding is not very different from that contained in the original *Agenda*.

However, compared with 1992, the mood at the UN was much more somber because of the failures of the organization in Somalia, Rwanda and Bosnia. So the *Supplement* also notes that implementation can be 'complicated' because of a lack of support from member states and it calls for more attention to be devoted to the 'timing and modalities' of returning peacebuilding functions to local actors so as to preserve any gains that have been made. This of course is an important issue that remains under-researched. The focus of the rest of the section on peacebuilding is on two types of situations that might require international attention.

The first is where there is already a significant international presence in a country. Here it is envisaged that a strong role for a peace operation will not be problematic though it is pointed out that it is important that the timing of the transfer of responsibilities back to local control should not be unduly affected by institutional or budgetary considerations at the UN. How realistic this is, given the organization's perennial economic problems and the absence of consensus in the Security Council is debatable. The more difficult situation, the document argues, is when peacebuilding is needed but where there is no strong international presence on the ground. In such situations the hope is that the UN Secretary-General, acting on his general mandate under the UN Charter, could play an early warning role and can initiate discussions with the state concerned about what measures could be taken. This seems to be a restatement of what Hammarskjold called preventive diplomacy.

Unlike the original *Agenda*, the *Supplement* seems no longer interested in inter-state peacebuilding and is focused entirely on armed conflicts within a single sovereign state. However, it still concentrates only on the structural dimensions of peacebuilding. Soon after the *Supplement* the UN established a number of peacebuilding offices. The first was in Liberia (UNOL), mandated to support the peace process in that country following the elections of July 1997. This was followed by offices in Guinea-Bissau in 1999, and the Central African Republic and Tajikistan in 2000 (Teran 2007).

Although the *Supplement* was the most significant restatement of the UN's interest in peacebuilding, a number of other documents were issued by the organization around the same time that seem to reveal a consolidation of the concept of peacebuilding around four pillars: security, development, democratization and human rights (Chetail 2009). So *An Agenda for Development* (United Nations, 1994) claims 'peace-building offers the chance to establish new institutions, social, political and judicial, that can give impetus to development' and goes on to argue that through a stronger emphasis on social justice and land reform states 'in transition can use peace-building measures as a chance to put their national systems on the path of sustainable development' (par. 23). The *Agenda for Democratization* (Boutros-Ghali 1996) notes that 'the entire range of United Nations assistance, from support for a culture of democracy to assistance in institution-building for democratization, may well be understood as a key component of peace-building' (par. 46). We should also note the *Inventories of United Nations Peacebuilding Activities* (United Nations 1996) and *Peacebuilding Capacity* (United Nations 2006) undertaken by the organization.

The next major UN document to address peacebuilding was the Brahimi Report of 2000 (United Nations 2000). This was a comprehensive review of peace operations established by the UN Secretary-General to try to learn the lessons from the challenges and failures of the 1990s. It expands and deepens previous statements on peacebuilding by pointing out, inter alia, the need to deal with spoilers and notes the desirability of complementing peacebuilding with action against corruption and effective action against diseases (including HIV/AIDS). Brahimi approves the idea that the UN should develop a stronger peacebuilding capacity. In fact it proposes that the UN should become the focal point for such international activity (par. 44). It also endorses a 1998 Security Council Resolution that encouraged the Secretary-General to explore the creation of peacebuilding structures at the UN by proposing that the 'Executive Committee on Peace and Security discuss and recommend to the Secretary-General a plan to strengthen the permanent capacity of the United Nations to develop peace-building strategies and to implement programmes in support of those strategies' (par. 47). The Report also makes three other recommendations to improve UN peacebuilding. The first is to allocate some money at the start of a deployment for quick impact projects. Secondly, there should be a 'doctrinal shift' in the use of civilian police and human rights experts to strengthen the rule of law and respect for human rights. Lastly, disarmament, demobilization and reintegration (DDR) work should be funded through the assessed budgets of peace operations in their first year to speed up this work and reduce the dangers of a return to armed conflict.

In fact the high failure rate of peace processes has been a particular problem. According to Murthy (2007: 47) this is as high as 50 per cent within five years. Other problems were also clear, with critics noting a 'strategic deficit' and poor coordination within and between governments when it came to thinking about peacebuilding (Smith 2004). The *Responsibility to Protect* report was also less than complimentary about practice to date and stated:

> Too often in the past the responsibility to rebuild has been insufficiently recognized, the exit of the interveners has been poorly managed, the commitment to help with reconstruction has been inadequate, and countries have found themselves at the end of the day still wrestling with the underlying problems that produced the original intervention action.
>
> (International Commission on Intervention and State Sovereignty 2001: par. 5.1)

In order to try to deal with such problems the UN realized it had to try to give a stronger sense of direction to its work in this area and so at the end of 2005 it agreed to establish a new Peacebuilding Commission. Its 31 members reflect the multi-dimensional nature of peacebuilding in that it includes seven representatives each from the Security Council (including the P5), ECOSOC and the General Assembly as well as the top five financial and military contributors to the organization. The World Bank and the IMF are not members, though they participate in meetings of the Commission. Both had become accustomed to intervening in the economies of states such as Namibia, Cambodia, Rwanda and Bosnia to promote neo-liberal policies (see Paris 2002). The World Bank, in particular, has made significant strides in recent years in developing a post-conflict policy.

The main functions of the Commission are to: promote best practice; improve the coordination of actors engaged in this work; advise governments who want assistance with peacebuilding tasks; and enhance the attention and the funding given to peacebuilding at the international level. The first three states to obtain assistance were Sierra Leone, Burundi and Guinea-Bissau. To help with its work the Commission has established a Working Group on Lessons Learned. There is also a Peacebuilding Support Office in the Secretariat to offer strategic advice and policy guidance to the Commission. This is headed by an Assistant Secretary-General for Peacebuilding Support (currently Judy Cheng-Hopkins from Malaysia).

The Peacebuilding Commission as established was a weaker version of the one proposed in the *In Larger Freedom* report (Annan 2005), that was itself based on a document from the High Level Panel on Threats, Challenges and Change (United Nations 2004: Part 3). It was diluted because there was a desire to get a consensus from member states and this meant accommodating the views of governments that were not so enthusiastic about this proposed initiative. After some hard negotiations the final version of the Commission had more members, was more cumbersome, had a smaller staff and a lower capacity, and was less dynamic than the one the Secretary-General originally wanted (see Berdal 2009; Miall 2007; Murthy 2007). It also has to rely on voluntary contributions to the Peacebuilding Fund, and has very few powers of its own. One study criticizes it for being 'unwieldy' and for being slow to engage with civil society actors (Lambourne and Herro 2008).

The mandated five-year review of the Commission resulted in a 2010 report entitled *Review of the United Nations Peacebuilding Architecture* (United Nations 2010). Its findings offered even more ammunition to critics for it concluded that the 'threshold of success' established in 2005 had not been achieved and it called for improvements to be made in nearly all aspects of the Commission's work. Its recommendations called for: more genuine national ownership; greater civil society involvement; better relationships with the main UN bodies and with international financial organizations; more flexibility; stronger regional development; a stronger field identity; more ambition; a more effective communication strategy; improved status; better performance; more empowerment; and a stronger Support Office. The *Review* stated that it wanted to be a 'wake-up call' for the Commission (par. 174).

The current state of UN peacebuilding

The emergence of peacebuilding theory and practice has been one of the most interesting developments in peace and conflict research in the past generation. There seems little doubt that it is a strategy that is likely to increase in importance in the years ahead, and just as peacekeeping was the UN's most important innovation in peace and security in the first fifty years of its existence, peacebuilding could become its most important contribution in the next fifty years. Like peacekeeping it has developed in an unplanned and *ad hoc* manner, which might be one reason why it remains a concept that is hard to define. There have also been some positive features of practice to date in places such as Namibia, El Salvador and Mozambique. Tharoor (1995–6: 54) argues that such cases 'cannot lightly be dispensed with'. Yet too often supporters of peacebuilding have been put in the awkward position of favoring more interventions whilst admitting that they have not been undertaken very well in the past. This is like the customer in a restaurant who complains that the food was not very nice and the portions were too small.

There is no doubt that there is a close affinity between peacebuilding and the liberal approach to peace and conflict. Indeed, any peace strategy that promotes democracy, human rights, the respect for the law and a less restricted economy is going to contain strong traces of liberal thinking. None of these ideals seem inappropriate or contemptible in themselves and yet the liberal approach to peacebuilding has become the target of a number of critical studies (see, for example, Mac Ginty 2011; Paris 1997, 2010; Richmond 2009, 2011). There are undoubtedly good grounds for being skeptical about some of the grander claims made by liberal peace thinkers. It can be an approach that is insensitive to gender issues (Enloe 2004; Porter 2007). The same is true of class divisions. It is also notoriously blind to the power of ethnic and national identity. Liberal peacebuilding can also promote an unwarranted solidarist view of global issues in a world which has still stubbornly pluralist (Ramsbotham 2000). Nor is this the first time that liberalism is been behind a grand scheme to transform intra-state conflicts. Those who remember the Walt Rostow style modernization ideas of the early 1960s might be excused a shudder of *deja vu* when they read about a quote attributed to Francis Fukuyama where he hoped that 'someday Somalia would look like Norway. It's called progress' (Pfaff 2011: 69).

Yet there is a need to be cautious in characterizing peacebuilding practice since 1988 as 'liberal' in an uncritical manner. There are several reasons for this. The first is that it underestimates differences of approach within the liberal paradigm. Crudely put, the US approach is different from that of the EU, and both are different from the one adopted by the UN. The UN is very state-centric in its attitude to peacebuilding, whereas the EU is more post-Westphalian (Richmond et al. 2011). Nor is the UN a liberal organization in the way the EU could claim to be. Even within the UN we have noted peacebuilding practice has been influenced by a lack of consensus between the west and states such as China and Russia. Berdal (2009: 160) has argued that the creation of the Commission has actually 'reinforced divisions and tensions within the UN body politic' between the powers and between the North and the South. One of the major fault lines that has developed at the UN is that between the western democracies and states such as Russia and China who are more likely to resist any erosion of sovereignty. This is bound to affect the ability of the UN to create and sustain peacebuilding operations.

Dobbins et al. (2005) note that UN missions tend to have a smaller footprint and a lower profile than US-led missions. They are not as reliant on hard power, cost less and are not accompanied by the 'grandiloquent' rhetoric that is so characteristic of US deployments. They also have a higher success rate in promoting effective peacebuilding. After studying 16 cases between 1945 and 2005, Dobbins et al. (2005: xxv) provisionally note of 'the eight UN-led cases, seven are still at peace', whereas of 'the eight US-led cases, four are at peace'. The US has been 'slow to learn from its own past interventions (such as in Somalia) and to take advantage of the principles of peacebuilding best practice being developed by the UN' (Lambourne and Herro 2008: 275–6).

It should also be noted that if the way to strengthen peacebuilding is to put more emphasis on grass roots empowerment and civil society, then the strongest support for these ideas might come from the western liberal tradition. So Murthy (2007: 48) notes how it is governments such as the US that have pressed most for a stronger role for NGOs and local stakeholders during peacebuilding.

Furthermore, although peacebuilding has been heavily influenced by liberal ideas this does not mean the strategy has been implemented in accordance with these ideals. As W. Andy Knight (2003: 242) points out, such implementation 'suffers from vagueness and a general failure to distinguish properly between the ideal and the reality on the ground'. The 'reality on the ground' might not always be supportive of liberal beliefs and might involve complicity in developments that are far from liberal because of power considerations, self-interest or short-term/low-cost thinking. These might include empowering corrupt and undemocratic leaders or creating a rentier class in post-agreement societies. Tolerance is a sound liberal principle, but not when it involves acceptance of criminal networks or of human rights abusers (Teran 2007). In such cases we have peacebuilding that is liberal in its inspiration but not in its implementation. One does not have to be a realist to appreciate the warning that governments espousing liberal ideals may be using them as a cover for less altruistic motives.

A second feature of peacebuilding as it has evolved through the UN is its strong focus on structure-centered analysis. As we have already noted, the corollary of this is that there has been a relative disinterest in actor-centered approaches. Strategies such as reconciliation, truth recovery, inter-communal dialogue, building empathy and reducing prejudice do not receive much attention in official peacebuilding doctrine even though the UN and other actors might do such work under other headings. This bias in favor of structural change might be a more general characteristic of peacebuilding doctrine. As far back as the article where Galtung introduced the concept he recognizes that his approach 'does not take sufficiently into account the importance of attitudes, sentiments, emotions' (Galtung 1976). However, he hoped that a better peace structure will in itself induce more positive feelings and attitudes.

A final feature of how the concept of peacebuilding has evolved is its association with UN peace operations that are characterized by two important features: the focus is on the role of external actors and the interventions involve some highly invasive interventions. The close association of peacebuilding and peacekeeping at a very early stage of its development might have been justified on pragmatic grounds. However, it helped to form an impression that peacebuilding was something introduced by external actors into a violent conflict and that it was linked to the international deployment of military forces. In other words, it is something the 'international community' visits on others. So the archetypal peacebuilding cases that have received the most attention in the literature are operations in places such as Somalia, Liberia, Haiti, Bosnia Herzegovina, Afghanistan and Iraq. Important instances such as Northern Ireland, the Baltic states, Macedonia and South Africa tend to be ignored (see, for example, Miall 2007). Here the peace process was led by local actors and the level of international involvement was less invasive and forceful; more like peace support than peacebuilding. As a result they come closer to the criterion set by Lederach (1997) that good peacebuilding practice should be elicitive rather than prescriptive. By underestimating these examples we could be trying to learn positive lessons about peacebuilding from the wrong cases.

References

Annan, K. (2005) *In Larger Freedom: Towards Development, Security and Human Rights for All*, New York: United Nations, A/59/2005.

Appiah, K.A. (2004) 'The election and America's future', *New York Review of Books,* Vol. LI, No. 17, November 4, 2004, p. 6.

Berdal, M. (2009) *Building Peace After War,* Adelphi Papers 49: 407, London: Routledge.

Boutros-Ghali, B. (1992) *An Agenda for Peace*, New York: United Nations.

Boutros-Ghali, B. (1995) *A Supplement to An Agenda for Peace*, New York: United Nations.

Boutros-Ghali, B. (1996) *An Agenda for Democratization*, New York: United Nations.

Chandler, D. (2002) *From Kosovo to Kabul (and Beyond): Human Rights and International Intervention*, London: Pluto Press.

Chetail, V. (2009) 'Introduction: Post-conflict Peacebuilding – Ambiguity and Identity', in Chetail, V. (ed.) *Post-Conflict Peacebuilding: A Lexicon*, Oxford: Oxford University Press.

Cutillo, A. (2006) *International Assistance to Countries Emerging from Violent Conflict: A Review of Fifteen years of Interventions and the Future of Peacebuilding*, New York: International Peace Academy.

Dobbins, J. et al. (2005) *The UN's Role in Nation-Building: From the Congo to Iraq*, Santa Monica: Rand Corporation.

Doyle, M.W. (1983) 'Kant, liberal legacies and foreign affairs', *Philosophy and Public Affairs* 12: 205–235.

Doyle, M.W. and Sambanis, N. (2000) 'International Peacebuilding: A Theoretical and Quantitative Analysis', *American Political Science Review* 94: 779–801.

Enloe, C. (2004) *The Curious Feminist* Part 3, Berkeley: University of California Press.

Fisher, R.J. (1993) 'The Potential for Peacebuilding: Forging a Bridge from Peacekeeping to Peacemaking', *Peace and Change* 18: 247–250.

Galtung, J. (1969) 'Violence, Peace and Peace Research', *Journal of Peace Research* 6: 167–191.

Galtung, J. (1976) 'Three realistic approaches to peace: peacekeeping, peacemaking and peacebuilding', *Impact of Science on Society* 26: 103–115.

Galtung, J. (1985) 'Twenty-five Years of Peace Research: Ten Challenges and Some Responses' *Journal of Peace Research* 22: 129–140.

Goulding, M. (1993) 'The evolution of United Nations peacekeeping' *International Affairs* 69: 451–464.

Harbottle, M. (1980) 'The strategy of third party interventions in conflict resolution', *International Journal* 35: 118–131.

Hoffmann, S. (1996) *The Ethics and Politics of Humanitarian Intervention*, Notre Dame: University of Notre Dame Press.

International Commission on Intervention and State Sovereignty (2001) *The Responsibility to Protect*, Ottawa: International Development Research Centre.

Knight, W.A. (2003) 'Evaluating recent trends in peacebuilding research', *International Relations of the Asia-Pacific* 3: 241–264.

Kumar, K. (ed.) (1997) *Rebuilding Societies After Civil War*, Boulder: Lynne Rienner.

Lambourne, W. and Herro, A. (2008) 'Peacebuilding Theory and the United Nations Peacebuilding Commission: Implications for non-UN Interventions', *Global Change, Peace and Security* 20: 275–289.

Lederach, J.P. (1997) *Building Peace: Sustainable Reconciliation in Divided Societies*, Washington DC: United States Institute of Peace.

Mac Ginty, R. (2011) *International Peacebuilding and Local Forms of Resistance: Hybrid Forms of Peace*, Basingstoke: Palgrave.

Mayall, J. (2000) 'Democracy and international society', *International Affairs* 76: 61–75.

Maynard, K. (1999) *Healing Communities in Conflict*, New York: Columbia University Press.

Miall, H. (2007) 'The EU and the Peacebuilding Commission', *Cambridge Review of International Affairs* 20: 29–45.

Murthy, C.S.R. (2007) 'New Phase in UN Reforms: Establishment of the Peacebuilding Commission and Human Rights Council', *International Studies* 44: 39–56.

Paris, R. (1997) 'Peacebuilding and the Limits of Liberal Internationalism', *International Security* 22: 54–89.

Paris, R. (2002) 'International Peacebuilding and the "mission civilisatrice"', *Review of International Studies* 28: 637–656.

Paris, R. (2010) 'Saving liberal peacebuilding', *Review of International Studies*, 36: 337–365.

Pfaff, W. (2011) 'How much progress have we made?', *New York Review of Books* LV111: 8, pp. 69–71.

Porter, E. (2007) *Peacebuilding: Women in International Perspective*, London: Routledge.

Pugh, M. (ed.) (2000) *The Regeneration of War-Torn Societies*, Basingstoke: Macmillan.

Pugh, M. and Cobble, M. (2001) 'Non-nationalist Voting in Bosnian Municipal Elections: Implications for Democracy and Peacebuilding', *Journal of Peace Research* 38: 1 27–47.

Ramsbotham, O. (2000) 'Reflections on UN Post-settlement Peacebuilding', in Woodhouse, T. and Ramsbotham, O. (eds) *Peacekeeping and Conflict Resolution*, London: Frank Cass, pp. 169–189.

Ramsbotham, O. and Woodhouse, T. (1996) *Humanitarian Intervention in Contemporary Conflict: A Reconceptualization*, Cambridge: Polity Press.

Reychler, L. and Paffenholz, T. (eds) (2001) *Peacebuilding: A Field Guide*, Boulder: Lynne Rienner.

Richmond, O.P. (2009) 'Beyond Liberal Peace?', in Newman, E., Paris, R. and Richmond, O.P. (eds) *New Perspectives on Liberal Peacebuilding*, Tokyo: United Nations University Press.

Richmond, O.P. (2011) *A Post-Liberal Peace*, London: Routledge.

Richmond, O.P., Bjorkdahl, A. and Kappler, S. (2011) 'The Emerging EU Peacebuilding Framework: Confirming of Transcending Liberal Peacebuilding', *Cambridge Review of International Affairs* 24: 37–41.

Roberts, A. (1993) 'The United Nations and International Security', *Survival* 35: 3–30.

Rupesinghe, K. (1998) 'Coping with internal conflicts: teaching the elephant to dance', in Alger, C.F. (ed.) *The Future of the United Nations System: Potential for the Twenty-First Century*, Tokyo: UN University Press.

Schivelbusch, W. (2001) *The Culture of Defeat: On National Trauma, Mourning, and Recovery*, London: Granta.

Sisk, T.D. (2001) *Peacemaking in Civil Wars: Obstacles, Options and Opportunities*, Kroc Institute Occasional Paper 20. Notre Dame: University of Notre Dame.

Smith, D. (2004) *Towards a Strategic Framework for Peacebuilding: Getting Their Act Together*, Oslo: Ministry of Foreign Affairs.

Snyder, J. (2000) *From Voting to Violence: Democratization and Nationalist Conflict*, New York: W.W. Norton.

Spielmann, M. (1986) 'If Peace Comes – Future Expectations of Israeli Children and Youth', *Journal of Peace Research* 23: 51–67.

Teran, N.S. (2007) *Peacebuilding and Organized Crime: The Cases of Kosovo and Liberia*, Swiss Peace Working Paper 1/2007, Berne: Swiss Peace Foundation.

Tharoor, S. (1995–6) 'Should UN Peacekeeping go "Back to Basics"', *Survival* 37: 52–64.

United Nations (1994) *An Agenda for Development*, New York: United Nations, A/48/935.

United Nations (1996) *An Inventory of Post-Conflict Peacebuilding Activity*, New York: United Nations.

United Nations (2000) *Report of the Panel on United Nations Peace Operations*, New York: United Nations, A/55/305.

United Nations (2004) *A More Secure World: Our Shared Responsibility*, Report of the High Level Panel on Threats, Challenges and Change, New York: United Nations.

United Nations (2006) *Inventory United Nations Capacity in Peacebuilding*, New York: United Nations.

United Nations (2010) *Review of United Nations Peacebuilding Architecture*, New York: United Nations, A/64/868.

Wheeler, N.J. (2000) *Saving Strangers: Humanitarian Intervention in International Society*, Oxford: Oxford University Press.

3

THE LIMITS OF PEACEBUILDING THEORY

Gerald M. Steinberg

Academic interest in and research focused on peace studies and peacebuilding has grown steadily in recent decades, producing a myriad of articles in scholarly journals, books, conferences, workshops, and university programs dedicated to this field. Researchers, practitioners, and officials of funding agencies – government and private – are naturally drawn to the hope or promise for finding a cure for the scourge of war, both between states and within states.

However, in direct contrast to the growth of what has been cynically called 'the peace industry', the situation on the ground remains quite grim. Few stable agreements have been implemented, and many of the major post-Cold War international and ethno-national conflicts continue. Where the violence has subsided, this can often be attributed to a major use of force, as in Sri Lanka and East Timor. In Kosovo, a large peacekeeping presence has provided some stability, but the evidence indicates that enmity between societies and populations remains significant. Conflicts in central Africa include periodic outbursts of extreme violence, Cyprus remains divided, relations between India and Pakistan are volatile, and the Israeli–Palestinian conflict continues to simmer, escalating periodically into wider warfare, as in Gaza in December 2008. And while a few conflicts seem to have been settled, such as Northern Ireland and Angola, the factors involved are unclear and have been not convincingly generalized.

To some degree, the enormous disconnect between the ongoing investment in academic peacebuilding, on the one hand, and the dismal outcomes on the other, can be explained by the enthusiasm of the would-be peacemakers. Many of the theories, models, papers, books, simulations, etc. under the banner of political conflict resolution are guided, written, and produced by researcher-practitioners with strong personal commitments to peace.

As will be shown in this chapter, advocates and enthusiasts often underestimate the fundamental differences between societies – particularly the behavioral and normative distinctions between liberal pluralist democracies and groups dominated by an intolerant ideological, nationalist or religious framework. The social-psychological approach to peace generally assumes the existence of a common foundation based on shared human values. Contact theory, dialogue, cross-cultural communications and interaction, as well as forgiveness, reconciliation, and even quasi-legal arguments (or at least legal discourse) are among the main dimensions used in this approach, from which mutual understanding and compromise are expected to flow (Ellison and Powers 1994).

Similarly, the approaches based on democratic peace theories, which are used to justify the liberal interventionist policies pursued by the US and Europe, have also produced meager results. The creation of stable democratic institutions and accompanying political cultures based on pluralism and tolerance has proven very illusive. As in the case of the social-psychological models, the enthusiasts have greatly overstated the likely impacts, and underestimated the obstacles.

While the Hobbesian state of nature and 'war of all against all' is ideologically anathema to hopeful peacemakers and their academic supporters, the evidence overwhelmingly demonstrates the validity of this framework for many conflict situations. The sources of violent identity conflict – in the form of inter-ethnic and inter-religious and similar disputes – remain as intense in the twenty-first century as they were thousands of years ago. Harold Saunders, a former senior diplomat in the US State Department and a strong supporter of the social-psychological approach to peace, observed that 'until relationships are changed, deep-rooted human conflicts are not likely to be resolved' (Saunders 1999: 31). But none of the current theories and models have been demonstrated as reliable means for changing political relationships or the Hobbesian condition, leaving conflict management based on deterrence and defense as the best alternatives to the distant hopes for peace.

Applying social-psychology to international conflict

Attempts to develop consistent and successful models for international peacemaking and peacebuilding have a long history, but few long-term successes. Indeed, the most peaceful periods of history have generally been due to the dominance of major empires – thus the terms and sometimes the nostalgia for *pax Romana*, *pax Britannica* and even the Cold War, when the US and the Soviet Union divided the world and generally controlled conflicts, preventing them from spiraling out of control. These imperial periods of peace reflect the Hobbesian model of the *Leviathan* (1660) – the superpower, or powers, who impose international order.

In contrast, Immanuel Kant's model of *Perpetual Peace* (1795) argued that the Hobbesian state of nature could be overcome through a combination of republican governments accountable to their citizens, international law to regulate state behavior, and economic interdependence to create interests in maintaining peace and avoiding the costs of war. This model developed by Kant and his followers evolved into democratic peace theory, as embodied in the League of Nations experiment, and then refined in the establishment of the United Nations. The Kantian model is also considered the foundation of the European Union, which has prevented a return to violence on this continent for six decades. While Western Europe has been an important exception as a zone of peace, the efforts to export the European experience to other regions have not succeeded. (The starting conditions in post-World War II Europe – the total defeat of the Axis powers and the long occupation of Germany by the Allied powers – were unique, and not applicable to other conflict regions and conditions.)

Going beyond Hobbesian realism and Kantian republican internationalism, new approaches to peacebuilding, based on social-psychological theories, emerged towards the end of the Cold War. This coincided with the emergence of social-psychology as an academic discipline and the basis of both individual therapy and the manipulation of social policies. Academics became enthusiastic supporters of this approach, including Kelman (2000), Kriesberg (2001), and Lederach (1997), joined by practitioner-diplomats such as Burton (1969), Montville (1989, 1993), Saunders (1999, 2001), and many others. This path to peace based on or centrally supported by dialogues, peace camps, and basic human contact, has led to large-scale funding from governments and major foundations.

Much of this activity is reinforced by professional and personal accolades and awards, accompanied by high media profiles. Audiences are drawn to experts promising hope for 'breakthroughs', and by messages of conciliation and images of peace.

However, this enthusiasm has not been accompanied by empirical results. Despite numerous workshops, dialogues, peace camps for youth, joint textbook writing exercises, and other forms of personal and group interaction in Sri Lanka, the Balkans, Cyprus and the Arab–Israeli contexts, peacebuilding efforts have not produced the desired impact. These conflicts either continue to rage, or have been ended (perhaps temporarily) by force, and not via agreement based on compromise and understanding. Northern Ireland appears to be a singular exception, but even here, the evidence that contact and dialogue were central causes in this outcome is unclear.

Indeed, as will be demonstrated below, the methodological dimension of the behavioral and empirical research necessary to measure impacts of social-psychological models in international conflict has been neglected, to understate the situation. In many cases, the mere fact of a contact event taking place – such as a summer camp or theater group with Israelis and Palestinians, workshops involving Serbs and Kosovars, or a track-two conference – is considered to be significant and sufficient, in and of itself. In other examples, anecdotes and impressions substitute for measurements of results.

In scholarly articles on attitude change and reframing in such conflicts, the measurements are often based on observing small groups during short periods of interaction, and the impacts are difficult to discern. Furthermore, the claims that these impacts can be extrapolated to the macro-level of societies, or to the leaders and decision makers, are also based more on enthusiasm than on careful and critical examination of the evidence. The results of 'meta studies' which attempt to integrate a number of inconclusive small-scale analyses involving limited groups, are highly ambiguous (Pettigrew and Tropp 2000; Maoz 2011).

In addition, assertions built on the foundations of contact theory in peacebuilding are generally not falsifiable, meaning that analyses do not include a counter-hypothesis which allows for the possibility of refutation. Many of the conclusions based on workshops, simulations and other forms of interaction that claim success in attitude change among participants, did not consider or measure the impact of alternative explanations and factors. In case studies such as on Northern Ireland, whose authors claim that people-to-people interaction was central in resolution of conflict, the claims of success for the social-psychological interventions (Fitzduff 1996, 2002) erase the other factors that might explain the results, such as economic dimensions, or suppression of terror by military force. Similarly, the 1979 Egyptian–Israeli peace treaty was negotiated by Sadat and Begin in the aftermath of the 1973 war that left both countries badly damaged, and without the assistance of peacebuilding workshops and dialogues (Stein 1989).

The following analysis focuses on the evolution of these efforts, examining the theoretical assumptions, as well as the efforts to apply them in specific conflict situations and environments. Evaluation methodologies, to the extent that these exist, will also be considered.

As will become clear, despite the enthusiasm of its supporters, the empirical results have been relatively meager. There is little if any evidence for most of the claims that international conflicts have been fundamentally transformed as a result of the social-psychological approach to peacebuilding. In some cases, these well-intentioned efforts have resulted in counterproductive outcomes by adding to the intensity of the conflict, reifying negative stereotypes and one-sided narratives, and leading to increased violence. Images of implacable hostility are strengthened when participants in dialogues reject the legitimacy of the other side, or repeat stereotypes and conflict-promoting narratives (Hamburger 1994; Hanssen 2001).

Origins: Allport's contact hypothesis

In 1954, Gordon W. Allport (1954) developed the 'contact hypothesis', arguing that through direct interpersonal and intergroup communications, as well as shared experiences, racial prejudice in the United States could be overcome. According to this theory, success required the following conditions: equal status, shared objectives, ability to develop significant social relations; and wider societal support. Through such interactions, negative stereotypes resulting from social, economic, religious and other barriers could be replaced by discovery of common human traits and values in 'the other' (Amir 1976).

Allport's model led to the development of strategies of intergroup contact in efforts to eliminate prejudice and ethnic tensions through attitude changes (often measured through surveys and observation). In the early stages, this approach relied on casual interactions, meaning that they were largely unstructured, and the simple act of bringing together members of different groups (primarily Americans from different racial and ethnic groups) was expected to promote attitude transformation and the removal of prejudice.

In efforts to apply and measure the impacts and outcomes, the main variables included time (short and isolated interactions of a few hours or perhaps days, summer camps of a few weeks, and more intensive repeated interaction over months or years, in different settings); the degree of functionalist interaction (from integrated sports teams and theater groups, to joint economic enterprises); and the age of the participants (children and teenagers are deemed to be more receptive to long-term attitude change than adults) (Rothbart and John 1985).

Early efforts to apply Allport's approach can be seen in some aspects of US–Soviet negotiations during the Cold War, particularly after the 1962 Cuban Missile Crisis brought the two superpowers to the brink of mutual nuclear destruction. During the arms limitation talks that followed, which resulted in the 1972 SALT and ABM treaties, the host diplomats in Vienna and Helsinki arranged for cultural events and river cruises that enabled the negotiators to mix casually and communicate informally.

This unstructured interaction was perceived as a means of breaking down cultural and political barriers between the two sides and thereby reducing fears while promoting greater flexibility (Voorhees 2002; Newhouse 1973). The development of epistemic communities of scientists and arms controllers, based on common experiences, perspectives and professional ties, as postulated by Emanuel Adler (1992), is seen to have contributed to this process.

However, a detailed examination of the evidence raises numerous questions regarding the causes and factors that led to the agreements. During this period, the roles of unofficial or 'back-channel' communications channels and strategic calculations were central to the successful negotiations, and suggest that the interpersonal relations and epistemic links played a secondary role, at most (Kissinger 1979, 1982).

Furthermore, social interactions involving elites and officials from the US and the Soviet Union in the context of formal negotiations are not readily applicable to instances of civil war or violent ethno-national or religious conflicts, in which there is often no framework for interaction between the masses of any kind. (The absence of bridges linking elite contacts with mass interactions in the context of peacebuilding efforts, and the implications of this situation, will be examined below.)

Taking a different approach, beginning in the 1960s, John Burton, an Australian diplomat, began to apply 'needs theory' and rational problem-solving approaches to peace efforts. Political conflict is explained as resulting from conditions in which universal human needs, such as security, identity, or acceptance, are absent. This approach was distinguished from traditional theories of international negotiation, which focused on state and interest-based conflict, as well as power relationships. According to Burton (1969, 1987), international conflict would be resolved through processes and agreements that satisfied these basic human needs.

Herbert Kelman, a social-psychologist at Harvard University, adopted and expanded Burton's model, combining it with Allport's contact hypothesis to international conflict (Ruggiero and Kelman 1999). (Kelman was the Harvard Professor of Social Ethics, a position previously held by Allport.) Unlike Burton, Kelman had no training in international relations and no diplomatic experience, but used his personal and family experience to argue that the group dynamics methodologies developed by psychologists such as Kurt Lewin, and combined with Burton's models, were the keys to resolving protracted international conflicts (Kelman 2004).

As a social-psychologist, Kelman's analysis was far removed from both Hobbes and Kant, and based on an intense, if empirically unsupported belief that 'a long-term resolution of the conflict requires development of a transcendent identity for the two peoples that does not threaten the particularistic identity of each. … each side perceives the other as a source of some of its own negative identity elements, especially a view of the self as victim and as victimizer.'

To overcome 'the negative interdependence of the two identities', Kelman brought Israeli and Palestinian elites to problem-solving workshops beginning in the 1970s. The goal was to develop 'positive elements in the relationship' through 'equal-status interactions that provide the parties the opportunity to "negotiate" their identities …' (Kelman 1999). Through the Program on International Conflict Analysis and Resolution (PICAR), he expanded the workshop approach to other ethno-national conflicts. In this framework, current and former government officials, military commanders, top journalists, academics and other policy makers and molders of public opinion were brought together. The personal interactions, building on the contact theory and Burton's framework, were combined with exercises focusing on the perceived conflict issues.

Although elite workshops, dialogues and similar activities were conducted for more than thirty years, the results have not been examined independently or systematically, and contributions towards peace, if any, cannot be demonstrated empirically. Instead, these projects expanded regardless of the outcomes due to the ability of Kelman and his counterparts to generate a great deal of enthusiasm and publicity, which were central to receiving significant funding. Major foundations and governments made generous grants, expecting that these activities would produce important breakthroughs towards resolving protracted international conflicts. Such activities are sold as the means 'to replace the typical conflict frame of win–lose with a win–win frame' (Maoz 2004a: 233).

Academics, such as Ronald Fisher (1983, 1989, 1997a, 1997b, 2001), Azar (1990, 2002) and many others, as well as former diplomats, including Montville (1990a) and Saunders (1999), received funding to hold dialogues involving officials and molders of elite opinion related to the Arab–Israeli conflict, Sri Lanka, Northern Ireland, the Balkans, Cyprus, Sierra Leone, and many other regions.

In parallel, law school faculty entered the field of international negotiation, also promoting elite dialogues and workshops, couched in the discourse of law and legal philosophy. As in the case of social-psychologists, the law-based theories and models assumed, without analysis or evidence, that they could simply transfer conflict amelioration techniques and experience from family, business and other contexts to international political and identity conflicts. In 1983, Professor Roger Fisher founded the Project on Negotiation (PON) within the Harvard Law School, and with William Ury, published its manifesto, *Getting To Yes: Negotiating Agreement Without Giving In* (1981), which combined the tools of rational decision making, social-psychology and contact theory. Like Kelman's PICAR program, PON also began raising funds and conducting workshops related to a number of international and ethno-national conflicts, including the Middle East.

Pre-negotiation and transformation of elite perception

Theories of attitude change as a key part of conflict resolution are inherently linked to stages of the transformation process, with a particular emphasis on the pre-negotiation phase. As Schiff (2008: 389) has noted, 'the pre-negotiation process is designed to change the beliefs and expectations of decision-makers, thereby enabling them to consider options entailing negotiations and compromise. A change in beliefs and expectations, or the absence thereof, is assumed to be critical for the success or failure of subsequent negotiations' (citing Bercovitch 1991; Druckman and Hopmann 1989; Zartman 1996).

Pre-negotiation in ethno-national conflicts is expected to begin after significant events, such as a major war resulting in a mutually hurting stalemate. Other models consider the potential for positive changes in the form of mutually enticing opportunities, leading to pre-negotiation (Stein 1989; Zartman 1989; Mitchell 1996). At this stage, the conflicting parties, often with the assistance of a mediator, begin to consider alternatives to the ongoing zero-sum conflict, and signal a willingness to explore compromise win–win outcomes.

In the pre-negotiation stages, analysts such as Mitchell (1996) emphasize the importance of developing 'internal ripeness' for compromise and attitude change at the societal level. Schiff (2008: 389) observes that '[t]he required change in the beliefs and expectations is effected through several functions', including 'establishing mechanisms that facilitate perceptual changes', building mutual trust, and granting legitimacy.

The process of transforming a 'winning mentality to a conciliating mentality', to use Zartman's terminology (1989), is often seen as requiring active third-party involvement. Third parties – diplomats or academic practitioners, for example – assume activist roles, seeking 'to provide the setting, create the atmosphere, establish the norms, and offer occasional interventions that make it possible for such a process to evolve' (Kelman 1992: 65 cited by Schiff 2010; Maoz 2005). In structured frameworks, the cross-group interactions are intentionally controlled and manipulated in order to 'influence perceptions, opinions, and reactions' (Maoz 2004a).

In another variation, track-two dialogues are a form of unofficial or semi-official diplomacy, in which elites and opinion leaders from opposing sides in international conflicts meet to discuss substance. As Schiff (2010) has shown, the objective of such activities is 'to trigger changes in relationships and perceptions that are essential for disputants to recognize the necessity of an official negotiation process, especially in ethno-national or identity conflicts' (citing Davidson and Montville 1981: 145–157).

The participants are expected to focus on 'developing strategies, influencing public opinions, and organizing human and material resources in ways that might help resolve the conflict' (Montville 1991: 262; Saunders 1999, 2001). 'The assumption is that if the conflicting parties overcome their psychological obstacles to negotiation, they will consent to meet for official negotiations and will conduct such negotiations on the basis of shared interests, which is an essential element in conflict resolution' (Schiff 2010 citing Burton 1969, 1987; Kelman 1987; Montville 1990b).

Many of the properties associated with ripeness, pre-negotiation and associated contact-based peacebuilding activities remain ambiguous. In the Sri Lankan and Israeli–Palestinian frameworks, for example, the fact that dialogues between officials or elites were taking place was used to claim ripeness. When these discussions broke down, and violent conflict resumed or increased, the absence of impact from dialogues and other contact-related activities became clear.

In some cases, third-party involvement has gone beyond indirect encouragement of dialogue. For example, after failing to persuade top Israeli and Palestinian leaders to meet and 'overcome their psychological obstacles' under his direction, Kelman took the role of practitioner-scholar to an extreme by meeting directly and publically with PLO leader Yassir Arafat in 1983. Kelman gained a great deal of publicity for himself by publishing his 'professional analysis' in an academic journal, claiming that Arafat had changed, and was signaling a readiness for peace. To Israeli and other skeptics, Kelman explained 'the continuing ambiguity and inconsistency of these signals' (including ongoing terror attacks) as resulting from 'political and psychological' factors. 'Analysis of Arafat's cognitive style and image of the enemy, as revealed in two lengthy conversations with the author, reinforces the hypothesis that he has the capacity and will negotiate an agreement with Israel, based on mutual recognition and peaceful coexistence, if offered necessary incentives and reassurances' (Kelman 1983: 203). In this way, Kelman placed himself directly at the center of the Israeli–Palestinian relationship, substituting his personal aspirations and hopes for those of the protagonists, in a highly counter-productive manner. Twenty years later, after failed peace efforts and extensive violence, nothing remained of Kelman's 'academic' analysis of Arafat (Ross 2004) and Israeli contacts were largely confined to fringe groups (Seliktar 2009: 13–14).

Among the reasons for such direct involvement, academic practitioners often refer to the need for symmetry in power relations in order to change attitudes in conflict situations, based on Allport's emphasis on equal status. In this framework, third parties are encouraged to act as artificial power balancers by aiding the weaker parties in order to promote attitude change and other peacebuilding processes (Rouhana and Korper 1997; Maoz 2004b). Among some researchers in the field of peacebuilding, this emphasis is reinforced by post-colonial ideology in which power is associated with aggression, and weakness is linked to morality and victimhood (Steinberg 2007).

However, assessing relative power is highly subjective, and the conflicting parties compete to present themselves as weak and threatened by the power advantage of the other, in order to gain the support of third parties. Different forms of power include military capabilities, including standing armies, advanced technology, and asymmetric warfare; economics, demographics, alliances, and 'soft power' dimensions. With the exception of extreme cases, such as South Africa under apartheid, there are no reliable and accepted measures for comparing between these dimensions. As a result, peacebuilding models that give significant weight to perceived power imbalances, as well as efforts to intervene in order to offset such perceptions, are highly problematic.

Bottom-up approaches and people-to-people (P2P) programs

As the number and extent of peacebuilding workshops and dialogues increased, without noticeable reductions in intergroup violence, some analysts recognized that the narrow focus on elite activities was insufficient to resolve protracted religious, ethno-national and other forms of identity conflicts. To supplement the elite or top-down exchanges, bottom-up forms of interaction and contact were developed in order to change social attitudes and perceptions at the societal levels. Theorists argued that without extensive support for concessions and compromises with the enemy, agreements among leaders would be readily undermined by 'spoilers' and would not stand the test of time.

This diagnosis led to efforts to promote the wider societal transformations viewed as necessary for resolving religious, ethno-national and other forms of identity conflicts, in the form of unofficial diplomacy, and 'people to people' (P2P) or grass-roots activities. Such processes were expected to create the broad empathy and understanding necessary to cut across the divisions, thereby, according to the theory, promoting collective attitude changes necessary for peace (Chigas 2007: 559–560).

A number of P2P workshops were held after the Rwandan genocide, bringing Hutus and Tutsis together 'to promote psychological healing from the traumatic effects of the genocide as well as skills in promoting healing in others ... [and] more broadly, a more positive orientation toward members of the other group' (Staub and Pearlman 2000). Similar programs were held in the context of the East Timor and other ethno-national conflicts.

During the Palestinian–Israeli Oslo Process (1993–2000), P2P was given a central role in peacemaking, with funding from the governments of Norway, the US, European governments and elsewhere. 'Its goal was to cultivate grassroots contacts between Israeli and Palestinian civil societies and lay the foundations for a culture of peace and coexistence. People-to-People appeared in the context of an attempt to change the dehumanized and stereotyped perceptions of "the other" society and nurture empathy, personalization and recognition of each others' goals and needs' (Perlman and Nasser-Najjab 2006). According to one study published in 2004, over 275 'contact programs' involving Jewish and Arab–Israelis were being conducted in this period, and designed to involve different age groups, professions, etc. (Abu-Nimer 2004: 406). Activities included sports encounters, joint theater and art-oriented programs, 'peace radio' stations, and other formats.

A number of non-governmental organizations (NGOs) and quasi-autonomous NGOs (QUANGOs) promoting similar agendas often received funding to hold P2P workshops and dialogues, including PRIO (Peace Research Institute Oslo) which is supported by the government of Norway, and Search for Common Ground, which is based in the United States. The organizations involved, as well as their funding agencies, tend to promote themselves and advertise their achievements, without independent evaluation.

Despite the extent of such activities, no concrete and measurable impact has been discerned. Peacebuilding based on P2P and unofficial diplomacy share many of the limitations found in the elite level application of contact theory in the context of intense identity conflicts and violence. Attitude changes of individuals are difficult to measure, time-limited, and generally confined to a very small group of self-selected participants. There are fundamental and inherent problems in transforming micro-level changes in perceptions, attitudes, and policy positions towards the conflict, to the extent that they occur, into macro-level political changes (Schiff 2010 citing Burton 1987; Kelman 2000, 2002; Azar 2002; Fisher and Kelman 2003; Fisher 2007).

Many P2P programs placed a particular emphasis on bringing together students from opposing sides in international conflicts, in order to equip the next generation with the tools for conflict resolution, as imagined in the social-psychological approach (Connolly, Fitzpatrick, Gallagher and Harris 2006). Harvard Law School's 'Middle East Negotiation Initiative' includes a major negotiation skills training program for Jewish and Arab students (Harvard PON 2012).

The 'Seeds of Peace' program was one of the largest (in terms of number of participants) and most publicized youth-oriented P2P projects based on the contact hypothesis. Its founding paralleled the 1993 Oslo agreements (the Declaration of Principles) between the Israeli and the Palestinian leadership. The stated objective was 'to give Arab and Israeli youngsters the opportunity to look at the world afresh, to rise above the hatreds of their elders, and to develop a shared desire to create a new world free of hostility and violence' (Richard Solomon in Wallach 2000: ix).

This framework involved bringing 'hundreds of youngsters from very different backgrounds living, playing, and working together for three weeks in the beautiful woods of Maine' (Wallach 2000: ix). In the three-week program, campers were expected to discover 'how much they have to gain by building the friendships that are the seeds of a constructive future'. The interactions involved sporting events (teams were composed of participants from the opposing sides) as well as daily 'coexistence sessions' where 'the youngsters argue about their positions and vent their anger and frustration…'. Ignorance and misinformation were to be replaced by 'mutual understanding and humanized relationships', discovering a 'shared human reality that transcends differences in background'.

Repeating the claims of the contact hypothesis, Seeds of Peace leaders declared: the simple fact of living with youngsters from the other side 'does much to dispel prejudice' (Wallach 2000: x). If each camper could '"make one friend" with a camper from among the "enemy"', the effort was deemed a success. Stereotypes would break down 'when you actually learn to like them, share personal secrets, or find common ground' (Wallach 2000: xi).

As is the case with many such programs, no methodology was applied to assess results (see the generalized analysis below). Organizers declared that 'the Seeds of Peace program has received remarkable results. Almost everyone who learns about this program finds Seeds of Peace inspiring. Even hardened politicians, skeptical diplomats, and world-weary journalists find themselves sensing a more hopeful future ...' (Wallach 2000: ix).

However, in the absence of detailed evidence of success and systematic evaluation, such claims cannot be taken at face value. Indeed, as the conflicts continue at many levels, the impacts of such programs are difficult to discern. The inspiration to overcome differences and make peace, inculcated during two decades of programming – the earliest participants are now adults – and involving thousands of individuals had no measurable impact on the conflicts. Even if hundreds, or even thousands of individuals had undergone significant and long-lasting attitudinal changes, these failed to influence millions or tens of millions of citizens on the two sides of the numerous conflicts.

Reconciliation, forgiveness and peacebuilding

A further extension of the bottom-up social-psychological and contact hypothesis approach to peacebuilding is reflected in the application of theories of victimhood, forgiveness and reconciliation in international conflict. In a skeptical observation, Hermann (2004: 40) notes that 'the most salient term that conflict-resolution experts have recently elaborated ... is that of "reconciliation" ... as the panacea that can rescue us from the shortcomings of the theories and practical blueprints for getting from war to peace'.

The Truth and Reconciliation Commission, applied during the transition from apartheid in South Africa, is often cited as a highly successful demonstration. Under this mechanism, individuals on all sides of the conflict were given 'the chance to express their regret at failing to prevent human rights violations and to demonstrate their commitment to reconciliation. ... Guilt for wrongdoing needs to be translated into positive commitment to building a better society – the healthiest and most productive form of atonement' (South Africa Ministry of Justice 1995). Expanding from this experience, various forms of 'truth and reconciliation' processes have been proposed and, in some cases, applied to a variety of other peacebuilding efforts, including Rwanda, the Balkans, and Colombia (Hayner 2001; Schaap 2007).

This approach is an extension of the collective (rather than elite-based) people-to-people approach to attitude change in international conflict resolution, with a particular emphasis on claims of historical injustice and efforts to promote forgiveness and reconciliation. Joseph Montville (1989) wrote of a 'healing function' to reverse the impact of 'victimhood' and trauma among populations involved in political conflicts. 'After well over a decade as a practitioner [in the US State Department] and theorist in political conflict resolution, the author is convinced that healing and reconciliation in violent ethnic and religious conflicts depend on a process of transactional contrition and forgiveness between aggressors and victims which is indispensable to the establishment of a mutual acceptance and reasonable trust. This process depends on joint analysis of the history of the conflict, recognition of injustices and resulting historic wounds, and acceptance of moral responsibility where due' (Montville 1993: 112).

Similarly, Lederach (1997) published a model of peace based on 'truth (open expression of the past); mercy (forgiveness); justice (restitution and social restructuring); and peace (common future, well being, and security for all the parties)'. Kelman (1999) revised his social-psychological approach by publishing a model of 'positive peace' which incorporated reconciliation.

Amidst a myriad of definitions, Maoz (2004a: 225) sought to bring clarity to the concept: '[r]econciliation is a cluster of cognitive and emotional processes through which individuals, groups, societies and states come to accept relationships of cooperation, concession and peace in situations of former conflict' (Azar et al., 1999; Staub and Pearlman 2000; Bar-Tal 2000; Bar-Tal and Bennink 2004; Maoz 2000; Miari 1999; Kriesberg 1998). Public acts and ceremonies, highlighting the reconciliation theme, are important elements in many models (Bargal and Sivan 2004). But, Hermann questions the degree to which leaders are able to 'repent or forgive for the body politic they represent' (2004: 43).

Furthermore, the context of South African apartheid was unique, with universally acknowledged injustices, and most attempts to generalize from this case ignore the details. In contrast, in most international, ethno-national and religious conflicts, such as in Northern Ireland, Cyprus, the Middle East, the Balkans, Armenia and Azerbijan, Turks and Kurds, etc., each group claims victimhood and their respective narratives attribute aggressor status to the enemies. These labels, and the processes of forgiveness and building of trust, then become additional arenas for conflict.

Thus, as Hermann (2004) demonstrates, 'the notion of reconciliation cannot serve as the key concept for cracking the enigma of peacemaking and peace stabilizing'. The definitions and frameworks are highly variable, making 'reconciliation little more than a buzzword, an amenable but loose framework for different contents depending on the user's disciplinary affiliation, cultural background, or the particularities of the cases at hand' (Hermann 2004: 41).

In practice, and given the differences in historical narratives and perceptions of justice, the attempts to implement such processes can be counterproductive, themselves generating additional conflict rather than the reverse (Schimmel 2004; Hamburger 1994; Hanssen 2001).

Beyond enthusiasm: Downsizing expectations

Efforts to apply contact hypothesis and wider social-psychological theories to peacebuilding begin with the premise that conflict resolution techniques used in families and business disputes are readily transferable to complex, protracted and violent ethno-national and religious conflicts. This transfer erases the Hobbesian 'state of nature' and inherent anarchy of international relations, as well as the degree to which collective religious, ethnic and other affinities and hatreds are fundamentally different from other conflict frameworks. This reality cannot be overcome primarily through dialogue, understanding and 'talking to the enemy', whether at the elite or grass-roots levels.

In examining this approach, Pettigrew (2011: 185) acknowledges that 'institutions and societies are social systems and, as such, are more than the sum of their individual parts. Moreover, macro-units, too, have unique properties of their own … For instance, when psychoanalysts discuss the individual's proclivities for aggression and violence and then extrapolate these insights onto the problems of war and societal violence, they are committing a gross example of the compositional fallacy'.

However, such honest assessments are unusual, and in many cases, many proponents of contact-based peacebuilding, in its various forms, substitute enthusiasm for independent, systematic and falsifiable evaluation methodologies necessary to test the claims and results of related activities. And in the cases in which rigorous evaluations are used to measure attitude change among participants, the results are very limited (Maoz 2004b, 2011). As in the case of public opinion polls and similar techniques, the degree to which questionnaires and interviews provide meaningful measures of political attitudes in a conflict situation is the subject of intense debate.

Beyond the question of reliability, most evaluations, including those provided by Maoz, only seek to measure attitude changes at the particular time of the contact activity, and do not provide any indication of long-term impacts. These are found to generally erode over time, in what is known as the 'sustainability' problem in applying the contact hypothesis.

In addition, most studies of attitude change in protracted political conflicts were based on artificial situations, in which different groups were brought together under laboratory conditions (Hanssen 2001). Results claimed in these situations have not been duplicated among general populations, or in 'natural' settings involving cross-cultural communication and interaction (Hanssen 2001; Dixon et al., 2005; Maoz 2004b). Analyses have shown that new friends from 'the other side' are regarded as special and atypical, while the group stereotypes and generalizations remain (Hamburger 1994).

The self-selection of participants in people-to-people dialogues and workshops in conflict environments is another limitation that is generally overlooked. Volunteers for such frameworks are predisposed towards communication with and positive images of 'the other' from the beginning, while others without these views are not interested in, and are generally not invited to participate in these frameworks (Hermann 2004; Hanssen 2001).

Elite-based processes focusing on attitude change involving decision makers and opinion leaders – politicians, journalists, academics, teachers, etc. – are designed to overcome these limitations through micro- to macro-level 'spillover'. But there is little evidence for such spillover and general impact confidence building (Steinberg 2004). The meager impacts on peacebuilding from hundreds of workshops, dialogues, people-to-people activities, and similar efforts to effect attitude change, validates these observations.

In contrast, Northern Ireland stands out as an example that would seem to demonstrate that under certain circumstances, extensive contact activities at different levels can contribute significantly to peacebuilding. Fitzduff (1996, 2002) and others point to thousands of contact programs promoting 'pre-political dialogue', in which participants exchanged views on 'issues of mutual concern'. Elites from the opposing communities engaged in 'tough dialogues' to prepare their constituencies for compromise. Initiative 92 'received over five hundred submissions from people and groups in Northern Ireland'. Churches facilitated tolerance through social action, 'shared Bible study groups, inter-denominational worship, joint services and demonstrations following murders, participation in cross-community justice groups, setting up inter-denominational clergy groups and inviting clergy of other denominations to preach in their churches'. In parallel, business groups and trade unions promoted similar agendas and activities (Fitzduff 2002; Church and Visser 2001; Pollak 1993; Nelson 2000; Cairns 2000; O'Halloran and McIntyre 1999).

The claims made by Fitzduff (2002) and others that these activities were the fundamental reasons for success are not supported by rigorous and falsifiable analysis. Indeed, as Mac Ginty (2010) has noted, the periodic eruption of cross-group violence, years after the 1998 referendum (seen as the official end of the conflict), reflects ongoing grievances, 'persistent low-level intergroup hate crime … and growing sectarianism'. In the absence of detailed evaluations based on appropriate methodologies in order to attribute cause and effect, such conclusions are subjective and do not provide guidance in applying the techniques in other conflicts. Many factors were at work in Northern Ireland, including wide-spread economic incentives involving the European Union (Dougal 2005), as well as intense British military actions and the policies of the Irish Republic and the US Government in bringing pressure on the IRA to end its use of violence and accept compromise. Based on this evidence, the rational actor model can explain a great deal of the policies and changes in the Northern Ireland peace process.

At the same time, there is also no basis for excluding the possibility of significant impacts from the cross-community dialogues and cooperative projects in Northern Ireland. Widespread changes in attitudes, perceptions and stereotypes can be considered necessary, although not sufficient and perhaps also not primary conditions for the reduction in violence and promotion of peace efforts in protracted identity conflicts. Clearly, far more detailed, systematic and falsifiable evaluations are needed in order to reach substantive conclusions regarding the impact of contact-related processes in protracted identity conflicts.

In dealing with such complex environments, with many variables and very little information on processes, academics from different disciplines would be well advised to proceed with caution. As noted in the case of Kelman and others, enthusiasm has blinded many observer-practitioners to the need for systematic, appropriate and independent evaluation methodologies. As in all areas of academic endeavor, theories such as peace studies, international negotiation, and diplomacy require methods that can distinguish useful, if modest results, from barren and even counterproductive efforts.

However, in voicing these criticisms, it is also important not to exaggerate them. The reality of intractable conflict in many regions does not exclude a positive role for dialogues, particularly in pursuing the less ambitious but more realistic objective of conflict management within the Hobbesian framework. In such situations, in which intense core disputes over territory, history, power, and justice continue, a ceasefire based on mutual deterrence can be supported by dialogue and 'agreeing to disagree' on narratives. Perhaps this is a more realistic view of Northern Ireland, and may explain the situation in Cyprus, Ngorno-Karabakh, and relations between Israel and the Palestinian West Bank. Through cross-cultural communications, workshops, low-profile joint economic enterprises, track-two discussions, and similar exercises, shaky ceasefires can be strengthened and extended. While short of peace treaties that mark the 'end of conflict', such limited aspirations replace messianism with more realistic goals.

After a long career in international negotiation, Harold Saunders (1999: 4–5) urges fellow diplomats and would-be peacemakers to focus on 'the human dimension'. This is still important advice, if taken in a broader context. The failed history of peacebuilding clearly shows that in the context of intense and protracted conflict, the 'common human dimension' is insufficient to make the transition from war to peace. But with a more modest agenda, accompanied by rigorous evaluation methodologies, diplomats, academics and practitioners might play a positive role in helping to manage ethnonational, religious and other forms of identity conflicts.

Acknowledgement

With thanks to Dr. Amira Schiff for her comments on an earlier draft, and to Joshua Bacon for his assistance.

References

Abu-Nimer, M. (2004) 'Education for Coexistence and Arab-Jewish Encounters in Israel: Potential and Challenges', *Journal of Social Issues* 60: 405–422.

Adler, E. (1992) 'The Emergence of Cooperation: National Epistemic Communities and the International Evolution of the Idea of Nuclear Arms Control', *International Organization*, 46: 101–145.

Allport, G.W. (1954) *The Nature of Prejudice*, Cambridge, MA: Perseus Books.

Amir, Y. (1976) 'The Role of Intergroup Contact in the Change of Prejudice and Ethnic Relations', in P.A. Katz (ed.) *Towards the Elimination of Racism*, New York: Pergamon.

Azar, E.E. (1990) *The Management of Protracted Social Conflict: Theory and Cases*, Hampshire, UK: Dartmouth Publication.

Azar, E.E. (2002) 'Protracted Social Conflicts and Second Track Diplomacy', in J. Davies and E. Kaufman (eds) *Second Track / Citizens' Diplomacy—Concepts and Techniques for Conflict Transformation*, Lanham, MD: Rowman and Littlefield.

Azar, E., Mullet, E., and Vinsonneau, G. (1999) 'The Propensity to Forgive: Findings from Lebanon', *Journal of Peace Research* 36(2): 169–181.

Bargal, D. and Sivan, E. (2004) 'Leadership and reconciliation', in Y. Bar Siman Tov (ed.) *From Conflict Resolution to Reconciliation*, Oxford: Oxford University Press.

Bar-Tal, D. (2000) 'From intractable conflict through conflict resolution to reconciliation: Psychological analysis', *Political Psychology*, 21, 351–365.

Bar-Tal, D. and Bennink, G.H. (2004) 'The Nature of Reconciliation as an Outcome and as a Process', in Y. Bar Siman Tov (ed.) *From Conflict Resolution to Reconciliation*, New York: Oxford University Press.

Bercovitch, J. (1991) 'International mediation and dispute settlement: Evaluating the conditions for successful mediation', *Negotiation Journal*, 7: 17–30.

Burton, J.W. (1969) *Conflict and Communication*, London, UK: Macmillan.

Burton, J.W. (1987) *Resolving Deep-Rooted Conflict: A Handbook*, Lanham, MD: University Press of America.

Cairns, E. 'The Role of the Contact Hypothesis in Peacemaking in Northern Ireland: From Theory to Reality', paper presented to The Andre Salama International Workshop for Research on Peace Education, Haifa, May 2000.

Chigas, D. (2007) 'Capacities and Limits of NGO's as Conflict Managers', in C. Crocker, F.O. Hampson and P. Aall (eds) *Leashing the Dogs of War: Conflict Management in a Divided World*, Washington DC: United States Institute of Peace Press.

Church, C. and Visser, A. (2001) *Single Identity Work,* Northern Ireland: United Nations University/INCORE.

Connolly, P., Fitzpatrick, S., Gallagher, T. and Harris, P. (2006) 'Addressing diversity and inclusion in the early years in conflict-affected societies: A case study of the Media Initiative for Children – Northern Ireland', *International Journal for Early Years Education*, 14: 263–278.

Davidson, W.D. and Montville, J.V. (1981) 'Foreign Policy According to Freud', *Foreign Policy*, 45: 145–157.

Dixon, J., Durrheim, K., and Tredoux, C. (2005) 'Beyond the Optimal Contact strategy: A reality check for the contact hypothesis', *American Psychologist*, 60: 697–711. Online. Available HTTP: <http://www.psych.lancs.ac.uk/people/uploads/JohnDixon20071008T153013.pdf> (accessed 17 January 2012).

Dougal, J. (2005) 'Curse of sectarianism still paralyses North', *Irish Times*, 23 November.

Druckman, D. and Hopmann, P.T. (1989) 'Behavioral Aspects of Negotiations on Mutual Security', in P.E. Tetlock et al. (eds) *Behavior, Society, and Nuclear War, Vol. 1*. New York: Oxford University Press.

Ellison, C.G. and Powers, D.A. (1994) 'The contact hypothesis and racial attitudes among Black Americans', *Social Science Quarterly*, 75: 385–400.

Fisher, R. and Ury, W. (1981) *Getting to Yes: Negotiating Agreement Without Giving In*, New York: Houghton Mifflin Harcourt.

Fisher, R.J. (1983) 'Third-Party Consultation as a Method of Conflict Resolution: A Review of Studies', *Journal of Conflict Resolution*, 27: 301–334.

Fisher, R.J. (1989) 'Prenegotiation Problem-Solving Discussions: Enhancing the Potential for Successful Negotiation', in J.G. Stein (ed.) *Getting to the Table: The Processes of International Prenegotiation*, Baltimore, MD: Johns Hopkins University Press.

Fisher, R.J. (1997a) *Interactive Conflict Resolution*, Syracuse, NY: Syracuse University Press.

Fisher, R.J. (1997b) 'Interactive Conflict Resolution', in W. Zartman and J.L. Rasmussen (eds) *Peacemaking in International Conflict,* Washington DC: United States Institute of Peace Press.

Fisher, R.J. (2001) 'Cyprus: The Failure of Mediation and the Escalation of an Identity Based Conflict to an Adversarial Impasse', *Journal of Peace Research*, 38: 307–326.

Fisher, R.J. (2007) 'Assessing the Contingency Model of Third-Party Intervention in Successful Cases of Prenegotiation', *Journal of Peace Research*, 44: 311–329.

Fisher, R.J. and Kelman, H.C. (2003) 'Conflict Analysis and Resolution', in D.O. Sears, L. Huddy, and R. Jervis (eds) *Political Psychology*, New York: Oxford University Press.

Fitzduff, M. (1996) *Beyond Violence: Conflict Resolution Processes in Northern Ireland,* Tokyo: United Nations University Press.

Fitzduff, M. (2002) *Beyond Violence: Conflict Resolution Processes in Northern Ireland*, New York: United Nations University Press.

Hamburger, Y. (1994) 'The Contact Hypothesis Reconsidered: Effects of the Atypical Outgroup Member on the Outgroup Stereotype', *Basic and Applied Social Psychology*, 15: 339–358.

Hanssen, A.F. (2001) 'A Test of the Racial Contact Hypothesis from a Natural Experiment: Baseball's All Star Voting as a Case', *Social Science Quarterly*, 82: 51–66.

Harvard University Law School, Program on Negotiation (PON) (2012) 'Video: Professor Robert Mnookin leads negotiation skills training for Jewish and Arab students in Israel', Online. Available <http://www.pon.harvard.edu/daily/international-negotiation-daily/video-professor-robert-mnookin-leads-negotiation-skills-training-for-jewish-and-arab-students-in-israel/> (last accessed 9 April, 2012).

Hayner, P.B. (2001) *Unspeakable Truths: Facing Challenge of Truth Commissions*, New York: Routledge.

Hermann, T. (2004) 'Reconciliation: Reflections on the Theoretical and Practical Utility of the Term', in Y. Bar Siman Tov (ed.) *From Conflict Resolution to Reconciliation,* New York: Oxford University Press.

Hobbes, T. (1660) *Leviathan*. Online. Available HTTP: <http://oregonstate.edu/instruct/phl302/texts/hobbes/leviathan-contents.html> (accessed 17 January 2012).

Kant I. (1795) *Perpetual Peace: A Philosophical Sketch*. Online. Available HTTP: < http://www. constitution.org/kant/perpeace.htm> (accessed 27 March 2012).

Kelman, H.C. (1983) 'Conversations with Arafat: A social-psychological assessment of the prospects for Israeli–Palestinian peace', *American Psychologist*, 38: 203–216. Online: Available <http://www.wcfia.harvard.edu/node/892> (last accessed 9 April 2012).

Kelman, H.C. (1987) 'The Political Psychology of the Israeli–Palestinian Conflict: How Can We Overcome the Barriers to a Negotiated Solution?', *Political Psychology*, 8: 347–363.

Kelman, H.C. (1992) 'Informal Mediation by the Scholar/Practitioner', in J. Bercovitch and J.Z. Rubin (eds) *Mediation in International Relations: Multiple Approaches to Conflict Management*, New York: St. Martin's Press.

Kelman, H.C. (1999) 'The Interdependence of Israeli and Palestinian National Identities: The Role of the Other in Existential Conflicts', *Journal of Social Issues*. Online. Available HTTP: <http://findarticles.com/p/articles/mi_m0341/is_3_55/ai_58549262/?tag=content;col1> (accessed 18 January, 2012).

Kelman, H.C. (2000) 'The Role of the Scholar-Practitioner in International Conflict Resolution', *International Studies Perspectives*, 1: 273–288.

Kelman, H.C. (2002) 'Interactive Problem Solving as a Tool for Second Track Diplomacy', in J. Davies and E. Kaufman (eds) *Second Track / Citizens' Diplomacy—Concepts and Techniques for Conflict Transformation*, Lanham, MD: Rowman and Littlefield.

Kelman, H.C. (2004) 'Continuity and change: My life as a social psychologist', in A.H. Eagly, R.M. Baron, and V.L. Hamilton (eds) *The social psychology of group identity and social conflict: Theory, application, and practice*, Washington DC: American Psychological Association.

Kissinger, H. (1979) *White House Years*, New York: Little, Brown and Company.

Kissinger, H. (1982) *Years of Upheaval*, New York: Little, Brown and Company.

Kriesberg, L. (1998) *Constructive Conflicts: From Escalation to Resolution*, Lanham, MD: Rowman & Littlefield.

Kriesberg, L. (2001) 'Mediation and the Transformation of the Israeli–Palestinian Conflict', *Journal of Peace Research*, 38: 373–392.

Lederach, J.P. (1997) *Building Peace: Sustainable Reconciliation in Divided Societies*, Washington DC: United States Institute of Peace Press.

Mac Ginty, R. (2010) 'Hybrid Peace: The interaction between top down and bottom up peace', *Security Dialogue*, 41: 391–412.

Maoz, I. (2000) 'Power relations in intergroup encounters: A case study of Jewish-Arab encounters in Israel', *International Journal of Intercultural Relations*, 24: 259–277.

Maoz, I. (2004a) 'Social-cognitive aspects in reconciliation', in Y. Bar Siman Tov (ed.) *From Conflict to Reconciliation*, Oxford: Oxford University Press.

Maoz, I. (2004b) 'Coexistence Is in the Eye of the Beholder: Evaluating Intergroup Encounter Interventions Between Jews and Arabs in Israel', *Journal of Social Issues*, 60: 437–452.

Maoz, I. (2005) 'Evaluating the Communication between Groups in Dispute: Equality in Contact Interventions between Jews and Arabs in Israel', *Negotiation Journal*, 21: 131–146. Online. Available HTTP: http://peach.haifa.ac.il/images/4/4d/Maoz.NegJournal.pdf (accessed 18 January 2012).

Maoz, I. (2011) 'Does contact work in protracted asymmetrical conflict? Appraising 20 years of reconciliation-aimed encounters between Israeli Jews and Palestinians', *Journal of Peace Research*, 48: 115–125.

Miari, M. (1999) 'Attitudes of Palestinians toward Normalization with Israel', *Journal of Peace Research* 36: 339–348.

Mitchell, C. (1996) 'Cutting Losses: Reflections on Appropriate Timing', Working Paper 9, Virginia: Institute for Conflict Analysis and Resolution, George Mason University. Online. Available HTTP: <http://icar.gmu.edu/wp_9_mitchell.pdf> (accessed 17 January 2012).

Montville, J.V. (1989) 'Psychoanalytic Enlightenment and the Greening of Diplomacy', *J. Amer. Psychoanal. Assn* 37: 297–318.

Montville, J.V. (1990a) *Conflict and Peacemaking in Multiethnic Societies*, Lanham, MD: Rowman and Littlefield.

Montville, J.V. (1990b) 'The Arrow and the Olive Branch: A Case for Track Two Diplomacy', in V.D. Volkan II, J.V. Montville, and D.A. Julius (eds) *The Psychodynamics of International Relationships*, Lexington, MA: Lexington Books.

Montville, J.V. (1991) 'Transnationalism and the Role of Track-Two Diplomacy', in W.S. Thompson and K.M. Jensen (eds) *Approaches to Peace: An Intellectual Map*, Washington DC: United States Institute for Peace Press.

Montville, J.V. (1993) 'The Healing Function in Political Conflict Resolution', in D.J.D. Sandole and H. van der Merwe (eds) *Conflict Resolution in Theory and Practice: Integration and Application*, Manchester: Manchester University Press.

Nelson, J. (2000) *The Business of Peace: The Private Sector as a Partner in Conflict Prevention and Resolution*, London: International Alert, Council on Economic Priorities and The Prince of Wales Business Leaders Forum. Online. Available HTTP: <http://www.international-alert.org/resources/publications/business-peace> (accessed 17 January 2012).

Newhouse, J. (1973) *Cold Dawn: The Story of SALT*, New York: Holt, Rinehart and Winston.

O'Halloran, C. and McIntyre, G. (1999) *Inner East Outer West: Addressing Conflict in Two Interface Areas*, Belfast: Belfast Interface Project.

Perlman, L. and Nasser-Najjab, N. (2006) 'The Future of People-to-People', *Palestine–Israel Journal of Politics, Economics and Culture*. Online. Available HTTP: <http://www.pij.org/details.php?id=394> (accessed 28 December 2011).

Pettigrew, T.F. (2011) 'Toward Sustainable Psychological Interventions for Change, Peace and Conflict', *Journal of Peace Psychology*, 17: 179–192. Online. Available HTTP: <http://dx.doi.org/10.1080/10781919.2010.536758> (accessed 17 January 2012).

Pettigrew, T.F. and Tropp, L. (2000) 'Does intergroup contact reduce prejudice? Recent meta-analytic findings', in S. Oskamp (ed.) *Reducing prejudice and discrimination*, Mahwah, NJ: Erlbaum.

Pollak, A. (1993). *A Citizens Inquiry: The Opsahl Report on Northern Ireland*, Dublin: Lilliput Press.

Ross, D. (2004), *The Missing Peace: The Inside Story of the Fight for Middle East Peace*, New York: Farrar, Straus, and Giroux.

Rothbart, M. and John, O.P. (1985) 'Social categorization and behavioral episodes: A cognitive analysis of the effects of intergroup contact', *Journal of Social Issues*, 41, 81–104.

Rouhana, N.N. and Korper, S.H. (1997) 'Power asymmetry and goals of unofficial third party intervention in protracted intergroup conflict', *Peace and Conflict: Journal of Peace Psychology*, 3: 1–17.

Ruggiero, K.M. and Kelman, H.C. (1999) 'Introduction to the Issue', *Journal of Social Issues*, 55: 405–414.

Saunders, H.H. (1999) *A Public Peace Process: Sustained Dialogue to Transform Racial and Ethnic Conflicts*, New York: St. Martin's Press.

Saunders, H.H. (2001) 'The Virtue of Sustained Dialogue Among Civilizations', *International Journal on World Peace*, 18: 35–44.

Schaap, A.W. (2007) 'Reconciliation as Ideology and Politics', *Constellations: An International Journal of Democratic and Critical Theory*, 15: 249–264.

Schiff, A. (2008) 'Pre-negotiation and its Limits in Ethno-National Conflicts: A Systematic Analysis of Process and Outcomes in the Cyprus Negotiations', *International Negotiation*, 13: 387–412.

Schiff, A. (2010) 'Quasi Track-One Diplomacy: An Analysis of the Geneva Process in the Israeli–Palestinian Conflict', *International Studies Perspectives*, 11: 93–111.

Schimmel, S. (2004) *Wounds Not Healed by Time: The Power of Repentance and Forgiveness*, Oxford: Oxford University Press.

Seliktar, O. (2009) *Doomed to Failure?: The Politics and Intelligence of the Oslo Peace Process*, Santa Barbara: ABC-CLIO.

South Africa Ministry of Justice (1995), *Promotion of National Unity and Reconciliation Act 34 of 1995*. Available online <http://www.justice.gov.za/legislation/acts/1995-034.pdf> (accessed 9 April 2012).

Staub, E. and Pearlman, L.A. (2000) 'Healing, Forgiveness, and Reconciliation in Rwanda: Project Summary and Outcome'. Online. Available HTTP:<http://www.theworld.com/~gubin/Rwandafiles/Tempfinal.htm> (accessed 18 January 2012).

Stein, J.G. (1989) 'Getting to the Table: The Processes of International Prenegotiation', *International Journal,* 44: 231–236.

Stein, K. (1990) *Heroic Diplomacy*, London: Routledge.

Steinberg, G.M. (2004) 'The Centrality of Confidence Building Measures: Lessons from the Middle East', in D. Carment and A. Schnabel (eds) *Conflict Resolution: Rhetoric and Reality*, NY: Lexington Books.

Steinberg, G.M. (2007) 'Postcolonial Theory and the Ideology of Peace Studies', *Israel Affairs*, 13: 4, 786–796.

Voorhees, J. (2002) *Dialogue Sustained: The Multilevel Peace Process and the Dartmouth Conference*, Washington DC: United States Institute of Peace Press.

Wallach, J. (2000) *The Enemy Has a Face: The Seeds of Peace Experience*, Washington DC: United States Institute of Peace Press.

Zartman, W.I. (1989) 'Pre-negotiation: Phases and Functions', *International Journal*, 44: 237–253.

Zartman, W.I. (1996) 'Bargaining and Conflict Reduction', in E.A. Kolodziej and R.E. Kanet (eds) *Coping with Conflict after the Cold War*, London: Johns Hopkins Press, pp. 271–290.

PART II

Approaches and cross-cutting themes

4

GENDER AND PEACEBUILDING

Maria O'Reilly

Introduction

International intervention in conflicted and post-conflict societies in the post-Cold War era has been characterised by a growing international consensus regarding the aims and methods of managing, resolving and/or transforming contemporary conflict (Richmond 2004). Leading states, international organisations, international financial institutions and other key peacebuilding actors focus on (re)building a 'liberal peace' through the reconstruction of liberal polities, economies and societies (Bellamy and Williams 2004: 4–5; Paris 1997; 2004). This growing consensus on achieving peace through liberalisation has triggered major changes in the conduct of peace operations, and critical reflections in peace and conflict studies on the nature and quality of peace being (re)built in the aftermath of war. In parallel, a slow but positive shift can be detected in policymaking rhetoric regarding the gender-specific consequences of armed conflict and violence, coupled with a gradual acknowledgement of the importance of integrating a gender-perspective in the development and implementation of peacebuilding interventions. The need to undertake 'gender mainstreaming' has been articulated in international policy pronouncements and programme guidelines produced by major peacebuilding actors, most notably the UN whose adoption of Security Council Resolution 1325 called for the broad participation of women in peacebuilding and post-conflict reconstruction, acknowledged that conflict is a gendered experience, argued that sustainable peace entails the full and equal participation of women in decision-making, and affirmed a belief that women can play an important role in peace processes. Despite these developments, women often remain marginalised from official peace processes, the issue of gender equality is rarely prioritised in the design and implementation of peace agreements and post-conflict reconstruction programmes, and war crimes of gender violence are generally not adequately addressed in transitional justice processes. This situation points to the need to explore the ways in which (re)building peace may (re)construct gendered forms of domination, injustice and insecurity in transitional societies, rather than empowering women (and marginalised men) to achieve political, economic and social transformation in the aftermath of war.[1]

This chapter explores the gender dynamics of war-fighting and peacebuilding, providing an overview of feminist perspectives on war and peace. I begin by outlining feminist approaches to international relations (IR) and introducing gender as socially constructed and performative. Then, I highlight the ways in which gendered discourses and practices play a key role in the legitimisation, conceptualisation and production of contemporary warfare. As is shown, war is a deeply gendered and gendering social practice, reliant on the construction and reproduction of dominant masculine and submissive feminine identities ('tough men' and 'tender women') in ways that create and sustain inequalities between and among women and men. Following this, I explore feminist scholarship on post-conflict peacebuilding, highlighting the fact that although the aftermath of war often provides an opening in which gender relations can be transformed, in many cases gendered hierarchies of power are (re) constructed and maintained in the transition from 'war' to 'peace', with women relegated to a subordinate position within the transitional society. This outcome is linked to masculinist understandings of peace as a *process* and as an *outcome* by both international and local actors. I then highlight how feminists have responded to these issues, before pinpointing the need to explore how local expressions of gendered agency and resistance emerge in response to international peacebuilding interventions. Such research would spotlight how women reclaim agency and political subjectivity in the aftermath of conflict, in ways that reiterate or transgress dominant models or understandings of gender being (re)constructed in post-war settings.

Feminist approaches to international relations

Feminist approaches to IR have introduced *gender* as a relevant empirical category and theoretical tool for analysing global power relations as well as a normative standpoint from which to construct alternative world orders (True 2001: 231). Despite significant variations in epistemology and methodology, the key concern of feminist theory is to explain the unjustified asymmetry between women's and men's social and economic positions, and to seek prescriptions for ending it (Tickner 2001: 11). Feminists begin from 'the politics of the personal, in which women's subjectivities and experiences of everyday life become the site of the redefinition of patriarchal meanings and values and of resistance to them' (Weedon 1997: 5). Jill Steans (2006: 27) has identified core tasks necessary to 'gender' the discipline: a) to point to the exclusions and biases of mainstream IR; b) to make women visible as social, economic, and political subjects in international politics; c) to analyse how gender inequalities are embedded in daily practices of international relations; d) to empower women as subjects of knowledge by building theoretical understandings of international relations from the position of women and their lived, embodied experiences; e) to elucidate ways that 'masculinities' and 'femininities' are forged, shaped, and reproduced in relation to global processes and forces; and f) to highlight specific sites and manifestations of gender relations outside of the Western context and address the racialised and colonised dimensions of international relations. These tasks involve approaching 'gender' as a *variable* in international relations, as *constitutive* of international relations, and/or as a *transformative* way of knowing international relations, in each case challenging the assumptions of mainstream theories and helping to construct new 'gendered' theories of global politics (True 2001: 232).

One of the most significant contributions made by feminist IR scholars is their insistence that 'gender makes the world go round' (Enloe 2000a: 1–18), permeating all aspects of public and private life (Tickner 1997: 614) and implicated in various constructions of identity (e.g. race, class, nationality, sexuality, etc.) via symbolic and cultural practices (Hutchings 2008b: 101). Gender refers not to *essential/biological* differences between women and men but to *asymmetrical social constructions* of masculinity and femininity (True 2001: 236), binary oppositions which are often used to 'naturalise' the inferior status of 'women' (Tickner 2001: 16). Through the processes of *gender symbolism*, *gender structure*, and *individual gender*, gendered social life is produced (Harding 1986: 17–18). Characteristics such as power, autonomy, rationality, and public become stereotypically associated with masculinity; their opposites (weakness, dependence, emotion, and private) are associated with femininity (Tickner 1997: 614). Gender roles and identities are produced and perpetuated through complex power relations – both a *material* effect of the way in which power takes hold of the body and an *ideological* effect of the way power 'conditions' the mind (Squires and Weldes 2007: 187). Gender is thus not something humans *acquire*, but something we *do*; it exists only so far as it is ritualistically and repetitively performed (Lloyd 1999: 15; Stone 2005; Butler 1990). Through the enactment of particular political, economic and social roles in war-fighting and peace-making, understandings about what it means to be a man or a woman, masculine or feminine, are constructed and reproduced in ways that challenge and/or reinforce gendered hierarchies of power (Butler 1990). Applying a 'feminist' or 'gender lens' (Peterson and Runyan 1999) to the study of war and peace therefore means analysing how the categories of 'woman' and 'man' are historically and contextually produced (Butler 1990), highlighting the differential impact this has on women's and men's lives and suggesting possibilities for gender norms to be transgressed or transformed.

Gender and war

The crucial role that gender plays in international relations is especially evident in discourses and practices of war and political violence, illustrating the centrality of socially constructed gender roles to the war/defence system and therefore to the production of contemporary war and political violence. As Goldstein (2001) has demonstrated, war is a gendered activity, reliant on the construction of a male–female duality that marginalises gender diversity through socialisation. Thus, women and men are forced into separate categories (despite individual diversity) as society focuses on the modest biological tendencies that make *most* men better suited than *most* women to fight in conflicts and maintain national security. This happens because most men are averse to soldiering and killing therefore gender identity is used as a tool to persuade men that fighting is a 'masculine' quality (Goldstein 2001: 264–266). With few exceptions, militaries are traditionally exclusively male realms characterised by archetypal masculine norms, with military service functioning as a rite of passage to manhood (Segal and Wechseler Segal 1983: 165). It has even been argued that war has never *only* been an instrument of policy; rather war is 'an assertion of masculinity' and a method by which men 'assert their own glory' (Van Creveld 2001: 161–167). War is bound up with particular behaviours (e.g. autonomy, risk-taking, courage and endurance), practices (e.g. combat, technical mastery), and values (e.g. honour, rationality), that are traditionally associated with masculinity (Goldstein 2001; Barrett 1996). Various authors have argued that there is a causal or constitutive relationship between masculinity and war – masculinity can be viewed as the key *cause* of war or as a *product* of the war system, or the relationship between masculinity and war may be interpreted as *mutually constitutive* and *mutually reinforcing* (Hutchings 2008a: 390–391).

Women too have played an integral role in conflict and security, whether as mothers, wives, girlfriends, peace activists, camp followers, prostitutes, or munitions workers (Enloe 1983). Yet their role is principally designated as non-combatants (Elshtain and Tobias 1990: ix). Jean Bethke Elshtain has explained that popular understandings of war have evolved around our dominant symbols of male fighters and women non-combatants as the 'Just Warrior' and 'Beautiful Soul'. Through these stereotypes, societies have generally understood war as the man's sphere, whilst peace has long been regarded as a women's issue. Male violence is thus portrayed in war as rational, public, rule-governed and sanctioned, whereas female violence is understood as irrational, private and disorderly (Elshtain 1995: preface). Buttressing the self-consciously 'masculine' warrior ethic is the construction of the female gender as a nurturing, feminine 'other'. Dominating, aggressive behaviour in men is complemented by passive, nurturing behaviour in women (Chapkis 1988: 107–109). Women have often been charged with making the trauma of combat more bearable by symbolising 'normal' life, witnessing male bravery, and helping to boost morale by providing soldiers with something to fight for and protect (Dombrowski 1999: 3). The distinction between war and peacetime is sharpened by the use of gender categories that feminise normal life and masculinise combat. Consequently, the normally unlawful exercise of killing is made easier to accomplish because soldiers can view killing as a legitimate act in the abnormal circumstances of wartime (Goldstein 2001: 302).

Gender plays a key role in the legitimisation and conceptualisation of contemporary violence (Hutchings 2008a). As Shepherd notes, gender narratives – in intersection with constructions of race, class, sexuality etc. – are central to the production of a recognisable and legitimate narrative of war, and to the framing of certain responses, actions and attitudes as permissible (while prohibiting others) (Shepherd 2006: 19–41). *Ad bellum*, the case for war is often made through narratives that focus on the need to protect 'vulnerable' or 'powerless' 'womenandchildren' (Enloe 1990) from abuse by violent/ oppressive men – in the case of Afghanistan, for example, western military intervention was framed in colonialist terms as a case of 'white men saving brown women from brown men' (Spivak, quoted in Abu-Lughod 2002: 784). *In bello*, the distinction between combatant and civilian is also constructed through gendered discourses that construct most men as legitimate and most women as illegitimate targets of violence (Kinsella 2004; Gardam 1993). Although the civilian/combatant distinction makes men more likely to be killed by enemy forces and less likely to be rescued by humanitarian aid workers (Carpenter 2003), for feminists the larger problem is not only that the principle of non-combatant immunity puts women's *and* men's lives at risk by providing the enabling conditions for wars to be fought and legitimised as 'just' and 'humane', but also that it both relies upon and reinforces gendered forms of violence, subordination and oppression (Sjoberg 2006a, 2006b). Via the 'logic of masculinist protection' (Young 2003), states construct women as 'the protected' while men are assigned the role of actual or potential 'protectors' or 'defenders', authorised to utilise the state's legitimate force (Stiehm 1982: 367). However, the reality of contemporary warfare undermines the construction of women as 'protected civilians' – women have been specifically targeted for forced displacement, physical and sexual violence as part of deliberate strategies to destabilise communities (El Jack 2003: 3), prompting feminists such as Claudia Card (1996) to conceive of war as an 'international protection racket' in which violence against women is an ever-present threat. Alarmingly, the wartime rape of women (and men) is prevalent in many contemporary conflicts and has become institutionalised – wartime rape and sexual violence is now understood not as a 'mere' *by-product* of war that results from the 'natural'/'biological' need to satisfy 'uncontrollable' (hetero)sexual desire (Brownmiller 1976), but is rather a *weapon* utilised to punish, torture, and humiliate the 'enemy', to assert dominance and control over a territory and its population, and is always connected to wider gendered relations of power (Baaz and Stern 2009; Enloe 2000b; Goldstein 2001; Hansen 2000; Stiglmayer 1994).

The dominant narrative of war (as found for example in news reports, policy documents, and cultural texts such as novels, films and monuments, etc.) often constructs women in essentialist terms as weak, vulnerable, and/or helpless victims of aggression/abuse – as grieving mothers and widows, as desperate refugees, as traumatised victims of rape and sexual violence, etc. – and men as heroic warriors and protectors of women. Such simplistic thinking denies women agency and overlooks the important roles that women play in both conflict and in peacebuilding processes – as combatants, peace activists, bearers of ethnic/national identities, as heads of households tasked with ensuring their family's physical and economic survival and with maintaining a semblance of everyday life, etc. It is also inaccurate – although it is true that women are adversely affected by war, men can also be victims, while women have also been perpetrators of violence (see e.g. Carpenter 2006; Moser and Clark 2001; Sjoberg and Gentry 2007). Furthermore, the danger of such essentialist thought obscures the fact that gender roles and identities are in constant flux, particularly during wartime (Moser and Clark 2001; Meintjes et al. 2001). While wars often have a catastrophic impact on women's (and men's) lives, they also destabilise traditional gender roles and identities and create opportunities after conflict to overturn unequal power relations and achieve gender justice and equality (ibid). Thus, as Abeysekera (cited in Reilly 2007: 1644) argues, transitional moments offer 'an opportunity to consolidate some of the more positive changes that occurred as a result of the conflict [including] ... opening up new spaces of life and work for women'. Consequently, the challenge for contemporary peacebuilders is not only to understand how the construction of hierarchical gender roles and identities is entangled in conflict – in its emergence, escalation, de-escalation and settlement – but also how to make use of the transformative potential of peacebuilding processes to effect the social, economic and political changes required to achieve positive peace for both women and men, in ways that contest rather than reaffirm gendered inequalities and exclusions in post-conflict societies.

Gender and peace

In spite of the opportunities presented in the aftermath of conflict to reconfigure gender roles and identities in more equitable terms, feminist scholars point out that many women in post-conflict societies continue to be politically, economically, and socially marginalised, and suffer from widespread gender-based violence and discrimination. The 'post-war moment', Zarkov and Cockburn (2002) point out, often remains a 'continuum of conflict' in which women's insecurity is generally maintained and sexual inequality regularly becomes institutionalised. As Lori Handrahan (2004: 430) argues, once a ceasefire is called, and the 'official' conflict has subsided, women's insecurity often becomes 'so prevalent that it becomes invisible and accepted as the norm'. There is generally no aftermath of conflict for women (Meintjes et al. 2001: 1–17) – instead a 'post-war backlash' often occurs, manifest by a continuation of aggression endured during wartime, new forms of violence, and restrictions placed on social, economic, and political activity (Pankhurst 2007: 3–4; Turshen 2001: 84). Women in post-conflict societies frequently experience an increase in trafficking, prostitution, domestic violence, female slavery, 'honour killings' and rape (Handrahan 2004: 434), making clear-cut distinctions between 'pre-war', 'wartime' and 'post-war' periods difficult to pin down. Worryingly, these problems are connected not only to a reassertion of pre-conflict national patriarchy (Turshen 2001) but also to the post-conflict arrival of international patriarchy from international peacebuilding actors who, in Handrahan's (2004: 436) view, often demonstrate an 'aggressive refusal' to seriously consider gender issues in the design and implementation of post-conflict reconstruction programmes. It appears that dominant models of post-conflict peacebuilding and reconstruction often work to *(re)embed* rather than adequately *contest* gendered forms of inequality and domination in post-conflict zones. Whilst the liberal peace circles around principles that are supposedly 'gender-neutral', in reality the promotion of democracy, human rights, and the rule of law does not necessarily ensure gender equality and security, a fact that has long been identified by feminist critiques of liberalism and the public–private divide (Reilly 2007: 159; see e.g. Lister 1997; Pateman 1989; Phillips 1991; Young 1990) and more recently by researchers within feminist security studies (for an overview see Sjoberg and Martin 2010).

The negative outcome of many peacebuilding exercises can be attributed firstly to the marginalisation of women from high-level decision-making, in particular their exclusion from official negotiations on peace agreements and subsequent post-conflict reconstruction frameworks (Chinkin and Paradine 2001; Bell and O'Rourke 2007), and secondly to the lack of recognition afforded to the role that women already play in informal peacebuilding activities (Porter 2007). Masculinist understandings of peace as a *process* – which does not necessarily require the involvement of women at formal peace negotiations – must therefore be challenged in order to achieve gender justice and equality in transitional contexts. Furthermore, there is a need for narrow gendered notions of peace as an *outcome* – e.g. signified by the cessation of public but not private violence, and/or by the (re)construction of a liberal state in which women are equal under the law but marginalised in political, economic and social life – to be contested. McKay and Mazurana (cited in Reilly 2007: 164) for instance argue that peace should incorporate 'gender justice, demilitarization, the promotion of non-violence, reconciliation, the rebuilding of relationships, gender equality, women's human rights, the building of and participation in democratic institutions, and sustaining the environment'. More expansive visions of peace than currently conceived within orthodox peacebuilding literature are necessary to achieve positive peace in transitional contexts, encompassing efforts to confront violence within the 'private sphere' and to tackle gendered patterns of discrimination and inequality, so that material gains for both women and men can be secured. The challenge is, on the one hand, to make visible the gender-biased ideas, meanings and perspectives that are constructed and reproduced within dominant peacebuilding theories, policies, and practices, and on the other, to (re) envisage alternative ways of achieving peace in conflicted and post-conflict societies in ways that challenge gendered forms of exclusion/marginalisation, that affirm women's agency, and that challenge threats or enactments of direct and structural violence at both micro (e.g. family, household) and macro (e.g. society, state) levels.[2]

Feminist responses

A variety of responses to the challenge of deconstructing and reconstructing peacebuilding in theory and practice have emerged from feminist scholars and activists. Liberal feminists espouse a *rights-based* approach, drawing for example on UN Security Council resolutions on women, peace and security (UNSCRs 1325, 1820, 1888, 1889 and 1960) and international instruments such as the Beijing Platform for Action, Beijing Declaration and the Convention of the Elimination of All Forms of Discrimination Against Women (CEDAW) to argue that women have a right to equal and meaningful participation in all levels of conflict prevention, management and post-conflict reconstruction interventions, and that a gender perspective must be integrated into peacebuilding both in policy and practice (Strickland and Duvvury 2003). UNSCR 1325 has been particularly helpful in this respect, enabling feminists at both grassroots and elite levels, within non-governmental, governmental and international agencies and organisations to pursue claims for gender justice and security in a variety of post-war contexts.[3]

Other feminists have sought to challenge the negation of women's roles in peacebuilding by arguing from a standpoint perspective that women have a *distinctive contribution* to make to peace, having been socialised more than men to be 'relational thinkers' (Brock-Utne 1989: 15) who generally privilege an 'ethic of care' over an 'ethic of justice', and human relationships over abstract principles (Gilligan 1982). The practice of mothering, encompassing as it does the protection, nurturing and social training of children, and the maternal thinking it gives rise to have been held to provide the foundation for peace (Ruddick 1990; see also Boulding 1992; Reardon 1993). It is argued that 'adding' women's voices and experiences to peace processes and post-war institutions will result in the nurturing of peaceful relationships and in militarism being challenged, making peace more likely to be sustainable. However, the standpoint perspective has been criticised by 'black' and 'Third World' feminists for ignoring the diversity of women's experiences of domination and discrimination and for overlooking the differences that exist *between* women because of the way that gender intersects with other structures of identity such as race/ethnicity, class, nationality, sexuality, dis/ability, etc. (Collins 2000; Yuval-Davis 1997, 2006). The existence of *multiple standpoints* is increasingly recognised, as is the need for feminist perspectives of peace to emerge through constant negotiation among women.

Accordingly, a politics of 'transversalism' has been advocated to enable women to create networks of solidarity across racial/ethnic/national/class and other divides, to campaign *as women for women* as a way to challenge gendered inequalities and (re)create more peaceful and emancipatory societies (Cockburn 1998, 2002). Transversal politics involves engaging in dialogue, using techniques of 'rooting' and 'shifting' – centring on one's own experiences whilst being empathetic to the differential positionings of the other individuals and collectivities – to make possible discussion and political activism (Yuval-Davis 1997: 88–92). In affirming difference, opposing essentialist views of identity, acknowledging injustices, and ensuring that all voices are heard and given equal weight in decision-making (Cockburn 1998: 224–229), the transversal approach recognises that peacebuilding processes are marked by many different subjectivities, that women (and men) are differentially situated within particular social structures and therefore that individual lives are characterised by diverging degrees of power(lessness) and (in)security. It therefore provides a helpful method through which women can reach out to 'others' across divides and to push for the (re)construction of a positive, sustainable peace that is characterised by gender justice and equality.

Whilst liberal, standpoint and transversal feminist perspectives have spotlighted the benefits of, and possibilities that emerge from, making women integral to peacebuilding efforts, critical feminist scholars have problematised the tendency of key peacebuilding actors to 'add women' to existing policy frameworks without challenging hegemonic notions of peace and the impact of peacebuilding policies on the ground. Thus Sandra Whitworth (2004) argues that while the UN has embraced gender mainstreaming in peacekeeping missions, it has also silenced more radical questions that feminists have raised such as the deployment of peacekeeping forces and performances of militarised masculinities in post-conflict settings, a response which has created insecurities for local populations (see also Higate and Henry 2004, 2009). Meanwhile, poststructural feminists have begun to explore the constitutive relationship between gender and international peacebuilding, noting how the peacebuilding policies are conceptualised, legitimised and ultimately made possible through the discursive construction of gender (e.g. Shepherd 2006; Krasniqi 2007). They note that international peacebuilding actors tend to privilege certain kinds of gender roles and identities to mobilise support for international intervention. Stereotypes of women as potential/actual victims of violence in need of masculine protection by foreign interveners are often found in the policies, statements and reports of organisations such as the UN, resulting in the reproduction of patriarchal relations of power. Worryingly, after 9/11 feminist discourse was often invoked to legitimise neo-colonial wars in Iraq and Afghanistan in the name of 'women's rights', 'democracy' and 'security' (Ayotte and Husain 2005; Ferguson 2005; Shepherd 2006). This points to the need to spotlight the politics of cultural representation, to consider how neo-colonial attitudes inform both feminism and western peacebuilding interventions – whether, as Väyrynen (2010: 148) suggests, 'peacebuilding is a form of imperialist subject-constitution that renders the subaltern women as mute as ever'. It also highlights the importance of examining the responses and forms of resistance that the liberal peace has generated, by listening to the oppositional voices and actions of individual women, women's groups and movements (see e.g. Al-Ali and Pratt 2009; Tickner 2002).

Future directions

There remains a need to develop feminist accounts of how local expressions of gendered agency and resistance emerge within specific contexts of international intervention, to highlight how women reclaim agency and political subjectivity in response to peacebuilding projects, in ways that reiterate or transgress dominant models or understandings of gender. Women in post-conflict societies often demonstrate resistance to their representation as passive victims by, for example, creatively negotiating, modifying, resisting, and/ or embracing peacebuilding policies and practices for their own ends, by opening up productive questions about how their states, societies and communities should best deal with legacies of mass violence and profound loss, and by engaging in forms of political activism that resist attempts to forget, suppress or contain traumatic memories of violence. This is in spite of a liberal peace project that seeks to discipline, regulate and control the emotions, attitudes and behaviour of 'conflict prone' individuals and populations, to 'manage' their agency and capacity for thought and action. There is a need to recover the 'subjugated knowledges' (Spivak 1988: 272) and agency of women subjected to myriad forms of *gendered* violence – whether 'epistemic' (ibid.), direct, structural, cultural (Galtung 1990, 1971), or normative (Butler 1999, 2004a, 2004b) violence – during war and/or in 'peace'. Such research will provide a challenge to gendered forms of inequality, subordination or oppression currently tolerated within post-conflict settings, and help contribute to the transformation of gendered relations of power in ways that improve the material conditions of women's (and men's) lives in the aftermath of conflict.

Acknowledgements

Research for this chapter was supported by the Economic and Social Research Council (grant number ES/G013993/1).

Notes

1 The majority of studies on peacebuilding overlook gender – Väyrynen (2004, 2010) is a notable exception.
2 See Birgit Brock-Utne (1989) for an overview of direct and indirect violence committed or threatened within micro or macro domains.
3 For an assessment of UNSCR 1325 and its implications for women's activism see Special Issue of *International Feminist Journal of Politics*, Vol. 13, No. 4, 2011.

References

Abu-Lughod, L. (2002) 'Do Muslim Women Really Need Saving? Anthropological Reflections on Cultural Relativism and its Others', *American Anthropologist*, 104(3): 783–790.

Al-Ali, N. and N. Pratt (2009) *What Kind of Liberation? Women and the Occupation of Iraq*, Berkeley: University of California Press.

Ayotte, K.J. and M.E. Husain (2005) 'Securing Afghan Women: Neocolonialism, Epistemic Violence, and the Rhetoric of the Veil', *National Women's Society Association Journal*,17(3): 112–133.

Baaz, M.E. and M. Stern (2009) 'Why Do Soldiers Rape? Masculinity, Violence, and Sexuality in the Armed Forces in the Congo (DRC)', *International Studies Quarterly*, 53(2): 495–518.

Barrett, F.J. (1996) 'The Organizational Construction of Hegemonic Masculinity: The Case of the US Navy,' *Gender, Work & Organization*, 3(3): 129–142.

Bell, C. and C. O'Rourke (2007) 'Does Feminism Need a Theory of Transitional Justice? An Introductory Essay,' *International Journal of Transitional Justice*, 1(1): 23–44.

Bellamy, A.J. and P. Williams (2004) 'Introduction: Thinking anew about peace operations', *International Peacekeeping*, 11(1): 1–15.

Boulding, E. (1992) *The Underside of History: A View of Women Through Time,* Newbury Park: Sage.

Brock-Utne, B. (1989) *Feminist Perspectives on War and Peace Education,* New York: Pergamon Press.

Brownmiller, S. (1976) *Against Our Will: Men, Women, Rape,* Harmondsworth: Penguin.

Butler, J. (1990) *Gender Trouble: Feminism and the Subversion of Identity,* London: Routledge.

Butler, J. (1999) *Gender Trouble,* New York and London: Routledge Press.

Butler, J. (2004a) *Precarious life: the powers of mourning and violence,* London: Verso.

Butler, J. (2004b) *Undoing Gender,* New York and London: Routledge.

Card, C. (1996) 'Rape as a Weapon of War,' *Hypathia,* 11(4): 5–18.

Carpenter, R.C. (2003) '"Women and Children First": Gender, Norms, and Humanitarian Evacuation in the Balkans 1991–95', *International Organization,* 57(4): 661–694.

Carpenter, R.C. (2006) 'Recognizing Gender-Based Violence Against Civilian Men and Boys in Conflict Situations,' *Security Dialogue,* 37(1): 83–103.

Chapkis, W. (1988) 'Sexuality and Militarism,' in E. Isaksson, ed., *Women and the Military System,* London: Harvester, pp. 107–109.

Chinkin, C. and K. Paradine (2001) 'Vision and Reality: Democracy and Citizenship of Women in the Dayton Peace Accords,' *Yale Journal of International Law,* 26: 103–178.

Cockburn, C. (1998) *The Space Between Us: Negotiating Gender and National Identities in Conflict,* London: Zed Books.

Cockburn, C. (2002) 'Women's organization in the rebuilding of Bosnia-Herzegovina,' in D. Zarkov and C. Cockburn, eds., London: Lawrence & Wishart.

Collins, P.H. (2000) *Black Feminist Thought: Knowledge, Consciousness and the Politics of Empowerment,* New York and London: Routledge.

Dombrowski, N.A., ed., (1999) *Women and War in the Twentieth Century,* London: Garland.

El Jack, A. (2003) 'Gender and Armed Conflict,' *BRIDGE (development – gender) Overview Report,* Brighton: University of Sussex.

Elshtain, J.B. (1995) *Women and War,* London: Basic Books.

Elshtain, J.B. and S. Tobias, eds., (1990) *Women, Militarism & War: Essays in History, Politics and Social Theory,* Maryland: Rowman & Littlefield.

Enloe, C. (1983) *Does Khaki Become You? The Militarization of Women's Lives,* London: Pluto Press.

Enloe, C. (1990) 'Women and Children: Making Feminist Sense of the Persian Gulf Crisis,' *The Village Voice,* 25 September.

Enloe, C. (2000a) *Bananas, Beaches and Bases: Making Feminist Sense of International Politics,* London: University of California Press.

Enloe, C. (2000b) *Maneuvers: The International Politics of Militarizing Women's Lives,* Los Angeles: University of California Press.

Ferguson, M.L. (2005) '"W" Stands for Women: Feminism and Security Rhetoric in the Post-9/11 Bush Administration', *Politics and Gender,* 1(1): 9–38.

Galtung, J. (1971) 'A Structural Theory of Imperialism,' *Journal of Peace Research,* 8(2): 81–117.

Galtung, J. (1990) 'Cultural Violence,' *Journal of Peace Research,* 27(3): 291–305.

Gardam, J. (1993) 'Gender and Non-Combatant Immunity,' *Transnational Law and Contemporary Problems,* 3(2): 345–370.

Gilligan, C. (1982) *In A Different Voice: Psychological Theory and Women's Development,* Cambridge, MA: Harvard University Press.

Goldstein, J.S. (2001) *War and Gender: How Gender Shapes the War System and Vice Versa,* Cambridge: Cambridge University Press.

Handrahan, L. (2004) 'Conflict, Gender, Ethnicity and Post-Conflict Reconstruction,' *Security Dialogue,* 35(4): 429–445.

Hansen, L. (2000) 'Gender, Nation, Rape: Bosnia and the Construction of Security,' *International Feminist Journal of Politics,* 3(1): 55–75.

Harding, S. (1986) *The Science Question in Feminism,* Ithaca, NY: Cornell University Press.

Higate, P. and M. Henry (2004) 'Engendering (In)security in Peace Support Operations,' *Security Dialogue,* 35(4): 481–498.

Higate, P. and M. Henry (2009) *Insecure Spaces: peacekeeping, power and performance in Haiti, Kosovo and Liberia,* London: Zed Books.

Hutchings, K. (2008a) 'Making Sense of Masculinity and War,' *Men and Masculinities,* 10(4): 389–404.

Hutchings, K. (2008b) '1988 and 1998: Contrast and Continuity in Feminist International Relations,' *Millennium*, 37(1): 97–105.

Kinsella, H.M. (2004) 'Securing the Civilian: sex and gender in the laws of war,' in M. Barnett and R. Duvall, eds., *Power and Global Governance*, Cambridge University Press, pp. 249–272.

Krasniqi, V. (2007) 'Imagery, gender and power: the politics of representation in post-war Kosova,' *Feminist Review*, 86: 1–23.

Lister, R. (1997) *Citizenship: Feminist Perspectives*, Basingstoke: Macmillan.

Lloyd, M. (1999) 'Performativity, Parody, Politics,' *Theory, Culture & Society*, 16(2).

Meintjes, S., A. Pillay and M. Turshen, eds., (2001) *The Aftermath: Women in Post-Conflict Transformation*, London and New York: Zed Books.

Moser, C. and F.C. Clark (2001) *Victims, Perpetrators or Actors: Gender, Armed Conflict and Political Violence*, London and New York: Zed Books.

Pankhurst, D. (2007) *Gendered Peace: Women's Struggles for Post-War Justice and Reconciliation*, New York and London: Routledge.

Paris, R. (1997) 'Peacebuilding and the limits of liberal internationalism,' *International Security*, 22(2): 54–89.

Paris, R. (2004) *At Wars End: Building Peace After Civil Conflict*, Cambridge: Cambridge University Press.

Pateman, C. (1989) *The Sexual Contract*, Stanford: Stanford University Press.

Peterson, V.S. and A. Sisson Runyan (1999) *Global Gender Issues*, Boulder, CO: Westview Press.

Phillips, A. (1991) *Engendering Democracy*, Cambridge: Polity Press.

Porter, E. (2007) *Peacebuilding: Women in International Perspective*, Abingdon and New York: Routledge.

Reardon, B.A. (1993) *Women and Peace: Feminist Visions of Global Security*, New York: State University of New York.

Reilly, N. (2007) 'Seeking gender justice in post-conflict transitions: towards a transformative women's human rights approach,' *International Journal of Law in Context*, 3(2): 155–172.

Richmond, O.P. (2004) 'UN Peace Operations and the Dilemmas of the Peacebuilding Consensus,' *International Peacekeeping*, 11(1): 83–102.

Ruddick, S. (1990) 'The Rationality of Care,' in J.B. Elshtain, and S. Tobias, eds., *Women, Militarism & War: Essays in History, Politics and Social Theory*, Maryland: Rowman & Littlefield, pp. 229–253.

Segal, D.R. and Wechseler Segal, M. (1983) 'Changes in Military Organization,' *Annual Review of Sociology*, 9: 151–170.

Shepherd, L.J. (2006) 'Veiled references: Constructions of gender in the Bush administration discourse on the attacks on Afghanistan post-9/11,' *International Feminist Journal of Politics*, 8(1): 19–41.

Sjoberg, L. (2006a) *Gender, Justice and the Wars in Iraq: A Feminist Reformulation of Just War Theory*. Oxford: Lexington.

Sjoberg, L. (2006b) 'Gendered Realities of the Immunity Principle: Why Gender Analysis Needs Feminism,' *International Studies Quarterly*, 50(4): 889–910.

Sjoberg, L. and C.E. Gentry (2007) *Monsters, Mothers, Whores: Women's Violence in Global Politics*, London and New York: Zed Books.

Sjoberg, L. and J. Martin (2010) 'Feminist Security Theorizing', in Robert A. Denemark, ed., *The International Studies Encyclopedia*, available at < http://www.isacompendium.com/subscriber/tocnode?id=g9781444336597_yr2011_chunk_g97814443365978_ss1-11>. Last accessed 30 January 2012.

Spivak, G.S. (1988) 'Can the Subaltern Speak?' in C. Nelson and L. Grossberg, eds., *Marxism and Interpretation of Culture*, Urbana: University of Illinois Press, pp. 271–313.

Squires, J. and J. Weldes (2007) 'Beyond Being Marginal: Gender and International Relations in Britain,' *British Journal of Politics and International Relations*, 9(2), 185–203.

Steans, J. (2006) *Gender and International Relations*, Cambridge: Polity Press.

Stiehm, J.H. (1982) 'The Protected, the Protector, the Defender,' *Women's Studies International Forum*, 5(3/4): 367–376.

Stiglmayer, A. (1994) ed., *Mass Rape: The War Against Women in Bosnia-Herzegovina*, Lincoln: University of Nebraska Press.

Stone, A. (2005) 'Towards a Genealogical Feminism: A Reading of Judith Butler's Political Thought,' *Contemporary Political Theory*, 4(1): 4–24.

Strickland, R. and N. Duvvury (2003) *Gender Equity and Peacebuilding: From Rhetoric to Reality*, Washington DC: International Center for Research on Women.

Tickner, J.A. (1997) 'You Just Don't Understand: Troubled Engagements Between Feminists and IR Theorists,' *International Studies Quarterly*, 41: 611–632.

Tickner, J.A. (2001) *Gendering World Politics: Issues and Approaches in the Post-Cold War Era*, New York: Columbia University Press.

Tickner, J.A. (2002) 'Feminist Perspectives on 9/11,' *International Studies Perspectives*, 3(4): 333–350.

True, J. (2001) 'Feminism,' in Burchill et al., eds., *Theories of International Relations*, Basingstoke: Palgrave.

Turshen, M. (2001) 'Engendering relations of state to society in the aftermath,' in Meintjes et al., *The Aftermath: Women in post-conflict transitions*, London: Zed Books, pp. 78–96.

Van Creveld, M. (2001) *Men, Women & War*, London: Cassell Military.

Väyrynen, T. (2004) 'Gender and UN Peace Operations: The Confines of Modernity,' *International Peacekeeping*, 11(1): 125–142.

Väyrynen, T. (2010) 'Gender and Peacebuilding,' in O.P. Richmond, ed., *Palgrave Advances in Peacebuilding: Critical Developments and Approaches*, London: Palgrave Macmillan, pp. 137–153.

Weedon, C. (1997) *Feminist Practice and Poststructuralist Theory*, Oxford: Blackwell.

Whitworth, S. (2004) *Men, Militarism and UN Peacekeeping: A Gendered Analysis*, Boulder: Lynne Rienner.

Young, I.M. (1990) *Justice and the Politics of Difference*, Princeton: Princeton University Press.

Young, I.M. (2003) 'The Logic of Masculinist Protection: Reflections on the Current Security State,' *Signs: Journal of Women in Culture and Society*, 29(1): 1–25.

Yuval-Davis, N. (1997) *Gender and Nation*, London: Sage Publications.

Yuval-Davis, N. (2006) 'Intersectionality and Feminist Politics,' *European Journal of Women's Studies*, 13(3): 193–209.

Zarkov, D. and C. Cockburn (2002) 'Introduction,' *The Postwar Moment: Militaries, Masculinities and International Peacekeeping in Bosnia and the Netherlands*, London: Lawrence & Wishart.

5

RELIGION AND PEACEBUILDING[1]

Mohammed Abu-Nimer

Introduction

The fields of religious peacebuilding in general and interfaith dialogue in particular have grown tremendously in the last two decades. Peacebuilding scholars and practitioners have been advocating for a more central role for religious peacebuilding interventions. The primary argument for such calls is based on the assumption that religious identity is a key influence on protracted conflict dynamics, especially in areas in which political parties have managed to manipulate their community's identity in ways that place their religious differences at the core or center of the conflict. For example, in the case of post-Saddam Iraq, certain Shia, Sunni, and American political leaders have often cited that religious differences between Shia and Sunni are the root causes of this conflict. Thus reframing the conflict from power sharing, center and periphery, rich elites and poor masses into uni-dimensional religious differences between Shia and Sunni has provided international and local civil society groups with the opportunity and opening to begin emphasizing the need for interfaith and intrafaith dialogue programs in post-Saddam Iraq. Such activities were not allowed and did not exist in Iraq prior to the war.

Similar realities have existed in Egypt; religious differences simply were not part of the Egyptian public political narrative. However, in the last two decades, with the rise of Islamic movements and the clashes between the Mubarak regime and the Islamic Brotherhood, some organizations have begun to introduce interfaith dialogue programs and are calling for religious pluralism.[2] In Israel/Palestine, the rise to power of Hamas and the Jewish religious right, since the late 1980s, has opened the gates for interfaith dialogue programs that aim to ameliorate the theological ignorance of Arabs and Jews in Palestine and Israel (Abu-Nimer, Khoury and Welty 2007). In Sri Lanka, the conflict between the Tamil ethnic minority and the Sinhalese majority has always been framed around the issues of power sharing and resource distribution. However, in the last two decades, a few local and international NGOs have begun promoting interfaith dialogue between Sinhalese Buddhist and Tamil Hindus, as well as between

Christians and Muslims. These interfaith dialogue programs have been funded mainly by American and European donors.

At the academic level, new programs are being launched focusing on peacebuilding within religions contexts. Journal articles are also being published in an attempt to theorize and conceptualize the practice of interfaith peacebuilding. It is clear that a subfield is being formed and shaped even within the northern academic institutions (Appleby 2011).

The rapid development of religious peacebuilding initiatives raises basic questions on future trends, and on areas that religious peacebuilding has not yet developed or addressed. Specifically, what cutting edge initiatives are emerging? What issues has religious peacebuilding failed to address? What are its future possible directions? How can religious peacebuilding be better integrated with other forms of conflict resolution?

This chapter focuses on some of the above questions, based on reflections derived from the author's practice in this field over the last twenty years, and his work in conflict areas such as Sri Lanka, Palestine/Israel, Egypt, Mindanao, Chad, Niger, and the US. Interfaith dialogue and religious peacebuilding can be a key factor in unlocking the deep-rooted conflicts in many of the above identity-based conflict areas. In such contexts, conflict dynamics have evolved in ways that local and outside forces have managed to reframe or manipulate the religious identities of the main conflict parties. Identity politics has produced a significant portion of various local communities who view their relationship with the other communities through the lens of their religious identities. In fact, when asked to articulate the issues involved in the conflict, members of these communities may rely on religious texts to justify their current and historical positions towards the other. For example, a Buddhist monk in Sri Lanka may believe that the island belongs to the Sinhalese majority as part of his belief system that Buddhism in Sri Lanka is an authentic and pure version of Buddhism. Similarly, in the last two decades, more Muslims and Jews in Israel and Palestine have begun framing their conflict through their respective religious identities and affiliations. Thus, one hears frequent citation of scripture in justifying the right to the Holy Land, and the need to be more faithful to one's religion and faith as a way to resolve the conflict. Conflict dynamics that rely on religious affiliation require that peacebuilding practitioners and activists learn how to engage with their local communities through their faiths rather than through humanist or secular sets of peacebuilding values and methods.

Accomplishments and challenges

Obviously, the field of religious peacebuilding has developed a great deal in the last two decades, especially with the leadership of institutions like the Religion and Peacemaking Center at the United States Institute of Peace, the World Parliament of Religions, and other international and regional institutions. The accomplishments of religious peacebuilding can be easily reviewed in evaluation reports and case studies published in journals and other media, such as the groundbreaking work of Scott Appleby (2000), David Little (2007), Gopin (2002), Swidler (1998), and Johnston and Sampson (1995) to name a few. In most of these documentations of success, the religious peacebuilding programs' contributions can be classified in a few main categories:

- *Breaking negative stereotypes*: The majority of the interfaith dialogue programs focus on breaking existing negative stereotypes. Due to a lack of contact between members of conflicting groups, whole generations often grow up without learning the basics about the other faith group. As a result, negative stereotypes are constructed in the minds of community members. Thus, for example, religious peacebuilding programs often build their interventions on the assumption that when they provide basic information about Islam to Christians in the US, the participants' understanding of Islam will grow and act as a counterforce to endorsement of religious violence. The same principles are followed by religious peacebuilding programs designed between the Tamil and Sinhalese communities in Sri Lanka.

- *Humanizing the other*: Religious peacebuilding programs have certainly contributed to the process of humanizing the other or the enemy in war zone areas such as Israel/Palestine. Jewish participants in interfaith dialogue groups learned that Muslim prayers can be peaceful and deeply spiritual too, as can the call for prayer. When religious scriptures and beliefs are deployed to justify acts of dehumanization, religious peacebuilding has provided effective countermeasures to the dehumanization of the enemy.

- *Advocating for justice and human rights*: In civil war and violent conflict contexts, religious peacebuilding activists have also initiated campaigns to confront oppressive policies and systematic violations of human rights. For example, in Sri Lanka in 2007, the Anti-War Front, led by a number of religious leaders, joined the campaign to fight against Sri Lankan government and LTTE (Liberation Tigers of Tamil Eelam) violations of human rights.[3] In Mindanao, Philippines, many bishops and clergy from the Catholic Church have actively engaged in opposing the 'all out war' launched by President Estrada in 2000 against the Moro Islamic Liberation Front (MILF). There are many other examples illustrating the active role that religious peace activists have taken in opposing violence and advocating for basic equal rights for all communities in conflict areas (Dyck 2001).

- *Supporting nonviolent resistance*: Joining and adopting nonviolence resistance campaigns and ideologies requires major commitments from clergy and leaders. When examining religious peacebuilding in various conflict areas, it is clear that religious actors have participated in fewer initiatives and have had less involvement in such campaigns than the previous three categories of action. For example, in conflict areas such as Sri Lanka, Palestine and Israel, Egypt, and Sudan there is a large number or segment of the religious leadership who have been co-opted by political elites or regimes. Thus, the mainstream religious institutions tend to be among the last forces to join nonviolence resistance campaigns that call for reforms or change of political regimes. For example, Al Azhar's religious leadership (one of the most influential Islamic religious institutes in Egypt) waited for a long time before they formally declared their endorsement of the Egyptian revolutionary groups. Similarly, the Coptic Church in Egypt carefully observed the unfolding of the revolutionary events before they stood against the regime. The Buddhist institutions in Sri Lanka have continued to support the war against the Liberation Tigers of Tamil Eelam (LTTE) and the government's 'policies of nationalization' since the 1980s. Only a few monks broke away from the establishment and joined the nonviolent action campaigns of 2007. In another example, both the Catholic Church and black pastors in the Washington DC area have endorsed 'Occupy DC', and have maintained ongoing linkages with the movement's young leaders, providing them with spiritual support and endorsement.[4]

Obviously, there are many other contributions emanating from interfaith dialogue and religious peacebuilding. However, due to the limited scope of this chapter, the remaining sections will focus on the shortcomings and possible future directions of this emerging field. It should be noted that these limitations or gaps exist across the board, in violent and nonviolent conflict contexts, and that these limitations are not associated with one specific organization, country, or program.

Operating on the fringes

Religious peacebuilding actors still operate on the fringes of peacemaking and peacebuilding, which themselves operate on the fringes of real-politik or government policy making. Obviously, there are internal and external factors that have obstructed the development and situating of the field into a more mainstream arena or gaining access to the policy making and academic centers of power.

Some of the factors that have prohibited religious peace actors from gaining a role in these circles include:

1   The western cultural assumption that religion and faith have to be kept outside of political and academic institutions in order to protect public and private spheres and to maintain scientific objectivity.
2   The assumption that most, if not all, conflicts are mainly about resources and not about religious identity. Thus there is no need to involve religious actors in policy discussions related to conflicts.
3   A great deal of the funding allocated to peacebuilding is being generated by various governmental agencies (within the context of relief and development or to counter radicalism). Thus, for practitioners there is a lack of incentive/support to focus on religious peacemaking.
4   The emerging field of religious peacebuilding has not yet developed a comprehensive understanding, nor tools and approaches that are unique to religious peacemaking. Today, what practitioners call 'religious peacemaking' is still strongly tied into secular and humanist approaches and tools of peace and conflict resolution mechanisms and techniques.

To counter the marginalization of religious peacebuilding, scholars and practitioners need to explore more ways to strategically place their work (language, discourses, and strategies) closer to the centers of power in their own communities and contexts.

No evaluation mechanisms to trace impact

Similar to the peace and conflict resolution field, religious peacemaking has not yet developed systematic methods to capture its micro or even macro effects or impact. A majority of the evidence provided by practitioners and evaluators depends on anecdotal data and lacks comprehensive and systematic designs.

The above challenge does not mean that practitioners cannot trace how participants in one workshop of interfaith dialogue have been affected by the workshop and have transformed their interpersonal and individual relationships. On the contrary, such measurements of impact at the individual level have been utilized by evaluators. However, evaluators of interfaith dialogue still struggle on how to measure and trace the impact of interfaith dialogue workshops on the wider political reality, or even to capture the cumulative influence of all interfaith activities in one specific region. In fact, the religious peacemaking field has not developed systematic/empirical answers to its core questions of: What is unique about religious peacebuilding approaches and tools? What conditions and factors are needed for interpersonal, organizational, and societal changes to take place as a result of religious peacebuilding interventions? Why does it work and how does it work?

For example, in 2010 the author, with a team of practitioners, conducted a workshop with Iraqi interfaith dialogue facilitators. Considering the harsh realities of Iraq at that time (suicide bombing and deep sectarian divides between Shia and Sunni), the trainees were amazingly courageous and open to learning new skills and implementing these tools. Each of the 15 trainers had completed several workshops and trained other community members in interfaith dialogue and pluralism. Thousands of people have been affected and touched by their activities, especially because it also involved the showing of the film *The Imam and the Pastor* (FLT Films 2006). The positive impact of these workshops at the individual level of attitudes and perceptions is beyond any doubt. The author has witnessed the testimony of hundreds of individuals on the transformative impact that such workshops have had on them. Saleh al Tae, an Iraqi facilitator in his mid-60s, who cried when watching the film, took it on himself to bring interfaith dialogue into this community. Al Tae has organized a number of interfaith dialogue meetings in the Baghdad area around the screening of this film and has integrated it as part of the ongoing activities of a local Iraqi Association for Intellectual Revival.[5]

Three years after the Iraqi interfaith program was completed, the same Iraqi communities are still living in fear and anxiety, and their sectarian divides are growing. We have no measures to detect the effect of these workshops and programs at these levels or scales of violence. Nevertheless, those who participated are all 'believers' that the participants benefited and have transferred their knowledge and skills to their communities.

Another example, the Forum for Intercultural Dialogue (FID) has operated in Egypt for 15 years and has conducted hundreds of workshops and trainings for Christians and Muslims in all districts of Egypt. Hundreds of their graduates/participants have been active in the Egyptian revolution. They have published many books and other publications on interfaith dialogue and pluralism in Egyptian society. Despite that, we have very little evidence of their contribution to Egyptian macro politics and to the Egyptian discourse of tolerance and coexistence between religious groups. Nevertheless, despite the random explosion of sectarian violence in Egypt every few months, many believe that forums like this have had an impact on Muslim–Christian relations in Egypt. The same applies to Israeli–Palestinian interfaith peacebuilding. Certain peacebuilders and donors believe that it is effective despite the macro deterioration of Arab–Jewish relations in Israel and Palestine.

Several factors contribute to explaining the above status of the field:

1 Peacebuilding scholars and practitioners have no specialized research to design more systematic evaluation mechanisms for interfaith or religious peacebuilding.
2 The majority of interfaith officers who implement these programs are not professionally trained in program design and implementation and are not trained in basic monitoring and evaluation techniques. Thus, they are not aware or capable of adjusting their programs at the outset to be designed to capture micro or macro impact.
3 Although the donors demand impact measures, in most cases donors and implementers neglect to allocate resources to systematic macro or micro evaluation. Evaluation in interfaith dialogue is not taken seriously by many practitioners or even donors.

A limited presence in academic institutions

Peace and conflict resolution programs around the world have grown tremendously. Today there are over 500 undergraduate and over 15 graduate programs in this field in the US alone. This rapid growth in academic degrees has flooded the job market with Master degree graduates, yet there are a limited number of jobs. Nevertheless, within the peace and conflict resolution field, there is little emphasis on religious peacemaking. For example, in the leading six academic institutions in the US, one cannot find more than one or two courses on religion and peace in each institute. There is one graduate program that has developed a certificate or specialization on this topic and only one PhD program has been developed.[6]

Academic institutions have yet to embrace religious peacebuilding as an integral part of their institutional structure or academic offerings. Nevertheless, there are a few Endowment Chairs for Religious Peacemaking, but they lack the funding and capacity to promote the academic offering at their institutions.[7]

Some factors that can help in understanding the above reality include the following. First, peace and conflict resolution programs are themselves categorized, and perceived or labeled, by other departments as 'soft sciences', 'soft power', 'naïve', etc. So it is thought that including religious peacemaking in their curricula might 'tarnish' the image within and outside the academic institutions. Second, the academic institutions and their rigid disciplinary divisions have made it difficult for religious peacebuilding to establish itself as a separate or integrated discipline. Third, religion in the western cultural context is perceived as a sensitive and private matter; thus attempts to discuss it in the public sphere risk causing sensitivities. This obstacle affects all other areas too; however, in academic and government institutions which protect public space, introducing religious and faith frameworks can become very challenging. Many academic institutes do not talk about 'our God' and definitely not Allah in the classroom.

A consensus on the need to protect children from religious pluralism

Despite the flourishing of religious peace programming, an overwhelming majority of these programs are still targeting adults and community members, especially clergy.

All religious groups and sects continue to protect their children from 'education for religious pluralism'. Sunday schools rarely invite a Muslim to talk about his/her faith; similarly Muslims in their religious schools or Friday schools do not, for example, get a Christian, a Jew, or a Buddhist monk to explain their faith principles and practices.

In Mindanao, Philippines, when the author suggested that Muslim and Christian clergies should bring guest speakers to their religious schools, or have a priest come to the mosque to speak to the Muslim children, both sides were furious, contending that such an act would provoke their communities and confuse the children further. The same reality exists in the US; the majority of religious schools avoid bringing clergy or speakers from other faith groups to interact with their children and enrich their interfaith education. In Baltimore in 2007, at a Quaker meeting, a participant explained this phenomenon: 'The process of religious brainwashing and dogmatization cannot be completed if other faith perspectives are brought in the process.'

This, of course, relates to trends and is not meant to be a generalization applied to all the religious groups or programs. There are a number of pioneer interfaith programs that target children's education for religious pluralism. However, those tend to be the smallest in scale and the least accessible. This situation can be explained, first, in that religious clergy in most faith groups are still operating as the gatekeepers of their faiths and feel that their communities have entrusted them with their children; second, there is a general assumption that children need to know their faith first and should not be confused with different doctrines before they have formulated their own religious identities, especially in conflict areas in which religious identity is being manipulated by politicians and parties to fuel the ongoing conflict dynamics. A Christian pastor explained his opposition to inter-religious programming: 'Children are limited in their capacity to process more than one religious doctrine. Let us educate [i.e., indoctrinate] them first until they are adults. Then they can deal with other faith groups.'

Obviously, religious peacebuilding programs need to be developed more and even be integrated as part of the formal and informal educational curriculum. Such programs can be the best prevention against religious-based violence in any diverse community.

Mainstreaming gender in religious peacebuilding

Although some progress has been made in introducing women's experiences and perspectives in the peacebuilding field (primarily due to the efforts of international organizations such as the UN and its agencies, USAID, DFID, World Bank, etc.) in inter-religious peacemaking, the majority of the programming and the organizations themselves continue to be male-dominated (both in perspective and physically). There are few women-led programs in interfaith dialogue. In Israel and Palestine, there is a women's interfaith group that has operated since 2002, in addition to the network established by the United Religious Initiative (URI). But there are few other programs led by women. In general, there is simply very little leadership access for women in interfaith dialogue circles. For example, after two years of working with religious peacebuilding and pluralism in the Islamic Quranic schools of Chad and Niger, the author, along with the implementing team, was granted access to the women's Quranic schools. However, the clergy would not allow or promote the participation of the women of their community in interfaith dialogue meetings, certainly not as panelists or facilitators.

Some of the factors that influence this reality include, first, religious institutions themselves are still structurally dominated by men. In most faith groups, males are still the gatekeepers of the faith and its rituals. The male clergy speaks for the faith and conducts its ceremonies. Second, interfaith dialogue is often defined as a space to talk about political or community relations problems, and such themes, in many societies, have been defined by social norms as a male domain and have excluded women from the conversation. Third, for various reasons, donors seem not to push this agenda enough in their funding of religious peacebuilding. Very few specific grants are made for women and interfaith dialogue.[8]

Religious peacebuilding is lacking in reaching out to the media

Like the peace and conflict resolution field, religious peacebuilding has not invested enough resources in developing strategies and approaches to handle or reach out to media outlets. Observing the Arab revolutions in which youth and media constitute the primary engines behind the protest, it is obvious that, for any peacemaking program to become effective, it has to establish creative ways to present itself through the media.

There are many religious stations or satellite programs – in fact there are too many of them in both the northern and southern hemispheres. There is no shortage in the number of faith-based media outlets that are fully devoted to the promoting of a single religious message. In the US alone, millions of people watch religious programming on a weekly basis. Religious media programming has also become a major outlet for Islamic Da'awa (Calling) throughout the Muslim world.

The reality that few interfaith programs are being aired or initiated may be explained, first, by the fact that existing religious media outlets are themselves part of the problem of religious war-making. They are mainly devoted to propagating one faith and themselves to the exclusion of other faith groups. They are often supported by certain religious exclusionist agenda.[9] Second, public media outlets are similar to government and academic institutions in most cases (especially in the western hemisphere which separates religion and faith from public life). Thus, dealing with religious identities in any form becomes a sensitive issue for these media outlets. Third, religious peacemaking is not the most attractive source of news. A group of 'religious men' debating or answering questions about their faith does not make headlines. Thus, it is more challenging to break into the mainstream media that often seek 'sensational events'.

Considering the above reality, it is clear that interfaith dialogue organizations have to specifically target faith-based media programming (the most influential industry in religious indoctrination). New programs on religious pluralism and peace can be the focus of such religious peacebuilding, especially in conflict zone areas.

Interfaith dialogue between talk and action

Scholars and practitioners have identified the paradox of 'action versus talk' as part of dialogue group dynamics and models (see Thistlethwaite 2012; Arinze 2002; McCarthy 1999; Smock 2002; Cox and Philpott 2003; Barnes 2001; Schoem and Hurtado 2001; Abu-Nimer 2002, 1999). Participants who belong to minority groups tend to call for action as a criteria for measuring the success of dialogue groups. However, members of the dominant majority tend to be satisfied or comfortable with gaining a deeper understanding of the conflict and the perspective of minority members (Abu-Nimer 1999; Hubbard 2001).

The interfaith dialogue field of practice did not escape these dynamics; in fact the majority of interfaith dialogue interaction tends to focus on similarities and emphasizes the inter-religious unity between the various faith groups. Such a strategy obviously calls for harmony and avoids calls for actions in which the status quo is challenged by the interfaith group members collectively, or even on an individual basis. For example, Palestinian members of interfaith groups repeatedly complained that their dialogue experiences were exclusively focusing on talk and getting to know the other faith. When they insisted on some actionable interventions by the group, such as confronting the Israeli soldiers at the checkpoints, joining demonstrations against the settlers, or signing petitions in their communities, the majority of the Israeli group's members opposed and expressed their discomfort in joining such activities (Abu-Nimer 2007).

Several factors can explain the smaller numbers of interfaith dialogue groups that call and engage in actions rather than focusing solely on talking and raising awareness. Firstly, sponsorship of interfaith organizations tends to be associated with the dominant majority in the organizations. For example, American Jewish organizations and donors are primarily supportive of interfaith dialogue between Israelis and Palestinians; Sinhalese majority-dominating organizations are often the ones who call for interfaith activities and programs. Similarly, Catholic churches and institutions are the primary initiators of interfaith dialogue activities in the Philippines; and white Christian churches are the main groups that promote interfaith dialogue in North America. Secondly, carrying out action-oriented activities as a result of an interfaith dialogue process requires the participants to get out of their 'comfort zones', especially for those who enjoy certain privileges due to their group affiliation. This process is potentially painful and demands higher risk taking, and individuals who decide to engage in action are more likely to pay a heavier price or cost (in their own social circles) than those who resist engaging in such actions.

Interfaith dialogue programs have tended to emphasize harmony models and only a few programs have explored the need to pursue action and concrete tangible linkages to social justice issues. Such exploration is essential for the future development of the field of inter-religious peacebuilding.

Integrating/coordinating/networking with social and political movements for justice and peace

In many conflict areas, the majority of inter-religious peacebuilding activities are consciously framed as nonpolitical or carried out by actors who are not part of the existing social and political peace movements. For example, in Israel/Palestine, there are a number of interfaith dialogue groups and organizations whose organizers, when interviewed, did not perceive themselves as a part of the Israeli–Palestinian peace movement (Abu-Nimer 2007). In fact, they deliberately disassociated themselves from such movements. Also, the peace movement leaders did not see them as partners who could take a stand against occupation or for economic and social justice. This alienation from existing peace movements is a reality that characterizes many interfaith peacebuilding groups, partly due to the lack of awareness of these religious actors of the need to link with other social change leaders in order to support a collective process of change. This lack of connection can be based on, firstly, a lack of professional capacity among the religious actors, and the nature of interfaith dialogue programs is that they tend to be operated by faith-based initiatives or individuals who have had little professional training as community developers or peacemakers. Also, they tend to lack the strategic and in-depth understanding of the conflict in which they operate. They are mainly motivated by faith. Strategic alliances are not part of their faith-based planning or programming, but rather the contrary is often the case. Secondly, in many instances, interfaith initiatives are de-politicized because they tend to be supported by the establishment and dominant majority organizations. This inability to bridge the ideological differences between existing social and political movements has also been cited by social movement leaders in their explanations for why they do not reach out to interfaith dialogue groups to join their campaigns.[10]

In this context, we should make a clear distinction between religious peacebuilding that focuses on dialogue and cultural and religious exposure programs versus those religious peacebuilding organizations that support advocacy and nonviolent resistance. The second group does not shy away from partnering with peace and protest movements, while the first group often avoids any institutional linkages to such groups (Abu-Nimer et al., 2007).

For example, the Israeli government will support interfaith programs (not financially, but certainly ideologically), while Palestinian organizations support nonviolence resistance and social justice movements. A similar distinction can be made among African American and other minority groups in the US versus the middle upper class establishment organizations in American society that tend to support apolitical interfaith dialogue.

In Egypt, the Al Azhar Institute leadership who attempt to represent moderate Islamic voices and other Christian religious groups, stood on the line or in the middle (between protestors and the government of Mubarak) for too long before they joined the social nonviolence movements in the Arab world. Religious organizations that support interfaith dialogue often operate within the realm of the establishment.[11]

Developing systematic linkages and coordinating with local and regional political and social movements is a crucial step for interfaith religious peacebuilding to effectively contribute to social and political change in context. In fact, such structural links can counter the tendency of interfaith initiatives to serve the interests of the dominant majority, especially when the dialogue model claims to be apolitical or educational.

Conclusion

Although interfaith religious peacebuilding is a rapidly emerging field, there are certain steps that can enhance its future professional advancement. Some of these steps include, firstly, initiating an annual international conference that could be sponsored by the Religious Peacebuilding Practice and Study Association. The creation of such an association can certainly promote the presence of the field in both academic and policy circles. Secondly, by launching a Journal of Religious Peacebuilding. Such a journal could provide a space for scholars and practitioners to explore theories, methodologies, and applications of religious peacebuilding worldwide. A refereed journal would certainly advance the status and visibility of religious peacebuilding in the field of peace and conflict resolution. Thirdly, initiating a worldwide Network for Religious Peacebuilding which could become an umbrella professional network for practitioners of religious peacebuilding to advance the field and systematically connect people. Through this, practitioners and activists could engage in local, regional, and even international activities of advocacy and professional development.

Notes

1 This chapter is based on a conference presentation for the Religion and Peacemaking Center, United Stated Institute of Peace (USIP), Washington, DC: 9 November 2011.
2 The Coptic Evangelical Organization for Social Services (CEOSS) launched one of the few interfaith programs in the mid-1990s.
3 See A. Balaya Bedamu, Rata Nobedamu by Prayathna Sabha, National Anti-War Front (Sri Lanka) and Håemasiri Abåevardhana (2007). The same idea was confirmed in an interview with Catholic Priest Anura in Colombo, July 2007 (interview completed as part of an assessment report on Sri Lanka).
4 Rev. Carroll Baltimore, President of the Progressive National Baptist Convention, recited a closing prayer at a meeting of prominent coalition African American pastors who have teamed up with leaders of 'Occupy Wall Street' to launch a new series of actions that they consider part of Rev. Martin Luther King Jr.'s unfinished legacy. Rev. Ben Chavis, former head of the National Association for the Advancement of Colored People, said, during a news conference at the National Press Club in Northwest Washington, 'If Dr. King were alive today, he would be part of Occupy Wall Street' ('Black pastors link Occupy Wall Street to MLK', Hamil Harris, *Washington Post* 12/14/2011). Similarly, Catholic activists prepared to march with Occupy DC protesters when 'Catholic United', an organization that touts itself as a group designed to promote justice and the common good, first unveiled a symbolic golden calf at an 'Occupy Wall Street' march in October 2011. According to Rev. Jennifer Butler, executive director of Faith in Public Life, the golden calf is a symbol of idolatry – in this particular case, its greed and love of money – in Jewish, Christian, and Muslim traditions ('Catholics United readies golden calf for Occupy DC march', Katie Rogers, *Washington Post* 12/15/2011).
5 The film was screened in Baghdad between November 2010 and October 2011, personal communication with Saleh Al Tae, January 10, 2012.
6 Emory University was developing a PhD program in religious peacemaking.
7 See such Endowment Chairs in George Mason University; American University; Notre Dame University among others.
8 One exception is that, in 2011, the United States Institute for Peace (USIP) funded a special workshop on peace and dialogue in Turkey for Muslim women. WWW.USIP.Org
9 The '700 Club' is a classic example of such agenda exclusion and promotion of religious fanaticism in the American media and public. There are many other examples from all faith groups.
10 A similar reality also exists in the US. For example, few religious groups joined the Occupy Wall Street movement despite the possible shared agenda that can be found between religious peacebuilding programming and the movement. See previous example of religious groups in the Washington DC area, who joined the Occupy Wall Street movement.
11 There are many examples from Arab and Muslim countries; Catholic and Protestant churches in many African and Latin American countries; and the mainstream Buddhist institutions in Sri Lanka and their position on peace and protest against the war.

References

Abu-Nimer, M. (1999) *Dialogue, Conflict Resolution, and Change: Arab Jewish Encounters in Israel*, New York: SUNY.

Abu-Nimer, M. (2002) 'The Miracles of Transformation Through Interfaith Dialogue: Are you a believer?' in Smock, D. (ed.) *Interfaith Dialogue and Peacebuilding*, Washington DC: United States Institute of Peace Press.

Abu-Nimer, M., Khoury, A., and Welty, E. (2007) *Unity in Diversity: Interfaith Dialogue in the Middle East*, Washington DC: United States Institute of Peace Press.

Appleby, S. (2000) *The Ambivalence of the Sacred: Religion, Violence, and Reconciliation* (Carnegie Commission on Preventing Deadly Conflict), New York: Rowman Littlefield.

Appleby, S. (2011) Presentation to USIP Workshop on Religious Peacebuilding, 9 November.

Arinze, F. (2002) *Religions for Peace: a call for solidarity to the religions of the world*, New York: Doubleday.

Barnes, M.A. (2001) 'Between Rhetoric and Reticence: Theology of Dialogue in a Post-Modern World', in Singh, D. and Schick, R. (eds) *Approaches, Foundations, Issues and Models of Interfaith Relations*, Delhi: Henry Martin Institute of Islamic Studies, 134–153.

Cox, B. and Philpott, D. (2003) 'CFIA Task Force Report: Faith Based Diplomacy', *The Brandywine Review of Faith and International Affairs*, 1(2): 31–40.

Dyck, D. (2001) 'Islam and Christianity as Sources of Conflict and Resources for Peace on the Island of Mindanao in the Philippines: A Case Study of Two Interfaith Peace-building Initiatives', in Singh, D. and Schick, R. (eds) *Approaches, Foundations, Issues and Models of Interfaith Relations*, Delhi: Henry Martin Institute of Islamic Studies, 470–499.

FLT Films (2006) 'The Iman and the Pastor: A documentary from the heart of Nigeria', Initiative for Change. Online. Available http://www.fltfilms.org.uk/imam.html. Last accessed 20 June 2012.

Gopin, M. (2002) 'The Use of the Word and Its Limits: A Critical Evaluation of Religious Dialogue as Peacemaking', in Smock, D. (ed.) *Interfaith Dialogue and Peacebuilding*, Washington DC: United States Institute of Peace Press.

Hubbard, A. (2001) 'Understanding Majority and Minority Participation in Interracial and Interethnic Dialogue', in Abu-Nimer, M. (ed.) *Reconciliation, Justice and Coexistence*, Lanham: Lexington Books.

Johnston, D. and Sampson, C. (eds) (1995) *Religion: The Missing Dimension of Statecraft*, Oxford: Oxford University Press.

Little, D. (2007) *Peacemakers in Action: Profile of Religion in Conflict Resolution*, New York: Tenenbaum Center.

McCarthy, K. (1999) 'Reckoning with Religious Difference: Models of Interreligious Moral Dialogue', in Twiss, S.B. and Grelle, B. (eds) *Explorations in Global Ethics: Comparative Religious Ethics and Interreligious Dialogue*, Boulder, CO: Westview Press.

Schoem, D. and Hurtado, S. (eds) (2001) *Intergroup Dialogue: Deliberative Democracy in School, College, Community, and Workplace*, Michigan: University of Michigan Press.

Smock, D. (ed.) (2002) *Interfaith Dialogue and Peacebuilding*, Washington DC: United States Institute of Peace Press.

Swidler, L. (1998) *Theoria-Praxis: How Jews, Christians and Muslims Can Move Together from Theory to Practice*, Bondgenotenlaan: Peeters.

Thistlethwaite Brooks, S. (ed.) (2012) *Interfaith Just Peacemaking: Jewish, Christian, and Muslim Perspectives on the New Paradigm of Peace and War*, New York: Palgrave Macmillan.

6

RECONCILIATION

Emma Hutchison and Roland Bleiker

Introduction

Peacebuilding and reconciliation are intrinsically linked. The former refers to the broad process of establishing order and stability after conflict. The latter deals more specifically with the deep societal wounds that inevitably open up after war and other traumatic events. Antagonisms are often so entrenched and societies so divided that initial peacekeeping and peacebuilding missions can, at best, stop the conflict and start the reconstruction process. Add to this that prevailing approaches often focus on immanent tasks: providing security, building institutions, safeguarding the rule of law and implementing democratization (Cousens and Kumar 2001; Mac Ginty and Richmond 2009; Pugh 2000; Richmond 2008; Richmond 2011; Richmond and Franks 2009).

Providing security and building institutions is undoubtedly important to peacebuilding, particularly in the early days. But a stable order cannot be reached unless the psychological sources of conflict are addressed too: the residues of violence and death that linger long after open hostilities have ceased and that can, at any moment, break into the open again.

Reconciliation engages these deep-seated wounds of conflict. It is thus an important part of peacebuilding activities. But this is where agreements end. The very nature of reconciliation is hotly debated and constantly contested (see Norval 1998). Intensive discussions surround the role of testimonies and 'truth telling', the redemptive power of listening, the offering of remorse or the possibility of commemorating past injustices in politically inclusive, 'agonistic' ways. There are major debates between those advocating forgiveness and those emphasizing the need to bring culprits of past crime to justice. Or there are numerous suggestions about how to introduce and institutionalize non-discriminatory, pluralistic types of political arrangements (see Gobodo-Madikizela 2002; Hayner 2001; Honig 1996; Minow 1998; Schaap 2005; Tully 1995, 1999).

The purpose of this chapter is to highlight and explore one issue that unites all of these various approaches and debates: the crucial but all too often neglected role of emotions. We begin by outlining the central role emotions play in the context of conflict and post-conflict situations. Although the ensuing implications are increasingly recognized, there are still major obstacles to understanding the importance of emotions. To deal with these obstacles we stress the need to view emotions not just as private reactions, but as socio-political forces that contribute to the construction of identity and community. Once seen as such, emotions can then be acknowledged for the central role they play in the reconciliation process. A first important step here consists of recognizing that fear and anger often prevail after conflict. The results are antagonistic forms of identity and community that further fuel rather than solve conflict. Prevailing approaches, particularly those that stress the security and institutional dimensions of peacebuilding, are designed to manage such political residues of fear, anger and resentment. Doing so is undoubtedly important, particularly in the aftermath of a major conflict. But it is not enough to create a political environment that allows divided societies to overcome ideas about justice that centre around retribution or revenge.

We thus argue for the need to see reconciliation as a way of recasting the emotional legacies of conflict. Central here is an attempt to legitimize compassion and empathy as active components of the reconciliation process. Some scholars already recognize the importance of this process. Two examples: Andrew Schaap attributes positive emotions a central role in reconciliation processes that work in transformative, rather than merely restorative, ways (see Schaap 2005); John Paul Lederach (2005: 5) sees peacebuilding at its most important and its most promising in a society's capacity to transcend violence by creatively mobilizing a certain level of moral imagination.

A brief chapter cannot possibly provide an exhaustive account of the role that emotions play in processes of reconciliation. Doing so would inevitably have to entail engaging the unique circumstances that surround each conflict and the subsequent attempts to restore peace. We merely identify and explore the type of emotional and political mind-sets with which existing conflicts can be understood and managed more successfully. Our suggestions are thus primarily of a conceptual nature. We advance them by drawing and elaborating on our previous collaborative theoretical work (most notably Hutchison and Bleiker 2008 and Bleiker and Hutchison 2008) and on a range of individual empirical studies in which we examined peacebuilding and reconciliation in several concrete situations, such as Korea, Timor Leste, Sri Lanka and Bosnia or in the context of terrorism (for instance Bleiker 2008 and Hutchison 2010).

Approaching emotions and reconciliation

Reconciliation deals with the residues of conflict and trauma: events that have brought pain and suffering to a great number of people. Every conflict is different. But all of them – from civil wars to terrorist attacks – leave deep emotional wounds. Scholars who deal with trauma have examined the numerous ways in which the lives of survivors have become uprooted and altered in irreconcilable ways. This process goes well beyond physical scars and beyond feelings of fear and anger that inevitably accompany death and suffering. Less obvious emotional scars are just as deep, in part because conflicts often defy our capacity to reason: a traumatic event is simply too powerful to be comprehended through the type of reasoning we acquire during the normal course of our lives. The result is a deep sense of emotional dislocation (see Caruth 1996; Edkins 2003; Humphrey 2002: 11–25; Scarry 1985: 4–11).

Nowhere are these emotional scars more obvious than in the relationship between victims and perpetrators of a conflict. How can the gap between them ever be bridged? And yet, this is precisely the key task of a reconciliation process. Testimonies in truth commissions, for instance, are meant to bring victim and perpetrator together in an effort to heal and forgive (see Gobodo-Madikizela 2002: 12–20; Norval 1998: 251–6). But even when such commissions work well, as was arguably the case of South Africa, much is still required to diminish on-going feelings of fear, mistrust, betrayal, discrimination and stereotyping (see Halpern and Weinstein 2004: 570).

Emotions, then, are central to the reconciliation process. Few would dispute this observation. And yet, relatively little is known about how exactly emotions can introduce a healing process into communities of fear and anger. Or so argues Pumla Gobodo-Madikizela (2002: 8), a clinical psychologist and former member of the South African Truth and Reconciliation Commission. While placing great value on the work of the Commission, she nevertheless stresses that the Commission failed in addressing a crucial issue: the feelings and sensibilities that were associated with the telling, listening, giving of apologies and asking for forgiveness. Gobodo-Madikizela identifies a pattern that goes far beyond the reconciliation process in South Africa.

Prevalent scholarly approaches to politics and reconciliation pay far too little attention to emotions. And there are good reasons for why this is the case. For one, emotions have traditionally been seen as purely private and irrational phenomena. Historically perceived to encapsulate women's 'dangerous desires', emotions were thought to be feelings or bodily sensations that overtook us, distorting thought and the ability to make 'rational' and ethical judgement (Seidler 1998; see also Elster 1999). The task of public policy and rational decision making was thus to keep emotions away. 'Justice' must be free of passion, it was believed, because it is emotion that distorts judgement and impels people to perform irrational acts of violence and harm (see Homes 1995; Jamieson 1992).

Emotions as socio-political forces

A first major task thus consists of challenging these deeply held modern beliefs that draw a clear line between emotions and reason. Individuals make both rational and emotional judgements. In fact, perceptions, reflections and choices often involve an inseparable mixture of emotional and rational processes (Nussbaum 1995).

Even more importantly, emotions are more than mere personal reactions. They play an important social and political role. Individual experiences of conflict and trauma, for instance, can translate into collective experiences, and thus into political formations. This process plays a crucial role in shaping processes of reconciliation.

Individual feelings emerge from and are constitutive of the social and institutional processes that bind society together. This is why numerous scholars, particularly in fields such as psychology, sociology and philosophy, advocate an understanding of emotion as derived from a social context rather than internal psychological conditions alone. Particular experiences evoke particular emotions, yet it is these emotional responses that are shaped through patterns of communication and language, and more broadly, through socialization into particular historically grounded ways of being (see Nussbaum 2001: 107–9, 175–81; Shilling 1997: 197–8). Seen from such a vantage point, emotions are less manifestations of our individual nature but more expressions of 'the type of social relations in which we live' (Burkitt 1991: 2). This is the case because emotions help us to make sense of our self. They situate us in relation to others and the world that surrounds us. By framing forms of personal and social understanding, emotions are inclinations that lend individuals to locate their identity within a wider collective.

Particularly significant for processes of reconciliation is that emotions play a key role in constituting the kind of identity attachments that bind communities together. Such forms of emotional identity can emerge despite – or rather as a direct response to – the feelings of pain, solitude and fragmentation that are engendered by conflict. Traumatic events can pull people together, giving them a common purpose. Injury and death – or what one scholar calls a 'culture of pain' (Morris 1993) – can therefore become instrumental to the constitution of a community and the sense of collective identity that emerges in the wake of trauma (see Ahmed 2004; Berezin 2001, 2002; Fierke 2004; Nash 2003; Scheff 1994).

Communities of fear and anger

If emotions do indeed play a significant role in constituting identities and political communities, then emotions can and must be seen as central to how conflicts are generated, viewed and solved. If scholars and politicians have a better understanding of the role that emotions play in these processes, then they would also be able to employ emotions more effectively in attempts to promote healing and reconciliation in the aftermath of trauma.

Such a recognition leads to an obvious question: what type of emotional identities and communities tend to emerge after conflict and how can they be transformed into more peaceful or at least non-violent ones?

Post-conflict societies are not simply divided by the pain of past or continuing injustices, but also by the feelings that accompany traumatic histories and memories. Significantly, these emotions – fear, anger, resentment – often extend to broader social relations. This is not simply the case for those who have survived or witnessed trauma first-hand, but it is also true of society more generally. Fear and anger can be passed down, transcending the structures and boundaries within the wider social or communal sphere, and can influence perceptions of the world and of others. Phenomena that are feared also engender anxiety, because they threaten (see Ahmed 2004: 78–9; Furedi 2004, 2005: 122–5; Holmes 2004).

Community attachments based on fear and anger almost inevitably lead to volatile political environments. It is often only a matter of time until resentment spills over into an open conflict. In a worst case scenario the result is a cycle of violence from which it becomes almost impossible to escape. Examples here range from parts of the Middle East to Sudan and Northern Ireland. Breaking through such cycles of violence requires engaging the emotional grievances that often drive and fuel conflict in the first place.

We do not suggest that fear and anger have no place in processes of political reconciliation. Such emotions should, indeed, be of central concern. Recognizing fear and anger brings them into the public sphere, and in so doing incorporates them into processes that aim to placate feelings of revenge and create a culture of healing and collaboration (Muldoon 2008; Govier 2002). But when fear and anger remain unacknowledged and unaddressed they can easily recreate a culture of anxiety and resentment. They can then risk becoming objects of short-term political manipulation.

Prevailing approaches to peacebuilding are often not sufficiently attuned to deal with the emotional dangers that accompany communities of fear and anger. Providing security and stability tends to be seen as a more urgent and important task. Psychological issues are seen of a lower priority – as aspects of reconciliation that can be dealt with later in the peacebuilding process. This is why in many parts of the world, the social dislocation wrought by traumatic events is often countered immediately with political projects that immediately restore a sense of community, security and order (see, for instance, Edkins 2003: 9–16, 215–33). This is understandable, of course. Security in post-conflict situations is of prime importance. And so is the need to reconstruct a political order and community. But hastily conceived efforts to restore order can easy reconstitute – even if unknowingly – the very exclusions and prejudices that were responsible for generating the conflict in the first place (Schaap 2005: 13–15).

Recasting emotional reconciliation

Reconciliation deals with the emotional residues that linger underneath and beyond the institutional dimensions of peacebuilding. No matter how secure and democratically ordered a post-conflict society is, it is unlikely to achieve lasting stability if the underlying emotional sources of conflict remain unaddressed.

Needed, then, is a certain recasting of reconciliation – one that explicitly takes into account the role that emotions play in conflict and post-conflict situations. We concentrate on one particular but important aspect of this process: how an alternative, less divisive sense of identity and community can be constructed following experiences of trauma. Establishing such a conception of community is admittedly a challenge. It would involve an understanding of trauma's impact – both at a personal and social level – and attempt to put into practice strategies that promote empathetic and humanizing ways of reconciling past grievances. Doing so is to acknowledge that the prevailing institutionalized models of reconciliation and healing are not enough. Indeed, as Gobodo-Madikizela suggests (2002: 13–14), strategies that foster 'humane connections' between victim and perpetrator need to be sought if forgiveness is to become strong enough to overcome deep-seated feelings of anger and revenge. Halpern and Weinstein (2004: 579–82), likewise, speak of how perpetrators might empathetically engage or identify with victims. Doing so, they stress, is essential to find non-violent ways of working through the differences that keep traumatized and divided societies apart.

Before such strategies can be implemented in an institutionalized setting one must face difficult questions concerning how individuals and groups divided by conflict can initially be brought together, and thus how personal and collective feelings of fear and outrage can be transformed into emotions that may help to confront and ameliorate conflict: optimism and hope. We do not imply here that victims can completely forget and let go of their pain. Nor do we suggest that anger and frustration will necessarily fade away. What we do stress, though, is that some form of emotional 'turning point' in conflict must be reached before divided societies can successfully cultivate new ways of thinking about trauma and envisage the possibility of establishing a harmonious or at least non-violent order (see Gobodo-Madikizela 2002: 15; Schaap 2006: 7, 87,90–4).

A scheme of emotional healing seeks to recast political reconciliation in terms of the psychological and emotional harms that divided societies inevitably endure. Underpinning an emotionally sensitive model of social healing is the notion that societies need to acknowledge and work through not only the various emotions associated with first-hand experiences of trauma, but also the collective forms of emotions that feed into or fuel disingenuous perceptions of others, thus keeping a society divided. Important here is the basic recognition that prevailing, 'official' ways of thinking about trauma necessarily generate particular feelings – both individually and collectively. These forms of 'social emotion' – what Andrew Ross (2005: 45) has called 'affective energies' – can at least partially shape the forms of collective agency that can either help to ameliorate or perpetuate conflict. Fear and anger, for instance, fuel the mind-sets that prevent individuals and groups divided by conflict from coming together to acknowledge and attempt to heal each other's pain (for an example, see Bar-Tal 2001). If divided societies are to come together and start a process of healing, then there need to be strategies in place that allow individuals and groups to negotiate past grievances, and to reflect upon how their memories and emotions force the past into the politics of the present.

Legitimizing compassion and empathy

Considering the linkages between emotion and reconciliation inevitably leads to a more concrete question: what kind of emotions are most likely to facilitate the collective reckoning with and healing of trauma?

Particular emotions, such as empathy and compassion, may help to generate a social space conducive to the collective acknowledgment and attempted healing of trauma (see Gobodo-Madikizela 2002; Halpern and Weinstein 2004; Schaap 2006: 3–4). Empathy generally involves the ability to identify with (to at least some degree) the experiences and situation of another. Scholarly writings often suggest that empathy is key to reconstructing social relationships and communal bonds after mass violence and trauma. The respective reasoning behind this is that individuals and groups divided by conflict must be able to see the situation from the complex perspective of another, one who has been traditionally considered an adversary. In so doing the suffering and trauma of others may 'resonate emotionally', thereby providing an understanding of how another feels and why they may feel the things they do (Halpern and Weinstein 2004: 579–82). Victims and perpetrators may, as Gobodo-Madikizela (2002: 23) contends, be able to see each other as above all 'human'. This recognition may then lead to processes of re-humanization – of both victim and perpetrator – and in turn inspire the agency needed to successfully embrace reconciliation. Of course, implicit within this approach is that a form of empathetic identification – with the suffering other – can help to break down the antagonisms that caused the initial conflict. Feelings of empathy – and perhaps similarly, sympathy and compassion (see Whitebrook 2002) – may therefore prompt the shared understanding that is needed to take responsibility of, and in turn, resolve the conflict for the betterment of all.

The question of how to foster particular kinds of emotions – those that may help to ameliorate conflict and create a culture of forgiveness – also prompts broader questions concerning how the conflict and ensuing trauma is considered, and thus represented, in the wider social sphere. Practices of representing trauma and its emotions – whether they are fear and anger, guilt and remorse – inevitably become sources of identity. They often define communities in a divisive way, creating a sense of safety and unity in juxtaposition to a hostile and threatening outside. Countering such tendencies, a process of reconciliation that sees emotions as both part of the social fabric and as forms of knowledge and judgement would attempt to work through the feelings and perceptions that accompany destructive social relations. It would articulate identity and notions of community in less disparaging ways. A political process of healing would attempt to place fear and anger in context, thus drawing more actively upon feelings of compassion and empathy in order to articulate and realize a more respectful relationship between identity and difference.

The emotional value that individuals and groups attribute to their traumatic memories and the social influence these emotions then exert therefore also needs to be recognized – even if, as is often argued, individuals and groups may have to break with the past in order to unify and move on. Central here are the emotions associated with traumatic events and the manner in which they become collectively remembered and commemorated. We have already stressed how prevalent approaches to politics tend to emphasize and collectively engage emotions such as fear, anger and hatred, consequently leading to the reconstitution of antagonistic and belligerent conceptions of identity and community. Yet, how trauma is represented and commemorated are fundamental to such conceptions, for particular understandings of history can work to delineate and close off boundaries of community (see Bell 2003: 69–71; Megill 1998: 46–51; Misztal 2004: 75–7). These processes have already been uncovered and discussed at length within reconciliation literatures (for example, see Norval 1998; Schaap 2005). Scholars advocate the active engagement with, and institutionalization of, multiple histories. They speak of 'counter memory' (Booth 1999: 249–68; Misztal 2004: 77–81), 'counter memorials' (Norval 1998: 259–61) and 'minority histories' (Chakrabarty 2000), seeking to unify community by including recollections of trauma that differ from the official and widely accepted story of what happened in the past.

Conclusion: Implementing emotional reconciliation

We have sought to demonstrate that emotions are essential to the task of moving societies from conflict-prone patterns towards a culture of healing and reconciliation. A first major step in this process consists of simply recognizing the social and political influence that emotions can exert. Their influence is particularly strong in the aftermath of a conflict. This is why scholars and politicians require a systematic understanding not only of the feelings associated with first-hand experiences of trauma, but also of the manner in which these affective reactions can spread and generate collective emotions that decisively shape peacebuilding processes.

Conflict and trauma can generate powerful emotions, such as fear, anger, mistrust and betrayal, which can in turn bind societies and communities together by generating cultures of fear, anger, resentment and anxiety. Rather than initiating a much needed process of healing after atrocity and trauma, such reactions can easily generate fear of and intolerance towards difference, thus establishing new cycles of violence and hatred. Prevailing approaches to peacekeeping and peacebuilding are not necessarily equipped to deal with these tasks. Their purpose is often to deal with immanent and seemingly more important challenges: providing security, building institutions, creating democratic accountability and generating economic progress. All these aspects are undoubtedly crucial but they cannot lead to a genuinely stable and peaceful society unless one also addresses, in an active and political way, the deep emotional wounds that inevitably exist after protracted conflicts.

How is one to overcome feelings of fear, injustice and betrayal that linger after conflict? How is one to generate an open and trusting environment through which adversaries can confront each other in a non-threatening and transformative way?

We suggested that dealing with these challenges requires reframing reconciliation more consciously in terms of engaging emotional processes of personal and social healing. By providing an inclusive space – one where victims, witnesses and perpetrators can come together and visualize each other's emotional pain – we suggest that emotional understanding can help to dissolve, or at least attenuate, numerous underlying tensions. In this sense, trauma's emotions may open up possibilities for political transformation.

Our suggestions have inevitably been abstract. We do not have the space here to elaborate how they have worked – or how they could work – in concrete political situations. We were, thus, at best able to pinpoint a number of important conceptual points.

The practical consequences of our conceptual suggestions cannot easily be summarized. But they would certainly consist of stressing that the task of politicians, diplomats and mediators is – or at least ought to be – to create a space where grievances can be freely expressed, and corresponding emotions can be collectively and empathetically worked through. At stake here is not simply the suspension or cessation of violence, but also, and crucially, that adversaries are encouraged to come together in the hope that their relations can be realized anew. Once again, this is not to suggest that the emotions of direct victims can be instantly transformed. Rather, the aim would be to draw out and work through the collective, politicized forms of emotion that may unknowingly constitute animosity and divisive political relations. During times of violence the need for such a space becomes pertinent. Indeed, it would provide the conditions through which present-day politics and associated configurations of community can be reconsidered in light of injustices and exclusions (see Schaap 2006: 98–101). Being able to stop and critically reflect upon what has led events to be as they are is therefore fundamental (see Campbell 2005; Jabri 2005). Recognizing the profoundly emotional and damaging nature of violence and ensuing trauma may provide an impetus to do so. The ensuing process would involve leaders in politics and the media becoming more aware of the implications involved in the proliferation of fear and suspicion. Rather than constructing community and formulating policy around fear alone, the strategy we propose suggests that feelings of vulnerability can be considered in a political enabling way. Indeed, the sense of contingency that ensues after trauma – the sense of insecurity – can be thought as creating a space for political change.

References

Ahmed, S. (2004) *The Cultural Politics of Emotion*, Edinburgh: Edinburgh University Press.

Bar-Tal, D. (2001) 'Why Does Fear Override Hope in Societies Engulfed by Intractable Conflict, as It Does in the Israeli Society?', *Political Psychology*, 22(3): 601–27.

Bell, D.S.A. (2003) 'Mythscapes: Memory, Mythology, and National Identity', *British Journal of Sociology*, 54(1): 63–81.

Berezin, M. (2001) 'Emotions and Political Identity: Mobilizing Affection for the Polity', in Goodwin, J., Jasper, J.M. and Polletta, F. (eds), *Passionate Politics: Emotions and Social Movements*, Chicago: University of Chicago Press, pp. 83–98.

Berezin, M. (2002) 'Secure States: Towards a Political Sociology of Emotion', in Barbalet, J. (ed.), *Emotions and Sociology*, Oxford: Blackwell, pp. 33–52.

Bleiker, R. (2008) *Divided Korea: Toward a Culture of Reconciliation*, Minneapolis and London: University of Minnesota Press.

Bleiker, R. and Hutchison, E. (2008) 'Fear No More: Emotions and World Politics', *Review of International Studies*, 34(1), 115–135.

Booth, J.W. (1999) 'Communities of Memory: On Identity, Memory, and Debt', *American Political Science Review*, 93 (2): 249–68.

Burkitt, I. (1991) *Social Selves: Theories of Social Formation of Personality*, London: Sage.

Campbell, D. (2005) 'The Onto-politics of Critique', *International Relations*, 19(1): 127–34.

Caruth, C. (1996) *Unclaimed Experience: Trauma, Narrative, and History*, Baltimore: Johns Hopkins University Press.

Chakrabarty, D. (2000) *Provincializing Europe: Postcolonial Thought and Historical Difference*, Princeton: Princeton University Press.

Cousens, E.M. and Kumar, C. (eds) (2001) *Peacebuilding as Politics: Cultivating Peace in Fragile Societies*, Boulder, CO: Lynne Rienner.

Edkins, J. (2003) *Trauma and the Memory of Politics*, Cambridge: Cambridge University Press.

Elster, J. (1999) *Alchemies of the Mind: Rationality and the Emotions*, Cambridge: Cambridge University Press.

Fierke, K.M. (2004) 'Whereof We Can Speak, Thereof We Must Not Be Silent: Trauma, Political Solipsism and War', *Review of International Studies*, 30(4): 471–91.

Furedi, F. (2004) *Therapy Culture: Cultivating Vulnerability in an Uncertain Age*, London: Routledge.

Furedi, F. (2005) *Politics of Fear: Beyond Left or Right*, London: Continuum.

Gobodo-Madikizela, P. (2002) 'Remorse, Forgiveness, and Rehumanization: Stories from South Africa', *Journal of Humanistic Psychology*, 42(1): 7–32.

Govier, T. (2002) *Forgiveness and Revenge*, London: Routledge.

Halpern, J. and Weinstein, H.M. (2004) 'Rehumanizing the Other: Empathy and Reconciliation', *Human Rights Quarterly*, 26(3): 561–83.

Hayner, P.B. (2001) *Unspeakable Truths: Confronting State Terror and Atrocity*, New York: Routledge.

Holmes, M. (2004) 'The Importance of Being Angry: Anger in Political Life', *European Journal of Social Theory*, (7)2: 123–32.

Homes, S. (1995) *Passions and Constraint: On the Theory of Liberal Democracy*, Chicago: University of Chicago Press.

Honig, B. (1996) 'Difference, Dilemmas, and the Politics of Home', in Benhabib, S. (ed.), *Democracy and Difference: Contesting the Boundaries of the Political*, Princeton: University of Princeton Press, pp. 257–77.

Humphrey, M. (2002) *The Politics of Atrocity and Reconciliation: From Terror to Trauma*, London: Routledge.

Hutchison, E. (2010) 'Trauma and the Politics of Emotions: Constituting Identity, Security and Community after the Bali Bombing', *International Relations*, 24(1), 65–86.

Hutchison, E. and Bleiker, R. (2008) 'Emotional Reconciliation: Reconstituting Identity and Community After Trauma', *European Journal of Social Theory*, 11(3): 385–403.

Jabri, V. (2005) 'Critical Thought and Political Agency in Time of War', *International Relations*, 19(1): 70–8.

Jamieson, K.H. (1992) *Dirty Politics: Deception, Distraction, and Democracy*, New York: Oxford University Press.

Lederach, J.P. (2005) *The Moral Imagination: The Art and Soul of Peacebuilding*, Oxford: Oxford University Press.

Mac Ginty, R. and Richmond, O.P. (eds) (2009) *The Liberal Peace and Post-war Reconstruction*, London: Routledge.

Megill, A. (1998) 'History, Memory, Identity', *History of the Human Sciences*, 11(3): 37–62.

Minow, M. (1998) *Between Vengeance and Forgiveness: Facing History After Genocide and Mass Violence*, Boston: Beacon Press.

Misztal, B.A. (2004) 'The Sacralization of Memory', *European Journal of Social Theory*, 7 (1): 67–84.

Morris, D.B. (1993) *The Culture of Pain*, Berkeley: University of California Press.

Muldoon, P. (2008) 'The Moral Legitimacy of Anger', *European Journal of Social Theory*, 11(3): 299–314.

Nash, K. (2003) 'Cosmopolitan Political Community: Why Does It Feel So Right?', *Constellations: An International Journal of Critical and Democratic Theory*, 10(4): 506–18.

Norval, A.J. (1998) 'Memory, Identity and the (Im)possibility of Reconciliation: The Work of the Truth and Reconciliation Commission in South Africa', *Constellations: International Journal of Critical and Democratic Theory*, 5(2): 250–65.

Nussbaum, M.C. (1995) 'Rational Emotions', in *Poetic Justice: The Literary Imagination and Public Life*, Boston: Beacon, pp. 53–78.

Nussbaum, M.C. (2001) *Upheavals of Thought: The Intelligence of Emotions*, Cambridge: Cambridge University Press.

Pugh, M. (ed.) (2000) *Regeneration of War-Torn Societies*, New York: St. Martins.

Richmond, O.P. (2008) *Peace in International Relations,* London: Routledge.

Richmond, O.P. (2011) *A post-Liberal Peace*, London: Routledge.

Richmond, O.P. and Franks, J. (2009) *Liberal Peace Transitions*, Edinburgh: Edinburgh University Press.

Ross, A.A.G. (2005) *Affective States: Rethinking Passion in World Politics*, PhD dissertation, Baltimore: Johns Hopkins University.

Scarry, E. (1985) *The Body in Pain: The Making and Unmaking of the World*, New York: Oxford University Press.

Schaap, A. (2005) *Political Reconciliation*, London: Routledge.

Schaap, A. (2006) 'Agonism in Divided Societies', *Philosophy and Social Criticism*, 32(2): 255–277.

Scheff, T.J. (1994) *Bloody Revenge: Emotions, Nationalism and War*, Boulder, CO: Westview Press.

Seidler, V.J. (1998) 'Masculinity, Violence and Emotional Life', in Bendelow, G. and Williams, S.J. (eds), *Emotions in Social Life: Critical Themes and Contemporary Issues*, Routledge: London, pp. 193–210.

Shilling, C. (1997) 'Emotions, Embodiment and the Sensation of Society', *Sociological Review*, 45(2): 195–219.

Tully, J. (1995) *Strange Multiplicity: Constitutionalism in an Age of Diversity*, Cambridge: Cambridge University Press.

Tully, J. (1999) 'The Agonic Freedom of Citizens', *Economy and Society*, 28(2): 161–82.

Whitebrook, M. (2002) 'Compassion as a Political Virtue', *Political Studies*, 50(3): 529–44.

7

THE POLITICS OF MEMORY AND PEACEBUILDING

Marc Howard Ross

Introduction

Collective memory is increasingly discussed as an important feature of large group behavior and it is useful to consider how the politics of memory plays a crucial role in peacebuilding efforts. The focus on memory here is less about the memory of individuals than with the memory of groups especially those involved in long-term, often violent, conflicts. My main goal is to offer a theoretically and empirically useful way to consider collective memory's role in ethnic conflict and its relevance to peacebuilding. This chapter has two parts: the first asks four questions about the nature of collective memory relevant to the dynamics of mobilization and mitigation in contemporary conflict; the second offers six lessons for peacebuilding. The argument is built around two central premises: that the construction of collective memories is a social and political process, and that present needs shape what is told and retained about the past and help explain both continuities and changes in memory over time. Because the content of collective memories and the uses of the past change, we need to focus on the forces that move them in a more or less inclusive direction.

Four questions about collective memory

(1) What is collective memory and how is it conceptualized? The *what* problem examines several puzzles in the identification of collective memory in the study of ethnic conflict and peacebuilding; (2) Who makes up the collectivity that shares, nourishes, and modifies these memories? The *who* problem focuses on the identification of relevant units of analysis given the absence of formal group boundaries with membership criteria; (3) What are the mechanisms by which collective memories are maintained, communicated and transformed? The *mechanism* problem asks how individuals and groups come to hold, invoke and transmit collective memories; (4) How are collective memories an important foundation for collective action? The *action* problem asks how and when are memory and identity mobilized to produce collective action in the name of the group.[1]

What is collective memory?

Collective memories have both cognitive and affective components. They are about emotionally salient events and persons in the past that have particular relevance to how a group understands itself and the challenges it faces in the present and future. These accounts are not simply historical details about the past but are central in conveying social, political, and moral lessons. A starting point for some authors is the difference between what is often referred to as history which is about facts, specific events and truth (as positivists use the term)—an 'objective' past that can be found in documents and other artifacts such as archaeological evidence and popular memory. In contrast, others emphasize how people understand the past and situate it in social frameworks (Olick, Vinitzky-Seroussi, and Levy 2011). The significance of a more subjective understanding of the past is located in popular narratives and memories as experienced through the eyes and mind of participants in the events and their descendants (Olick, Vinitzky-Seroussi, and Levy 2011). Despite real limits to this distinction, it can serve as a useful starting point. Yet the limits are important too for both historical accounts and collective memory should be understood as selective narratives that include plausible explanations about the past found in culturally accessible locations such as in school texts, films, commemorative events, family stories, and the sacred places that are emotionally significant for groups.

One complicated issue is the extent to which there needs to be consensus over the content of collective memories to be considered truly 'collective'. We can certainly identify events, persons and groups in many societies about which many people have clear memories either from direct experience or from learning about them from others. At the same time, because many people remember the 'same' large-scale events, there is invariably significant diversity in what exactly is remembered and the specific emotions associated with these memories that are linked to the social diversity in who is remembering what. As a result, we can ask what is the same about memories of the 'same event' when they are remembered differently.

Consider four examples from American history about which there are many strong beliefs and emotions: the founding of the United States, the Civil War, World War II, and the Vietnam War. Two of these events are beyond the personal experiences of Americans alive today or their immediate ancestors, while the two twentieth-century wars are in the living memory of most Americans either through their own experiences or the accounts of family members and friends. If we ask the extent to which there is consensus around the memories about these events we would find that there is high consensus in how Americans think about the founding of the country in the late eighteenth century and in their understanding of WWII, but significant differences in both the content and emotions concerning the Civil War and Vietnam. For example, the specific memories of the American Civil War and the lessons they have drawn from them are generally quite divergent in the north and the south and among whites and blacks, and there are changes over time as well (Blight 2001). Yet I suggest all four of these events are relevant to the study of collective memory even though in two of the cases there is low consensus around the content and emotions associated with them. The key point is that most Americans have some knowledge and feelings about all four of these events as opposed to people living in Central Asia or Central Africa.

The same question arises when we ask what it is that people in the same culture share (Ross 2009b). People who share a culture are not identical in all of their beliefs and behaviors, meaning that there is within-group diversity in any cultural community. Cultures are not membership groups like labor unions or states that provide membership or identity cards that allow us to quickly know if someone is in one or not included. By themselves shared beliefs or common actions do not tell us all we want to know about shared cultural identity. People may hold common views or engage in similar actions but consider themselves part of very different cultural traditions. Conversely, people who are part of the same culture may hold diverse views on many issues or engage in very different behaviors. Anthropologist Robert LeVine (1984), building on Clifford Geertz (1973), argues this is not a problem since culture is best understood as a shared system of meaning—what some describe as a mutually intelligible frame or worldview— not particular practices or specific beliefs. This means that while there is significant within-cultural variation in the thoughts, feelings, and behaviors, what people share are common systems of meaning—and understandings of the symbols and representations they communicate and that accompany a shared cultural identity (LeVine 1984: 68).

Memories, like culture, are formed and persist through social interaction as Maurice Halbwachs, the French sociologist, argued in his still-influential analysis of collective memory (Halbwachs 1995 [1950]). He showed how social structure produces and shapes institutions and interpersonal networks that frame worldviews and organize narratives forming shared accounts of key events and personalities. This perspective stresses social frameworks and specific practices—especially rituals and commemorative activities as Halbwachs emphasized that reinforce the acquisition, retention and power of memories of past events (Fogu and Kansteiner 2006; Lebow 2006; Middleton and Edwards 1990; Olick 1999; Olick and Robbins 1998). Controlling narratives and defining their content affects what is then remembered and what is forgotten by a group. Post-modern analyses such as Hobsbawm and Ranger's (1983) notion of 'the invention of tradition' emphasize the constructed and changing nature of the past and memories about it, and make us aware that important national holiday celebrations such as July 14, Bastille Day in France, or July 12, marking the Battle of the Boyne for Protestants in Northern Ireland, were not widely celebrated until more than a century after the events themselves. Similarly, the memories surrounding important historical figures and places are rarely stable and can change a good deal over time (Schwartz 1991, 1997, 2000).

What this means is that we should think of collective memories as socially constructed accounts that change in response to contemporary needs and to shifts in political events and social conditions. At the same time Schudson (1989) reminds us that there are limits to the ways that the past can be reconstructed because available materials are structured and finite, limiting individual choice. As a result, once the past is enshrined in certain ways, it is hard, but not impossible, to alter.

To study how people think about the past, historians Rosenzweig and Thelen (1998) asked a national sample of Americans what the past means to them and how they use it. The answers they received support Halbwachs' notions about the role of social structure in shaping what people know about the past and how the memories are shaped. Their data emphasize the importance of personal—and especially family—networks in providing both cognitive and emotional accounts about the past, invariably beginning with personal connections to it and working outward and connecting distant events and people in highly personal ways. For them, the past that most people easily relate to grows out of personal links through which more distant events are filtered. They also find that group identities matter in filtering the past and how it is used. For example, Blacks are more likely to refer to their ancestors collectively—not just referring to family members—and to see their own histories as a microcosm of the group experience much more than Whites do.

In sum, memories that matter are cognitive and affective; there is variation in content within and between groups even when people share mutually intelligible frames and meanings to interpret events; events and people who can be connected cognitively and emotionally to one's own life experiences are the most significant ones to most people; racial and ethnic identities sometimes play an important role in memory; written history and school textbooks are not as salient as accounts from family and friends; personally experienced historical sites and museums are more important in developing collective memories than school texts and many media presentations which are variously seen as either distant or biased (Rosenzweig and Thelen 1998).

Who shares collective memories?

This question can be asked in two different ways which produce two different answers. If we begin with a particular group of people—large or small—we can ask what memories they hold in common. Second, we can start with individuals and ask which memories they share with others. Which approach to collective memories is of interest, depends on what questions one is asking.

The first is most relevant if one is interested in the collective memories found in groups of family members or those in local communities, work groups, among gender groups or age cohorts as well as larger collectivities such as those defined in terms of ethnic, racial and national identities. The larger point is that all human groups of whatever size and makeup will have certain collective memories with which a large proportion of their members are familiar, just as they have cultural frameworks and systems of meaning to make sense of them. Memories of certain kinds of events and people such as prominent political events like some elections, assassinations, coups d'état, and wars are widely shared. So are traumatic natural and human-made disasters. There are also acts of bravery and heroism and sporting and entertainment events common to large numbers of people in the same generation or country. At the same time, there will be internal diversity among people in large collectivities such as religious or national groups that results in variation in the content and affect of shared collective memories and in the intensity with which they are held.

In contrast, starting with individuals rather than a group will show that no one shares *all* his or her memories with other people, and even those that are shared are not shared with the same people and no others because people operate in multiple social worlds through multiple social networks in their lives. While an initial reaction might be that if the memories are not all the same within a group, they are not really collective, a more nuanced reflection would be that with all collective memories there are some parts for which there is widespread consensus and high agreement in content while there are other parts about which there are differences in emphasis and even outright disagreement. For some this poses a crucial methodological barrier. However, this is the messy reality of social life and the diversity of social networks makes identifying collective memories difficult but does not mean that they are not worth understanding.

What are the mechanisms by which collective memories are held, invoked and transformed?

This is a large question that can be answered from a variety of theoretical and disciplinary perspectives. I focus here on the social mechanisms and the widespread agreement that (1) social and individual mechanisms are connected, as Halbwachs first argued, and (2) that social dynamics are central to understanding the salience and accessibility of individual memories both of which are crucial to understand the content and structure of the collective memories and their relevance for peacebuilding.

The social sources of collective memory creation and retention are wide-ranging and not always easy to categorize. The most obvious one is the small face-to-face worlds in which people live. Family, school, peer group, and work settings matter, as the large literature on socialization has documented for decades. For example, Devine-Wright and Lyons (1997) found that emotions associated with historically sacred sites in Ireland differed across political groups in significant ways and argued that '[p]laces seem to act as cues for social memories for different groups' (1997: 44). What must be emphasized is that in addition to the cognitive and affective learning in social contexts, people share 'theories' about the world, groups in it, and core assumptions about the motives of insiders and outsiders and how they are likely to behave in particular situations. I refer to these as psychocultural interpretations that prioritize and shape beliefs and actions particularly in high stress, ambiguous situations such as high conflict and violence settings (Ross 2007).

Direct and indirect personal experiences are a common, crucial way that memories are created and reinforced.[2] For example, Rosenzweig and Thelen's (1998) data show that learning about an event, such as World War II or the Civil Rights movement, through an older family member or friend is a crucial transmission channel. One reason is that such sources are trusted more highly than sources such as history books or the media. We should not be surprised to learn this for it is the way that many traditional cultures transmitted important information for generations.

The mass media clearly matter in both transmitting and reinforcing memories although we should recognize that claims about mass media impact often greatly outrun solid evidence for them. Still, we can safely say that there are now enough studies to support the proposition that the media matter in *what* we think about and *how* we think about it—the process of agenda-setting (Iyengar 1991). However, not all media messages are equally relevant. Only some create powerful memories for people and heighten the likelihood of their long-term retention. Prominent among these are unexpected, traumatic ones where the media images are retained for and often transmitted across generations (Dayan and Katz 1992). Dayan and Katz emphasize the ceremonial aspects of media events and how they communicate a yearning for togetherness and fusion that are especially relevant in high intensity situations. Live media coverage of historical events, often occasions of state, can transfix a nation or the world and collectively experiencing them in small groups of family and friends then reinforces their emotional intensity and shared perception of reality (1992: 177).

A very different mechanism is direct participation in actions that can have significant effects on memory creation and reinforcement for individuals and groups. Verba (1961) found strong support for the participation hypothesis, the idea that once people engage in a behavior they are more likely to be emotionally invested in it. Such events are then more likely to be remembered, in part to justify the energy and resources the individual or group invested in an action in the first place.[3] This mechanism often operates by getting people to take small steps—attending a meeting, signing a petition, donating a small amount of money—which make them more committed to a cause. Of course, this is contrary to the widespread belief, at least in western culture, that to get people to do (or remember) something they first need to be persuaded that it is important.

How are collective memories mobilized to produce collective action?

Collective memories, even when they are deeply felt, don't explain group mobilization in any simple way. Rather, the emotions and beliefs contained in the memories need to be translated into actions—a process that concretizes the connections between the memories about the past, and what should be done in the present.[4] Making sense of how this is accomplished in different contexts is challenging because it is unlikely that there is one simple pattern of linkage. Collective memories are not isolated fragments but larger aggregations organized in ways that highlight, emphasize and frame particular perspectives and privilege certain versions of the past while playing down or ignoring others that shape present and future action that render some behaviors more plausible than others. This framing emphasizes a particular worldview that makes certain courses of action seem reasonable and others less attractive although it would be simplistic to believe that worldviews directly cause action themselves.

Three conceptual tools—narratives, ritual expressions and enactments, and symbolic landscapes—are especially important here and can be a useful part of successful peacebuilding in societies with strong memories of previous intense hostility and trauma. In settings with high polarization, distrust, and strong collective memories of intergroup hostility, peacebuilding activities must address how former enemies view each other and create room to coexist. To accomplish this is an important step in the development of more inclusive frameworks that envision a peaceful shared future and what it means for people's daily lives. Narratives, ritual expressions and enactments, and symbolic landscapes can be viewed as *aides mémoires* in the development, reinforcement and transmission of collective memories (Ross 2007, 2009a). Often these are used to emphasize exclusive accounts and practices that reinforce polarization, but because they are constructed, peacebuilding can mobilize them to develop more inclusive memories and views of the future that promote peacebuilding.

Narratives are explanations for events—large and small—in the form of short, common sense accounts (stories). They are often communicated through expressions and enactments which may be mundane, everyday, or special, activities such as religious practices, music, film, theater, paintings, language use, statues, museum presentations, memorials, public monuments, clothing, or flag displays that symbolically connect the past and present. What is crucial to remember is that they are infused with strong emotions communicating far more than historical facts. Narratives meet many needs and people are especially likely to rely upon them when they are disoriented and struggling to make sense of events in situations of high uncertainty and stress in societies coming out of conflict. In this way narratives become key linkage mechanisms connecting people across time and space as they draw on shared memories (Volkan 1988).

Repetitive cultural rituals are a powerful way to create and strengthen narratives and collective memories and while they are often presented as timeless, rituals are regularly invented and reinvented to meet present fears and needs (Connerton 1989; Hobsbawm and Ranger 1983). Participation in a wide range of activities such as festivals and commemorative ceremonies is important in Connerton's analysis which emphasizes that rites are not merely expressive; rites are not merely formal; and rites are not limited in their effect to ritual occasions (1989: 44). In addition, rituals commemorate continuity and in so doing shape communal memory (1989: 48). Invented rituals sometimes begin long after the events they mark. In addition, '[r]itual is not only an alternative way of expressing certain beliefs, but that certain things can be expressed only in ritual' (Connerton 1989: 54). As such, they can be a significant barrier to intergroup reconciliation and reinforce prior differences but when they are recast in more inclusive terms, rituals offer a powerful way to express new relationships.

A society's symbolic landscapes communicate and frame social and political messages through public spaces imbued with emotional significance that express a society's core values and honor heroes through images, objects and other expressive representations (Cosgrove 1998). Some are sacred sites, but not necessarily religious ones. These landscapes frame social and political messages, communicate power and belonging through how they represent inclusion and exclusion, hierarchy, and portray dominant and subordinate groups in particular ways. They can create and transmit collective memories as well as help change them over time. These sites represent group identity and when certain rituals take place on them, they can enhance a narrative's emotional significance. Examples of this connection abound in group holidays and rituals that emphasize a link between the present and past, inviting us to consider: Who is present and who is absent in public representations? What are the qualities of those people and objects portrayed in it? Who controls the representations and to what extent are they contested? How is hierarchy portrayed and what qualities are associated with particular positions within a society's hierarchy?

Inclusion and exclusion are powerfully expressed through the expansion or restriction of a society's narratives, rituals and its symbolic landscapes. Exclusion of groups from the symbolic landscape is a clear denial of belonging. In contrast, a more inclusive symbolic landscape can powerfully communicate mutuality and a shared stake in society. It renders the previously unseen visible, gives voice to those once voiceless, or publicly identifies what was previously invisible. Inclusion offers powerful messages that can help reshape relations among those who once fought bitterly, offering acceptance and legitimation that can both reflect and promote changes in intergroup relationships. Through inclusion, groups can more easily develop a shared identity that helps mourn past losses and expresses hopes and aspirations for a joint future.

Collective memories and peacebuilding

Given the importance of collective memories, they must be an integral part of any peacebuilding process in societies that have experienced protracted conflict and violence.

Creating new institutions is critical in such societies but by itself insufficient to build a durable peace. Given the role that long-term hostility and distrust fed by anger and feelings of exclusion play in intergroup conflict, the emotional side of relationships and long-term memories about them must be included in peacebuilding efforts. At the same time, it is the case that collective memories are often sources of conflict exacerbation rather than the opposite. Yet because social processes can modify collective memories, there is also the potential to add to, modify, and repackage them in ways that lower hostility and distrust and promote intergroup cooperation. Central to peacebuilding are inclusion, acknowledgment, focus on a shared future, the identification of common interests, and positive experiences that reward peacebuilding initiatives. Addressing collective memories can play a role in each of these as peacebuilders set to work.

Collective memories are rarely directly malleable and simply telling people they are wrong is rarely productive. Rather, they shift and even change when lived experiences change and as people begin to view each other in less suspicious and distrustful ways. As a result, peacebuilding is likely to have its greatest effect on collective memories when it improves the short and medium-term rewards resulting from the operation of new institutional arrangements and addresses the emotional needs of members of all communities so that the benefits of peace are apparent and past differences are not viewed as inevitable predictors of future conflicts.

With this framework in mind, I close by offering six suggestions about how the politics of memory might be addressed and incorporated into peacebuilding processes.

1 *Increase inclusiveness.* During periods of intense conflict collective memories of groups—even in the same society—are exclusive and highly differentiated. Peacebuilding must find ways to bridge these differences among former enemies in ways that begin to develop more inclusive and shared understandings of the past, present and future. Narratives, rituals, and symbolic landscapes all should be part of this process.

2 *Acknowledgment matters.* Groups building new relationships invariably feel very vulnerable. It is crucial that peacebuilders do not try to assign blame to entire groups for a previous conflict. There should be no rush to develop a common narrative about the past as any group will feel this as denial of their own past, drawing attention to what is lost and harden, rather than weaken, fears about what peacemaking entails. Although it seems paradoxical, it is better for groups to mutually acknowledge their differences in interpretations of past events than be obliged to reject what they still believe.

   Acknowledgment is not the same as acceptance. Acknowledgment recognizes differences in interpretations or experiences without necessarily approving them. It entails risks, however, and for that reason mutual acknowledgment is far more effective as a joint action than a unilateral effort. One barrier is that acknowledgment is fraught with high risks when it is viewed in zero-sum terms. For example, Kelman (1999) points out that Israelis and Palestinians often fear that acknowledging the other's political right to exist is a denial of one's own rights and this same dynamic is seen in many other situations as well.

   Acknowledgment of joint rights becomes very problematic in the case of resources such as land, water, minerals or government positions that are perceived as limited so that the more one side controls then the less the other can have. Sacred areas such as holy sites are particularly difficult to share and some writers describing this problem contend that it may be impossible in the immediate aftermath of long-term conflict (Hassner 2009). At the same time, there are a number of sites that are historically sacred to more than one group that have been shared over long periods of time, so sharing is not necessarily impossible—just hard to achieve.

3 *Focus on a shared future and the identification of joint interests.* Unless a conflict ends in the military victory of one side over the other, peacebuilding has to focus on the joint needs of the former opponents. The recent and even the distant past is not a place to begin since it will only emphasize differences. The present and the future need to be the focus of attention in ways that stress common needs and mutual gains to establish confidence and trust that cooperation is better than conflict and that each side will stick to an agreement. An obvious example is the promise of safer and more prosperous life for children that parents on all sides wish for after overt conflict and violence. When this is successful, negative mutual images and the memory of past suffering can be more easily compartmentalized and past events are less likely seen as a prologue to future ones. This strategy is not to deny the past, but to 'contain' it.

4 *Moving away from polarized, simplistic stereotypes of former opponents.* Rather than promote a narrative that demonizes an out-group and portrays conflict with them as inevitable, the identification of common interests requiring cooperation can help. It would encourage the construction of more nuanced mutual images as people learn that there are among their former opponents those with whom one can undertake joint, cooperative actions, and identify goals and interests. In the same way that interest differences can be tied to specific time periods, extreme negative images can be compartmentalized as well.

5 *Develop common rituals and expressions.* Expressive culture can be a central feature of peacebuilding. Typically divided and strife-torn societies are characterized by exclusive rituals and symbolic expressions in each community that accentuate distinctiveness. Obvious examples include religious practices, holidays, songs, language choices, heroes, flags, emblems, banners and festivals. What is missing are common expressions that bring members of each community together. Following wars what one side celebrates is often a cause for another to mourn. In Northern Ireland, for example, Protestant celebrations of the Battle of the Boyne mark their triumph over Britain's Catholic monarch and symbolize their centuries of domination over the island's Catholic majority. In Israel, Independence Day marks the founding of the state for Jews in 1948 while Land Day marks the 'Nakba', the Palestinians' loss of their homes, fields and expulsion into exile at the same time.

Sometimes former enemies successfully develop common rituals and expressions that mark a change in their relationship. In recent decades we can find a number of examples in the changed relationship between Germany and its neighbors. Perhaps most iconic is the 1970 photo of German Chancellor Willy Brandt falling to his knees in an apparently spontaneous gesture of humility and penance at the site of the Warsaw Ghetto uprising after laying a wreath. At Verdun, the site of a ten-month long basically inconclusive 1916 WWI battle in

Northern France where 306,000 French and German soldiers died and half a million more were wounded, is today a memorial site emphasizing the folly of this and similar European wars, although it once was a French symbol of resistance against the invading German army. In 1984, French President François Mitterrand and German Chancellor Helmut Kohl participated in a moving reconciliation ceremony at the battlefield holding each other's outstretched hands while laying a wreath together to mark the casualties both sides suffered.

6 *Create inclusive symbolic landscapes.* In divided societies sacred sites, public rituals, memorials, monuments and museums are dominated by the more powerful group while the weaker ones are often absent or invisible in these places and events. Peacebuilding needs strategies that move them in more inclusive directions. One way to do this is the modification of previously exclusive sites and the broadening of the representations on them. For example, in Pretoria, the National Museum and other South African museums now call what was known as the Second Boer War (1899–1902), the South African War and point out that a significant number of Blacks were involved in it in various capacities and some 30,000 lost their lives. In the United States, 25 years after the Civil War, the government granted permission to southern states to build memorials to their fallen soldiers at Gettysburg, the site of the war's bloodiest battle in 1863. Veterans from the two sides began to hold joint reunions and reenactments and after 1900 former Confederate soldiers could be buried in Arlington National Cemetery. Only in very recent decades have sites of slavery in both the north and south been marked and the long-forgotten stories of events on them begun to be told.

Notes

1 There is an additional dimension that is worth thinking about but that I do not consider here which is, 'Why and how does the intensity of collective memories vary across individuals, cultural groups, and over time?' The *intensity* problem asks how and why not all collective memories are equally salient for all people in a group. Initially I would suggest that there are two very different answers to the question of why there is invariably within-group variation in the intensity and meaning of collective memories. One is that collective memories serve the interests and goals of different people and subgroups. This answer emphasizes how interests motivate action and define meanings; the second is that identities are at the core of engagement in collective memories and that particularly when identities are threatened, people protect them through rituals and symbolic expressions that the lessons from collective memories reinforce.

2 By indirect personal experiences I am referring to those experienced through a person close to an individual rather than the individual.

3 The argument is also consistent with dissonance theory which makes a similar argument that engaging in an action makes a person or group more committed to it.

4 Any full explanation would also need to consider opportunity structures and resources that promote or inhibit action as well.

References

Blight, D.W. (2001) *Race and Reunion: The Civil War in American History*, Cambridge and London: Belknap/Harvard.

Connerton, P. (1989) *How Societies Remember*, Cambridge: Cambridge University Press.

Cosgrove, D.E. (1998) *Social Formation and Symbolic Landscape*, Second Edition, Madison: University of Wisconsin Press.

Dayan, D., and E. Katz (1992) *Media Events: The Live Broadcasting of History*, Cambridge: Harvard University Press.

Devine-Wright, P., and E. Lyons (1997) 'Remembering Pasts and Representing Places: The Construction of National Identities in Ireland', *Journal of Environmental Psychology*, 17: 33–45.

Fogu, C., and W. Kansteiner (2006) 'The Politics of Memory and the Poetics of History'. In *The Politics of Memory in Postwar Europe*, eds. R.N. Lebow, W. Kansteiner and C. Fogu, Durham and London: Duke University Press. 284–304.

Geertz, C. (1973) 'Thick Description: Toward an Interpretive Theory of Culture.' In *The Interpretation of Cultures*, ed. Clifford Geertz. New York: Basic Books. 3–30.

Halbwachs, M. (1995) [1950] *La memoire collective*, Paris: Albin Michel.

Hassner, R.E. (2009) *War on Sacred Grounds*, Ithaca and London: Cornell University Press.

Hobsbawm, E. and T. Ranger, eds. (1983) *The Invention of Tradition*, Cambridge: Cambridge University Press.

Iyengar, S. (1991) *Is Anyone Responsible? How Television Frames Political Issues*, Chicago: University of Chicago Press.

Kelman, H.C. (1999) 'The Interdependence of Israeli and Palestinian National Identities: The Role of the Other in Existential Conflicts', *Journal of Social Issues* 55(3): 581–600.

Lebow, R.N. (2006) 'The Politics of Memory in Postwar Europe'. In *The Politics of Memory in Postwar Europe*, eds. R.N. Lebow, W. Kansteiner and C. Fogu, Durham and London: Duke University Press. 1–39.

LeVine, R.A. (1984) 'Properties of Culture: An Ethnographic View'. In *Culture Theory: Essays on Mind, Self and Emotion*, ed. R.A. Schweder and R.A. LeVine. Cambridge: Cambridge University Press. 67–87.

Middleton, D. and D. Edwards (1990) 'Introduction'. In *Collective Remembering* eds. D. Middleton and D. Edwards. London: Sage Publications. 1–22.

Olick, J.K. (1999) 'Collective Memory: The Two Cultures', *Sociological Theory* 17: 333–48.

Olick, J.K., and J. Robbins (1998) 'Social Memory Studies: From "Collective Memory" to the Historical Sociology of Mnemonic Practices', *Annual Review of Sociology* 24: 105–40.

Olick, J.K., Vinitzky-Seroussi, and D. Levy (2011) 'Introduction'. In *The Collective Memory Reader*, eds. J.K. Olick, Vinitzky-Seroussi and D. Levy. Oxford and New York: Oxford University Press. 3–62.

Rosenzweig, R. and D. Thelen (1998) *The Presence of the Past: Popular Uses of History in American Life*, New York: Columbia University Press.

Ross, M.H. (2007) *Cultural Contestation in Ethnic Conflict*. Cambridge: Cambridge University Press.

Ross, M.H. (2009a) 'Cultural Contestation and the Symbolic Landscape: Politics by Other Means?' In *Culture and Belonging in Divided Societies: Contestation and Symbolic Landscapes* ed. M.H. Ross. Philadelphia: University of Pennsylvania Press. 1–24.

Ross, M.H. (2009b) 'Culture in Comparative Political Analysis'. In *Comparative Politics: Rationality, Culture and Structure*, eds. M.I. Lichbach and A.S. Zuckerman. Cambridge: Cambridge University Press.

Schudson, M. (1989) 'The present in the Past Versus the Past in the Present', *Communication* 11: 105–13.

Schwartz, B. (1991) 'Social Change and Collective Memory: The Democratization of George Washington', *American Sociological Review* 56: 221–36.

Schwartz, B. (1997) 'Collective Memory and History: How Lincoln Became a Symbol of Racial Equality' *The Sociological Quarterly* 38 (3): 469–96.

Schwartz, B. (2000) *Abraham Lincoln: Forge of National Memory*, Chicago and London: University of Chicago Press.

Verba, S. (1961) *Small Groups and Political Behavior: A Study of Leadership*, Princeton: Princeton University Press.

Volkan, V.D. (1988) *The Need to Have Enemies and Allies: From Clinical Practice to International Relationships*, Northvale, NJ: Jason Aronson.

PART III

Disciplinary approaches to peacebuilding

8

INTERNATIONAL RELATIONS THEORY AND PEACEBUILDING

Dominik Zaum

Peacebuilding research more generally, and theorising about peacebuilding in particular, has been a genuinely interdisciplinary endeavour, and has brought together contributions from comparative politics, sociology, economics, political economy, anthropology, and international relations. Many of these have made major – at times controversial and contested – contributions to the peacebuilding debates and practices. These include the importance of state-building (Paris 2004); the difficulty of transitioning from narrow elite settlements (or closed access orders) to open, peaceful societies (North, Wallis and Weingast 2009; de Waal 2009: 99–113); and the economic causes of civil war (and by implication peace) (Collier and Hoeffler 2004: 563–95). This chapter examines what International Relations (IR) theory has contributed to the 'reading' and 'doing' of peacebuilding, that is to interpreting contemporary peacebuilding practices ('reading') and to our understanding of what peacebuilding interventions work and why, and what key obstacles to effective peacebuilding efforts are ('doing'). Both the interpretation of and engagement in peacebuilding are complex, multi-faceted practices that cannot be captured in their entirety in a short chapter. Reading peacebuilding can involve amongst other things situating peacebuilding within wider global practices, normatively evaluating peacebuilding practices, or critically engaging with the objectives of peace-builders. Doing peacebuilding involves anything from deciding on peacebuilding interventions in the first place; to peacebuilding programming and a concomitant understanding of what might work and what might not in particular circumstances; to the structures and resourcing of peacebuilding efforts. Theory – though not necessarily IR theory – can contribute to all of these.

To keep the discussion focused and the chapter reasonably readable, the focus here is therefore on the following. First, with regard to reading peacebuilding, the chapter examines what IR theory has contributed to the debate on liberal peacebuilding, as this paradigm and the extensive critique of it have been the dominant lenses through which peacebuilding efforts have been read. While sceptical about the contribution of the liberal peace debate to the reading – and understanding – of contemporary peacebuilding practices, it argues that IR theory has made important contributions to both the liberal peace argument, and to the critical engagement with the liberal peace. Second, with regard to doing peacebuilding, the chapter examines what IR theory has contributed to the understanding of what works and does not work in peacebuilding interventions, and to what the key challenges to successful peacebuilding, understood narrowly as the avoidance of conflict recidivism,[1] are. It argues that overall our understanding of what contributes to the successful consolidation of peace has remained limited,[2] as is consequently the contribution that IR theory has made to this endeavour. However, important insights into what works in peacebuilding, such as the contribution that peace operations can make to the implementation of peace agreements, come from IR theory's insights into the role of security dilemmas. Theory on its own however, can only provide new perspectives and avenues of investigation, it cannot provide evidence for what works and what does not. Ultimately, our knowledge of peacebuilding practices can only improve if theoretical claims are empirically tested in a systematic fashion. The limited insights that IR theorising has offered into the understanding of peacebuilding are the result of a characteristic of research into peacebuilding more generally; there is a paucity of rigorous empirical research, especially comparative research.

Before examining these two questions in more detail, it is worth highlighting three apparent limitations to evaluating the contribution of IR theory, in particular to reading and doing peacebuilding: its overlap with different disciplines of social science, its focus on the international, and the limited explicit engagement with peacebuilding in mainstream IR theory.

First, similar to peacebuilding, IR itself has rather blurred disciplinary boundaries, overlapping and drawing on insights from within international law, international political economy, international development, history, and sociology, to name only the most obvious ones. This makes it problematic to attribute particular theoretical claims uniquely to IR theory. Various conceptions of international order are advanced by different IR theories, and the causal mechanisms that different theories identify often draw on these different disciplines: Kenneth Waltz famously highlights the role of microeconomic theory in his development of structural realism and his claims about the effects of anarchy on state-behaviour (Waltz 1979). Similarly, are claims about the peacebuilding effects of democracy and democratisation insights from the domestic application of democratic peace theory (which is generally considered to be part of IR theory),[3] or should they be attributed to democratic theory and comparative democratisation scholars? The work of individual theorists has also at times been shaped by their own personal and professional experiences, as Martti Koskenniemi (2000: 17–34) has highlighted with regard to Hans Morgenthau, whose understandings of the role of power and law in international relations were substantively shaped by his experience as a lawyer in the dying days of Weimar Germany.

Second, the main focus of IR theory – explaining the structures and dynamics of international order – is not an obvious place to start to look for insights for peacebuilding debates, which are generally concerned with the transformation of the structures and dynamics of domestic order that fuelled violence in the first place. There are, undoubtedly, good reasons for which IR theory might offer a useful lens for understanding peacebuilding practices and challenges. Peacebuilding has become an important preoccupation of major international and regional organisations, and of powerful states that have increasingly institutionalised it in their policy-making machinery. Global norms, especially human rights norms, have been regularly invoked

Table 8.1 Articles on peacebuilding and related topics in leading IR theory journals, 1991–2011

	EJIR	Int. Organi- zation	Int. Security	Int. Studies Quarterly	Review of Int. Studies	Security Studies	World Politics	Total
1991–1995	0	0	0	2	0	0	1	3
1996–2000	0	1	2	0	0	0	2	5
2001–2005	0	2	0	2	2	0	4	10
2006–2011	2	1	3	6	9	3	3	27
Total	2	4	5	10	11	3	10	45

to justify peacebuilding interventions. Processes of globalisation mean that peacebuilding has important regional and global dimensions, i.e. through regional conflict dynamics (as in West Africa and the Balkans) (Pugh and Cooper 2004), and the role of global flows of licit and illicit resources and their implications for peacebuilding (Ballentine and Nitzsche 2005). However, the focus of IR on international dynamics and actors raises the danger that the actions and motives of these actors become the predominant focus of peacebuilding theory, at the expense of understanding local perceptions of peacebuilding, local interests, local politics, and their interactions with external peacebuilding aims and practices. The extent to which the influence of IR theory on peacebuilding debates has indeed held the focus until recently predominantly on the role of international actors and structures will be discussed in more detail below.

Finally, despite the prominence of peacebuilding as an international practice, there has only been limited explicit theoretical engagement, especially by mainstream IR, with peacebuilding, though a range of prominent IR theorists such as Robert Keohane (2003: 275–98) and Stephen Krasner (2006: 85–120) have over the last decade engaged with normative questions related in particular to the right to intervene, that touch on the peacebuilding debate. One indicator of this is the noted absence of peacebuilding scholarship in the major IR theory journals. A quick database search of article topics in leading IR theory journals (Table 8.1) suggests that throughout the first two decades of the post-Cold War period, the discussion of peacebuilding in some of the leading journals remained very limited, even as peacebuilding and associated practice like state-building and stabilisation have become prominent international practices that have absorbed substantial resources, and have been increasingly institutionalised at both the international and national level.[4]

As the increase in articles on peacebuilding after 2001 suggests, only in the aftermath of the 9/11 attacks, and the subsequent wars in Afghanistan and Iraq (both of which have been extensively examined through a peace- and state-building lens) did IR theory properly 'discover' peacebuilding. Until then, theoretical peacebuilding debates largely remained the preserve of a few specialised journals.[5]

Reading peacebuilding: IR theory and the liberal peace debate

The 'liberal peacebuilding' label is most commonly associated with the notion that the establishment of liberal institutions – democracy, human rights, an open economy, and the rule of law – is a key condition for sustainable peace in societies affected by civil war (Chesterman, Ignatieff and Thakur 2005; Dobbins, Crane, Jones, Rathmell, Steele and Teltschik 2005; Barnett 2006: 87–112). While this belief in the beneficial causal effects of liberal institutions has been at the core of the liberal peace argument, it has often been used in a looser way, and interventions characterised by one or more of three liberal characteristics have been associated with liberal peacebuilding:

- liberal agency, that is interventions conducted by liberal, Western states;
- motivation by liberal objectives, i.e. addressing large-scale human rights violations; and
- interventions justified and shaped by liberal causal beliefs that the promotion of liberal-democratic political institutions, 'good' governance, and economic liberalisation are central to bringing peace and prosperity to conflict-affected countries.

The liberal peacebuilding paradigm emerged very much as a 'reading' of the international peacebuilding practices that emerged in the aftermath of the Cold War: theory very much followed and tried to catch up with practice. The development of this paradigm, first termed 'liberal internationalism' by Roland Paris in 1997, was an attempt to make sense of the practices of international organisations and Western states in conflict-affected countries as diverse as Cambodia, El Salvador, Bosnia, or East Timor. IR theory has contributed to this reading in four ways.

First, the liberal peace paradigm focuses on the role of liberal international norms, in particular human rights norms (Donnelly 1998: 1–24) and norms associated with an international responsibility to protect, in shaping the practices of states and international organisations. In that regard, the liberal peace paradigm reflects the wider 'social turn' in IR scholarship, and a growing focus on both the regulatory and constitutive functions of norms in international order.[6] A range of scholars have theorised the roles of liberal norms on peacebuilding (Paris 2004; Zaum 2007), arguing that accounts relying on motivations of self-interest and traditional understandings of national security are insufficient to understand both the proliferation of peacebuilding interventions, and the particular forms that they take. These investigations into the functions of norms have on the one hand focused in particular on their role in justifying peacebuilding interventions, arguing for a normative shift in the aftermath of the Cold War towards a 'solidarist' consensus that has elevated humanitarian and human rights concerns on the international policy agenda, challenging traditional conceptions of sovereignty and non-intervention (Chesterman 2001; Gheciu and Welsh 2009: 121–46; Wheeler 2000). On the other hand, they have theorised the role of norms in shaping peacebuilding practices, and examined how liberal norms have both shaped the objectives of peacebuilding efforts, and through the purported causal effects of liberal institutions on peace-consolidation (an issue discussed in more detail below in the context of doing peacebuilding) have provided institutional blueprints that have informed peacebuilding practices.

Second, and linked with this, has been a wider discussion about the nature of state sovereignty amongst IR theorists, which has shaped both debates about the rights to and restrictions on international peacebuilding interventions into the domestic affairs of states, and about the 'kind' of sovereignty that underpins sustainable peace and stability in diverse and divided societies. The liberal peace paradigm has focused on the implicit social contract considered to be the basis of political authority, and has attempted to conceptually 'unbundle' the different dimensions of sovereignty (Tin-bor Hui 2004: 83–103). Krasner (1999), for example, identifies four different dimensions of sovereignty (international legal sovereignty, Westphalian sovereignty, domestic sovereignty, and interdependence sovereignty). Normative liberal peacebuilding theory has generally tied the legal protections offered by sovereignty to the attainment of particular – liberal – forms of domestic sovereignty, problematizing state–society relations, and the relationship between internal and external dimensions of sovereignty (Biersteker and Weber 1996; Krasner 1999; Philpott 2001).

The third contribution of IR theory to peacebuilding has also been in the domain of normative theory and the question of liberal agency. It addresses the question of which states have the authority to interpret whether a state should enjoy or has forfeited the protections that sovereignty is traditionally seen to offer, in particular the right to non-intervention. Rather than on the character of the state at risk of intervention, these arguments focus on the normative qualities of the intervenors, and in particular the purported superior moral and deliberative qualities of democratic states. Drawing on Rawls (1999) *Law of Peoples*, Robert Keohane (2003) for example has argued that such authority should rest with liberal states because of their open and accountable institutions. More prominently, the Princeton Project on National Security, led by prominent liberal scholars Anne-Marie Slaughter and John Ikenberry (2006), argued for the establishment of a League of Democracies to authorise military interventions in situations where the veto of non-democratic states would prevent the use of force against countries guilty of substantial human rights violations. Based on the explicit assumption that democracies would view security challenges similarly and therefore would agree when such a situation merited an intervention (a heroic assumption in light of the experience in the UN Security Council over Iraq just earlier in 2002/3); this proposal was as close as one can get to the universalist liberalism at the heart of the critique of the liberal peacebuilding paradigm.

IR theory's fourth contribution is to the critical reading of this peacebuilding paradigm. A full discussion of the criticisms of the liberal peace is beyond the scope of this chapter (for a good overview, see Campbell et al. 2011; Chandler 2010), and it suffices to say here that at the core of the criticisms of liberal peacebuilding have been two claims in particular. The first is normative, and argues that the promotion – or imposition – of liberal institutions in conflict-affected countries by Western states and international organisations is normatively questionable as, like colonial and imperial rule, it denies autonomy to those subject to such state-building interventions (Bain 2003). The second is that the specifically liberal character of these state-building interventions has caused many of the pathologies suffered by the affected countries (Jahn 2007; Richmond 2011).

A comprehensive discussion of these critiques is beyond the scope of this chapter.[7] However, it is worth noting two wider problems that IR theory's contribution to the reading of peacebuilding has posed more generally.

The first is that both the claims of the liberal peacebuilding paradigm, and key claims of its critics, inconveniently lack empirical support. Thus, the causal claims made for the pacifying effects of democratisation and free markets have been found wanting, as studies have shown that not only democratising countries but also countries subject to the International Financial Institution's liberalisation programmes are more prone to the outbreak of conflict.[8] Similarly, the notion that state- or institution-building should take priority over both political and economic liberalisation, advanced for example by Roland Paris in his seminal 2004 book, has been qualified by more recent investigations into the tensions between state- and peacebuilding (Call 2008).

In addition, both the liberal peacebuilding paradigm and its critics assert the existence of a coherent liberal peacebuilding project. It is assumed that all those participating in this project – western countries, international organisations, and western NGOs – have similar (liberal) normative commitments, shared motivations for their engagement, shared objectives, and similar understandings of the impact of liberal institutions. This not only assumes a degree of coherence and consensus within liberal thought on peacebuilding, but also that external peace-builders act for liberal reasons. This is at best weakly supported by the empirical evidence. States and international organisations engage in peacebuilding for a variety of reasons and motives, not all of them liberal, and many shaped by institutional or national self-interests. Not all actors necessarily share the same causal beliefs about the pacifying effects of liberal institutions, and have different perspectives on the source of conflict and the obstacles to peace which inform a focus on different institutional 'fixes', and at times competing priorities.

Over the last two decades, the justifications advanced for peacebuilding interventions have also changed, raising further doubts about the existence of a solidarist consensus governing peacebuilding practices. While justifications for peacebuilding interventions in the 1990s were mostly advanced in cosmopolitan terms, through references to universal human rights and notions of sovereignty as responsibility; the first decade of the 21st century witnessed an increased reliance on justifications based on narrower understandings of national and international security – a development particularly pronounced in the aftermath of 9/11.[9] While such security concerns surely also informed earlier peacebuilding interventions in Central America, the Balkans, or West Africa, the first decade of the 21st century witnessed the further securitisation of peacebuilding interventions, and the growing emphasis on their contribution to the national security of the intervener highlights the distinctly non-liberal motivation of peacebuilding interventions.

A second, and arguably more profound negative impact of IR theory on the reading of peacebuilding has been the privileging of the international dimension of peacebuilding over local dimensions. This has affected both the liberal peacebuilding paradigm and its critics to a similar degree. Thus, both the proponents and the critics of liberal peacebuilding have focused on the motives and practices of international actors, rather than on local perspectives on peacebuilding,[10] and have construed local actors as passive recipients of either international largesse and wisdom, or ill-conceived policies and exploitative practices. As a result, the debate around peacebuilding has often rooted both success and failure in the prescriptions of the liberal peacebuilding model, rather than in the complex interactions of local and international actors.[11]

The importance of the local dimension of peacebuilding and of the interactions in particular between interveners and the elites of recipient countries has been increasingly recognised in empirical investigations of the consequences of peacebuilding interventions (Berdal and Zaum 2012). In addition, some of the most recent efforts that have critically engaged with some of the problems of the previous theoretical literature on peacebuilding have highlighted the importance of local resistance to and adaption of the peacebuilding prescriptions of external intervenors, and the consequent emergence of 'hybrid' orders (Mac Ginty 2011). This development in the literature provides a necessary corrective to the rather uncritical focus on the international dimension of peacebuilding. In both theoretical and empirical investigations of peacebuilding, however, the perspective of those at the receiving end of peacebuilding interventions, who could provide essential insights into the workings and wider consequences of these hybrid orders for their daily lives, and who mostly live in the global South, are largely missing. The influence of IR theory (a discipline still largely dominated by mostly male scholars from the global North), has arguably reinforced this imbalance.

Doing peacebuilding

Generally, our knowledge of how to 'do' peacebuilding – of the tools available to consolidate peace in conflict-affected societies – is sketchy. As Bruce Jones and Molly Elgin-Cossart (2011: 13) note,

> Until very recently, academic study has focused on the causes of conflict rather than policy interventions. Donors themselves, and international institutions, have spent more time on policy, but rarely with good research design or method. Thus only a smattering of instruments has been studied systematically.

It is therefore unsurprising that IR theory's contribution to doing peacebuilding has been limited. However, two important contemporary peacebuilding practices – the deployment of peacekeeping forces and the promotion of democratic institutions – have been influenced by insights from IR theory, namely the security dilemma, and democratic peace theory.

Security dilemma

The security dilemma is one of the central concepts of international relations, especially neo-realist theories (Booth and Wheeler 2007; Jervis 1978; Waltz 1979). At the heart of the security dilemma is the condition of uncertainty about the motives of other actors. This uncertainty means that even defensive actions to increase one's own security can be interpreted as a threat by others and result in actions to counter this perceived threat. A desire to increase one's security has thus paradoxically, made one less secure.

In international relations, the security dilemma is generally associated with anarchy – the absence of centralised authority – as this reinforces states' uncertainty about the motives of other states. While IR theory has applied the concept of the security dilemma to the international realm, the condition of uncertainty and the logic of the security dilemma can also be present in domestic settings, and can be particularly important in the context of civil wars and situations where the state either does not act as a reasonably neutral arbiter between different societal groups but is captured by one of them (and hence seen as a threat by others), or is too weak to monopolise violence and enforce rule-governed interactions (Posen 1993: 27–47).

The security dilemma is one of the key obstacles to cooperation between actors under conditions of uncertainty and lack of trust, and especially for neo-realist IR theorists it has been a central obstacle to the creation of institutions that could help states to realise mutual gains through cooperation. Domestically, security dilemmas are at the heart of weak institutions in the aftermath of conflict: histories of conflict and low levels of trust and interaction between different groups make the interpretation of their actions more difficult, fuel uncertainty about their motives, and limit their ability to cooperate. Conflict-affected countries tend to lack strong institutions that can help to mitigate the risks of cooperation. Overcoming security dilemmas and their consequences is therefore at the heart of peacebuilding efforts.

In the context of peacebuilding, two ways of addressing security dilemmas stand out: inclusive political settlements, especially through power-sharing; and the role of external third parties in overcoming information and trust problems between conflict parties, and thereby facilitating cooperation between them. Inclusive political settlements involving all relevant parties to a conflict are an important contributor to the prevention of conflict recidivism (Call 2012; Hartzell and Hoddie 2007). However, this is an insight from the comparative politics literature, rather than IR theory. IR theory, however, has contributed to the understanding of the role of third parties, in particular international organisations, in overcoming security dilemmas in the context of the implementation of peace agreements.

One of the first to examine the challenge that security dilemmas pose to peacebuilding was Barbara Walter (1997: 335–46), in her work on barriers to civil war settlement. Walter identified the difficulty of conflict parties to commit to disarmament and demobilisation of their forces because of uncertainty about the commitment of other conflict parties to peace. In the absence of credible security guarantees, Walter suggests, the risk of such a commitment is too high for individual conflict parties. From this arises an important role for external actors: they can, through the provision of peacekeeping forces, provide the security guarantees that enable conflict parties to credibly commit to disarmament, demobilisation, and the participation in post-war institutions.

A range of quantitative and qualitative studies have subsequently examined the role that peacekeeping forces can play in helping to consolidate peace, and have found that their deployment can substantially reduce the risk of conflict recurrence (Doyle and Sambanis 2006; Page-Fortna 2008). Central to this has been the ability of peacekeeping forces to provide a credible guarantee to conflict parties that their participation in a peace accord will not leave them exposed and vulnerable to attacks.

Democratic peace theory

The existence of a 'democratic peace' has been amongst the most influential theoretical claims of IR theory of the last 30 years. It is rooted in the recognition that democratic states have rarely, if ever, gone to war with each other, and has associated this absence of conflict with the character of democratic institutions. Democratic institutions are argued, first, to impose a degree of restraint on governments through the checks and balances of democratic institutions. Second, democratic institutions are said to have a preference for the non-violent resolution of conflicts domestically, which they externalise in their relations with other democracies, who therefore mutually recognise each other as similarly restrained.[12]

Both scholars and policymakers have quickly applied the logic of the democratic peace not only to inter-state relations, but also to civil conflict, and democratisation has become a central part of the democratic peacebuilding paradigm. Hence, it has been argued that democracy helps to stabilise divided societies, as it provides an institutional framework that allows for the non-violent resolution of conflicts between different societal groups, and gives them all a stake in the state.[13] The UN and many states have continued to emphatically embrace democracy as a central element in ending civil conflicts. In the words of then-UN Secretary-General Kofi Annan (1998),

> in the absence of genuinely democratic institutions contending interests are likely to seek to settle their differences through conflict rather than through accommodation … Democratization gives people a stake in society. Its importance cannot be overstated, for unless people feel that they have a true stake in society lasting peace will not be possible and sustainable development will not be achieved.

These strong claims for democratisation have been challenged by a growing number of scholars pointing to the record of post-conflict democratisation efforts, and arguing that democratic competition can deepen the conflict between different groups and rekindle conflict (Paris 2004; Snyder 2000). These findings, however, have so far failed to fuel a fundamental re-think with regard to the promotion of democratisation as an instrument for peacebuilding. The strong normative commitment to democracy amongst many states and institutions involved in peacebuilding has complemented the contentious causal claims derived from democratic peace theory in shaping peacebuilding practice. IR theory has thus shaped peacebuilding practice, but has not made a major contribution to understanding what works and what does not when it comes to promoting sustainable peace. To the extent that there has been a debate around democratisation from this perspective, it has mostly focused on issues such as the timing of elections, and the character of electoral systems, as some systems are recognised to have a greater likelihood to promote inclusion, or generate renewed conflict.[14] These, however, are issues on which IR, and IR theory in particular has little to say.

Conclusion

In the words of Michael Doyle and Nicholas Sambanis (2006: 1), the record of peacebuilding efforts since the end of the Cold War has been 'mixed at best'. A similar assessment can be made about IR theory's contribution to reading and doing peacebuilding.

As the discussion has shown, IR theory has clearly shaped both peacebuilding practices and our understanding of these practices in important ways. However, these influences have not necessarily contributed to more effective practices, and a better understanding of them. IR theory's contribution to the liberal peacebuilding debate has for a long time kept the focus on the international aspects of peacebuilding, in particular the role of external actors and their policies. While this raised important normative and policy questions, in the long run it impoverished the debate by either focusing on the technicalities of peacebuilding such as donor coordination problems, or by advancing a very inward-looking debate about the problems of liberalism. The growing recognition that external intervenors normally lack the power to lastingly impose their institutional solutions on conflict-affected societies, and that the observable outcomes tend to reflect complex negotiations and trade-offs between the interests and ideals of diverse local and international actors, and are in this sense 'hybrid', reveals the limitations of much of the liberal peacebuilding debate of the last decade. If hybridity becomes the baseline for understanding peacebuilding, it raises important and interesting questions about how the nature of international–local interactions shape outcomes, which peacebuilding processes can transform or reinforce existing power structures, or how divisions between external peacebuilding actors create political spaces that local elites can exploit in their resistance to international peacebuilding policies. The dynamics of globalisation mean that peacebuilding inevitably has regional and international dimensions, and IR theory can help to both inform and understand peacebuilding practices and dynamics. For this, though, it needs to be less normatively driven and engage more with the messy and complex realities on the ground.

Notes

1 For a thoughtful criticism of such a narrow understanding of peace, see Oliver Richmond (2005) *The Transformation of Peace*, Basingstoke: Palgrave Macmillan.

2 The 2011 World Development Report puts a more positive gloss on this, emphasising the complexity of the causes of conflict. See World Bank (2010) *World Development Report 2011: Conflict, Security, and Development*, Washington DC: World Bank.

3 As reflected in the notorious claim, so often uncritically misquoted in undergraduate essays, that 'the absence of war between democratic states comes as close as anything we have to an empirical law in international relations' (J. Levy (1989) 'The Causes of War: A Review of Theories and Evidence', in P.E. Tetlock, J.L. Husbands, R. Jervis, P.C. Stern, and C. Tilly (eds.), *Behavior, Society, and Nuclear War*, Vol. 1, New York: Oxford University Press, 70).

4 A Web of Science search covered the following journals: *European Journal of International Relations, International Organization, International Security, International Studies Quarterly, Review of International Studies, Security Studies, and World Politics*, and covered the period from 1991 to 2011. It searched for the following topics: 'peacebuilding' OR 'peace-building' OR 'statebuilding' OR 'state-building'. While not comprehensive, this quick review gives a good indication of the very limited discussion of peacebuilding in mainstream IR theory journals. As the search term also included related terms such as 'state-building', which in some of the literature are used synonymously with historical processes of state formation, and as the search results also include short review articles, the results displayed here might even overstate the substantive engagement with peacebuilding by IR theory.

5 In recent years, the peacebuilding debate has generated its own dedicated journals, such as *Peacebuilding, Journal of Intervention and Statebuilding*, and the *Journal of Peacebuilding and Development*, the latter of which is more practice-oriented.

6 See for example M. Finnemore (1996) *National Interests in International Society*, Ithaca: Cornell University Press; P.J. Katzenstein ed., (1996) *The Culture of National Security: Norms and Identity in World Politics*, New York: Columbia University Press; J.G. Ruggie (1998) *Constructing the World Polity: Essays in International Institutionalization*, London: Routledge; A. Wendt (1999) *Social Theory of International Politics*, Cambridge: Cambridge University Press.

7 For such a critique, R. Paris (2010) 'Saving Liberal Peacebuilding', *Review of International Studies*, 36(2): 337–65.

8 On the IFIs, see C. Hartzell and M. Hoddie, with M. Bauer (2010) 'Economic Liberalization via IMF Structural Adjustment: Sowing the Seeds of Civil War?', *International Organization*, 64(2): 339–356; S. Woodward (2012) 'The IFIs and Post-conflict Political Economy', in M. Berdal and D. Zaum (eds.), *The Political Economy of Post-conflict Statebuilding: Power after Peace*, Abingdon: Routledge. On democratisation, see in particular L.E. Cederman, S. Hug, and L.

Krebs (2010) 'Democratization and Civil War: Empirical evidence', *Journal of Peace Research*, 47(4): 377–94; M. Mann (2004) *The Dark Side of Democracy: Explaining Ethnic Cleansing*, Cambridge: Cambridge University Press.

9 See for example George W. Bush's Inaugural Address of 20 January 2005: '[t]he survival of liberty in our land increasingly depends on the success of liberty in other lands. The best hope for peace in our world is the expansion of freedom in all the world'.

10 On local perspectives, see for example, Mac Ginty (2011); B. Pouligny (1999) 'Peacekeepers and Local Social Actors: The Need for Dynamic, Cross-cultural Analysis', *Global Governance*, 5(4): 403–24.

11 Amongst the most notable examples of this are W. Bain (2006) 'In Praise of Folly: International Administration and the Corruption of Humanity', *International Affairs*, 82(3): 525–38; and Jahn (2007).

12 See for example M.E. Brown and S. Lynn-Jones eds., (1996) *Debating the Democratic Peace*, Boston: MIT Press.

13 See for example R.J. Rummel (1995) 'Democracy, Power, Genocide, and Mass Murder', *Journal of Conflict Resolution,* 39(1).

14 For example B. Reilly (2008) 'Post-Conflict Elections: Uncertain Turning Points of Transition?' in A.K. Jarstad and T.D. Sisk (eds.), *From War to Democracy: Dilemmas of Peacebuilding*, Cambridge: Cambridge University Press, 157–81; A. Reynolds ed., (2002) *The Architecture of Democracy: Constitutional Design, Conflict Management, and Democracy*, Oxford: Oxford University Press.

References

Annan, K. (1998) Report of the Secretary General, *The causes of conflict and the promotion of durable peace and sustainable development in Africa*, New York: United Nations, paras. 77–78.

Bain, W. (2003) *Between Anarchy and Society: Trusteeship and the Obligations of Power*, Oxford: Oxford University Press.

Ballentine, K. and H. Nitzsche eds., (2005) *Profiting from Peace: Managing the Resource Dimensions of Civil War*, Boulder: Lynne Rienner.

Barnett, M. (2006) 'Building a Republican Peace: Stabilizing States after War", *International Security*, 30(4): 87–112.

Berdal, M. and D. Zaum eds., (2012) *Power after Peace: The Political Economy of State-Building*, Abingdon: Routledge.

Biersteker, T. and C. Weber eds., (1996) *State Sovereignty as Social Construct*, Cambridge: Cambridge University Press.

Booth, K. and N. Wheeler (2007) *The Security Dilemma: Fear, Cooperation, and Trust in World Politics*, Basingstoke: Palgrave Macmillan.

Call, C. with V. Wyeth eds., (2008) *Building States to Build Peace*, Boulder: Lynne Rienner.

Call, C. (2012) *Why Peace Fails: The Causes and Prevention of Civil War Recurrence*, Washington DC: Georgetown University Press.

Campbell, S., D. Chandler, and M. Sabaratnam eds. (2011) *A Liberal Peace? The Problems and Practices of Peacebuilding*, London: Zed.

Chandler, D. (2010) *International Statebuilding: The Rise of Post-Liberal Governance*, London: Routledge.

Chesterman, S. ed., (2001) *Civilians in War*, Boulder: Lynne Rienner.

Chesterman, S., M. Ignatieff, and R. Thakur eds., (2005) *Making States Work: State Failure and the Crisis of Governance*, New York: UN University Press.

Collier, P. and A. Hoeffler (2004) 'Greed and Grievance in Civil Wars', *Oxford Economic Papers*, 56(4) 563–595.

Dobbins, J., K. Crane, S.G. Jones, A. Rathmell, B. Steele, and R. Teltschik (2005) *The UN's Role in Nation-Building: from the Congo to Iraq*, Santa Monica: Rand Corporation.

Donnelly, J. (1998) 'Human Rights, a New Standard of Civilisation?', *International Affairs*, 74(1): 1–24.

Doyle, M. and N. Sambanis (2006) *Making War and Building Peace: United Nations Peace Operations*, Princeton: Princeton University Press.

Gheciu, A. and J. Welsh (2009) 'The Imperative to Rebuild: Assessing the Normative Case for Post-conflict Reconstruction', *Ethics and International Affairs*, 23(2): 121–146.

Hartzell, C. and M. Hoddie (2007) *Crafting Peace: Power Sharing Institutions and the Negotiated Settlement of Civil Wars*, University Park: Pennsylvania State University Press.

Ikenberry, G.J. and A.M. Slaughter (2006) *Forging a World of Liberty under Law: US National Security in the 21st Century*, Princeton, NJ: Woodrow Wilson School of Public and International Affairs, 27 Sept.

Jahn, B. (2007) 'The tragedy of liberal diplomacy: democratization, intervention, state-building, Part I and II', *Journal of Intervention and Statebuilding*, 1(1): 87–106, and 1(2): 211–229.

Jervis, R. (1978) 'Cooperation under the Security Dilemma', *World Politics*, 30(2): 167–214.

Jones, B. and M. Elgin-Cossart (2011) *Development in the Shadow of Violence,* Report on the Future Direction of Evidence on Issues of Fragility, Security, and Conflict, Geneva, 22 September.

Keohane, R. (2003) 'Political authority after intervention: gradations in sovereignty', in J.L. Holzgrefe and R. Keohane (eds) *Humanitarian Intervention: Ethical, Legal, and Political Dilemmas*, Cambridge: Cambridge University Press, 275–298.

Koskenniemi, M. (2000) 'Carl Schmitt, Hans Morgenthau and the Image of Law in International Relations', in M. Byers (ed.) *The Role of Law in International Politics*, Oxford: Oxford University Press, 17–34.

Krasner, S. (1999) *Sovereignty: Organized Hypocrisy*, Princeton: Princeton University Press.

Krasner, S. (2006) 'Sharing Sovereignty: New Institutions for Collapsed and Failing States', *International Security* 29(2): 85–120.

Mac Ginty, R. (2011) *International Peacebuilding and Local Resistance: Hybrid Forms of Peace*, Basingstoke: Palgrave Macmillan.

North, D., J. Wallis, and B. Weingast (2009) *Violence and Social Orders: A Conceptual Framework for Interpreting Recorded Human History*, New York: Cambridge University Press.

Page-Fortna, V. (2008) *Does Peacekeeping Work? Shaping Belligerents' Choices after War*, Princeton: Princeton University Press.

Paris, R. (1997) 'Peacebuilding and the Limits of Liberal Internationalism', *International Security*, 22(2): 54–89.

Paris, R. (2004) *At War's End: Building Peace After Civil Conflict*, New York: Cambridge University Press.

Philpott, D. (2001) *Revolutions in Sovereignty: How Ideas Shaped Modern International Relations*, Princeton: Princeton University Press.

Posen, B. (1993) 'The Security Dilemma and Ethnic Conflict', *Survival*, 35(1): 27–47.

Pugh, M. and N. Cooper, with J. Goodhand (2004) *War Economies in a Regional Context: Challenges of Transformation*, Boulder CO: Lynne Rienner.

Rawls, J. (1999) *The Law of Peoples*, Cambridge MA: Harvard University Press.

Richmond, O.P. (2011) *A Post-Liberal Peace*, Abingdon: Routledge.

Snyder, J. (2000) *From Voting to Violence: Democratization and National Conflict*, New York: Norton.

Tin-bor Hui, V. (2004) 'Problematizing Sovereignty: Relative Sovereignty in the Historical Transformation of State-Society Relations', in M.C. Davis, W. Dietrich, B. Scholdan and D. Sepp (eds.), *International Intervention in the Post-Cold War World: Moral Responsibility and Power Politics*, London: M.E. Sharpe, 83–103.

de Waal (2009) 'Missions without end? Peacekeeping in the African political marketplace', *International Affairs*, 85(1): 99–113.

Walter, B. (1997) 'The Critical Barrier to Civil War Settlement', *International Organization*, 51(3): 335–364.

Waltz, K. (1979) *Theory of International Politics*, New York: MacGraw-Hill.

Wheeler, N.J. (2000) *Saving Strangers: Humanitarian Intervention in International Society*, Oxford: Oxford University Press.

Zaum, D. (2007) *The Sovereignty Paradox: The Norms and Politics of International Statebuilding*, Oxford: Oxford University Press.

9

SOCIAL PSYCHOLOGY AND PEACEBUILDING

Shelley McKeown

Introduction

It is undeniable that intergroup conflict is an important societal issue; it depletes our resources and threatens our survival. Whilst in an ideal world the end of conflict would lead to peace, the course of history has shown that this is unlikely to be the case. Take the Cold War as an example; despite its end a 'fierce new assertion of nationalism and sovereignty emerged with the result that the world is now threatened by intergroup conflicts based on brutal ethnic, religious, social, cultural, or linguistic strife' (Boutros-Ghali 1992). Given the maintenance and re-emergence of conflict and the intractability of some such as those in Cyprus and Northern Ireland it is of vital importance to understand how to build peace and improve intergroup relations. Within this chapter I will outline how social psychology has contributed to peacebuilding in terms of understanding and improving intergroup relations, real-world applications and what it still has to offer.

Social psychology is a diverse subject area but at the most basic level is 'an attempt to understand and explain how the thoughts, feeling and behavior of individuals are influenced by the actual, imagined or implied presence of others' (Allport 1985: 3). So what has this got to do with peacebuilding? It is widely accepted that the origins of social psychology are heavily rooted in war (Gibson 2011). This is evidenced in some infamous social psychological studies which grew out of a desire to understand social influence. Take for example the Milgram (1963) obedience study which was inspired by World War II. In this study Milgram wished to understand why Nazi guards carried out such atrocities against the Jews. Milgram did not believe that it was due to evil per se but rather that certain social situations and influences may lead to this obedient behaviour. Milgram's study was a milestone in social psychological research, demonstrating that even the most well-intentioned individuals can be influenced to cause severe harm to others.

> With numbing regularity good people were seen to knuckle under the demands of authority and perform actions that were callous and severe. Men who are in

everyday life responsible and decent were seduced by the trappings of authority, by the control of their perceptions, and by the uncritical acceptance of the experimenter's definition of the situation, into performing harsh acts.

Milgram (1965: 74)

Henri Tajfel was another social psychologist whose experiences of being a Jew in Nazi Germany during World War II led to his interest in understanding group membership. Tajfel and his colleague John Turner developed one of the most famous social psychological theories: social identity theory. The theory explains how group membership and subsequent social comparisons may lead to negative out-group attitudes which, under certain conditions, can result in intergroup conflict.

As well as understanding how and why conflict occurs, social psychologists have also been involved in understanding how to improve intergroup relations. This has been to inform theory as well as practical interventions aimed at building peace in conflicted societies. A number of theories have been developed to determine under what circumstances identity and contact can lead to improved relations between groups. One of the most renowned is the contact hypothesis which claims that bringing groups in conflict together under favourable circumstances can lead to prejudice reduction. Social psychologists have also been involved in designing and evaluating peacebuilding interventions such as inclusive education, contact interventions, problem-solving workshops and media interventions, throughout the world.

Given the diversity of social psychology, its contribution to peacebuilding is wide and varied. Social psychologists examine both interpersonal and intergroup processes and this is translated into the study of factors which prevent and factors which encourage peace. In their overview of social psychology and peace, Cohrs and Boehnke (2008) outline four areas in which social psychology has contributed to peace.

- *Obstacles to negative peace*: This refers to research which examines the existence and maintenance of social inequality and social injustice. For example Social Dominance theory; this is outlined in more detail later in this chapter.
- *Catalysts of negative peace*: This refers to understanding how to reduce violence and aggression both at the interpersonal and intergroup level. This includes interventions such as those aimed at preventing genocide and mass violence.
- *Obstacles to positive peace*: This refers to the processes which are responsible for maintaining social injustice and social inequalities. Cohrs and Boehnke use research examples such as ethnic discrimination and the role of ideologies in maintaining social injustice.
- *Catalysts of positive peace*: The authors describe catalysts of negative peace as the processes which encourage and maintain social justice and equality such as the advancement of positive peace and non-violence.

Cohrs and Boehnke outline these distinctions and the relevant literature in more detail in their paper. The remainder of the chapter will be divided into four broad sections. The first will outline social psychology and understanding intergroup relations, the second social psychology and improving intergroup relations, the third social psychology's real-world applications to peacebuilding and the fourth what social psychology still has to offer for peacebuilding. Inevitability these sections overlap and not everything regarding social psychology and peacebuilding is included. I have made these arbitrary distinctions simply for the ease of the reader (and the writer!).

Understanding intergroup relations

I would like to argue that only when we understand intergroup behaviour can we truly understand how to build peace. At the most basic level social psychologists interested in intergroup relations want to answer three main questions.

- *Why do people form groups?* A key interest is to understand how and why groups are formed, what factors influence group productivity and different types of group leadership. Understanding these enables us to determine the functions of being part of a group and the result of group membership on behaviour.
- *Why do people behave differently in groups?* Social psychologists are also interested in why individuals behave differently in groups. Research on social influence, in particular conformity and obedience, highlight the importance of the social situation on behaviour. Importantly, social psychologists look to both interpersonal and intergroup factors to understand why people behave differently in groups.
- *Why do groups develop in-group love and out-group hostility ... sometimes apparently without real conflict of interest?* To understand why groups develop in-group favouritism and out-group negativity, social psychologists have a range of research areas which they can call upon. These include the development of attitudes, aggression and prejudice as well as theories on intergroup relations. This allows for a better understanding of how negative intergroup relations occur.

In summary, much if not almost all of the social psychological literature can be related to the understanding of intergroup relations. Whilst this is the case I would now like to focus on theories which have been developed specifically to explain the emergence of intergroup conflict.

Social psychological theories of intergroup relations

Early psychological theories focused heavily on the role of the individual as an explanation for intergroup conflict. The psychodynamic approach, developed from the work of Freud and later by Bion and Klein, suggests that loyalty towards a group leader and early childhood experiences explains the likelihood to be involved in intergroup conflict. Authoritarian personality theory (Duckitt 1989) on the other hand, argues that an individual's fascistic characteristics are the trigger. Moving from the sole focus on the individual, other theories have recognised the role of the group in explaining intergroup conflict. For example relative deprivation theory (Davis 1959) suggests that when one feels deprived relatively, not necessarily absolutely, compared with another group this can lead to conflict. Similarly, realistic group conflict theory (Levine and Campbell 1972) suggests conflict is a result of scarce resources. Related to this, social dominance theory (Sidanius and Pratto 1999) claims every society has a dominant group and one or more subordinate groups and that this has been the case since 'the beginning' – evolution. Social dominance theory argues that it is through maintaining these social hierarchies that conflict can occur. Terror management theory (Greenberg et al. 1986) takes a different viewpoint on why conflict occurs. This theory suggests that it is our survival instinct and our wish to maintain our cultural worldview and boost mortality that leads us to associate more positively with those who have the same views as ourselves. This is because it is argued that those who do not hold the same cultural worldview as us threaten our mortality.

One of the most acclaimed theories to explain the relationship between the individual and the group is social identity theory (Hogg 2006). In contrast to the previously mentioned theories, social identity theory suggests that there is a fundamental difference between interpersonal and intergroup processes such that intergroup processes cannot be explained by interpersonal processes alone. Tajfel (1978) defines social identity as 'that part of an individual's self-concept which derives from his/her knowledge of his/her membership of a social group (or groups) together with the value and emotional significance attached to that membership' (Tajfel 1978). According to social identity theory (SIT) we tend to divide our world into social categories and define ourselves in terms of the group we feel we belong to. These social categories can be based upon such concepts as nationality, race, gender, social class and occupation (Terry et al. 1999). SIT argues that in order to promote psychological distinctiveness, groups compare themselves to others through social comparison processes.

Ed Cairns once explained group formation to me through an experience he had at the airport. Imagine this scenario:

> You are travelling alone at the airport waiting for a flight. Everyone is going about their own business and you are reading the paper. All of a sudden the dreaded words 'Flight delayed' appear on the screen. You look around to express your dismay and for the first time you recognise the other passengers who must be on your flight, the airport is busy but they are the people with the angry faces. You join a queue to collect your refreshment vouchers at the allocated desk and you can feel tensions rising amongst the other passengers. You begin to chat and express your frustrations to those around you. From behind you hear a man shouting 'This is a disgrace, you think they could have told us sooner and why haven't we received an explanation for this delay? What on earth is going on?' This person soon takes a leader role and vows to get some answers for the delayed passengers and marches up to the airline representatives. You find yourself chatting with other passengers and deciding the plan of action you should take as a group, i.e. those who have been delayed. To think, only 10 minutes ago you did not know any of these people yet you are now planning some form of collective action. You have now become a member of a group.

SIT explains how this group membership can lead to conflict. Through social comparison processes groups compare themselves with other groups. This process may lead to in-group love and out-group derogation and result in increased self-esteem (Rubin and Hewstone 1998). Conflict can be a consequence of group membership when direct confrontation is viewed as the only option to increase self-esteem. This is most likely to be the case where it is not possible to leave the group, where the situation is unstable and where the group situation is viewed as illegitimate.

Each of these theories adds an interesting and different dimension to the understanding of intergroup conflict. By understanding how conflict occurs we can then try to understand how to improve intergroup relations with the ultimate aim of informing practice and policy to help to build peace. The advantage that social psychology has is that it is rooted in theoretical groundwork (Vollhardt and Bilali 2008). This means that social psychologists face the challenge of trying to integrate theory, research and practice with the hope of implementing practical interventions to improve intergroup relations. In the next part of this chapter I will outline some social psychological theories developed to explain how to improve intergroup relations.

Improving intergroup relations

There have been a number of theories developed to explain how to improve intergroup relations. Firstly I will outline several approaches based upon social categorisation processes including recategorisation, decategorisation and salient categorisation. Secondly I will focus on the role of improving intergroup relations through prejudice reduction based upon the contact hypothesis.

Whilst social identity formation can lead to categorisations and comparisons resulting in intergroup conflict, new social categorisations can help to improve intergroup relations. The three models outlined below differ but at the same time share some similarities with the effectiveness of each being highly dependent upon contextual processes. This is particularly true when considering the problem of generalisation and different contact experiences of minority and majority groups (Hewstone et al. 2002). Nevertheless each model has important implications for societies wishing to improve intergroup relations and build peace.

- *Recategorisation* (common in-group identity): In recategorisation, representations of group memberships are transformed from two separate groups to one more inclusive group of a superordinate category. This is often referred to as a common in-group identity. The development of this identity occurs with accompanying depersonalisation and subgroup salience (Dovidio et al. 1997). Research has demonstrated that a common in-group identity can lead to more positive intergroup attitudes and reduce intergroup bias. Criticisms of this model include that a common in-group identity may 'be short-lived, or unrealistic in the face of powerful ethnic and racial categorizations' (Hewstone et al. 2002: 590). Furthermore, in societies with continuing conflict a superordinate identity may be viewed as threatening, making it unlikely especially for minority groups to join. Hewstone et al. argue that this can actually lead to an increase in intergroup prejudice.
- *Decategorisation*: The process of decategorisation encourages original group boundaries to be de-emphasised. This enables group members to view out-groupers as individuals. Brewer and Miller state that 'with personalisation, category identity becomes subordinate to individual identity, rather than vice versa' (1988: 318). It is argued that viewing members of the out-group in a more

personalised way should reduce prejudice by reducing category salience. This is in contrast to viewing others as simply 'us versus them'. Research has shown that this multiple categorisation approach can lead to reduced prejudice. This is because individuals are no longer viewed in terms of simplistic social categories such as British versus Irish.

- *Salient categorisation*: Salient categorisation refers to making group membership salient on two dimensions simultaneously, for example ethnicity and nationality rather than one or the other. Primarily this model deals with concerns about the generalisation of intergroup contact between groups in conflict beyond the contact situation. Hewstone and Brown (1986) argue that it is important to keep intergroup identities salient whilst fostering intergroup contact. This model is problematic because research has shown that when identity salience is high it can be associated with intergroup anxiety, intergroup bias and distrust (Islam and Hewstone 1993). As a result it is argued that contact needs to be both intergroup and interpersonal to be most effective (Hewstone 1996).

These three models demonstrate that it is possible to encourage positive intergroup relations through different social categorisation processes. This is important for peacebuilding because it outlines that processes such as developing a superordinate common in-group identity may have a positive effect. For example in South Africa the development of the Rainbow Nation brings together a top-down approach of living together for one and for all. In contrast, Northern Irish society has seen the development of a potential common in-group identity – Northern Irish. This has, however, been mostly used by those on the ground and has not filtered up into the government with political parties mostly catering for those who define their identity as British or Irish. Building peace therefore needs to encourage group commonality where possible.

In addition to the role of social categorisations to improve intergroup relations one of the most renowned ways of reducing intergroup prejudice with the hope of building peace has been through encouraging intergroup contact, usually based upon the premise of the contact hypothesis.

In its simplest form, the *contact hypothesis* states that bringing conflicted groups together, under favourable conditions, can help to reduce intergroup prejudice and in turn foster positive community relations (Allport 1954).

> Prejudice (unless deeply rooted in the character structure of the individual) may be reduced by equal status contact between majority and minority groups in the pursuit of common goals. The effect is greatly enhanced if this contact is sanctioned by institutional supports (i.e., by law, custom or local atmosphere), and provided it is of a sort that leads to the perception of common interests and common humanity between members of the two groups.
>
> Allport (1954: 281)

It has been argued that conditions outlined by Allport are important if intergroup contact is to improve intergroup relations and have the maximum effect (Pettigrew 2008).

Support by local authorities and institutions is suggested to be important in order to facilitate effective intergroup contact (Pettigrew 1998). For example social institutions should set a clear example in which their policies should promote integration and equality. By doing this the creation of a new social order can be facilitated.

Equal status refers to within and not outside the contact situation (Pettigrew 1998). This is important as many conflicts are centred on a minority/majority problem. Pettigrew (1998: 66) argues that equal status is 'difficult to define and has been used in different ways'. To encourage equal status, the contact situation should address perceived inequality or superiority but should also be realistic. Equal status implies equal ability especially in relation to pursuing common (superordinate) goals.

Prejudice is reduced through the active pursuit of *common goals* (Pettigrew 1998). For example research has shown that taking part in team sports can produce this effect and even more so with winning (Pettigrew 1998). According to Allport 'The nub of the matter seems to be that contact must reach below the surface in order to be effective in altering prejudice. Only the type of contact that leads people to do things together is likely to result in changed attitudes' (1954: 276). When groups have common goals it is important that this leads to cooperation between groups.

In the classic Robbers' Cave Experiment, Sherif et al. (1961) found that intergroup *cooperation* resulted in more favourable out-group attitudes. This experiment involved twenty-two 5th grade boys who were taking part in a summer camp in 1954. The boys were split into two groups (Eagles and Rattlers) and over a one-week period only interacted with their own group. The camp leaders organised activities in which the two groups would compete (e.g. football, tug-of-war). During this time the competition between the groups became violent leading to group flags being burnt, cabins being raided and food fights breaking out. The camp leaders used various techniques to try to bring the groups together including positive propaganda and contact through non-competitive activities (e.g. watching movies) but these did not work, it was only cooperative action that had a positive effect. The organisers arranged for a camp truck to break down and both groups were needed to pull it uphill. It was only then that intergroup friendships began to develop. Recent research on cooperative learning amongst different racial and ethnic groups further supports this idea. Weigel et al. (1975) examined biracial learning and cross-race friendships and found that working together led to more intergroup friendship formation. Inclusive education in Northern Ireland has produced similar findings.

The contact hypothesis has been hailed as one of the most successful theories in social psychology (Dovidio et al. 2003). Although commentators generally agree that optimal contact (i.e. contact that fulfils Allport's conditions) helps to reduce intergroup prejudice, what constitutes effective contact is often debated (Maoz 2002). Some argue that not all of the conditions outlined by Allport (1954) need to be met for contact to work as they simply facilitate the effect (Pettigrew, 2008). Further, that contact occurring in situations lacking optimal conditions can still have a positive outcome (Pettigrew 1998). Other commentators have argued that contact failing to fulfil the conditions of the contact hypothesis is unlikely to reduce intergroup prejudice (Hewstone and Brown 1986). Adding to the debate, in their recent meta-analysis, Pettigrew and Tropp (2006) found that studies which claimed to involve optimal contact produced more positive effects. At the same time the authors also reported that those studies which did not state a use of the key conditions still showed a reduction in prejudice following contact.

In addition to examining how contact works, research has focused on determining the mechanisms which mediate the contact–attitude relationship. For example Sherif et al. (1961) showed that cooperative interdependence was a direct mediator of behaviour and attitude change. Researchers have established a variety of mediators associated with successful intergroup contact such as intergroup anxiety (Stephan and Stephan 1985), forgiveness (Tam et al. 2007), trust (Tam et al. 2009) and group salience (Voci and Hewstone 2003).

Research has also been conducted to determine the moderating mechanisms which help to distinguish when contact works. It is argued that contact will only be effective if a positive attitude is generalised to the out-group as a whole, rather than to one person viewed as an exception to the rule. Further this should be accompanied by personalisation in which category membership needs to be made less salient in contact situations to ensure positive experiences. It is suggested that the two perspectives of category salience and personalisation can be integrated by increasing category salience over time (Pettigrew 1998). Other moderators such as social and religious identification (Cairns et al. 2006) and group membership salience (Brown et al. 1999) have been found to play an important role in the contact–attitude relationship.

Recently, Pettigrew's reconceptualisation of the contact hypothesis suggested the inclusion of intergroup friendship formation as a fifth condition. This has led to research examining different types of friendships which can encourage positive contact effects. These include: direct friendship, indirect or extended contact and imagined contact. Direct friendship with an out-group member can lead to generalisation of positive attitudes to the out-group as a whole (Turner et al. 2007). Indirect contact such that knowing that an in-group friend has an out-group friend has also been found to lead to the generalisation of positivity to the out-group (Turner et al. 2008). More recently commentators have shown that simply imagining having an out-group friend can promote more positive intergroup attitudes (Turner and Crisp 2010).

Research on the contact hypothesis is wide and varied. What is evident is that its key principles are of vital importance for bringing conflicted groups together and building peace. The work of social psychologists has continued to develop the theory to understand the best conditions for prejudice reduction. This research has been used to inform real-world applications of intergroup contact and interventions devised to build peace all over the world.

Real-world applications

As we are only too aware, intergroup conflict can result in high levels of segregation and negative intergroup attitudes leaving little opportunity for groups to come together naturally. Consequently, many conflicted societies adopt programmes and policies to encourage intergroup contact with the hope of improving intergroup relations and preventing the continuation or re-emergence of intergroup conflict. The processes involved in bringing together groups in conflict are dependent upon the historical context of the society involved. For example in some societies, such as South Africa and the US, racial segregation was forced through laws. In these circumstances it was a priority to firstly end policies of segregation and allow racial groups to come together naturally. For other societies, such as Northern Ireland, segregation has been self-serving in that groups self-segregate rather than being forced to. In both types of societies the bringing together of groups to improve intergroup relations has been a priority. To do this, different approaches have been used such as story-telling projects, truth and reconciliation commissions and inclusive education. Whilst intergroup dialogue has been encouraged in many societies, a large number of projects have simply aimed to bring groups in conflict together with the hope of improving intergroup relations. In her research, Ifat Maoz (2011) has argued that there are five main models used in Israel to attempt to build peace between Israeli and Palestinian youth. These models are outlined in more detail as follows:

- *Co-existence*: This model aims to promote mutual understanding in line with the contact hypothesis. It emphasises intergroup similarity and tends to ignore the group differences.
- *Joint projects*: Similar to co-existence, the joint projects model promotes mutual understanding but additionally focuses on doing things together.
- *Confrontation*: The confrontational model derives from Social Identity theory and focuses on the strive for social and political change.
- *Narrative story-telling*: This model is both confrontational and co-existence in nature. It encourages both interpersonal and intergroup interactions between groups through story-telling.
- *Rehumanisation*: The final model suggested by Maoz focuses on the rehumanisation of the out-group. This is evidenced in work in bi-lingual and bi-national schools.

Maoz takes a critical approach to examining the effectiveness of these interventions. Whilst some contact is better than no contact at all, questions have been raised regarding the true impact short-term interventions can have in the face of intractable conflicts.

Although these models have been outlined in the context of Israel they encompass the types of interventions which have been introduced in conflicted societies worldwide. Social psychologists have been involved in developing and evaluating many of these interventions. As the research in this area is vast, I will briefly outline and focus on inclusive education, contact interventions and interventions taking place beyond the West.

Inclusive education

One of the major tools to build peace has been through inclusive education with the hope of building peace. Harris (2010: 11) defines peace-education as 'the process of teaching people about the threats of violence and strategies for peace'. Social psychologists have been involved in evaluating the effects of inclusive education. This is important in order to aid understanding in what is most effective for building peace.

Inclusive education is argued to be 'underpinned by broad variations' of the contact hypothesis (Donnelly and Hughes 2006: 493). The success of inclusive education is often, therefore, down to individual schools and their (in)correct implementation of the conditions of the theory. For societies such as the US and South Africa the development of inclusive education involved the removal of legislation preventing different racial groups from being educated together. In other societies inclusive education was developed to establish a shared space in which the groups in conflict can be educated together such as bi-lingual schools in Israel/Palestine and religiously integrated schools in Northern Ireland.

Longitudinal research in the US demonstrates that desegregated education has largely produced positive results (Pettigrew 2004). In Northern Ireland, similar findings have been evidenced. In a comparison of pupils attending integrated and segregated schools, Stringer et al. (2000) found that pupils who attended integrated schools reported higher levels of intergroup contact than those attending segregated schools. More recently, from data obtained through a random sample of the Northern Irish Life and Times (NILT) survey (1996–2007), Hayes and McAllister (2009) found that those who attended integrated schools were significantly more likely than those who didn't to have more intergroup contact through friendship and residency. The authors also reported that those who attended integrated schools were more likely to be optimistic compared with those attending segregated schools, when considering future relations in Northern Ireland. In a comparative study of bi-lingual/bi-national education in Israel and integrated education in Northern Ireland, Donnelly and Hughes (2006) outline the importance of culture and context in determining effectiveness.

Whilst inclusive education throughout the world has attracted much research attention in its attempt to build peace there have been other interventions put in place which have been designed and evaluated by social psychologists.

Contact interventions

Due to high levels of political violence and group segregation, many conflicted societies, such as Croatia, Northern Ireland and Cyprus, have introduced various interventions aimed to encourage intergroup contact and dialogue with the hope of improving intergroup relations.

One example of this is problem-solving workshops. These workshops are designed to bring together conflicting groups and encourage dialogue to help to resolve the conflict. Kelman and colleagues have been involved in the development of these workshops since the 1970s. In his 1997 paper, Kelman outlines the impact these workshops have had in Israel/Palestine. These workshops have also been adopted in other societies including Cyprus (Broome 1997). Problem-solving workshops are based upon social psychological assumptions that there must be intergroup dialogue and understanding before reconciliation can take place. 'It follows that social-psychological insights are complementary to political analysis, in that while conflict often arises out of objective and ideological differences, its escalation and intractability are typically the result of psychological and social factors' (Fisher 2001: 28). Advocates of problem-solving workshops demonstrate that they can lead to more positive attitudes towards group members, although there is debate as to whether this is generalised to out-group members as a whole.

Similar to contact schemes and problem-solving workshops in Israel/Palestine, intergroup contact initiatives and peace-making programmes have taken place in Northern Ireland. In the beginning these were referred to as holiday schemes as they took children away from troublesome areas of Northern Ireland during the marching season (Robinson and Brown 1991). In the years since, holiday schemes have developed and now include a range of cross-community programmes focusing on interpersonal and intergroup development as well as leadership. These schemes typically involve bringing young people from both sides of the divide together to engage in intergroup dialogue and understanding. McKeown and Cairns (2012) in their review of peace programmes in Northern Ireland highlight the role of such schemes for conflicted societies. The authors argue the importance of these interventions as a way to counteract negative conflict experiences as well as try to prevent the continuation or re-emergence of intergroup conflict. Whilst they have been found to have an immediate positive effect, concerns have been raised regarding their long-term impact.

Beyond the West

Beyond contact interventions and inclusive education, social psychologists have also been involved in peacebuilding on the ground in societies torn by mass killings and genocide. Much research has examined for example the integration of child soldiers in Uganda (Veale and Stavrou 2003). In addition new research is examining the effects of intergenerational transmission on children growing up in war-torn societies (Lapwoch 2012). Working alongside NGOs it is hoped that this research will help to build peace and inform interventions to improve intergroup relations in these societies.

Continuing research has also been examining the effects of media on peacebuilding. Elizabeth Levy Paluck has used radio programmes and dialogue to improve intergroup relations in countries including Rwanda and the Democratic Republic of Congo. Within these studies Paluck has argued the importance of media-based interventions in conflicted societies. In one study in Rwanda it was found that a year of listening to a radio programme promoting independent thought led to changes in attitudes, norms and behaviours (Paluck and Green 2009). This was compared with a control group who listened to a radio programme about HIV and Aids prevention.

The future of social psychology and peacebuilding

What has become clear in this chapter is that social psychology has played an important role in peacebuilding and will continue to do so. The diversity of social psychology itself and the vast amount of research being conducted into peacebuilding is far beyond the remit of this chapter but I do hope I have at least convinced you of the importance of social psychology.

I also want to convince you that the work of social psychology and peacebuilding is far from over. One of the key inspirations to continue the social psychological study of peace is to try to improve intergroup relations based on rigorous scientific findings. Through conducting reviews and analyses, social psychologists will continue to inform policy makers and practitioners of the most effective means of peacebuilding. Vitally, social psychologists will continue to work on the theoretical frameworks which are important to understand how and why conflict occurs, which can then be used to devise the most effective peacebuilding strategies. To do this we need to work together as researchers and practitioners because building peace is not a one model fits all and what works in one society may not work in another or even worse may exacerbate the situation.

Further, social psychology has an important role in understanding what peace actually is. The UN defines a culture of peace as:

> an integral approach to preventing violence and violent conflicts, and an alternative to the culture of war and violence based on education for peace, the promotion of sustainable economic and social development, respect for human rights, equality between women and men, democratic participation, tolerance, the free flow of information and disarmament.
>
> (United Nations General Assembly 1999)

It is important that social psychology works towards a greater understanding of what it means to improve intergroup relations and build peace. For example based upon the above definition, does peace simply represent the absence of explicit group conflict, shared education and space and social equality? If so, it could be argued that it is possible to achieve a culture of peace whilst groups live separate lives. Evidence for this comes from recent social psychological research which has been examining intergroup relations on the ground. Studies have shown that even in racially and religiously mixed spaces people remain highly segregated at the individual level. This is evidenced through the use of space in settings including cafes, beaches, schools and universities. Further, studies examining implicit and explicit attitudes demonstrate that even in the absence of conflict and promising peace agreements, the deep-seated antipathies for the out-group can remain. I would argue therefore that it is important through peacebuilding to achieve a truly shared society where individuals live and work together in harmony. The problem that peace-builders face is that for many societies the harsh reality is that segregation between groups exists primarily because it works (Shirlow and Murtagh 2006).

Given the nature of conflict and its constant changing and re-emerging it is important to continue to work towards peace. This is vital not only in war-torn societies but also in post-conflict societies because the absence of war does not automatically mean the presence of peace. Mac Ginty et al. (2007) outline in detail the evidence for no war no peace in Northern Ireland. The authors argue that top-down peace agreements need to be met with localised aspirations for peace and that more needs to be done to counteract the societal divisions and attitudes which occur on the ground. Thus the work of social psychologists in peacebuilding needs to continue and develop to work with individuals and groups living in conflicted societies.

References

Allport, G.A. (1954) *The Nature of Prejudice*. Reading, MA: Addison-Wesley.

Allport, G.W. (1985) 'The historical background of social psychology'. In: Lindzey, G. and Aronson, E. (eds), *Handbook of Social Psychology*. New York: Oxford University Press, pp. 1–46.

Boutros-Ghali, B. (1992) *An Agenda for Peace: Preventive Diplomacy, Peacemaking and Peace-keeping* Document A/47/277 – S/241111, 17 June 1992 (New York: Department of Public Information, United Nations). Available online http://www.un.org/Docs/SG/agpeace.html. Last accessed 25 June 2012.

Brewer, M.B. and Miller, N. (1988) 'Contact and cooperation: When do they work?' In: Katz, P.A. and Taylor, D.A. (eds), *Eliminating racism: Profiles in controversy*. New York: Plenum, pp. 315–326.

Broome, B.J. (1997) 'Designing a collective approach to peace: Interactive design and peace support workshops with Greek-Cypriot and Turkish-Cypriot communities in Cyprus', *International Negotiation*, 2(3): 381–407.

Brown, R., Vivian, J., and Hewstone, M. (1999) 'Changing attitudes through intergroup contact: the effects of group membership salience', *European Journal of Social Psychology*, 29(5–6): 741–764.

Cairns, E., Kenworthy, J., Campbell, A., and Hewstone, M. (2006) 'The role of in-group identification, religious group membership and intergroup conflict in moderating in-group and out-group affect', *British Journal of Social Psychology*, 45(4): 701–716.

Cohrs, J.C. and Boehnke, K. (2008) 'Social psychology and peace: An introductory overview', *Social Psychology*, 39: 4–11.

Davis, J.A. (1959) 'A formal interpretation of the theory of relative deprivation', *Sociometry*, 22(4): 280–296.

Donnelly, C. and Hughes, J. (2006) 'Culture, Contact and Context: Integrated Schools in Northern Ireland and Israel', *Comparative Education*, 42(4): 493–516.

Dovidio, J.F., Gaertner, S.L., and Kawakami, K. (2003) 'Intergroup Contact: The Past, Present, and the Future', *Group Processes & Intergroup Relations*, 6(1): 5–21.

Dovidio, J.F., Gaertner, S.L., Validzic, A., Matoka, A., Johnson, B., and Frazier, S. (1997) 'Extending the benefits of recategorization: Evaluations, self-disclosure, and helping', *Journal of Experimental Social Psychology*, 33(4): 401–420.

Duckitt, J. (1989) 'Authoritarianism and group identification: A new view of an old construct', *Political Psychology*, 10(1): 629–640.

Fisher, R.J. (2001) 'Social-psychological processes in interactive conflict analysis and reconciliation'. In: Mohammed, A.-N. (ed.), *Reconciliation, Justice, and Coexistence: Theory & Practice*. Lanham, MA: Lexington Books, pp. 25–45.

Gibson, S. (2011) 'Social Psychology, War and Peace: Towards a Critical Discursive Peace Psychology', *Social Psychology and Personality Compass*, 5(5): 239–250.

Greenberg, J., Pyszczynski, T., and Solomon, S. (1986) 'The causes and consequences of a need for self-esteem: A terror management theory'. In: Baumeister, R.F. (ed.), *Public self and private self*. New York: Springer-Verlag, pp. 189–212.

Harris, I. (2010) 'History of Peace Education'. In: Solomon, G. and Cairns, E. (eds), *Handbook on Peace Education*. Hove: Psychology Press, pp. 11–12.

Hayes, B. and McAllister, I. (2009) 'Education as a mechanism for conflict resolution in Northern Ireland', *Oxford Review of Education*, 35(4): 437–450.

Hewstone, M. (1996) 'Contact and categorization: Social psychological interventions to change intergroup relations'. In: Macrae, C.N., Stangor, C. and Hewstone, M. (eds), *Stereotypes and stereotyping*. New York: Guilford Press, pp. 323–368.

Hewstone, M. and Brown, R.J. (1986) 'Contact is not enough: An intergroup perspective on the "contact hypothesis"'. In Hewstone, M. and Brown, R. (eds), *Contact and conflict in intergroup encounters*. Oxford: Basil Blackwell, pp. 1–44.

Hewstone, M., Rubin, M., and Willis, H. (2002), 'Intergroup bias', *Annual Review of Psychology*, 53(1): 575–604.

Hogg, M.A. (2006) 'Social Identity Theory'. In: Burke, P.J. (ed.), *Contemporary Social Psychological theories*. California, CA: Stanford University Press, pp. 111–136.

Islam, M.R. and Hewstone, M. (1993) 'Dimensions of contact as predictors of intergroup anxiety, perceived out-group variability, and out-group attitude: an integrative model', *Personality and Social Psychology Bulletin*, 19(6): 700–710.

Kelman, H.C. (1997) 'Group processes in the resolution of international conflicts: Experiences from the Israeli–Palestinian case', *American Psychologist*, 52, pp. 212–220.

Lapwoch (2012) 'What did we do in the war mummy? Intergenerational transmission of knowledge about war in Northern Uganda'. Paper presented at the Northern Ireland branch British Psychological Society Conference, Northern Ireland.

Levine, R.A. and Campbell, D.T. (1972) *Ethnocentrism: theories of conflict, ethnic attitudes and group behaviour*. New York: Wiley.

Mac Ginty, R., Muldoon, O., and Ferguson, N. (2007) 'No war, no peace: Northern Ireland after the agreement', *Political Psychology*, 28(1): 1–12.

Maoz, I. (2002) 'Is there contact at all? Intergroup interaction in planned contact interventions between Jews and Arabs in Israel', *International Journal of Intercultural Relations*, 26: 185–197.

Maoz, I. (2011) 'Contact in protracted asymmetrical conflict: Twenty years of planned encounters between Israeli Jews and Palestinians'. Paper presented at the International Conference of Political Psychology, Istanbul.

McKeown, S. and Cairns, E. (2012) 'Peace-making youth programmes in Northern Ireland', *Journal of Conflict, Aggression and Peace Research*, 4: 69–76.

Milgram, S. (1963) 'Behavoiral study of obedience', *Journal of Abnormal and Social Psychology*, 67: 371–378.

Milgram, S. (1965) 'Some Conditions of Obedience and Disobedience to Authority', *Human Relations*, 18(1): 57–76.

Paluck, E.L. and Green, D.P. (2009) 'Deference, dissent, and dispute resolution: An experimental intervention using mass media to change norms and behavior in Rwanda', *American Political Science Review,* 103: 622–644.

Pettigrew, T.F. (1998) 'Intergroup contact theory', *Annual Review of Psychology*, 49(1): 65–85.

Pettigrew, T.F. (2004) 'Justice Deferred A Half Century After Brown v. Board of Education', *American Psychologist*, 59(6): 521–529.

Pettigrew, T.F. (2008) 'Future directions for intergroup contact theory and research', *International Journal of Intercultural Relations*, 32(3): 187–199.

Pettigrew, T.F. and Tropp, L.R. (2006) 'A meta-analytic test of intergroup contact theory', *Journal of Personality and Social Psychology*, 90: 751–783.

Robinson, A. and Brown, J. (1991) 'Northern Ireland children and cross-community holiday projects', *Children & Society*, 5(4): 347–356.

Rubin, M. and Hewstone, M. (1998) 'Social identity theory's self-esteem hypothesis: A review and some suggestions for clarification', *Personality and Social Psychology Review*, 2(1): 40–62.

Sherif, M., Harvey, O.J., White, B.J., Hood, W.R., and Sherif, C.W. (1961) *Intergroup cooperation and competition: The Robbers Cave experiment*. Norman, OK: University Book Exchange.

Shirlow, P. and Murtagh, B. (2006) *Belfast: Segregation, violence and the city*. London: Pluto Press.

Sidanius, J. and Pratto, F. (1999) *Social Dominance: An Intergroup Theory of Social Hierarchy and Oppression*. New York: Cambridge University Press.

Stephan, W.G. and Stephan, C. (1985) 'Intergroup anxiety', *Journal of Social Issues*, 41: 157–176.

Stringer, M., Wilson, R., Irwing, P., Giles, M., McClenahan, C., and Curtis, L. (2000) *The impact of schooling on the social attitudes of children*. Belfast: Integrated Education Fund.

Tajfel, H. (1978) *Differentiation between different social groups: studies in the social psychology of intergroup relations*. London: Academic Press.

Tam, T., Hewstone, M., Cairns, E., Tausch, N., Maio, G., and Kenworthy, J. (2007) 'The impact of intergroup emotions on forgiveness in Northern Ireland', *Group Processes & Intergroup Relations*, 10(1): 119–135.

Tam, T., Hewstone, M., Kenworthy, J., and Cairns, E. (2009) 'Intergroup Trust in Northern Ireland', *Personality and Social Psychology Bulletin*, 35(1): 45–59.

Terry, D.J., Hogg, M.A., and White, K.M. (1999) 'The theory of planned behaviour: Self-identity, social identity and group norms', *British Journal of Social Psychology*, 38(3): 225–244.

Turner, R.N. and Crisp, R.J. (2010) 'Imagining intergroup contact reduces implicit prejudice', *British Journal of Social Psychology*, 49(1): 129–142.

Turner, R.N., Hewstone, M., Voci, A., Paolini, S., and Christ, O. (2007) 'Reducing prejudice via direct and extended cross-group friendship', *European Review of Social Psychology*, 18(1): 212–255.

Turner, R.N., Hewstone, M., Voci, A., and Vonofakou, C. (2008) 'A test of the extended contact hypothesis: The mediating role of intergroup anxiety, perceived ingroup and outgroup norms, and inclusion of the outgroup in the self', *Journal of Personality and Social Psychology*, 95(4): 843–860.

United Nations General Assembly (1999) *UN Programme of Actions on a Culture of Peace*, A/53/243, 13 September.

Weigel, R.H., Wiser, P.L., and Cook, S.W. (1975) 'The impact of cooperative learning experiences on cross-ethnic relations and attitudes', *Journal of Social Issues*, 31(1): 219–244.

Veale, A. and Stavrou, A. (2003) *Violence, reconciliation and identity: The reintegration of Lord's Resistance Army Child Abductees in Northern Uganda*, Institute of Security Studies, South Africa. Monograph No. 92.

Voci, A. and Hewstone, M. (2003) 'Intergroup contact and prejudice toward immigrants in Italy: The mediational role of anxiety and the moderational role of group salience', *Group Processes and Intergroup Relations*, 6: 37–54.

Vollhardt, J. and Bilali, R. (2008) 'Social psychology's contribution to the psychological study of peace: A review', *Social Psychology*, 39: 12–25.

10

ANTHROPOLOGY AND PEACEBUILDING

M. Anne Brown

Introduction

This chapter offers a reflection on what anthropology as a tradition of scholarship and debate, but perhaps most pertinently as a history of engagement across deeply problematic conceptions of otherness and encounters with difference and power, offers to contemporary peacebuilding. The journey of modern anthropology, from at least the nineteenth century to now, can be deeply instructive for peacebuilding; what could be called the 'errors' of this complex field of reflection may be as useful as its insights; its epistemological struggles and methodological comportment might offer as much as its studies of particular places to our understanding of how we live and relate to each other as human beings and societies. Let me note, however, that I am writing here not as an anthropologist but as someone working on questions of peacebuilding (or peace formation) who has been inspired and influenced by the work of anthropologists. This chapter then does not seek to provide a systematic or critical overview of the state of the art of anthropology and its potential contribution to peacebuilding; the categories and tropes discussed are not necessarily those that an anthropologist might choose but those that have been important to me when grappling with challenges posed by questions of working against violence.[1]

It is useful to frame a discussion of anthropology's potential contribution by briefly sketching some of the elements of peacebuilding. Broadly understood, peacebuilding seeks to remedy the underlying causes of violent conflict and transform the long-term relationships between those in conflict. It is less a settled field of practice and reflection, however, than a number of things sitting awkwardly together: a difficult terrain of experience; a body of conceptual models and practices around statebuilding; an assemblage of hopes and humanitarian ideals; a more longstanding, rich, but often disparate collection of practice and theoretical approaches and critiques.[2] It remains also what those living with violent conflict or its legacy are doing to restore their collective lives.

From the most basic perspective, the effort to build peace is a raw terrain thrown up by the encounter with violence. The questions which peacebuilding raises emerge, in this sense, from 'the face of the victims' (Goenawan Mohamad in Brown 2009: 16) and the perpetrators (Zulaika 2004: 418). Arguably, they make up some of the most enduring and fundamental questions about how we live together – questions about the patterns of suffering we inflict on each other, the ways violence works in and on our collective lives and institutions, and the ways we might then undo or put aside violent histories and their legacy. These questions fundamentally concern our patterns of global exchange as well as particular communities and states. How do we rebuild our collective lives in ways that do not tear us or others apart? How does someone live with a neighbour who might have betrayed her, or whom she might have betrayed? Or, more positively, what is living well together? What has been made possible by this ripping away of the former status quo – might this be a moment of possibility and a kind of liberation? Violent conflict can bring us up against the limits of the usual categories of understanding and theory; it can pose the bewilderment of 'how can this be': a question not always satisfied by socio-political analysis (Zulaika 2004: 418; Gaita 1999: 39). Importantly, we are brought to these limits not only through atrocity or despair but also through people's capacity, at times, for endurance, creativity, imagination, humour and compassion (Lederach 2005; Nordstrom 2004).

While the causes of a violent conflict might be identifiable at the macro level, serious violence can change everything. Violence emerges from particular socio-political contexts, but 'high levels of violence and direct experience of atrocities' (Lederach 1997: 18) become their own drivers of action, embedding conflict in complex patterns of inter-generational trauma, betrayal and distrust. Moreover, cultural, social and economic dynamics can be reshaped by embedded violence. Peacebuilding efforts thus frequently occur at the most difficult disjunctures of people's collective and subjective existence – when earlier social and political institutions are fragmenting, trust is undermined, fundamental values are in doubt, basic forms of control (including control over one's own body) violated, and perhaps new forms of control, power and access to wealth, rooted in direct violence, asserted. However useful general answers to the questions raised by such dynamics might be, actual responses to violent conflict and efforts to rebuild in its wake need to be wrought from the realities and relationships on the ground.

Given the complexity of such challenges, peacebuilding can be understood inclusively as that spectrum of efforts by which people seek to restore life to their relationships, communities and institutions, their social, political, cultural and economic orders in the face of violence (Lederach 1997). This approach to peacebuilding does not place it in a temporal sequence (after the cessation of violent conflict); those engaged are not necessarily from elsewhere (although they may include external parties) and come from many different walks of life. As the work of Carolyn Nordstrom or Volker Boege among others make clear, there are always people within conflict situations working to make and expand places of peace, however small (Nordstrom 1997, 2004; Boege 2006, 2011) as well as those supporting these efforts.

Following its formal introduction into the United Nations agenda in 1992,[3] peacebuilding has also become a notable UN and multilateral activity, and so an intense focus of international diplomatic, organizational and research endeavour. Peacebuilding in this context is understood in a temporal sequence, as 'post-conflict reconstruction', after the steps of preventive diplomacy, peacemaking and the military enterprise of peacekeeping. Military intervention is seen to 'clear a space' for peacebuilding to become possible and, while this can be essential for a large-scale international operation, it may also 'shape the space' of peacebuilding conducted through this route. Peacebuilding understood in this context is premised on external intervention; the questions dominating it become ones of how international interventions should best be conducted. As well as the strong emphasis on the optimistically named post-conflict reconstruction, this orientation to peacebuilding is also inevitably one formed through the offices of 'the capital', whether that is New York or the local capital, rather than the street, the market or the hamlet. Peacebuilding as an activity of the 'international community' has thus become closely associated with the activities of (generally elite) international political entities and the resources they can command – it has gained its international prominence and purchase through such activities.

There are more fundamental differences between these two broad approaches (the first indicated only very broadly) than distinctions between 'bottom up' and 'top down' points of departure. Nevertheless, it is important that in practice these different orientations also jostle along side by side, productively or not. Peacebuilding efforts represent a wide range of activities; in any given instance, these efforts can offer much of value. Oliver Richmond's outline of four generations of peacebuilding theory and practice offers a useful categorization in this context (Richmond 2010). The focus in this chapter, however, is on some of the trends shaping the most dominant of these 'generations', the liberal peacebuilding of international peacebuilding missions.

Liberal peacebuilding

International peacebuilding missions represent a particular, if heterogeneous, kind of answer to the questions of peacebuilding. Such missions are a mix of humanitarian, political and security responses to violent conflict, but they are also profound and extensive interventions into the political and social relations of others – others who are almost invariably 'less developed'. The orientation of international peacebuilding missions continues to be shaped in important ways by the historical moment of their emergence as a formal UN activity: at the end of the Cold War, in a (historically recently achieved) era when wars were not centred in (or encouraged by) Europe and the great powers, framed by liberal triumphalism (Paris 2004) and coloured by a reimagining of war (Kaldor 1998). After the end of the Cold War, armed conflict was seen as being of a 'new' kind and level of barbarism and irrationality, in putative contrast to the 'logic' of the Cold War, World Wars I and II and the Clausewitzian wars of the nineteenth and twentieth centuries. In contrast to conventional wars between states, the savagery and fluidity of the 'new wars' were no longer the monopoly of states driven by *raison d'etat*, 'but events in interzones – the places where weak states had withdrawn or collapsed' (Richards 2005: 2). The interzones became identified as 'violence-prone areas' given almost inherently to violence (Das and Kleinman 2000).

In this context it is not surprising that building or strengthening states, ideally in as short a time-frame as possible, has come to dominate much of the UN peacebuilding agenda (Paris 2004). The international community has worked on the understanding that the broad forms and ideals of the liberal state offer the best overall framework for the management of conflict and the pursuit of order, security, justice and economic well-being (e.g., see Jeong 2005). This reflects the continuing strength of liberal conceptions of a range of public goods (democracy, human rights, justice etc.) and, pragmatically but powerfully, that we work from what we (think we) know and from what is to hand – liberal statebuilding offers a set of drawing-board plans. Liberal statebuilding (and the 'liberal peace', Duffield 2001; Mac Ginty 2010) draws also, however, from the notion that the liberal state represents the fundamentally rational and ordered alternative to what is cast as the unruly violence of non-state forms of social order ('the state of nature' of 'violence-prone areas') or totalitarian repression.

Major liberal peacebuilding interventions carry models of idealised social, political and economic relations, based on particular conceptions of liberal market statehood that frequently bear little relation to the political, social or economic realities on the ground, or the governance values and practices of the populations where they are introduced (Nixon 2006). The process of institutional transfer tends almost inevitably to be top down. This in part is a way of managing the complexity of the field of operation but it also reflects institutionally embedded assumptions (sometimes more a default position than a positive understanding) about how political community, including the state and its institutions, takes shape. In effect, it is presumed that the basic elements of the liberal state are universal and inherently rational, and that its architecture can be 'delivered' from elsewhere and take effective root.

Thus answers to the difficult questions of peacebuilding in any particular case are treated as substantially already known. The challenge is recast as a technocratic one (how these answers can be implemented) and more amenable to policy-making from distant capitals. At best, as Martin Krygier and Whit Mason, writing about the efforts to transpose rule of law arrangements, note, this outlook confuses a 'state of affairs, the rule of law, with particular and contingent means thought apt to achieve it, and then it elevates the latter as though they were the former … Law-constrained social relations are general, perhaps even universal, goods; particular institutions are merely attempts to attain them' (2008: 3). Mechanistic approaches to institutional transfer infer that arriving at the answers does not need to overly involve those living the questions. While there is analysis of local political struggles, these are often seen at a level of elite generality and framed within a background narrative of 'violence-prone areas' (Das and Kleinman 2000; Richards 2005).

In this conceptual orientation local societies, local cultures and local politics tend to figure primarily as the site of the problem. It is the local state that has failed, the local society that is dysfunctional and the local culture that is corrupt. This reifies the society and effectively reduces the need for explanations that engage more deeply with the field of local, national and international interaction (Das and Kleinman 2000). Thus the Balkans figures as a site of 'ancient hatreds', implicitly beyond comprehension (Richards 2005). This approach opens the way for outcomes such as the Dayton Accords, a peace settlement that has embedded division through the specific structures by which electoral democracy has been institutionalized. Similarly, conflict in parts of the Pacific Island region is seen through the lens of the area being an 'arc of instability' populated by 'tribal and warlike' people where 'nothing works'. Melanesian culture itself becomes the problem. Not only does this homogenize significant difference across the region, but also the difficult relations between local societies and global forces with which Melanesians grapple are reduced to expressions of an essentialized Melanesia. If Melanesian culture is to blame for the lack of fit between community values and state mechanisms and between subsistence economics and the economic basis of state operations, rapid urbanization, growing inequality, international resource stripping and so on, 'then those of us who are also part of these interactions – the former colonisers, the regional powers and neighbours, the international agencies, the traders … have no role, responsibility or place' in these conflicts (Brown 2008: 196–7). There is a sharp polarization generated here: 'culture' is what happens locally; peacebuilders are the carriers of universal values, rational norms and ideal types. This is their legitimacy and authority. This dichotomy establishes a powerful and potentially damaging field of relationship with local actors, which those working within must struggle to move beyond.

Anthropology, in its focus, its methods and its own chequered history, offers at least a partial antidote to these characteristics of liberal peacebuilding. To the focus on abstract models of supposed worldwide applicability and the dichotomy of 'ideal type state' versus 'failed state' so popular in some branches of political science (Moe 2012) an anthropological orientation brings a 'jeweler's-eye' (Marcus and Fischer 1986: 15) to what is actually occurring in particular sites and local contexts. To the emphasis on elite politics and technocratic delivery it offers investigation of how the dynamics of violent conflict – and efforts to work against it – are embedded in the everyday life and the dynamics of communities, institutions and sites of exchange. To the reification of culture, the institutionally embedded lack of self-awareness and the overlooking of local peacebuilding, an anthropological orientation offers critical reflection on the interaction of local and global actors, whether dealing in weapons, pursuing approaches to peace or engaged in research as observer and/or observed.

Culture, context and relationships

Anthropology represents the effort to see and understand practices, including those generating or sustaining violent conflict, within the lived world of their own social contexts. Contexts are multidimensional and heterogeneous; they can be predominantly local and within the scope of face-to-face relations, but even the most apparently isolated can be deeply marked by the criss-crossing of multiple global and regional transactions, of power, goods, imageries. It is widely recognized that violent conflict is waged across societies and that 'the complex and specific intersections of the local and global' (Mitchell 2000: 205) or 'the distorted relationship between daily, face-to-face relations and large scale identities produced by nation-states' (Appadurai in Das and Kleinman 2000: 3) form the context of much contemporary war and violence. The 'time-honoured methods of empathic and engaged witnessing, however, of "being with" and "being there"' (Scheper-Hughes and Bourgois 2004: 27) that are anthropology and ethnography's stock in trade enable this insight to be pursued in concrete terms. Panning out beyond a focus on elites 'to locate war within the precise social contexts from which it springs' (Richards 2005: 4), anthropological analyses of conflict seek to offer more locally engaged approaches to investigating the causes or the processes which sustain and embed violent conflict in people's everyday experience (Milne 2010; MacLeod 2007). For supporting the emergence of more peaceful political orders, countering or undoing the social forces driving violent conflict is far more important than military dominance – and for this, contextual knowledge is vital. 'External attempts to promote … "peace" … will succeed only when local notions of social order are accommodated' and engaged, if not necessarily accepted (MacLeod 2007: 73).

Anthropological accounts also, fundamentally for peacebuilding, pay attention to the ways people build and rebuild their collective lives in the context of violence, whether they are sustaining violence, surviving it, or taking steps to craft less destructive social and political orders (Lederach 2005; McWilliam 2005; Nordstrom 1997). The local generation of socio-political order and conflict management can provide alternative pathways to peaceful relations to those promoted by liberal statebuilding or represent the dynamic negotiation and incorporation of re-interpreted liberal norms (Brown and Gusmao 2012; Mac Ginty 2011; Cummins 2010). 'Such reconfigurations can pose obstacles to peace and stability, but they can also be creative and generative' (Moe 2012). As a number of anthropologists of violence argue, carefully investigating the 'black box' of 'violence-prone areas' is essential to supporting efforts to create peace (Richards 2005; Das and Kleinman 2000).

Almost mirroring the notion of social context is that of culture. Anthropology is often popularly defined as the study of other cultures; its focus on culture and the recognition and appreciation of cultural difference are perhaps the most obvious contributions that anthropology offers peacebuilding. There is nothing simple about the idea of culture and the various things we mean by it; like other lode-star terms culture is an elastic, evocative and sometimes treacherous word. We can talk about global culture, corporate culture, Fataluku culture or Polynesian culture.[4] The term can work as a reified catch-all explanation that stops discussion (and a partner to 'violence-prone area') or an invitation to go more deeply into the matrix of social relationships and meaning from which people act. The history of its use, along with the history of anthropology itself, is caught in the long wave and undertow of colonialism. This history resonates powerfully in the polarization, touched on above, repeatedly drawn between the hoped-for universalism and rationality identified with the modern state and what are by contrast cast as the fractured customs, traditions and cultures of supposedly less enlightened societies (Smith 1999).

Despite these problems, culture remains a vital term. Culture can be understood as people's ways of life and ways of making shared sense of their (or our) world or worlds: a dynamic matrix of values, practices, implicit and explicit shared understandings. It is an 'ongoing creative process' involving the social ordering of space, time and relationships, including relationships between the material and non-material world, between genders, and between the self, others and groups. One person can, and generally will, be a living part of different, even contesting, cultures. The idea of context draws attention to the intersecting trajectories traversing the local and binding it elsewhere; it emphasizes the dynamic interconnectedness of things, even while focusing on the specific network being probed. The idea of culture might suggest that difference matters and point to what can be the profound power of even subtle difference, particularly in the experience of the self in relation to others, the natural world and the moral or non-material universe. Different cultures are different 'answers to a fundamental question: What does it mean to be human and alive? ... [These answers] collectively comprise our human repertoire for dealing with all the challenges that will confront us as a species ...' (Davis 2009: 19) including that of transforming violent and destructive structures and relationships.

The exploration of culture produces, generally, an increased awareness that collectively and subtly we form the world to a profound extent; that the world of our experience is not given. Clearly there is debate about where and how thresholds might be drawn, but that is not the point here. Anthropological accounts of life repeatedly demonstrate this simple, but in practice not easily grasped, insight – that even though what we share as human beings in the world runs throughout and shapes our ways of working with the questions of life, the differences remain significant. Differences are far from absolute, but nor, despite the ongoing and costly destruction of indigenous cultures, do they seem to be going away. Moreover, the nature of the difference can be entirely unexpected – we often do not realize that we operate according to a certain mode of grasping the world until we stumble across an alternative. While we may accept in principle that we shape our reality, it is extremely difficult to comprehend the extent, subtlety and logic of differences that can be in play without seriously engaging with at least careful accounts of other ways of life.

The active awareness of culture offers an antidote to the naïve universalism that continues to characterize much peacebuilding. Not such that we are open to an imagined relativist tumult but rather to the recognition that we are engaged in a slow exchange with each other and across cultures, among other gulfs. An awareness of culture highlights our own ethnocentrism; it offers awareness not just of others – those whose societies we are arriving in – but of ourselves, not as neutral bearers of universal truth, but as carriers of a mixed bag of 'tools' and of histories that we may not grasp well ourselves. (How well do we understand the interdependencies of political, social, economic and technological shifts that enabled the very recent crystallization of public goods that currently define the workings of the liberal state?) We are part of a dialogue and an exchange in which we all have things to learn, including about how we might disentangle entrenched patterns of violence (Brown 2009). An awareness of culture and context is the recognition that the matrix of relationship and meaning within which people are operating is fundamental to working with them on significant political and social change. It is also fundamental to recognizing what people and communities are already doing to work against violence – at the least not to undermine those efforts (Boege 2011). Such an approach could be regarded as an anthropological orientation within peacebuilding.

An anthropological orientation is arguably fundamental to working against violence. Peacebuilding aims at reworking political community and relationships in ways that enable political and social structures and processes to deal with – and transform – the causes and effects of embedded violence. As noted above, the questions raised by such efforts go well beyond the institutional architecture of the state and penetrate all the dimensions of people's collective lives, including relationships with sources of meaning, value and order (Lederach 2005). It is vital, then, that external peacebuilders seek a genuine appreciation of and engagement with how people locally understand and enact 'community'. Not to do so risks erecting an order and language of political life that marginalizes people from their new institutions or creates institutions open to capture by social forces not seen or understood by the international agencies. There are too many examples of both dynamics, from Somalia to Bosnia (Krygier and Mason 2008). Not only are such efforts unlikely to be successful in instituting peace, they offer neither substantive democracy nor liberalism. The effort to establish the rule of law is a central element of many peacebuilding missions. But how is justice understood, how is it 'experienced, perceived, conceptualized, transacted and produced' (Hinton 2011: 1) in the places and to the people affected by the violence? If the justice processes pursued by the international community are largely alien and unrecognizable to the participants and their communities there seems little reason to expect these processes to contribute to establishing a sense of accountability on the ground. Effective legal institutions are not in and of themselves the source of justice; rather, they work to uphold justice because they are embedded in networks of mutual exchange with the societies of which they are part. 'To pluck out of this dense thicket of institutions, cultures, traditions, mores and practices, merely the formal rules or architecture of legal institutions is simply to pick at leaves' (Krygier and Mason 2008: 11).

This is not to suggest that only what counts as justice (or political community) in the local society is relevant, that local processes are necessarily sufficient or desirable, or that there are not divisions within the societies concerned about the forms of justice needed. International state or societal actors also have a legitimate and important voice in justice processes following armed conflicts. International and regional norms are far from irrelevant; given that most armed conflicts have international dimensions, international actors may bring vital insights into the causes of and responsibilities for the conflict, as well as the ability to reach and constrain key figures. But as Alexander Hinton has noted in a discussion of international transitional justice processes, justice is 'frequently assumed to be something almost transcendent and universal, epitomized by due process, legal rights, and international norms' (Hinton 2011: 1). This assumption renders invisible the complexities and messiness of how a sense of justice is negotiated and established, or not, within societies, but also between them and international bodies after entrenched violence or mass atrocity. If we are concerned with peacebuilding, having the patience to stay with these complexities, or to know when to step aside from them, is critically important. The patience to take local realities and their interactions not only seriously, but as of fundamental importance, is the strength of anthropology. The nature of the engagement is then where peacebuilding steps beyond the concerns of anthropology.

Similarly, the drive to 'build a state' can fail in significant ways to engage with how political order, legitimacy, accountability and participation are understood and enacted for people in the societies at stake. To take the example of East Timor, after the end of Indonesian control of the territory in 1999, the international community and the returning East Timorese diaspora saw the task ahead of them as building a state 'from nothing' (Hohe 2002a). East Timor was repeatedly seen as constituted by an absence that had to be filled. Since the region was to become an independent state the absence of state institutions was important. It did not, however, equate with the absence of political community. The complex forms of local sociality and agency that had substantially enabled survival and resistance in the face of Indonesian military occupation (McWilliam 2005) were effectively excluded from consideration, except as 'folklore' (Hohe 2002b) or as an obstacle to liberal values. This overlooking of culture, context and therefore of local agency has profound political consequences. Once categorized in such terms, there was little need for sustained engagement on the part of either international agencies or the East Timorese elite with the broader population about the nature of the state of which they were to be part, beyond a training role. 'The Transitional Administration built institutions based on the assumption that there were no strong concepts and ideas existing on the local level, and that the population just had to be "taught" democracy' (Hohe 2002b: 570; Mac Ginty 2011). Nevertheless, as ethnographies are making clear, local societal actors are negotiating the tensions and hybridizations between governance approaches in East Timor (e.g., Yoder 2007; Palmer and De Carvalho 2008; Cummins 2010; Brown and Gusmao 2012).

An anthropological orientation offers peacebuilding deeper curiosity about the cultures at work in these and other cases, appreciation of the fertile possibility of different pathways to social goods, awareness of the contingent and constructed nature of our own social arrangements, and a recognition that modern configurations of the individual in the market state are not the only, or necessarily the best, ways of creating viable political community (even if they were always achievable, e.g., see Nixon 2006). Such orientations in international institutional policy-making could help avoid the profound 'overlooking' and occlusion that characterizes and undermines much international peacebuilding. Greater awareness of the social world, however, does not thereby resolve the complexity and messiness of the challenges peacebuilding throws down, rather it deepens immensely the resources available with which to work, and highlights the need for greater humility. Such shifts would constitute a subtle revolution in the framework of relationships by which the dominant approaches to peacebuilding are pursued: away from the delivery of already known truths from us to them, towards being part of fallible and sometimes difficult exchanges about how we live together without entrenching violence. We all have things to offer and to learn in such exchanges.[5]

Anthropology's journey

The history of modern anthropology tracks a long course through approaches to peoples and places identified as elsewhere, other and different. In this context it has itself been implicated in violence. Modern anthropology emerged as a discipline in the context of colonialism (Clifford 1988). In keeping with the categories of race, gender and nature prevalent in scientific European discourse of the time, a substantial portion of nineteenth and earlier twentieth century anthropological writing – European or American – portrayed civilization as a ladder of progress, with 'other' cultures (and races), particularly indigenous cultures, appearing as bounded, discrete examples of 'primitive' stages of human development, preserved in isolation. The wealth of anthropological output across this long period cannot be reduced to variations on the ladder of progress and there have always been counter-trends. Nevertheless, by virtue of its objectification of other cultures, much early anthropological writing helped articulate what was essentially a global political interaction which justified the violent domination of others and appropriation of their lands and resources.

The use of anthropological tropes in the colonization of Australia is a vivid case in point (Stanner 1969). According to this enactment of international power relations, Indigenous Australians were in a 'state of nature' – 'mankind in the chrysalis stage' (Sir James Frazer in Stanner 1969: 35). The Hobbesian or Lockean versions of the idea of the social contract as the basis of the state played a critical role as a litmus of 'civilization'. Not having entered into the social contract that constituted the state Aboriginal Australians were cast as a 'people without politics' (Lauriston Sharp 1958, in Hiatt 1984: 4) and without law. The imperial powers of Europe by contrast represented the most developed point in a natural trajectory of human civilization. Assimilation into the 'white' races could only be of benefit; 'the superior races have a right, because they have a duty ... to civilise the inferior races' (Ferry 1885, in Cowie 1986: 47). Similarly in North America, contemporary accounts drew on social contract theory to both vaunt an ideal model of the state and replace the long, violent history of conquest and destruction of Indigenous Americans 'with the captivating picture of the inevitable and benign progress of modern constitutionalism' (Tully 1995: 78).

A 'long-lasting Hobbesian bias' was deeply entrenched in anthropology (Richards 2005: 12). Thus, in the Pacific Islands region, Polynesian societies were regarded as superior to the Melanesians, because their centralized, hierarchical and hereditary political order appeared closer to the nineteenth-century version of British constitutional monarchy and strong class stratification. The violence of colonization was seen as inherently civilizing and a necessary part of pacification; indigenous violence in Melanesia was depicted as the mindless savagery of the state of nature (Jolly 1996: 177). While such approaches are no longer current in anthropological writing, they continue to resonate in contemporary assumptions that the central task for fragile regions is to successfully reproduce the institutions and trajectories of the 'modern' world. The approaches of modernization theories remain potent.

The ladder of progress and its variants structured not only images of others, but of how the colonizing powers understood themselves in relation to others. 'The "idea" of the West became a reality when it was re-presented back to indigenous nations through colonialism' (Smith 1999: 64). Moreover the division of the European researcher from the primitive subject of research was not only the observed 'fact' of the time, but embedded in the very grounds of knowing itself, as anthropological research, drawing from the contemporary epistemology of the natural sciences, drew a categorical distinction between knower and known. The subject of research was constituted as passive, inert and fixed, just as the researcher was the active seeker of truth (Smith 1999). It was '[o]ne of the major assumptions upon which anthropological writing rested until only yesterday, that its subjects and its audience were not only separable but morally disconnected, that the first were to be described but not addressed, the second to be informed but not implicated …' (Geertz 1988: 132).

Among its effects, such constructions of anthropological knowledge promoted a concept of culture as fixed, discrete and thereby 'pure' (its authenticity depended on this isolation) and distinct from the dynamic, reason-seeking individual. As Clifford Geertz suggests in the quote above, this is a construction of knowledge that makes moral recognition and dialogue across the division of subject and object of knowledge, if not impossible, then a narrative paradox. Anthropologists have (largely and painfully) worked their way past these constructions of knowledge, culture and people. Anthropological writing provides a broad scope of powerful critiques of parochial universalisms and progress as a metanarrative. The movement of historical events, debates across the human and natural sciences, political struggles, including decolonization struggles and the increasingly assertive voices of 'primitive peoples' and others breaking into these solipsistic knowledge practices and onto all the variously constituted world stages have enabled these shifts, but the methods and processes of anthropological research themselves have also contributed, perhaps significantly.

The methodologies of attention and careful observation over time brought into view the violence of colonial domination and shed greater light on the operation of power, including in the production of knowledge (e.g., Stanner 1969). This strengthened critical elements from within and beyond the discipline. The anthropologists' 'audience' began to sense its own implication in, and relationship with, the unfolding accounts of other lives. 'Being with and being there' have brought increasing moral recognition of those others, or increasing articulation of this recognition, in their train. Grasping the other as implicitly an upturned mirror of the self can over time turn on its head to become a de-naturalizing of the self and deconstruction of its certitudes, enabling 'the sophisticated reflection by the anthropologist about herself and her own society that describing an alien culture engenders' (Marcus and Fischer 1986: 4). Drawing attention to this effect in Ruth Benedict's war-time study of Japan, *The Chrysanthemum and the Sword*, Clifford Geertz notes '[a]t the close, it is … us that we wonder about. On what … do our certainties rest?' (Geertz 1988: 121–2).

Meanwhile, the epistemological gulf of the positivist methodologies becomes the search for the proper distance between researcher and subject (Scheper-Hughes and Bourgois 2004: 26) or the nuanced distance of irony. For anthropology, irony functions as awareness of the complexity and sometimes intense moral ambiguity of working across differences or divisions of culture, power and (particularly in conflict situations) suffering and safety (Geertz 2000: 30; Scarry 1985). Without giving up on knowledge, irony involves a wry recognition of the constancy of mistake and misreading, of the precariousness of our understanding of complex human dynamics and the need to carry our shared knowledge with lightness and humility (Marcus and Fischer 1986; Geertz 2000; Zulaika 2004). Moving from the mechanistic application of models, irony involves the active recognition that there is much we do not know, and that some of it will be critical to the issues at hand. Such recognition can open a space for dialogue. Joseba Zulaika's account of talking with Spanish villagers following a series of ETA assassinations in the late 1970s suggests that for probing violence and the potentials for peace, key dimensions of knowledge are created in the process of conversation across division – the divisions that violence creates or reveals. 'The other cannot be thematised: we must speak to him, not just about him' (Zulaika 2004: 418). While this insight is central to conflict resolution and certain approaches to peacebuilding (e.g., see Lederach 2005) it has had little impact on the central trends of liberal peacebuilding. This move to grasp a dimension of knowledge in relationship is potentially a key contribution of an anthropological orientation to peacebuilding. Anthropological research is not simply an account of somewhere else: it has become the story and struggle of a journey towards others, of more or less disturbing encounters, of reflection on what is often the scarred tissue of meeting across division or difference. It is a journey and a meeting that is not an account of the primitive, the bizarre or the failed but an extended reflection on the mysteries and dilemmas of the shared human condition. It is a journey from which peacebuilding needs to learn.

Conclusion – Paying attention

While anthropology might have moved on, discursive categories shaped in the forge of the long colonial encounter – about the nature of culture, tradition and the drive to modernity, the goals of development, the form and trajectory of civilization, us and them – remain implicitly embedded in much political and social science and policy writing and continue to structure liberal peacebuilding in 'violence-prone areas'. Good governance, including restraints upon violence, for example, is repeatedly identified with Western liberal mechanisms for representation, accountability and security; what others might offer to these or associated social and political goods tends to be discounted. State building as a form of peacebuilding is often applied as if practices of the individual and the state, the public sphere of the state, zones of toleration and associated models of rationality and systems of accountability were simply there, waiting for the dark accretion of tradition and history to be swept away. But these discursive architectures cannot simply be 'delivered'; they are complex, hard-working achievements of culture, not naturally existing givens. This is not to suggest that the structures, institutions and practices of the democratic state do not have much to offer regions struggling with violent conflict, or that democratic governance does not have fundamental elements and ideals that are widely generalizable, even if the actual institutions may not be. It is rather that the actual structures and processes needed will always be concrete and embedded in the specificities of this place, this context, this contested history, this set of struggles and demands, and oriented to the needs of these people. For this, locally led innovation and deep engagement with the textures of peoples and places are required.

Underpinning the awareness of culture and context that anthropology offers peacebuilding is a basic methodological pillar and an ethic: an ethic of attention. It is not a heroic ethic, but it nevertheless has real implications for policy (although they become clearer around concrete policy-making) as for theory and practice. In peacebuilding, such an ethic might involve the effort to understand and be aware of others in their own terms, even when those terms do not altogether make sense to you, if you do not know what to do with them, or if they simply do not fit with your priorities. Meas Nee's retelling of his experiences in Cambodia (1996) offers a powerful request for such attention and, following the devastation of the killing fields, for the space not to 'develop' for a time, but simply to sit with others. Carolyn Nordstrom's *A Different Kind of War Story* (1997) provides accounts of how some communities in Mozambique understood what brought the war to them, how to take the war out of people and how to prepare for war. For bearers of international peacebuilding agendas much in these descriptions might make little sense. Nordstrom's accounts in these instances make no judgements; they are a careful listening and retelling – an act of respect and at the same time an observing of the texture of distance; we are not others, differences are real. For peacebuilders too, an ethic of attention might require not rushing to judgement or answers unless compelled by genuine need; it might require at times holding open an uncomfortable space, rather than trying to bring about an inevitably superficial and weak conformity to abstract principles formulated elsewhere. This is far from moral vacuity (and it is not always moral issues at stake) but recognition of the need for long engagement and exchange. There may be more value in starting from where we are, even if that place is uncomfortable, messy and troubling, than moving quickly to premature resolution in an abstract truth or an imported institution lacking local legitimacy (Brown 2009: 71). Uncomfortable spaces can allow room to observe and to listen and for others to speak.

Notes

1 Anthropological writing contains a wealth of work on particular regions of the world relevant to peacebuilding. Specific fields, notably legal anthropology, also engage with peacebuilding in particular regions or more generally, e.g., Thomas Carothers' 2006 edited volume, *Promoting*

the Rule of Law Abroad: In Search of Knowledge (Washington D.C.: Carnegie Endowment for International Peace). More general anthropological works dealing with violent conflict and peacebuilding include A.L.H. Hinton's 2011 anthology, *Transitional Justice*; with K.L. O'Neill (2009) *Genocide*; and *Genocide: An Anthropological Reader* (Durham, N.C.: Duke University Press), J.V. Milne (2010) 'Method, Theory and Ethnography in Peace and Conflict Studies' in O.P. Richmond (ed.) *Palgrave Advances in Peacebuilding* (Basingstoke: Palgrave, 74–98); P. Richard's 2005 anthology *No Peace No War*; N. Scheper-Hughes and P. Bourgois' 2004 anthology *Violence in War and Peace*; Das, Kleinman, Ramphele and Reynolds' 2000 anthology *Violence and Subjectivity*; and Sponsel and Gregor's 1994 edited volume *The Anthropology of Peace and Non-Violence*.

2 See Richmond (2010) 'A Genealogy of Peacebuilding' for a different, more elaborated identification of different 'generations' of peacebuilding.

3 With the publication of *An Agenda for Peace,* by the then UN Secretary General, Boutros Boutros Ghali.

4 Mark Pedelty (2004: 403), writing about war correspondents, notes, 'reporters are a community in and of themselves. They work together, play together, and often, live together. They share an integrated set of myths, rituals and behavioural norms. They are, in short, a culture'.

5 See Volker Boege (2011) 'Hybrid Forms of Peace and Order on a South Sea Island' for a positive example of this.

References

Benedict, R. (2005) *The Chrysanthemum and the Sword: Patterns of Japanese Culture*, Boston: Houghton Mifflin.

Boege, V. (2006) *Bougainville and the Discovery of Slowness: an Unhurried Approach to State-Building in the Pacific (ACPACS Occasional Paper No. 3)*. Brisbane: ACPACS.

Boege, V. (2011) 'Hybrid Forms of Peace and Order on a South Sea Island: Experiences from Bougainville (Papua New Guinea)' in *Hybrid Forms of Peace: From Everyday Agency to Post-Liberalism*, O.P. Richmond and A. Mitchell (eds), Basingstoke: Palgrave Macmillan.

Brown, M.A. (2008) 'Custom and Identity: Reflections on and Representations of Violence in Melanesia' in N. Slocum-Bradley (ed.) *Promoting Conflict or Peace through Identity*, Surrey: Ashgate.

Brown, M.A. (2009) *Human Rights and the Borders of Suffering: the Promotion of Human Rights in International Politics*, Manchester: Manchester University Press.

Brown, M.A. and Gusmao, A. (2012) 'Looking for the Owner of the House: Who is Making Peace in Rural East Timor?' in *Hybrid Forms of Peace: From Everyday Agency to Post-Liberalism*, O.P. Richmond and A. Mitchell (eds), Basingstoke: Palgrave Macmillan.

Clifford, J. (1988) *The Predicament of Culture: Twentieth Century Ethnography, Literature and Art*, Cambridge: Harvard University Press.

Cowie, H.R. (ed.) (1986) *Imperialism and Race Relations*, Melbourne: Nelson.

Cummins, D. (2010) 'Democracy or "Democrazy": Local Experiences of Democratization in Timor-Leste', *Democratization*, 17(5): 899–919.

Das, V. and Kleinman, A. (2000) 'Introduction', in Das, Kleinman, Ramphele and Reynolds, (eds) *Violence and Subjectivity*, Berkeley and Los Angeles: University of California Press.

Davis, W. (2009) *The Wayfinders: Why Ancient Wisdom Matters in the Modern World*, Toronto: Anansi Press.

Duffield, M. (2001) *Global Governance and the New Wars: the Merging of Security and Development*, London: Zed Books.

Gaita, R. (1999) *A Common Humanity*, Melbourne: Text Publishing.

Geertz, C. (1988) *Works and Lives: The Anthropologist as Author*, Stanford, CA: Stanford University Press.

Geertz, C. (2000) *Available Light: Anthropological Reflections on Philosophical Topics,* Princeton and Oxford: Princeton University Press.

Hiatt, L.R. (1984) 'Aboriginal Political Life'. *The 1984 Wentworth Lecture*, Canberra: Australian Institute of Aboriginal Studies.

Hinton, A.L.H. (2011) 'Towards an Anthropology of Transitional Justice', in A.L.H. Hinton (ed.) *Transitional Justice: Global Mechanisms and Local Realities after Genocide and Mass Violence,* New Brunswick, NJ: Rutgers University Press.

Hohe, T. (2002a) 'The Clash of Paradigms: International Administration and Local Political Legitimacy in East Timor', *Contemporary Southeast Asia,* 4(3), 569–589.

Hohe, T. (2002b) 'Totem Polls: Indigenous Concepts and "Free and Fair" Elections in East Timor', *International Peacekeeping,* 9(4), 69–88.

Jeong, H.-W. (2005) *Peacebuilding in Postconflict Societies: Strategy and Process,* Boulder: Lynne Rienner.

Jolly, M. (1996) 'Women ikat raet long human raet o no? Women's rights and domestic violence in Vanuatu', *Feminist Review,* 52: 169–190.

Kaldor, M. (1998) *New and Old Wars: Organised Violence in a Globalised Era,* Stanford: Stanford University Press.

Krygier, M. and Mason, W. (2008) 'Interpersonal Violence, the Rule of Law and its Enforcement', paper delivered at the Ninth Annual Global Development Network Conference, Brisbane, 29 January–5 February, 2008.

Lederach, J.-P. (1997) *Building Peace: Sustainable Reconciliation in Divided Societies,* Washington: USIP Press.

Lederach, J.-P. (2005) *The Moral Imagination: The Art and Soul of Building Peace,* Syracuse: Syracuse University Press.

Mac Ginty, R. (2010) 'Hybrid Peace: The Interaction Between Top-Down and Bottom-Up Peace', *Security Dialogue,* 41(4): 391–412.

Mac Ginty, R. (2011) 'Hybrid Reconstruction: the Case of Waad in Lebanon' in O.P. Richmond and A.Mitchell (eds) *Hybrid Forms of Peace: From Everyday Agency to Post-Liberalism,* Basingstoke: Palgrave Macmillan.

MacLeod, A. (2007) 'Police Reform in Papua New Guinea', in M.A. Brown (ed.) *Security and Development in the Pacific Islands,* Boulder, CO: Lynne Rienner.

Marcus, G.E and Fischer, M.M.J. (1986) *Anthropology as Cultural Critique,* Chicago and London: University of Chicago Press.

McWilliam, A. (2005) 'Houses of Resistance in East Timor: Structuring Sociality in the New Nation', *Anthropological Forum,* 15(1): 27–44.

Milne, J.V. (2010) 'Method, Theory and Ethnography in Peace and Conflict Studies' in O.P. Richmond (ed.) *Palgrave Advances in Peacebuilding,* Basingstoke: Palgrave, 74–98.

Mitchell, J. (2000) 'Violence as continuity: violence as rupture – narratives from an urban settlement in Vanuatu' in S. Dinnen and A. Ley (eds) *Reflections on Violence in Melanesia,* Canberra: Hawkins Press / Asia Pacific Press.

Moe, L.W. (2012) 'Hybrid and Everyday Political Ordering: Constructing and Contesting Legitimacy in Somaliland', *Journal of Legal Pluralism,* forthcoming.

Nee, Meas with Healy, J. (1996) *Towards Restoring Life: Cambodian Villages,* Sydney: Overseas Service Bureau.

Nixon, R. (2006) 'The Crisis of Governance in New Subsistence States,' *Journal of Contemporary Asia,* 36(1): 75–101.

Nordstrom, C. (1997) *A Different Kind of War Story,* Philadelphia: University of Pennsylvania Press.

Nordstrom, C. (2004) *Shadows of War,* Berkeley and Los Angeles: University of California Press.

Palmer, L. and De Carvalho, D. (2008) 'Nation-building and Resource Management: the Politics of "Nature" in Timor-Leste', *Geoforum,* 39: 1321–1332.

Paris, R. (2004) *At War's End, Building Peace after Civil Conflict,* Cambridge: Cambridge University Press.

Pedelty, M. (2004) 'War Stories: The Culture of Foreign Correspondents' in N. Scheper-Hughes and P. Bourgois (eds) *Violence in War and Peace: An Anthology,* Oxford: Blackwell.

Richards, P. (2005) 'New War, An Ethnographic Approach' in *No Peace, No War: An Anthology of Contemporary Armed Conflicts,* Ohio and Oxford: Ohio University Press and James Currey.

Richmond, O.P. (2010) 'A Genealogy of Peace and Conflict Theory' in O.P. Richmond (ed.) *Palgrave Advances in Peacebuilding, Critical Developments and Approaches,* Basingstoke: Palgrave Macmillan.

Richmond, O.P. and Mitchell, A. (eds) (2012) *Hybrid Forms of Peace: From Everyday Agency to Post-Liberalism,* Basingstoke: Palgrave Macmillan.

Scarry, E. (1985) *The Body in Pain: The Making and Unmaking of the World*, New York: Oxford University Press.

Scheper-Hughes, N. and Bourgois, P. (2004) 'Making Sense of Violence' in N. Scheper-Hughes and P. Bourgois (eds) *Violence in War and Peace: An Anthology*, Oxford: Blackwell.

Smith, L.T. (1999) *Decolonizing Methodologies, Research and Indigenous Peoples*, London, New York, Dunedin: Zed Books and the University of Dunedin Press.

Stanner, W.E.H. (1969) 'After the Dreaming', *The 1968 Boyer Lectures*, Sydney: Australian Broadcasting Commission.

Tully, J. (1995) *Strange Multiplicity: Constitutionalism in an Age of Diversity*, Cambridge: Cambridge University Press.

Yoder, L.M. (2007) 'Hybridising Justice: State-Customary Interactions over Forest Crime and Punishment in Oecusse, East Timor', *Asia Pacific Journal of Anthropology*, 8(1): 43–57.

Zulaika, J. (2004) 'The Anthropologist as Terrorist' in N. Scheper-Hughes and P. Bourgois (eds) *Violence in War and Peace: An Anthology*, Oxford: Blackwell.

11

ECONOMISTS AND PEACEBUILDING

Jurgen Brauer and Raul Caruso

Introduction

On 7 June 1919, two days after his 36th birthday, John Maynard Keynes resigned from the United Kingdom's Treasury team at the Paris Peace Conference, who were negotiating what was to become the Treaty of Versailles, signed on 28 June 1919. The details of Keynes' already lofty intellectual stature and of the political environments in Britain, France, and the United States at the time can be gleaned from Robert Skidelsky's, and from numerous other, biographies of the man.[1] Upon his resignation, Keynes penned a small book, published in 1920. Called *The Economic Consequences of the Peace*, he prefaced it as follows:[2]

> The writer of this book was temporarily attached to the British Treasury during the war and was their official representative at the Paris Peace Conference up to June 7, 1919; he also sat as deputy for the Chancellor of the Exchequer on the Supreme Economic Council. He resigned from these positions when it became evident that hope could no longer be entertained of substantial modification in the draft Terms of Peace. The grounds of his objection to the Treaty, or rather to the whole policy of the Conference towards the economic problems of Europe, will appear in the following chapters. They are entirely of a public character, and are based on facts known to the whole world.
>
> J.M. KEYNES
> KING'S COLLEGE, CAMBRIDGE,
> November, 1919

Thereupon, Keynes lay out, in so compelling a fashion that neither his argument nor his evidence have ever seriously been challenged, the case for why the allies' Terms of Peace to be imposed on Germany were physically and financially impossible to fulfill. The whole of the book can be read in a single, focused three-hour session, but many a reader will do it in less time than that, succumbing to Keynes' passionate loosening of an avalanche of striking, overwhelming, and eventually mind-numbing specificity: One begins to skip the painful detail of how the victors intend to punish the loser.

147

Keynes writes (Keynes 1920: 250–251):

> If we take the view that for at least a generation to come Germany cannot be trusted with even a modicum of prosperity, that while all our recent Allies are angels of light, all our recent enemies, Germans, Austrians, Hungarians, and the rest, are children of the devil, that year by year Germany must be kept impoverished and her children starved and crippled, and that she must be ringed round by enemies; then we shall reject all the proposals of this chapter, and particularly those which may assist Germany to regain a part of her former material prosperity and find a means of livelihood for the industrial population of her towns. But if this view of nations and of their relation to one another is adopted by the democracies of Western Europe, and is financed by the United States, heaven help us all. If we aim deliberately at the impoverishment of Central Europe, vengeance, I dare predict, will not limp. Nothing can then delay for very long that final civil war between the forces of Reaction and the despairing convulsions of Revolution, before which the horrors of the late German war will fade into nothing, and which will destroy, whoever is victor, the civilisation and the progress of our generation.

Such were 'the economic consequence of the peace' indeed: restrictions on world trade, hyper-inflation, the depression years in the United States and in Europe, the rise of Hitler, the pogrom that became the Holocaust, and war on such a calamitous scale that 'the horrors of the late German war will fade into nothing.' How prescient.

Even though it be true that Keynes' efforts at sanity failed, one cannot think of a more dramatic demonstration of what good economists have ever done for peace.

Alas, in late 1944, Henry Morgenthau, then-Secretary of the United States Treasury, advocated a 'harsh peace' for Germany. His eponymous Morgenthau Plan advocated the partitioning of Germany. He proposed to strip it of its most valuable assets in the West—the coal deposits and the iron and steel industry in the Ruhr area—thereby to deprive the nation of its industrial prowess. Morgenthau willed the complete pastoralization of Germany, reducing the people of the geographic heartland of Europe to mere tillers of the land.

Franklin Roosevelt and Winston Churchill agreed to this plan, in modified form, on 16 September 1944. News of the agreement leaked, however, and led to a redoubling of Germany's albeit already doomed war effort. Following Victory Day, then, Germany's remaining factories were dismantled, parts, machinery, and equipment were shipped abroad, patents expropriated, research forbidden, and—in a mad dash—useful engineers and scientists were spirited out of the country just as soon as any of the Allies could lay their hands on them.[3] The German economy duly collapsed and so did Europe's other postwar economies. It looked as if Keynes' *Economic Consequences of the Peace* might be repeated yet again.

Eventually, saner heads prevailed. In the waning moments of the European war, the American presidency changed hands. Roosevelt had died, and Truman assumed the Presidency on 12 April 1945. Morgenthau's term as Secretary of the Treasury ended on 22 July 1945. Even as the deindustrialization of Germany proceeded as planned, in a famous speech delivered in Stuttgart on 6 September 1946, Truman's new Secretary of State, James Byrnes, took a dismal view of the effects. So did former president Herbert Hoover, in a series of reports penned in 1947. As Germans scraped by on starvation diets, Stalin's Soviet Union was a rising power. Already it held eastern Germany and, as from 24 June 1948, it was to blockade the Western allies' rail and road access to the partitioned Berlin, prompting them to fly in relief supplies and sharply escalate the incipient Cold War. The writing on the wall seemed clear: an economically strengthened, resurgent Germany could either be part of a new Western alliance or else be incorporated into a Soviet one. As in the 1920s, it was feared that hungry mouths would flee to those who promised to feed them.

In July 1947, Truman thus came to abolish the punitive measures imposed on Germany, and his new Secretary of State, General George C. Marshall (Byrnes had resigned his post in January that year) formulated what would become the eponymous Marshall Plan, in effect from 1948 to 1952. Not blind to its political purpose, a strange kind of peace economics had been crafted, for which Marshall would be awarded the Nobel Peace Prize in 1953.

So there we have the peace economist, in the person of Keynes, and peace economics, or at least nonwar economics, in the person of Marshall. This sets the stage for two strands one might investigate: one concerning a flurry of books by prominent economists on the problem of peace, the other, a flurry of activity by bureaucrats and politicians to secure it. Among the former are such famed names—among economists at least—as Arthur Pigou, Kenneth Boulding, and Lionel Robbins, Englishmen all, each penning one or more books detailing their thoughts on the matter.[4] Among today's luminaries, economics Nobel Laureate Joseph Stiglitz, together with co-author Linda Bilmes, is probably the outstanding voice regarding the cost of war, at least US-related wars.[5] Indeed, about a dozen economics Nobel Laureates, Stiglitz among them, grace the board of Economists for Peace and Security in the United States. As happened to Keynes, politics mostly ignores them. But, again as with Keynes, this does not render their views false.

On the bureaucratic-political side of things, the single most often told story is that of Jean Monnet and Robert Schuman. Like Keynes, Monnet participated in the Paris Peace Conference in 1919, in Monnet's case as an assistant to the French delegation. Like Keynes, he envisioned a pan-European economic cooperation zone. Like Keynes, he would be disappointed. Despite this, the French appreciated his good efforts and awarded him with the post of Deputy Secretary-General of the newly-founded League of Nations. Monnet was but 31 years old.[6] He resigned four years later to devote himself to international business and finance in a private capacity but resurfaced during the early World War II years in positions of high influence in France, Britain, and the United States, urging Roosevelt to get on with an industrial armaments plan, the success of which led Keynes to credit him with shortening the war by a year.[7] Together with Robert Schuman—the Franco-German-Luxembourgian statesman, French Minister of Finance, of Foreign Affairs and two-time Prime Minister of France—plans were crafted and introduced for what with many a twist and turn would become today's European Union. These plans were wholly based on a vision of a pan-European economic union, so intricately interconnected, so tightly woven, so strongly bound, that European war would no longer be thinkable, nor indeed feasible.

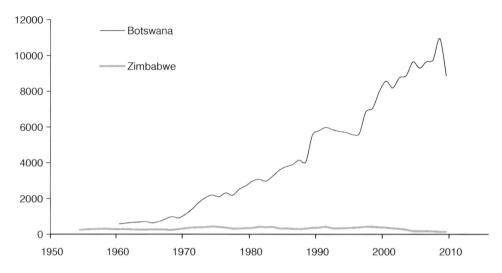

Figure 11.1 Inflation and purchasing power parity-adjusted per capita GDP, Botswana and Zimbabwe (I$; base year = 2005).

Source: Extracted from Heston, Summers, and Aten (2011)

Defense, conflict, and security economics

As an academic discipline, what has economics ever done for peace? Plenty, it turns out, even if the modern-day economics profession, certain luminaries notwithstanding, does not seem much interested in the topic. But just one comparative chart illustrates why the profession, and others, should care: perpetual peace pays; perpetual violence costs (Figure 11.1).

It is not that Botswana has been free of economic troubles, but that its peaceful politics do not impede its economic advancement. The same of course cannot be said about its neighbor, Zimbabwe.

A brief history: in the post-World War II era, *defense economics* might be dated with the arrival of Robert McNamara in the Pentagon as US Secretary of Defense. Defense economics deals with economic aspects of managing the defense sector and includes topics such as military R&D, procurement, and the defense industry (e.g., Gansler 1980; 1989), military manpower and the debate over moving from conscription to an all-volunteer force (e.g., Ash, Hosek, and Warner 2007; Poutvaara and Wagener 2007), the use of game theory to understand the implications and to devise strategies to manage the then-ongoing nuclear arms race between the United States and the Soviet Union (e.g., Schelling 1960), and alliance theory, the theory of how alliances arise and function (Olson and Zeckhauser, 1966). The key idea is that defense economics deals with aspects internal to the defense establishment. However, this soon gave rise to extensions, such as debates over whether military R&D leads to civilian sector 'spin-offs' (e.g., Ruttan 2005), whether military spending stimulates otherwise underperforming developing economies (Benoit 1973), and studies on the economic effects of military expenditure on national economies even in economically advanced countries. For instance, military bases and arms manufacturers are unevenly distributed across the geography of the United States so that taxes raised in some states benefit other states. Geographically uneven military expenditure, in turn, can skew recruitment of military-related construction, engineering, scientific, consulting, and other work and therefore affect local and regional labor markets. Defense economics thus soon attracted independent, academic economists studying the wider beneficial or adverse local, regional, or economy-wide effects of military expenditure per se. The field might well be said to have broadened into *military economics* (e.g., Smith 2009).

With the ending of the Cold War in the late 1980s, a series of brutal civil wars broke out during the 1990s, not only but especially in Africa, and led to an increased interest in *conflict economics*. Inasmuch as investments by international financial institutions such as the World Bank Group and the International Monetary Fund were placed at risk, conflict economics, based on academic work by Jack Hirshleifer in particular,[8] became a catchall and a euphemism. As a catchall, it broadened the scope of academic work to consider any type of conflict between and among diverging interests. As such, conflict includes conflict within families, between firms and employees, firms and their suppliers, firms and their customers, conflict between vested interests for public sector largesse, and so on. Hirshleifer applied a 'contest success function', a mathematical description of the likelihood of succeeding in a contest, or conflict. Anderton and Carter's (2009) *Principles of Conflict Economics* textbook is a reflection of this, as is *The Oxford Handbook on the Economics of Peace and Conflict*, edited by Garfinkel and Skaperdas (2012). Yet, conflict economics is also a euphemism as, in practice, much of what conflict researchers address is highly violent, shockingly brutal, endemically entrenched, and sometimes genocidal. Violence economics would be a better term. The much-cited article by Paul Collier (1999) understates matters: the cost of violence is far more than the 2.2 percent growth reduction per conflict year he estimated at the time. As World Bank Group president Robert Zoellick notes in his foreword to the *World Development Report 2011*, 'Not one low-income country coping with these problems [of weak governance, poverty, and violence] has yet achieved a single Millennium Development Goal'.[9]

Although there already existed a long-standing literature on the economics of terrorism, in the wake of the attacks of 11 September 2001 in the United States, economists paid increasing attention to forms of politically motivated violence other than war and civil war and, with it, to the cost of security beyond traditionally understood defense. *Security economics* (Brück 2005) emerged and then further branched to encompass aspects such as high-seas piracy and virtually any security-related cost borne by firms and private households in consequence of violence or the threat thereof. Thus, security economics has begun to sidle up to the economics of crime, a well-established field of study. But huge outlays on security in the private and public sectors are also the result of defensive, deflective, or avoidance behavior, that is, prevention. Security amounts to risk management. Security becomes insurance. And yet, although insurance may bring some peace of mind, security is not peace, and security economics is not peace economics.

Peace economics

The primary distinguishing characteristic of peace economics lies in its normative aspect (Caruso 2010): how *should* the world look like, and what can be done to bring about a progressively more stable, peaceful state of the world? We thus define our subject matter as follows: *peace economics* concerns the economic study and design of political, economic, and cultural institutions, their interrelations, and their policies to prevent, mitigate, or resolve any type of latent or actual violence or other destructive conflict within and between societies. This normative character has been emphasized, among others, by Isard (1994), Arrow (1995), and Coulomb, Hartley, and Intriligator (2008). Peace economics is ecumenical in welcoming a variety of intellectual approaches. For example, within the orthodox domain of rational choice theory, one might study the conditions under which individuals choose to allocate time and other resources to constructive or destructive ends and attempt to determine just which switch in degree or kind would call forth a corresponding switch in behavior. For example, it is well established that individuals may fall into violent behavior because of poor or unjust economic conditions.[10] An economist might then be concerned with the natural, political, economic, and cultural conditions that shape an individual's motivation and means to engage in violent or otherwise destructive behavior. This example is positive— it describes the 'What is' state of affairs—and is filed under the rubric of conflict or security economics. What pushes the example into peace economics is the normative aspect: to design institutions and policies that prevent, mitigate or resolve actual and potential violence or other destructive conflict by influencing individuals' choice behavior in favor of peace-creating habits. Peace economics thus embraces the view that behind the veil of positivism there lies a distinct normative view of the world.

Peace economics is not unlike engineering. The point is not merely to describe why bridges collapse or remain standing. Rather, the point is to derive and then apply principles such that only bridges will be built whose likelihood of collapse is near zero. Bridges are constructed in varying environments and to varying specifications. These include the type of soil in which a bridge is anchored, the wind velocities it is subject to, and the traffic it is expected to bear. Likewise, societies large and small operate in varying and constantly changing environments. To fulfill their economic purpose—the assurance of the livelihood of their population—they need to be built to varying specifications. Among these are the construction of institutions and policies that prevent, or at least minimize, unproductive (that is, wastefully destructive) contest.[11]

Post-World War II, Kenneth Boulding put matters succinctly: 'The economic problem of reconstruction is that of *rebuilding the capital of society* … Reconstruction is merely a special case of economic progress. If we are to understand its problems thoroughly, we must examine *what is meant by economic progress* and try to discover how it comes about' (our emphases).[12] By 'capital' Boulding means assets, things that in time yield income based on these assets. Human capital, of which formal education is an example, is one such asset. During periods of violence, its accumulation is delayed and its stock is depreciated or destroyed. Human capital needs to be rebuilt. Physical and financial capital are other forms of assets that need to be (re)constructed. Thus, peace economics becomes the centerpiece of development economics, and—as Boulding maintains—of all of economics, for which society does not wish to progress further? For Boulding all economics *is* peace economics and all economists *are* peace economists.[13] Without development, there is no stable peace; without stable peace, there is no long-term progress. Prosperity is a necessary (but not sufficient) condition for peace, and peace is a necessary (but not sufficient) condition for prosperity.

Following from the previous point one issue, among others, pertains to the concept of stability. Like an engineer who wants to build a stable bridge, peace economists want to establish stable, peaceful social systems. Boulding (1978) differentiates among stable (continuous) war, unstable war (war punctuated by occasional peace), unstable peace (peace punctuated by occasional war), and stable (continuous) peace. In medieval Genoa, for example, a strategy of mutual deterrence adopted by rival clans continuously generated mutual increases in military might. But in the long term, their arms race equilibrium became unstable, leading Genoa first to social unrest and then to civil war (Greif 2006). As in game theory, peace economics is concerned with the conditions that underpin the existence, uniqueness, and stability of social systems. Evidently, social systems are unstable, or else they would not oscillate between war and peace. Hence, the virtuous cycle of peace and prosperity is vulnerable to breakdown, to reversal, and one objective of peace economics is to identify and to mend vulnerabilities in the system.

Peace economics takes the positive approach as its starting point—one does need to describe, 'What is'—but then pushes into the normative arena. Rather than standing aloof from application to policy, peace economics invests in application to policy. One example comes from the debate on the 'democratic peace' versus the 'capitalist peace' in which the statistical evidence by now appears to favor the latter. A normative implication is to let matters of political governance take care of themselves and instead attend to promote economic freedoms: a people who trade and prosper fight more rarely, regardless of the political arrangements of their societies.[14]

Peace economics for the twenty-first century

Conceptual framework

In a recent article, two researchers write that 'peace agreements are fragile' (Bove and Smith 2011: 257). Indeed, depending on how one measures, between one-quarter to one-half of all recent civil wars that ended in peace flared up again within a few years' time as war. Like engineering bridges, peace economics is not primarily about the prevention of failure (in the sense of 'keeping the lid on a boiling pot of water') but about the creation of stable structures of peace. It is about invulnerability, irreversibility, and about the foolproof, unconditional viability of peaceful social systems.

We can now outline our conceptual framework, and the role of peace economics within it, as follows. We define any community of any size as a social system. It consists of natural, political, economic, and cultural domains. Violence is one way by which any domain and the social system as a whole can be threatened. We apply Galtung's distinction between negative and positive peace (Galtung and Jacobsen 2000). The former refers to the *absence* of direct violence, the latter to the absence of indirect or structural violence, that is, the *presence* of conditions that eliminate the causes of violence and establish enduring peace. With low levels of negative peace in any domain (that is, with high levels of violence), the system can become infected, vulnerable, and 'tip' into becoming unsustainable. It can collapse. To be sustainable, the system must be designed to be less vulnerable. Now define positive peace as social system sustainability (positive peace = social system sustainability). Characterized by immunity to threat, sustainability requires a threshold level of inoculation where threat atrophies to mere nuisance.[15] In principle, sustainability and its threshold can be measured with positive peace or wellbeing indicators of which there are very many, even if not universally agreed upon as yet. It is true that successful efforts at building positive peace will be measured by lowered levels of violence, but the focus of positive peace does not lie with suppression of that which is destructive; rather, it lies with the upliftment of that which is constructive. The reason for this is that negative peace may result from mere repression of violence (which itself can be violent), leaving underlying causes of violence unaddressed. In contrast, positive peace redresses latent causes of violence to make violence superfluous and even unthinkable.

Negative peace, positive peace, and social system sustainability thus are linked within a common conceptual framework. The objective is to obtain hysteresis—a ratchet-effect—at each stage of successful institution and policy building so that there is no going back.[16] At each stage, achievements are locked in. They become irreversible. System performance variability is reduced, an ever-higher degree of stability is achieved, until a threshold is crossed and an invulnerable end-state of a stable, peaceful social system is obtained. Peace economics enters this framework because of the definition we gave it. It concerns the economic study *and design* of political, economic, and cultural institutions, their interrelations, and their policies to prevent, mitigate, or resolve any type of latent or actual violence or other destructive conflict within and between societies.

Challenges

Here, we delineate three challenges for peace economics. First, peace economics must provide better measures of positive peace. Second, peace economics must re-engage in the discussion about what counts as economic progress. Third, peace economics must recover and reclaim its own visibility within economics!

Measurement of a phenomenon depends upon the definition of the phenomenon itself. Thus definitions of peace range from cease-fires to the establishment of just societies. Some definitions emphasize the negation of a status (especially of war); others highlight positive components of a peaceful environment. With Galtung, we refer to the first as negative peace and to the latter as positive peace. Both need to be measured, but the measures needed are different. Measurement of negative peace and its effects can refer to a counterfactual state of the world wherein violence or other destructive conflict did *not* take place. For example, negative peace is, for now, the conceptual basis of the Global Peace Index (GPI), developed by the Institute for Economics and Peace (IEP), in Sydney, Australia. Presently, the GPI is a combined score consisting of measurements of 23 indicators mostly related to the absence of or threat to peace. This includes, for example, factors such as levels of violent crime, military expenditure, and weapons availability. But the ultimate goal is to develop a comprehensive and coherent set of positive peace (social sustainability) measures. Once an initial set of such measures exists, the operational key will be scalability. If indicators are overly community-specific, it is unlikely that they can be generalized across all communities. But if they are too general, they may not speak to local perceptions of and needs for peace. A way around this is to start with top-level indicators, common to all communities, and then scale down to community-specifics by way of 'satellite' measures that may only be partially comparable across communities. Because of their training related to data and data analysis, peace economists can make a useful contribution here.

A second issue relates to Boulding's warning about 'what is meant by economic progress', as some varieties of progress can lead to the very chaos and violence that genuine economic progress is meant to prevent. As the International Monetary Fund has belatedly learned, economic growth at all cost will not do. For example, questions about equity of progress invariably enter the picture.[17] At any given point in time, the state of a social system is the outcome of past interactions among natural, political, economic, and cultural domains. It follows that the economic study of institutions and policies has to take things into account that exceed the usual, narrow boundaries of economics. This makes peace economics a branch of economics enriched by contributions from many fields of study such as philosophy, politics, mathematics, psychology, sociology, and ecology. Unlike orthodox economics, peace economics is not obsessed with narrowly applying rational choice theory and its tools. Peace economics neither denies that orthodoxy can be relevant and useful, but nor does it view orthodoxy as the only way forward. Interdisciplinarity makes peace economics part of a broader peace science (Isard 1988).

Third, peace economics needs to recover and reclaim its standing within economics itself. In this regard, it is helpful to list an alphabetized sample of great economists who have devoted considerable effort to think and write about the economics of peace, often in book-length treatments. It includes Kenneth Arrow, Kenneth Boulding, F.Y. Edgeworth, John Kenneth Galbraith, John Harsanyi, Michael Intriligator, Walter Isard, John Maynard Keynes, Lawrence Klein, Wassily Leontief, Friedrich List, Karl Marx, Roger Myerson, Douglass North, Mancur Olson, Vilfredo Pareto, A.C. Pigou, David Ricardo, Lionel Robbins, Thomas Schelling, Joseph A. Schumpeter, Adam Smith, Werner Sombart, Joseph Stiglitz, Jan Tinbergen, Thorstein Veblen, Léon Walras, and Knut Wicksell—a surprisingly diverse assembly (at least to those steeped in the field). Nonetheless, workaday economists today do not appear much concerned with questions of peace. A charitable interpretation is that perhaps they really do believe, as Boulding implied, that all economics *is* peace economics. Still, if the relevance of a subfield in economics is attested to by inclusion in the *Journal of Economic Literature* (JEL) classification scheme, then something is amiss. Work related to peace economics is captured mainly in subject codes D74 (conflict; conflict resolution; alliances), D78 (positive analysis of policymaking and implementation), and H56 (national security and war). As yet, there is no descriptor for peace economics as we have defined it. Nevertheless, peace economists today can count on a growing number of specialized outlets that consider their work, including the *Journal of Conflict Resolution* (since 1956), the *Journal of Peace Research* (since 1964), *Conflict Management and Peace Science* (since 1973), *Defence and Peace Economics* (since 1990), *Peace Economics, Peace Science, and Public Policy* (since 1993), the *Economics of Peace and Security Journal* (since 2006), and the *International Journal of Development and Conflict* (since 2011). A number of *Handbooks* are available, and textbooks will follow soon. Peace economics is a growing field of study.

Summary

In sum, we assert that while founded on positive precepts, peace economics is particularly distinct for its normative character. Its focus lies on an economic understanding and putting in place political, economic, and cultural structures that would prevent any type of violent conflict and its adverse consequences. In a nutshell, peace economics is about the contribution of economic science to peacebuilding.

Notes

1 Skidelsky (1983).
2 Keynes (1920); also see Keynes (1922).
3 The story goes that when Soviet and US warplanes met in the skies over Korea, during the Korean war, the pilots were mutually perplexed about the similarity of the aircraft, the MIG15 and the F86. It appears both jets were designed, in no small part, by postwar access to German documents as well as post-Nazi scientific, engineering, and design refugees/migrants, one part having gone West, the other East. Ample documentation is available on the internet but see, e.g., the illustration in Budiansky (2004, p. 372). Much the same was true of rocketry and nuclear engineering; see Rhodes (1995) or search for "Operation Paperclip" and "Operation Osoaviakhim," respectively.
4 Pigou (1921); Boulding (1945); Robbins (1950). See Coulomb (2004) for a history of economic thought on war and peace.
5 Stiglitz and Bilmes (2008).
6 Although routinely described as "an economist," Monnet received no economics training, nor in fact any post-secondary formal education at all.
7 Mayne (1991, p. 117). It is difficult to find an original source for the statement attributed to Keynes, but one source may be http://www.larouchepub.com/other/2000/cheminade_fdr_monnet_2724.html#fnB1 [accessed 14 October 2011] which, in turn, references Mönick (1970).
8 See, e.g., the essays in Hirshleifer (2001).
9 Relatedly, only in 2009 did the United Nations General Assembly (UNGA) see fit to acknowledge that the Millennium Development Goals are impossible to fulfill in the absence of peace. To quote: "Although the linkage between armed violence and development is not explicit in the Millennium Development Goals, they offer entry points for development agencies to consider. Objectives such as reducing poverty, ensuring maternal health and promoting education are all associated with effective armed violence prevention and reduction initiatives. Nevertheless … there is no Millennium Development Goal that specifically deals with conflict, violence and insecurity" (UN General Assembly, 5 August 2009, item #33, p. 11, A/64/228).
10 A classic reference is Gurr (1970).
11 On productive and unproductive entrepreneurship, see Baumol (1990). On the economics of destruction see, e.g., Vahabi (2011).
12 Boulding (1945, pp. 4, 73).
13 Interestingly, Léon Walras nominated himself for the 1906 Nobel Peace Prize. He was convinced that the study of economics was a means to promote the peaceful fraternity of states.
14 See, e.g., Gartzke (2005); Human Security Report Project (2011, chapter 2).
15 Note our choice of "inoculation" and "immunity" over the more common term "resilience." Resilience is a biological term that refers for instance to an ecosystem's ability to bounce back and recover after collapse. In psychology, resilience likewise refers to a post-traumatic "come back." But one does not want individuals and societies to collapse in the first place; one wants immunity to collapse so that resilience will not be necessary.
16 Hysteresis is the dependence of a system state on its own history.
17 See, e.g., Del Castillo (2008); Brauer and Dunne (2012).

References

Anderton, C.H. and Carter, J.R. (2009) *Principles of Conflict Economics: A Primer for Social Scientists*, New York: Cambridge University Press.
Arrow, K. (1995) 'Some General Observations on the Economics of Peace and War', *Peace Economics, Peace Science, and Public Policy*, 2(2): 1–8.
Ash, B.J., Hosek, J.R., and Warner, J.T. (2007) 'New Economics of Manpower in the Post-Cold War Era', in T. Sandler and Hartley, K. (eds) *Handbook of Defense Economics*, 2, Amsterdam: Elsevier.

Baumol, W.J. (1990) 'Entrepreneurship: Productive, Unproductive, and Destructive', *Journal of Political Economy*, 98(5): 893–921.

Benoit, E. (1973) *Defense and Economic Growth in Developing Countries*, Boston, MA: Heath & Co., Lexington Books.

Boulding, K.E. (1945) *The Economics of Peace*, New York: Prentice-Hall.

Boulding, K.E. (1978) *Stable Peace*, Austin, TX: University of Texas Press.

Bove, V. and Smith, R.P. (2011) 'The Economics of Peacekeeping', in D.L. Braddon and K. Hartley (eds) *Handbook on the Economics of Conflict*, Cheltenham, UK: Elgar, pp. 237–264.

Brauer, J. and Dunne, J.P. (2012) *Peace Economics: A Macroeconomic Primer for Violence-Afflicted States*, Washington DC: United States Institute of Peace Press.

Brück, T. (2005) 'An Economic Analysis of Security Policies' *Defense and Peace Economics*, 16(5): 375–389.

Budiansky, S. (2004) *Air Power*, New York: Viking.

Caruso, R. (2010) 'On the Nature of Peace Economics', *Peace Economics, Peace Science, and Public Policy*, 16(2), Article 2.

Collier, P. (1999) 'On the Economic Consequences of Civil War', *Oxford Economic Papers*, 51(1): 168–183.

Coulomb, F. (2004) *Economic Theories of Peace and War*, London: Routledge.

Coulomb, F., Hartley, K., and Intriligator, M. (2008) 'Pacifism in Economic Analysis: A Historical Perspective', *Defense and Peace Economics*, 19(5): 373–386.

Del Castillo, G. (2008) *Rebuilding War-Torn States: The Challenge of Post-Conflict Economic Reconstruction*, Oxford: Oxford University Press.

Galtung, J. and Jacobsen, C.G. (2000) *Searching for Peace: The Road to TRANSCEND*, London: Pluto Press.

Gansler, J.S. (1980) *The Defense Industry*, Cambridge, MA: MIT Press.

Gansler, J.S. (1989) *Affording Defense*, Cambridge, MA: MIT Press.

Garfinkel, M.R. and Skaperdas, S. (eds) (2012) *The Oxford Handbook of the Economics of Peace and Conflict*, New York: Oxford University Press.

Gartzke, E. (2005) 'Economic Freedom and Peace', in J. Gwartney and R. Lawson (eds) *Economic Freedom of the World: 2005 Annual Report*, Vancouver, BC: Fraser Institute, pp. 29–44.

Greif, A. (2006) *Institutions and the Path of the Modern Economy: Lessons from Medieval Trade*, New York: Cambridge University Press.

Gurr, T. (1970) *Why Men Rebel*, Princeton, NJ: Princeton University Press.

Heston, A., Summers, R. and Aten, B. (2011) Penn World Table Version 7.0, Center for International Comparisons of Production, Income and Prices at the University of Pennsylvania (May 2011).

Hirshleifer, J. (2001) *The Dark Side of the Force: Economic Foundations of Conflict Theory*, New York: Cambridge University Press.

Human Security Report Project (2011) *Human Security Report 2009/2010: The Causes of Peace and the Shrinking Costs of War*, New York: Oxford University Press.

Isard, W. (1988) *Arms Races, Arms Control, and Conflict Analysis*, New York: Cambridge University Press.

Isard, W. (1994) 'Peace Economics: A Topical Perspective', *Peace Economics, Peace Science, and Public Policy*, 1(2): 6–9.

Keynes, J.M. (1920) *The Economic Consequences of the Peace*, London: Macmillan and New York: Harcourt edition available at http://www.econlib.org/library/YPDBooks/Keynes/kynsCP.html [accessed on 14 October 2011].

Keynes, J.M. (1922) *A Revision of the Treaty*, London: Macmillan.

Mayne, R. (1991) 'Gray Eminence', in D. Brinckley and C. Hackett (eds) *Jean Monnet: The Path to European Unity*, New York: St. Martin's Press, pp. 114–128.

Mönick, E. (1970) *Pour mémoire [par] Emmanuel Mönick*, Paris: Mensil, impr. Firmin-Didot.

Olson, M. and Zeckhauser, R. (1966) 'An Economic Theory of Alliances', *Review of Economics and Statistics*, 48(3): 266–279.

Pigou, A.C. (1921) *The Political Economy of War*, London: Macmillan.

Poutvaara, P. and Wagener, A. (2007) 'Conscription: Economic Costs and Political Allure', *Economics of Peace and Security Journal*, 2(1): 6–15.

Rhodes, R. (1995) *Dark Sun: The Making of the Hydrogen Bomb*, New York: Simon & Schuster.

Robbins, L. (1950) *The Economic Problem in Peace and War*, London: Macmillan.

Ruttan, V.W. (2005) *Is War Necessary for Economic Growth? Military Procurement and Technology Development*, New York: Oxford University Press.

Schelling, T. (1960) *The Strategy of Conflict*, Cambridge, MA: Harvard University Press.

Skidelsky, R.J.A. (1983) *John Maynard Keynes: A Biography*, London: Macmillan.

Smith, R.P. (2009) *Military Economics: The Interaction of Power and Money*, New York: Palgrave Macmillan.

Stiglitz, J.E. and Bilmes, L.J. (2008) *The Three Trillion Dollar War: The True Cost of the Iraq Conflict*, New York: Norton.

Vahabi, M. (2011) 'The Economics of Destructive Power', in D.L. Braddon and K. Hartley (eds) *Handbook on the Economics of Conflict*, Cheltenham, UK: Elgar, pp. 79–104.

12

SOCIOLOGY AND PEACEBUILDING

John Brewer

Introduction

It is ironic that the discipline of sociology, so closely associated historically with the study of the problem of order, has concentrated on studying war rather than peace. Sociological analyses of organized violence in late modernity abound (most recently see Malešević 2010). However, the changing nature of organized violence today (on which see Kaldor 1999), which is simultaneously witnessing ever more sophisticated forms of weaponry and the return to de-technological war, in which the machete is the favoured weapon of genocide, has both increased the proclivity to violence in late modernity and its level of barbarity and atrocity. There has been a collapse in the distinction between civilian and combatant, and the human body has become a battle site, on which is inflicted moral depravities not witnessed since pre-modern times. While this has led some sociologists to query the very nature of late modernity and its commitment to Enlightenment values (for example Bauman 1989; 1998), it has had a profound impact on the subject matter of the discipline of sociology by encouraging what elsewhere I have called a second wave cognitive revolution (see Brewer and Hayes 2011: 7–10). If the first wave in the 1960s focused on the rediscovery of social meaning and *Verstehen*, in such forms as social phenomenology, ethnomethodology and cognitive sociology, the second wave today addresses notions like risk, vulnerability, suffering, emotion, forgiveness, hope, anger, revenge, reconciliation and, now, peace. This second wave is not solely down to the reintroduction of genocide as an experience in late modernity, but the reinvigorated sociological analysis of new forms of organized violence has implicated the development of the sociology of peace processes.

Individual sociologists have been contributing to the field of peace studies for a very long time. It is worth recalling that the founder of this new field in the 1960s, Johan Galtung, was originally a sociologist; and for people of my generation he will always be remembered for having written a famous textbook on mathematical sociology (the imprint of which is still felt on his use of equations and formulae and his logical approach in peace studies, see Galtung 2008). Significant contributions to peace studies, both as a field of practice and a theoretical subject, have been made by sociologists, such as Lee Smithey (2011) and, more notably, John Paul Lederach, whose well-known models for peacebuilding (for example, Lederach 1997; 2005) have inspired others to apply them in actual cases (see Knox and Quirk 2000). Sociology pioneered the idea of 'divided society' as a way of capturing the structural dynamics behind zero-sum conflict and Brewer (2003) and Oberschall (2007) used case studies to reflect on how this kind of society inevitably implicates but also constrains peacebuilding. Individual sociologists have worked on the role of memory in peace processes (Brewer 2006), on forgiveness (Misztal 2010; 2011), truth and truth recovery (Lundy 2011) and transitional justice more widely (Elster 2004), and on the potential for religious peacebuilding (Brewer, Higgins and Teeney 2011), amongst many other things.

However, for all the work of sociologists as individuals, there has not been an attempt to develop a sociological perspective on peace. The sociology of peace processes is undeveloped. This is despite the huge potential of the discipline for understanding the nature and dynamics of post-conflict societies. This neglect is partly the result of disciplinary closure, which has seen peace studies, political science and international relations dominate the field, but it also lies in a misunderstanding of the nature of peace, which is thought primarily to describe the process by which accords, agreements and pacts are negotiated at the regime level to bring an end to problematic politics.

Peace, however, is a very interdisciplinary concept. The philosopher and ethicist Avishai Margalit (2010) has problematized the concept of peace by referring to those peace accords that on moral grounds ought *not* to have been negotiated – since they enshrine human indignity – as 'rotten compromises' (he has in mind the Munich and Yalta Agreements). The discipline of economics has long worked on the effects of violence in civil war and the impact of 'war economies' on the potential for peace (Keen 1998), and we now recognize the importance of strong economies for statebuilding during peace processes (see Collier 2008). Even theology has contributed to the conceptualization of peace through efforts at understanding the scriptural basis to advocating forgiveness and reconciliation at the political level (Shriver 1995; Torrance 2006) and between nations (Amstutz 2004), and the writings of David Herbert (2003) from within religious studies stress the link between religion, civil society and peace. There is now an established subfield of peace criminology, and both law and religious studies (on the latter see Philpott 2007) contribute to our understanding of transitional justice after conflict. The second wave cognitive revolution in sociology has also opened this discipline up to engagement with peace and a nascent sociology of peace processes is emerging.

The sociology of peace processes

This new field in sociology – an infant entrant into the analysis of peace processes – is difficult to characterize with any definitiveness because of its novelty, and I am in a difficult position in doing so because I am so closely associated with pioneering it, but I suggest there are three ways in which it can be mapped: by its substantive, conceptual and analytical foci.

Addressing first its substantive focus, the sociology of peace processes draws on key ideas within the discipline of sociology as they pertain to an understanding of the meaning of peace and the processes that help consolidate and strengthen peace agreements. This work has been summarized by Brewer (2010a) and covers the relevance to peace processes of sociological ideas on emotions, gender, civil society, memory, citizenship, truth, victimhood and globalization, amongst others (on the ideas of social capital and spiritual capital as they relate to peace see Brewer, Higgins and Teeney 2011; on social capital see Leonard 2004). The claims that Brewer makes in *Peace Processes: A Sociological Approach* are that sociologists have not applied these ideas in the past to an understanding of peace processes and that analysts of peace processes have tended to either overlook them completely or ignore the sociological take on them. Of course, there are a number of sociologists exempt from this complaint, in that, in particular, people like Jon Elster (2004) and Thomas Scheff (1994) have applied ideas from the sociology of emotions to help understand the problems around the management of emotions following conflict, such as those around negative emotions, like anger, hate and revenge, and the cultivation of positive ones around empathy, forgiveness, hope, reconciliation and the like. And there are some advocates of the liberal model of peace in international relations and peace studies that are opening up to some of these ideas, notably civil society (especially Paris 2004), although not yet to sociology's particular emphasis.

It has to be admitted, however, that sociologists in other fields have not yet awakened to the potential of their ideas for understanding peace processes. We await, for example, masculinity theorists becoming attuned to the import of their ideas for understanding the deconstruction of violent masculinities amongst ex-combatants and to the development of non-violent masculinities in post-conflict societies, although the sociological writings of John Brown Childs (2003) on gang violence are relevant here. Similarly, sociologists of religion offer no understanding of the dynamics of religious peacebuilding. The reduction of the sociology of religion to the sociology of secularization tends to inhibit the ability of sociologists of religion to see it playing a positive role in society, which is why the specification of religious peacebuilding is done either by mainstream sociologists from outside the sociology of religion (such as Beck 2010; Brewer, Higgins and Teeney 2011) or by non-sociologists. The same must be said for the area of women and peacebuilding, which is burgeoning, advances in which are made almost entirely from outside the sociology of gender (for some exceptions see Lentin 1997; Wallace, Haerpfer and Abbott 2009), although feminist sociologists have made a significant contribution to our understanding of repressed victimhood, especially as it affects women (for example Lentin 1999). To prove the point about the sociology of gender, however, perhaps the best contribution to the topic of repressed victimhood has been by the feminist historian Urvashi Butalia (2000).

The second way to characterize the sociology of peace processes is through its conceptual contribution. I have in mind here the way in which sociology broadens our conceptualization of peace processes. I earlier referred to the way in which peace is inherently perceived as a political process. I mean this in two ways. A peace process is thought to describe the negotiations at the regime level through which an accord or agreement is negotiated to bring an end to problematic politics; and the consolidation of the agreement afterwards is itself represented as a political process involving the introduction of good governance structures and statebuilding. That 'distorted politics' may reside in social processes like racism, ethnicity, structural inequality, and zero-sum conceptualizations of social identity, does not seem to affect the assumption that once problematic politics is resolved and good governance structures are implemented, the process of societal healing follows on naturally. This assumption is naive. Sociology is useful for alerting us to the distinction between what elsewhere (Brewer 2010a: 200–4; Brewer, Higgins and Teeney 2011: 34ff) I have called the political and social peace processes.

Conflict resolution studies, politics and international relations, for example, can lay claim to expertise on the political peace process, namely, the negotiation process at the regime level that results in the accord and the process of statebuilding thereafter. However, good governance structures like democratic forms of political representation, new forms of inclusive voting systems, a new constitution, institutional reform of the polity and the economy, the introduction of human rights law and bill of rights, and the like, are insufficient on their own to address the social peace process. By this is meant the process of societal healing, that is, the restoration of broken relationships, the development of a sense of community and shared responsibility for the future. Reconciliation is part of this, but so too is compromise, empathy, trust and forgiveness. These tend not to be the concerns of the liberal model of peacebuilding and the good governance approach, which neglects such things in preference for the focus on the political peace process. The social peace process forms the area of expertise of the sociology of peace processes.

The conceptual focus of the sociology of peace processes therefore offers an advance by supplementing existing approaches through broadening our attention towards a range of matters that go to define and shape the social peace process. These include the problem of interpersonal accommodation after conflict, the question of what healing means at the societal level, how compromise at the level of interpersonal social relations works, what forgiveness means and whether or not third-party forgiveness – people, mostly politicians, forgiving on others' behalf – is feasible, the new forms of memory work needed to move society on from the conflict and the appropriate level of social and political change needed to permit ongoing social cleavages to be structurally reproduced in non-violent ways, amongst other things.

In other writings I have suggested that one way to understand the sorts of issues that constitute the social peace process is through a series of policy dilemmas that go toward defining the sociological dynamic to peace processes (see Brewer 2004, 2011). I referred to these as a series of policy tensions, problems and imperatives or needs. There are the tensions between truth and reconciliation, and between justice and peace; the problems of victimhood, and of remembrance and commemoration; and the policy imperatives to assist the social reintegration of former combatants, the need to develop a programme of citizenship education for the new society, as well as finding ways to extenuate the mundane over the sense of crisis during the travails of the peace process. These pose serious challenges for policymakers but I suggested their resolution was equally important for the eventual success of the peace process as all the institutional reform in the political peace process associated with good governance and statebuilding.

My own empirical research deals with some of the policy concerns in the social peace process. I lay all this out for reasons which will become apparent shortly. For example, I have recently published research as the principal investigator arising from a four-year Economic and Social Research Council-funded project (RES-000-23-1258) on the contribution of civil society to peacebuilding, which addressed the role of the churches to Northern Ireland's peace process as the illustrative case (see Brewer, Higgins and Teeney 2011). I am principal investigator on a five-year £1.26 million

Leverhulme-funded programme of research – begun in 2009 – on compromise amongst victims of conflict, addressing Northern Ireland, South Africa, Sri Lanka, Sierra Leone, Colombia and contemporary Spain, which also includes a project on witness evidence at truth commissions (www.abdn.ac.uk/compromise-conflict). And I am involved in a project as principal investigator on the contribution of religion to the social well-being of ex-combatant prisoners in Northern Ireland, funded by the Northern Ireland Association of Mental Health.

I state this as a way of laying down a complaint, for, unfortunately, there is not much work of this sort going on in sociology – or at least it is fragmented along with sociology's disciplinary boundaries and hived off into new interdisciplinary subfields like memory studies, victimization studies, transitional justice studies, and the like. Sociology is an exporter discipline infusing many of these interdisciplinary fields. Part of the problem in establishing the sociology of peace processes as the conceptual focus for analysing the social peace process is not so much hostility from outsiders but persuading sociologists that their discipline has something to contribute in the face of its disciplinary fragmentation, to which the new field of the sociology of peace processes might be thought itself to contribute. Thus, rather than proffering possible answers to the questions raised above about the social peace process, I prefer in this short chapter to address the third contribution of the sociology of peace processes, its analytical focus, which goes some way to explaining how a disciplinary perspective enhances the analysis of peace processes.

A sociological perspective on peace processes

Sociology has ceded the analysis of peace processes to other disciplines in large part because a perspective on such matters that is identifiably sociological is difficult to conceive and there is resistance to the fragmentation of the discipline that the topic is thought to reinforce. While it is feasible to imagine various formulations of such a perspective – it is hardly necessary to limit it to just one – in what follows I proffer a personal view that locates the analysis of peace processes at the centre of what Charles Wright Mills (1959) calls the sociological imagination. This expands upon the approach I developed in my book *C. Wright Mills and the Ending of Violence* (Brewer 2003), which I applied to understand the emergence and development of the peace processes in Northern Ireland and South Africa. I take the opportunity in this chapter for the first time to link this perspective to arguments developed in the two books that followed next in the trilogy, *Peace Processes: A Sociological Approach* (Brewer 2010a) and *Religion, Civil Society and Peace in Northern Ireland* (Brewer, Higgins and Teeney 2011). What follows is therefore a thoroughgoing sociological perspective representing ideas I have been struggling with for the last ten years, although necessarily addressed here briefly due to the limited space available.

Negotiated peace settlements represent only one way in which conflict is pacified. Post-conflict societies are of three types. One type is based on conquest, involving military victory for one group and defeat for others, such as in colonization and contemporary Sri Lanka; another is based on cartography, as map makers redraw territorial boundaries to partition the groups into separate nation states or devolved regions, keeping warring factions apart, as occurred following the deconstruction of the former Yugoslavia; the third is based on compromise as erstwhile protagonists negotiate a second best deal in which they give up on first preferences for the sake of peace, represented by all those modern societies where peace agreements have settled long-standing conflicts, such as Northern Ireland and South Africa.

This typology coheres around three axes that usefully capture the scale of the problems faced by compromise societies based on negotiated peace deals. The first is territorial integrity/spatial separation, describing the extent to which, post-conflict, erstwhile protagonists share a common nation; the second is relational distance/ closeness, referring to the level to which former enemies share common values; the third is cultural capital/cultural annihilation, describing the extent to which parties retain their cultural capital and resources following conflict. This is represented in Figure 12.1. This captures the nature of the problems faced by post-conflict societies based on compromise, represented diagrammatically in the circle within the figure, for they can involve protagonists without relational closeness, where all parties retain their cultural capital and resources, and have to share common territory.

This means that peace processes must find ways in which all the social cleavages that once provoked the conflict can be reproduced, following the peace agreement, now in non-violent ways, when there are few common values and senses of shared identity, and where no group is vanquished to the point of cultural annihilation but each have kept their resources and power. The political peace process that delivered the negotiated settlement and monitors conformity to all the good governance structures and institutional reforms afterwards is not capable on its own of dealing with the full range of issues that compromise post-conflict societies face.

The political peace process can, of course, deliver much. Good governance is important. A strong economy, effective statebuilding, the introduction of human rights law and effective institutional reform can eliminate problematic politics. But Figure 12.1 highlights that despite good governance, social cleavages persist in post-conflict societies based on negotiated peace accords. There can be few shared values, or at least, small differences appear large, social distance remains, and former enemies live side-by-side as neighbours, sharing territory while remaining members of groups that retain their labour power, political clout and cultural legitimacy, even if occasionally only by means of a strong international diaspora. All this is to say that attention to the social peace process becomes critical after a successful political peace process.

The stability of the compromise represented by the negotiated peace agreement depends as much on success in managing the social peace process as on the introduction of all the reforms represented by good governance structures and human rights law. Public policy attention therefore needs to be directed toward the policy dilemmas and problems that shape the social peace process around victimhood, remembrance, the reintegration of ex-combatants, the development of citizenship education, new forms of memory work and memorialization and questions of justice and truth. All this has to be done at the same time as the potential threat of renewed violence is managed to avoid the return to war by spoilers and dissidents stuck on their first preferences or profiting from the war economy. In other words, reconciliation does not end with the success of the political peace process; it only really starts then. It is hardly a surprise, therefore, that negotiated peace agreements are fragile, for they leave untouched the task of societal healing that only really begins once the political peace process opens up the space for

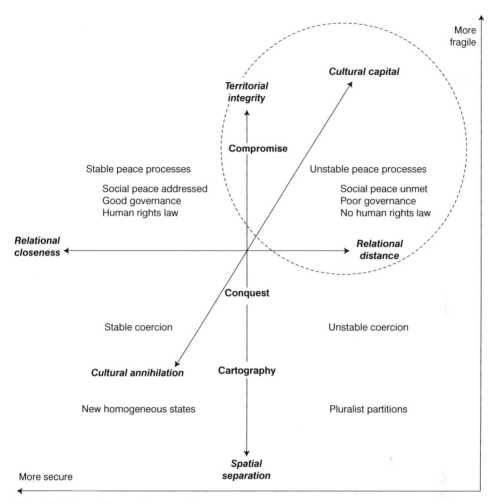

Figure 12.1 Types of post-violence society

dealing with the task of interpersonal compromise free from the sound of guns or the cut of machetes.

One way to represent the issues confronting the social peace process is by utilizing the famous contrast between negative and positive peace (see Galtung 1996). Negative peace describes processes that bring about an end to violence. Positive peace refers to social transformation, in which questions of inequality, injustice and social redistribution are addressed. In the social peace process, negative peace needs to be maintained by managing the threat of renewed violence while pushing onward to implement positive peace, the very fact of which may persuade some to return to war because they resist the idea of social transformation. The policy dilemmas in the social peace process thus involve tight balancing acts. For example, they involve managing the needs of both victims and ex-combatants, implementing truth recovery and encouraging new forms of memory work that do not make victims arbiters of the future, and balancing the contrasting demands of restorative and retributive notions of justice, as well as dealing with the social cleavages that mark the social structure as unequal and in need of social redistribution, while maintaining the economic strength that permits successful statebuilding. Policies that encourage interpersonal compromise and accommodation across the divide have to exist alongside those that permit victims dignity and recognition. This is a fine balancing act indeed.

Post-conflict societies that neglect social redistribution, no matter how successful their political transition, face the problem of frustrated expectations, for they often leave the same level of disparity across the social cleavages as in the past. Failure to address positive peace therefore offers a severe test of the capacity of the political peace process to desensitize the conflict by democratically translating it in institutional ways through new forms of governance. In some cases, dissidents resist the institutionalization of the conflict and return to violence, such as in Northern Ireland. This explains why activists in South Africa, for example, complain that they now experience class apartheid rather than racial apartheid.

The social peace process is thus about social transformation, the political peace process conflict transformation. Put another way, the political peace process introduces negative peace, the social peace process positive peace. This is why both sets of distinctions are critical to a sociological perspective on peace processes, as represented in Table 12.1.

Political peace processes rarely concern themselves with the bottom left cell of the table (positive/political), for peace agreements rarely address social transformation, or, at least, the success of the institutional reforms in embedding new political values and democratic practices is dependent on the extent to which the new state, in conjunction with civil society and grassroots groups, also work in the top left cell (positive/social). Similar sorts of co-operation are required to negotiate ceasefires (negative peace), where peacemaking in both of the right-hand cells involves civil society and political groups working to stop the killings, although rarely together or in co-ordination.

It is worth emphasizing that the cells are not hermetically sealed. As noted above, the relationship between the variables is recursive. Positive peace is only feasible once negative peace has been won; with the violence over, the real job of positive peacemaking can take top priority (although always being mindful to manage the threat of renewed violence). The social and political peace processes enable each other; the social peace

Table 12.1 Peacemaking in practice

	Positive	*Negative*
Social	Involves civil society and grassroots groups working in areas of expertise to focus on social transformation and societal healing, whether in pre- and/or post-agreement phases.	Involves civil society and grassroots groups working in areas of expertise to focus on conflict transformation by intervening as mediators in specific instances of violence and/or campaigning to end the violence generally.
Political	Involves political parties, negotiators and politicians incorporating social transformation and societal healing into the terms of the accord and/or using the new political structures to address social transformation and societal healing.	Involves political parties, negotiators and politicians negotiating ceasefires and campaigning for all factions to desist from killing.

process can be used as a conflict reduction strategy (top right-hand cell) preparing the space for political negotiations (bottom two cells), and a successfully negotiated peace accord gives civil society and grassroots groups the opportunity to address the range of issues involved in social transformation and societal healing (top left-hand cell), safe within a secure context established by the accord, where political freedoms, the rule of law and human rights pertain. There should be constant movement, therefore, between the cells, up, down and across, and collaboration between the new state, civil society and the grassroots in making these transitions.

Civil society here includes women's groups, whose contribution to peacebuilding is internationally recognized through the United Nations Development Fund for Women, as well as the churches, faith-based NGOs, trades unions, community development groups, human rights bodies and the like, all of whose contribution to peace needs to be celebrated in addition to that of militant groups, politicians, political mandarins, civil servants and advisers who negotiate deals in the political peace process (see Bew, Frampton and Gurruchaga 2009, for an analysis of 'talking to terrorists' in Northern Ireland and the Basque Country which focuses only on the latter set of people). This reinforces the earlier argument that the substantive focus of the sociology of peace processes draws on sociological ideas about gender, civil society, religion, emotions and the like as they pertain to peace.

I contend that this conceptual apparatus, substantive focus, and set of ideas exemplifies the sociological imagination. Charles Wright Mills is remembered as the first progenitor of this phrase but it is bandied about in sociology almost constantly to the point where it means everything and thus ultimately nothing. I employ it here in the sense that Mills used it. He argued that sociology should be concerned with a subject matter that is historically specified, by which he meant located in real time and space, referring to real events, people and processes. In doing this, sociology needed to show the intersection and connection between four dimensions, the social structure, individual personal biography, history and the political process. This gives social reality a three-dimensional quality. First, social reality is simultaneously microscopic, based around individuals' personal worlds, and macroscopic, in that the institutional and structural order of society impacts on people's personal milieux. Social reality is also simultaneously historical and contemporary, in that present structures, circumstances, events, processes and issues have a historical relevance that may impact on their current form and future development. Thirdly, reality is simultaneously social and political; society is deeply impacted by the operation of power within the nation state and beyond and politics affects both the social structure and the personal biographical worlds of people, and is in turn affected by them.

The sociological imagination therefore involves a co-ordination of personal biographical experience, social structural conditions, historical forces and political power and looks at the intersection of them all. In Mills's words (1959: 143), the lives of individuals cannot be adequately understood without reference to the institutions (political and social) and historical forces within which their biography is enacted, and societies are composed in part of the biographical experiences, both historical and contemporary, of the people they comprise. One reflection of this intersection, stressed most by Mills, is the interaction between 'personal troubles' and 'public issues'. The indissolubility of the individual and social structure ensures that people's private 'troubles' transfer into public issues that transcend local and personal environments to affect society generally (such as divorce and unemployment). Conversely, public issues can become private troubles to affect the individual and shape their biographical experiences (such as fear of crime, anxiety over redundancy, and the consequences of high mortgage rates for homeowners).

It is possible to distil the sociological imagination into a set of guidelines for examining and understanding peace processes that go toward defining what a sociological perspective on such matters might look like. These are as follows.

- A sociology of peace processes should not offer a grand theory or universal schema to understand peace processes in the abstract, but is restricted in its applicability to historically specified cases that exist in real time and space;
- It is necessary to locate specified peace processes in their historical past, to establish whether historical factors continue to shape the form and context of the process (such as the legacy of colonialism or historical wrongs, real or imagined);
- Any account of the emergence, development and progress of the peace process in historically specified cases must focus on the intersection between the social structure, individual biographical experience and the political process;
- This means in practice that it is necessary to:
  - Identify the social structural conditions, and changes to long-established patterns of structural differentiation, both nationally and internationally, which affect the potential for conflict transformation in the political peace process and social transformation in the social peace process;
  - Outline the events and developments within the political peace process, nationally and internationally, which have altered the political dynamics of the conflict, and accordingly affect both conflict transformation and social transformation;
  - Chart the influence of individual biographical experience on the political and social peace processes, by examining (a) the effect of key individuals who have exploited the moment and whose strategies for change and political mobilizations bear upon peace; and (b) the experiences of ordinary people in taken-for-granted settings whose interests and values make them open to mobilization in the political peace process and to interpersonal compromise and accommodation in the social peace process;
- It is important to show the interaction between local personal milieux and the social structure, by exploring how ordinary people experience the structural and political changes to their local setting, and whose response to which affects progress in the political and social peace processes;
- The dialectic between 'personal troubles' and 'public issues' needs to be highlighted in both the conflict and post-conflict phases. For the pre-agreement phase, it needs to be shown how the broad social conflict translates into 'personal troubles', which themselves transform into 'public issues', and vice versa, and how this affects the wish to end violence and the will to make peace. For the post-agreement phase it needs to be shown how this dialectic presents itself as a series of issues in the private and public spheres, which define and shape the problem of societal healing.

There is no opportunity here to apply this perspective to specific peace processes (although see the cases of Northern Ireland and South Africa in Brewer 2003), but it is indicative that a sociological perspective can be developed for the analysis of peace processes that captures the very kernel of the sociological imagination. It is a truism that sociology exists always between God and chance. That it is to say, miracles and accidents can happen that affect peace processes but mediating between them is the discipline of sociology, which rejects mono-causal accounts of peace processes to offer a whole-rounded approach drawing on social structural conditions, politics, history and individual biographical experience.

Conclusion

The arguments in this chapter have been an attempt at proselytization, for which I offer no apology. I am hoping to convince sociologists of the need to develop a sociological perspective on peace processes and analysts from other disciplines that sociology has much to add. The chapter is programmatic in outlining the potential that lies in such an approach rather than descriptive of a large body of work already done. What sociology can achieve is immense; what it has done so far is quite limited. What it can achieve, in short, is the broadening of our understanding of the meaning of peace, expert attention on the social peace process, by which is meant the question of societal healing that is left as a problem of interpersonal accommodation *after* the political peace process has worked, and sensitivity toward a series of issues as vitally important to the success of the peace process as any set of institutional reforms. Analysts of peace processes from other disciplines need to open their eyes to matters beyond politics and sociologists to start applying their special insights to what will be an enduring problem in the twenty-first century given the proliferation of new forms of organized violence in late modernity.

References

Amstutz, M. (2004) *The Healing of Nations*, Lanham: Rowman and Littlefield.
Bauman, Z. (1989) *Modernity and the Holocaust*, Cambridge: Polity Press.
Bauman, Z. (1998) *Globalization: The Human Consequences*, Cambridge: Polity Press.
Beck, U. (2010) *A God of Our Own*, Cambridge: Polity Press.
Bew, J., M. Frampton and I. Gurruchaga (2009) *Talking To Terrorists*, London: Hurst.
Brewer, J. (2003) *C. Wright Mills and the Ending of Violence*, Basingstoke: Palgrave.
Brewer, J. (2004) 'Justice in the context of racial and religious conflict', *Logos*, 41: 80–103.
Brewer, J. (2006) 'Memory, truth and victimhood in post-trauma societies', in G. Delanty and K. Kumar (eds), *The SAGE Handbook of Nations and Nationalism*, London: Sage, 214–24.
Brewer, J. (2010a) *Peace Processes: A Sociological Approach*, Cambridge: Polity Press.
Brewer, J. (2010b) 'Dealing with emotions in peacemaking', in S. Karstedt, I. Loader and H. Strang (eds), *Emotions, Crime and Justice*, Oxford: Hart, pp. 295–316.
Brewer, J. and B. Hayes (2011) 'Post-conflict societies and the social sciences: a review', *Contemporary Social Science*, 6: 5–18.
Brewer, J., G. Higgins and F. Teeney (2011) *Religion, Civil Society and Peace in Northern Ireland*, Oxford: Oxford University Press.
Brown Childs, J. (2003) 'Places of sense/senses of place: gang violence, positive cultures leadership and peacemaking', in T. Bamat and M. Cejka (eds), *Artisans of Peace*, Maryknoll: Orbis Books, pp. 226–55.
Butalia, U. (2000) *The Other Side of Silence*, London: Hurst.

Collier, P. (2008) 'Postconflict economic policy', in C. Call (ed.) *Building States to Build Peace*, London: Lynne Reinner, pp. 103–18.

Elster, J. (2004) *Closing the Books*, Cambridge: Cambridge University Press.

Galtung, J. (1996) 'Violence, peace and peace research', *Journal of Peace Research*, 6: 167–96.

Galtung, J. (2008) *50 years: 25 Intellectual Landscapes Explored*, Bergen: Transcend University Press.

Herbert, D. (2003) *Religion and Civil Society*, Aldershot: Ashgate.

Kaldor, M. (1999) *New and Old Wars*, Cambridge: Polity Press.

Keen, D. (1998) *The Economic Functions of Violence in Civil Wars*, Oxford: Oxford University Press.

Knox, C. and P. Quirk (2000) *Peace Building in Northern Ireland, Israel and South Africa*, Basingstoke: Macmillan.

Lederach, J.P. (1997) *Building Peace*, Washington: United States Institute of Peace Press.

Lederach, J.P. (2005) *The Moral Imagination*, Oxford: Oxford University Press.

Lentin, R. (1997) (ed.), *Gender and Catastrophe*, London: Zed Books.

Lentin, R. (1999) 'The rape of the nation', *Sociological Research Online*, 4, accessed online www. socresonline.org.uk/socresonline/4/2/lentin.html (20 October 2011). Webpage no longer operational.

Leonard, M. (2004) 'Bonding and bridging social capital: the view from Belfast', *Sociology* 38: 927–44.

Lundy, P. (2011) 'Paradoxes and challenges of transitional justice at the "local" level', *Contemporary Social Science* 6: 89–106.

Malešević, S. (2010) *The Sociology of War and Violence*, Cambridge: Cambridge University Press.

Margalit, A. (2010) *On Compromise and Rotten Compromises*. Princeton: Princeton University Press.

Mills, C.W. (1959) *The Sociological Imagination*, Oxford: Oxford University Press.

Misztal, B. (2010) *The Challenges of Vulnerability*, Basingstoke, Palgrave.

Misztal, B. (2011) 'Forgiveness and the construction of new conditions for a common life', *Contemporary Social Science*, 6: 39–54.

Oberschall, A. (2007) *Conflict and Peace Building in Divided Societies*, London: Routledge.

Paris, R. (2004) *At War's End*, Cambridge: Cambridge University Press.

Philpott, D. (2007) 'What religion brings to the politics of transitional justice', *Journal of International Affairs* 61: 93–110.

Scheff, T. (1994) *Bloody Revenge*, Boulder: Westview.

Shriver, D. (1995) *An Ethic for Enemies*, Oxford: Oxford University Press.

Smithey, L. (2011) *Unionists, Loyalists and Conflict Transformation in Northern Ireland*, Oxford: Oxford University Press.

Torrance, A. (2006) *The Theological Grounds for Advocating Forgiveness in the Sociopolitical Realm*, Belfast: Institute of Contemporary Christianity.

Wallace, C., C. Haerpfer and P. Abbott (2009) 'Women in Rwandan politics and society', *International Journal of Sociology*, 38: 111–25.

13

HISTORY AND PEACEBUILDING

Anthony Oberschall

Introduction

When violent conflicts end – whether it be war between states or internal war – institutions and routines for cooperation among the adversaries are necessary for building lasting peace: shared governance; economic reconstruction; justice for victims and perpetrators of crimes; settlement for refugees and forcefully displaced persons; law, order and security issues such as integration of combatants into civilian life and curbing criminal gangs.

Historical memory, truth, justice and reconciliation for peacebuilding are intertwined in a complex fashion, sometimes advancing in lockstep but sometimes clashing. When amnesty is a condition for peace making, it blocks some victims' quest for justice and truth. Truth commissions and war crimes trials uncover historical truths which offend and threaten some. They deny the truths, claim justice is partisan, and rally behind the accused who are celebrated saviors and heroes. In the short term, some demand justice and historical truth for reconciliation; for others it deepens divisions and derails peacebuilding. In the longer term, collective narratives about conflict and adversaries are embedded in family and community memories, popular culture (movies, murals, graffiti, songs, videos, public celebrations), history and social studies instruction in schools, and collective myths endorsed by political and religious leaders and parties.

In the large topic of peacebuilding and history, I examine five limited propositions:

1 Conflict amplifies hostility, negative stereotypes, threat perception, historical falsehoods and incompatible collective myths.
2 Professional historians possess a method for non-partisan historical inquiry that converges on truth and challenges exaggerations, falsehood, and collective myths.
3 History instruction in schools is controlled by governments and community groups more interested in promoting patriotism and other causes than historical truth about group relations. In some instances, during reconciliation, political leaders sponsor non-partisan and non-confrontational history writing and instruction for schools.

4 The impact of school history instruction on students' attitudes and behaviors in inter-group reconciliation has been little studied, and probably is positive but limited.

5 Historical information and knowledge disseminated via the world wide web is double-edged, with lots of opinion, falsehood and misinformation available side by side with primary sources and sophisticated analyses. The popular open source encyclopedia Wikipedia is based on good-faith collaboration and rules promoting cooperation, and can produce non-partisan narratives for contentious history topics.

The use of history by conflict actors

Violent conflicts leave deep psychological and emotional scars that impede cooperation among adversaries. Prior to violent conflict in divided societies, most people have live-and-let-live ethnic interactions. Animosity and distrust between ethnic groups do exist, even outright hostility in some circles. These attitudes and beliefs mirror experiences of discrimination and domination, rivalry, oppression and historical wrongs, and they and their memories persist in folk narratives, family histories, artistic and intellectual works, school and religious instruction, and other manifestations of ethno-national culture. But in peace times, people are busy getting on with their lives, and memories and animosities do not preoccupy them. In a national sample of over 4,000 Yugoslavs before the break-up in the mid-1990s, two-thirds reported good and satisfactory ethno-national relations in their neighborhoods and workplaces, and less than 10 percent chose 'bad' and 'very bad' (Yugoslav Survey 1990: 25); only 7 percent believed the country would break up and six out of ten asserted that the 'Yugoslav' affiliation was important for them.

During conflict, politicians, media personalities and intellectuals mobilize their supporters with massive nationalist hate propaganda which demonize opponents, spread fear of attack, and justify aggression against other ethnics in the name of legitimate self-defense. In Yugoslavia, in the first post-communist democratic elections in 1990 before the break-up, in the media as well as election rallies, speakers gave vent to exaggerated nationalist rhetoric and hostile attacks on other nationalities (Woodward 1995: 124). A content analysis of a random sample of political and mass media communications made by Vojislav Seselj, a prominent Serb nationalist leader, on Serb–Croat, Serb–Muslim and Serb–Albanian relations during the Serb–Croatian war in 1991–94 indicates that close to a half advocated aggression against other nationalities and rejection of compromise and conflict management, about 40 percent of messages featured one or more 'threats against Serbs', and about 20 percent the victimization of Serbs by other peoples, nations, international organizations and foreign states. In these claims, references to history were commonplace (Oberschall 2012: 176–9). History was invoked also to press territorial and statehood claims. On behalf of a Greater Serbia as the principal successor state to Yugoslavia, Seselj claimed that the Kosovars should go back to Albania because almost all of them, or their parents, migrated to Kosovo during the Italian occupation in World War II. Bosniaks do not deserve a separate state because the Muslim majority there are not a distinct nation; they are Serbs who converted to Islam under the Turks. The highly inflated and disputed figures on ethnic killings in World War II were used by all national activists to prove historical victimhood and to justify pre-emptive attacks. Nationalist xenophobic propaganda was effective in the Yugoslav break-up. The political scientist Bogdan Denitch (1996: 81) recalled that 'Everyone was traumatized by all the talk of World War Two atrocities…even those who seemed immune to nationalism.'

Although such propaganda is not a total fabrication of history, it is full of historical falsehoods and exaggerations which magnify threat, fear and distrust, and resonate with folk stereotypes and animosities in ethno-national relations. The Serb nationalist mobilization orchestrated by Milosevic in the media and in huge nationalist and religious rallies and pageants, featured prominently the medieval Kosovo battle centered on the Serb martyrdom that saved Christianity from the Turks. For Serb nationalists, the historic battle legitimized the reassertion of Serb hegemony in Kosovo. The manipulation of history for justifying ethnic aggression and political power is not limited to speech, print and media. History is objectified in physical artifacts, like religious buildings, places of pilgrimage, battlefields, cemeteries, monuments, museums, street and place names, dress, music, parades, festivals, celebrations and the like. To change history, or rather opportunistically reinvent history and eradicate historical memory, artifacts are destroyed and new ones created.

The dismemberment of Yugoslavia shows that history is manipulated, and in some cases totally invented, for the delegitimation and destruction of institutions and group relations and for building new nation-states and institutions. During conflict, shared culture and history get discredited and separate, divisive and hostile cultural and historical narratives become entrenched. After years of ethnic violence and xenophobic propaganda, the restoration of live-and-let-live cooperation is problematic. Mistrust, animosity, avoidance and ethnic separation become the dominant folk beliefs and sentiments, and behaviors in ethnic relations. The experience of displaced persons who returned home after the fighting in Bosnia and Croatia is that pre-war friendships and neighborly relations were not resumed, and recrimination and interpersonal conflict over betrayal and in-group solidarity were avoided by keeping apart (Stover and Weinstein 2004). All national groups felt victimized by the war and considered their group to be the greatest victim. Denial of war crimes and other criminal behaviors by their nationality and preserving a positive national image was achieved with collective self-deception: biased memories, embellishment of particular events, omission or downplaying crimes by own nationality, rationalizations (the others started it, everybody did it, it was self-defense). The researchers called the process of collective denial 'a fertile ground for collective myth making' (Stover and Weinstein 2004: 149). In Vukovar, Serbs and Croats had created an opposed narrative and interpretation of the same events: the onset of causes of war; what happened during the war; the end of the war, and the aftermath of war (Stover and Weinstein 2004: 146, 239). There was no possibility of conducting a reasoned discourse about the war, history, guilt and responsibility, and nationality relations.

Similar behaviors occur in other divided societies. In their tortured negotiations, in their media, as reflected in public opinion studies and the pronouncements of political leaders, the Israelis and the Palestinians do not share the same vocabulary about their tragic, disputed history. Are suicide bombers martyrs or terrorists? Are the occupied territories the historic land of Israel, Judea and Samaria? Is the West Bank an 'occupied' or a 'liberated' territory? Do the state of Israel and cities like Tel Aviv actually exist, which the Palestinian maps do not show? Did the Palestinians flee their homes during the 1948 war or were they driven out by force and prevented from returning after the fighting stopped? Is unregistered Arab land held under customary right 'absentee, abandoned property' that the Israelis can seize? And what is Jerusalem? For the Palestinians, Jerusalem is the old city; they regard only about 10 percent of the surrounding area claimed by Israel as Jerusalem. Many Palestinians deny that there ever was a Jewish temple (Solomon's Temple) at the Temple Mount, which they call the Haram al Sharif (Noble Sanctuary). Most Israelis believe that the Palestinian claim to East Jerusalem as their capital is unjustified. Many Israelis believe that when Jews started to immigrate to Palestine there were hardly any Arabs living there, and that Jewish settlers returning to the homeland after centuries created an egalitarian society in the wilderness, in empty land (Oberschall 2007: chapter 5). According to Meron Benvenisti (1995: 200), a long-time vice mayor of Jerusalem, the Israelis and Palestinians have created self-serving collective myths that block understanding and conflict management: 'Myths are the building blocks from which a society constructs its collective self-image…to rouse people to action, to live dreams, to blur ugly lies, to cope with unpleasant reality, to find consolation and to channel hatred…myths are not illusions; they are a jumble of real and legendary events … the minute they are absorbed, they become truer than reality itself. Many aspire to shatter myths, to force people to confront objective truth…the attempt to rip away the façade cannot succeed because it amounts to an attack on the collective self-identity. It will therefore be met with anger.'

A positive role for professional historians

In Sarajevo, Belfast, Jerusalem, Mostar, Nicosia and other divided cities, in public spaces, schools and places of worship, on facades, separation walls, with graffiti, murals, posters, parades, flags, marches, celebrations, songs and chants, in the media and in public speeches, ethno-national and religious myths that divide are displayed and re-enacted. The question for peacebuilders is: Can a truthful, balanced and non-partisan history weaken self-serving partisan myths and contribute to peaceful ethno-national relations? Is an objective, non-partisan history at all possible? Has non-partisan history been written by adversaries in deeply divided societies? Has it had an impact beyond narrow professional and educated circles? Has it changed history instruction in schools, media discourse, popular culture and folk beliefs about the past?

Two methods of inquiry for knowledge and truth have proven to be sound: scientific inquiry and the adversarial method in justice for determining guilt and innocence. In the scientific method, every step is public, transparent, documented, verified, and subject to replication. Recognition and fame, financial interest, national prestige, rivalry and other reasons may motivate scientists, as they do others, but such interested, biasing and arbitrary factors are controlled. It is peer review, i.e. evaluation and replication by other scientists, that forms the collective judgment and verdict of what is accepted as knowledge in the science community. The core of the method is to probe and test nature with hypotheses, both those the scientist believes to be true and those he believes are mistaken, and to examine all evidence in an unbiased manner, whether or not it favors or contradicts a particular hypothesis. The scientific method has been spectacularly successful.

The adversarial method in the criminal justice system rests on the conviction that for getting at truth in human affairs the strongest case for both sides should be made by advocates, and that a third, non-interested party (judges or jury) decides truth beyond reasonable doubt. Innocence is presumed until guilt is proven. Both sides have access to the same and to all pertinent facts, are bound by the same rules on evidence and trial procedure enforced by an impartial judge. Truth emerges by vigorous probing and cross-examination of the material facts and human testimony, with false, unreliable, contradictory and ambiguous evidence discarded, and conjectures based on faulty evidence made implausible. Trial errors are appealed to a higher court. Like all institutions, justice is vulnerable to human error, yet the adversarial method has been widely accepted as the unbiased path to truth in human affairs.

Starting with Leopold Ranke in the nineteenth century, academic historians applied a mixture of the scientific and the adversarial method to historical scholarship using rigorous investigation of primary sources, unbiased weighing of evidence, probing the authenticity of eyewitnesses and plausibility of hearsay accounts, testing evidence for forgery and fabrication, questioning the validity of cause–effect claims, minimizing confirmation bias by pursuing a number of hypotheses and explanations, and making their work and conclusions completely transparent with citations and bibliographies enabling independent peer review, as in natural science (Evans 1999: chapter 1). The historian's craft was in time augmented by specialized sciences, e.g., carbon dating, and new disciplines such as forensic anthropology. As in justice and science, there remain differences in interpretation which are debated in professional circles. New evidence does get discovered and can lead to new ideas and hypotheses, and thus rethinking and rewriting of history. But ad hominem attacks and allegations of bias based only on rejection of conclusions, typical in politics, are unacceptable in the professional community for settling questions of historical knowledge and truth.

In the 1970s and later, the humanities and some social sciences came under the influence of post-modernism which claimed that those who have power control the writing of history and determine what historical truth is. Post-modernists deny the possibility of objective, non-partisan knowledge and truth in human affairs. Women, Afro-Americans, gays and lesbians, scholars from the Third World, and other groups claiming oppression charged that the biased narratives of the dominant majority had excluded their contributions, hopes and aspirations, leaders and heroes, and that only members of an oppressed group are capable of writing an unbiased account of their history. The argument that knowledge itself is ethnocentric and gender specific makes all history contested and arbitrary. There can be no reconciliation through shared, non-partisan history, written jointly by adversaries.

Arthur Schlesinger Jr. (1992: 72) critiqued the cult of ethnicity in recent American history writing in textbooks and in advocacy history and concluded that 'history as a weapon is an abuse of history.' He exposed the claim that Western civilization courses were instances of cultural capitalism. He disputed the idea that history is not an intellectual discipline but social psychological therapy to raise self-esteem, race and ethnic consciousness, and group pride. Richard Evans (1999: 191–2) wrote that 'While historians are certainly swayed…by present moral or political purposes in carrying out their work, it is not the validity or desirability of these, but the extent to which their historical arguments conform to the rules of evidence and the facts on which they rest, by which they must stand or fall in the end.' He showed that post-modernism's hyper-relativist principles resulted in shoddy and false history.

Evans himself participated in a dramatic demonstration that historical truth and falsehood could be determined 'beyond reasonable doubt.' In the famous holocaust denial trial Irving versus Lipstadt (www.holocaustdenial.net/trial/judgement), the trial turned on how historians use historical evidence. Irving, the holocaust denier and plaintiff, argued in post-modernist fashion that facts in any complex human enterprise contain inconsistencies, gaps and uncertainties and that different interpretations of the same events are normal and legitimate. The defense hired Evans, the well-known historian of modern Germany, who with the help of many graduate students checked hundreds of quotes and citations Irving had made. They established that Irving had practiced deliberate manipulation of data and deception, such as omission of contrary evidence, fabricating and altering quotes, and doctoring the historical record. These were not random errors and sloppy scholarship but consistently stacked the evidence in favor of holocaust denial. Irving vigorously cross-examined Evans and other researchers for his defense, and tried to cast doubts on their methods and findings, without success. British judge Charles Gray on April 11, 2000, concluded that the defense proved beyond reasonable doubt that Irving had created a body of data that was not truthful, and proved it in seventeen instances that were at the core of contention about the holocaust. Gray also concluded that the fabrication and intentional omission of evidence, bias and advocacy, claiming to be scholarship, can be distinguished from sound scholarship and rational argument, using the same methods of proof as in a criminal trial for determining the guilt or non-guilt of the defendant.

The most telling proof that non-partisan history about contentious events and interpretations could be written by members of adversary nationalities and ethnic groups jointly is from the former Yugoslavia. An international group of historians (Ingrao and Emmert 2009), calling itself the Scholars' Initiative, organized a dozen research teams, from all the successor states of Yugoslavia, Europe and the United States. They challenged the competing nationalist narratives and memory about the break-up of Yugoslavia, divisive myths, falsehoods and omissions, rationalizations (e.g., all sides sinned equally, we were the only/the main victims, they massacred their own to draw international attention), and post-war politicians' manipulation of public memory and denial of responsibility. The Scholars chose twelve major topics at the core of the Yugoslav break-up and wars, e.g., the dissolution of Yugoslavia, the fate of minorities, ethnic cleansing and war crimes, Kosovo under Milosevic, the war in Kosovo. The teams composed of Croats, Serbs, Bosniaks, Kosovars, Slovenes and outsiders, after much research and debate, wrote cohesive and non-partisan histories of each. Unlike other attempts at contentious history, these were unified essays, not parallel accounts from the perspective of this and that adversary.

To be sure, because state archives and many documents were yet inaccessible, the histories had limitations that future research would correct, but that is true of all history writing and all knowledge. The historians had available to them the voluminous records of the International Criminal Tribunal for the former Yugoslavia (ICTY). Politicians, nationalists and the public have charged the ICTY for being biased, but that accusation refers to indictments – some alleged war criminals from a nationality have been indicted and tried, whereas others alleged to have committed similar crimes have not – not to the actual conduct of the trials themselves. The ICTY trials are thorough. The trial of Milomir Stakic (icty.org: IT-97-24), physician and director of the Prijedor community health center, member of the Crisis Committee that orchestrated the ethnic cleansing, killings and the detention camps for non-Serbs, lasted one year, February 2002 to May 2003. The prosecution presented 37 witnesses, and 19 witness statements in 80 sitting days, and the defense countered with 38 witnesses and 7 witness statements in 67 sitting days. In total, 1,448 exhibits were admitted in evidence. Stakic was charged with specific counts of crimes against humanity, murder, extermination, deportation, inhumane acts, persecutions, and two counts of genocide. His defense claimed that the camps were only transit centers for the protection and assistance of families who wanted to leave Prijedor. Attempts to intimidate prosecution witnesses were numerous. Thirty-four witnesses were granted protective measures, e.g. facial and voice distortion, testifying in closed session, pseudonyms, and redaction of testimony. All witnesses and experts were vigorously cross-examined by skilled lawyers, much more vigorously than is the case at scholarly conferences, and that record surely benefits the writing of non-partisan, truthful history.

Stakic was sentenced to 20 years to life.

History instruction in schools

In a chapter titled 'Living together and hating each other' (Ingrao and Emmert, 2009: chapter 11) the authors reflected on rewriting history for reconciliation. History and memory sustain national and ethnic identity. The shared past gives meaning to 'who we are' and 'why we belong together'. History texts and artifacts objectify group identity and legitimize the political regime. Powerful political and psychological forces perpetuate the status quo of partisan history. The team notes examples of group resistance to the break-up and to war, and of cross-national assistance, that have been omitted from the regime-sponsored histories of the conflicts. Rewriting history brings truth into the open; unfortunately truth is troubling and is denied by some. A non-partisan narrative can promote healing and reconciliation if it supersedes victimization narratives and collective myths. This has not happened yet in the Yugoslav successor states. Despite many initiatives and funding by international bodies (the European Association of History Educators, Organization for Security and Cooperation in Europe, institutes and foundations) education reform in history and geography has received scant support from ministries, the public, teachers and politicians. In Bosnia, all three nationalities display a 'shameful and consistent attempt to justify present divisions by tracing them back thorough history' (Ingrao and Emmert 2009: 410).

Non-partisan history writing and instruction in schools is highly problematic everywhere. Frances Fitzgerald (1980: 47) studied US history school-texts of the 1950s through the 1970s and concluded that 'history textbooks for elementary and secondary schools are not like other kinds of histories…they are essentially nationalistic histories… they are written not to explore but to instruct – to tell children what their elders want them to know about their country. This information is not necessarily what anyone considers the truth of things.'

Fifteen years after Fitzgerald, James Loewen (1996) revisited American history school-texts, which continued to perpetuate national myths and were crammed with facts. The message to students was that history is a long sequence of facts to be memorized, not an inquiry and disciplined reflection about the past. Loewen focused on ten collective myths, like the 'Gone with the Wind' inspired history of Reconstruction in the South after the Civil War, and confronted them with what the best historical scholarship offered. Though his and Frances Fitzgerald's books were bestsellers, their combined impact on school text-book history has been minimal.

The deepest political and cultural wounds in US political discourse have arisen from the Vietnam War. A mass of information is available about the war, from news reporting, the *Pentagon Papers*, Congressional hearings, archives, documents released under the Freedom of Information Act, writings by soldiers, and the like, and highly regarded professional histories have been written about it. These sources and writings have not trickled down to public schools. Frances Fitzgerald found that school history-text coverage was inaccurate and misleading. James Loewen was astonished by the degree of avoidance of the war in school texts, which he discussed in a chapter titled 'Choosing not to look at the war in Vietnam'. David Hunt (1996) studied eleven school-texts about the war and found them limited and confusing. These school narratives coexist with folk views of the war based on Hollywood films like 'Rambo' and 'Apocalypse Now'. Looking at folk beliefs and media, Joseph Cox (1996) finds that the Vietnam War narratives are by and large a celebration of heroic idealism that taps into the myth of American exceptionalism and divinely justified national purpose. Such narratives matter for US foreign policy. The pollster Daniel Yankelovich (2005) found that President Bush's framing of the Afghanistan and Iraqi wars as a moral crusade against evil, which was blessed by God, resonated favorably with the public.

History teaching in the US about the Vietnam War has not made for the healing of wounds and reconciliation. Conservative patriots claim the war was won on the ground by the military and that the working class youth who served honorably were betrayed at the home-front by anti-Vietnam war hippies, leftists, elitist media, and college educated draft dodgers. Anti-war liberals believe the war was Cold War ideology driven, unnecessarily brutal and destructive of American and Vietnamese lives, promoted by deception and lies, and prolonged to save the reputations of political leaders, national security intellectuals and military brass. Half a century ago, the historian Henry Steel Commager concluded that 'There is no reason to suppose that the compulsory study of American history … makes good citizens' (quoted in Fitzgerald 1980: 178). That is still the case, and one might add, there is no reason to suppose that history in public schools makes 'informed citizens about their history and government' and 'open minded citizens'.

The impact of school history instruction on student behavior

Most countries have a more centralized education system than the US, which enables governments and professional associations to control and influence school curricula, including enlisting history writing and instruction for peacebuilding. After the punitive and humiliating Versailles Treaty following World War I which fueled nationalist revenge in Germany, starting with De Gaulle and Adenauer, the leaders of Germany and France after World War II instituted policies of reconciliation through their governments, professional associations and civic bodies for changing their historical adversarial relationship to cooperation. At the core of reconciliation were economic, political and security interests like the Steel and Coal community and military alliance against the Soviet threat. On the cultural front, to alter negative stereotypes, hostility and threat perception, universities established relations under a conference of rectors; twin-city partnerships were formed; a Franco-German commission of secondary school teachers instituted changes in the history and geography curricula; pupil exchange partnerships were started; Franco-German intellectual associations were formed under the leadership of public intellectuals like Alfred Grosser and Theodore Heuss. Symbolic acts of reconciliation such as De Gaulle's state visit to West Germany in 1962 and the Franco-German friendship treaty of 1963 advanced the transition from enmity to amity. Successful Franco-German reconciliation became the dynamic for the larger European Community and the European Union (Dicht, 1984). Building a shared culture and history was continued when President Mitterrand and Chancellor Kohl joined hands at the Verdun military cemetery on September 22, 1984. Five French and five German historians were commissioned in the Elysee Treaty of 2003 to write a text on contemporary history (since 1945) for secondary schools in both countries.

Reconciliation was also at the center of German foreign policy with Israel and European states like Poland and the Czech Republic. It necessitated accepting responsibility for injurious and destructive actions and commitment to historic truth by all sides. It was only partly accomplished with the Czechs because vocal Sudeten Germans expelled in 1945 insist on compensation and right of return. In the 1970s, East–West détente made it possible for Germany and Poland to settle disputed borders and the status of the Germans expelled after the war. German acceptance of responsibility under the Social Democrats was symbolized by Chancellor Willy Brandt's silent kneeling at the Warsaw uprising memorial in 1970 (Long and Brecke 2003: 21). Starting in 1972, a German Polish Textbook Commission made up of professional historians met twice a year and examined 26 topics for study, rewriting and inclusion in school texts. Though initially opposed by the Christian Democrats (CDU), textbook cooperation continued after the CDU came to power in 1982, and reconciliation and cooperation for a mutually acceptable history curriculum became the lasting policy of both countries (He 2009: 79–92).

In recent decades academic historians and school history teachers have forged Europe-wide bonds about history writing and teaching, in organizations like the European Association of History Educators (euroclio.com) and publications like the *International Journal of Historical Teaching and Research,* which safeguard scholars' autonomy and promote non-partisan methodology, dialogue and collaboration among historians from former adversaries as a tool of reconciliation (Barkan 2009). There is little research about what the impact of non-partisan, more truthful teaching of history is for changing negative stereotypes, hostile community narratives and other cultural obstacles to reconciliation. In Northern Ireland, since 1990, an addition to partisan and sectarian history in schools has been exposing each side to how the other side frames and understands the same historic events, and there have been initiatives for more shared curriculum changes by the UNESCO Center at the University of Ulster (www.ulster.ac.uk/unesco). In one study, 253 secondary school students were probed in depth on what sense they made of such parallel presentation. The students understood the other side better and believed such instruction reduced prejudices and stereotypes; nevertheless they clung to their respective community narratives and fitted new facts learned into those narratives (Barton and McCully 2009).

Looking over peacebuilding efforts through non-partisan history, history texts and instruction in several countries, it appears that reconciliation starts when political elites pursue shared material, political and security interests with adversaries after violent conflicts. Changing the culture of enmity and teaching non-partisan histories to school children become part of the broader process of conciliation and cooperation, but do not drive it. When political elites do not reconcile, as in Bosnia, cultural reconciliation also fails, stereotypes, animosity and strained inter-ethnic personal relations persist. When the peace making keeps failing, as between Israelis and Palestinians, even modest initiatives by citizens for an understanding of each other's historical narratives remain limited and vulnerable. Research on textbooks shows that they reflect a culture of enmity and opposites, for example, Jewish immigrants to Palestine are 'pioneers' for the Israelis and 'gangs' and 'terrorists' for the Palestinians; heroes of one side are monsters of the other; maps eliminate the cities and towns of the other; the texts delegitimize each other's rights, history and culture (Bar-On and Adwan 2006: 311–12). School-texts are just the tip of a cultural iceberg of hate and vilification. According to Palestinian Media Watch, which monitors Palestinian Arabic media and schoolbooks, in a Hamas children's TV program, a Mickey Mouse-like character urges Palestinian children to murder Jews (www.palwatch.org). In opposition to such hostility and partisanship, with the help of international sponsors, some Israeli and Palestinian teachers and historians affiliated with the Peace Research Institute in the Middle East created parallel historical narratives, in Arabic and Hebrew, of several contentious historic events such as Jewish immigration into Palestine and the 1948, 1967 and 1973 wars, tested their use and taught them to their 15–16-year-old students (vispo.com/PRIME/learningeachothershistoricalnarratives). Although the Israeli Ministry of Education and the Palestine Authority at first supported this Israeli–Palestine textbook project, this modest initiative was banned by both in 2010. The two leaders knew that 'the disarmament of history can happen only after the disarmament of weapons, but one can prepare for it'. There was no disarmament of weapons, and the disarmament of history was torpedoed.

History and the web

The internet is replacing print as a source of information, for history and other subject matter, and that is happening especially for students at all ages. The internet has made available archives, documents and other historical raw data as well as professional publications, which has been of great help to professionals and amateur historians, students writing papers and history buffs. At the same time, the world wide web is filled with advocacy, falsehood, fabrication, opinion and pseudo-scholarship that presents itself as objective fact and analysis. There are no gatekeepers or peer reviewers to separate junk from knowledge. Because search engines maximize advertising and profits, not sound knowledge, unsophisticated users have to sort out sound sources from a multitude of junk, a task that they may not know how to do.

Many turn to Wikipedia, a web-based free encyclopedia written collaboratively by a large number of anonymous volunteer contributors under the supervision of Wiki management (Reagle 2010). Wiki is based on the principle of an open source system, or crowd sourcing. Its rules evolved from original anarchy which proved vulnerable to vandals who secretly alter, delete and manipulate text. Wiki's culture of good faith collaboration is based on a neutral, non-partisan point of view; avoids personal attack; uses verifiable, published, reliable sources; rules out original research; and forbids nullifying the editing of others without prior discussion. Many elect to contribute on a particular topic, but the final text is based on discussion and agreement of all the collaborators. Postings are anonymous and no one gets credit. Without agreement, nothing gets posted. When they cannot agree and compromise, a Wiki management committee mediates between the adversaries, and when that fails, an Arbitration Committee acts like a quasi-court and decides what gets posted. These experienced editors supervise the process and ensure that edits cumulate into improvements on the topic. The rules constrain collaborators to conform to elements of the scientific inquiry and of adversarial method – on neutrality (eliminates confirmation bias), on verifiable, published sources (rules of evidence), on Socratic debate and consensus among the contributors (akin to peer review). Because Wiki requires consensus, on contentious historical topics in divided societies it fits a peacebuilding frame more than much school-text writing does, and it is inimical to partisan, advocacy history.

There are hundreds if not thousands of contentious historical topics in Wikipedia. To get a sense for how Wiki matches up with conventional sources, like school texts, I checked the entry for the 'Gaza War' in October 2009, a topic that I had recently researched for a scholarly publication. It was a long text of many pages with over a hundred citations, and the editors cautioned that 'the neutrality of this article is disputed'. Many teams of collaborators had contributed to the article; there were about 60 contested items, and a log of lengthy debates was made public in numbered archives. For instance archive 35 had debates on the inclusion of the photo of an infant victim of uncertain identity without a named source, and archive 66 recorded a debate about calling the 'war' a 'massacre'. Archive 50 debated whether there was evidence that Hamas had used ambulances and hospitals as a shield for fighters – a violation of the Geneva Convention. Another team discussed how to present the discrepant casualty numbers and classification of deaths from the fighting, and decided to publish the Israeli and the Palestinian figures side by side, without a verdict on which was more truthful. In these disputes, some took the Palestinian position, and others the Israeli position. By and large, with the help of Wiki supervisors, these disputes were resolved. Because of the rule about the use of verifiable, published, and respected sources, the bulk of the text mirrored the news reporting of the prestigious international news media: the BBC, the *Guardian*, the *New York Times, Jerusalem Post*, al-Jezeera, international NGOs, and not extremist, partisan and biased sources. My conclusion is that Wikipedia produced an account of the Gaza War that an attentive reader and viewer of the international media got during the war and the immediate period preceding and following it. It is a non-partisan account that raises questions of violations of the Geneva Conventions and crimes against humanity by both adversaries, and the lack of wisdom of their leaders. If the Wiki record on other controversial history topics is similar, then the on-line encyclopedia is a good place to get basic, non-partisan information and sources and for starting a deeper, more academic history. Though cumbersome and slow, Wiki supervised crowd sourcing avoids the anarchy and unreliability of the world wide web.

References

Bar-On, D. and Adwan, S. (2006) 'The Prime Shared History Project', in *Educating Toward a Culture of Peace*, Charlotte, NC: Information Age Publishing, pp. 311–312.

Barkan, B. (2009) 'Historians and Historical Reconciliation', *American Historical Review*, 114(4): 889–913.

Barton, K. and McCully, A. (2009) 'When history teaching really matters: Understanding the impact of school intervention in students' neighborhood learning in Northern Ireland', *International Journal of Historical Teaching and Research*, 8(1): 28–46.

Benvenisti, M. (1995) *Intimate Enemies*, Berkeley: University of California Press.

Cox, J. (1996) 'American War Myths' in Slabey, R. (ed.) *The United States and Vietnam: From War to Peace*, Jefferson CO: McFarland, pp. 177–89.

Denitch, B. (1996) *Ethnic Nationalism*, Minneapolis: University of Minnesota Press.

Dicht, R. (1984) 'Die Versoehnung ist kein Grund zur Selbstzufriedenheit' in Manfrass, K. (ed.) Paris-Bonn: Eine dauerhafte Bindung schwieriger Partner/Sigmaringen, Jan Thorbecke Verlag.

Evans, R. (1999) *In Defense of History*, New York: Norton.

Fitzgerald, F. (1980) *America Revised*, New York: Vintage.

He, Y. (2009) *The Search for Reconciliation*, Cambridge: Cambridge University Press.

Hunt, D. (1996) 'Images of the Viet Cong' in Slabey, R. (ed.) *The United States and Vietnam: From War to Peace*, Jefferson CO: McFarland, pp. 51–68.

Ingrao, C. and Emmert, T. (eds) (2009) *Confronting the Yugoslav Controversies*, Washington DC: United States Institute of Peace.

Loewen, J. (1996) *Lies My Teachers Told Me: Everything Your American History Teacher Got Wrong*, New York: Touchstone Books.

Long, W. and Brecke, P. (2003) *War and Reconciliation*, Massachusetts: MIT Press.

Oberschall, A. (2007) *Conflict and Peace in Divided Societies*, London: Routledge.

Oberschall, A. (2012) 'Propaganda, hate speech and mass killings' in Dojcinovic, P. (ed.) *Propaganda, War Crimes Trials and International Law*, London: Routledge, pp. 176–9.

Reagle Jr., J. (2010) *Good Faith Collaboration: The Culture of Wikipedia*, Massachusetts: MIT Press.

Schlesinger Jr., A. (1992) *The Disuniting of America*, New York: Norton.

Stover, E. and Weinstein, H. (2004) (eds) *My Neighbor, My Enemy: Justice and Community in the Aftermath of Mass Atrocity*, Cambridge: Cambridge University Press.

Woodward, S. (1995) *Balkan Tragedy*, Washington DC: Brookings Institution.

Yankelovich D. (2005) 'Poll Positions', *Foreign Affairs*, 84 (5): 2–16.

Yugoslav Survey (1990) 'Public opinion survey on the Federal Executive Council's social and economic reform', *Yugoslav Survey* (Belgrade), March 31, pp. 3–26.

14

QUANTITATIVE APPROACHES

Patrick M. Regan

The study of conflict management and peace has a long tradition in the social sciences, much of it driven by definitional debates about what peace means or the analysis of specific cases where efforts to achieve a peaceful resolution of a conflict have been successful (e.g., Wallensteen 2009; Fortna 2008; Hartzell and Hoddie 2007). We know enough about the processes of trying to generate peaceful outcomes to actually engage in the debates and discussions taking place in this volume. My contribution is to try to advance the study of peace, peacebuilding, peacekeeping, and other forms of control over the tendency toward armed conflict by pushing the way we study peace in a different direction. I think we are best served by looking for general patterns in the data across a large sample of cross-national or cross-cultural environments, and to use those observed patterns to draw inference about what works, under what types of conditions, and in what time frames. Put differently, I'm going to make the case for the quantitative study of peacemaking that relies on data that is systematic, replicable, and broadly generalizable.

In this volume you will undoubtedly get a sufficient description of the more traditional view of how to study peace processes, so I will not try to recreate those arguments in a form of point–counterpoint, but rather take on the role of advocacy for a method. My argument will be rooted in a simple assumption that the similarities among different cases of conflict and conflict management are at least as revealing to us as are the differences. The approach that I will advocate also relies on our understanding of typical cases, or what you might think of as the 'on average' principle. I accept that there might not even be an average case out there, so the prescriptions for policy will of necessity have to deviate from this estimated average. But while there might not be a case that falls precisely on the 'average' line, the whole idea of an average operates from the premise that each randomly picked conflict – or peacebuilding effort – is very much like others that we observe. Indeed this is often an unspoken assumption of a traditional analysis of peacebuilding or any other political outcome. It is important, I believe, to at least consider ex ante that any individual case is average. Alternatively it might take a bit of hubris to think that any one case that any one scholar is analyzing is sufficiently different from the average case that it demands their devoted attention. If we accept that on average each individual case is, well, about average on any number of dimensions, then we are better off understanding the conditions for building peace in the average case and looking for the idiosyncratic only after understanding what typically happens. The case study approach is less able to identify the typical.

Having spelled out my basic assumption that is at the foundation for studying the peacebuilding process from a quantitative perspective, let me put my argument into context. Generating or sustaining peace is a complex process that takes considerable acumen on the part of those negotiating or implementing an agreement, as well as the combatants who have to commit to the solution. Since the end of World War II, there have been upwards of 200 civil wars and some quite serious interstate wars that required the efforts of the world community and its institutions to secure and maintain peace (Themner and Wallensteen 2011; Wayman and Sarkees 2010). These conflicts range from the wars in Korea, Vietnam and Afghanistan to the genocides in Rwanda, Darfur and Sudan. The Congo, Somalia, the Philippines, Sri Lanka and the civil wars in Central America add to the range of brutal wars for which making peace was critical. Smaller wars also dot the landscape of armed conflicts in the past 60 years, such as wars in Burma or India. Some have ended with victory by one side or the other, some through negotiated settlements that required the implementation of complex state-building agreements, and some seem to either grind on for decades or peter out of their own accord. The increasingly common outcome is a negotiated resolution.

One of the problems of generating the knowledge from which we can draw inference about what works and when, is made difficult by the diversity in size, demographics and brutality of the civil wars in the twentieth century. If a scholar were to choose any two, four, or six wars, say wars that ended in a negotiated settlement under the auspices of an international peace process, there would be many, many more wars with similar characteristics left on the table. Inferences about the 200+ wars would be drawn from the six chosen by the analyst. Any inferences that inform our understanding of the effect of an attempt at managing the conflict would be skewed by the case selection. There is of course value to this approach, value that we usually wrap up in notions like high internal validity or process tracing. It is just a bit harder to draw broadly generalizable inferences from a few selected observations.

Internal versus external validity

Without turning this into a chapter on research designs, internal validity is a way to think about how clear or certain we are about the relationship among observed behaviors within a particular event, say the peacebuilding efforts in a specific civil war. By focusing heavily on internal validity, we might learn something about the makeup of an interposition force, the character of the leadership under stressful conditions that worked or didn't, or maybe something about how a particular rebel force reacted to pressures or demands. On the other hand, a focus on external validity provides a way to think about how portable or generalizable are the inferences of our research. We might, for example, learn that democracies are more willing to negotiate amnesty than non-democracies, or that the size of the rebel forces influences the type of peacebuilding arrangements that are required to sustain peace. If we consider one type of post-war program, Disarmament, Demobilization and Reintegration (DDR), and think about the difference between questions of internal and external validity, the point becomes easy to grasp. I should also make clear that these are not mutually exclusive categories, where you either have only internal validity or external validity, but rather shades of grey where a scholar tries to maximize on one at the expense of the other. In the ideal world of social science we would be able to maximize on both dimensions simultaneously. Differing research strategies make this joint maximization rather difficult, so we tend to choose.

Consider, for example, studies designed to assess the United Nations' efforts to Disarm, Demobilize, and Reintegrate former combatants in the process of post-conflict peacemaking. The end of a war must result in the dissolution of opposing armies, particularly rebel armies, because competing centers of authority are in many ways the sine qua non of a civil war (Regan 2000). So the question becomes one of how to best organize and implement DDR programs that ensure stable and long-lasting peace.

One approach might be to look at, say, four cases where the UN organized DDR programs in the aftermath of a civil war. Let's assume that two of these four were pretty successful; the other two didn't fare so well. A scholar who adopts a case study approach to understanding DDR success would look closely at these four cases, paying particular attention to those aspects of the design, implementation, and possibly personnel that would be expected theoretically to account for the success or failure of the program. By comparing these components across the cases of failures and successes, the researcher could provide some insight into what appeared to work and what did not in the course of the design and implementation phases of the DDR program. At the end of this study we might know, with a high level of confidence, that some condition was associated with success and some other with failure, at least in these four cases. Now let us for a moment assume that the population consisted of forty cases in which the UN organized DDR programs. This sample of 10 percent of the total should make one wonder how things played out in the other 90 percent of possible observations that the researcher could have chosen to analyze. A fundamental problem is that absent a solid research design we just don't know and it is an unreasonable demand on a scholar to acquire intimate details on all 40 cases, so inferences get drawn from a sample that might mask as much as it might help illuminate (Most and Starr 1989).

Another approach to this same puzzle would be to ask how DDR programs work in all 40 cases. If you adopt this strategy a number of the variables that might be of interest to the other scholar – leadership characteristics, specific behaviors, etc. – would be too cumbersome to measure across the range of possible observations, so the most important variables would tend to be more general. Theory will also point to this range of things that are linked to DDR success, such as the size of the UN contingent, the size of the country into which they are deployed, the number of fatalities in the war, and whatnot. In each instance these are easily measureable variables in ways that leadership decisions are not. This quantitatively oriented scholar would look for patterns in the data associated with various characteristics of the conflict and the DDR efforts; variables that were statistically significant would be the primary tool for drawing inferences. Now the scholar adopting this approach would – or should – also include in the sample all the other wars that did not generate a UN peacekeeping effort with a DDR program, so what this approach would tell us is, given a set of characteristics of the conflict and any DDR efforts, how likely it is that DDR contributed to a stable and enduring peace. High on external validity, a bit weaker on internal validity, and importantly what the quantitative approach will point to is a probabilistic understanding of the relationship among the efforts of the UN and the stability of peace as an outcome (Most and Starr 1989).

Knowledge generation and policy making

In my wont to take the life of a scholar seriously and that of a peace researcher very seriously, I see two arenas into which the efforts of a social scientist can contribute to peace through contributions where our understanding of the social-political world should lead to action that tries to make the world better. The key, however, is to have solid information about how the world works and why.

Let me look at the quantitative approach to studying peacebuilding from two perspectives: theoretical development and the implications for policy articulation. If either a quantitative or a qualitative approach provided a better foundation, it should show up in how we use the results of our studies. I'll start with the efforts to articulate sound policy from the results of our social science research.

Imagine that you are a policy maker confronted with an ongoing civil war that appears to be reaching a point where an end is in sight and some form of post-conflict arrangements have to be articulated. Regardless for whom you make policy – the country at war or some external, but interested country – you have an interest in long-term stability associated with the end of the war. If you were new to the job or to the subject of civil wars, you might consider that this one particular war was just your average civil war, one that just happens to be winding down as you take over the reins. So in effect you are asked to dip into the pool of civil wars and develop a policy that will help secure the peace, possibly using DDR through the United Nations. You would have a couple choices for how to proceed, one being to pick a conflict that looks rather similar to this one; the other to see what happens 'on average' across the range of civil wars.

By the 'average' conflict, I simply mean one that is in an average country with national wealth that is about average with the rest of the countries that experienced civil war, the number of soldiers fielded by the government and the rebels were not remarkably different than other civil wars, and the numbers of killed were, well, average. Human rights violations, while probably not great, were at about the same frequency of other civil wars, and the size or geography of the particular country was not out of the ordinary. If you defined the average country that had a civil war, there would be a rather large group of all the countries that congregated around this point and most would be unremarkable from the next. Granted, critical things like language or the dominant religion might differ, as might the concentration of cultural groups, but these factors, too, can be described at some level by the average characteristics. The alternative to thinking about the average country with the average conflict is to consider this one particular case to be something of an outlier, a country that is significantly different enough on these structural or contextual conditions to make it stand out in a crowd. An outlier is by definition not your average case, but also by definition most cases are closer to the average than to an outlier. In fact, an outlier moves the average toward that one odd case, so in theory without outliers the grouping around the average might be tighter.

So if you wanted to understand what types of policies are most successful in generating an enduring and stable peace, would you look for the most similar conflict that was successfully managed and see if the current one is sufficiently similar to generate a coherent policy, or would you ask about what worked in the average conflict? I think the best money is on asking about the conditions for success in the average conflict and then working from the average toward the specific rather than from the specific to the average. Here's why.

The core of this really goes back to the idea of internal versus external validity and how we benefit more or less by one strategy over the other. The way I think about things is that we only know a case is an outlier after we have already explored many of the common features that it holds with other observations that we might have access to. And since in general the very idea of an average exists because there are many, many aspects of any set of observations that are more similar than different, most conflicts will look more alike than different, at least on a number of critical dimensions. So randomly picking from that pool of civil wars is likely to come up with the average civil war. Now if the similarities among civil wars are sufficiently numerous to allow us to think about two – or maybe 50 – different wars as somewhat analogous cases, then knowing what works on average is the way to go. In this pool of wars, moreover, there are likely to be some that ended because of war weariness, some with external interventions, some as a result of victory, and some through negotiated agreements. This average pool of wars with somewhat different endings will likely have resulted in a range of successful outcomes, providing us with the opportunity to observe how war ends and whether the role of UN DDR programs, if any, are linked to the durability of peace. The ability to generalize from a large number of observations provides a wonderful starting point for the policy maker.

Since we all know that any one civil war, just like almost any one individual, is not going to represent the precise average, a policy maker should tinker with prescriptions derived from this average estimate to best construct a policy, but she can now do so with a solid starting point. This isn't too terribly different from the seasoned blackjack player who goes into the game knowing a lot about the distribution of cards in the deck, and with some adroit attention to detail, can get a sense of the distribution of cards that remain obscured in the dealer's hand once some cards have been revealed in the deal. It is not that difficult to figure out that on average there are not enough face cards remaining to make a wager a logical step. There always remains the probability that a face card would show on the next round, but the good gambler works on the on-average principle. These are also the people that the casinos try to remove from the premises because they beat the odds more often than not. Playing with human life and playing blackjack are not in the same realm, but the principle for thinking about the best strategy is based on the same underlying understanding of probabilities. The good card player generalizes from the broad patterns to the specific hand. I think the good policy maker should do the same.

If what appeared to work – on average – was a form of a DDR program in conflicts that have killed no more than, say, a thousand people, in a country of 20 million with an economy that has the potential to address critical grievances, then you could judge such a country against the one that is currently demanding attention. Alternatively, if countries of the size and character that the policy maker is struggling with have an equal chance of stability with or without the involvement of the UN and DDR programs, then the choice becomes not *how* to design a good program but *whether or not* you should. Other factors that were not used to generate the average relationship might be required to answer this question. Important, also, is the ability to gauge the magnitude of the effect of DDR on the stability of peace in a manner that allows for a probabilistic estimate, in effect combining a statistical and substantive inference about possible outcomes.

From a policy perspective the implications for a systematic, quantitative approach to studying peacemaking are rather stark and I am surprised that this methodological direction is not more frequently utilized. There is, however, another way to think about the value of systematic analysis in our research, and one that most of us take as our primary objective: theory building.

Many of us ask questions about social-political events because we want to know how things work or why sometimes good outcomes are obtainable even though under some conditions they are not. Put differently, we want to know the causal processes behind events that shape the world we live in. Issues of war and peace might have a greater impact on how we live than almost any other social or political behaviors, and therefore it behooves us to understand why wars happened, what we can do to stop or ameliorate the consequences of them, or to help regain the stability and dignity of the human condition. Theory driven by logical connections and empirical verification is central to this enterprise.

If developing a theoretical understanding of cause and effect on issues of war and peace are so important, then it requires that I account for why a particular method of research provides greater clarity to the outcome we all seek. So next I make the case that studying peacemaking by resort to large N statistical analysis will allow us to make advances in knowledge beyond what other approaches permit.

Knowledge generation and theory development

I like to think that generating knowledge is an incremental process. The folk wisdom idea of a light bulb suddenly going on borders on nonsense, at least as a practical metric. Even the literal light bulb going on – Edison's discovery of the incandescent bulb – was a result of many, many experiments in trying to get a filament design that would sustain the burning process and provide sufficient light. When he finally found it the light bulb went off, but it took him a long time to come up with the right material and the appropriate configuration. The lubricant WD40 is named after the number of tries it took to get the chemical mixture right (WD40 Inc. 2012). If it had only taken ten tries we might be using a product called WD10, but we're not. The same is true in social science, though we have an even harder task in that we cannot experiment in the sense that other sciences can. Almost any of the physical or medical sciences can create a control group and an experimental group; the task is then to observe the effects of the experiment relative to the control. We can't just start two wars and try to make peace in one so we can judge a policy relative to how the other war is playing out. So the social science task is made more difficult by our struggles to control for, say, the effects of DDR programs – or any other form of treatment.

So one question is how do we best draw inference from our research without the ability to experiment or control certain aspects of an environment just so that we can directly observe the effects of our explanatory condition. Both the case study and the statistical approach allow for some form of controls, but my point is not that there are ways to do science effectively without experiments, but rather that some approaches are better than others in providing a way to draw inferences while controlling for potentially confounding factors. As scientists we want to know what variables most often affect the outcome of interest with what magnitude of effect and under what types of controlled conditions. We would love to be able to create experiments but ethical obligations and practical modalities make this a particularly dicey path to travel.

The questions are really rather simple and to some degree the answers get muddled to the extent that we make the analysis complex. A chemist might want to know about the parameters of a particular bonding process as temperature rises. The chemical bonding might involve a complex process but the test involves observations of the chemical changes as the temperature is varied. Most other aspects of the environment can be controlled in the lab. The process of making peace out of war is complex, but our ability to observe certain aspects of that process – or the putative cause and effect – need not be. For example it might not require a complex investigation of the qualities of a peacekeeping leadership to understand the influence of the size of the effort on the durability of the peace. At the margins the acumen of the ranking member may be important but that skill might be dwarfed by the sheer numbers of peacekeepers. An effort to look too closely at one aspect may obscure the other. The process of doing statistical analysis involves developing simplified models that can provide for us a way to observe the effects of variation on some dimensions while we control for conditions associated with others. Simplicity and clarity is one key to doing the analysis. And if theory points to the inclusion or exclusion of variables in the model, then the tests should allow us to evaluate actual outcomes in light of our expectations. When successful, we learn things about the theoretical roots of peacemaking efforts.

The science of quantitative versus qualitative approaches

If theory and policy prescriptions are imperative, their importance is magnified to the extent to which we have confidence in the inferences we make and the policy prescriptions we proffer, which is in turn a function of our ability to confirm and reconfirm our results. We could barely imagine engineers or the policy community acting on one study that offered, say, a new way to generate energy. Rather, scientists in different labs would attempt to confirm the results of the study under similar and alternative sets of conditions. If results could not be confirmed, the original analysis may be called into question. One potential explanation might be that the science was contaminated because of local environmental conditions. The breakthrough with cold fusion technology is but one such example, where one path-breaking study could not be replicated and the idea of cold fusion energy reverted back to a conceptual idea (Fleischmann and Pons 1989). Fortunately for our pocketbooks, and our expectations, the scientific ethos took on the task of subjecting the original set of experiments to replication. None were able to do so. Other examples, such as the initial 'star wars' program under President Reagan's tenure allegedly did not follow such a well-honed path where science determined the veracity of some of the technology. Critics charged that the tests were falsified or manipulated and in the end the idea of a nuclear umbrella proved to be a chimera, and an expensive one at that (GAO 1994).

That same type of rigor of replication should be critical, maybe more critical, in the social sciences because we deal with such consequential behaviors as armed conflict.

One of the critical differences between more traditional forms of social science research and that which I advocate is the ability to replicate results, and in part to control for the confounding influence of the environment, which in our case can often be the scholar carrying out the research. The somewhat recent banking meltdown provides but one example where the interest of the scholars got in the way of their ability to draw inference from evidence (Iceland banking evaluations). As the extent of the risk to global banking was becoming clear, a number of economists came to non-replicable conclusions about banking stability, just shortly before the world's banking system collapsed; they all earned considerable sums of money for doing so. Teams of well-schooled scholars proclaimed the banks of Iceland to be sound, stable and well capitalized (Mishkin and Herbertson 2008). My point is that it is difficult to take the subjective out of social science and replication provides for us one critical way to maintain objectivity.

Replicability requires that the procedures taken to generate and analyze the data are transparent, and at least in theory could be redone under the same procedures by a different scholar and she would arrive at similar results. Now maybe the procedures in the initial study were mistaken and therefore the results are not valid, but that is what replication would uncover. In a more traditional case study approach, replication becomes nearly impossible because the subjective interpretation of the evidence – often texts or statements – is most often not systematic, at least in the sense that a second scholar could recreate the thinking that went into the initial inference. Let me explain by way of example, and again using DDR as the subject.

Replication requires that one scholar could reproduce the evidence and analysis of a particular research article, including coding the data and estimating the strength of the relationships among explanatory factors. A key part of this resides in the generation of the data. When I start a data generating process the first thing I do is design a set of coding rules and a coding form. I really ask myself just what type of data would be required for me to test the core part of my argument. With the coding rules and form in hand, I pretest these instruments on sources that would not be part of the primary data. For example, if my study were to range from 1990 to 2010, I might pretest on observations prior to 1990. Only after the coding instruments make sense do I begin coding data from sources that will constitute the data to be analyzed, and as I do this, I have a coder who engages in inter-coder testing. I target 10 percent of all the observations to be subjected to inter-coder reliability testing. A reasonable question might be 'so how does this matter?'

First, if I know that I could take two coders, give them the same coding rules and sources, and they could come up with the same coded values on each variable, say, 95 percent of the time, then I already have a metric for judging the reliability of that part of my research, something that a case study specialist simply cannot do. Second, and equally importantly, if some other scholar wants to replicate my work, the coding rules are available and I know that they work, at least on average, something like 90+ percent of the time. The other scholar may think that the sources I used have biased my results and therefore my inferences and that is perfectly fine. She can take my coding instruments and subject other sources to the same coding regime and confirm (or not) the results of my study. Alternatively the other scholar may think that my coding rules were not the best and she can manipulate the rules that guide particular coding decisions. In short, replication – or the ability to replicate – is built into the process.

So if we take a study of DDR and we want to know the program's effect on long-term stability, given local resistance, job training, land usage and other contextual factors, we have to have data across all post-war situations, some of which had DDR programs and others that have not. In those instances where DDR programs were set up, the data associated with them would be provided (presumably) by the UN. But data on local resistance to the DDR program or the peace arrangements would have to be coded, as might the existence of job training programs in non-DDR post-conflict environments. Right at this point there is considerable deviation from a more traditional case study approach in that the population of post-conflict environments would be used. If we clearly delineated the rules that determined our cases for inclusion or exclusion and set out clear coding rules of those conditions for which data has to be coded, everything about the study could be replicated. To reiterate an earlier point, such a study as this might have higher external validity than internal validity, but it is important that the results can stand up to scrutiny so that any inferences are on much more solid ground. In the end not only are policy inferences easier to make, but so too are the intellectual refinements and testing required to advance our understanding.

Good science requires replication and extension, without it we cannot tell the difference between random errors associated with our research design and implementation and the results of a causal process. Many will be familiar with the great fanfare that ushered in the cold fusion experiments in the 1980s. The world thought that the advent of limitless energy was on the horizon. Lots of money was thrown at the question but cold fusion died a cold death because something about the science could not be replicated. The same requirements for replication should be important for social and political research. If one study finds a strong relationship between DDR programs and stable peace and that study is based on a small sample and non-replicable methods, the results could be a fluke, they could be the result of faulty research, or they could be correct and form the basis for future policy. But if policy makers are going to commit to the policy they should have confidence that the results from which they formulate policy can be supported. Replication is everything.

Replication is not only important for the policy maker trying to articulate or calibrate policy to secure peace, but also important for the scholar trying to advance on our understanding of peacebuilding efforts. You can take any number of quite visible topics in the physical or social sciences to observe the role of replication in theoretical development. Two stand out. The democratic peace proposition started with early theorizing that was eventually tested empirically in 1972 after the scientific community had finally generated the systematic data to engage in empirical testing (Small and Singer 1972; Chan 1984). The formulation of the democratic peace argument changed dramatically over the next twenty years as new scholars took to task different parts of the theoretical and empirical puzzle. By the turn of the twenty-first century, presidents and prime ministers were touting the value of the democratic peace as they formulated policy. The war in Iraq, the Palestinian elections of 2006, and the new political institutions in Afghanistan have each been lauded from a democratic peace perspective. Today we know a lot more about the dynamics of that peace and its theoretical limitations in large part because of the ability to test, replicate and retest the core tenets of the arguments. Another turn on this can be seen in our understanding of how different fats contribute to heart disease and failure. We learned that saturated, then unsaturated, then polyunsaturated and finally transfats were bad for our hearts. The changing explanation for the effects of fats on heart performance was not necessarily shoddy science but rather the result of scientific progression. As each argument was tested and refined, we moved closer to a robust understanding about how what we eat influences how long we get the opportunity to eat. Good science matters a lot and now the fast food restaurants have stopped selling you French fries made with transfats. I would posit that the same holds for understanding some of the complex relationships involved with how the world community can work to resolve conflict and generate long-lasting peace among former warring parties. This would be a real accomplishment and will be accelerated to the extent that we employ good scientific methods.

Importantly, replication is not a research requirement that applies well to qualitative studies. It is not that qualitative scholars are not serious or systematic, but rather that the decisions that they take to draw inference are generally not replicable, in part because those choices are often less transparent and based on subjective criteria. If replication is such a critical aspect of the science from both a theoretical and policy perspective, then this liability is one that needs to be considered carefully as we begin to formulate our research strategies.

The putative shortcoming of quantitative approaches

Many critics will lament the relative lack of systematic knowledge gained from the somewhat recent emphasis on the scientific approach to understanding political decisions and they use this as rationale for thinking that the approach isn't worth the effort. Put differently, the Holy Grail of politics, let alone peacebuilding, remains elusive and the quantitative method provides no more purchase on finding it than a good case study does. I would suggest that a relative judgment of past accomplishments is the wrong standard to impose because neither have we found the Grail as a result of the plethora of case study material devoted to any one issue. Instead we should focus on the contributions to theoretical development, even if those contributions are incremental and in increments that are quite small at times. From this standard both approaches to the study of peacemaking are vital to the overall objective of figuring out how the world community can contribute to the betterment of the people who reside in this community. But each particular methodological orientation must be evaluated on how it can contribute, how theory is advanced or retarded, and how inferences of use to the policy community can be advanced.

These types of demands on knowledge generation are certainly not unique to the study of peacebuilding, nor to political science more generally, but it is mostly in the realm of political science that we even debate the merits of differing methodological approaches. Most social sciences, many if not most businesses, almost all betting houses, and certainly all insurance companies have long ago figured out that the search for systematic patterns provides the most robust estimates of the relationships of interest to them. Even the bankers and investment houses that swindled the world economy up through 2008 knew all too well that by understanding the systematic patterns in the data on risk they could make billions, and that as long as they could also control the implementation, they had a good gig going. The big house of cards appears to have fallen apart on efforts to shield what they knew were bad bets from otherwise good people. The patterns in the data, moreover, told them how to do so.

To my mind we will learn much more about how to organize and implement policies to sustain peace after war by adopting research strategies that compel us to think about systematic variation and replication under broadly cross-national conditions. I understand the costs that are borne in doing so but I also think that the benefits in the form of theoretical development and policy articulation are well worth those costs. In the scheme of things, and recognizing that a qualitative and quantitative approach can serve a common goal, I ask myself the simple question of how the sequence of knowledge acquisition can affect the articulation of coherent and adroit policy. If I were making the policy I would want to know first the general trends that exist in the data on a cross-national basis. In effect I would want to know what works on average and under what conditions. At the same time I would also want to know whether the current country that I was dealing with is 'average' or an 'outlier'. Both of these answers would come from the systematic data, and largely only from systematic data. Having that information under my belt I would turn next to a regional expert who could elucidate some of the more nuanced conditions and characteristics associated with the one specific conflict that is the source of the policy debate. The fine-grained story would be useful for policy making even if the country was an 'average' country facing an 'average' threat from an 'average' rebel force, but it might be critical if this country was clearly identified as an outlier. The policy maker would only know what nuances to look for after she understood what worked, when and why, on average.

References

Chan, S. (1984) 'Mirror Mirror on the Wall', *Journal of Conflict Resolution*, 28: 617–48.

Fleischmann, M. and Pons, S. (1989), 'Electrochemically induced nuclear fusion of deuterium', *Journal of Electroanalytical Chemistry*, 261(2A): 301–8.

Fortna, V.P. (2008) *Does peacekeeping work?: Shaping belligerents' choices after civil war*, Princeton, NJ: Princeton University Press.

GAO (1994) *Ballistic Missile Defense: Report to the Chairman, Subcommittee on Federal Services, Post Office and Civil Service*, Washington DC: Committee on Governmental Affairs, US Senate.

Hartzell, C. and Hoddie, M. (2007) *Crafting Peace: Power-Sharing Institutions and the Negotiated Settlements of Civil War*, State College, PA: Penn State Press.

Mishkin, F.S. and Herbertson, T.T. (2008) *Financial Stability In Iceland*, Reykjavik: Iceland Chamber of Commerce.

Most, B.A. and Starr, H. (1989) *Inquiry, Logic and International Politics*, Columbia, SC: South Carolina Press.

Regan, P.M. (2000) *Civil Wars and Foreign Powers*, Ann Arbor: University of Michigan Press.

Small, J.D. and Singer, M. (1972) *The Wages of War*, New York: Wiley.

Themner, L. and Wallensteen, P. (2011) 'Armed Conflict, 1946–2010', *Journal of Peace Research*, 48(4): 525–536.

Wallensteen, P. (2009) *Understanding Conflict Resolution*, London: Sage Press.

Wayman, F. and Sarkees, M. (2010) *Resort to War, 1816–2007*, Washington DC: CQ Press.

WD40 Inc. (2012) http://www.wd40.com/about-us/history/. Accessed 22 June 2012.

PART IV

Violence and security

15

SECURITIZATION AND PEACEBUILDING

Necla Tschirgi

Peacebuilding is a compelling but highly loaded and contested concept. Despite relentless examination and searing critiques in the last two decades, its enduring power raises an interesting question. What is it about peacebuilding that generates strong reactions from its proponents and detractors alike? This chapter offers an answer to that question by examining the conflicting agendas that have come to be pursued under the deceptively benign term of peacebuilding. In specific, it focuses on the strong nexus between security and development that undergirds peacebuilding and the growing concerns over the securitization of peacebuilding.

Peacebuilding defies a single definition. Efforts to craft a universally acceptable definition have led nowhere (Barnett et al. 2007). While it is generally agreed that peacebuilding is an endogenous process, in most contemporary conflict contexts international actors have come to play an important role. In this chapter, peacebuilding is narrowly and explicitly used to refer to the international peacebuilding agenda. The activities, strategies and goals pursued by international actors in the name of peacebuilding have ranged from grassroots development projects to ambitious statebuilding and stabilization operations.[1] The concept's expansive breadth in the highly fluid post-Cold War international environment has led to its appropriation by diverse actors with differing interests and agendas.

In the 1990s, the concept of peacebuilding emerged as a way to link development and security—two fields of study and practice that had developed on separate tracks since the end of World War II. The concept offered a new paradigm for international actors to think about post-Cold War challenges and opportunities by positing that human well-being (both in terms of socio-economic development and personal security) needed to be promoted simultaneously as the basis for sustainable peace. Peacebuilding challenged the traditional, state-centric views of security by taking people, rather than states, as the referent of security and by moving beyond a narrow focus on military security to consider issues such as poverty and socio-economic development as central to creating the foundations for peace.

Expectations for a more peaceful world in the wake of the Cold War era were short-lived. Within a decade, there was a tidal change in peacebuilding discourse and policy. Largely driven by national security concerns after 9/11, the post-Cold War peacebuilding discourse was steadily overtaken and altered by other priorities. This chapter argues that in the immediate post-Cold War years, peacebuilding was firmly grounded in the concept of liberal peace and was integrally related to human security. Although it was recognized that conflicts in the periphery had ramifications for international peace and security, these were not construed as a direct threat to the security of the global system or to the vital security interests of its dominant members. After 9/11, as state-centric security concerns re-asserted their dominance, influential voices in the academic and policy communities came to see peacebuilding as a sub-set of the international security agenda. Nonetheless, the liberal peacebuilding agenda continues to co-exist with its latter-day more securitized version. The heated debates stemming from the tensions and contradictions between these two competing strands are the subject of this chapter.

The concept of securitization informing the following analysis comes from the work of Buzan, Waever and de Wilde (1998) who provide a useful framework for understanding how certain issues are construed as an existential threat and are assigned a security status through an inter-subjective and politically constructed process. According to Buzan et al. (1998), '"Security" is the move that takes politics beyond the established rules of the game and frames the issue either as a special kind of politics or as above politics. Securitization can thus be seen as a more extreme version of politicization.' An issue becomes *securitized* when it is presented as an existential threat requiring emergency measures outside the bounds of normal politics. The security quality of an issue is not dependent on the issue itself but the way in which it is presented and received in the public realm. Thus, there is a particular logic to securitization: an issue is identified in a *speech act* by *securitizing actors* who declare *a referent object* to be *existentially threatened* and call for the adoption of *emergency measures* to counter this threat. Not all efforts to securitize an issue are successful since effective securitization is not decided by the *securitizer* but by the audience of the *security speech act*. In short, as defined by Buzan et al., securitization is a deliberate and contested act that is informed by and serves a particular set of interests. Recognizing the political construction of securitization, this chapter investigates the extent to which peacebuilding has been successfully securitized in the last two decades and the broader implications of that effort.

The chapter consists of three sections. The first reviews the emergence of liberal peacebuilding at the United Nations and the multilateral arena in the aftermath of the Cold War. The second section examines the impact of 9/11 on the peacebuilding agenda with the launch of the Global War on Terror (GWOT) and the counter-insurgency strategies put into place following the US-led wars in Afghanistan and Iraq. Following the heightened international interest in fragile states after 9/11, the third section analyzes the ramifications of the growing conflation of peacebuilding with statebuilding to ascertain whether this is likely to promote 'secure development' or to further 'securitize peacebuilding.' Finally, the concluding section offers some reflections on the future of peacebuilding in light of the competing agendas that claim to advance peace—albeit through very different visions.

Post-Cold War peacebuilding: At the nexus of security and development

Peacebuilding is not a new concept; it dates back to Johan Galtung's pioneering work in the 1970s. However, it found a particularly fertile environment at the end of the Cold War. For almost fifty years, the world's attention was focused primarily on preventing the outbreak of nuclear war between two heavily armed power blocs. The end of the Cold War and the collapse of the Soviet Union opened up new possibilities for international action on a broader range of issues threatening peace and security, including intra-state conflicts and civil wars. Specifically, it allowed the United Nations, which was largely paralyzed during the Cold War, to start playing a more active role in promoting peace and security. The promise of the new peacebuilding agenda was that the international community would intervene collectively—as a 'third party'—to help resolve violent conflicts and to support peacebuilding without the shadow of Cold War politics or in pursuit of the narrow national interests of individual states.

The impetus for peacebuilding came from multiple sources, but found its strongest expression at the United Nations. The UN provided the rationale as well as the operational principles for peacebuilding as the concept went through various iterations in the following two decades. In the UN's landmark report, *An Agenda for Peace* (UN 1992), it was introduced as part of a series of tools at the UN's disposal including preventive diplomacy, peacemaking, peacekeeping and post-conflict peacebuilding and was defined as post-conflict action 'to identify and support structures which will tend to strengthen and solidify peace in order to avoid a relapse into conflict.' Subsequently, in *An Agenda for Development* (UN 1994) and the *Supplement to An Agenda for Peace* (UN 1995), the term was expanded to encompass the full spectrum of activities ranging from conflict prevention to post-conflict re-construction. Despite the differences in emphasis, what united the emerging peacebuilding discourse was the search to bridge the sharp divide between development and security that had characterized the Cold War international system. Peacebuilding provided a useful construct allowing analysts, policymakers and practitioners to explore the links between people-centered development and security in countries grappling with violent conflict.

In the internal conflicts of the 1990s where the boundaries between war and peace were blurred, humanitarian relief, peacemaking, peacekeeping and peacebuilding became closely interlinked. At the United Nations, many programs and agencies became involved in a variety of civilian activities to restore peace, prevent a relapse into conflict, and facilitate the transition to development. Concurrently, the UN's traditional peacekeeping operations increasingly became multi-dimensional. Outside the UN, donors, multilateral institutions and international NGOs assumed new roles in conflict-affected countries. The OECD's Development Assistance Committee played a critical role in placing conflict prevention and peacebuilding on the agenda of the donor community and donors followed suit by developing a variety of new tools, instruments and mechanisms to respond to intra-state conflict. Alongside institutional reforms, the 1990s saw significant innovation and experimentation in terms of new policies, programs and funding mechanisms to address the multi-faceted challenges of peacebuilding in countries at different phases in their transition from conflict to peace (Tschirgi 2004; Cutillo 2006; Baranyi 2008).[2]

Given the range of governmental and non-governmental actors assuming new roles in conflict contexts, peacebuilding interventions were highly fragmented, ad hoc and supply driven. Nonetheless, there was an emerging consensus that peacebuilding required concerted multilateral action to assist nationally-led efforts at the intersection of peacemaking, peacekeeping and post-conflict reconstruction. From the late 1980s through the mid-1990s, there was a succession of peace operations from Namibia and Cambodia to Guatemala and Bosnia. By the end of the decade, the Brahimi Report (UN 2000) stated:

> The Security Council recognizes that peacebuilding is aimed at preventing the outbreak, the recurrence, or the continuation of armed conflict and therefore encompasses a wide range of political, development, humanitarian and human rights programmes and mechanisms. This requires short and long-term actions tailored to address the particular needs of societies sliding into conflict or emerging from it. These actions should focus on fostering sustainable development, the eradication of poverty and inequalities, transparent and accountable governance, the promotion of democracy, respect for human rights and the rule of law and the promotion of a culture of peace and non-violence.

Without unduly romanticizing it, it can be argued that the promise—if not the reality—of the first decade of international peacebuilding was to bring multilateral approaches to address deep-rooted sources of conflict through broad-based, people-centered and multi-dimensional efforts. The peacebuilding agenda of the 1990s had a strong liberal orientation—promoting political and economic liberalization as the ideal path in transitioning from war to peace.

Despite its ambitious liberal aspirations, the international community's track record in building liberal peace was quite meager. Many conflict-affected countries failed to get on a path to peace and development while others lapsed or relapsed into conflict. Yet, time and again international and multilateral forces proved inadequate to deal with the resurgence of violence. In each case, the dual imperative for security and development was put to the test. The tensions between the civilian and military dimensions of peacebuilding came to a head in the Balkans when conventional military forces from NATO became involved alongside the United Nations.

The Balkan wars started with the dissolution of Yugoslavia. After brief armed confrontations, Slovenia and Croatia achieved their independence while the civil wars in Bosnia and Herzegovina and Kosovo waged on without relief. The war in Bosnia and Herzegovina lasted from 1992 until October 1995 when a United Nations Protection Force (UNPROFOR) was established to monitor the ceasefire that would allow for peace negotiations to take place. Following the Peace Agreement in Paris on 14 December, the UN established the International Police Task Force (IPTF) and the UN Civilian Office in Bosnia-Herzegovina (UNMIBH) which lasted until 31 December 2002. Meanwhile, having already deployed Operation Deliberate Force during the fighting, NATO established and deployed the 60,000-strong Implementation Force (IFOR) to enforce the accord's military provisions. Primarily responsible for UN activities related to law enforcement and police reform, UNMIBH cooperated closely with the NATO-led IFOR and its successor, the multinational Stabilization Force (SFOR). Thus, Bosnia and Herzegovina saw the emergence of a division of labor between the NATO-led military operations and the UN-led civilian operation which would subsequently be replicated in Kosovo.

Following Yugoslavia's disintegration, Albanian Kosovars accelerated their armed resistance to Serbian rule. When diplomacy and economic sanctions failed to reverse the steady plunge into war, NATO initiated a bombing campaign in March 1999 which lasted almost three months. In June 1999, the Security Council passed a resolution asking member states to establish 'a security presence' to deter hostilities, demilitarize the Kosovo Liberation Army (KLA) and facilitate the return of refugees. It also authorized an international civil presence in Kosovo—the United Nations Interim Administration Mission in Kosovo (UNMIK)—which marked the end of the NATO intervention. While UNMIK established its presence on the ground, a 50,000-strong NATO-led multinational Kosovo Force (KFOR) arrived to provide security. The Security Council vested UNMIK with authority over the territory and people of Kosovo. The Mission was asked to perform basic civilian administrative functions, promote the establishment of substantial autonomy and self-government, facilitate a political process to determine Kosovo's future status, coordinate humanitarian and disaster relief, support the reconstruction of key infrastructure, maintain civil law and order, promote human rights, and assure the return of all refugees and displaced persons.

As has been noted, 'NATO's intervention in Kosovo in 1999, and the resulting effort to assist the fleeing communities and then to help reconstruct the province, has often been described as a key moment in the redefinition of civil–military relations in the context of peacebuilding. The political leaders who launched NATO's military campaign heralded it as the first humanitarian war, prompted by the international community's revulsion at the grave human rights violations taking place' (Gheciu 2011: 99). Although UNMIK was expected to work closely with the NATO-led KFOR, the legal relationship between the KFOR and UNMIK was never clearly defined. 'In other words, the peacebuilding machinery established under UN auspices took the form of a network of institutions with no clear, hierarchical common structure for the system as a whole. [As a result] questions of coordination and coherence between civil and military responses to peacebuilding challenges were put forcefully on the agenda' (Gheciu 2011: 99). Moreover, NATO's involvement in humanitarian relief and reconstruction activities led to suspicion among the NGO community. 'The NGO community repeatedly expressed serious concern about "an extreme politicization and militarization of aid", involving the delivery of aid to the local population for particular political objectives and by the same actors who had been directly involved in war' (Gheciu 2011: 100).

What is noteworthy about the two Balkan cases is the resort to NATO's military power alongside multilateral civilian peacebuilding efforts. With few exceptions, the international community had relied primarily on limited and under-resourced UN peace operations throughout the 1990s. Driven largely by Europe's interest in stopping the wars on its own continent, the international engagement in the Balkans was more robust and indeed became the precursor of what transpired after 9/11, with the introduction of external military forces outside the UN's peacekeeping operations and driven by a hard security agenda.

Some critical theorists argue that even in the 1990s peacebuilding was basically a tool to control disorder in regions of conflict in the post-Cold War, market-oriented liberal global order (Duffield 2001). However, this is an overly-monolithic reading of the tremendous surge of support for peacebuilding among a wide range of governmental and non-government actors. Indeed, a closer look at the sea change in international policy discourse and practice after 9/11 covered in the next section reveals the differences in the peacebuilding agenda of the 1990s and the decade since 2001.

Peacebuilding in the shadow of counter-terrorism and counter-insurgency

The decade of the 1990s was an uncertain interregnum in terms of global peace and security. Although the threat of a major global confrontation dissipated, the world confronted a range of lesser security challenges and transnational threats. The security studies literature of the period reflects both a deepening and widening of the concept of security, and growing contestation of the state-centric, post-Westphalian security paradigm (Buzan and Hansen 2007). Given the fluid security context, traditional security institutions assumed new roles as reflected in the rapid expansion of UN peacekeeping and NATO's engagement in the Balkans. There was a growing interdependence between military and civilian actors in response to the protracted no-war, no-peace contexts that characterized post-Cold War conflicts. While this raised some concerns about the increasing militarization of aid and the closing off of humanitarian space, both in discourse and practice there was widespread commitment to conflict prevention and liberal peacebuilding as common priorities for the international community.

The events of 9/11 radically changed the global security calculus for the United States as well as its key allies. Following the concerted terrorist attacks on US soil, terrorism was *securitized* as an existential threat by the US government, unleashing a chain of events that led to two international wars and untold death and destruction. The two wars and the resultant need for stabilization and reconstruction catapulted peacebuilding into a different security arena. According to the securitization framework of Buzan et al. (1998: 23–24), an issue becomes *securitized* when it is presented and accepted as an existential threat that requires emergency measures outside the normal bounds of politics. This is indeed what happened in the United States after 9/11 as political and military leaders and intelligence experts declared that the US and its people were existentially threatened by terrorism which required emergency military action. This was widely accepted by the public, opening the door to the US intervention in Afghanistan and the US-led Global War on Terror (GWOT). While the international community was hesitant to embrace the US *speech act*, the radical change in US policies toward conflict-affected areas had important ramifications for international peacebuilding since GWOT and peacebuilding intersected in multiple ways—in Afghanistan, Iraq and beyond.

In Afghanistan, with the collapse of the Taliban regime, it quickly became clear that military force could not address that country's deep-rooted problems that required a broad mix of humanitarian, human rights, development and security strategies. However, the overriding goal for the US intervention was to eliminate al Qaeda in Afghanistan. As a result, the US military led Operation Enduring Freedom (OEF) concentrated on counter-terrorist operations against al Qaeda and the residual Taliban elements throughout the country, while a small international force of some 5,000 troops were deployed to provide security in the capital (Dobbins et al. 2003). The US initially opposed an international stabilization force beyond Kabul, not least because the administration 'viewed Afghanistan as the opening campaign in a larger war against terrorism. US policy makers did not want to tie down significant numbers of US forces or logistical capacities in Afghanistan' (Dobbins et al. 2003: 133).

Meanwhile, following the Bonn agreement in December 2001, the UN initiated an ambitious 'nation-building' project in Afghanistan with the establishment of UNAMA, the UN's political mission in Afghanistan, and the deployment of the international security assistance force (ISAF) which was put under NATO command in August 2003. As Barnett Rubin (2008: 39) has noted, 'In Afghanistan, there was from the start a contradiction between the security objectives of the US and the security imperatives of state building and the political process.' These contradictions were never resolved—leading peacebuilding in Afghanistan to be labeled 'an oxymoron' (Williams 2011: 119). More than ten years after the US military intervention and with a major surge of US forces in 2010 to deal with continuing insurgency, the Afghan case represents the extreme paradox of a massive peacebuilding effort amidst military operations guided by a separate security mandate.

Yet, the Afghan case is not unique. In March 2003, while the situation in Afghanistan remained extremely precarious, the US launched a full-fledged war on Iraq. Although it is still too early to assess the full impact of the Iraq war, at a minimum it was instrumental in draining vital political attention and resources from Afghanistan. As a result, a decade after the US intervention, the country remains in tatters. And despite the killing of Osama bin Laden in May 2011, the US military forces are scheduled to stay in Afghanistan until the end of 2014. In short, the future of nation-building and peacebuilding in Afghanistan remains an open question.

Meanwhile, the US war in Iraq led to a decade of instability, insecurity and destruction following the overthrow of the Saddam Hussein regime. Despite widespread opposition to the US invasion, the United Nations reluctantly assumed an active role with the end of major combat operations. The United Nations Assistance Mission in Iraq (UNAMI) was given the dual task of facilitating a political process while assisting with humanitarian relief and development aid. Specifically, Security Council Resolution 1546 (2004) mandated UNAMI to play a leading role in convening a national conference to select a Consultative Council; advise and support Iraq's independent electoral commission, interim government and the transitional National Assembly on elections; promote national dialogue and consensus-building on drafting a national constitution; advise the government in developing effective civil and social services; contribute to the coordination and delivery of reconstruction, development, and humanitarian assistance; promote the protection of human rights, national reconciliation, and judicial and legal reform in order to strengthen the rule of law in Iraq; and advise and assist the government on initial planning for the eventual conduct of a comprehensive census. These, of course, are similar to the peacebuilding activities that the UN and other international actors had been engaged in throughout the 1990s. Yet, there was a major difference. UNAMI (like UNAMA) had to operate under the shadow of massive military operations led by the United States, rather than as part of multilateral UN peacekeeping operations.

Indeed, until the withdrawal of its combat troops in December 2011, the US exercised paramount control in Iraq especially during the period 2003–2007 when there was an armed insurgency. The gravity of the insurgency led the US to develop its counterinsurgency strategy, known as COIN. The striking feature of COIN is its incorporation of peacebuilding practices into a counter-insurgency and counter-terrorism strategy. As Sarah Sewall notes in her introduction to the COIN Field Manual (United States Army-Marine Corps 2007: xxiii), 'Today, counterinsurgency and counterterrorism operations are often conflated in official US statements, and COIN has become an increasingly common conceptual framework for the global struggle against terrorism.'

The UN's role in Afghanistan and Iraq has been studied extensively and its shortcomings documented in great detail. The UN missions in both countries cannot be understood in isolation from the concurrent military operations and the larger security agenda pursued by the US and its allies. The UN's involvement in Afghanistan and Iraq has cast a dark shadow on the international peacebuilding project by not only violating the principle of third party interventions that had characterized post-Cold War peacebuilding, but also by promoting a peacebuilding paradigm dependent on external coercion as well as concurrent counter-terrorism and counter-insurgency operations. COIN's work on the ground has been particularly problematic for peacebuilding. Eschewing a military strategy targeting insurgents, COIN has adopted a population-centered approach whereby civilian protection 'becomes *part of* the counterinsurgency's mission, in fact, the most important part' (United States Army-Marine Corps 2007: xxv). Thus, in Sewall's words, COIN 'incorporates stability operations, also known as peace support operations, reconstruction and nation building. Just recently, these were considered a separate category of military activity closely associated with multinationals or United Nations peacekeeping operations in which force is rarely used' (United States Army-Marine Corps 2007: xxiii).

Afghanistan and Iraq constitute a category by themselves and should not be seen as representative of the peace operations and peacebuilding efforts undertaken in other conflict-affected or post-conflict countries. Yet, the post-9/11 securitization agenda has had broader ramifications for peacebuilding.

Peacebuilding and statebuilding: Securing or securitizing development?

The most direct impact of 9/11 on international peacebuilding has been the emergence of a security-oriented stabilization and statebuilding agenda which contrasts sharply with the human-centered, development-oriented agenda of the 1990s. In the last decade, peacebuilding has increasingly become conflated with stabilization and statebuilding in so-called 'failed', 'fragile' or conflict-affected states. Thus, examining the stabilization and statebuilding agenda offers important insights into the competing approaches to peacebuilding that co-exist today.

State failure was already on the international agenda in the 1990s following the break-up of Yugoslavia, the collapse of Somalia and armed challenges to weak governments throughout Africa. While policymakers and academics recognized the external ramifications of state failure, initially the focus was primarily on its internal security, political and governance dimensions and different approaches to strengthening state capacities (Paris 2004). Thus, the OECD-DAC's path-breaking report, *Helping Prevent Violent Conflict* (1997, 2001), repeatedly referred to 'failed or collapsed states' or 'states in crisis' and 'crisis of state legitimacy' but did not make any reference to statebuilding, and stabilization referred to economic policies. The *Guidelines* called for strengthening the state, engaging with the state, and co-operating with the state and national authorities.

As Call and Cousens (2008) have noted, '[h]istorically, international peacebuilding efforts tended to neglect state building in favor of emphasis on social relations among conflicting groups or economic determinants of peace…They tended to assume state capacity as a given and did not problematize contestation over state design, form, or function.' State failure gained special prominence after 9/11 as a peace and security issue. The 2002 US National Security Strategy clearly stated, 'America is now threatened less by conquering states than we are by failing ones' (US NSS 2002). Other countries and institutions quickly followed suit in identifying state failure and its antidote, statebuilding, as key challenges because of increased security threats—especially terrorism—emanating from state fragility.

The new focus on statebuilding was largely (but not entirely) motivated by externally-driven security interests and was accompanied by a new wave of scholarship and policy initiatives. For example, in 2004, the Report of the UN Secretary-General's High Level Panel on Threats, Challenges and Change (UN 2004) argued that 'in an era when dozens of States are under stress or recovering from conflict, there is a clear international obligation to assist States in developing their capacity to perform their sovereign functions effectively and responsibly.' In his follow-up report, *In Larger Freedom*, UN Secretary General Kofi Annan (2005) underscored the interdependence between development, security and human rights, and affirmed:

> Sovereign States are the basic and indispensable building blocks of the international system. It is their job to guarantee the rights of their citizens, to protect them from crime, violence and aggression, and to provide the framework of freedom under law in which individuals can prosper and society develop. If States are fragile, the peoples of the world will not enjoy the security, development and justice that are their right. Therefore, one of the great challenges of the new millennium is to ensure that all States are strong enough to meet the many challenges they face.

However, governments and national security institutions saw state failure as a direct security threat. The 2008 UK National Security Strategy stated, 'In the past, most violent conflicts and significant threats to global security came from strong states. Currently, most of the major threats and risks emanate from failed or fragile states … Failed and fragile states increase the risk of instability and conflict, and at the same time have a reduced capacity to deal with it' (UK 2008: 14). The 2008 US National Defense Strategy (US 2008) made a similar argument:

> The inability of many states to police themselves effectively or to work with their neighbors to ensure regional security represents a challenge to the international system. Armed sub-national groups, including but not limited to those inspired by violent extremism, threaten the stability and legitimacy of key states. If left unchecked, such instability can spread and threaten regions of interest to the United States, our allies, and friends. Insurgent groups and other non-state actors frequently exploit local geographical, political, or social conditions to

establish safe havens from which they can operate with impunity. Ungoverned, undergoverned, misgoverned, and contested areas offer fertile ground for such groups to exploit the gaps in governance capacity of local regimes to undermine local stability and regional security.

From both a longer-term development perspective and from a heightened security perspective, statebuilding emerged as a key priority. Yet, the implications of statebuilding for peacebuilding are far from simple. Statebuilding and peacebuilding can collide in various ways to undermine peace (Call and Cousens 2008; Newman 2010). Indeed, just as Cold War imperatives led to strategies in support of regime stability at the expense of state consolidation, the post-9/11 focus on statebuilding has had mixed consequences. On the one hand, it has generated greater attention to, and additional resources for, conflict-affected and fragile states. On the other hand, it has led to a hierarchy of security priorities with selected countries receiving the lion's share of resources that are not necessarily targeted to address long-term developmental or human-security needs. Given the range of actors involved in conflict-affected countries in the last twenty years, there are multiple approaches to peacebuilding and statebuilding which tend to pull in different directions. Although many donor governments began to adopt 'whole of government' strategies and the so-called '3D' approach to ensure greater coherence between their diplomacy, defense and development policies, the tensions between competing priorities have not been easy to resolve.

For example, the OECD-DAC's adoption of the *Principles for Good International Engagement in Fragile States & Situations* in April 2007 was an important policy development. The ten principles were aimed to maximize the positive impact of international engagement in fragile states while minimizing unintentional harm. The principles explicitly recognized the links between political, security, and development objectives, and focused on statebuilding as an objective. However, the OECD-DAC (2007) also noted:

> The challenge for governments involved in fragile states is to establish clarity on and coherence in objectives. These objectives are likely to differ among the departments involved … Therefore, ministries may promote national interests rather than the interests of a partner country, which, from the perspective of development co-operation, is problematic. When dealing with the problems of precarious statehood—and in particular the wide range of potential threats emanating from them—the issue therefore is how governments determine their priorities for engagement in fragile states. From the perspective of the OECD-DAC, the question more specifically is where development outcomes should rank *vis-à-vis* trade, counter-terrorism, national defence and other political objectives of donor countries.

Indeed, the tug of war between competing agendas remains one of the key challenges facing international peacebuilding in the post-9/11 context. Defense departments and national security agencies view conflict and state fragility primarily as a security issue, and thus approach statebuilding and peacebuilding instrumentally from a stabilization perspective. Meanwhile, development actors take a longer-term approach rooted in the concept of sustainable peace. In a speech on fragile states on 8 January 2009, World Bank President Robert Zoellick made a strong plea for the international community to focus on 'securing development—bringing security and development together first to smooth the transition from conflict to peace and then to embed stability so that development can take hold over a decade and beyond' (World Bank 2009). He added, '[o]nly by securing development can we put down roots deep enough to *break* [his emphasis] the cycle of fragility and violence.' In identifying the ten priorities for 'securing development', Zoellick focused first and foremost on 'building legitimacy of the state.' His definition of legitimacy corresponded closely to the longer-term peacebuilding agenda by emphasizing delivery of basic services and strengthening of local authorities.

Zoellick is not alone in his call for 'securing development.' In the last few years, there has been a proliferation of new research, policy development and programming primarily by development actors that are grounded in a socially-constructed understanding of statebuilding. Among influential policy reports, three deserve special attention since they reflect the orientation of the development community. These are OECD DAC's *Supporting Statebuilding in Situations of Conflict and Fragility,* the World Bank's *World Development Report 2011: Conflict, Security and Development* and UNDP's *Governance for Peace: Securing the Social Contract.* Recognizing that aid to fragile and conflict-affected states accounts for 30 percent of global official development assistance flows while low-income fragile or conflict-affected countries have consistently failed to achieve a single Millennium Development Goal, these reports focus primarily on the developmental consequence of conflict and fragility. The reports are complementary in seeking a new framework for development programming in situations of fragility and conflict based on concepts of legitimate and responsive institutions, inclusive political processes and resilient state–society relations. Meanwhile, the International Dialogue on Peacebuilding and Statebuilding (composed of 36 donor as well as recipient countries and multilateral organizations) held its Fourth High Level Forum on Aid Effectiveness in Busan in November 2011 and adopted the 'New Deal for Engagement in Fragile States.' The New Deal involves five peacebuilding and statebuilding goals (legitimate politics, security, justice, economic foundations, and revenues and services) as a guide to national and international efforts in conflict-affected and fragile states. The Dialogue itself is a concerted effort to overcome the tensions between the peacebuilding and statebuilding agendas.

However, aligning the two agendas in conflict-affected and fragile states becomes particularly challenging in light of transnational threats such as terrorism, organized crime and piracy that continue to preoccupy governments and national security institutions. A recent example serves to illustrate this point. The 2011 World Development Report (World Bank 2011: 44) describes the West Africa Coast Initiative (WACI) which is a joint program by the UNODC, UN Office for West Africa, UN Department of Political Affairs, and Interpol to combat illicit drug trafficking, organized crime, and drug abuse in the region. WACI 'comprises a comprehensive set of activities targeting capacity-building, at both national and regional level, in the areas of law enforcement, forensics, border management, anti-money-laundering, and the strengthening of criminal justice institutions, contributing to peacebuilding initiatives and security sector reforms.' WACI is a security-oriented initiative. Whether it will also contribute to peacebuilding depends greatly on how it is designed and implemented and the extent to which it promotes human security. But it can also undermine peacebuilding if it creates another level of security institutions divorced from local priorities and needs. The needs in conflict-affected and fragile states are immense. Initiatives like WACI can be a mixed blessing—securing peacebuilding or securitizing peacebuilding.

Whither peacebuilding?

The preceding analysis traced the evolution of international peacebuilding over the last two decades to demonstrate the multiple and conflicting agendas that are currently subsumed under the term peacebuilding. There is broad agreement that peacebuilding resides at the nexus of development and security. However, the interpretation of whose security is at stake and how security and development should intersect varies greatly.

In the 1990s, peacebuilding had a distinctly liberal orientation, but it was largely people-centered and prioritized longer-term development based on a country's unique circumstances. While scholars and practitioners challenged liberal internationalism and the type of peace being promoted around the world, the focus remained squarely on the conflict-affected countries. What happened after 9/11 was the resurgence of the state-centric security agenda, which has appropriated peacebuilding as part of an external security agenda. Although different actors and institutions continue to use the terms peacebuilding, nation-building, stabilization and reconstruction, there are significant differences of emphasis in terms of their basic principles, short-term and long-term strategies and ultimate goals.

At the moment, there are two parallel tracks of peacebuilding. On the one hand, the United Nations, regional organizations and various humanitarian and development actors are actively engaged in multi-dimensional peace operations in a range of countries that are of relatively minor geo-strategic or economic interest for powerful international actors. On the other hand, in other places, most prominently Afghanistan and Iraq, peacebuilding has been instrumentalized to serve a larger security agenda. The tensions between the two tracks play themselves out at different fora where multilateral humanitarian impulses confront national security priorities. However, just as the end of the Cold War and 9/11 created entirely new environments for peacebuilding, the Arab Spring has unleashed new dynamics that will severely test the promises and premises of international peacebuilding as it has evolved in the last twenty years. It remains to be seen whether we will witness the re-invigoration or the gradual demise of international peacebuilding as the link between security and development.

Notes

1 The terms peacebuilding, reconstruction, nation-building, stabilization, statebuilding have, unfortunately, come to be used interchangeably. There are significant conceptual, political and practical differences between them which are only partially covered in this chapter.
2 International peacebuilding has never been a monolithic enterprise. This section exaggerates the consensus within 'mainstream' peacebuilding in order to contrast it with 'securitized' peacebuilding.

References

Annan, K. (2005) *In Larger Freedom: Towards Security, Development and Human Rights For All*, New York: United Nations.
Baranyi, S. (ed.) (2008) *The Paradoxes of Peacebuilding Post-9/11*, Vancouver: UBC Press.
Barnett, M., Kim, H., O'Donnell, M., and Sitea, L. (2007) 'Peacebuilding: What Is in a Name?' *Global Governance: A Review of Multilateralism and International Organizations*, 13(1): 35–58.
Buzan, B. and Hansen, L. (eds) (2007) 'Volume Four: Debating Security and Strategy and the Impact of 9-11', *International Security*, Thousand Oaks: Sage Publications.
Buzan, B., Waever, O., and de Wilde, J. (1998) *Security: A New Framework for Analysis*, Boulder: Lynne Rienner.
Call, C.T. and Cousens, E.M. (2008) 'Ending Wars and Building Peace in War-torn Societies', *International Studies*, 9(1): 1–21.
Cutillo, A. (2006) 'International Assistance to Countries Emerging from Conflict: A Review of Fifteen Years of Interventions and the Future of Peacebuilding', IPA Policy Paper, New York: International Peace Academy, Online. <http://www.ipacademy.org>. Last accessed 23 June 2012.
Dobbins, J., McGinn, J.G., Crane, K., Jones, S.G., Lal, R., Rathmell, A., Swanger, R.M., and Timilsina, A.R. (2003) *America's Role in Nation-Building: From Germany to Iraq*, Santa Monica: RAND.
Duffield, M. (2001) *Global Governance and the New Wars: The Merging of Development and Security*, New York: Zed Books.
Gheciu, A. (2011) 'Divided Partners: The challenges of NATO–NGO Cooperation in Peacebuilding Operations', *Global Governance*, 17(1): 95–113.
Newman, E. (2010) 'Peacebuilding as Security in 'Failing' and Conflict-Prone States', *Journal of Intervention and Statebuilding*, 4(3): 305–322.
OECD (1997) *DAC Guidelines on Conflict, Peace and Development Co-operation*, Paris: OECD.
OECD (2001) *DAC Guidelines: Helping Prevent Violent Conflict*, Paris: OECD.
OECD (2007) 'Whole of Government Approaches in Fragile States', Online. <www.oecd.dac/dataoecd/15/24/37826256pdf>. Last accessed 23 June 2012.
Paris, R. (2004) *At War's End: Building Peace after Civil Conflict*, Cambridge: Cambridge University Press.
Rubin, B. (2008) 'The Politics of Security in Postconflict Statebuilding' in C.T. Call and V. Wyeth, *Building States to Build Peace*, Boulder: Lynne Rienner.
Tschirgi, N. (2003) 'Peacebuilding as the Link between Security and Development: Is the Window of Opportunity Closing?' IPA Policy Paper, New York: International Peace Academy.
Tschirgi, N. (2004) 'Post-Conflict Peacebuilding Revisited: Achievements, Limitations, Challenges' IPA Policy Paper, New York: International Peace Academy.
United Kingdom (2008) *National Security Strategy*, Norwich: Her Majesty's Stationery Office.
United Nations (1992) *An Agenda for Peace: Preventive Diplomacy, Peacemaking and Peace-keeping (Report of the Secretary-General pursuant to the statement adopted by the Summit Meeting of the Security Council on 31 January 1992)*, A/47/277-S/2411, New York: United Nations.
United Nations (1994) *An Agenda for Development: Report of the Secretary-General*, A/48/935, New York: United Nations.
United Nations (1995) *Supplement to An Agenda for Peace: Position Paper of the Secretary-General on the Occasion of the Fiftieth Anniversary of the United Nations*, A/50/60-S/1995/1, New York: United Nations.
United Nations (2000) *Report of the Panel on United Nations Peace Operations (Brahimi Report)*, A/55/305-S/2000/809, New York: United Nations.
United Nations (2004) *A More Secure World: Our Shared Responsibility. Report of the High-level Panel on Threats, Challenges and Change*, New York: United Nations.
United States (2008) *National Defense Strategy*, Washington DC: Department of Defense.
United States Army-Marine Corps (2007) *US Army-Marine Corps Counterinsurgency Field Manual*, Chicago: University of Chicago Press.

Williams, M.J. (2011) '(Un)Sustainable Peacebuilding: NATO's Suitability for Postconflict Reconstruction in Multiactor Environments', *Global Governance,* 17(1): 115–134.

World Bank (2009) 'Securing Development' by World Bank President Robert B. Zoellick, a presentation at USIP, Online. <http://siteresources.worldbank.org/NEWS/Resources/ RBZUSIPSpeech010809.pdf>. Last accessed 21 January 2012.

World Bank (2011) *World Bank Development Report 2011: Conflict, Security and Development,* Washington, D.C.: World Bank.

16

SECURITY SECTOR REFORM

Mark Sedra

Introduction

In 2003, Afghan President Hamid Karzai described the Western-backed security sector reform (SSR) process in his country as the 'basic pre-requisite to [sic] recreating the nation that today's parents hope to leave to future generations' (quoted in Hodes & Sedra 2007: 51). Such bold statements by both recipient political leaders and donor officials are now routine in states undergoing war-to-peace transitions. It reflects a consensus in the international development and security policy over the importance of SSR 'for the consolidation of peace and security, in preventing countries from relapsing into conflict and in laying the foundations for sustainable peace' (UNSG 2008: 3). But it also conceals the rather poor record of achievement of this model of security assistance, which has given rise to a growing chorus of critiques calling for fundamental changes in how it is conceived and applied.

The fundamental dilemma facing SSR can be summarized as a 'conceptual–contextual divide' (Chanaa 2002). The core principles and desired outcomes of SSR, despite being widely embraced in the Western donor community, have rarely been applied effectively in practice. In fact, most SSR programs conform to the SSR model in name only, instead practicing the type of 'train-and-equip' security assistance that the developmentalized SSR model was supposed to render obsolete.

Three dominant schools of thought have emerged to explain the failings of the SSR model and chart a future path for it: the monopoly, 'good enough' and hybrid schools. The key theme or variable that unites and divides the schools is their positions on the role of the state. The monopoly school, perhaps the dominant of the three in the policy community, adopts a state-centric, technocratic approach to reform that prioritizes the installation of Western-oriented state structures. Advocates of the monopoly school hold that the key to advancing stabilization and peacebuilding in transition states is more robust institutions, a thicker state capable of assuring a monopoly of force. The reason for the failings of the SSR model, according to this school, has been the insufficiency of donor resources, coordination, political capital and time.

The 'good enough' school also sees the end-point of the SSR process as a state, but not necessarily an idealized Western state with a full monopoly of force, but rather a mediated 'good enough state' that meets the minimum criteria of Weberian statehood. It eschews long-term strategic planning, opting instead for incremental, iterative programming that favors short- and medium-term interventions as a means to build momentum for more conventional and comprehensive reform strategies. It is amenable to engaging with non-state and alternative security and justice structures, but as a temporary or transitional measure to buy time for political and security conditions to align for more statist solutions. It is a pragmatic, ad hoc approach that seeks to combine recognition of immediate on-the-ground realities, with long-term liberal aspirations to actualize at least some of the ambitious prescriptions of the orthodox SSR model.

The more radical of the three schools, the hybrid school, argues that the liberal-oriented, Weberian state is out of place in most peace- and state-building contexts. By characteristically ignoring the multiple layers of informal and non-state authority that exist on the ground, SSR interventions miss an opportunity to promote sustainable security, stability and peace. The hybrid model does not reject the state, but holds that it should work alongside rather than replace existing security, justice and governance structures that are effective and legitimate. The problem with SSR interventions for the hybrid school is not the insufficiency of donor resources being brought to bear, but its rigid state-centrism and apolitical outlook, which tends to ignore political and power dynamics. To be successful, SSR must be less normative, less state-centric and more attuned to local realities. The hybrid model advocates a more flexible and moderated form of the liberal peace capable of accommodating alternative norms and types of authority. It envisions co-governance arrangements between state and non-state authority, not as a temporary measure, but as a permanent feature.

This chapter will describe the emergence and evolution of the SSR concept in the peace- and state-building fields, emphasizing the discordance between its rapid, albeit flawed, conceptual development and its poor record of achievement. It will then outline the three major schools of thought concerning future directions for the model – the monopoly, 'good enough' and hybrid schools – concluding with some thoughts on the future of the SSR concept in peacebuilding theory and practice.

The emergence and evolution of SSR

With the end of the Cold War and the changing geopolitical climate, space opened in the international security policy arena for new thinking on security assistance. Development actors entered that space empowered by new research that identified a direct causal link between security and poverty reduction. The World Bank's seminal *Voices of the Poor* study, which surveyed over 60,000 poor women and men from 60 countries, crystallized that security-development nexus, with respondents identifying insecurity as one of the paramount obstacles to escaping poverty (Narayan & Petesch 2002). The advent of the human security paradigm, which sought to shift the object of security policy and assistance from the state to the individual, would further set the stage for the emergence of the SSR concept. Not only was the nascent SSR model human- rather than regime-centric, but also it was holistic, governance-focused and rooted to core Western liberal principles like democratic civilian control, gender equality, transparency, accountability and respect for human rights. It would become a cornerstone of the liberal peace- and state-building projects.

SSR was a reaction to the perceived excesses and inequity of Cold War-era security assistance in developing countries, which was conceived by donors in the Western and Eastern blocs as an instrument of realpolitik, not a tool to provide an enabling environment for development (Cooper & Pugh 2002). The 'hard' security assistance of the Cold War typically assumed two forms, assistance to security forces and security-related economic aid, and focused on 'transmitting military or policing skills and facilitating the sale of equipment to the security forces' (DFID 2000: 63). The manner in which the security sector of the recipient country was governed and how it treated its population was a secondary, if not irrelevant concern.

The term 'security sector reform' was coined in a 1998 speech by then UK Secretary of State for International Development Clare Short (Short 1998). It was Short, the head of a development agency, not a security institution, who would help redefine international security assistance and firmly embed the concept in the global policy lexicon. Exemplifying the perceived importance of SSR in their core mandate, DFID argued in a 2000 report that 'development expenditure in the social and economic sectors may not bear fruit unless the security sector fulfills its legitimate functions relatively efficiently and effectively' (DFID 2000: 3). The barriers separating the security, development and political spheres appeared to be breaking down. However, the SSR model's development lens would, as time passed, clash with traditional security modes of thinking.

Although the UK played an indispensable role in shepherding the SSR model onto the global stage, the OECD and the UN would be instrumental in elaborating its doctrine and affixing it to the peace- and state-building projects. The 2007 *OECD DAC Handbook on Security System Reform* stands as the core reference document in the field. It lays out the core liberal principles of SSR and some generic guidelines and lessons to actualize them. According to the handbook:

> Donors should engage in SSR with three major overarching objectives: i) the improvement of basic security and justice service delivery, ii) the establishment of an effective governance, oversight and accountability system; and iii) the development of local leadership and ownership of a reform process to review the capacity and technical needs of the security system.
>
> (OECD DAC 2007: 10)

By 2011, most major Western donor states endorsed the *OECD DAC Handbook* in whole or in part, and offered, as an outgrowth from it, their own specific SSR policies. Significant variances did exist in SSR approaches among donors, due to differing legal and security traditions as well as capacities and interests, but the core SSR principles enshrined in the handbook were widely endorsed.

Whereas previous forms of security assistance were delivered in silos or compartments, focusing on 'hard' or coercive security institutions, like the army, police and intelligence services, SSR views the sector as an integrated, holistic system that encompasses related civilian structures and capacities like judicial bodies, oversight structures and civil society organizations. More specifically, the security sector can be defined as encompassing all bodies authorized to use force, such as the armed forces and police; intelligence agencies and security services; civil management and oversight bodies, including line security ministries, legislative committees and national security advisory bodies; judicial and public security structures such as the judiciary, corrections systems, and human rights commissions; non-statutory security bodies comprising private security companies and militia groupings; and civil society actors, most notably NGOs and the media (UK Government 2003: 3).

According to the logic of SSR, institution-specific assistance will deliver meager results if not coordinated with reform activities across the security and justice architecture. For instance, even the best-trained police would be hard-pressed to perform their jobs effectively in the absence of functional courts and prison systems. Of course, delivering donor aid and support across such a wide spectrum of fields and functions requires a level and depth of expertise that no single donor agency can offer, necessitating joined-up or whole-of-government strategies. It would become clear to donors over time that implementing SSR demanded a rather fundamental shift. As Lilly et al. state, 'security sector reform implies in some respects as many changes in donor practice in terms of improvements in coherence and co-ordination as it does in aid recipient countries' (Lilly et al. 2002: 1).

While the *OECD DAC Handbook* and other core policy documents in the SSR canon pay homage to the underlying political demands of social engineering security systems of developing and conflict-affected states, they still treat the project largely as a technical exercise, which, if endowed with the right level of resources, leadership and coordination can achieve transformative change. This premise was reinforced by some of the formative early experiences with SSR implementation. The SSR model cut its teeth in the post-Communist transition states of Eastern Europe and post-Apartheid South Africa. The design of the orthodox SSR framework was influenced by the lessons learned from those cases, which were positive in many respects. The positive outcomes from these experiences were, paradoxically, problematic for the development of the SSR concept because those early cases were not representative of the type of challenging environments that the SSR model would principally be deployed to confront as it matured. The states of the former Eastern Bloc and post-Apartheid South Africa featured highly favorable conditions for SSR: they had stable security environments; strong elite consensus for reform; decisive domestic leadership; and high levels of institutional and human capacity. These were contexts that already featured strong states, with some Western liberal democratic foundations. In the case of the Eastern European states, there were powerful incentives for reform of the security institutions in the form of prospects for NATO and European Union membership. Most contemporary conflict-affected states where SSR is applied feature none of these conditions. It may be possible to apply a highly formulaic, technical and apolitical strategy in contexts featuring ideal conditions for change, but where those conditions are absent, as they have been in cases like Afghanistan, the Democratic Republic of Congo and Timor-Leste, conventional SSR approaches have struggled.

The 'conceptual–contextual divide'

In her influential 2002 paper on *Security Sector Reform: Issues, Challenges and Prospects*, Jane Chanaa identified a 'conceptual–contextual divide' as one of the principal challenges facing the SSR model. The model, in her view, had not been adequately adapted to the particular challenges and conditions of dominant reform contexts. A decade later, that divide had become more of a chasm. While the core principles of the concept have been steadily mainstreamed in donor thinking on peace- and state-building, little progress has been made to develop more effective tools and strategies to apply it in practice. Lacking the means to drive the social engineering implied in the SSR model, donors have tended to revert in practice to more conventional types of security assistance. Donor programs may still be labeled SSR, couched in the rhetoric of liberal democratic governance and change, but in practice they typically comprise Cold War-era train-and-equip activities. A familiar pattern emerges in many SSR contexts: SSR programs are constructed under the façade of the orthodox SSR model, but as the complex and difficult realities of the local context, and the model's inability to adapt to them, become apparent, donors revert to their train-and-equip comfort zone. This can be understood as a 'slide toward expediency', as donors have time and time again abandoned their lofty SSR ambitions in favor of more achievable and expedient 'hard' security goals (Sedra 2006).

There is wide consensus on a number of specific dilemmas facing the SSR model, which reflect the conceptual–contextual divide. The first relates to the economic sustainability of the project. At its core, the SSR model seeks to create Weberian state structures conforming to liberal democratic principles in contexts that typically lack the necessary political traditions or resources to support them. SSR recipient states tend to be chronically weak, politically fragmented and impoverished with deep human and institutional capacity deficits. Building stable institutions in such contexts is, even if feasible on political grounds, a generational project requiring intensive and extensive donor support. Such long-term investment at the levels required is rarely forthcoming, and in the wake of the global financial crisis and the streamlining of Western government spending (including development budgets) will likely be even less so over the coming decade. The construction of unsustainable formal security structures that local governments cannot afford without massive and largely open-ended external subsidies, can have the effect of undermining peace and stability. For instance, the security sector constructed for Afghanistan with Western, principally US, funds is widely accepted to be unsustainable, with Afghanistan's 2006 Interim Poverty Reduction Strategy Paper admitting that '…the international community has imported models of security forces that impose costs Afghanistan may not be able to sustain' (IMF 2006: 27). Considering that in 2010, Afghan state security expenditures were equivalent to more than double the country's domestic revenues, the Afghan government indeed has no hope of sustaining its security institutions – even with record setting revenue increases – without massive external subsidies for the foreseeable future.[1] This situation is particularly ominous because there are numerous examples in modern Afghan history of security institutions and whole regimes collapsing in response to the withdrawal of external rents, the eruption of conflict being a characteristic result (Sedra 2009). In the Afghanistan case, as in other SSR cases, flawed reforms could do harm, undermining rather than consolidating peace.

The difficulty of encouraging local ownership is the second dilemma facing SSR. According to the OECD, 'the most critical task facing countries embarking on SSR processes is to build a nationally-owned and led vision of security' (OECD DAC 2005: 12). It has long been accepted that donor-imposed development strategies and assistance are counterproductive. As Joseph Stiglitz notes: 'Policies that are imposed from outside may be grudgingly accepted on a superficial basis, but will rarely be implemented as intended' (quoted in Donais 2009: 119). However, what constitutes local ownership and how to measure it is not always clear. A distinction can be made between regime and national level ownership, with the latter largely expressed and exercised through civil society groupings (Goodhand & Sedra 2007: 54). To meet the ownership requirement for successful SSR, donors tend to cultivate a narrow stratum of like-minded elites, often Western-educated technocrats, whose constituency in the government and wider society is precarious. This hardly meets the seemingly broad-based standard of ownership espoused by the orthodox model. As a result, 'the emerging SSR agenda has tended to reflect donor understandings and priorities, and it is no stretch to suggest that from a donor perspective, the entire SSR enterprise has been about making "their" security institutions look more like "our" security institutions' (Donais 2009: 119). In practice, donor approaches on ownership have been more about getting locals to buy into their agenda, rather than enabling them to develop locally relevant and sustainable strategies.

The third dilemma of the model relates to the donor approach to informal and non-state structures, actors and norms. SSR is rigorously state-centric and seems to assume that it is operating on a societal blank slate. The model either ignores non-state 'layers of security and justice provision' or seeks to actively dismantle them, usually under the pretext that they threaten liberal values and the state's monopoly of force (Baker & Scheye 2007: 504). This approach conflicts with the reality that non-state structures tend to enjoy higher levels of legitimacy in many reform contexts than do states. In Africa, for instance, customary courts adjudicate up to 90 percent of public disputes (Baker & Scheye 2007: 512). Customary law and non-state security structures provide extensive services to large segments of the population in scores of conflict-affected states, from the Solomon Islands, Timor-Leste and Nepal, to Afghanistan, Iraq and Mozambique (see Jackson 2011: 1809; Baker & Scheye 2007: 512).

The *OECD DAC Handbook* recognized that a 'balanced approach to supporting state and non-state [security and justice] provision' is needed with the understanding that 'programmes that are locked into either state or non-state institutions, one to the exclusion of the other, are unlikely to be effective' (OECD DAC 2007: 11). Two years later, another OECD report, this time charting the 'results and trends from the publication and dissemination' of the handbook reaffirmed that 'a holistic, governance-focused approach to democratic oversight and accountability also requires engaging… different non-state actors from civil society groups to armed non-state actors in security and justice delivery.' Despite such clear recognition, there are few examples of donors effectively engaging non-state structures (Lawrence 2012). For instance, in Haiti commercial security enterprises provide extensive security services across the country, employing more personnel than the Haitian National Police, yet domestic and international stakeholders have invested surprisingly few resources in developing cooperative arrangements and regulation frameworks for the commercial sector (Burt 2012). The SSR model continues to float above existing realities on the ground rather than engaging them head on to improve service delivery.

Issues of coordination have also presented a major dilemma to SSR implementation. The enthusiasm for comprehensive and integrated programming for peace- and statebuilding projects has not evaded the SSR community. The SSR model prioritizes the establishment of mechanisms and modalities that encourage and institutionalize coordination and cooperation among domestic and external stakeholders. In reality, however, many donors have experienced trouble coordinating their own agencies and departments in SSR missions, let alone achieving some level of strategic and programmatic coherence with donor partners and local actors. As Paul Jackson (2011: 1811–12) states:

> …SSR usually consists of a rather mixed group of ad hoc policies and initiatives that do not lead to a coordinated approach to dealing with partner countries. The lack of a comprehensive strategy effectively means that SSR in practice too frequently consists of a series of small uncoordinated programmes delivering 'traditional' development and security activities but renamed and rebadged as SSR.

The reality is that different donors bring different capacities and interests to the table in SSR missions that are not always easily reconcilable. Often the result is disjointed and even contradictory SSR programming that can result in resource wastage and even instability.

Emerging schools of thought

The challenges and setbacks experienced by donors in the application of SSR have given rise to some trenchant critiques of the model. The early critiques manifested as debate over the nomenclature of SSR. Many in the field lobbied for changes in terminology, shifting, for instance, to security sector transformation over 'reform' in order to highlight the immense scale of the concept and to shed the apparent normative baggage associated to the notion of reform. The OECD moved to replace the 'sector' designation in SSR with 'system', to emphasize the holistic, systemic and interconnected nature of the process. These debates though were about more than semantics; they reflected a growing unease about the direction of the concept, its growing scope, and its policy–practice gap. Over time more nuanced critiques would coalesce into distinct schools of thought, of which three can be defined.

Louise Andersen (2011) identifies two distinct models of SSR – the monopoly and hybrid models – that reflect growing intellectual and policy tensions in the field. They are referred to here as schools of thought, given that the hybrid model is still early in its conceptual elaboration and neither model has been fully operationalized. A third school of thought is also added called the 'good enough' school, which, on a policy spectrum, would lie between the other two. Using navigation as a metaphor to explain the positions of the schools, the monopoly school supports an acceleration in the speed with only minor deviations in course; the 'good enough' model seeks an alteration in route with roughly the same destination; while the hybrid model demands a 90-degree turn and a whole new destination. One could potentially add a fourth school to this list: the train-and-equip school. The SSR skeptics that comprise this school primarily emanate from the traditional security and defense policy communities, who support the restoration of Cold War-era train-and-equip policies, unencumbered by liberal considerations of governance, human rights or human security. The approach appeared to gain momentum after the 9/11 attacks, leading to the securitization of many SSR programs. However, this chapter will confine itself to critiques that seek to engage, reorient and rework the SSR model rather than jettison it outright.

Monopoly school

As Andersen puts it, '…the key question confronting the SSR agenda is whether a conventional state monopoly on violence is required to ensure democratic governance, rule of law and other liberal values, or whether other – hybrid or non-state – forms of security and justice provision may be more in tune with local realities and preferences and thus more legitimate and sustainable' (Andersen 2011: 5). The monopoly school is convinced of the former and believes that only through the establishment of a strong state conforming to liberal norms can sustainable peace be consolidated. For the most part, the school adheres to SSR doctrine as laid out in documents like the *OECD DAC Handbook*. It does not deny the 'conceptual–contextual divide' that has afflicted SSR, but argues that it stems from the failure of donors to adequately apply the model as designed, because of a lack of either capacity, resources or political commitment. Thus, addressing the dilemmas of SSR should not 'involve re-examining the underlying assumptions of the model but designing newer technocratic solutions to problems – bigger budgets, more time, better planning and better technical knowledge of staff' (Jackson 2011: 1812). The real problem is that SSR in its purest form was never really tried.

Where the school does deviate slightly from the orthodox SSR path is in its emphasis on institutionalization as the precursor to deep liberalization. This strategy 'remains within the confines of the wider liberal template and endorses a sequential approach based on the assumption that a certain minimum of state capacity has to be in place before extensive reforms aimed at controlling or curbing the power of the state can be pursued' (Andersen 2011: 12). The end state of the monopoly school is the same as that of the orthodox SSR model, even if the sequencing to achieve it may have been recalibrated.

The onus to improve the performance of the SSR model is largely placed on the donors, who, as the school's critique goes, have to do a better job in designing SSR strategies, integrating their activities and ensuring that adequate resources are invested. A key step for donors, according to the monopoly school, is 'to include local actors in the SSR process' (Hänggi & Scherrer 2008: 497). To the monopoly school, recipient populations are the object or target of reforms, bystanders in the process. The role of donors is to ensure that 'local actors are efficiently trained and resourced to continue' the work that donors conceived and launched 'during the period of external presence' (Schnabel & Ehrhart 2006: 5).

Prioritizing institutionalization and 'the quintessential Weberian task of balancing the effectiveness and legitimacy of security forces' (Paris & Sisk 2009: 16), the monopoly model is unabashedly state-centric. It is skeptical of calls to recognize non-state authority because of the potential deleterious consequences for Western human rights norms and because it may encumber the state from consolidating its monopoly of force. It is a linear, top-down, normative approach that equates the sequential development of the state with peacebuilding. All roads lead to the state for the monopoly model.

'Good enough' school

Those in the 'good enough' school believe that 'premature and overly formulaic or prescriptive interventions…may insufficiently account for local contextual factors and yield uneven outcomes' (Colletta & Muggah 2009: 427). They still believe that SSR is the *sine qua non* of peacebuilding and state-building but that current approaches 'sometimes gloss over heterogeneous and complex ground realities' (Colletta & Muggah 2009: 427). Rather than being linear and normative in its approach like the monopoly school, the 'good enough' school is pragmatic and iterative. It eschews grand normative strategies in favor of incremental, ad hoc initiatives that build towards more comprehensive outcomes. They accept that 'operationalizing a holistic approach is essentially impossible, and probably not desirable' (Ball & van de Goor 2011: 14). While the 'good enough' school advocates scaling back the high ambitions of the SSR model and injecting it with greater flexibility, it is still fundamentally state-centric and aligned to the liberal peace.

Unlike the hybrid school, which questions the statist and liberal core of the SSR model, the 'good enough' school holds that the successful application of SSR is more a matter of timing, sequencing and scale of interventions. As Colletta and Muggah (2009: 439) argue, measures are needed 'to create space for [SSR] participants to understand and ultimately participate in conventional security promotion'. In other words, the atmosphere in the immediate aftermath of conflict is simply not ripe for conventional or orthodox SSR interventions; during that tenuous period, interim stabilization measures are needed to sustain a 'holding pattern' and 'buy time' for the political, security and economic conditions to align in favor of SSR (Colletta & Muggah 2009: 431). They could include anything from the formation of temporary security forces and the launching of community dialogue processes to neighborhood watch arrangements.

Members of this school support the empowerment of non-state security structures, but as a transitional or interim mechanism on the long and circuitous road to statehood. That state will invariably be less sophisticated and developed than those of the West, featuring rudimentary, low-tech governance structures that are nonetheless 'good enough' to meet basic Weberian and liberal standards. While advocating community-based strategies that take into account local methods and knowledge, not to mention politics and traditions, agency in the process still lies with exogenous actors although in a slightly mediated form. The 'good enough' school lowers expectations for the process and endows it with greater flexibility, but the goal and core principles do not stray far from the orthodox model. While the monopoly school may argue that the 'good enough' school is influenced by a 'bigotry of low expectations', the hybrid school would complain that it is still too state-centrist and not contextualized and grounded enough.

Hybrid school

The hybrid school holds that 'effective SSR programming…needs to be based on a realistic assessment of how existing forms of security and justice are provided at the local level rather than on a normative idea of how it ought to be provided' (Andersen 2011: 444). The crux of the school's critique of the orthodox SSR model centers on the role of the state and how non-state security and justice actors are engaged. According to Baker and Scheye (2007: 505), two of the main proponents of the hybrid school:

SSR is typically premised on two fallacies, which are the product of its state centric approach. The first fallacy is that the nature and resources of the post-conflict and fragile state are capable (or could ever be made capable in the intermediate term) of delivering the reforms proposed. The second is that the post-conflict and fragile state is in practice the main actor in security and justice.

Contrary to notions of a 'blank slate', scores of non-state norms, structures and actors – whether community, tribal, kinship, sectarian or commercial in character – that provide security and justice services exist within recipient societies. For instance, Bruce Baker identifies eleven types of police organizations other than state police commonly providing local security in Africa: informal anti-crime groups, religious police, ethnic/clan militias, political party militias, civil defense forces, informal commercial security groups, formal commercial security groups, state-approved civil guarding, local government security structures, customary policing and courts, and restorative justice committees (Baker 2007). SSR tends to ignore these real security providers despite their effectiveness and legitimacy, both of which tend to exceed that of the state. The appeal of these mechanisms to populations stems from their 'physical, linguistic and cultural accessibility; legitimacy; efficacy; timeliness of decisions; low transactional costs; support for restitution and restorative justice rather than punishment and incarceration; and degree of participation afforded to disputants' (Baker & Scheye 2007: 512). Conversely, state structures in the aftermath of conflict tend to be weak and ineffective at best, and corrupt and predatory at worst.

One of the underlying assumptions of both the monopoly and 'good enough' schools is that the state is the only actor capable of building peace and addressing conditions of insecurity and instability in an effective, legitimate and equitable fashion. Not only are non-state structures capable of playing this role, but also they often emerge as a reaction to the state's inability to do so.

The hybrid school does not wholly reject the state, but nor does it see it as the irreducible culmination of political change and development. Rather it envisions the creation of co-governance arrangements between state and non-state actors with the ultimate goal of improving security and justice delivery to individuals and communities (Lawrence 2012). In a sense the hybrid school brings SSR back to its human security roots. While conventional SSR approaches speak of people-centered approaches only to settle for the expansion of state coercive capacity, the hybrid model begins and ends with human security.

It is important to remain cognizant of the fact that since 'we are dealing with a large range of agencies, non-state security and justice is far from being an homogenous group that can be readily demonised or romanticised' (Baker & Scheye 2007: 513). It is no panacea for insecurity, instability and societal division and faces a number of distinct problems around issues like human rights, accountability, minority discrimination, and corruption. Indeed, 'the type of security provided by localized, informal security systems is often based on discriminatory practices that favour armed groups, local elites and patriarchal systems of rule' (Andersen 2011: 15). These problems though are not exclusive to the non-state sphere, but are common facets of post-conflict and developmental states. One could in fact argue that by virtue of their place within local communities, non-state bodies 'may be more amenable to the preservation of human rights and the delivery of an accountable service, for they more accurately reflect local beliefs and needs and are regarded by local people to be more legitimate'(Baker & Scheye 2007: 517). Moreover, the approaches supported by the monopoly and 'good enough' schools similarly have the potential to inadvertently produce illiberal outcomes, in those cases through the creation of an overbearing or predatory state.

There are a number of myths surrounding non-state structures that the hybrid school seeks to debunk. One surrounds the capacity of non-state actors to reform. There is an assumption that traditional non-state actors, norms and structures by virtue of their embedded cultural and historical role in communities are static and unchanging. Quite to the contrary, they are constantly evolving and adapting in response to shifting cultural, political and historical dynamics. We have seen in places like Afghanistan that non-state traditional actors have been able to collaborate with the state, whether it is in the form of the public recording of community *shura* (local council) decisions or the employment of tribal self-defense militias to backstop formal security forces. There is ample room for co-governance and complementarity between the state and non-state; the latter is hardly incapable of reform. Another dominant myth is that these structures are irrevocably hostile to the state and innately view it as a competitor. In reality, it is difficult 'to distinguish sharply between state and non-state justice and security systems' in many conflict-affected states (Baker & Scheye 2007: 513). They invariably 'inter-penetrate, mingle, and merge' (Baker & Scheye 2007: 514). It is not uncommon to see leaders of non-state bodies hold official positions within the state or at least influence it. Governance in many post-conflict societies can be conceived as a continuum where there is no neat line demarcating state and non-state.

One particular role that the state can play in societies where there are complex, multi-layered security, justice and governance structures, is as an accountability body 'to monitor, license, and regulate the activities of non-state service providers' (Baker & Scheye 2007: 519). Rather than strengthening the administrative and coercive power of the state directly through conventional state-building practices, donors can 'extend the scope of state control into areas where its influence is limited by means of negotiating relations of sovereignty with existing non-state providers of security' (Albrecht et al. 2010: 82). By supporting hybrid, co-governance arrangements, donors can indirectly foster an alternative type of monopoly of force, one based on a network of partnerships and compacts between state and society rather than on the hegemony of a central state.

The hybrid school draws on a number of recent problematic SSR cases. A 2011 RAND Corporation study reflecting on the legacy of the US intervention in Afghanistan candidly concluded:

> The case of Afghanistan ... shows that Western models for forces and ministries may not work in countries with very different societies, requirements, and resources. The ability to understand this fact and to derive reasonable plans for developing and fielding host-nation forces that take the unique context of the country into account will be a critical capability.
>
> (Kelly et al. 2011: 20)

As the RAND Corporation report recognized, blindly importing alien Western institutions and norms into transition states without taking into account the local context, is a fraught and futile exercise with few success stories to draw upon. It is also costly. One can calculate a 'double cost' in a state-centric approach, the cost of both dismantling non-state structures and erecting new state bodies to replace them (Lawrence 2012). The hybrid school seeks to unshackle SSR from this normative and state-centric bias, to focus on issues of people-centered service delivery.

Conclusions

SSR is a concept in transition, if not in crisis (Sedra 2007). Its high, some say unrealistic ambitions, have rarely been translated into positive change on the ground in conflict-affected environments. The model's poor record has caused many analysts to 'raise questions about how far SSR is actually possible in the real world' (Jackson 2011: 1805). Despite more than a decade of case study experience and 'notwithstanding the considerable enthusiasm for such activities, there is thin evidence that DDR or SSR yield effective outcomes during (or after) the transition from war to peace' (Colletta & Muggah 2009: 446). The model is based on an increasingly contested premise, that liberal norms and Weberian statehood are 'universally achievable' or even 'desirable' in post-conflict transition countries (Andersen 2011: 14). Even if the orthodox SSR model were technically feasible, it may not be a politically possible context.

The uncomfortable reality for many security sector reformers is that recipient actors often don't want what donors are selling. In a 2011 report for the OECD, Ball and van de Goor note that consultations with recipient governments in a range of countries undergoing internationally-supported SSR projects strikingly revealed that 'despite the rhetoric…governments in Guinea-Bissau, Nepal and Timor Leste are clearly not interested in "SSR", either as an analytic tool or an operational concept' (Ball & van de Goor 2011: 24). The same could likely be said of many other recipient governments that have been treated as passive actors in international experiments with social engineering. They may pay lip-service to the concept under donor duress, but have little interest in investing scarce political capital and human resources in its implementation.

The schools of thought detailed in this chapter offer different diagnoses and remedies for the problems facing SSR. All three see SSR as a key facet of peacebuilding and even the actualization of a liberal peace, although to very different degrees. According to the monopoly school the problem is that orthodox SSR has never really been tried. To members of the 'good enough' school, immediate post-conflict environments are simply not ripe for SSR, whether because of instability, insecurity or political divisions. By adopting more pragmatic, 'bottom-up' and 'area-based approaches to security promotion' in the short term, they can 'create space for participants to understand and ultimately participate in conventional security promotion' over the long term (Colletta & Muggah 2009: 446). The hybrid school sees the orthodox SSR model as too state-centric, normative, apolitical and acontextual. Instead of seeking to impose formal state structures and liberal principles in environments of fragmented authority, the process should 'work with multiple authorities in order to maximize their strengths and minimize their weaknesses' (Baker 2007: 217).

In many ways the future of SSR comes down to two fundamental issues: the role of the state and the capacity of Western donors to actualize transformative change in line with the liberal peace. Is the state the sole actor capable of providing stability, security and good governance, or can hybrid arrangements, engaging alternative norms and non-state governance structures, better deliver peace and security to local populations? This is an open and controversial question. As Jackson (2011: 1818) states, 'critics of the liberal peace approach, and by implication the orthodox approach to SSR, concede that what is really required is a rebalancing of external regulation and internal voice that could lead to an effective state that is locally accountable.' There is, however, heavy division among critics on what role non-state structures can and should play in this rebalancing.

What has become less controversial in recent years is the perspective that Western donors have limited capacity to transform nation-states and re-make them in the liberal, Western image. The growing skepticism of the Western peace- and state-building projects is no longer confined to the academic community, but has gained momentum in mainstream policy circles, limiting enthusiasm in Western capitals for protracted overseas engagements. Whether as a result of the difficult experiences in Afghanistan and Iraq, declining US global leadership or the international financial crisis, the appetite for massive external interventions is lessening. Without the political will for long-term state-building projects, the almost neo-colonial orthodox SSR model will appear even less viable. As Michael Ignatieff has observed about today's Western state-builders: 'no imperialists have ever been so impatient for quick results' (2003: 115). That Western impatience and cost and risk aversion appears set to increase in this era of fiscal austerity and shifting global power. But, if you support the hybrid school, that may be a good thing, as donors look for less costly, locally-owned and more sustainable outcomes.

Note

1 Figures taken from the website of the General Budget Directorate of the Afghan Ministry of Finance. Access at: http://www.budgetmof.gov.af/ [accessed on 17 June 2010].

References

Albrecht, P., Stepputat, F. and Andersen, L. (2010) 'Security Sector Reform. The European Way', in M. Sedra (ed.) *The Future of Security Sector Reform*, Waterloo: Centre for Governance Innovation.

Andersen, L. (2011) *Security Sector Reform and the Dilemmas of Liberal Peacebuilding*, DIIS Working Paper 2011: 31, Copenhagen: DIIS.

Baker, B. (2007) 'Nonstate Providers of Everyday Security in Fragile African States,' in L. Anderson, B. Møller and F. Stepputat (eds) *Fragile States and Insecure People? Violence, Security, and Statehood in the Twenty-First Century*, New York: Palgrave Macmillan: 123–147.

Baker, B. and Scheye, E. (2007) 'Multi-layered justice and security delivery in post-conflict and fragile states', *Conflict, Security & Development* 7(4): 503–528.

Ball, N. and van de Goor, L. (2011) *The challenges of undertaking effective security and justice work*, Paris: Organisation for Economic Cooperation and Development.

Burt, G. (2012) *From Private Security to Public Good: Regulating the Private Security Industry in Haiti*, CIGI SSR Issue Paper No. 9, Waterloo, ON: Centre for International Governance Innovation.

Chanaa, J. (2002) *Security Sector Reform: Issues, challenges and prospects*, Adelphi Paper 344, Oxford: International Institute for Strategic Studies.

Colletta, N. and Muggah, R. (2009) 'Context matters: interim stabilization and second generation approaches to security promotion', *Conflict, Security & Development*, 9(4): 425–453.

Cooper, N. and Pugh, M. (2002) *Security-sector transformation in post-conflict societies*, Conflict Security and Development Group Working Papers, London: King's College.

DFID (2000) *Security Sector Reform and the Management of Military Expenditure: High Risks for Donors, High Returns for Development,* London: United Kingdom Department for International Development.

Donais, T. (2009) 'Inclusion or Exclusion? Local Ownership and Security Sector Reform', *Studies in Social Science,* 3(1): 117–131.

Goodhand, J. and Sedra, M. (2007) 'Bribes or bargains? Peace conditionalities and "post-conflict" reconstruction in Afghanistan', *International Peacekeeping,* 14(1): 41–61.

Hänggi, H. and Scherrer, V. (2008) 'Towards an Integrated Security Sector Reform Approach in UN Peace Operations', *International Peacekeeping,* 15(4): 486–500.

Hodes, C. and M. Sedra (2007) *The Search for Security in Post-Taliban Afghanistan,* IISS Adelphi Papers, No. 391, London: Routledge.

Ignatieff, M. (2003) *Empire Lite: Nation-Building in Bosnia, Kosovo and Afghanistan,* London: Vintage.

IMF (2006) *Islamic Republic of Afghanistan: Interim Poverty Reduction Strategy Paper – Summary Report,* IMF Country Report No. 06/195, Washington DC: International Monetary Fund.

Jackson, P. (2011) 'Security Sector Reform and State Building', *Third World Quarterly,* 32(10), 1803–1822.

Kelly, T., Bensahel, N., and Oliker, O. (2011) *Security Force Assistance in Afghanistan: Identifying Lessons for Future Efforts,* Santa Monica: RAND Corporation.

Lawrence, M. (2012) 'Towards a Non-State Security Sector Reform Strategy', CIGI SSR Issue Paper No. 8, Waterloo, ON: Centre for International Governance Innovation.

Lilly, D., Luckham, R. and von Tangen Page, M. (2002) *A Goal Oriented Approach to Governance and Security Sector Reform,* London: International Alert.

Narayan, D. and Petesch, P. (2002) *Voices of the Poor From Many Lands,* Washington DC: World Bank.

OECD DAC (2005) *Security System Reform and Governance,* Paris: Organisation for Economic Cooperation and Development.

OECD DAC (2007) *Handbook on Security Sector Reform,* Paris: Organisation for Economic Cooperation and Development.

Paris, R. and Sisk, T. (2009) 'Introduction: understanding the contradictions of postwar statebuilding', in R. Paris and T. Sisk (eds) *The Dilemmas of Statebuilding: Confronting the Contradictions of Postwar Peace Operations,* New York: Routledge.

Schnabel, A. and Ehrhart, H. (2006) 'Post-conflict societies and the military: Challenges and problems of security sector reform', in A. Schnabel and H. Ehrhart (eds) *Security Sector Reform and Post-Conflict Peacebuilding,* New York: United Nations University Press.

Sedra M. (2006) 'Security Sector Reform in Afghanistan: The Slide Towards Expediency', *International Peacekeeping,* 13(1): 94–110.

Sedra, M. (2007) 'Security Sector Reform in Afghanistan and Iraq: Exposing a Concept in Crisis', *Journal of Peacebuilding and Development,* 3(2): 7–23.

Sedra, M. (2009) 'The Army, From Abdur Rahman to Karzai', in *Viewpoints Special Edition – Afghanistan, 1979–2009: In the Grip of Conflict,* Washington DC: Middle East Institute: 83–87.

Short, C. (1998) 'Security, Development and Conflict Prevention', Speech at the Royal College of Defence Studies, London, 13 May.

United Kingdom Government (2003), *Security Sector Reform Policy Brief,* London: Global Facilitation Network for SSR.

UNSG (2008) *Securing Peace and Development: The Role of the United Nations in Supporting Security Sector Reform. Report of the Secretary-General.* UN document no. A/62/659-S/2008/39. New York: United Nations.

17

DISARMAMENT, DEMOBILIZATION AND REINTEGRATION

Alpaslan Özerdem

Introduction

The focus of this chapter is the process of disarmament, demobilization and reintegration (DDR) of ex-combatants, which has been an integral part of the liberal peace responses around the world since the end of the Cold War (Kingma 2004; Leff 2008). According to the Escola de Cultura de Pau (ECP) (2009), in 2008 for example, 15 countries (Afghanistan, Angola, Burundi, Chad, Colombia, Côte d'Ivoire, Eritrea, Indonesia, Liberia, Nepal, Rwanda, Sudan, the Central African Republic, the DR Congo, and Uganda) were undertaking various DDR programmes. There were variations among them as to whether the DDR programmes were unilateral, bilateral or multilateral undertakings; or the process was part of a wider Security Sector Reform (SSR) process or not; or they were being undertaken after a complete cessation of conflict or there was a continued armed conflict; or they included the entire DDR process or just a particular phase; or they targeted armed opposition groups or distinguished between militias and paramilitary groups; or the caseload included a large number of child soldiers and female combatants; or the process was undertaken on the basis of strict eligibility criteria of disarmament or not. Any of these factors would be critical to the way DDR programmes are planned and implemented and such different typologies would all be helpful to understand the experience from the field. However, the approach in this chapter will be more at a conceptual level and the above-mentioned typologies and their applications will be referred to, if and when needed.

This chapter will present 'security' and 'development' approaches which are also referred to as minimalist and maximalist perspectives, respectively, as the two main schools of thought to draw up the main framework of its discussions on DDR (Muggah 2009). There is an important justification for this, as after more than two decades of DDR practice it is yet to be proven that the practice of DDR, especially in the way it is undertaken as part of the liberal peace agenda, is pertinent for the sustainability of peacebuilding processes. There is no conclusive research on the long-term impact of DDR programmes, but the research in Sierra Leone for example, shows that 'non-participants in DDR have reintegrated as successfully as participants' (Humphreys and Weinstein 2006: 39). Therefore, what constitutes the 'success' or 'failure' of DDR programmes becomes a key question to answer. From a security perspective, as will be explained in the next section, not taking part in future conflicts or in general, avoidance of relapsing into a conflict is considered as a success. However, the evidence indicates that it is questionable whether such an approach is capable of utilizing opportunities of DDR environments and enabling ex-combatants to become active, productive and peaceful members of their civilian communities (Shulhofer-Wohl and Sambanis 2010).

It is to address the key aspects of these two schools of thought that the chapter will first, focus on a number of key issues in the context of disarmament and demobilization with a specific reference to their impacts on the long-term reintegration prospects. The second part of the analysis will be dedicated to economic, social and political reintegration of ex-combatants in which the main focus will be the question of why contemporary DDR programmes often face major challenges in their implementation. Moreover, the analysis will underline that families and communities tend to play a much more significant role in reintegration than formal reintegration projects and programmes. Hence, this chapter makes a distinction between 'reintegration' which encapsulates the ex-combatant–community interaction in post-DDR contexts and reintegration as a phase of a DDR programme. The chapter will conclude with a set of recommendations on why social reintegration should be the priority area and why its conceptualization should incorporate the activities of economic and political reintegration.

However, before going any further it is important to remember that even in relatively small caseloads there tend to be large variations based on gender, age, disability, ethnicity, military ranking, education and vocational skills (DPKO 2010). In other words, ex-combatants are likely to have a wide range of needs, capacities and expectations, depending on these characteristics. Based on these demographic, social and cultural variations among ex-combatants, the opportunities and challenges that they might experience in the context of formal demobilization and reintegration programmes would also be different. The duration of service, combatants' particular roles, and tactics in combat are also necessary to bear in mind. In other words, the way that the conflict was fought and specific roles and experiences of the individual combatant have serious implications for their reintegration (Blattman and Annan 2008; Jennings 2009; Özerdem and Podder 2011).

Two schools of thought for DDR: Security and development

The United Nations Integrated Disarmament, Demobilization and Reintegration Standards (IDDRS) (2006) defines disarmament as the collection, control and disposal of small arms and light weapons and the development of responsible arms management programmes in a post-conflict context. Meanwhile, demobilization is defined as a planned process by which the armed force of the government and/or opposition or factional forces either downsize or completely disband. Having been demobilized and transported to their community of choice, the ex-combatants and their families would need to establish themselves in a civilian environment. Reinsertion assistance, which is intended to ameliorate the process, often includes post-discharge orientation, food assistance, health and educational support and a cash allowance. In many DDR programmes, reinsertion is undertaken as part of the demobilization phase, though in some cases it is a separate phase between demobilization and reintegration. Finally, reintegration is the process whereby ex-combatants and their families are integrated into the social, economic and political life of civilian communities.

The argument of why ex-combatants would need assistance and what might happen if they do not receive such a response is encapsulated by Collier's security risk perspective in which ex-combatants are seen as a security risk at both a micro and macro level (Collier 1994). According to the micro- and macro-insecurity framework, fear of personal violence and theft, namely micro-insecurity, may actually increase in the aftermath of an armed conflict for two basic reasons: first, the lack of an income source increases ex-combatants' propensity to commit crimes; and second, ex-combatants tend to be unskilled, except in the use of weapons, which awards them a comparative advantage in criminal activities. The macro-insecurity aspect on the other hand, argues that demobilization can increase macro-insecurity because ex-combatants can return to arms if their grievances and frustration continue to be neglected, causing insecurity at national, or even regional and global levels (Fitz-Gerald and Mason 2005). For example, Pouligny (2004: 15) considers the hasty disbanding of the Iraqi Army immediately after the 2003 invasion of the country by the US and its allies as one of the main reasons for 'the rapid proliferation of new militias and armed groups based on religious, ethnic and tribal lines'. Likewise, in West Africa some demobilized ex-combatants from Sierra Leone were re-recruited by armed groups in Liberia, while in the Côte d'Ivoire conflict there were ex-combatants from both Liberia and Sierra Leone (Özerdem 2008).

Meanwhile, the second school of thought on the relationship between DDR and peacebuilding can be coined as the development perspective (Berdal 1996). To explain this relationship Nübler (1997) utilizes the human resources approach in which ex-combatants are considered as a war-affected group with the potential to contribute to the general development in their community and country as a whole. Given that demobilized ex-combatants can sometimes form over 10 per cent of the workforce, their entry into productive activities can certainly contribute to economic development (Colletta et al. 1996). In addition to their skills and capacities, ex-combatants can also play a dynamic role in the development of new economic activities and employment opportunities. In Eritrea and Ethiopia for example, ex-combatants were relatively better educated than the general population (Ayalew and Dercon 2000).

Disarmament

As recommended in the Brahimi Report (2000) on the reform of UN peacekeeping operations, disarmament programmes are considered to be the first phase of an operation aimed at facilitating the rapid disassembly of fighting factions and reducing the likelihood of a resumption of conflicts. According to the IDDRS (2006), disarmament consists of four main phases: information collection and operational planning; weapons collection; stockpile management; and destruction. Experience strongly indicates that disarmament in war-to-peace transition situations seldom ensures a total collection and disposal of small arms and light weapons (SALW) and in fact, what is collected is often considered as the tip of the iceberg of the actual availability of SALW. In Afghanistan, the DDR process between 2003 and 2006 managed to collect only over 30,000 SALW and over 8,000 heavy weapons (Özerdem 2008). It is also important to remember that because of the conflict-affected countries' porous borders and the way such conflicts often have a strong regional dimension, a re-armament by belligerent groups would not be such a difficult task to achieve and a machete can also be a deadly weapon if the minds of people are not demilitarized. On the other hand, it is often argued that what the disarmament process signifies for the peacebuilding process in terms of the belligerents' commitment to the peace process is more important than the number of SALW collected. It is clear that disarmament is a necessary first step in establishing a secure environment, but it does not provide an automatic guarantee for a secure environment (Pugh 2000).

One of the key activities of disarmament, which tends to have a fundamental impact on all phases of the DDR process, is the establishment of individual eligibility criteria. In other words, who will be entitled to register as a combatant; what type of weapon as a minimum, would they need to hand in; and what criteria are required for proving that they really were a combatant. If the criteria for eligibility is too strict, as was the case in Sierra Leone, there may be many combatants who cannot include themselves in the process, for example, not all those involved in an armed group might have a weapon as they may have been 'wives' of combatants, messengers or cooks. On the other hand, if the eligibility criteria are lax and inadequately screened, as was the case in Liberia, many civilians may be registered as former combatants, adding an unsustainable financial burden to the process (Gleichmann et al. 2004).

In war-to-peace transitions which are initiated by negotiated settlement among a number of belligerent groups rather than cases where there is a clear 'victor', it is crucial that the disarmament is to be undertaken under the supervision of an impartial third party with full powers to inspect and investigate, and also enforce decisions. It would be particularly effective if this has been stipulated by an agreement between the belligerents and an impartial third party (Swarbrick 2007). Also, it is important to recognize the significance of weapons as a 'social norm' and 'economic value'. For example, in many conflict contexts, one of the key reasons that combatants join belligerent groups is its economic incentive through banditry, looting or regular wages. Meanwhile, as part of an armed group, particularly if this has started at a young age and lasted for a number of years, ex-combatants would be heavily relying on the social norms provided by being a member of that belligerent group and giving up the weapon would also mean giving up such social structures. It is in relation to such an identity and socio-economic transformation process that a 'social contract' perspective that addresses social, political and economic needs and aspirations of ex-combatants would be a right step forward for successful reintegration. In the formation of such a new 'social contract' between the post-conflict governance and ex-combatants, the presence of a neutral third party to facilitate the process is often critical as a means of trust and confidence building. However, this has become a thorny issue in the post-9/11 context where the international community has been intervening in conflict-affected environments such as Afghanistan and Iraq where it has itself been very much part of the conflict.

In addition to the planning factors discussed above, there are specific variables which have affected the success of disarmament efforts in Central America and Africa. These include the regional and local dynamics of the conflict, the distribution of weapons, the supply and demand for weapons, and the degree to which the 'weapons economy' is integrated into the wider economy and society (Pouligny 2004). For example, in some countries, the culture of the gun, which is often associated with masculinity, might also pose a difficult barrier to overcome; Afghanistan is illustrative of such an environment (Sedra 2002).

Demobilization

The main objective of a typical demobilization phase can be summarized as being to register, count and monitor the combatants and to prepare them for their discharge with identification documents. At the same time, it is necessary to gather the information required for their reintegration into the community (Gleichmann et al. 2004), and according to the IDDRS (2006) it is both a physical and a mental process. In addition to removing the symbols of a combatant's military life, such as their weapon, uniform and rank, demobilization activities can include a survey of combatants' needs and aspirations, medical examinations, counselling, reinsertion packages and transportation to the community of choice. Cantonment (sometimes termed assembly or quartering) might be used within demobilization if there is a considerable period of time needed before ex-combatants could return 'home' after their disarmament. In such contexts as Kosovo and Afghanistan, the demobilization phase was a matter of a few days, but in a number of African cases such as Angola, Liberia and Sierra Leone they were kept in cantonment areas for up to six months to a year (Özerdem 2008).

With or without a cantonment component, one of the most important aspects of the demobilization process is the registration and identification of each combatant. In some cases combatants may have no documentation and may not be able to read or write. Verification by comrades may then be necessary, or as is often the case, commanders provide a list of their combatants, or combatants come to the registration with a letter from their commanders. After such verification each combatant is often fingerprinted and photographed in order to produce an ex-combatant identity card that can be used in gaining access to reintegration benefits in subsequent programmes (Knight and Özerdem 2004).

In the registration of ex-combatants the following two scenarios are likely to happen, which can produce misleading information concerning the true scope of the caseload. First, in some cases combatants may not feel comfortable enough with the sustainability of the peace process, or being registered as an ex-combatant may pose a risk to their lives, for example, if they are going back to communities against whom they carried out atrocities. Consequently, there might be an under-registration of combatants. At the same time there might be false-registration by some civilians keen to be registered as ex-combatants in order to benefit from reintegration programmes. In some cases, the false-registration would result from belligerent groups' attempts to inflate the number of their combatants, thereby giving them enhanced political leverage in the peacebuilding process and so strengthening their patron–client relationship with the local population.

It should also be noted that demobilization occurs spontaneously in some post-conflict contexts, as was the case to some extent in Bosnia-Herzegovina. In the first stage of demobilization in the country, more than 400,000 ex-combatants who were largely not members of the regular army did not receive any reintegration assistance (Fitz-Gerald and Mason 2005). However, such self-demobilization is distinct from desertion and occurs when there is an environment in which combatants no longer have any formal obligation to be part of an armed group. It is sometimes the case that combatants are encouraged to desert by their commanders and comrades in order to reduce competition for the benefits of reintegration programmes. Some may even be coerced to desert, particularly female combatants and child soldiers if their presence is seen as a disadvantage for public relations purposes.

Another important component in the demobilization process is the provision of counselling in order to ensure that ex-combatants understand what benefits they can expect from the reintegration process and what their obligations are for the remaining part of the DDR process. Counselling and pre-discharge information on the challenges involved in the transition to civilian life is critically important, as it can be particularly problematic for those combatants who have been involved in warfare for a long time (Verhey 2001). For example, the Rwanda Patriotic Army (RPA) combatants were placed in 'solidarity camps' called *Ingando* where 'they received civic education and information on the government's policies'. The Rwandan government's 're-education' programme was a deliberate attempt to respond to the societal impact of the genocide, and included civilians too (Verwimp and Verpoorten 2004: 45).

The demobilization process comes to an end with the discharge of former combatants. Depending on whether cantonment is part of this process or not, the discharging of ex- combatants can be immediately after the conducting of registration and necessary surveys and checks, or when different groups are transported to their respective communities. The organization of transportation as part of the demobilization phase can be particularly important. Even if ex-combatants have the means of paying for their journey the transportation systems existing in the country may be inadequate or completely non-existent, especially if the DDR process is taking place in a very large country, as was the case in the Democratic Republic of Congo, Sudan, Mozambique or Angola. It would also be necessary to return ex-combatants to their communities in phases so that the absorption capacities of their receiving communities would not be over-pressurized. This is particularly important as receiving communities themselves are likely to be heavily affected by the conflict and trying to cope with post-conflict challenges with meagre resources.

Reintegration

The range of activities or services built into each reintegration programme differs in each case, however as Kingma (2004) notes, there exists a clear distinction between the different components of ex-combatants' reintegration: economic, political and social.

Economic reintegration

Economic reintegration is seen as a way in which 'to equip former fighters with productive skills and employment so that they can return to civilian life' (Ginifer 2003: 43) and is viewed as important for the short-, medium- and long-term objectives of the DDR process (Özerdem 2003). The economic reintegration initiatives continue to be the main approach and applications are undertaken by DDR programmes around the world. The conventional approach to economic reintegration would incorporate activities such as the provision of vocational training programmes, micro-enterprise development, labour-intensive public works, rehabilitation of agriculture, and employment opportunities through joining post-conflict security sector structures, etc.

However, the problem is that such economic reintegration programmes are often affected by a number of macro-economic factors such as structural adjustment programmes, economic reforms, economic stagnation, a narrow industrial base, labour market saturation, high inflation and high military expenditure. In other words, the demand side of employment and services from such newly created businesses and gained skills would be highly decisive in whether ex-combatants could actually end up in meaningful employment at the end of their training courses or whether their businesses could last in the medium to long term (Specker 2008). Moreover, so-called reintegration through the provision of a 3–6-month vocational training opportunity on a subject in which the ex-combatant might not have had much interest, often remains as an ideal. It is important to recognize that calling such undertakings 'reintegration' is often misleading as thousands of ex-combatants are left unemployed with no opportunities for meaningful livelihoods, as was the case in Kosovo and Afghanistan (Özerdem 2003; 2010).

Political reintegration

Political reintegration, 'the process through which the ex-combatant and his or her family become a full part of decision-making processes' (Kingma 2000: 28), forms an important component of the reintegration and peacebuilding process. Ex-combatants very often become involved with a military group because they identify with the politics of that group and oppose the politics of the government (Gomes Porto et al. 2007). Their effective political reintegration in the post-conflict environment is therefore instrumental to stability and security, as such reintegration should ensure they do not become a marginalized group and thus feel the need to return to arms. There are not many examples in DDR experiences that would incorporate specific political and social reintegration initiatives. The conventional thinking on such reintegration needs would be such that once ex-combatants are provided with opportunities of employment and livelihoods, the other two types of reintegration would happen in a more gradual way. In fact, it is also important to note that between these two types of reintegration, social reintegration gets the least attention from the DDR programmes, as political reintegration might be dealt with as part of wider negotiations and political settlements. In other words, the transformation of non-state armed groups into mainstream political parties in post-conflict contexts could be considered as a means of political reintegration, such as the cases of El Salvador (FMLN), Mindanao (MNLF), and Sudan (SPLA) (Özerdem 2008).[1]

Social reintegration

Effective social reintegration of ex-combatants is vital to the success of DDR programmes. Upon returning to their home communities, ex-combatants are faced with a dramatically changed and changing social landscape, one defined by violence and destruction, and it is in this environment that their reintegration takes place. This issue is ever more salient for ex-combatants creating homes in new communities. The need for effective social reintegration becomes increasingly apparent when one considers the fact that the identity of the ex-combatants and the community in relation to each other has undergone a transformation as a result of the conflict. Therefore, many suggest that the entire DDR process should focus on broader community development, engendering a balance between helping combatants and helping communities (Willibald 2006).

With such a conceptualization in mind, the community-located reintegration model puts an emphasis on structural aspects of the community and addressing the needs of the community in the absorption of ex-combatants. This is based on the argument that by simply focusing on the individual combatant, the challenges related to the wider social context where reintegration is taking place cannot be addressed. It is also crucial that the reintegration process recognizes and reinforces local reconciliation processes, since reintegrating ex-combatants in society can contribute to the overall strengthening of peace and to reconciliation in the long term through growing interaction among different groups and former warring factions. In other words, successful reintegration helps in building mutual confidence among former belligerent groups, thereby reducing the risk of renewed hostilities (DPKO 2010).

Community-focused programmes are a rarity in contemporary DDR responses and when undertaken they are often planned, led and financed by external actors, while communities tend to participate in a limited way which is often no more than being beneficiaries. In other words, community-centred reintegration can be described as a community-located approach which carries out such projects for communities and ex-combatants without any significant involvement by them in the process. For example, the literacy programmes for ex-combatants in Afghanistan were opened to other illiterate groups in their receiving communities, and in Sierra Leone and Liberia there were ad-hoc reconstruction initiatives of schools and health clinics for communities, which centred on the needs of communities as well as ex-combatants (Leff 2008; Maclay and Özerdem 2010). However, they were all responses from international and national actors rather than being initiatives which originated from the decision-making of communities and the mobilization of their resources and capacities, which could be defined as a community-based approach (Asiedu 2010). Therefore, it is important to make the distinction between community-located and community-based reintegration programmes.

In the social reintegration of ex-combatants, the role of the receiving family and community is imperative, and there are a number of key issues in the way that the re-connection between ex-combatants and the context that receives them could be re-established. The first issue to be borne in mind is the level of mistrust and fear that may be the case between ex-combatants and receiving communities in certain war-to-peace transition environments such was the case in Sierra Leone and Liberia. In Cambodia, many Khmer Rouge combatants were often not accepted back into society and were afraid of revenge (Verkoren 2005). The experience of armed conflict and its impacts in terms of fear, resentment or hatred would need to be addressed by building bridges between these two war-affected groups. It is therefore essential that such a mistrust dimension is effectively addressed through the encouragement of community-based reintegration programmes which would bring communities and ex-combatants together for the satisfaction of their common physical, socio-political and economic needs (Ginifer 2003; Asiedu 2010). Therefore, the key issue that should be noted here is the possibility of returning 'home' not being a completely positive and welcoming experience for ex-combatants, as conflict-affected communities are often characterized by fragmentation and polarization in which the fighter has grown apart from civilian society (Nübler 1997; Annan 2009).

It is also important to note that even though family members and communities might not have negative feelings towards returning combatants, the way economic reintegration benefits tend to target them specifically can easily cause resentment and social divisions. The preferential treatment of ex-combatants by providing quotas for their recruitment in post-conflict security apparatuses and other economic reintegration programmes is often a source of resentment among other war-affected communities such as internally displaced persons, returnees and 'stayees' (Özerdem 2010). Therefore, by putting emphasis on both combatants and receiving communities through the social reintegration approach, there is a possibility of using reintegration assistance as a bridge between these two groups.

Without any doubt there is a clear recognition of the need of employment opportunities for ex-combatants' successful reintegration, but they often fall short in the provision of meaningful and sustainable livelihoods. This is partly because in conventional DDR programmes, the way that economic reintegration projects are planned and implemented often takes place in isolation from social reintegration issues. In other words, the issues, challenges and parameters of social and economic reintegration are viewed separately from each other. In fact, rather than compartmentalizing them as separate undertakings, economic reintegration projects such as vocational training and income generation activities could be considered as a means of social reintegration.

As part of transforming their identity from a combatant to citizen, former combatants should be able to take an active role in such decision-making mechanisms, which would create significant opportunities for social cohesion and reintegration. This would vary from voting in elections to taking an active role in the representation of communities in local institutional structures and wider political activities (Maclay and Özerdem 2010).

The 'justice' challenge would be another key priority area to be addressed in order to achieve the goal of social reintegration. This would have two main dimensions, as the issue of how to deal with crimes committed by combatants during the conflict and how they would relate to the challenge of law and order in post-conflict contexts. The former is a highly controversial issue as not dealing with it can cause serious resentment in communities. The objective of bringing justice to crimes committed by ex-combatants can also result in the breakdown of the peacebuilding process (Thiedon 2007; de Greiff and Duthie 2009). The option of a universal amnesty for ex-combatants is sometimes used as a measure of reintegration and reconciliation, as was the case in Uganda, but for those who experienced atrocities it is a highly unjust measure. In terms of respecting the rule of law and order, whether ex-combatants were involved in crime would be a decisive factor for their acceptance by communities and overall social reintegration. The identity of being an ex-combatant can be rather problematic as they seem to be the first group of people to be suspected of crimes committed in a post-conflict environment. For example, ex-combatants in Liberia often make reference to 'not being a troublemaker' in order to describe their intentions of good relations with communities (Bøås and Hatløy 2008).

Conclusion

This chapter has argued that contemporary 'economic reintegration' centred DDR programmes present limited opportunities for successful reintegration and it is misleading to consider the output as 'reintegration'. This is particularly important for a 'social contract' perspective through which ex-combatants would replace the social and economic value of arms with the structures, support and opportunities of civilian life. Such a social contract perspective is likely to demand a development approach to DDR rather than contemporary security-centred prioritization.

Moreover, compared with conventional combatant-centred programmes, a community-located reintegration approach is obviously an important step forward in DDR practice. However, it could only ensure a limited contribution to the actual reintegration of ex-combatants and the ownership of such programmes by receiving communities is a key factor for their cohesion with ex-combatants. Therefore, this chapter concludes that for effective reintegration, particularly in post-conflict contexts with deep and wide societal divisions, the community-based social reintegration approach would be the most comprehensive way of addressing ex-combatants' needs and aspirations.

Moreover, this chapter presents 'social reintegration' as the ultimate goal of an ex-combatant's reintegration into society and all other undertakings in terms of economic and political reintegration would need to be part and parcel of this objective. The main recommendation here is not to perceive DDR as a combination of separate phases taking place in a linear way but to use their sequential interaction through creative and innovative undertakings. By putting emphasis on the linkages between these three phases, it would be possible to adopt a 'reintegration-first' type approach in which reintegration challenges would be identified first and disarmament and demobilization would be undertaken accordingly. Otherwise, without a social reintegration approach in planning and implementing DDR programmes, many opportunities for bridging between former combatants and their receiving communities would be missed out and hence formal DDR programmes are likely to fall short in achieving the goal of 'reintegration'.

Note

1 FMNL: Farabundo Martí National Liberation Front. MNLF: Moro National Liberation Front. SPLA: Sudan People's Liberation Army

References

Annan, J. (2009) 'From "Rebel" to "Returnee": Daily Life and Reintegration for Young Soldiers in Northern Uganda', *Journal of Adolescent Research*, 24(6): 639–667.

Asiedu, V. (2010) 'Community-based Reintegration Programmes in Post-Conflict Environments: New Approach or Public Relations Gimmick? The Case of Sierra Leone'. Paper presented at PSA 2010 Conference. Edinburgh. 29 March 2010.

Ayalew, D. and Dercon, S. (2000) 'From the Gun to the Plough: the Macro- and Micro-Level Impact of Demobilisation in Ethiopia', in K. Kingma (ed.) *Demobilisation in Sub-Saharan Africa: The Development and Security Impacts*, New York: St. Martins, pp.132–171.

Berdal, M. (1996) *Disarmament and Demobilisation after Civil Wars, Adelphi Paper 303*. London: International Institute for Strategic Studies.

Blattman, C. and Annan, J. (2008) 'Child combatants in northern Uganda: Reintegration myths and realities', in R. Muggah (ed.) *Security and Post-Conflict Reconstruction: Dealing with Fighters in the Aftermath of War*. London: Routledge, pp. 103–126.

Bøås, M. and Hatløy, A. (2008) '"Getting in, getting out": militia membership and prospects for re-integration in post-war Liberia', *Journal of Modern African Studies*, 46(1): 33–55.

Brahimi, L. (2000) Report of the Panel on United Nations Peace Operations, Online. Available HTTP: <http://www.un.org/peace/reports_operations/docs/full_report.htm/> (accessed 4 July 2011).

Colletta, N., Kostner, M. and Wiederhofer, I. (1996) *Case Studies in War-to-Peace Transition: The Demobilization and Reintegration of Ex-Combatants in Ethiopia, Namibia and Uganda*. Washington DC: World Bank.

Collier, P. (1994) 'Demobilisation and Insecurity: A Study in the Economics of the Transition from War to Peace', *Journal of International Development*, 6(3): 343–351.

De Greiff, P. and Duthie, R. (eds) (2009) *Transitional Justice and Development: Making Connections*. New York: Columbia University Press.

DPKO (2010) *Second Generation Disarmament, Demobilisation and Reintegration (DDR) Practices in Peace Operations*. New York: United Nations.

Escola de Cultura de Pau (2009) *DDR 2009: Analysis of the World's Disarmament, Demobilization and Reintegration (DDR) Programs in 2009*. Online. Available HHTP: <http://escolapau.uab.cat/img/programas/desarme/ddr/ddr2009i.pdf> (accessed 20 November 2011).

Fitz-Gerald, A.M. and Mason, H. (eds) (2005) *From Combatant to Community: A Combatant's Return to Citizenship*, Shrivenham: Cranfield University.

Ginifer, J. (2003) 'Reintegration of Ex-Combatants', in M. Malan (ed.) *Sierra Leone: Building the Road to Recovery*, ISS Monograph Series 80.

Gleichmann, C., Odenwald, M., Steenken, K. and Wilkinson, A. (2004) *Disarmament, Demobilisation and Reintegration – A Practical Field and Classroom Guide*. Frankfurt: GTZ, NODEFIC, PPC, SNDC.

Gomes Porto, J., Parsons, E. and Alden, C. (2007) *From Soldiers to Citizens: The Social, Economic and Political Reintegration of UNITA Ex-Combatants*. Aldershot: Ashgate.

Humphreys, M. and Weinstein, J. (2006) *Disentangling of the Determinants of Successful Disarmament, Demobilization and Reintegration*. Online. Available HTTP: <DDR20% humphreys20%weinstein[1].pdf> (accessed 1 August 2011).

IDDRS (2006) *Integrated DDR Standards*. Online. Available HTTP: <http://www.unddr.org/index.php> (accessed 5 July 2011).

Jennings, K.M. (2009) 'The political economy of DDR in Liberia: A gendered critique', *Conflict, Security & Development*, 9(4): 475–494.

Kingma, K. (2000) 'Assessing Demobilisation: Conceptual Issues', in K. Kingma (ed.) *Demobilisation in Sub-Saharan Africa: The Developmental and Security Impacts*. Basingstoke: Macmillan Press.

Kingma, K. (2004) 'Demobilisation and Peace-Building in Southern Africa', in P. Bachelor and K. Kingma (eds) *Demilitarisation and Peace-Building in Southern Africa. Volume 1: Concepts and Processes*. Aldershot: Ashgate, pp. 133–162.

Knight, M. and Özerdem, A. (2004) 'Guns, Camps and Cash: Disarmament, Demobilisation and Reinsertion of Former Combatants in Transitions from War to Peace', *Journal of Peace Research*, 41(4): 499–516.

Leff, J. (2008) 'The Nexus between Social Capital and Reintegration of Ex-combatants: A Case for Sierra Leone', *African Journal on Conflict Resolution*, 8(1): 9–38.

Maclay, C. and Özerdem, A. (2010) '"Use" Them or "Lose" Them: Engaging Liberia's Disconnected Youth through Socio-Political Integration', *International Peacekeeping*, 17(3): 343–360.

Muggah, R. (ed.) (2009) *Security and Post-conflict Reconstruction: Dealing with Fighters in the Aftermath of War*. Abingdon: Routledge.

Nübler, I. (1997) *Human Resources Development and Utilization in Demobilization and Reintegration Programs*. Paper 7. Bonn: Bonn International Center for Conversion.

Özerdem, A. (2003) 'Vocational training of former Kosovo Liberation Army combatants: for what purpose and end?', *Conflict, Security & Development*, 3(3): 383–405.

Özerdem, A. (2008) *Post-war Recovery: Disarmament, Demobilisation and Reintegration of Former Combatant*. London: I.B. Tauris.

Özerdem, A. (2010) 'Insurgency, Militias and DDR as Part of Security Sector Reconstruction in Iraq: How Not To Do It', *Disasters*, 34 (Supp. 1) S40–S59.

Özerdem, A. and Podder, S. (eds) (2011) *Child Soldiers: From Recruitment to Reintegration*. Basingstoke: Palgrave Macmillan.

Pouligny, B. (2004) *The Politics and Anti-Politics of Contemporary "Disarmament, Demobilization & Reintegration" Programs*. Paris: Centre d'Etudes et de Recherches Internationales Sciences Po/ CNRS.

Pugh, M. (ed.) (2000) *Regeneration of War-Torn Societies*. London: Macmillan Press.

Sedra, M. (2002) *Challenging the Warlord Culture: Security Sector Reform in Post-Taliban Afghanistan*, Paper 25. Bonn: Bonn International Center for Conversion.

Shulhofer-Wohl, J. and Sambanis, N. (2010) *Disarmament, Demobilization, and Reintegration Programs: An Assessment*. Stockholm: Folke Bernadotte Academy.

Specker, L. (2008) *The R-Phase of DDR Processes: An Overview of Key Lessons Learned and Practical Experiences*. The Hague: Netherlands Institute of International Relations 'Clingendael'. Online. Available HTTP: <http://www.clingendael.nl/publications/2008/20080900_cru_report_specker.pdf> (accessed 5 June 2011).

Swarbrick, P. (2007) *Avoiding Disarmament Failure: The Critical Link in DDR – An Operational Manual for Donors, Managers, and Practitioners*, Geneva: Small Arms Survey.

Thiedon, K. (2007) 'Transitional Subjects: The Disarmament, Demobilization and Reintegration of Former Combatants in Colombia', *Transitional Justice*, 1(1): 66–90.

Verhey, B. (2001) 'Child Soldiers: Prevention, Demobilisation and Reintegration', World Bank Conflict Prevention and Reconstruction Unit. Online. Available HTTP: <http://lnweb18. worldbank.org/essd/essd.nsf/CPR/CPRNote3> (accessed 15 June 2011).

Verkoren, W. (2005) 'Bringing It All Together: A Case Study of Cambodia', in *Postconflict Development: Meeting New Challenges*, G. Junne and W. Verkoren (eds) London: Lynne Rienner pp.289–294.

Verwimp, P. and Verpoorten, M. (2004) '"What Are All the Soldiers Going to Do?" Demobilisation, Reintegration and Employment in Rwanda', *Conflict, Security & Development*, 4(1): 39–57.

Willibald, S. (2006) 'Does Money Work? Cash Transfers to Ex-Combatants in Disarmament, Demobilisation and Reintegration Processes', *Disasters*, 30(3): 316–339.

18

ZONES OF PEACE

Landon E. Hancock[1]

One of the more stable notions to come out of classical history has been the idea of sanctuary; defined as a place or a type of person which is held as inviolate and protected from harm. As described by Mitchell (2007b) this notion held through much of human history, though it was weakened somewhat with the advent of total war strategies in the early twentieth century. Despite this weakening, which included the decline of holy sites and special cities as sanctuaries, some forms of sanctuary—such as political asylum and, imperfectly, protection for clergy—did remain as viable practices (Mitchell 2007b).

Beginning in the 1980s a new sanctuary movement started in the Philippines, where it sprang from the EDSA People Power movement that toppled Ferdinand Marcos. According to Garcia (1997) the idea was inspired by a news report of a local community that had convinced leftist guerrillas to withdraw from their town and had, subsequently, prevented the military from occupying the town as well. This led directly to the creation of the first actual zone in Naga City. This zone, known as the Zone of Peace, Freedom and Neutrality (ZOPFAN), was declared in September 1988 and was followed by a number of other zones in the following two years in what is known as the first wave of Filipino ZoPs (Avruch and Jose 2007).

Following the relative success of the first wave of Filipino ZoPs, the use of territorial and communal-based forms of sanctuary both during and after civil conflicts began to grow. As Mitchell (2007b: 24) puts it, the end of the twentieth century saw 'a revival' of the use of local sanctuary in the midst of violent conflict, taking many forms; zones of peace, communities of peace, safe havens, truce corridors, days of tranquility and other forms of sanctuary were implemented, with varying levels of success, in conflicts around the world (Hancock and Iyer 2007). The basic characteristic of these sanctuaries, especially those based on communities or physical spaces, is that they are designed to produce negative peace by removing the threat and use of violence through the agreement of all warring parties. Beyond this basic characteristic, many ZoPs have expanded their activities into the realms of positive peace, seeking to create improved social relations, participatory governance and economic capacity. Thus, in many ways, zones of peace may be considered to be at the forefront of peacebuilding and conflict resolution, especially as they attempt to address both the cause and effect of violent civil strife.

This chapter will explore some of the current uses of ZoPs, indicating where they are entrenched as well as where their use may be seen as more innovative or exploratory. Following this I will examine the struggle for sanctuary and how the ZoPs movement, while born out of a desire for a cessation of violence, has extended its efforts well beyond this arena into realms of deliberative democracy, economic development and citizen peacebuilding.

Sanctuary defined: A ZoP's typology

Given the wide variety of ZoPs there can be some difficulty in creating a meaningful typology; one that is able to capture and categorize the different elements of ZoPs as they are actually used without doing damage to the wide variety of goals, methods and experiences undertaken by those seeking peace. Drawing from an earlier work (Hancock and Iyer 2007), I will use a temporal framework looking at ZoPs undertaken in the midst of violence, ZoPs undertaken as part of peacemaking and post-conflict peacebuilding and, finally, ZoPs whose use falls outside of these two main categories.

In the midst of violence

The most typically studied type of ZoP is that which has been created for the purpose of mitigating the effects of violence during a civil conflict. The two main areas where these types of zones have been created are the Philippines, where the idea originated, and Colombia which, arguably, has been home to the widest variety of zones of peace experiences, ranging from traditional locality-based zones to communities, *experiencias* (experiences) and supporting networks and NGOs. Other attempts at using zones of peace or safe havens have been made during the Bosnian civil war with the ill-fated UN safe havens (Mitchell 2007a), the *rondas campesinas* of Peru (Langdon and Rodriguez 2007), Operation Lifeline Sudan (Rigalo and Morrison 2007), Sri Lanka's Butterfly Peace Garden (Hancock and Iyer 2007) and the multiple use of Days of Tranquility for immunization and inoculation of children in the midst of civil conflicts (MacQueen et al., 2001).

In looking at these different instances of sanctuary at the local level it is important to note two primary categories: those zones or havens that are intended to last over an extended duration and those with either a limited duration or limited goals. The latter, typified by Days of Tranquility and Operation Lifeline Sudan are characterized by a limited temporal duration and often by their support by outside agencies seen as neutral to the conflict, such as the UN or UNICEF.

The former type of ZoP, typified largely by the many zones in the Philippines and Colombia, are characterized by a number of features. The first feature is that these zones are often created following some form of triggering event—usually an act of violence, that galvanizes the local population or, more infrequently, leads to outside intervention.

A second feature, which will be discussed in more detail below, is that many of the most successful zones of this type draw their strength from their grassroots orientation towards ownership and control. Most are governed by some form of participatory democracy and, in some places, have supplanted the existing local government, while in others, they exist alongside the official local government (Mitchell and Rojas 2012; Rodriguez 2012; Rojas, 2007; Valenzuela 2009).

A third feature present in many, if not most, of the grassroots-driven ZoPs is their multifaceted approach to conflict mitigation and peacebuilding. Unlike top-down oriented zones, which tend to limit themselves to ameliorating violence, grassroots-driven zones focus on a wide array of projects, beginning with mitigating violence, but also including increased democratic representation, educational initiatives, economic initiatives and social and cultural activities. As Mitchell and Rojas (2012) and Rodriguez (2012) show, these efforts can lead to tensions with existing state authorities. Additionally, Avruch and Jose (2007) note that where local efforts are welcomed, and supported, government sponsorship carries its own price; often leading to dissention as to how to use newly acquired resources.

The fourth feature I will detail here—there are many other possibilities—is the necessity for any local peace zone to negotiate 'buy-in' or acceptance of the zone's existence with relevant armed actors. This feature will also be covered in more detail below, but essentially involves continuous negotiations with local representatives of different armed actors to ensure that the neutrality of the zone is respected by both sides and gives assurances to each side that the zone will not become a base of support for the other side (Mitchell and Hancock 2007; Neumann 2010; Rojas 2007; Sanford 2003; Valenzuela 2009).

Despite the promise that ZoPs can create an environment of sanctuary for many local communities in the midst of conflict, these types of zones—while the most prolific—also tend to be the most fragile. Whenever an armed group—whether pro- or anti-government—feels that a particular zone is thwarting its ability to control a region or is providing aid to its enemies, there is little that unarmed peasants can do to stop them taking action against it. Additionally, some ZoPs in Colombia have been displaced or destroyed merely because their location sits upon a valuable route for drug trafficking or other profitable activity (Mitchell and Rojas 2012). Finally, these fragile zones almost always run up against government opposition due to their direct challenge to governmental authority. In situations like these governments may attempt to coopt the ZoPs, as they did in the Philippines and Colombia; create their own zones, as they did with the southern *rondas* in Peru; or, as was also done in Colombia, to meet the ZoPs with hostility and declare that those who reject the control of the government must, by necessity, be part of the insurgents and should be treated as enemies of the state (Mitchell and Rojas 2012). These responses can bring significant challenges to the success and even existence of peace zones and, as we will see below, are the basis for continuing tensions between local peacebuilding efforts and national-level peacemaking.

Post-conflict peacebuilding

A second area where zones of peace—or ZoP-like entities—have been used is in post-conflict environments. Initial examinations of this temporal slot parsed out the use of ZoPs as devices for peace implementation in places like Zimbabwe, Yugoslavia or Aceh (Hancock and Iyer 2007; Iyer and Mitchell 2007; Mitchell 2007a) and separately considered their use as peacebuilding devices for addressing post-conflict violence and deprivation in places like El Salvador and Northern Ireland (Chupp 2003; Hancock 2007; 2012). Both types of ZoPs are important for our examination, but recognition of their inherent differences is necessary in order to understand when and why each type of zone can be considered successful and what kinds of challenges each type of zone faces.

The use of ZoPs as a post-conflict peacebuilding device was pioneered by local activists on the southern coast of El Salvador. As detailed elsewhere by Lopez-Reyes (1997), Chupp (2003) and Hancock (2007), the Local Zone of Peace (LZP) was formed by 43 communities in 1995 in response to increasing civil violence following the repatriation of Salvadoran youth who had become gang members while living in the US (Hancock 2007: 107). In the decade and a half that the LZP has been in operation, it has expanded from its original 43 communities to encompass 146 communities engaging in a variety of social, cultural and economic activities designed to address the needs of its local communities. Current and past activities have included their inaugural *culture of peace program* (Chupp 2003) which set the methods and goals for the rest of their activities, sustainable agricultural programs, youth internet and radio programs, tattoo-removal programs for ex-gang members, disaster-relief and rebuilding programs, and economic cooperatives for generating products and moving them to market (Hancock 2007).

The growth and success of the LZP has led in a number of directions, some actualized and others as possibilities. One of the more interesting possibilities was the proposal by Timor-Leste's President, Dr José Ramos-Horta, to create 46 post-conflict peace zones as a method of peacebuilding and development for that war-ravaged country.[2] Although this project did not come to fruition it provides an ambitious blueprint for the innovative use of peace zones to rebuild war-torn societies. Other outcomes of the LZP project have been expanded partnerships between its projects and the Salvadoran government, including collaboration with the Ministry of Education to increase basic literacy for low-income adults and a proposal to expand parts of the LZP model to other regions of the country.

A second area which could be classified as a post-conflict zone of peace is the Suffolk–Lenadoon interface in Belfast, Northern Ireland. Throughout the violent upheaval known as the Troubles, a majority of the violence between Protestant Unionists and Loyalists and Catholic Nationalists and Republicans took place on the interfaces between their working class enclaves in Belfast. As a result of this violence many of the interfaces between the communities were dotted by barriers, known euphemistically as peacelines, and remain sites of intense economic deprivation as well as flashpoints for periodic violence (Boal 1996; Jarman 2005; Shirlow and Murtagh 2006). In 1996 community activists from each side of the interface began to meet and, eventually, created both the Suffolk–Lenadoon Interface Group (SLIG) and its economic arm, the Stewartstown Road Regeneration Project (SRRP). Almost alone among the many projects seeking to address either political and criminal violence or economic deprivation, SLIG and SRRP have integrated their efforts in a recognition that economic development requires good inter-community relations and that good inter-community relations cannot be built in an atmosphere of economic deprivation (Hancock 2012).

As a method of peace implementation, zones of peace themselves have only been used once: in the ill-fated attempt to create peace zones in Aceh between *Gerakan Aceh Merdeka* (GAM) and the Indonesian government (Iyer and Mitchell 2007). Elsewhere these safe zones have been discussed under the nomenclature of disarmament, demobilization and reintegration (DDR) efforts undertaken by local parties or the international community—often under the guidance of the UN (Hancock and Iyer 2007). The key elements of these ZoPs are similar to those outlined for limited duration or temporary zones undertaken in the midst of violence; namely an effort to keep the parties within the zone safe from violence and the necessity of achieving agreement from all warring parties to support this aim. One major difference between DDR zones and the temporary zones discussed above is the goal of such zones in assisting a transition from conflict to peace—rather than just providing an interlude in the fighting. In order to ensure success of this mission, DDR scholars and practitioners have come to realize that much more needs to be done than was traditionally envisaged.

DDR efforts, once limited to gathering forces together, collecting their arms, demobilizing them and, finally, providing individuals with minor resources and training, are beginning to expand their repertoire of activities. Recognition that ex-combatants suffer from physical and psychological illnesses, and that they can be stigmatized upon their return to society have led to the inclusion of other 'R's such as repatriation, resettlement, reception and, at times, reconciliation; each designed to more fully reintegrate ex-combatants into society and to give them a sense of place and a stake in the ongoing peace process. The hope behind the expansion of 'R's is that, with a stake in the process, ex-combatants will be less likely to return to fighting if, and often when, political gains either evaporate or shift against their favor (Knight and Özerdem 2004; Theidon 2009; Wessells, 2004).

One important element of this vision of DDR is the alignment that it has with elements of traditional ZoPs, whether those created during conflicts or in post-conflict environments. Like El Salvador's LZP and SLIG's efforts, newer DDR programs seek to more fully integrate former combatants through multiple avenues, including social, psychological and economic initiatives designed to ensure a positive experience for both the ex-combatant and for the society to which he or she returns. Unlike the more comprehensive post-conflict ZoPs, DDR programs still tend to focus more of their energy at the individual level, and especially on the ex-combatant, rather than on the entire community (Kingma 2002).

Preventive deployments?

As in an earlier analysis (Hancock and Iyer 2007) we continue to find uses of ZoPs which sit outside of the temporal framework or represent innovative uses of that framework. Some notable examples include Operation Lifeline Sudan, days of tranquility in the Salvadoran and Somali civil wars for health inoculations, the Butterfly Peace Garden in Sri Lanka and the protection of sacred sites and religious artifacts advocated by the Zones of Peace International Foundation (ZOPIF). More recent research and activism have proposed the use of zones of peace along the Haitian–Dominican border as a preventive measure (cf. Warfield and Jennings 2012).

In addition, a number of other initiatives have been taken that resemble ZoPs created in conflict or post-conflict zones, but instead of operating in environments which have suffered from civil violence, these zones seek to create peace or address inequality in urban areas of the United States. One of the earliest was the Harm Free Zone (HFZ) initiative, piloted by the US NGO, Critical Resistance as a method of self-policing communities and reducing reliance on what they called the 'prison industrial complex'. The goals of the HFZ are to build community autonomy, abolish the prison industrial complex and 'transform our ways of treating each other' by addressing the harms that individuals do to themselves and their communities and by redressing those harms within the community.[3] Other groups, such as Sista II Sista, in Brooklyn, New York and Spirit House in Durham, North Carolina are listed as participating in the HFZ movement as late as 2009, but as of 2011, no longer advertise doing so. This may be because the HFZ movement, like other ZoP movements, requires that both relational and structural elements be addressed; a goal that may be out of reach for many smaller communities embedded within larger societies.

The struggle for sanctuary

As we transition from description to discussion, this section will highlight some of the many challenges local communities face when attempting to either create or sustain a zone of peace. Some of these challenges are internal, while others are external, but both types must be successfully met in order for any particular zone to be successful, or to even survive in the long run.

Internal challenges

Like any other community organization, a zone of peace needs to have a high level of internal cohesion and buy-in into the mission, direction and goals of the whole. Many ZoPs, especially those created in the midst of violence, come about as a result of some triggering event that shocks the community and brings it together. The transformation from the initial activist impulse into social change requires a great deal of coordination, discussion and agreement from the larger community. In many ZoPs there is a core cadre of leadership, but decisions are rarely taken without agreement or consensus amongst the larger community. One of the main goals for any cadre is to ensure that there is sufficient buy-in from the community (or communities) that make up the zone. In locales as different as Northern Ireland and Colombia, core cadre members used participatory processes to ensure that all members of the community had the chance to discuss and approve of the creation of the ZoP as well as its goals, programs and general operation (Hancock 2012; Serna 2002).

Using a participatory process can, at times, slow decision-making, but it does have important benefits that provide internal strength to any peace community or ZoP. One of these is the sense of individual agency that involving the community in decision-making processes gives. This sense of agency is, I believe, one of the characteristics that makes grassroots-oriented zones more likely to survive, and thrive, as compared with instances where the impetus for the zone comes from outside the community. However, in order to preserve that sense of agency for the largest possible number of individuals in the zone means that the goals and programs of the zone will need to be able to accommodate the aspirations of various constituencies in the zone. This drive for agency, alongside the recognition by these communities that their problems extend far beyond physical violence perpetrated by outsiders—or themselves—is one of the main reasons that grassroots-oriented zones engage in a wide variety of peacebuilding and development-oriented activities. Many authors detail the wide variety of activities undertaken by ZoPs both in and out of conflict zones, including educational activities, job training, economic initiatives, public relations campaigns and the creation of parallel governance structures just to name a few (Avruch and Jose 2007; Neumann 2010; Rodriguez 2012; Rojas 2007; Valenzuela 2009). The Colombian peace community of San José de Apartadó, has gone so far as to create its own university in partnership with 15 local communities.[4]

The continuous work on cohesion does not, in every case, lead to success in the face of external pressure or even internal dissent. As discussed by Mitchell and Rojas (2012), Colombia's initial ZoP, the Constituent Assembly of Mogotes, fell victim to a combination of internal division and external pressures. The internal division was the resurgence of traditional conservative forces, which, alongside pressures from the Catholic Church and the Colombian government, have managed to sideline the activities of the Constituent Assembly, even if it has not been disbanded (Mitchell and Rojas 2012).

One of the more important tools that peace communities use to support their internal cohesion is their attention to creating cultures of peace. The idea of creating a 'culture of peace' in opposition to existing cultures of violence is one that has arisen in a number of different locales and can be expressed as an explicit program (cf. Chupp 2003) or merely as an aspiration to incorporate peaceful methods of conflict management into everyday life. In places like Mindanao or San José de Apartadó, the culture of peace is seen as an intentional rejection of the existing cultures which tend to glorify war and extol the virtues of vengeance (Alther 2006; Iyer 2004).

The main difficulty that ZoPs have is a general lack of resources. Most ZoPs in places like the Philippines, Colombia, El Salvador and other developing countries operate on a shoestring budget, if that, and can, at times become hostage to foreign funders or governmental restrictions. As shown by Rodriguez (2012), recent Colombian initiatives have attempted to bring peace communities under government control by dictating how they use government-disbursed funds. Additionally, community groups in Northern Ireland have traditionally had difficulties in securing funds unless they focus primarily on inter-communal relationships rather than on the economic development issues they often feel are important to addressing the underlying causes of conflict (Hancock 2012). In the Philippines the designation of several ZoPs as Special Development Areas made them eligible for governmental funding; which positively affected some zones, but proved detrimental to others when the new resources created conflicts over how they should be directed, shattering the ZoPs' hard-won internal cohesion (Avruch and Jose 2007: 61).

By contrast, the two post-conflict ZoPs, in El Salvador and Belfast, have made concerted efforts to maintain control over their own funding sources. When the LZP was declared in 1998, it also created its own US-based NGO, the Fund for Self-Sufficiency in Central America (FSSCA), located in Texas and managed by José (Chencho) Alas, a prime mover in the creation of the zone (Hancock 2007: 109). The FSSCA has expanded beyond the LZP, renaming itself Eco-viva and working on a number of projects throughout Central America. However, it maintains its relationship with the LZP, soliciting funds and overseeing visits from US-based groups seeking to assist the region. Likewise SLIG has broadened its funding base from the UK's Community

Relations Council, which oversees much of the peace-oriented funding provided to the province by the UK, EU and US. SLIG has gone directly to large foundations, such as the Atlantic Philanthropies, in order to circumvent what they see as onerous regulations and red tape imposed by governmental funding agencies (Hancock 2012).

While ZoPs face many difficulties from within and, as we will see below, from without, many of their greatest strengths are drawn from their internal cohesion. Despite the fact that this cohesion is difficult to achieve and to maintain, it provides the basis for carrying out the many programs that assist the community to create sanctuary and achieve positive peace.

External realities

The main external reality for many ZoPs is that they are located in local communities with limited resources. They often face up to groups that are far larger, both in terms of numbers and in terms of monetary wealth and coercive force, and challenge their power to exact compliance. Adhering to our temporal framework, I will first discuss the main challenge faced by ZoPs in the midst of conflict, followed by the main challenge that ZoPs in the midst of conflict share with those in peace implementation and post-conflict arenas. Given that most, if not all, ZoPs that fall outside of these two areas are created by external agents, there is little need to examine their external challenges as separate from what has been covered above.

The main external challenge faced by ZoPs in the midst of conflict is the threat and use of violence against the citizens of the zone. By declaring neutrality, rather than taking sides, ZoPs in the midst of conflict run high risks of violence by both sides—as well as by their shadow proxies—and have often suffered for this resistance. In San José de Apartadó, the number of villagers killed by armed actors since the declaration of the zone in 1997 is just under 200, including the massacre of eight people in 2005 (San José de Apartadó 2011). The kinds of resistance put forth by external actors ranges from the violence just described to pressures from the state to either participate in the creation or maintenance of local armed militias or to provide intelligence for use by state forces or insurgent groups (Hancock and Mitchell 2012). Mitchell and Rojas (2012) outline the kinds of tensions that have existed between the Colombian government and local zones of peace, especially under the 'democratic security' policies of President Uribe. Three of these policies appeared to directly target the efforts of local ZoPs to remain neutral and to work for peace in their own communities. Specifically they called for the creation of military or police posts in every municipality throughout the country; the creation of local forces of armed peasants; and for the creation of a network of 'informants' who would be paid to supply intelligence and information about suspected insurgents (Mitchell and Rojas 2012). These three 'democratic security' policies point to a key area of tension between local ZoPs and the state centered around the disputation over control, sovereignty, and the extent to which local communities may dictate to or restrict the actions of the state. The problem is that the very definition of the state—as understood since Westphalia—is that it is the only entity with a monopoly over the use of force and it should have undisputed control over this force within its borders. The existence of ZoPs in the midst of conflict as places which typically bar all armed actors from their territory sets up a situation in which police and the military—who are ostensibly responsible for public safety—are barred from performing their duties.[5] When coupled with the tendency taken by many states following the 9/11 attacks in the US to describe conflicts in more Manichean terms, what one sees in Colombia is the equation of a desire for neutrality with the suspicion that 'neutrals' are really 'sympathizers' with insurgent forces. In fact, as Mitchell and Rojas (2012) indicate, statements by government ministers—and President Uribe himself—allude to this belief, indicating that the desire for neutrality by San José de Apartadó was 'a signal' that they supported the FARC.[6]

A second challenge for many ZoPs, both during and following conflicts, is their lack of resources and, at times, the withdrawal of state resources from regions that do not support government policies. In Colombia and, to a lesser extent, Northern Ireland, agencies charged by the government with overseeing national and international resources have attempted to direct those resources towards specified goals. For Colombia, part of the goals were to ensure that peacebuilding projects remained within the scope of governmental and World Bank requirements, creating extraneous reporting requirements and forcing local peacebuilding efforts to compete with each other for limited funds. As Rodriguez (2012) notes, this level of centralized control over access to funding has resulted in programs that become more and more dislocated from the needs of the local communities that they are supposed to serve. An additional problem relating to this control over resources is the fact that peace communities which resist governmental oversight gain no access to these resources.

In Northern Ireland the issue of control of access to funding is less severe; but issues regarding the aim and scope of programs required by the Community Relations Council (CRC) remain. The most contentious of these for local groups is the CRC's main requirement that funds should be primarily for improving community relations rather than solely for development. As explored in more depth elsewhere, this requirement has created difficulties because of the inability of local communities to address what they see as structural problems which contribute to continuing violence on Belfast's interface zones (Hancock 2012). The only interface zone which appears somewhat immune to these funding requirements is SLIG, which has been able to garner significant international attention and funding with its successful mix of community relations and economic development. This success story is similar to the LZP in El Salvador, which circumvented a lack of resources from the central government by creating their own US-based NGO to solicit external grants and other types of aid (Hancock 2007).

Despite the hardness of these external realities, the fact is that many peace sanctuaries continue to be founded and many of them continue to thrive. They do this without many external resources and, often, when facing hostility from forces of the state, paramilitary forces, or even criminal gangs. While some of these forces won't hesitate to use violence, others attempt to assert their authority in a more traditional fashion, by controlling resources or access to those resources. Like their need for control over core principles, goals and content of their programs, ZoPs benefit from some level of control over their own resource streams, with those ZoPs having either no resources or their own resources generally achieving more longevity and success than those ZoPs which are dependent upon national or international sources for a majority of their resources and funding. This reality accentuates the importance of grassroots ownership and control over the ZoP and the fact that abrogating this control often leads to the failure of the ZoP, or at least to the failure of its ability to meet the needs of its constituents.

Beyond sanctuary

Overall what we have seen in examining the 'state of the art' with respect to Zones of Peace is that despite their many challenges—both internally and externally—they remain a viable method for peacebuilding and development both during and following violent conflicts. It is also apparent from many analyses of ZoPs that the most successful are those which engage in a wide variety of activities to engender positive peace as they attempt to address issues of violence and a lack of negative peace. As discussed above, part of this may stem from a need to take into account the many goals of different members or constituencies within the zone, but another part likely stems from the recognition that violence does not stem from poor relationships alone, but also results from structural violence creating a deprivation of basic needs for things beyond security. ZoPs which address issues of structural violence through peacebuilding activities have the effect of also addressing the deprivation of 'higher order' needs by providing avenues for individual and communal agency in addressing perceived problems of a lack of resources, education and control over their own destinies.

The strength of the tie between grassroots control and peacebuilding activities is such that, in comparison with temporary zones controlled from above, one would have to recommend that most, if not all, ZoP efforts should attempt to follow a bottom-up orientation towards governance and should allow themselves as broad a remit of activities as the community itself feels is necessary. This recommendation should be followed despite the very real tension that exists between local and national efforts (covered below) because the greatest strength of any ZoP appears to lie in its community and the cohesion that comes from a sense of local ownership and control. As Avruch and Jose (2007) warn us, even well-intentioned attempts by national governments to support ZoPs can undermine their survivability if, through their assistance, they undermine the cohesion that grassroots ownership brings.

The need for and strength of grassroots ownership and control is one source of the second major issue that must be addressed by many, if not all, zones of peace: the continuing tension between local control over initiatives and the desire for central control by authorities outside of the ZoP. In conflict zones this has largely to do with the desire of the ZoP to exclude armed actors, whether incumbent or insurgent, and the inevitable tension this creates between those groups who insist they are acting in the best interests of the community and the voice of the community rejecting this claim. In post-conflict ZoPs this tension has more to do with control over resources and the direction of peacebuilding and development efforts. In many places ZoPs face the unenviable choice between accepting state help and direction or proceeding with very little in the way of support, but retaining their neutrality. For most, the best path remains to 'go it alone' whenever possible and to deal with national-level agencies whenever forced to. Thus far, only a few post-conflict ZoPs have been able to harness enough resources from beyond the state to avoid this Hobson's choice; but some examples from Colombia, most notably San José de Apartadó, have shown how even conflict-ZoPs may be able to gather regional and international resources in order to sustain themselves.[7]

Despite these difficulties, one can note that the move beyond sanctuary towards positive peace and development shows the powerful potential of ZoPs to change their own environment. Zones of peace are not a panacea for peacebuilding and development. They do not equalize power with the state, or with insurgents in conflict zones, seeking to assert their authority, either military or otherwise. But they do provide a mechanism to take a principled stand against the kinds of violence, both direct and structural, that continue to deny people in conflict-troubled areas the opportunity for peace, development and the fulfillment of basic needs. Because of this, zones of peace remain a powerful tool for the oppressed, the persecuted and the forgotten in these societies.

Notes

1 With thanks to Christopher Mitchell for helpful comments.
2 For more information on the intent of Dr. Ramos-Horta's initiative see: http://www.zonesofpeace.org/zones.html.
3 For more detail see the Harm Free Zone General Framework at http://harmfreezone.org/framework.pdf.
4 This university is known as either the University of the Peasant or the University of Resistance. See http://vimeo.com/13418712 for more information.
5 This theoretical argument ignores the reality, particularly in Colombia, that much of the violence committed against the citizens of these zones is committed by forces allied to the state.
6 From the President's March 20, 2005 remarks in Cerpa.
7 Most notably, San José de Apartadó has been supported by Fellowship of Reconciliation, an interfaith peace organization, which has sent unarmed accompaniment missions to the peace community since 2002. For more on their work with the peace community, see http://www.forcolombia.org/peacecommunity. Last accessed June 27, 2012. For more on unarmed accompaniment see Coy (2011).

References

Alther, G. (2006) 'Colombian Peace Communities: The Role of NGOs in Supporting Resistance to Violence and Oppression', *Development in Practice*, 16: 278–291.

Avruch, K. and Jose, R.S. (2007) 'Peace Zones in the Philippines', in Hancock, L.E. and Mitchell, C.R. (eds) *Zones of peace*, Bloomfield, CT: Kumarian Press.

Boal, F.W. (1996) 'Integration and Division: sharing and segregating in Belfast', *Planning Practice & Research*, 11: 151–158.

Chupp, M. (2003) 'Creating a culture of peace in postwar El Salvador', in Sampson, C., Abu-Nimer, M. and Liebler, C. (eds) *Positive approaches in peacebuilding: A resource for innovators*, Washington DC: Pact Publications.

Coy, P.G. (2011) 'Nonpartisanship, interventionism and legality in accompaniment: Comparative analyses of Peace Brigades International, Christian Peacemaker Teams, and the International Solidarity Movement', *International Journal of Human Rights*, 1–19.

Garcia, E. (1997) 'Filipino Zones of Peace', *Peace Review*, 9: 221–224.

Hancock, L.E. (2007) 'El Salvador's post-conflict peace zone', in Hancock, L.E. and Mitchell, C.R. (eds) *Zones of peace*, Bloomfield, CT: Kumarian Press.

Hancock, L.E. (2012) 'Belfast's Interfaces: Zones of Conflict or Zones of Peace?' in Mitchell, C.R. and Hancock, L.E. (eds) *Local Peacebuilding and National Peace: Interaction Between Grassroots and Elite Processes*, London, New York: Continuum.

Hancock, L.E. and Iyer, P. (2007) 'The nature, structure and variety of "peace zones"', in Hancock, L.E. and Mitchell, C.R. (eds) *Zones of peace*, Bloomfield, CT: Kumarian Press.

Hancock, L.E. and Mitchell, C.R. (2012) 'Between Local and National Peace: Complimentarity or Conflict?', in Mitchell, C.R. and Hancock, L.E. (eds) *Local Peacebuilding and National Peace: Interaction Between Grassroots and Elite Processes*, London, New York: Continuum.

Iyer, P. (2004) 'Peace Zones of Mindanao, Philippines: Civil Society Efforts to end Violence', *Steps Towards Conflict Prevention*, Collaborative Learning Projects.

Iyer, P. and Mitchell, C.R. (2007) 'The Collapse of Peace Zones in Aceh', in Hancock, L.E. and Mitchell, C.R. (eds) *Zones of peace*, Bloomfield, CT: Kumarian Press.

Jarman, N. (2005) *BIP Interface Mapping Project,* Belfast: Institute for Conflict Research and the Belfast Interface Project.

Kingma, K. (2002) 'Demobilization, Reintegration and Peacebuilding in Africa', *International Peacekeeping,* 9: 181.

Knight, M. and Özerdem, A. (2004) 'Guns, Camps and Cash: Disarmament, Demobilization and Reinsertion of Former Combatants in Transitions from War to Peace', *Journal of Peace Research,* 41: 499–516.

Langdon, J. and Rodriguez, M. (2007) 'The Rondas Campesinas of Peru', in Hancock, L.E. and Mitchell, C.R. (eds) *Zones of peace,* Bloomfield, CT: Kumarian Press.

Lopez-Reyes, R. (1997) 'Establishing Salvadoran zones of peace', *Peace Review,* 9: 225.

MacQueen, G., Santa-Barbara, J., Nuefeld, V., Yusuf, S. and Horton, R. (2001) 'Health and peace: Time for a new discipline', *Lancet,* 357: 1460.

Mitchell, C.R. (2007a) 'Comparing Sanctuary in the Former Yugoslavia and the Philippines', in Hancock, L.E. and Mitchell, C.R. (eds) *Zones of peace,* Bloomfield, CT: Kumarian Press.

Mitchell, C.R. (2007b) 'The Theory and Practice of Sanctuary: From Asylia to Local Zones of Peace', in Hancock, L.E. and Mitchell, C.R. (eds) *Zones of peace,* Bloomfield, CT: Kumarian Press.

Mitchell, C.R. and Hancock, L.E. (2007) 'Local Zones of Peace and a Theory of Sanctuary', in Hancock, L.E. and Mitchell, C.R. (eds) *Zones of peace,* Bloomfield, CT: Kumarian Press.

Mitchell, C.R. and Rojas, C. (2012) 'Against the Stream: Colombian Zones of Peace under Democratic Security', in Mitchell, C.R. and Hancock, L.E. (eds) *Local Peacebuilding and National Peace: Interaction Between Grassroots and Elite Processes,* London and New York: Continuum.

Neumann, H. (2010) 'Reframing Identities and Social Practices Despite War', *Peace Review,* 22: 184–191.

Rigalo, K. and Morrison, N. (2007) 'Operation Lifeline Sudan', in Hancock, L.E. and Mitchell, C.R. (eds) *Zones of peace,* Bloomfield, CT: Kumarian Press.

Rodriguez, M. (2012) 'Colombia: From Grassroots to Elites: How some Local Peacebuilding Initiatives Became National in Spite of Themselves', in Mitchell, C.R. and Hancock, L.E. (eds) *Local Peacebuilding and National Peace: Interaction Between Grassroots and Elite Processes,* London and New York: Continuum.

Rojas, C. (2007) 'Islands in the Stream', in Hancock, L.E. and Mitchell, C.R. (eds) *Zones of peace,* Bloomfield, CT: Kumarian Press.

San José de Apartadó (2011) *Urgent Appeal: Help for Colombia, Protection for San José de Apartadó* [Online]. Peace Direct. Available: http://www.insightonconflict.org/2011/05/urgent-colombia-san-jose-de-apartado/. Last accessed June 27, 2012.

Sanford, V. (2003) 'Peacebuilding in a War Zone: The Case of Colombian Peace Communities', *International Peacekeeping,* 10: 107–118.

Serna, M.L.G. (2002) 'Mogotes Municipal Constitutent Assembly: Activating "popular sovereignty" at a local level', *Accord: Owning the Process: Public Participation in Peacemaking,* 4, 74–77.

Shirlow, P. and Murtagh, B. (2006) *Belfast: segregation, violence and the city,* London and Ann Arbor, Pluto.

Theidon, K.S. (2009) 'Reconstructing Masculinities: The Disarmament, Demobilization, and Reintegration of Former Combatants in Colombia', *Human Rights Quarterly,* 31: 1–34.

Valenzuela, P. (2009) *Neutrality in internal armed conflicts: experiences at the grassroots level in Colombia.* Originally presented as the author's thesis (doctoral), Uppsala University.

Warfield, W. and Jennings, Y.R. (2012) 'A ZoPs Approach to Conflict Prevention', in Mitchell, C.R. and Hancock, L.E. (eds) *Local Peacebuilding and National Peace: Interaction Between Grassroots and Elite Processes,* London and New York: Continuum.

Wessells, M. (2004) 'Psychosocial Issues in Reintegrating Child Soldiers', *Cornell International Law Journal,* 37: 513–525.

19

PEACEBUILDING, LAW AND HUMAN RIGHTS

Christine Bell

Introduction: Law and the politics of peacebuilding

Human rights violations are an inter-connected part of contemporary intra-state conflict. They are both structural causes of conflict and symptoms of conflict (Parvleliet 2009). Addressing such violations is therefore an integral part of any peacebuilding process. The project of post-conflict peacebuilding generally includes substantial reform of law and legal institutions. Peace settlements tend to provide for human rights in the form of bills of rights, incorporation of international instruments, reform of policing and criminal justice apparatus, together with an array of new national human rights institutions. This provision aims to stop human rights violations and ensure that in the future such abuses cannot take place. Human rights provisions aim to restrict untrammelled and abusive use of power, in particular with regard to the use of lethal force. Although neutral in coverage, human rights provisions, at their heart, touch on how power is allocated and exercised as between the protagonists to the conflict. Such provision cannot be conceived of as 'additional' to the political reforms at the heart of any peacebuilding project; but must be understood as a vital component of those reforms to be supported or resisted by parties to the conflict depending on their support for or resistance to the transition from conflict and depending on the new balance of power.

Law as subject and object of change

A complex relationship exists between using law and legal institutions to enforce human rights protection as part of a peacebuilding project and the need to rehabilitate the concept of law, legal institutions and the rule of law itself. During a conflict, law will have been used and abused as a tool of war and any faith in the notion of the rule of law or confidence in law and legal institutions will have been severely damaged (Bell, Campbell and Ní Aoláin 2004). A key part of the peacebuilding project will be to rebuild these institutions and to attempt to renew confidence in the rule of law as a potential restraint on future abuses of power. Law will not merely be the subject of change; it will be the object of change. Part of the complexity of peacebuilding in this area, therefore, is the difficultly of using law and legal institutions as tools of peacebuilding whilst simultaneously building credibility in these institutions as a peacebuilding end.

International law and the lack of 'fit'

Matters are further complicated when one considers the regulatory role of peacebuilding by international law. Two international legal regimes are of particular relevance, international human rights law and international humanitarian law. Significant controversy exists with regard to which of these regimes applies during conflict, and also to which regime applies to what peacebuilding tasks and actors post-conflict. To explain briefly, humanitarian law comprises a set of standards which applies when armed conflict has reached a certain threshold. It aims to apply basic standards of humanity to limit the worst excesses of the conflict in order to protect civilians, occupied peoples, or prisoners of war. While the project of 'humanizing' armed conflict is to some extent a strange one, the law is based on the assumption that parties to conflict may have a strong mutual self-interest in ensuring the protection of vulnerable populations rooted in the concept of reciprocity. Traditionally this body of law applied only to international armed conflict between two states. Since the 1970s, however, it has been extended by new international legal standards, judicial rulings, and customary international law deriving from the practice of states to apply in some part to conflicts arising within states.[1] This body of law claims to regulate both the practice of states and the practice of non-state combatants; however, it only applies if certain conflict thresholds are met. Human rights law, on the other hand, was created for times of peace. Nevertheless, it was also assumed that it could have some relevance to times of war. International human rights law makes provision for states to enter 'derogations' from certain of its provisions in times of war or national emergency threatening the life of the nation.[2] This provision sets up a compromise with states whereby some exceptions to human rights law are permitted but the circumstances permitting exception are limited to instances where the state faces a serious and violent threat and both threat and scope of limitations are technically susceptible to review by international bodies. The two regimes, therefore, potentially overlap with reference to the regulation of intra-state conflict and post-conflict environments but the emphasis, purpose, and scope of the protection they provide is different.

The additional difficulty with regard to how these legal regimes relate to peacebuilding is that neither regime was really designed with contemporary intra-state armed conflict in mind. Contemporary intra-state conflict typically involves states and their non-state opponents, who typically are not formally organized into armies, both often using high levels of violence, including targeting of civilians in a political context in which distinctions between civilian and combatant are difficult. Neither do the relevant legal frameworks – separately or considered as a whole – explicitly address key legal dilemmas of peacebuilding. For example, they do not provide for any balancing of demands for accountability for the worst atrocities of the conflict, with a peacebuilding task that typically revolves around trying to bring all the protagonists of conflict away from violence and into a set of new political and legal institutions. Neither do they contemplate international actors taking part in institutions of domestic governance.

The last two decades of peacebuilding practice have therefore required creative applications and interpretations of these international legal regimes so as to provide guidance to peacebuilders. However, this process of creative revision makes it difficult to view relevant international law as a straightforward tool for the regulation of peacebuilding. Rather, it too is a tool that becomes reshaped and remoulded in the process of attempting to regulate peacebuilding dilemmas.

This chapter briefly illustrates how these dynamics affect the process of peacebuilding. A wide definition of peacebuilding is adopted to include all those initiatives to build peace that arise during conflict and peace processes, are provided for in a peace settlement, and take place post-conflict.

Law and conflict

International law governing conflict within states operates to manage and limit that conflict regardless of why it is being waged and stays neutral as to the cause or ends of the conflict. It applies regardless of how just or unjust the ends of the conflict are. States tend to stay signed up to international human rights conventions and subject to their enforcement mechanisms throughout a conflict. Of course, they will often enter derogations and make provision for emergency legal regimes in which their human rights commitments are suspended. Humanitarian law, which applies to situations of conflict, only applies once a certain threshold of conflict is met. Common article 3 of the Geneva Conventions 1949 applies to armed conflict not of an international character, setting down some minimum standards for its conduct, in particular with regard to treatment of persons not involved in the conflict. Protocol II 1977 to the Geneva Conventions applies to non-international armed conflict between the armed forces of a state and 'dissident armed forces or other organized armed groups which, under responsible command, exercise such control over a part of its territory as to enable them to carry out sustained and concerted military operations and to implement [the] Protocol.' However, the conflict level must be more than that of Common article 3.

In contemporary intra-state conflict, the Common article 3 and Protocol II thresholds of conflict will only be met in some conflicts some of the time. Whereas states are sometimes surprisingly willing to admit the application of human rights law in principle, they are often unwilling to admit the application of humanitarian law. Humanitarian law applies whether the state admits the existence of a conflict or not. It might be thought that its application would be attractive to states given that in some respects, for example use of lethal force, its standards are looser than that of human rights law. However, states resist its application because it involves states admitting to a fairly high level of internal armed conflict and its application is viewed by states as admitting the effectiveness of non-state armed actors, even though the legal standards themselves outline that no status is conferred on such actors by admission that they apply. These implicit admissions run counter to preferred state narratives of the violence as one against 'terrorists' or even akin to a massive crime wave. States prefer to view such conflict as governed under 'ordinary' criminal law, often amended through emergency law provisions and, if subject to any international legal regime, within the framework of international human rights law (see generally Gross and Ní Aoláin 2006). However, there are consequences to the attempt to wage conflict not just through the use of violence but using the framework of the 'normal' criminal justice system. Prosecuting of the conflict can often involve police as well as the army, the normal courts, and prisons, and this taints the criminal justice system in the eyes of non-state opponents as a tool of conflict and source of human rights abuses rather than a neutral safeguard of the rule of law.

International human rights bodies continue to articulate and attempt to enforce human rights law during conflict. International human rights mechanisms such as the periodic reporting mechanism of treaty-bodies, or their complaint or case mechanisms, continue through conflict and will evaluate whether the domestic legal system is protecting rights or itself is part of the problem. However, human rights enforcement mechanisms – of limited effectiveness at the best of times – often appear to be powerless to ameliorate the conflict and do not engage directly with the need to stop the conflict. International humanitarian law applying to non-international armed conflict has no legal enforcement machinery; enforcement is the responsibility of all signatory states. However, the International Committee of the Red Cross plays a monitoring role that aims to promote and ensure enforcement of the relevant Conventions.

Because conflicts revolve around particularly widespread and egregious violations of human rights and humanitarian laws and the standard enforcement machinery of individual complaints and periodic reporting are often inadequate to the urgency or scale of the situation, many conflict situations tend to receive additional *ad hoc* or specialized attention. This attention can be from the international human rights machinery of the United Nations or relevant regional organizations such as the Council of Europe or the African Union. United Nations Special Rapporteurs, International Commissions of Inquiry, and special committees of experts all may play a role in documenting human rights and humanitarian law abuses and are often followed up with diplomatic pressure. The effectiveness of these bodies varies, depending on how a state calibrates the international reputation costs of continuing with abuses as against what they understand to be the domestic existential costs of moving from conflict-related abuses. As regards non-state actors, human rights mechanisms tend to focus on states as it is only state parties that commit to treaties. *Ad hoc* bodies may use a combination of human rights and humanitarian law and comment also on the acts of non-state actors, which are also likely to be relevant to the state's defence of its violations. Whether these interventions affect the actions of non-state actors depends on the extent that these actors care about their international reputation, which itself may depend on whether they hold themselves out in the international domain as having some connection to a representative base. The less the non-state group has a political base and aspirations to international recognition, the less human rights standards will have a compliance pull.

Despite the apparent failure of international human rights and humanitarian law to limit the conflict and their silence as to the rights and wrongs of the conflict itself, it can provide a resource for later peacebuilding efforts. First and foremost, the existence of these bodies of law, and the international machinery to enforce them, mean that violations of human rights and humanitarian law are ever more likely to be thoroughly and authoritatively documented throughout a protracted conflict, or, in cases of short, sharp conflict, soon after it has ended. Investigations usually provide some clear documentation of the patterns of abuse and an authoritative articulation of how the law applies and whether particular acts of conflict were lawful or unlawful during the conflict. Should a peace process develop, these accounts will be useful for mediation efforts and to understand how the conflict's worst excesses affect the day-to-day life and security of persons. This understanding is vital to designing peace settlements that will be effective in ending violence. For example, a human rights agreement signed at an early stage of the peace process in El Salvador was an effective inhibitor of conflict because its terms were fashioned with good knowledge of when and how human rights violations, such as disappearances, took place and were able to be targeted at these violations themselves but also at the practices that enabled them.[3] Provisions, for example, prohibited arrests for political activities, arrests at night, arrests by persons not properly identified, and arrests for which reasons were not given. Moreover, there is some evidence that human rights standards and mechanisms may limit the worst excesses of the conflict, acting as a 'damper' not just on state violence but all forms of violence (Campbell and Connolly 2006). It is possible that monitored human rights commitments can contribute to creating the 'mutually perceived hurting stalemate' that is vital to the parties as they move towards peace negotiations (Zartman 1985).

Human rights advocacy can also create a resource in civil society. Increasingly the attempt to enforce human rights and humanitarian law involves the mobilization of a local civil society often linked into transnational networks (Bell and O'Rourke 2007). Human rights mechanisms provide a forum to such groups because the language and discourse of human rights can provide a space for such groups to intervene in political discourse without taking overt 'sides' as regards the conflict. The involvement of international actors in monitoring human rights violations can have a protective function, enabling civil society activism and local peacebuilding initiatives. Human rights monitoring can be important to local peacebuilding capacity and form a point of common platform across diverse groups. Connecting the conflict to international standards and mechanisms can also internationalize the conflict and build a network of international actors and 'friends' of the country who can later play a role in peacebuilding initiatives. For example, in Sri Lanka in 2002, a nongovernmental organization, the Working Group on Sri Lanka, brought in Ian Martin, a former Director of Amnesty International, to examine and make recommendations on the human rights situation relating to the conflict. As a peace process developed, Martin was appointed a Human Rights Advisor to the talks by the parties to the conflict, setting out provisions and even a road map for human rights protection. Although ultimately the peace process broke down, Martin was later involved in a mediation role as UN Secretary-General Special Representative in Nepal, where peace agreements with a substantial human rights component were negotiated between the government and Maoist opponents.[4] The example illustrates transnational connections that connect local communities with others in similar situations and with networks of international actors and how these connections work to diffuse peacebuilding and human rights innovations.

Law and peace negotiations

Once a formal negotiation is established, human rights protections can play an enabling and facilitative role. At a pre-negotiation or ceasefire stage, human rights protections and mechanisms often enter a process as part of the dynamic of limiting the conflict. Where non-state groups offer a ceasefire, the state – which retains the right to use 'legitimate' force – often offers protections against arbitrary use of its power – that is, human rights protections of fair trial, prohibition of lethal force, protection against arbitrary and unlawful killing. Often the text of ceasefire agreements can offer a way around the technical and political issues to which the international legal regime applies by incorporating the substantive standards into the text of the agreement itself, while avoiding any direct commitment to the international legal regime from which those standards derive. The human rights agreement in Guatemala, for example, included language limiting non-state violence drawn directly from humanitarian law, but addressed state concern about the legal application of humanitarian law by stating that it was not intended to apply.[5]

At a framework peace agreement stage, the central concern for the parties often concerns how power will be held and exercised in the future so as to address the competition over power and resources that has generated the conflict. Typically, what is being negotiated is in essence, if not in name, a constitutional framework. At this point, parties who have had very different views of human rights may find common ground in human rights language for quite different reasons. In South Africa, for example, as it became clear that a political shift from apartheid rule to multi-racial democracy was on the cards, the white population began to search for protection in a bill of rights, rather than minority rights protections. This coincided with an African National Congress (ANC) negotiating position which supported a bill of rights as part of a long-standing commitment to 'charterism'. In Northern Ireland, parties had quite different views of whether the police service should be entirely scrapped as illegitimate and unreformable or be maintained as the best police force in the world. Compromise was found on a commitment to a process of evaluation and change that stood to endorse neither position in favour of a programme of comprehensive re-structuring, founded on a set of human rights principles on which parties could agree, namely that the police force should be representative of those it served and should be accountable. In short, human rights protections at this point may facilitate agreement not because a party who has resisted human rights is suddenly converted to supporting a more human rights friendly approach, but because human rights become a way of articulating and addressing interests such as fear of discrimination and domination that underlie positions on what the borders and remit of the state should be. In place of seeking a separate state or form of government to ensure protection from discrimination and domination, human rights protections may start to serve this purpose.

Peace agreements, therefore, often begin to sketch a human rights agenda for change. They often provide human rights frameworks, such as ratification of international instruments and domestic bills of rights. They often provide principles and processes to ensure rule of law, reform of police, criminal justice, and prison regimes. They often establish a series of interlocking national institutions for promoting and protecting rights: human rights commissions, electoral commissions, media watchdogs, and gender bodies. These institutions aim to ensure that any new political institutions agreed to operate fairly. Often institutional provision is overlapping and somewhat chaotic as these institutions are relatively unproblematic to agree to, and so multiple institutions are 'thrown' at the problem of human rights protection. Often, rationalizing institutional provision becomes a post-conflict task.

Finally, peace agreements often address the issue of how to 'repair' some of the past. They make provision for return of refugees and displaced persons, including mechanisms for dealing with resultant property disputes. They address whether there will be a mechanism, such as a truth and reconciliation commission, to tackle the issue of past human rights abuses.

While international human rights standards inform peace agreement design, often their human rights provisions are quite specific to the conflict in question. Although human rights instruments talk in terms of requirements and un-negotiable principles, the concept of state implementation leaves room to negotiate over the means and mechanisms of implementation.

Role in post-settlement peacebuilding tasks

Post-settlement peacebuilding tasks often place rule of law reform at their centre. Reform of police, bringing armies under democratic civilian control, reducing the size of security forces, ensuring accountability, including complaints mechanisms, and processes of lustration – or weeding out – of human rights abusers are all central to ensuring that a ceasefire is maintained in the short term. Rule of law reform is also important to enabling transitions to democratic political structures. Fair legal processes aim to take the sting out of who is in power, ensuring that power is exercised fairly rather than in narrow, discriminatory clientele interests.

The implementation phase of any framework peace settlement also brings pressure for extended human rights commitments and mechanisms. While the issue of 'dealing with the past' is often seen as unhelpful to the early stages of transition from violent conflict, some capacity to reckon with the past and provide some form of accountability and of reparations often becomes understood to be vital to any future commitment to the rule of law. Increasingly, efforts to demobilize, demilitarize and reintegrate combatants, often involving some form of payment, while recognized as important are understood to create an inequity as regards their victims whose basic needs are often not met. Furthermore, while the short-term needs of peacebuilding may be rapid demobilization of troops, longer-term interests of peacebuilding, such as establishment of rule of law institutions, may require past human rights violations to be dealt with in some form. Truth and reconciliation commissions, forms of criminal process, vetting, and reparations schemes are all vital to peacebuilding and take place under the colour of law and international humanitarian and human rights standards. Again, these processes in practice often draw eclectically on human rights and humanitarian law, bypassing the problems of technical application by using them to frame inquiry in the mandate of the body established.

In recent years, however, the area of dealing with the past has been significantly complicated by the arrival of international criminal law. In 1998 the Rome Statute provided for the establishment of a permanent International Criminal Court (ICC) and the application of international criminal law where the state was unwilling or unable to prosecute those who had committed serious international crimes. While originally conceived as a response to inter-state conflict with antecedents that long preceded the peace agreement era, the ICC's eventual establishment took place against a backdrop of intra-state conflict and associated transitional justice developments. The Rome Statute provides a set of merged humanitarian and human rights standards applying over a range of conflict scales and both international and internal armed conflict. From its inception, most notoriously with the indictment of leaders of the non-state Lord's Resistance Army in Uganda, it has been used with respect to internal conflicts, generating controversy as to whether its existence enables or inhibits the emergence of peace processes. This body, with origins and genesis that had nothing to do with intra-state conflict or peacebuilding, now interfaces with and adjudicates on peace process compromises on amnesty. The Court's existence means that negotiated settlements must be conducted in the shadow of its remit.

Another relatively new peacebuilding human rights dilemma has entered the field with the increased international involvement in peacebuilding activities. The diversity and types of international involvement in peacebuilding functions has increased exponentially over the last two decades. The regional groupings and organizations who are actively involved in peacebuilding measures have proliferated; and they have continued to experiment and push their own mandates in terms of the types and degree of intervention they are prepared to undertake. Moreover, instances of intra-state conflict, which have also seen international armed conflict – Bosnia, Kosovo, Afghanistan and Iraq – have involved international administration and forms of externally prescribed and enforced peace settlement.

The more international organizations undertake forms of robust peacebuilding, for example using force or forms of international administration, the more they become capable of violating the rights of local populations. Yet, many of the international legal standards promulgated by international organizations such as the United Nations do not automatically apply to their own troops (for a review see Bell 2011: 350–4). Moreover, international instruments do not directly apply to non-state actors such as nongovernmental organizations and private security companies to whom peacebuilding tasks are increasingly 'contracted out'. Peacebuilders are often not held accountable at all, or are held accountable in their home state, which appears to local populations to constitute accountability to the wrong population in the wrong venue. A serious challenge in recent years has been how to handle the human rights abuses of a range of peacebuilders. This difficulty is particularly pressing because as peacebuilders face patterns of local resistance, their capacity for human rights violations and their apparent lack of accountability to local populations feed into local claims that the international implementers are acting illegitimately. Given that peacebuilding often involves the re-allocation of power, the battle for legitimacy is crucial to effective implementation. Accountability of the peacebuilders is not a matter of high principle that no-one be above the law, it is a pragmatic imperative.

Assessment of the contemporary context

The contemporary peacebuilding context addressed in this collection began around 1990 with the end of the Cold War. The last two decades have seen a steep learning curve with respect to how the relationship of human rights and peacebuilding is conceived and a Kuhnian paradigm shift in how the relationship is understood and managed. In the early 1990s, peacebuilding and human rights were viewed as different fields with different motivations, different ends and largely involving distinctly disconnected practices. Peacebuilding or conflict resolution focused on inclusion of the protagonists of conflict, removal of pre-conditions to negotiated solutions and some acceptance of the equality of protagonists to the conflict, at least for the purposes of negotiations. Human rights advocacy, in contrast, involved assertion of international norms, holding states to account as those responsible for protecting human rights, provided documentation that often showed that not all parties to conflict were equally 'bad', and continued to insist that human rights accountability should matter to peace settlement negotiation, terms, and implementation. As peacebuilding efforts moved from concern over reaching a peace agreement to implementing and sustaining settlement terms, human rights advocates began to see the potential of peace processes to institutionalize human rights protections over time, so the fields began to converge. Over time, an attempt to marry peacebuilding and human rights imperatives took place in an attempt to marry peace and justice. These approaches focused on how to manage the clashes of peacebuilding and human rights approaches, for example, through sequencing of transitional justice initiatives. This led to a fuller paradigm shift whereby an assumption of primacy of unconstrained negotiations against which human rights commitments had to be argued for was replaced by an assumption that human rights law applied and put certain matters – chiefly blanket amnesties – off limits. This paradigm shift can loosely be pinned to the year 2000 when the United Nations in particular nailed its colours to the mast as a 'normative negotiator', making it clear that it viewed negotiations as having a normative dimension and questioning the extent to which issues such as amnesty could be negotiated domestically, and the extent to which international law ruled out certain forms of amnesty in advance (see further UN Secretary-General 2004; Bell 2011: 342–3). The paradigm shift heralded a 'peace *and* justice' approach that appeared to hold out the possibility of uneasy compromise through creative institutional design. Over time, however, and in particular with the establishment and operation of the ICC, it now appears that the 'peace *and* justice' approach may be giving way to a 'justice *over* peace' approach in terms of the rhetoric of international organizations.

This recent shift in emphasis from 'peace *and* justice' to 'justice first and foremost' sits alongside increasing scepticism of what it is peace processes and settlements achieve. Scepticism arises at the level of the process itself: two decades on, peace agreements appear not to herald peace, but to beget new conflicts which need new peace agreements, or to push conflict across borders, or to take for ever to implement leaving countries in frozen conflicts where there is neither outright war nor a lived experience of peace. Scepticism also arises at the level of particular peacebuilding and human rights initiatives aimed at reconciling justice and peace. For example, mechanisms to 'deal with the past' such as truth commissions, once internationally supported, funded and encouraged, now are questioned in terms of what they deliver. Empirical evidence appears to cast doubt on whether the goals asserted for them are realized (see e.g., Thoms et al. 2008). The 'justice first' approach has been fuelled by angst over the appropriate and realistic goals of peacebuilding and human rights initiatives, but also by War on Terror priorities, which began to institute a 'backward' reframing of internal conflicts in terms of states (assumed to be legitimate) and terrorists (assumed to be illegitimate), and a turn towards emergency law regimes and a cautious or even hostile approach to negotiations and negotiated solutions to conflict.[6] These initiatives outlast the official end of the 'War on Terror'. Scepticism combined with the international War on Terror realignment have arguably resulted in a move away from negotiated ends to conflict and towards increased international intervention to impose and enforce the chosen ends of international actors. Peacebuilding now appears tilted away from indigenously negotiated solutions towards ever more explicit international requiring of a 'liberal peace'. Against this backdrop, the new primacy of 'justice' appears in a different light, not as the logical extension of human rights commitments but as enabling mechanisms such as the ICC to operate as merely one more tool in the international community's liberal peace armoury.

This new context poses the question of whether the era of peace settlements and innovative peacebuilding initiatives is in decline. Reviews of peace settlements (see Bell and O'Rourke 2010) and disturbing new events such as the Sri Lankan attempt to end its conflict with the LTTE militarily, appear to indicate it is. And yet, settlements continue to be negotiated, while stronger military intervention and 'victory' continue to leave peacebuilding tasks in their wake, with failed states themselves recognized to pose a 'war-on-terror' threat. As reflected in this volume, another response is needed and is emerging. Critical inquiry has questioned the extent to which internationally imposed peacebuilding is capable of being effective. In particular, criticism of 'liberal peacebuilding' questions whether a project of rolling out a set of democratic and rule of law institutions is possible or effective in societies in which all of the precursors of liberal democracy appear to be missing, namely common values and a common commitment to a common community in a commonly accepted territorial state. In particular, human rights and rule of law initiatives are at the centre of this critique because they seem to require the patterning of peacebuilding institution-building on the institutions of western liberal democracies such as elections, an independent judiciary, or bills of rights. These institutions may meet resistance from local power structures, including traditional justice systems, which are then viewed by international actors as an obstacle to the liberal peacemaking project rather than a resource. The more international actors attempt to 'enforce' peace and to implement a standard set of political and legal institutions, the more they can rub up against local resistance and the more the project appears paradoxical and self-defeating because it risks international actors transgressing against the very standards and values they are attempting to enforce. New approaches point to the need to consider local approaches to peacebuilding and justice as a resource which international approaches must work with rather than against.

Conclusion

In conclusion, some ways forward can be suggested. First, it is worth noting that the practice of peacebuilding can be demonstrated to have been fairly effective. On closer analysis, some of the figures which have been used to argue the failure of peace agreements demonstrate a practice that is fairly effective in reducing deaths in conflict – in over 75 per cent of cases (Suhrke and Samset 2007). It can also be argued that the disillusionment with particular peace and justice initiatives, such as truth commissions, owes more to international over-selling of the product and a failure to engage with and celebrate more diffuse, modest long-term goals.

I would argue that a way forward with regard to peacebuilding and human rights depends on a more nuanced understanding of peace and justice as essentially contested concepts (Gallie 1956), whose meaning must be constructed and agreed on at both international and domestic levels. International human rights standards must always be negotiated into any domestic context if they are to be effective. International human rights bodies enforcing standards in settled contexts increasingly view the process of international human rights enforcement not as a process of international imposition but as one of 'dialogue' between themselves and the domestic state.[7] Dialogue involves both sides – in this case the domestic and the international – talking and influencing each other. It views human rights as being authored not by international lawyers or by domestic states but in a process of negotiation between and among communities, between and among states, with cross-reference and dialogue between both those levels. Similarly, peacebuilding initiatives must always reckon with the normative claims of both the parties to the conflict and international community and acknowledge that dialogue and negotiation between the parties to a conflict does not happen in a normative vacuum in which those outside the conflict do not have an interest. The crucial question for the practice of peacebuilding and the practice of human rights implementation is whether dialogue over values of peace and norms of justice can prompt imaginative ways forward capable of assisting people to move from conflict to peace as 'sustainable fairness'. Current literature suggests embracing the hybrid nature of peace settlements and post-conflict terrain as incorporating a struggle over where values are appropriately authored and implemented – at international or local level (see e.g. Bell 2008; Boege, Brown, Clements, and Nolan 2008, 2009; Mac Ginty 2010, 2011; Schmeidl 2009; von Trotha 2009). There is no easy prescription or tool-kit for how to do this. The lessons that need to be learned relate less to how to develop 'best practice' tools and techniques and more to the apparently more esoteric question of how to recognize and enable this deeper dialogue in constructive ways.

Acknowledgement

I am indebted to Kasey L. McCall-Smith, for research assistance and comments on the chapter.

Notes

1 Geneva Convention for the Amelioration of the Condition of the Wounded and Sick in Armed Forces in the Field (1949), Geneva Convention for the Amelioration of the Condition of Wounded, Sick and Shipwrecked Members of Armed Forces at Sea (1949), Geneva Convention Relative to the Treatment of Prisoners of War (1949), and Geneva Convention Relative to the Protection of Civilian Persons in Time of War (1949); Protocol Additional to the Geneva Conventions of 12 August 1949, and Relating to the Protection of Victims of International Armed Conflicts (Protocol I) (1977); Protocol Additional to the Geneva Conventions of 1949, and Relating to the Protection of Victims of Non-International Armed Conflicts (Protocol II) (1977).

2 See for example, International Covenant on Civil and Political Rights (1960, Art. 4(1)): 'In time of public emergency which threatens the life of the nation and the existence of which is officially proclaimed, the States Parties to the present Covenant may take measures derogating from their obligations under the present Covenant to the extent strictly required by the exigencies of the situation, provided that such measures are not inconsistent with their other obligations under international law and do not involve discrimination solely on the ground of race, colour, sex, language, religion or social origin.'

3 Agreement on Human Rights (San José Agreement), 26 July 1990, Online, Available HTTP: <http://peacemaker.unlb.org/ > (accessed 8 February 2012).

4 See for example Comprehensive Peace Agreement between the Nepal Government and the Communist Party of Nepal (Maoist), 22 November 2006, Online, Available HTTP: <http://peacemaker.unlb.org/> (accessed 8 February 2012).

5 Article IX, Comprehensive Agreement on Human Rights, 29 March 1994, Online, Available HTTP: <http://peacemaker.unlb.org/> (accessed 8 February 2012).

6 See *Holder v. Humanitarian Law Project*, 561 US __, 130 S.Ct. 2705 (2010) (defining 'conflict resolution' tasks as capable of amounting to 'material assistance' to terrorists).
7 See *Al-Khawaja and Tahery v. UK*, Judgment of 15 December 2011, [2011] ECHR 2127; *R v. Horncastle*, [2009] UKSC 14.

References

Bell, C. (2008) *On the Law of Peace: Peace Agreements and the Lex Pacificatoria*, Oxford: Oxford University Press.

Bell, C. (2011) 'Post-conflict accountability and the reshaping of human rights and humanitarian law', in O. Ben-Naftali (ed.) *International Humanitarian Law and International Human Rights Law: Pas de Deux*, Oxford: Oxford University Press.

Bell, C. and O'Rourke, C. (2007) 'The people's peace? Peace agreements, civil society, and participatory democracy', *International Political Science Review*, 28(3): 293–324.

Bell, C. and O'Rourke, C. (2010) 'Peace agreements or "pieces of paper"? The impact of UNSC Resolution 1325 on peace processes and their agreements', *International and Comparative Law Quarterly*, 59: 941–80.

Bell, C., Campbell, C. and Ní Aoláin, F. (2004) 'Justice Discourses in Transition' *Social and Legal Studies*, 13(3): 305–28.

Boege, V., Brown, A., Clements, K. and Nolan, A. (2008) 'On hybrid political orders and emerging states: state formation in the context of "fragility"'. Online. Available HTTP: <http://www.berghof-handbook.net/documents/publications/boege_etal_handbook.pdf> (accessed 8 February 2012).

Boege, V., Brown, A., Clements, K. and Nolan, A. (2009) 'Undressing the emperor: a reply to our discussants'. Online. Available HTTP: <http://www.berghof-handbook.net/documents/publications/dialogue8_boegeetal_resp.pdf> (accessed 8 February 2012).

Campbell, C. and Connolly, I. (2006) 'Making war on terror? Global lessons from Northern Ireland', *Modern Law Review*, 69: 935–57.

Gallie, W.B. (1956) 'Essentially Contested Concepts', *Proceedings of the Aristotelian Society*, 56: 167–98.

Gross, O. and Ní Aoláin, F. (2006) *Law in Times of Crisis: Emergency Powers in Theory and Practice*, Cambridge: Cambridge University Press.

Mac Ginty, R. (2010) 'Hybrid peace: the interaction between top down and bottom up peace', *Security Dialogue*, 41(4): 391–412.

Mac Ginty, R. (2011) *International Peacebuilding and Local Resistance: Hybrid forms of peace*, Basingstoke: Palgrave Macmillan.

Parvleliet, M. (2009) 'Rethinking conflict transformation'. Online. Available HTTP: <http://www.berghof-handbook.net/documents/publications/parlevliet_handbook.pdf> (accessed 8 February 2012).

Schmeidl, S. with Karokhail, M. (2009) '"Prêt-a-porter states": how the McDonaldization of state-building misses the mark in Afghanistan'. Online. Available HTTP: < http://www.berghof-handbook.net/documents/publications/dialogue8_schmeidl_karokhail_comm.pdf> (accessed 8 February 2012).

Suhrke, A. and Samset, I. (2007) 'What's in a figure? Estimating recurrence of civil war', *International Peacekeeping*, 14: 195–203.

Thoms, O., Ron, J. and Paris, R. (2008) *The Effects of Transitional Justice Mechanisms: A Summary of Empirical Research Findings and Implications for Analysts and Practitioners*, Ottawa: Centre for International Policy Studies, University of Ottawa.

UN Secretary-General (2004) 'The rule of law and transitional justice in conflict and post-conflict societies', Report of the Secretary-General, 23 August 2004, New York, United Nations, UN Doc. A/59/565.

Von Trotha, T. (2009) 'The "Andersen Principle": on the difficulty of truly moving beyond state-centrism'. Online. Available HTTP: <http://www.berghof-handbook.net/documents/publications/dialogue8_trotha_comm.pdf> (accessed 8 February 2012).

Zartman, I.W. (1985) *Ripe for Resolution*, New York: Oxford University Press.

PART V

Everyday living and peacebuilding

20

EMPLOYMENT AND HOUSEHOLD WELFARE

Patrícia Justino and Ricardo Santos

Introduction

Countries recovering from violent conflict face considerable challenges in re-establishing the social contract between states and citizens, and the functioning of markets and social and political structures. This is largely due to the profound institutional transformations associated with violent conflict that affect the roles, attitudes and aspirations of those exposed to violence, all of which have significant implications for peacebuilding efforts.

Programmes of peacebuilding, peacekeeping and post-conflict economic recovery have been driven by and large by concerns with state security and state capacity (see UN 2004, 2005). This perspective has come under criticism in recent years due to insufficient attention paid to the social, economic and political dynamics of violence and conflict at the individual, household and community levels (Autesserre 2010; Justino 2009; Kalyvas 2008). Better data and improvements in micro-level research in conflict-affected countries have led to an increased focus of research and policy on the relationship between conflict and welfare outcomes among people affected by violence (see review in Justino 2012b).

This chapter makes use of this micro-level approach to analyse how processes of peacebuilding may be affected by welfare changes that take place during violent conflict. We focus for the most part on individuals and households, but discuss links with community-level processes in the final section of the chapter. We argue that the establishment of successful peacebuilding efforts is dependent on the understanding of two fundamental factors that shape the welfare status of those affected by violence: what happens to people exposed to violence, and what individuals and households do to protect lives and livelihoods in areas of conflict.

The chapter focuses mostly on one form of violent conflict – civil wars – defined as 'armed combat within the boundaries of a recognised sovereign entity between parties subject to a common authority at the outset of the hostilities' (Kalyvas 2007: 17). We concentrate on civil wars due to the scarcity of evidence at the micro-level of the impact of other forms of violent conflict. In what follows, we use the definition of peacebuilding provided by Boutros Boutros-Ghali during his time as UN Secretary General, as, 'action to identify and support structures which tend to strengthen and solidify peace to avoid a relapse into conflict' (United Nations 1994).

The chapter is organized as follows. The first section provides a general framework to understand the impact of violent conflict on the economic welfare of individuals and households in areas of violence. Section two discusses the choices, behaviour and strategies undertaken by people in areas of violent conflict to mitigate the effects of violence on their lives and livelihoods and the security of their families and immediate social networks. Section three discusses how the welfare effects of violent conflict may impact on peacebuilding efforts, and the significant but often overlooked implications of welfare adaptation strategies for the sustainability of peace and stability in post-conflict contexts. The fourth section concludes the chapter with a reflection of how these micro-level dynamic processes that take place during conflict can be addressed as part of peacebuilding strategies in communities affected by violent conflict. We focus on the importance of employment-generation policies and welfare-support measures that improve the long-term economic and social security of those living under violent conditions in ways that contribute to breaking cycles of poverty, war and instability.

What happens to households exposed to violence?[1]

Violent conflicts affect individuals and households through a variety of channels (Justino 2009). We discuss here key mechanisms underlying the relationship between violent conflict, economic welfare and employment that may impact on the long-term sustainability of peace and stability in local communities. These include changes in household composition, asset depletion and the effects caused by displacement.

Household structure and asset depletion

The first, most obvious impact of violent conflict is the destruction of life and the physical and mental disabling of individuals exposed to violence. Almost 750,000 people die as a result of armed conflict each year (Geneva Declaration Secretariat 2008). Nearly 15 million people were internally displaced by civil wars at the end of 2010 (UNHCR 2011). Death, injury and displacement affect not only combatants, but also civilians, often children, women and the elderly (World Bank 2011). These events are very traumatic experiences with considerable effects on the productive capacity of households and individuals living in contexts of armed violence. One direct consequence of violence on household structures is the increase in female-headed households, often widows (Kumar 2000; Schindler 2010).

Alongside the loss of household members, violent conflict results in severe asset depletion for many individuals, households and communities living in areas of violence. Houses, livestock and crops are valuable targets for armed groups looking for shelter, food and looting (Bundervoet and Verwimp 2005; Verpoorten 2005). Land is also a worthy asset for armed groups, as well as an indication of the wealth status of potential victims (Brockett 1990; González and Lopez 2007). The destruction of assets during conflict reduces considerably the income-generating capacity of households, which may be forced into undertaking low-return livelihood strategies (Brück 2004; Ibáñez and Moya 2009).

Violent conflict is associated with the depletion of not only physical, but also human assets (Justino 2012b). Recent empirical evidence has shown that violent conflicts result in largely negative and long-lasting nutritional and educational effects amongst children in war zones (see Alderman, Hoddinott and Kinsey 2006; Shemyakina 2006). The participation of young people in fighting may also in turn drive down levels of schooling and employment productivity, further reducing the accumulation of human capital assets among those exposed to armed violence (Blattman and Annan 2009). The destruction of individual and household assets is compounded further by damage to community assets such as infrastructure (roads, schools, health facilities, and other services) and organizations (social groups, youth organizations and so forth) (World Bank 2011).

Changes in physical and human capital accumulation may affect the sustainability of peace after the end of the war. On the one hand, the loss of physical and human capital during violent conflicts may push some households into permanent forms of destitution, exclusion and discontent that may result in persistent cycles of poverty and violence. Levels of exclusion and unemployment among young people are a popular explanation for the renewal of cycles of violence (Huntington 1996). The dynamics and aftermath of conflict might also benefit some groups that develop interests in the permanence of war economies (Keen 1997). On the other hand, recent research suggests that recruitment and exposure to armed violence may result in increased individual political participation and leadership amongst ex-fighters and those victimized by war (Blattman 2009; Bellows and Miguel 2006), which may well boost their income-generating opportunities. While a large focus has been placed on the 'spoilers' of peace, less attention has been paid to the forms of resilience and positive action that may emerge from situations of violence. The net impact of these micro-level effects on the sustainability of peace and stability remains under-researched.

Individual and household displacement

Displaced populations are at a particular risk of economic and social vulnerability given the severe reductions in social capital and assets that they experience (Ibáñez and Moya 2009). People tend to leave areas of violence for security reasons. But entire households and communities may also be forcefully displaced as a consequence of the strategies put into place by the contending parties in a violent conflict. Ibáñez and Moya (2009) describe some of the processes by which displacement reduces the means needed by households to attain their welfare and secure meaningful income-generating opportunities. In addition, displaced persons are likely to be victims of discrimination in areas of relocation, and find themselves unable to make use of previously acquired skills in new unfamiliar urban settings (Calderón, Gáfaro and Ibáñez 2011; Kondylis 2010).

The hardships faced by displaced people do not necessarily translate in the desire to return to original communities. Deininger, Ibáñez and Querubin (2004) find that households are unwilling to return to their place of origin when displacement was caused by distressing events or if security fears are still present. Raeymaekers (2011) finds that young Congolese show a preference to stay in receiving urban environments even if access to local jobs and other income-generating activities may be a considerable challenge. Tensions that generate from the relationship between displaced and hosting communities, from how displaced persons are assimilated into new communities (or original communities if they return), and from how their views and attitudes towards return to original locations are dealt with have enormous implications for peacebuilding and post-conflict reconstruction policies.

What do households do to protect lives and livelihoods in areas of conflict?

One of the key findings of a major ongoing research programme on conflict funded by the European Commission is that individuals and households in areas of violent conflict retain a large degree of agency when acting to secure their lives and livelihoods (see Justino 2012b).[2] Individuals and households exposed to violence formulate strategies that seek to mitigate the impacts of violence and conflict, even if some of this resilience may come with a cost when the strategies devised are unable to go beyond protecting current incomes while hindering future prospects. We discuss below three main strategies – risk mitigation, intra-household labour allocation and migration – that may have a significant impact on the sustainability of peace and stability.

Risk mitigation in conflict settings: Savings, buffer stock and subsistence strategies

Both in conflict and in peaceful settings, the ability of households to mitigate economic risk is largely determined by their capacity to manage their financial or quasi-financial assets. Livestock holdings are a particularly important form of savings in developing countries. However, livestock is not a secure asset in times of conflict since it can easily be stolen or killed. Livestock is also an important marker of wealth that may expose the owners to violence (Bundervoet 2006; Verpoorten 2005). Most households living in rural conflict areas have no option left but to resort to less risky subsistence activities in detriment of more rentable activities or off-farm employment (Brück 2004; Deininger 2003; McKay and Loveridge 2005). Despite its potentially negative long-term effects, in the immediate term subsistence and lower risk activities may be key to keeping people alive. This is because people living in areas of armed conflict are not only vulnerable to poverty and economic volatility, but are also vulnerable to violence. The interaction between these two levels of vulnerability may not go in the same direction (see theoretical discussion in Justino 2009). For instance, households that are poorer at the start of the conflict may well not be the worst affected by the direct and indirect impacts of violence. Wealthier households may be at higher risk if they have particular characteristics (ethnical and religious affiliation, geographic location or possession of assets that are attractive to armed groups) that may make them more prone to being targets of violence (Justino 2009). The levels and nature of vulnerability of a specific household also change during the course of the conflict in response to the economic, social and political transformations that take place, notably in terms of new community alliances or strategic decisions taken by the armed groups in control of the area of residence of the household (Justino 2009; Kalyvas and Kocher 2007). Post-conflict recovery and peacebuilding processes must therefore pay particular attention not only to the restoration of livelihood opportunities for the victims of violence, but also to the specific type of vulnerabilities that affect different population groups during the course of conflict. These may remain entrenched once the war is over when local processes of institutional transformation that emerged from the conflict remain in place despite formal peace agreements (Autesserre 2010; Justino 2012b).

Intra-household reallocation of labour and female economic participation

Violence affects the productive capacity of household members through killings, injuries, abduction and displacement, resulting in important re-structuring of intra-household labour allocations. This productive capacity may never be recovered if the household is unable to replace lost labour (see Justino and Verwimp 2008). Beegle (2005) finds that the Rwanda conflict resulted in reductions in farm labour and farming activity with detrimental effects on household consumption and income. Bircan, Brück and Vothknecht (2010) find that in conflict-affected countries, labour force participation stays below the long-term average during the first 10 years after the conflict. Labour productivity is also negatively affected by conflict and violence. Ibáñez and Moya (2009) find evidence for deterioration in the value and employability of the skills owned by displaced populations.

Interestingly, women's employment rates tend to increase during violent conflict, with important contributions to the economic stability of their households and communities where they live (Kumar 2000; Date-Bah 2003; El-Bushra and Sahl 2005). Women increase their participation in labour markets during conflict, and become household heads, because their partners have joined armed groups, have died or were injured during combat, or migrated or were displaced to avoid being targeted by violent groups. In a cross-country analysis of a sample of conflict-affected countries, Brück and Vothknecht (2011) show that aggregate female unemployment dropped from 12.3 per cent before conflict to 11.9 per cent during the conflict and 11.4 per cent after conflict. In contrast, total unemployment (men and women) increased from 9.1 per cent before conflict to 9.4 per cent during wartime. Similar evidence is found in country-level analyses (Calderón et al. 2011).

Children also become providers of labour in times of difficulty, both in contexts of violence and in peaceful settings affected by severe economic shocks. Children that are needed to replace labour may be removed from school, which may in turn deplete the household of their stock of human capital for future generations (Akbulut-Yuksel 2009; Shemyakina 2006). In a unique study, Rodriguez and Sanchez (2009) have tested directly the effect of war on child labour and find that violent attacks in Colombian municipalities by armed groups have increased significantly the inclusion of children in the labour market. They show that increased mortality risks, negative economic shocks and reduction in school quality due to violence are the main channels through which armed conflict leads to increased child labour.

Child labour during conflict may in turn be associated with youth unemployment in the post-conflict period. The presence of large numbers of youth was for a long time highlighted as one of the main factors explaining the outbreak of violence and conflict (Huntington 1996). The 'youth bulge' hypothesis has been dismissed more recently by Urdal (2004). However, the presence of large numbers of young people alongside weak economic performance, weak governance and low levels of education may increase the likelihood of violent outbursts (Urdal and Hoelscher 2009), which might in turn affect the success of peacebuilding efforts in the long term.

Non-forced migration

Migration is one of the possible coping strategies adopted by households in conflict settings (Czaika and Kis-Katos 2007). If some household members are able to leave conflict areas into more secure locations, remittances may take a possible key role in mitigating some of the negative effects of armed conflict on livelihoods and household welfare. Despite recent increases in the levels of remittances in conflict-affected countries (Goldring 2002), there is very limited information on how these are used by the households as coping strategies (Lindley 2007). Remittances have, however, the potential to be important mechanisms of household security both during and after conflict (Justino and Shemyakina 2010; Lindley 2007). Remittances can greatly affect labour force participation decisions of household members, in particular the decision to retain or enrol children in school, and consumption-smoothing strategies. In particular, there is evidence that remittances play a key role in female-headed households where the breadwinner was lost to conflict (or migrated himself). In this sense, remittances can be instrumental for households in avoiding poverty traps and maintaining socio-economic stability (Lindley 2007), both key factors in the long-term stability and economic recovery of households and communities affected by violent conflict.

Do changes in welfare and employment matter for peacebuilding?

The previous two sections have shown that the exposure of households to violence and conflict can have lasting detrimental effects on household welfare, pushing many into long-term poverty traps. Negative education and nutritional outcomes have particularly lasting effects (Akbulut-Yuksel 2009; Akresh and Verwimp 2008; Alderman, Hoddinott and Kinsey 2006). Although less studied, recent empirical evidence suggests that labour markets may constitute an important mechanism explaining the persistence of poverty traps among some households and the ability of other households to recover once the war is over. The resort to subsistence agriculture, limits to off-farm employment, asset depletion, and child labour are all common outcomes of conflict related to the operation, limitations and access to labour markets. The analysis in the previous section also demonstrates the large degree of agency exercised by individuals and households in areas of armed violence, and how these translate into the level and nature of the vulnerability and resilience they experience during and after the conflict.

Much is still to be understood regarding the impact of conflict on welfare and employment structures. But existing evidence strongly suggests that strengthening welfare support, local labour markets and employment conditions should be central concerns in peacebuilding and stability programming. In a report likely to shape the field of conflict, peacebuilding and development in the years to come, the World Bank states that: 'To break cycles of insecurity and reduce the risk of their recurrence, national reformers and their international partners need to build the legitimate institutions that can provide a sustained level of citizen security, justice and jobs – offering a stake in society to groups that may otherwise receive more respect and recognition from engaging in armed violence than in lawful activities' (2011: 8).

The evidence discussed in the sections above suggests however that providing security, justice and jobs is not only about preventing the emergence of peace 'spoilers', but also about protecting those that become vulnerable to the processes of violence and institutional change and supporting the positive roles that may emerge from conflict, such as women's economic participation, the positive effect of some forms of displacement on hosting communities or the positive role of new young leaders, among others. A better understanding of these important processes of vulnerability *and* resilience has important theoretical and policy implications. Theoretically, it provides important micro foundations to understand the duration and termination of violent conflict and the sustainability of peace processes, because as we have argued elsewhere, changes in levels of vulnerability and resilience feed into new norms of interaction and cooperation, as well as new institutional organization of local communities (Justino 2012b). At the policy level, understanding processes of both vulnerability and resilience is important for creating the space for internal and external peacebuilding interventions to engage with a range of actors, views and local realities.

These micro-level mechanisms are largely absent from most peacebuilding programmes, still largely concerned with issues of state security and state capacity, and limited notions of security. When welfare and employment concerns feature in peacebuilding programming, the focus is on either gaining the 'hearts and minds' of certain populations, or on providing alternative financial incentives for peace 'spoilers'. Severine Autesserre writes in her landmark book on the limitations of international peacebuilding in the Congo: 'The dominant international peacebuilding culture shapes the interveners' understanding of peace, violence, and intervention in a way that overlooks the micro-foundations necessary for sustainable peace. The resulting inattention to local conflicts leads to unsustainable peacebuilding in the short term and potential war resumption in the long term' (2010: 39–40).

International development assistance has focused more closely on the lives of the people affected by violence and in the restoration of local community relations. Humanitarian interventions are primarily concerned with restoring food security and health to those living in precarious situations, while the World Bank has strongly sponsored the implementation of community-driven development (CDD) efforts during the post-conflict reconstruction period as a way of strengthening social cohesion and building social capital (World Bank 2006). However, humanitarian intervention in post-conflict settings has long been criticized for its short-term horizon planning and absence of links to long-term development planning (see UNESCO 2011), while very limited rigorous evidence exists to date on the impact of CDD programmes on peacebuilding (see Barron, Diprose and Woolcock 2011).

One central issue in peacebuilding efforts worldwide, particularly since the convergence between peacebuilding programming and development strategies discussed elsewhere in this volume, is to support policy interventions that improve simultaneously the economic recovery of communities affected by armed violence, and sustain peace processes in the long term. These joint objectives require much more systematic strategic thinking to identify how individuals and households behave, react and relate to other households and communities in armed conflict settings and to understand the consequences of resulting violence on their welfare and adjustment behaviour. These are critical issues to the design of effective peacebuilding policies, capable of producing enduring effects.

Final reflections: Peacebuilding through economic welfare and employment support

The analysis above indicates the need for peacebuilding strategies to include a more systematic understanding of processes of both vulnerability *and* resilience that emerge during the conflict. We argue here that three important policy interventions emerge as central to the reduction of vulnerabilities and the support of forms of resilience that may impact positively on peacebuilding: education and skills acquisition, women's labour market participation and social assistance. We discuss also the importance of restoring community relations in the aftermath of violent conflict.

Education policy and skills acquisition

It has been widely acknowledged that creating conditions for the integration of conflict-afflicted households in labour markets, either via self-employment or otherwise, is key for successful peacebuilding policies. The World Bank in its World Development Report 2011 on *Conflict, Security and Development* suggests a series of measures to help 'transforming institutions to deliver [...] jobs', including the creation of business friendly environments, investments in basic infrastructure, the implementation of government employment-generation programmes and public works programmes, the provision of key agriculture assets, and supporting self-employment strategies through better market infrastructure and financial services.

One fundamental but overlooked mechanism that will ensure the success of employment-generation policies is the successful matching between the needs of employers and the skills of those looking for employment. These are severely affected by violent conflict due to the negative impact of conflict on educational attainments and the long-term accumulation of productive skills. Even limited exposure to violence (weeks or a few months) can lead to significant and long-lasting detrimental effects on individual human capital formation in terms of educational attainment, health outcomes and labour market opportunities (Akbulut-Yuksel 2009).

Children and young people are removed from school for a variety of reasons including soldiering (and abduction), household labour needs, insecurity fears, displacement, changes in returns to education, and the targeting of schools, teachers and students (Justino 2012a). Aid and reconstruction efforts are quick to re-establish basic education structures (UNESCO 2011). But children that lose out on school during the conflict may not necessarily benefit from these early, often short-term interventions, and will earn less, have worse job opportunities and poorer health than those that return to school. This not only affects their economic and social welfare, but also the opportunities available to their own children, creating cycles of deprivation and disenfranchisement that may persist for decades after the end of the conflict and may well reinforce structures for further violence (UNESCO 2011). Incentives for increased school attendance are not easily put in place, although some recent evidence suggests that social assistance programmes (see below) such as conditional and unconditional cash transfers may increase school attendance by reducing the need for child labour (Dubois, de Janvry and Sadoulet 2008). Remittances can play a crucial role in helping populations in post-conflict settings rebuild their livelihoods and recover their pre-war consumption levels, as well as keeping children in school (Lindley 2007).

Women's labour market participation and economic recovery

Violent conflict is associated with significant changes in the gender division of household labour. Increases in women's participation in the labour force during conflict and in its immediate aftermath have been registered by several countries including Bosnia, Cambodia, Colombia, El Salvador, Georgia, Guatemala, and Rwanda (Calderón et al. 2011; Kumar 2000; Date-Bah 2003). Many of these women are widows, and are particularly active in low-skilled jobs, and in the informal sector.

Despite this rise in female employment during conflict, women tend to lose their jobs once the conflict ends due to the return of men and societal pressures to go back to traditional roles (Date-Bah 2003; Kumar 2000). This is an unfortunate situation because women's economic empowerment is often associated with improvements in the welfare of their households and individual members (Duflo and Udry 2004; Hoddinott and Haddad 1991). Recent empirical evidence has also shown that gender economic equality is associated with a lower risk of inter-state conflicts (Caprioli 2003; Regan and Paskeviciute 2003).

Social assistance

Another important factor in the relationship between welfare outcomes and peacebuilding efforts is the protection of vulnerable population groups that are unable to benefit from economic recovery programmes. The standard approach to the provision of assistance to countries in conflict has been to focus on humanitarian aid and emergency relief, while less effort has been put into the use of compensatory policies, including safety net policies, cash transfers or other social security policies. Justino (2007), using state-level empirical evidence for India, shows that in the medium term, public expenditure on redistributive social transfers are effective means to reduce civil unrest and prevent the outbreak of violence in India. The role of social assistance policies in supporting household welfare in stressful circumstances is well known (Ahmad, Drèze, Hills and Sen 1991). But little other evidence exists on the role of social assistance policies in re-establishing livelihoods and social cohesion in post-conflict settings. This is an important though neglected area of focus for post-conflict economic and peacebuilding programming as household insecurity and competition for local governance in the supply of local public goods may well influence the sustainability of peace and the strength of potential for further violence in the future.

Creating enabling environments at the community level

The success of policies that target individuals and households is dependent not only on how those individuals and households respond to interventions, but also on the wider political, social and economic context in which they live. Violent conflicts break social cohesion and destroy the social fabric of communities (Colletta and Cullen 2000; World Bank 2011). Violent conflict may also affect the quality and functioning of institutions, the expansion of technology and social outcomes at community level (Acemoglu and Robinson 2006). Policies that strengthen community relations may play a central role in the successful implementation of employment-generating programmes and other welfare-supporting policies.

One important type of policy intervention is the integration of particular groups into society that may potentially have an interest in furthering violence. Walter (2004) and Sandler and Enders (2004) warn of the need for seeking the economic integration of former combatants. Castles and van Hear (2005) emphasize the importance of addressing the patterns of displacement and the patterns of resettlement during and after conflicts. Clark (2006) argues for the importance of integrating young people's political views and activities. This literature highlights not only the role of ex-combatants, refugees, internally displaced persons (IDPs) and young people as potential 'spoilers' of peace, but also their role as political actors in the promotion of peace in the post-conflict period. Despite fears around the role of former soldiers, refugees and youth in violence, these groups can have large positive impacts on processes of peacebuilding, due to their demographic weight, their exposure to the horrors of violence and their future leadership roles (Bellows and Miguel 2006; McEvoy-Levy 2006). Incorporating their views, fears and aspirations into peacebuilding programming is fundamental to the long-term success of such interventions.

A second key element in the restoration of community relations is the strengthening of community forms of conflict resolution. This is at the heart of most community-led development programmes with a focus on the protection of property rights and the regulation and, in some cases, creation or re-establishment of credit and insurance markets (see World Bank 2006; also Deininger 2003). The protection of property rights, especially pertaining to land, is critical and, if badly managed, can be one of the motives for the onset of violence (see discussion in Brockett 1990; Wood 2003). The importance of formalization is also stressed by Ibáñez and Moya (2009). This is not, however, a linear and straightforward process. Butler and Gates (2007) show that simply increasing property rights without complying to criteria of fairness and equity can in fact increase the level of conflict in society, since it may add to existing grievances. This is common to other types of local conflict resolution mechanisms (Barron, Diprose and Woolcock 2011).

Improving the levels of fairness and justice in community forms of conflict resolution, alongside improvements in education, support for women's economic participation and the provision of social assistance will go a long way to breaking cycles of poverty, destitution and violence.

Notes

1 The analysis in this section is based on the framework developed in Justino (2009).
2 See www.microconflict.eu. MICROCON is a collaborative programme of research among 23 research institutions in Europe, the USA, Latin America, South Asia and Africa, working on the micro-level analysis of processes of violent conflict from a multidisciplinary, empirical perspective.

References

Acemoglu, D. and Robinson, J. (2006) *Economic Origins of Dictatorship and Democracy*, Cambridge: Cambridge University Press.
Ahmad, E., Drèze, J., Hills, J., and Sen, A.K. (1991) *Social Security in Developing Countries*, Oxford: Clarendon Press.

Akbulut-Yuksel, M. (2009) *Children of War: The Long-Run Effects of Large-Scale Physical Destruction and Warfare on Children*, HiCN Working Paper no. 62.

Akresh, R. and Verwimp, P. (2008) *Civil War, Crop Failure and the Health Status of Young Children*, Working Paper 19, Households in Conflict Network.

Alderman, H., Hoddinott, J. and Kinsey, B. (2006) 'Long Term Consequences of Early Childhood Malnutrition', *Oxford Economic Papers*, 58 (3): 450–474.

Autesserre, S. (2010) *The Trouble with the Congo: Local Violence and the Failure of International Peacebuilding*, New York: Cambridge University Press.

Barron, P., Diprose, R. and Woolcock, M. (2011) *Contesting Development: Participatory Projects and Local Conflict Dynamics in Indonesia*, Yale: Yale University Press.

Beegle, K. (2005) 'Labor Effects of Adult Mortality in Tanzanian Households', *Economic Development and Cultural Change*, 53 (3): 655–683.

Bellows, J. and Miguel, E. (2006) 'War and Institutions: New Evidence from Sierra Leone', *American Economic Review*, 96 (2): 394–399.

Bircan, C., Brück, T. and Vothknecht, M. (2010) *Violent Conflict and Inequality*, HiCN Working Paper, no. 77.

Blattman, C. (2009) 'From Violence to Voting: War and Political Participation in Uganda', *American Political Science Review*, 103 (2): 231.

Blattman, C. and Annan, J. (2009) 'The Consequences of Child Soldiering', *Review of Economics and Statistics*, 92(4): 882–898.

Brockett, C.D. (1990) *Land, Power, and Poverty: Agrarian Transformation and Political Conflict in Central America,* Boston, MA: Unwin Hyman.

Brück, T. (2004) *Coping Strategies in Post-War Rural Mozambique*, HiCN Working Paper 2, Households in Conflict Network, www.hicn.org. Last accessed 27 June 2012.

Brück, T. and Vothknecht, M. (2011) 'Impact of Violent Conflict on Women's Economic Opportunities', in K. Kuehnast, C. de Jonge Oudraat and H. Hernes (eds) *Women and War – Power and Protection in the 21th Century*, Washington DC: United States Institute of Peace Press.

Bundervoet, T. (2006) *Livestock, Activity Choices and Conflict: Evidence from Burundi*, HiCN Working Paper 24, Households in Conflict Network, www.hicn.org. Last accessed 27 June 2012.

Bundervoet, T. and Verwimp, P. (2005) *Civil War and Economic Sanctions: An Analysis of Anthropometric Outcomes in Burundi*, HiCN Working Paper 11, Households in Conflict Network, www.hicn.org

Butler, C. and Gates, S. (2007) 'Communal Violence and Property Rights', paper presented at the third workshop of the Households in Conflict Network, Institute of Development Studies, Brighton, UK, 10–11 December.

Calderón, V., Gáfaro, M. and Ibáñez, A.M. (2011) *Forced Migration, Female Labour Force Participation, and Intra-household Bargaining: Does Conflict Empower Women?* MICROCON Research Working Paper 56, Brighton: MICROCON.

Caprioli, M. (2003) 'Gender Equality and State Aggression: The Impact of Domestic Gender Equality on State First Use of Force', *International Interactions*, 29(3): 195–214.

Castles, S. and Van Hear, N. (2005) *Developing DFID's Policy Approach to Refugees and Internally Displaced Persons,* Report to the Conflict and Humanitarian Affairs Department, Oxford: Refugee Studies Centre.

Clark, C. (2006) *Livelihood Networks and Decision-Making Among Congolese Young People in Formal and Informal Refugee Contexts in Uganda*, HiCN Working Paper 13, Households in Conflict Network, www.hicn.org. Last accessed 27 June 2012.

Colletta, N.J. and Cullen, M.L. (2000) *Violent Conflict and the Transformation of Social Capital: Lessons from Cambodia, Rwanda, Guatemala, and Somalia*, Washington DC: World Bank.

Czaika, M. and Kis-Katos, K. (2007) *Civil Conflict and Displacement: Village-Level Determinants of Forced Migration in Aceh*, HiCN Working Paper 32, Households in Conflict Network, www.hicn.org. Last accessed 27 June 2012.

Date-Bah, E. (2003) Introduction, in *Jobs after War: A Critical Challenge in the Peace and Reconstruction Puzzle*, Geneva: International Labor Office, pp. 1–29.

Deininger, K. (2003) 'Causes and Consequences of Civil Strife: Micro-Level Evidence from Uganda', *Oxford Economic Papers*, 55: 579–606.

Deininger, K., Ibáñez, A. and Querubin, P. (2004) *Towards Sustainable Return Policies for the Displaced Population: Why Are Some Displaced Households More Willing to Return than Others?*, HiCN Working Paper 7, Households in Conflict Network, www.hicn.org. Last accessed 27 June 2012.

Dubois, P., de Janvry, A. and Sadoulet, E. (2008) 'Effects on School Enrollment and Performance of a Conditional Transfers Program in Mexico', Department of Agricultural & Resource Economics, UC Berkeley, Working Paper Series.

Duflo, E. and Udry, C. (2004) 'Intrahousehold Resource Allocation in Côte d'Ivoire: Social Norms, Separate Accounts and Consumption Choices', Working Paper Series No. 10498, Cambridge, MA: National Bureau of Economic Research.

El-Bushra J. and Sahl, M.G. (2005) *Cycles of Violence: Gender Relations and Armed Conflict*, Nairobi and London: ACORD.

Geneva Declaration Secretariat (2008) *Global Burden of Armed Conflict*, Geneva: Geneva Declaration.

Goldring, L. (2002) 'Rethinking Remittances: Social and Political Dimensions of Individual and Collective Remittances', CERLAC Working Paper Series, University of York.

González, M. and Lopez, R. (2007) 'Political Violence and Farm Household Efficiency in Colombia', Selected Paper prepared for presentation at the American Agricultural Economics Association Annual Meeting, Providence, RI, 24–27 July.

Hoddinott, J. and Haddad, L. (1991) 'Household Expenditures, Child Anthropometric Status and the Intrahousehold Division of Income: Evidence from the Cote d'Ivoire', Discussion paper 155, Research Program in Development Studies, Woodrow Wilson School.

Huntington, S.P. (1996) *The Clash of Civilizations and the Remaking of the World Order*, New York: Simon & Shuster.

Ibáñez, A.M. and Moya, A. (2009) 'Do conflicts create poverty traps? Asset losses and recovery for displaced households in Colombia', *Research Working Papers*, Brighton: MICROCON.

Justino, P. (2007) 'Carrot or Stick? Redistributive Transfers versus Policing in Contexts of Civil Unrest', MICROCON WP 3, (http://www.microconflict.eu/publications/RWP3_PJ.pdf). Last accessed 27 June 2012.

Justino, P. (2009) 'Poverty and Violent Conflict: A Micro-Level Perspective on the Causes and Duration of Warfare', *Journal of Peace Research*, 46 (3): 315–333.

Justino, P. (2012a) 'Violent Conflict and Human Capital Accumulation', in *Elgar Companion to Civil War and Fragile States*. (eds) Graham Brown and Arnim Langer. Forthcoming.

Justino, P. (2012b) 'War and Poverty', in *Handbook of the Economics of Peace and Conflict*, Oxford University Press. (eds) Michelle Garfinkel and Stergios Skaperdas, Chapter 27. In press.

Justino, P. and Shemyakina, O. (2010) *Remittances and Labor Supply in Post-Conflict Tajikistan*, HiCN Working Paper 83.

Justino, P. and Verwimp, P. (2008) *Poverty Dynamics, Violent Conflict and Convergence in Rwanda*. MICROCON Research Working Paper 4, Brighton: MICROCON.

Kalyvas, S.N. (2007) *The Logic of Violence in Civil Wars*. Cambridge University Press.

Kalyvas, S.N. (2008) 'Promises and Pitfalls of an Emerging Research Programme: The Microdynamics of Civil War', in Stathis N. Kalyvas, Ian Shapiro and Tarek Masoud (eds), *Order, Conflict and Violence*, Cambridge University Press.

Kalyvas, S. and Kocher, M. (2007) 'How "Free" is Free-Riding in Civil Wars?', *World Politics*, 59 (2): 177–216.

Keen, D. (1997) 'A Rational Kind of Madness', *Oxford Development Studies*, 25 (1): 65–75.

Kondylis, F., (2010) 'Conflict displacement and labor market outcomes in post-war Bosnia and Herzegovina', *Journal of Development Economics*, 93(2), pp. 235–248.

Kumar, K. (2000) *Women and Women's Organizations in Post-Conflict Societies: The Role of International Assistance*, Washington DC: USAID.

Lindley, A., (2007) *Remittances in Fragile Settings: A Somali Case Study*, HiCN Working Paper no. 27, Households in Conflict Network (www.hicn.org)

McEvoy-Levy, S. (2006) *Troublemakers or Peacemakers? Youth and Post-Accord Peace Building*, Notre Dame, IN: University of Notre Dame Press.

McKay, A. and Loveridge, S. (2005) *Exploring the Paradox of Rwandan Agricultural Household Income and Nutritional Outcomes in 1990 and 2000*, Staff Paper 2005–06, Department of Agricultural Economics, Michigan State University, Michigan.

Raeymaekers, T. (2011) 'Forced Displacement and Youth Employment in the Aftermath of the Congo War: From Making a Living to Making a Life,' *MICROCON Research Working Paper*, no. 38.

Regan, P.M. and Paskeviciute, A. (2003) 'Women's Access to Politics and Peaceful States', *Journal of Peace Research,* 40(3): 287–302.

Rodriguez, C. and Sanchez, F. (2009) *Armed Conflict Exposure, Human Capital Investments and Child Labor: Evidence from Colombia*, HiCN Working Paper, no. 68 (November).

Sandler, T. and Enders, W. (2004) 'An Economic Perspective on Transnational Terrorism', *European Journal of Political Economy*, 20: 301–316.

Schindler, K. (2010) *Who Does What in a Household after Genocide? Evidence from Rwanda*, HiCN Working Paper 90, Households in Conflict Network (www.hicn.org). Last accessed 27 June 2012.

Shemyakina, O. (2006) *The Effect of Armed Conflict on Accumulation of Schooling: Results from Tajikistan*, HiCN Working Paper 12, Households in Conflict Network, www.hicn.org. Last accessed 27 June 2012.

UNESCO (2011) *The Hidden Crisis: Armed Conflict and Education*, Education for All Global Monitoring Report, Paris: UNESCO.

UNHCR (2011) *UNHCR Statistical Yearbook 2010*, United Nations High Commissioner for Refugees, http://www.unhcr.org/statistics. Last accessed 27 June 2012.

United Nations (1994) *An Agenda for Development: Report of the Secretary-General*, UN Doc A/48/935, 6 May.

United Nations (2004) *A More Secure World*, United Nations: New York.

United Nations (2005) *In Fuller Freedom*, United Nations: New York.

Urdal, H. (2004) *The Devil in the Demographics: The Effect of Youth Bulges on Domestic Armed Conflict, 1950–2000*, Social Development Papers – Conflict Prevention and Reconstitution, Paper no 14, World Bank.

Urdal, H. and Hoelscher, K. (2009) *Urban Youth Bulges and Social Disorder An Empirical Study of Asian and Sub-Saharan African Cities*, World Bank Policy Research Working Paper no 5110.

Verpoorten, M. (2005) 'Self-Insurance in Rwandan Households: The Use of Livestock as a Buffer Stock in Times of Violent Conflict', mimeo, KU Leuven, Belgium.

Walter, B.F. (2004) 'Does Conflict Beget Conflict? Explaining Recurring Civil War', *Journal of Peace Research*, 41 (3): 371–388.

Wood, E.J. (2003) *Insurgent Collective Action and Civil War in El Salvador*, Cambridge Studies in Comparative Politics. New York: Cambridge University Press.

World Bank (2006) *Community-Driven Development in the Context of Conflict-Affected Countries: Challenges and Opportunities*, Washington DC: World Bank.

World Bank (2011) *World Development Report: Conflict, Security and Development*, Washington DC: World Bank.

21

ORGANIC VERSUS STRATEGIC APPROACHES TO PEACEBUILDING

Sherrill Stroschein

Introduction

Many approaches to peacebuilding and assistance, or international 'helping', are grounded in an individualist perspective of social life. In this perspective, individual actors calculate their options and make strategic choices according to their individual goals. This calculation can produce conflict, as in the case of perceived 'security dilemmas' (Posen 1993; Fearon 1994) or it might provide a means for sustainable peace (Fearon and Laitin 1996), or for international actors to broker and preserve a peace (Walter 2002), by providing sanctions and incentives to influence preferred behavior. In the area of charitable assistance, the provision of resources to a group is understood to help them achieve their goals; only one group needs to be the focus of aid. While these individualist insights make some valuable contributions to the area of helping, they overlook the fact that social life is an inherently relational phenomenon. Communities at which intervention is aimed are comprised of *relations* between individuals (Petersen 2001; Varshney 2001), and it is a disruption of this web of relations that is constitutive of conflict. In addition, the provision of resources to one group can destabilize ongoing interactions between groups. In this relational, organic view, peacebuilding consists of reconstructing the mechanisms that facilitate sustained and peaceable interactions. Assistance to groups should reflect these dynamics. These interactions and mechanisms are often blind spots for those with an individualist view on these settings. In addition, efforts to provide humanitarian assistance to one group may disrupt the balance of this interaction, nullifying their potential contributions and increasing tensions between groups, unbeknownst to those trying to help.

In this chapter, I outline two examples of efforts by internationals to provide help in Romania during the 1990s. While well-intentioned, these efforts were informed by individualist, rather than organic premises – which proved disastrous for their efforts. In one instance, an effort by a Western NGO to broker an agreement between ethnic elites backfired as the elites were then punished from within their respective groups. Not only was the agreement rendered meaningless, but the elites also lost some legitimacy among their populations and the NGO suffered a public relations disaster; years later, the 'Neptun' incident (named after the sea resort where the agreement was signed) remains a joke in the country. Second, I will examine how a focus on humanitarianism can be coopted (Franks and Richmond 2008) by local actors and used as a weapon in their disputes with each other. In this instance, an effort by a Swiss NGO to build an orphanage became mired in a tense dispute regarding local ethnic demographics in Romania. Not only was the orphanage project a failure, but also the effort worsened tensions between Hungarians and Romanians for years to follow. Finally, I will close the chapter with an outline of some recommendations for how an organic perspective might better serve the success of such efforts.

Individualist views on peacebuilding

The liberal peace approach to peacebuilding (Paris 2004) is grounded in Western concepts emerging from the Enlightenment, including liberalism's focus on individuals (Mac Ginty 2011: 4). This kind of individualist paradigm produces a base assumption that individuals are the source of action in social life, and that they make calculated, often rational decisions about these actions – the theory of rational choice (Elster 1986: 2–4). These premises create two different models for peacebuilding in a conflictual or potentially conflictual setting. In the first model, an individual who is uncertain about the goals of another individual, and has reason to fear that individual, may find it rational to attack first. This premise, known within a local context as the 'security dilemma' (Posen 1993), implies that reducing uncertainty and fear between individuals should remove this incentive. Similarly, a group can be reduced to a unitary actor within these accounts, thus an identity group might attack another group first due to uncertainty and fear. For this reason, one frequent solution to peacebuilding problems is to provide 'credible commitments' between individuals or identity groups, to reduce fear and uncertainty (Fearon 1994; Walter 2002). These commitments are often understood to be enforced by external actors (Walter 2002). In this conception, external actors may help to reduce conflict by remaining in an enforcer, Leviathan role to ensure peace between individuals or groups – conceived of as strategic actors. This triad of an agreement between parties enforced by an external entity can be effective, because it reflects the logic that a hierarchical use of force is an effective means of maintaining order. However, it may imply a long-term commitment by internationals.

In the second model facilitated by individualist premises, there need not be an external enforcer present. Instead, the elites of each group maintain peace within a diverse setting by setting punishments for their 'subjects' (ordinary people of the same identity group) who harm individuals of the other group (Fearon and Laitin 1996). In an extreme conception of this model, interaction between groups may also be punished, due to the potential danger of conflict that they might imply. Strategic individuals are thus less likely to engage in peace-violating activities against the other group. Ongoing peace in this model is also facilitated by communication between the elites of each group, to reduce any potential uncertainty regarding their commitments to control their members. The logic of this model may be attractive to internationals, as it could imply a reduced involvement that rests upon empowering elites and supporting communication between them.

Both of these approaches can be frequently observed in peacebuilding practices. But there is an irony inherent in their use. The liberal framework of individualism and calculated decision making is often understood to empower individuals; however, both of these models involve strict hierarchies in which ordinary individuals are disempowered relative to external actors or to group elites. The notion of a creation or preservation of order relies on a hierarchical structure of enforcement, as opposed to bridging ties between groups (Varshney 2001).

The area of resource assistance reflects a similar problem. Assistance to one group may disrupt a delicate balance of interaction between groups. Moreover, attempts at providing resources may be coopted by local actors in battles with each other. An understanding of relational dynamics is crucial for successful efforts of 'helping' by internationals, as outlined in the following section.

Local interaction mechanisms versus strategic games

In a paradigm of rational, strategic individual actors, the scenarios by which they encounter each other in social life can be mapped using game theory (Elster 1986: 7–9; Morrow 1994). Game theory can evaluate the potential range of actions for individual actors in such encounters, by providing a matrix for the outcomes that emerge from the potential decisions of each. One of the premises of game theory is that individuals will try to maximize their utility, or the potential benefits that might accrue from an interaction, a fact that should make some joint outcomes more likely than others. Game theory could represent the first model of peacebuilding above by outlining the potential strategies of cooperation or defection from an agreement with or without a potential enforcer to show the effectiveness of the enforcer presence (see Walter 2002). For the second model above, game theory could demonstrate the calculations of ordinary people with regard to the sanctions enforced by their elites, or could also diagram potential interactions between elites of each group.

While there are some interesting insights that might be gained through this logical application of strategic theory to interaction, within game theory the interactions are grounded in a strict conception of individuality. Individuals might encounter each other in an interaction, but they are understood as having goals and preferences (perhaps originating from identities) that are fully attached to that individual and are separate from the interaction itself. In a similar logic, assisting one group with additional resources should improve their condition and facilitate maximizing their utility.

But such assistance does not take place in a vacuum. This independence of identities and interactions from resources and goals is almost never the case in the empirical world. In the absence of formal military intervention, local peace or conflict relies on local interactions (Roy 1994; Varshney 2001; Tilly 2003; Stroschein 2011). Without militaries or militias, violence is not an abstract threat directed from the center, but rather takes place at the local level, where perpetrators have actual access to each other such that harm can be committed. The local interactions that produce either conflict or coexistence have an organic character. The fact that there is more coexistence than conflict in mixed settings is due to an overwhelming practicality about the limits of those interactions, one that emerges organically (Mac Ginty 2011; Stroschein 2012). As noted by Mac Ginty, even deeply divided societies often find 'some sort of equilibrium' that is a product of local 'common sense' regarding the given fact of living together on the same territory (Mac Ginty 2011: 18). Those living in such settings have a concept of cultivating their 'quality of life' (Mitchell 2011: 1624). It is for this reason that there is more coexistence than conflict in mixed group settings.

Disruptions to these ongoing interactions may take place through an incursion by actors from outside of a local setting, such as militias or militaries (Stroschein 2005), or through international assistance to one group. Indeed, disruptions may also emerge organically, reflecting a spiral of negative interactions (Roy 1994; Brubaker 1996). While certainly not flawless, there are some self-correcting mechanisms inherent in the pragmatic stances that can emerge in such processes. Intervention by externals will be most successful if it facilitates these pro-coexistence interactions, rather than hindering them.

With attention to assumptions and theory, these kinds of local interactions are about relations, rather than about individuals (Mac Ginty 2011: 18; Stroschein 2012). Intervention that is grounded upon the premise that these settings are comprised of individuals acting strategically may mis-diagnose the problems and thus mis-apply potential solutions. Consider, for example, the model that coexistence emerges because elites coerce 'their' populations to behave using sanctions and incentives (Fearon and Laitin 1996). This model would imply that interveners should focus on influencing the actions of group elites to promote peace. This type of elite-based and hierarchical model for intervention is quite cost-effective and efficient, as it justifies a focus on simply a few individuals rather than on whole populations (Mac Ginty 2011: 10). Moreover, it is supported by the sound strategic logic of the model and thus appears to have solid theoretical grounding.

This individualist model, originating from economics, clashes with a more sociological approach that emphasizes relations. As outlined above, these local community settings reflect a *relational* character of ongoing interactions. In this context, *all* participants, rather than simply elites, 'work out shared agreements and tacit understandings in response to everyday contingencies' (Hall 1987: 6). The setting is one of a myriad of dynamic, incremental interactions across the society. As noted by Hall, order is negotiated in a social context, and is 'dynamic and changing because it is constantly reviewed' (Hall 1987: 6). Thousands of micro-transactions between ordinary individuals each day either promote or reduce peace (Pickering 2007: 2–3). The influence of elites on these interactions cannot be assumed to be as influential or as unproblematic as outlined in the strategic model. They must be filtered through these incremental and diffuse local interactions.

Nor is the influence of external actors necessarily as unproblematic as intended by those who wish to engage in help. These actions also must be filtered through the incremental and diffuse interactions taking place at the local level. In essence, interventions in such local contexts resemble trying to alter a machine that is already in motion, without a clear view of all of its moving parts. As noted by observers of peacebuilding operations, these efforts tend to produce a 'hybrid peace' that is the result of an additional interaction, one between international actors and those on the ground. In this inherently relational setting, 'no actor is able to unilaterally impose its will' (Mac Ginty 2011: 70), including international actors or elites. As noted by Pickering, international actors are simply one of six elements in a multilevel network model – and each element may interact with each of the others (Pickering 2007: 16, 47). In order to have a better sense of how interventions might interact with local ecosystems, it would be wise for internationals to have a strong sense of local context. Two examples of interventions in which more such understanding would have improved results are outlined below. The stories are outlined first, and a discussion of their implications appears in the section following them.

Ethnic elites and the NGO: The Neptun Sea Resort incident

The spring of 1993 witnessed several demonstrations by ethnic Hungarians regarding local government powers. These particular protests were about the government appointment of ethnic Romanian prefects at the head of two Hungarian-majority counties. The ethnic Hungarian party, the Democratic Union of Hungarians in Romania, or UDMR (RMDSz in Hungarian), also formally protested the decision in the central parliament, and was working on some proposals for increasing local government powers in a variety of forms, including potential autonomy (Stroschein 2012: 207). A violent riot between Hungarians and Romanians had also taken place in March 1990 in the town of Târgu Mureș, related to a conflict over language use and education (Stroschein 2011, 2012). In this context of general agitation, an NGO called the Project on Ethnic Relations (PER), based in Princeton, New Jersey, organized a meeting between Hungarian and Romanian elites at a resort called 'Neptun' on the Black Sea. The goal of the meeting was to obtain a signed agreement between elites that would demonstrate a commitment to work to reduce group tensions. It was the second of two meetings between these elites, with the first in February 1992.

In the logic of the elite-driven theory of ethnic relations outlined above (see Fearon and Laitin 1996), the meeting made good sense and was an attractive project for an NGO such as this one. An agreement between elites seemed to be the most efficient means to quell tensions between groups within the premises of an elite-driven framework. As outlined in the mission and strategies on the organization's website, it 'works with strategic elites, national and regional opinion leaders, government officials, and professionals on projects dealing with ethnic conflict, and helps them obtain expert advice' (Project on Ethnic Relations 2012). In arranging meetings between elites of groups, it intended to foster dialogue opportunities between them in a neutral environment. These are very reasonable premises for the work of an NGO, and the PER was indeed successful in arranging such dialogues throughout the region. The PER describes its work in Romania as representing 'some of its most notable achievements', and in these meetings 'agreements were reached between Romanian officials and leaders of the Hungarian community on a number of disputed issues' (Project on Ethnic Relations 2012).

Within the Hungarian party, the UDMR / RMDSz, however, a storm emerged following a report on the July 1993 PER meeting at the Neptun Sea Resort. Those individuals within the UDMR who had not been present at the meeting were incensed when news of an 'agreement' between some Hungarians and government representatives became public. One means by which they learned that the meeting took place was through an article in the *New York Times* by David Binder, praising the work of the PER in bringing the groups together. The Binder article included a (later corrected) reference to the Hungarian party as being an irredentist organization that wished Transylvania to be returned to Hungary (Binder 1993; Szabadság 1993c, 1993d). Such an error was not unusual in the Western press of the time, due to its simplistic approach to regional complexities. But it caused an outcry involving theories of conspiracy and an accusation that those meeting with the PER had caused irreparable damage to the Hungarian party in international circles. A public relations coup for the PER wreaked havoc for those who had participated in the 1993 meeting.

Even more thunderous and longstanding was the internal debate over the capacity in which these Hungarian individuals had taken part in the 'secret' meetings, and the nature of the agreements that had been claimed to be reached, particularly in English-language material on the PER. The accusations were initially spearheaded by the UDMR's honorary president László Tőkés,[1] but these were quickly joined by a number of others in the less moderate camp of the UDMR (Hargita Népe 1993a). Questions emerged regarding why the meetings had not been more transparent, and the three individuals who had participated were accused of falling under an undue influence of Romanian government officials. There was a particular focus on the kind of 'agreements' claimed to be reached, conducted without the full involvement with the UDMR membership, and whether these Hungarian individuals had brokered a secret arrangement with the Romanian government (Népújság 1993a). As the discussion evolved, these accusations escalated into those of a 'crisis of legitimacy' with elites acting on their own for the Hungarian party, including accusations of 'treason' (Hargita Népe 1993d; Szabadság 1993c).

The more moderate elements within the UDMR quickly put forth a response that there was 'no agreement' or formal declaration, and that the Hungarians who had been at the PER meeting were there in a 'personal capacity'. The response included a mention that the strongly-worded discussion of the success of the meeting was due to the Romanian elites wishing for some 'positive propaganda abroad'. A sharply-worded criticism was levied at the *New York Times*, for the Binder article containing 'a number of errors' (Hargita Népe 1993b; Szabadság 1993a). The three who had participated in the meeting had to make a public statement that the meetings were not secret and that they had not been negotiations (Hargita Népe 1993c; Szabadság 1993b).

The actions of the three Hungarian elites who had been involved in the PER meetings were then scrutinized in a meeting of the highest party membership, called to consider these events. Some of the more strident members of the party wanted them to resign as members of parliament, or to face some sort of punishments from the party, perhaps along ethics lines. While they were not removed from office, their actions were classified as a 'political mistake' that had brought harm to the party. It was also decided that actions and decisions would be more formalized within the UDMR, and that any potential agreements would need to be signed by the leadership, including by the honorary president, Tőkés (Szabadság 1993e, 1993f; Népújság 1993b; Hargita Népe 1993e, 1993f). In spite of these provisions, the more extreme wing of the UDMR continued to levy attacks, calling for resignations (Hargita Népe 1993g), and the resulting suspicion fostered increased fragmentation among the Hungarian party membership.

The orphanage incident

The city of Odorheiu Secuiesc/Székelyudvarhely lies in the Hungarian enclave in mountainous central Romania. During the 1990s, its population of 40,000 was approximately 97 percent Hungarian. Within the Hungarian ethnic community, the majority of the city's inhabitants are more precisely known as the Székely, a group that is part of a broader Hungarian identity. Throughout the 1990s, the town had fallen into a dispute with a Swiss NGO, Basel Hilft, regarding an orphanage that the NGO wished to build there. Soon after the revolution, the Swiss group had volunteered to contribute funds for a facility that local authorities understood would provide care for handicapped children in the region. In the course of the design and construction of the building, the Swiss NGO turned the administration of the property over to a Romanian group, and later chose to donate it to a group of Romanian nuns of a Greek Catholic order.

In the course of these changes, the future institution began to be described as an orphanage for children from throughout Romania, rather than for local children alone. Local authorities angrily disputed the change, arguing that they had understood the institute to be for children from their community, not from the rest of the country. They began to accuse the Swiss NGO and its Romanian counterparts of a plot to 'Romanize' or 'colonize' the community through the process of setting up an orphanage. Stories were spread in the local media that the children might be infected with AIDS (Weber and Andreescu 1997). Thus began a long dispute over the 'Cserehát' affair.

In 1996, the city authorities began a formal suit against the Romanian administrative group and the Greek Catholic order, attempting to halt progress on the institution. A local court official sealed the building. But by the spring of 1997, a court decision sanctioned the resumption of construction, and the nuns took up residence in the building in March. The arrival of the nuns upset a number of local inhabitants, and on April 18 a demonstration of several hundred local residents took place outside of the building. The crowd included the mayor as well as a local councilor (who was also a union leader) and church official, who made speeches against the efforts to go against the city's wishes on the building (Hargita Népe 1997a). In several meetings that followed, the representative of the Swiss NGO tried to add calm words to the situation, but the NGO had relinquished responsibility of the building to the religious order and was clearly rather unprepared for this unfolding of events. After a well-attended meeting on May 27 brought no resolution, on May 28 another demonstration was held (Hargita Népe 1997b).

This demonstration turned ugly. A crowd of a thousand to a few thousand local residents[2] angrily surrounded the building and broke inside, removing four Greek Catholic nuns living inside with physical force, and then locking the building behind them. While the nuns were not really harmed by the mob, they were threatened and frightened by them (Hargita Népe 1997c; Adevărul Harghitei 1997a, 1997b; Szabadság 1997; Weber and Andreescu 1997). Suspicions grew regarding the nature of the Swiss NGO and its source of funding, with the president of the county council in the neighboring enclave county making a public declaration that several questions regarding the NGO's activities and its relation to the Romanian religious order remained unanswered. The NGO found itself in the uncomfortable position of having to outline a detailed report on its motivations and the course of events for the local press (Hargita Népe 1997d, 1997f; Adevărul Harghitei 1997c). In spite of these efforts, suspicions remained, and the NGO's accounts were strongly disputed in the press by the former mayor (Hargita Népe 1997g).

Discussions years later with locals revealed continued Hungarian suspicions regarding the motivations behind the orphanage, with several noting it as a Romanian plot to change the local demographics. Given previous efforts by the communist regime to change these demographics by moving in outsiders, this perspective was plausible to many. At the same time, many Hungarians continued to formally frame the conflict as a property dispute, rather than as an ethnic dispute (Hargita Népe 1997e). This particular frame produced some more productive, though still tense, discussions over the next few months, and a standoff of sorts involving a government official took place in December. But over the next several years the matter was slowly worked out through the courts, with the orphanage eventually closing.

Organic versus strategic approaches

The stories above illustrate the way in which local interactions were disrupted by international interventions that were intended to help. Those who work for NGOs in the field soon learn that becoming aware of the local ecologies is crucial for viable 'helping' efforts (Huddleston 1999). In the story of the Neptun Sea Resort incident, there were two means by which the efforts at peacebuilding via elites created a scandal in which the Hungarian negotiators were attacked from within their party. First, there was a disjuncture between the NGO's desire to claim success by reaching an 'agreement' between the Hungarian and Romanian elites, and the need for locals to communicate with their constituents (Mitchell 2011: 1640). The Hungarian elites scrambled to claim that these were simply conversations taken in an informal capacity, directly counter to the NGO's claims in the English-language press. In addition, the effort to focus on elites, and to select those moderates who might be amenable to discussion, avoided the fact that the Hungarian party was (is) comprised of a diverse array of ideologies. The fact that the less moderate faction had not been part of the talks made them particularly keen to use the Neptun discussions as weapons against their more moderate opponents in the party, threatening that they should resign. These two facts raise questions regarding the legitimacy of such negotiations / agreements, and call into question the desirability of the elite-focused model for peacebuilding. Instead, an understanding of the diffuse and organic interactions that exist around and behind a few elites – forming an organic ecosystem of dynamic relations – should inform such peacebuilding attempts (Pickering 2007: 12; Mac Ginty 2011: 56–57). This type of scenario could be easily repeated in other settings, and could involve even more harm to those moderates involved in negotiations.

In the case of the orphanage incident, a well-intentioned effort by an NGO to create an orphanage for disadvantaged children in Romania went awry as it became a focal point in a local battle over demographics in a Hungarian enclave. At best, the NGO naively found itself in a situation that spun out of control. Local Hungarians instead tend to believe that its efforts to support an orphanage for ethnic Romanian children in the Hungarian enclave region were coopted (Franks and Richmond 2008: 81–82) by Romanian interests. In a context of strong ethnic cleavages, efforts at assisting one group may easily be coded by locals as part of that conflict, and can disrupt local interactions (Franks and Richmond 2008: 85). Both Hungarians and Romanians had become relatively used to the enclave remaining undisturbed, and thus a disruption to this status quo, no matter how innocent, became inflammatory. Even an orphanage could not escape this ongoing dynamic; international actors may imagine communities of moderates that do not emerge in practice (Franks and Richmond 2008: 86).

A crucial theme that emerges from both stories is the development of conspiracy theories around these NGO efforts. In the case of the orphanage, the NGO's attempts to outline its charitable intentions in the local press were viewed cynically by local Hungarians in light of their demographic concerns. Romanian-language newspapers demonstrated clear sympathy with the NGO, while the Hungarian-language local newspapers were full of suspicion regarding its activities. Similarly, the accusations levied from within the Hungarian party at those Hungarians who had attended the Neptun Sea Resort talks reflected a suspicion that they were being brought under 'undue influence' of Romanian officials. In this view, they could neither legitimately nor sincerely represent Hungarian interests.

These problems illustrate the need to approach interventions with a vision of a local ecosystem, in which well-intentioned moves can have unintended consequences. NGOs hoping to engage in peacebuilding or assistance activities should have an initial sense of the network of relations in a setting. Tracing out the potential relations in a setting, such as the relations between elites and non-elites, relations within a particular group between more and less moderate elements, and local demographic relations and historical practices should mitigate some of the potential pitfalls that can befall well-intentioned interveners. A view of assistance efforts to aid individual groups is not sufficient, as these groups do not exist in a vacuum, and assistance may disrupt local interactions. Moreover, a view of peacebuilding from an individualist, strategic perspective will mis-diagnose problems that are relational. Finally, NGOs should use this knowledge to consider where their goals may not align with those of the locals they wish to help, particularly in terms of publically claiming success through 'agreements' or through other metrics.

Conclusions

Local settings in which internationals may wish to intervene for 'helping' purposes are not arenas in which strategic individuals encounter each other. Instead, they are contexts full of diffuse relations and incremental interactions, many of which will be initially invisible to international actors. Interventions in local settings, whether for peacebuilding or resource assistance purposes, are like trying to alter a machine that is already in motion – and without a sense of all of its moving parts. In this chapter, I have outlined two stories of international interventions by NGOs in Romania during the 1990s that went awry due to some of these potential blind spots. While well-intentioned, these efforts were informed by individualist, rather than organic premises – which proved disastrous for their efforts. With a more relational approach to the local dynamics operating in settings of interest, NGOs and other international interveners will have greater power to avoid harm and provide real help.

Notes

1 Tőkés had gained a worldwide reputation as a key figure in the 1989 events that ended the previous regime.
2 Romanian sources tended to count around 500 participants.

References

Adevărul Harghitei (1997a) 'O nouă Golgată cu pecetea 'Corpului de Autoguvernare' din Odorheiu Secuiesc?', 30–31 May.

Adevărul Harghitei (1997b) 'Conflictul e artificial, dar intoleranţa etnico-religioasă e autentică!', 3 June.

Adevărul Harghitei (1997c) 'Nu mi-am putut imagina ca venind în România, să ajutăm nişte copii orfani, cu bani privaţi, să ajungă la ceea ce s-a întâmplat la Odorheiu Secuiesc', 12 June.

Binder, D. (1993) 'Romanians and Hungarians Building a Bit of Trust', *The New York Times*, July 20.

Brubaker, R. (1996) 'National Minorities, Nationalizing States, and External National Homelands in the New Europe', in Brubaker, R., *Nationalism Reframed: Nationhood and the National Question in the New Europe*, New York: Cambridge University Press: 55–76.

Elster, J. (1986) (ed.) *Rational Choice*, New York: New York University Press.

Fearon, J. (1994) 'Ethnic War as a Commitment Problem', paper presented at the American Political Science Association, New York, August 30–September 2 1994. Available at: http://www.stanford.edu/~jfearon/papers/ethcprob.pdf. Last accessed 27 June 2012.

Fearon, J. and Laitin, D. (1996) 'Explaining Interethnic Cooperation', *American Political Science Review* 90 (4): 715–35.

Franks, J. and Richmond, O. (2008) 'Coopting Liberal Peace-building: Untying the Gordian Knot in Kosovo', *Cooperation and Conflict* 43: 81–103.

Hall, P. (1987) 'Interactionism and the Study of Social Organization', *The Sociological Quarterly* 28 (1): 1–22.

Hargita Népe (1993a) 'Tőkés László sajtóértekezlete', 4 August.

Hargita Népe (1993b) 'Az RMDSz nevében tárgyalni cask az elnök mandátumával lehet', 5 August.

Hargita Népe (1993c) 'A megbeszélések nem voltak titkosak', 6 August.

Hargita Népe (1993d) 'Az Erdélyi Magyar Kezdeményezés RMDSz-platform közleménye', 12 August.

Hargita Népe (1993e) 'PER-per két vesztes féllel', 28 September.

Hargita Népe (1993f) 'Kerekasztalt javasol az RMDSz', 29 September.

Hargita Népe (1993g) 'Erdélyi Magyar Kezdeményezés RMDSz platform nyilatkozat', 8 October.

Hargita Népe (1997a) 'Székelyudvarhely: Élőlánc a Cserehaton', 19 April.

Hargita Népe (1997b) 'Székelyudvarhely: Még mindig feszült a hangulat a Cserehát miatt', 29 May.

Hargita Népe (1997c) 'Közlemény', 30 May.

Hargita Népe (1997d) 'Közlemény', 3 June.

Hargita Népe (1997e) 'Dészi Zoltán prefectus sajtónyilatkozata', 4 June.

Hargita Népe (1997f) 'Cyrill Bürgel levele: Az igazság a székelyudvarhelyi Szent Józef gyermekotthonról', 5 June.

Hargita Népe (1997g) 'Bürgel úr és a trójai faló', 7 June.

Huddleston, M. (1999) 'Innocents Abroad: Reflections from a Public Administration Consultant in Bosnia', *Public Administration Review* 59 (2): 147–58.

Mac Ginty, R. (2011) *International Peacebuilding and Local Resistance: Hybrid Forms of Peace*, Basingstoke: Palgrave Macmillan.

Mitchell, A. (2011) 'Quality / control: International Peace Interventions and "the Everyday"', *Review of International Studies* 37: 1623–45.

Morrow, J. (1994) *Game Theory for Political Scientists*, Princeton: Princeton University Press.

Népújság (1993a) 'Hullámverés az RMDSz-ben', 5 August.

Népújság (1993b) 'Állásfoglalás', 28 September.

Paris, R. (2004) *At War's End: Building Peace after Civil Conflict*, New York: Cambridge University Press.

Petersen, R. (2001) *Resistance and Rebellion: Lessons from Central Europe*, New York: Cambridge University Press.

Pickering, P. (2007) *Peacebuilding in the Balkans: The View from the Ground Floor*, Ithaca: Cornell University Press.

Posen, B. (1993) 'The Security Dilemma and Ethnic Conflict,' *Survival* 35: 27–47.

Project on Ethnic Relations (2012) *About PER*, Princeton, NJ: PER. Online. Available HTTP: < http://www.per-usa.org/1997–2007/brochure.htm > (accessed 5 February 2012).

Roy, B. (1994) *Some Trouble with Cows: Making Sense of Social Conflict*, Berkeley: University of California Press.

Stroschein, S. (2005) 'Examining Ethnic Violence and Partition in Bosnia-Herzegovina', *Ethnopolitics* 4 (1): 49–64.

Stroschein, S. (2011) 'Microdynamics of Bilateral Ethnic Mobilization', *Ethnopolitics* 10 (1): 1–34.

Stroschein, S. (2012) *Ethnic Struggle, Coexistence, and Democratization in Eastern Europe*, New York: Cambridge University Press.

Szabadság (1993a) 'Közlemény', 5 August.

Szabadság (1993b) 'Választóink érdekeit képviseltük', 6 August.

Szabadság (1993c) 'Visszatekintő tájékoztatás', 13 August.

Szabadság (1993d) 'Bizalomerősítés David Binder-módra (?)', 18 August.

Szabadság (1993e) 'Közlemény', 2 September.

Szabadság (1993f) 'Közlemény', 29 September.

Szabadság (1997) 'Éleződő konfliktus Székelyudvarhelyen', 2 June.

Tilly, C. (2003) *The Politics of Collective Violence*, New York: Cambridge University Press.

Varshney, A. (2001) 'Ethnic Conflict and Civil Society: India and Beyond', *World Politics* 53: 362–98.

Walter, B. (2002) Committing to Peace: The Successful Settlement of Civil Wars, Princeton: Princeton University Press.

Weber, R. and Andreescu, G. (1997) 'Evenimentele din Odorheiul Secuisesc, Raportul comitetului Helsinki Român', *22* (weekly newspaper), 1–10 November.

22

EDUCATION AND LEARNING

Patricia A. Maulden

Introduction

War and violence can break down established socio-cultural norms, values, and practices, normalizing aspects of violence in everyday and community life. When peace arrives, these non-violent concepts of legitimacy require review and perhaps reconceptualization or re-learning as part of building and sustaining peace. Education represents a process of individual empowerment, fostering the progression from one cognitive or affective state to another in a bottom-up rather than a top-down progression, requiring shifts in perceptions and an inner transformation. Change at the individual level can affect the family and household as well as the community levels. Empowerment, however, is socially-embedded agency and choice inextricably linked to values which reflect the wider community context (Snyder 2011: 182–3). That said, education and learning increase human capital or knowledge and cognitive skills as well as allowing individuals to use non-cognitive or affective skill, for example, attitude, motivation, and talent to enhance their productive capacities (Nübler 2000: 48–51). As they do so, they develop self-confidence, a sense of value as a contributing community member, and hope for the future, overriding the wartime doubt, hopelessness, and despair.

Issues regarding access, quality, and cost of education shadow not only the run-up to conflict but also the road back to peace. Collier (2001: 148–9) notes that lack of widespread educational opportunities for young men correlates with conflict potential, the less opportunity the greater the likelihood for conflict. On the other hand, the transition period following the signing of peace accords can present a 'window of opportunity' where educational reform sits at the center of post-conflict reconciliation and reconstruction agendas, for example, as in El Salvador, Guatemala, and Nicaragua in the 1980s and 1990s (Marques and Bannon 2003). As part of post-conflict development, however, educational reform can contribute to breaking the cycle of violence, refuel the previous conflict, or trigger a new one. This disparity occurs due to the overlap of education with many of the root causes of conflict. In other words, educational reform includes recognition of identity, cultural development, community survival, distribution of resources, access to political power, and ideological orientation (Degu 2005: 129–45). For example, to focus too heavily on political factors could impact on the distribution of educational resources as well as the ideological orientation of subsequent curricula. This might mirror the pre-war ways that many communities find abhorrent, setting up as part of reform a continuation of a contested past.

For societies emerging from civil war one of the main challenges becomes to move away from pre-war concepts and alignments toward a redefining of relationships from the political, the ethnic, the social, and the individual levels in ways that will foster nonviolence and increase social cohesion. Education is tasked with facilitating many of these desired changes in individuals, groups, and communities. In addition, education and educational reform become creating and sustaining powers behind the concept 'culture of peace' (de Rivera 2004: 535–42), meaning that education, particularly involving practices for the peaceful resolution of conflict, can serve to shift the pre-war or wartime norms, values, and practices toward nonviolent approaches to resolving differences. The culture or peace paradigm also includes, in part, sustainable development, human rights, gender equality, democratic participation, and tolerance (Boulding 2000). From this point of view, it is easy to see how, as in Central America, educational reform sits at the center of a much larger post-conflict agenda.

With these ideas in mind, education within communities and individuals becomes a more complex process, bringing in formal and informal approaches to knowledge and skills accumulation, critical thinking, and the ability to create peaceful relationships. This broad peace agenda must be operationalized within an environment where people continue to struggle with tension between tradition and modernity and boundaries erected to maintain power based on gender and age. The main goal underpinning the concept of education for all (UNESCO 1990) and the complexities listed above can be summarized as providing and maintaining a higher level of human security where the welfare of people at the community level remains paramount. That education acts as the transformative glue that holds the potential for human security together presents great opportunities but perhaps even greater challenges as will be explored throughout the remainder of this chapter.

Formal education

This section explores the roles that formal education (or schooling) can play in fostering peace as well as some of the constraints that can limit education's potential. As pointed out in the Introduction, education carries a heavy load of expectation in the process of stabilizing a negative peace (the absence of war) and consolidating a more positive post-conflict peace that encourages equity, opportunity, and individual dignity. During civil wars, formal education becomes almost impossible to maintain institutionally or to access personally. As a result, by the end of the war as was the case in Sierra Leone and Liberia, a generation of young people were left with little more than a year or two of schooling but yearning for a complete formal education or at least enough education and skills training to allow them to make an adequate living to support their families. As job insecurity feeds the potential for conflict, education, training, and subsequent employment give hope, dignity, and security to individuals and communities, strengthening a fragile peace. Government agencies or NGOs often make promises of education and training to ensure a better future but cannot fulfill them due to funding constraints, a dearth of qualified teachers, substandard school infrastructure, unavailable books and supplies, or simply a lack of political will. When this happens feelings of betrayal, anger, and hopelessness can lead to various levels of conflict, crime, and destructive behavior. In addition, if promises made are carried out but the economy remains stagnant and jobs nonexistent, similar negatives can be expected.

Formal education structures prior to the outbreak of civil war or violence often reinforced the social, cultural, economic, and political cleavages found in the larger society. Education was outside of many individuals' reach either for economic reasons or because of gender. In many places, education for girls and young women does not enter into the socio-cultural framework at all. When the war ends and NGOs come in to offer programs that are directed by women, with the mandate for inclusion of girls and women at all levels of programming, socio-cultural norms, values, and practices can and often do incorporate these values. Whether all forms of education programming are designed to encourage empowerment, however, remains an open question. One example would be the 'banking' approach to learning or the acquisition of a set store of knowledge (Freire 1999: 53–5) where information is a gift bestowed by the knowledgeable to those who know not. This model clearly defines the insiders (knowledgeable) and the outsiders (they who know not) and sets up or continues what Freire calls the 'structure of oppression.' In many cases, the structure of oppression and people's rejection of it played a role in generating civil war. Part of the peacebuilding agenda in the post-conflict environment involves transforming the oppressive structure to one that is more equitable and just. Education, both formal and informal, can play a key role in this process but does not in and of itself ensure the success of this endeavor.

Other perhaps more tangential consequences of education as it impacts peace could also be considered as potentially transforming. The day-to-day routine of schooling could aid in socialization, creating a sense of inclusion, gaining social value, and providing future social and economic benefits. Schools provide models of behaviors, values, beliefs, and attitudes that can guide individuals to adapt their own in response to what they see in a peaceful and positive environment. Equitable inclusion in educational opportunities allows individuals who may have previously been excluded to feel part of a larger community and valued in new ways. Attending school allows individuals to build social relationships, develop trust and self-confidence, and learn to participate and cooperate peacefully. These practices can be of extreme value throughout a person's life. Most communities place a high value on learning and subsequently on individuals who have earned an education (Dupuy 2008: 25–7). From a slightly different vantage point, education can impact peace through changing mindsets, cultivating a set of skills, promoting human rights, and the promotion of a culture inclusive of peaceful norms (Danesh 2006: 55–6). This could provide a framework through which individuals can 'create' peace in all aspects of their lives.

To this point, the approaches linking formal education and peace have been somewhat theoretical or best case scenarios. Using the example of Sierra Leone, the discussion now shifts to the impacts and reality of cost, policy, and tradition. Following the end of the civil war in Sierra Leone and culminating with the Truth and Reconciliation Report, education was placed front and center as an important peace dividend. There was an increase in enrollment of girls, partially subsidized by NGOs, and particularly boys who were former combatants. Over time, however, enrollment of boys remained somewhat steady but fewer girls attended as parents had to make economic choices regarding which child to send to school (Maulden 2007: 160–3). Human rights education has also proved challenging as has the focus on child rights as pushed by the NGOs. These concepts do not always line up with how life is lived in developing countries, for example concerning the value and necessity of child labor. In Sierra Leone (as well as Liberia) the saying goes, 'save the children, kill the parents' (Maulden 2011: 23). Child rights is seen to ignore child responsibilities, human rights bumping against traditional roles of parents and children. Discipline practices continue to include corporal punishment, most often lashes with a cane. In short, the notion of a 'culture of peace' through education has not as yet taken effect in Sierra Leonean schools as school violence is on the increase: knives brought to school, razor blades hidden in lunch bread, fights accompanying team sports, student rioting, teachers beaten, and vehicles burned (Paulson 2006: 343–5). These realities point to the lingering effects of violence that engulfed the country for so long as well as the limits of education, as yet not reformed, as a solution to social, economic, and cultural problems.

Finally, participants in formal education programs in the post-conflict environment are generally children and young people through the age of eighteen. That is not to say that individuals over the age of eighteen do not want or need additional education. Numeracy and minimal literacy skills could enhance earning power in the informal economy where most of the population in war-torn countries make their living. The education gap following war continues the cycle of poverty and despair among adults but they hope for better for their children. People of all ages hunger for education and increased skills as a way to better themselves in the world, and to gain dignity and self-respect. In other words, gaining an internal state of peace (Hicks 2011: 1) that can be extended outward to others.

Informal education

Informal or nonformal education includes seminars, workshops, skills training, apprenticeships, mentoring, technical training, and literacy and numeracy training for individuals not of official school age. Nonformal education can also focus on traditional or indigenous knowledge, not generally part of the 'knowledge hegemony' of either formal education structures or those supported by international agencies. Freire writes of 'problem posing' education that liberates through cognition and nonformal education types of transferals of information (1999: 60). Using this approach people reflect and act upon their world to transform it in an activation of the agent/structure dilemma. The popular education movement, as discussed by Lederach (1995: 25–7), presents a process of mutuality, for example students and teachers learning together, no one set of knowledge privileged over the other, an elicitive method that could break down barriers of power, gender, class. Regarding oral traditions or local knowledge, Verkoren (2008: 176–83) notes that traditional knowledge has not been captured in modern or formal education. There are many traditional methods of dispute resolution and practices to create peace among individuals and groups that over the war years have been dormant. Allowing these methods to become more widely known during the post-conflict period would certainly present an alternative framework for transformation that might resonate much more strongly with large segments of the population. Some international agencies respond more positively to the inclusion of tradition than do others but few if any change their program structure in significant ways to mutually engage with their program participants.

Immediately after the end of a civil war, internationally based organizations sponsor skills training, education, and other peace related formal and informal programs. They stay for a few years and then depart leaving the field clear for local ownership and expression of peacebuilding. Individuals trained in conflict resolution, family reunification, peace education, youth empowerment, gender equity, good governance, and livelihood strategies seize the opportunity to employ their efforts for the benefit of their communities. As they do so they also increase their feelings of self-worth, status in the community, and legitimacy as a positive influence in addition, of course, to having a paying job, no small thing in post-conflict settings. These benefits encourage former child soldiers, war victims, women, and youth in large numbers to become peacebuilding entrepreneurs – noting gaps in the peacebuilding market and creating programs and organizations to address those needs. As individuals and civil society groups organize to address particular concerns, not only do they meet some of their own basic needs but also fulfill the role of civil society in general – acting as intermediary between the individual and the state. The emphasis here is on the grassroots or civil society organizations started and maintained by individuals who would normally be outside of the civic power structure, who often experienced the full effects of war and are determined to work to prevent war's return (Omeje 2009). These individuals use their new knowledge and skills in ways that not only transform their own lives but the lives of their community members as well.

Except for the stipends and equipment given to former combatants, post-conflict benefits tend to be intangible. The distribution of these intangible benefits, however, presents an opportunity for increased community awareness through observations. Bourdieu (1992) describes the concept of *habitus* or the set of dispositions acquired through everyday training, watching, and learning. This set of dispositions or behaviors occurs within specific contexts or fields in which the social action takes place. After observing others' actions, individuals ascribe a meaning, either positive or negative, to what they have witnessed. Positive ascriptions become valued, modeled, and repeated, allowing the person to occupy part of the contextual space and possibly to feel a sense of legitimacy within that particular field or context. This dynamic facilitates learning similarly to the process suggested by Freire through action and reflection. Moving from the individual to the group, structuration theory (Giddens 1987) posits that social structures are reproduced by social practices across time and space, mentioned previously as the agent/structure dilemma. The theory does not imply that structures must be reproduced exactly or that humans have no capacity to alter what existed previously. The nexus of replication or change lies in the interaction between the individual social agent, the social structure, and the corresponding normative controls existent or emerging, for example, child rights, gender equity, reconciliation, transitional justice. These controls are sustained or altered through personal encounters, the process involving reflexivity (the action influencing the actor), routinization (approving and normalizing the action), and rationalization (structuring individual and socio-cultural norms, values, practices around the action). Within this process, rationalization sits at the intersection of reflexivity and routinization, or in the space where the individual and group find meaning and make sense of social actions and their effects. The meanings that emerge from social action can, of course, influence how much change in social action will occur in future. The reproduction of social practices and structures across time, as in the discussion above of *habitus* and structuration theory, does not imply recursion or a pattern repeating itself exactly. Social structures and practices do continue across time. They also, however, continue to change depending in part upon intervening variables. The role of informal learning offers an opening for transformation that can enlist individuals not part of the formal educational structure, increasing the potential for peace to be learned, practiced, and taught as part of every day life, certainly one of the goals of the peacebuilding paradigm.

Peace education

The previous sections focusing on formal and informal education explored the potential for peacemaking or peacebuilding on the individual, group, or community level. The basic idea focused on individuals transforming aspects of themselves through expanding and changing their cognitive and affective dimensions. In those discussions no direct mention was made of educating *for* peace (teaching conflict resolution techniques, for example) or educating *about* peace (examining the roots of the war, for example, to understand how best to develop a peaceful agenda) as proposed by Pepinsky (2000) and Salomon (2004). To expand this framework Harber and Sakade (2009: 174–5) add that the goal of educating for peace is to improve peaceful relations, the goal of educating about peace aims to promote awareness of peace and conflict, offering conflict resolution in the wider world. This ambitious agenda mirrors that of UNICEF's Global Campaign for Peace Education. Salomon also notes, however, that peace education in regions of intractable conflict confronts serious challenges such as conflicting collective narratives, shared histories and beliefs, grave inequalities, excessive emotionality, and unsupportive social climates (2004: 257–61). Peace education as so described fits into both the formal and informal educational sectors. Pepinsky and Harber and Sakade focus primarily on formal school settings, Salomon on formal school settings as well as off-campus programs, weekend workshops, summer camps, and community-based seminars.

Peace education serves several purposes, with varying implementation options depending upon epistemological foundations. All, however, conceptually link peace and education and operationalize this linkage programmatically. Freire's theories and praxis threads through them all, and each calls on United Nations sponsored documents and declarations for added legitimacy. The authors cited above also note the historical primacy of war studies and conceptualize peace education as a counter-measure. Ardizzone (2001: 16–19) goes further in her argument, aligning peace education with democracy, human security, promotion of global citizenship, and planetary stewardship. As with formal education at the center of a larger post-conflict agenda, as discussed previously, some theorists locate peace education at the center of a global agenda. Working in post-conflict countries and presenting a programming package based on a global agenda may, in some cases, prove a difficult sell. Most cultures have their own set of dispute or conflict resolution models, which are probably not incorporated into models developed outside of the country. One reason could well be that they are not known to policy planners, another that they are seen as unsuccessful in light of the recent war. From that point of view it would seem common sense that a new approach is not only warranted but also essential. This sets up an 'us and them' framework of interaction, 'us' possessing the better knowledge that 'they' need, a variation on the classic insider (who in reality could be considered an outsider) and an outsider (who is definitely an insider). This dynamic, although underpinned by liberating concepts from Freire, could turn out to be an example of the 'oppressor consciousness' transforming everything into an object of its domination (Freire 1999: 40). A harsh analysis to be sure but a cautionary tale nonetheless.

On the other hand, fieldwork in Sierra Leone, Liberia, and Burundi demonstrates that community-based peace education programs, both formal and informal, flourish. Primary school children learn mediation skills that they use with the police when a schoolmate or neighbor gets into trouble; secondary school students organize palaver (conflict) management programs similar to peer mediation programs, helping each other to solve problems at school that can include violence. Market women sought training in mediation and problem-solving to help them as they organize as well as to help them in their homes as they negotiate roles and task assignments with their husbands. Community members learn facilitation and dialogue techniques to approach a contested election in a more peaceful, and inclusive, way. These individuals are expanding their potential for peace in their everyday lives and are assisting others in their communities.

Conclusion

The chapter began with an overview of post-conflict challenges for communities and individuals, the difficulty in reforming education to meet the many demands placed upon it, and the role that education can play in the creation of peace. The formal education section explored the importance of education in bettering life conditions in the post-conflict environment; the individual benefits, economic and psychological, that can accompany education; and the limitations of education in creating a culture of peace. The informal education section examined additional educational opportunities and explored the closer processes of learning and change. The final section, on peace education, discussed theoretical models, the scope of influence, and some constraints faced by different approaches to educating for and educating about peace. The section concluded with a review of some of the community-based peace education observed during fieldwork.

The main point of education, setting aside structure, epistemological foundations, and scope of influence, remains learning. The loop model of learning can be explained as a three-level transition. For example, single-loop learning means that individuals reflect on experiences and decide to maintain the status quo, not thinking critically about an issue or changing a habit or practice, in other words not incorporating new thoughts or ideas into the day-to-day routine if they challenge what is standard practice. Double-loop learning occurs when something 'intervened' to shake up the usefulness or efficacy of former ideas and practices, causing deep thought and reflection to expand the range of possibilities and approaches. Triple-loop learning goes farther, rethinking assumptions upon which opinions, practices, and values are based, making changes where deemed necessary, and incorporating this strategy as standard practice, moving toward, as Bateson (1972) describes it, 'freedom from the bondage of habit'.

This pattern outlines the learning 'steps' that individuals can make as they engage with new concepts (gender equity) or practices (dialogue) and their influence or potential influence on the normal flow of everyday life. These are the cognitive and affective transformations mentioned in previous sections as experienced via education both formal and informal. The goal of post-conflict education, whether specifically peace education or not, really is freedom from the bondage of habit of violence and inequity. This process involves individual transformation that affects family, household, and community.

References

Ardizzone, L. (2001) 'Towards Global Understanding: The Transformative Role of Peace Education', *Current Issues in Comparative Education*, 4: 16–25.

Bateson, G. (1972) *Steps to an Ecology of Mind*, Chicago: University of Chicago Press.

Boulding, E. (2000) *Cultures of Peace: The Hidden Side of History*, Syracuse: Syracuse University Press.

Bourdieu, P. (1992) *Language and Symbolic Power*, Cambridge: Harvard University Press.

Collier, P. (2001) 'Economic Causes of Civil Conflict and Their Implications for Policy', in Crocker, C., Hampson, F., and Aall, P. (eds) *Turbulent Peace: The Challenges of Managing International Conflict*, Washington DC: United States Institute of Peace Press.

Danesh, H.B. (2006) 'Towards an Integrative Theory of Peace Education', *Journal of Peace Education*, 3: 55–78.

Degu, W.A. (2005) 'Reforming Education', in Junne, G. and Verkoren, W. (eds) *Postconflict Development: Meeting New Challenges*, Boulder, CO: Lynne Rienner.

de Rivera, J. (2004) 'Assessing the Basis for a Culture of Peace in Contemporary Societies', *Journal of Peace Research*, 41: 531–48.

Dupuy, K. (2008) *Education for Peace: Building Peace and Transforming Armed Conflict Through Education Systems*, Online. Available HTTP: <http://toolkit.ineeite.org/toolkit/INEEcms/uploads/1050/Education_for_Peace_Building_Peace.pdf> (accessed 26 November 2011).

Freire, P. (1999) *Pedagogy of the Oppressed*, New York: Continuum.

Giddens, A. (1987) *Social Theory and Modern Sociology*, Cambridge: Polity Press.

Harber, C. and Sakade, N. (2009) 'Schooling for Violence and Peace: How Does Peace Education Differ from "Normal" Schooling?', *Journal of Peace Education*, 6: 171–87.

Hicks, D. (2011) *Dignity: The Essential Role It Plays in Resolving Conflict*, New Haven: Yale University Press.

Lederach, J.P. (1995) *Preparing for Peace: Conflict Transformation Across Cultures*. Syracuse: Syracuse University Press.

Marques, J. and Bannon, I. (2003) *Central America: Education Reform in a Post-Conflict Setting, Opportunities and Challenges*, Online. Available HTTP: <http://www-wds.worldbank.org> (accessed 26 November 2011).

Maulden, P. (2007) 'Former Child Soldiers and Sustainable Peace Processes: Demilitarizing the Body, Heart, and Mind', unpublished dissertation, George Mason University.

Maulden, P. (2011) 'The Post-Conflict Paradox: Engaging War, Building Peace', in Charbonneau, B. and Parent, G. (eds) *Peacebuilding, Memory and Reconciliation: Bridging Top-Down and Bottom-Up Approaches*, New York: Routledge.

Nübler, I. (2000) 'Human Resources Development and Utilization in Demobilization and Reintegration Programmes', in Kingma, K. (ed.) *Demobilization in Sub-Saharan Africa: The Development and Security Impacts*, Basingstoke: Macmillan Press.

Omeje, K. (ed.) (2009) *War to Peace Transition Conflict Intervention and Peacebuildling in Liberia*, Lanham: University Press of America.

Paulson, J. (2006) 'The Educational Recommendations of Truth and Reconciliation Commissions: potential and practice in Sierra Leone', *Research in Comparative International Education*, 1: 335–50.

Pepinsky, H. (2000) 'Educating for Peace', *Annals of the American Academy of Political and Social Science,* 567: 157–69.

Salomon, G. (2004) 'Does Peace Education Make a Difference in the Context of an Intractable Conflict?', *Peace and Conflict: Journal of Peace Psychology,* 10: 257–74.

Snyder, A. (2011) 'Developing Refugee Peacebuilding Capacity: Women in exile on the Thai/Burmese Border', in Matyók, T., Senehi, J., and Byrne, S. (eds) *Critical Issues in Peace and Conflict Studies: Theory, Practice, and Pedagogy,* Lanham: Rowman and Littlefield.

UNESCO (1990) *World Declaration on Education for All: Framework for Action to Meet Basic Learning Needs,* Online. Available HTTP: <http://www.unesco.org/education/pdf/JOMTIE_E.PDF> (accessed 27 November 2011).

Verkoren, W.M. (2008) *The Owl and the Dove: Knowledge Strategies to Improve the Peacebuilding Practice of Local Non-Government Organizations,* Vossiuspers: Amsterdam University Press.

23

YOUTH

Siobhan McEvoy-Levy

Introduction

'Youth' is a fluid concept that changes over time and in relation to larger geo-economic and political developments as well as local factors such as patronage systems and gender norms (Jeffrey and Dyson 2008). While youth are defined with some minor variations by the United Nations, World Bank, and governmental aid agencies as between the ages of 12 and 29, local understandings of youth and adulthood can be different and determined by variables such as marital or job status. Of course, ideas about who is a child or a youth may also be manipulated for pragmatic peacebuilding purposes, including matching the perceived needs/desires of international actors (Shepler 2005). Still, a widely shared understanding of youth as a state of transition, and of the young needing guidance, can be discerned across contexts at the present time. Therefore, in this chapter, youth are defined as those people who are customarily considered 'not yet adults' by their societies.

The notion of 'youth' as a transitional state of development is not politically neutral, however. Rather, it reinforces adult territoriality – the tendency of adults to maintain some areas of knowledge and activity as adult-only preserves. Adult territoriality is demonstrated in traditional rites of passage as well as in modern ages of majority and enfranchisement. As justification for adult territoriality, youth are perceived as lacking knowledge and experience, less than rational, in need of protection, and sometimes, also, potentially dangerous. A self-serving form of adult idealism is to see the young as properly contained and protected in school and within family, and not active in the public spheres of politics or knowledge creation. Even when the young are economically active, as they are for survival in many parts of the world, when it comes to participation in serious political decision-making, adults are unwilling to give up that much influence, and are sometimes inclined to use violence to maintain it. Therefore, to be young means to have circumscribed, rationed and monitored access to knowledge and experience.

The boundaries constructed by adults to control the integration of the young into adult defined and controlled societies, including into communities of peacebuilders, are erected locally and internationally. They do sometimes erode or collapse, however. For example, during and after political violence (including war, violent revolution, terrorism, ethnic cleansing, and genocide) and related institutionalized segregation and oppression, those who are 'not yet adults' can be actors of note, posing both resistance and threat. Some traditional relationships between young and old may change. Youth in armed groups may temporarily call the shots, both literally and figuratively. The young / the next generation may become emotional political symbols of defeat, success, and hope for the future, as they are for both Israelis and Palestinians. Youth take to the streets using peaceful direct action, like Otpor in Serbia and the April 6 movement in Egypt, and also work more quietly in smaller groups for social justice and human rights. Young people consistently find multiple creative ways of resisting or subverting authority. So, despite the greater power of adult elites to police the boundaries of political action, those who are 'not yet adults' possess and utilize different forms of power as well, that they express through a range of armed conflict-related and strategic peacebuilding activities.

In this chapter peacebuilding is understood to mean activities that seek to prevent, manage and end direct violence and/or structural violence, and that seek to alter the systems of ideas and values that legitimize and promote physical violence and injustice. Whether this definition encompasses the goals or achievements of the multitude of organizations and agencies – local and international – that aim to 'do' peacebuilding in deeply-divided societies has been the subject of significant debate in the literature. But it is undisputed that many of those peacebuilding programs specifically target the young. 'Waging conflict nonviolently' – including political non-cooperation, human rights monitoring and advocacy, and civilian defense – is considered a key part of strategic peacebuilding by scholars in the field (Schirch 2004: 28). But programs oriented toward youth tend not to emphasize these aspects. More often, putting 'youth' and 'peacebuilding' together is interpreted as necessitating capacity building and educational efforts (see Kemper 2005). A multitude of locally-based inter-group contact and coexistence projects, as well as international and intercultural exchanges, identify youth as their key constituencies. They illustrate a belief in socializing children for a more peaceful future, a future that, ironically, previous generations of adults have failed to create. The aim of such initiatives is to decrease violence and increase justice through focusing on upcoming generations and fashioning a desired society by molding people for peace as they transition out of childhood and are 'not yet ¼ hardened' into adulthood (Galtung 2006: 261). But, *who* decides what this *peace* to-be-learned entails?

Critics of 'liberal' peacebuilding see it as an elitist, western-centric international political project (see, for example, Paris 2004; Newman et al. 2009). International peacebuilding often seems to favor pacification within the general population, prioritizing the prevention of direct violence while not pursuing justice, attacking some forms of culture as violent, but not others, and leaving structural violence systems intact while promoting neo-liberal economics and western-style democracy. Youth-targeted capacity-building programs of economic development, health care, and conflict resolution training are, like other aspects of the 'liberal' peace project, potentially subject to dynamics of orientalism and neo-imperialism. But, local, grassroots, 'culturally sensitive' forms of peacebuilding also often reinforce elder power and exclude youth and their interests.

Similar dynamics shape not just the structure of young people's engagement with peacebuilders and peacebuilding but also the *content* of peacebuilding programs oriented towards youth. In the nexus of international and local peacebuilding approaches, adults construct youth needs based on certain conceptualizations of youth development, and driven by certain underlying ideologies and pedagogies. Historically, the trend in peace education for youth has been toward promoting better inter-group understanding, empathy and peaceful coexistence, recognition of our common humanity and of the moral worth and rights of individuals and (sometimes) groups. But such well-meaning efforts can be counter-productive. Based on his experience working with young Israelis and Palestinians, Philip Hammack (2010), for example, critiques how contact theory-based programs engage with culture and identity in ways that reproduce rather than transform the conflict.

Building peace through children's education and training is an alluring, important, and, at the same time, problematic formula, therefore, in several ways. It may, unintentionally, reinforce the biased notion that young people are the source of social and political violence. Certainly, many young people find the power of a gun, Molotov or stone attractive, especially when the alternative is accepting real or perceived injustice, within systems of structural violence. But, overall most young people do not express their exclusion or dissatisfaction violently. Moreover, too often, the approach of teaching peace reproduces a hierarchical relationship between those who are 'not yet adults' and those who are, and often relies upon 'enlightened' adults as teachers and leaders and on the theories of adult experts. In this sense, even locally elicitive or indigenous peacebuilding can have its neo-liberal elements and may contribute to cycles of violence.

So, as an endeavor oriented towards youth, peacebuilding potentially faces a double legitimacy crisis – one related to the politics of peacebuilding itself and the other connected to the already subordinate power position of youth in relation to adults and within systems of structural violence. Central to this chapter is the understanding that peacebuilding as a field of practice is not revolution. It cannot swiftly or decisively resolve the contradictions and injustices of adult territoriality over knowledge creation or access to political decision-making power and the ideological space of peacebuilding, a territoriality that repeatedly shuts youth out. For practitioners, the politics of youth and peacebuilding, entails living with and working *within* such contradictions just described. For scholars, there is the also intimidating task of how to further explain and unravel them, while inevitably reflecting, partially creating, and strengthening the same contradictions. The chapter turns now to this unraveling process by exploring how youth have been constructed as a category for international intervention in recent academic and policy discourses and the challenges these different scripts pose for youth and peacebuilding.

Children and youth in war

Scholarly analyses in political science and international security which put young people at the center of the story of global politics only emerged quite recently (Brocklehurst 2006; Carpenter 2010; Kent 1995; Rosen 2005; Watson 2006, 2009). An important line of investigation was opened up by Helen Brocklehurst (2006) who examined how children are 'central to the practices of militarization and nationalization across the world and throughout history' (p. 171) and a significant political 'body' or 'group' in international relations (p. 172). George Kent analyzed the global political, economic and social contexts of children's lives and argued for expanding circles (local to international) of moral and legal responsibility for children's welfare (Kent 1995). R. Charli Carpenter (2010) examined discursive practices in transnational human rights campaigns that select some children over others for policy attention. Alison Watson (2009) looked at children in the international political economy (IPE), questioning the assumption that relations between states can be understood without considering children and childhoods. She notes that children are producers and consumers of goods, but they are not treated as actors in the IPE literature, and 'are not party to their self-sustenance as public political actors' or recognized within 'prevailing systems of knowledge creation' (p. 1). David Rosen argues that '[t]he child-soldier crisis is part of the contested domain of international politics in which childhood serves as a proxy for other political interests' (2005: 2). He examines the construction of the child in the narratives of humanitarian organizations and critiques their dehistoricized pleas about innocent child soldiers being brutalized in barbaric wars without precedent. In sum, this literature locates children and youth as politicized 'goods' or collectivities in international relations.

A second important script emerges from the large body of research on children in war that is rooted in legal and psychological perspectives and conducted by scholar-practitioners working on the prevention of child soldiering and the reintegration of child combatants. This work seeks to explain the roles of youth in violence and the impact of violence on them, and to promote better international child protection practices and rehabilitation processes (e.g. Barber 2008; Boothby et al. 2006; Brett and Specht 2004; Peters et al. 2003; Wessells 2009). More so than in the IR literature, youth are seen as agentic individuals, but viewed through a master narrative of blurred victim/perpetrators.

Others, however, are concerned with the impact of enemy child soldiers on the morale and fighting effectiveness of state militaries. Since the wars in Afghanistan and Iraq, such works have addressed the psychological costs and public diplomacy challenges of US militaries fighting children (Singer 2006) as well as why some young people become terrorists (Venhaus 2010). Militarized rationales for studying child soldiers, and youth generally, based on strategic concerns, such as that US soldiers will have to fight them, or that they will become political 'extremists', reflect the current politics of the 'war on terror'. They mark a shift in the location of children and war from being a primarily humanitarian issue to a security one as well. But a significant gap seems to exist in the lack of consideration of the young US and European veterans of the 'war on terror' as youth, who also often experience both psychological trauma and economic exclusion, and might provide either a resource or a challenge for post-war reconstruction or peacebuilding.

An academic literature focused directly on youth and peacebuilding (as a grassroots process and/or form of intervention) in internal and international conflicts emerged within the last decade (De Felice and Wisler 2007; Kemper 2005; Kurtenbach 2008; McEvoy-Levy 2001, 2006, 2011a, 2011b; Pruitt 2008; Schwartz 2010). The academic work on youth and peacebuilding builds upon research on child soldiers and social movements, as well as locally-focused ethnographic research that offer close analyses of youth and youth cultures in conflict zones (e.g. Boyden and DeBerry 2004; Collins

2004; Dauite et al. 2006; Hart 2006; Richards 1996; Shepler 2005; Sommers 2006a). These studies have helped develop a discourse of youth in conflict that emphasizes the complexity of the lived experience of war and political violence. They include analysis of the mechanisms of recruitment of youth to armed groups. But a greater focus is placed on the resilience, nonviolent coping strategies, care-taking, meaning-making and the social reproduction roles of young people, not just combatants, who are experiencing war.

Seeing youth as agents of change – at both the individual and collective levels – this literature argues that youth can be operationalized for either war or peace and that context and policy interventions matter. Some of these works attempt to provide a space where young people who would identify themselves as peacebuilders, whether they work within organizations or more organically out of specific socio-cultural contexts, such as hip hop and graffiti artists (including former child soldiers), and direct action organizers, attenders of binational schools, or critical youth workers, are more directly represented. They are included as case studies, as interviewees, and occasionally as authors and coauthors. This script also asserts the needs, rights and abilities of the young to participate in peace processes and the relative absence of socio-politically oriented youth programming (e.g. Kemper 2005; McEvoy-Levy 2006; Schwartz 2010). Some also utilize a peacebuilding lens to examine youth projects in situations where there is little direct political violence but still structural violence, like Australia, comparing them with those in a post-conflict context like Northern Ireland (Pruitt 2008). In general, though, the focus is international rather than transnational, emphasizes armed conflict and post-war reconstruction, and appears less interested in youth per se than in certain populations of youth in developing world countries and conflict zones.

Revolutions and thwarted transitions

Numerous policy and programming reports, toolkits and analyses of aid agencies, international organizations and NGOs are concerned with youth in conflict zones too (a useful literature review was compiled by Marc Sommers 2006b). The discourses of development and security policy are increasingly blurred in these policy documents and reports. They indicate increasing interest in youth at the higher international policy levels over the last two decades and most cite the 'youth bulge' (Urdal 2004). It is to this script, and its implications for peacebuilding, that the chapter now turns. It highlights two particular aspects that are relevant to peacebuilding in theory and practice, namely how the 'youth bulge' research has shaped an influential policy discourse about youth demographics as both a grand-scale threat and, perhaps contradictorily, as an opportunity for development.

Following 9/11, 'youth bulge' research, while already influential, attained increased traction and provided crucial material evidence for governments and international organizations to give attention to youth and release funds for youth programs. This point is underlined in a USAID technical brief:

> By the 2000s, all major development agencies, including USAID, as well as intelligence and security analysts, were paying attention to the role of youth in conflict. Numerous conflict resolution and prevention programs targeting

youth were designed on this premise to provide a counterweight to extremism – some excellent, others less so.

(USAID 2010)

Beyond actual data, however, there is also a discourse of the 'youth bulge' that influences contemporary international development and security thinking and practice. In this discourse youth are considered indicators of potential political instability. They are the 'demographic of insurgency' (Cincotta 2005) and inhibit successful democratic transitions (Cincotta 2008–09). To successfully transition to liberal democracy, countries need to 'grow up' but currently 'more than half the world's countries remain too young for comfort', according to Richard Cincotta (2008) who is a consulting demographer to the US National Intelligence Council. An interesting evolution in the script couches the youth risk in terms of a natural disaster: the concepts of a 'youthquake' and of youth as a 'massive demographic Tsunami' are attributed to an analyst at the Council on Foreign Relations (Benard 2008: 127).

The construction of youth as hostile power in international relations, can arguably be traced at least as far back as the early post-Cold War period and may also reflect earlier domestic fears of certain youth populations. Anne Hendrixson, for example, argues that an international discourse of Middle Eastern and African 'angry young men', birthed and supported through the 'explosive fertility' of their female counterparts ('veiled young women') mirrors an earlier domestic US discourse linking young males of color as 'superpredators' with female 'teenage welfare queens' (2004: 3). Certainly, some recent analysis of the challenge of youth in the Middle East offers stereotypes and tones of moral disapproval. An example of this narrative is provided by the director of the Rand Corporation's Middle East Youth Initiative:

> Many young people in the Middle East, especially the famously more volatile young males, are deprived of sensible activities, bereft of real hope for a happy and independent future, unschooled in practical modes of thinking, and sexually frustrated in their strict and puritanical societies. Many are hammered with the rousing appeals of radical preachers and ideologues. Others are simply bored and purposeless. Clearly this is not a promising recipe for social advancement.
>
> (Benard 2008: 127)

But quite differently from 1980s domestic US rhetoric demonizing the poor, the contemporary international development and security discourse on youth recognizes (even if sometimes only implicitly, as above) that economic marginalization contributes to youth demoralization and/or radicalism and not some inherent biological or moral flaw. At the same time, it is believed that youth dissatisfaction promotes authoritarianism because leaders can leverage a fear of instability, particularly among commercial elites, to maintain stability (Cincotta 2008).

In addition to presenting youth as a threat, a third interpretation of the 'youth bulge' script involves the idea of youth as a positive 'resource' for their societies as found in reports of aid agencies such as USAID, UNDP and DFID (see UNDP 2006; McLean Hilker and Fraser 2009). In the official development discourse, the 'youth crisis' script seems to be utilized with a lot of ambivalence, even described by one policy implementer as 'a double-edged sword' (USAID 2008). UNDP's Youth and Violent Conflict report notes in reviewing the trends in the literature:

> [T]he single most glaring gap in the research is the lack of attention to, and thorough documentation of, the positive contributions of young people in society. This translates into an increasing 'securitization' of the issue of youth. While it is often pointed out that youth should not be regarded as merely a negative force, this comment frequently appears to be an add-on, or an a priori disclaimer.
>
> (UNDP 2006: 18)

> While young people are seen as agents of violence, they are not necessarily identified as full actors in peace settings, and they are not recognized as having an active role as civil society actors, political constituents or participants in measures to redress violence. Young people are sometimes urged to be peacemakers, but they are seldom mentioned in responses to conflict through governance and political measures.
>
> (UNDP 2006: 33)

A related iteration of the significance of the youth bulge is found in a discourse of thwarted development. Seen within this frame, youth possess clear potential as a 'resource' for the positive development of their societies, but in many cases are instead unable to transition to the economic independence of adulthood, their individual transitions thwarted by structural constraints. Young people in the Middle East, for example, are viewed as a 'generation in waiting' (Dhillon and Yousef 2009). This analysis has also coined a new term for youth as a period of 'waithood', a combination of wait and adulthood. Yet, identifying 'waithood' as the problem arguably only nuances the threat discourse. Youth are presented as being only potentially threatening to states/order and the chief challenge is that youth are being stuck in transition (Salehi-Isfahani and Dhillon 2008; Dhillon and Yousef 2009) due to a combination of economic and political exclusion. If the situation is turned around, youth will be 'assets' for their societies, according to this perspective (Making Cents 2008). However, the development focus on youth is also often justified with reference to their large numbers, and/or to how 'waithood' may be a pathway to violence: 'They could be diverted into the terrorism track, into violence, political violence, and so on. That's the concern from an American point of view' (Setrakian 2007).

In the light of the 2011 revolutions in North Africa, it is interesting to ponder the differences between the contemporary development and demographic discourses about youth in waiting and earlier scholarship on revolution. Several different interpretations of youth and their roles quickly emerged during the so-called Arab Spring. By their soon-to-be-deposed leaders, youth were presented as young 'thugs' and 'terrorists'. On the other hand, close journalistic analyses of Tunisia and Egypt presented mass movements emerging from multiple small-scale 'counter-jihads' (Wright 2011), involving young actors, writers, artists, and musicians as well as more conventional political activists. Only time will tell how these stories are read in relation to fears of youth and 'youth bulges' and if they stimulate interest in youth activism as a form of peacebuilding. Suggesting perhaps that they will not, is the emerging perspective among US demographers that explain the North African uprisings not as youth bulge revolutions, but as uprisings related to a dissolving youth bulge effect as their societies age (Cincotta 2011). Their ultimate success, defined as stable liberal democracy, will be positively related to declining numbers of youth in this script.

The roles of youth in revolution have been considered in many earlier sociological and political science studies. In his introduction to the *Encyclopedia of Political Revolution*, Goldstone (1998: xxxvii) writes that 'regardless' of the movement 'their crucial basis is highly mobilizable young men and women with grievances against the state'. The complex politics and ultimate success, or eventual outcomes of these revolutions aside, a key factor in fomenting revolutions involves ideas. It is also recognized that the intellectual or ideological basis for revolutions may originate within, or be championed by, specific groups such as youth, as described, for example, by Michael Walzer (1999):

> Vanguard consciousness is the work of intellectuals somehow cut loose from the constraints of the old order – or of intellectuals who cut themselves loose. These are people, *usually young people*, who respond to the decadence of their world by withdrawing from it. They give up conventional modes of existence, conventional families and jobs; they choose marginality; endure persecution; go into exile.
>
> (Walzer 1999: 129, emphasis added)

The contemporary development and demographic/security focus is not on those who reject bourgeois status acquisition, of course, although many such young people are politically active within armed conflicts today (including for example young Israeli settlers creating illegal outposts in the West Bank). Instead, key objects of concern are those who cannot meet those needs – those without family, home and meaningful work or basic livelihood due to economic and political structures beyond their control. Empirically these gaps are real and their absence devastating to many of the world's youth. But, beyond the beliefs of radical Islamists, who may be feared as mass, and other potential terrorists who, ironically, make up only small numbers, minimal attention seems to have been given to the intellectual, ideological and political motivations of contemporary youth bulgers.

Conclusion: Further implications for peacebuilding research and practice

The discourses examined in this chapter represent not only different ways of seeing youth in relation to global geo-economics and politics but also different efforts to get youth on the international policy agenda. We know that policies are shaped not only by evidence but also by interpretations of and stories about evidence. An 'emerging paradigm' of 'emancipatory peacebuilding' (Theissen 2011: 115) will need to take further critical account of how youth are constructed in the discourses of international politics and development and challenge some of these stories. Over the last decade, these discourses have constructed young people not as revolutionaries but as victims of thwarted transition or potential terrorists, and not only as threats to states that cannot provide for their needs, but also as potential natural disasters able to overwhelm political life as we know it more generally. Such constructions of the challenge of youth make conflict management strategies more attractive and promote a momentum to contain rather than emancipate young people. Contradictorily, perhaps, the other interventions legitimized by these views of youth have the potential to be very intrusive, being designed to liberate trapped youth by correcting perceived defects of economy and culture, and sometimes based upon overly simplistic interpretations of the motives of the young shaped by religion and sexual drives. Even the thwarted development view that humanely focuses on youth marginalization, and sometimes places the blame on global structural violence, places youth on a trajectory for full political recognition only in the future and not in the present. Lastly, a clearly dominant story is that global order, understood as composed of stable liberal democracies, cannot be achieved until the numbers of young people decline. Such a finding can be easily interpreted to scapegoat youth for failed revolutions and failed reconstruction and peacebuilding plans.

To positively affect both youth and the prospects for peace in divided societies, proponents of emancipatory peacebuilding will be charged with transforming the fundamental and universal youth–adult hierarchies of political life, and without either revolution or social fabric-shattering wars. This is a lot easier said than done, but it at least entails engaging with the ideas of young people themselves. Among the important contributions that younger scholars, practitioners and policy professionals make is that they embody the arguments from the youth and peacebuilding literature that young people are not (only) politically significant because they can be helpless and/or dangerous. Moreover, they show how youth are not only significant as physical engines of mass movements but also as smaller-scale socio-cultural and ideological entrepreneurs bringing knowledge, perspective and hidden politics to the surface. Yet, while some of the authors whose work is discussed in this chapter (e.g. Schwarz and Pruitt) were themselves in their early 20s at the time of their writing, it is fair to say that the academic field of youth and peacebuilding is a largely adult preserve like any other. Adult territoriality is also a barrier to young people entering the professional youth policy world. As an example, a participant in a 2010 Washington DC symposium on youth and conflict noted the following: her superiors in a government aid agency wished that more young people would apply for employment, but they had also failed to notice that their job descriptions required 10 years of professional experience, excluding most young applicants.

The local content of peace programming would seem to benefit from critical pedagogies and practices that see youth as the teachers and leaders, rather than as followers or recipients of learning or resources. Certainly, as a general principle or aspiration, the idea of youth as agents of their own emancipation already shapes the identities of some youth development projects. Such projects may in themselves be considered too radical by international funders. But even when the influential ideas and methods are critical, and draw on social justice models that emphasize emancipation and radical critiques of structural violence at home and abroad, the theories and methods are still derived from so-called expert adult knowledge. They may pass one aspect of the peacebuilding legitimacy test (authenticity and grassroots responsiveness) but not the other (transforming adult territoriality).

Therefore, a challenge for emancipatory projects aimed at supporting peacebuilding is that they must induce adults to willingly give up power (at both the organizational and the wider society levels), so that youth can take up the leading roles through nonviolent means (that is, as part of a peacebuilding process rather than through revolutionary violence). However, the opposite dynamic – adult maintenance of power – has a strong pull. Emancipatory peacebuilding seems to prescribe for a contradiction, then, when applied to youth, for it requires youth to make revolutionary achievements without using (apparent) revolutionary means, that is, without using violence, and perhaps, as demonstrated by fears of 'youth bulges,' even without mass nonviolent protest.

References

Barber, B.K. (ed.) (2008) *Adolescents and War*, New York: Oxford.

Benard, C. (2008) 'Toy Soldiers. The Youth Factor in the War on Terror', in Gavin, M.D. (ed.) *A Work in Progress. The Prospects and the Potential of the World's Youth*, New York: International Debate Education Association.

Boothby, N., Strang, A. and Wessells, M. (eds) (2006) *A World Turned Upside Down. Social Ecological Approaches to Children in War Zones*, Bloomfield CT: Kumarian.

Boyden, J. and DeBerry, J. (eds) (2004) *Children and Youth on the Frontlines,* New York: Berghahn.

Brett, R. and Specht, I. (2004) *Young Soldiers: Why They Choose to Fight*, Boulder: Lynne Rienner.

Brocklehurst, H. (2006) *Who's Afraid of Children?: Children, Conflict and International Relations*, Aldershot: Ashgate.

Carpenter, C. (2010) *Forgetting Children Born of War: Setting the Human Rights Agenda in Bosnia and Beyond,* New York: Columbia University Press.

Cincotta, R. (2005) 'Youth Bulge, Underemployment Raise Risks of Civil Conflict', State of the World 2005 Global Security Brief #2, WorldWatch Institute. Online. Available HTTP: < http://www.worldwatch.org/node/76> (accessed 21 January 2012).

Cincotta, R. (2008) 'How Democracies Grow up: Countries with too many young people may not have a fighting chance at freedom,' *Foreign Policy*, February 19. Online. Available HTTP: < http://www.foreignpolicy.com/articles/2008/02/19/how_democracies_grow_up > (accessed 21 January 2012).

Cincotta, R. (2008–09) 'Half a Chance. Youth Bulges and Transitions to Liberal Democracy,' New Directions in Demographic Security, Wilson Center ECSP Report Issue 13: 10–18.

Cincotta, R. (2011) 'Tunisia's Shot at Democracy. What Demographics and Recent History Tell Us.' Online. Available HTTP: < http://www.newsecuritybeat.org/2011/01/tunisias-shot-at-democracy-what.html > (accessed 21 January 2012).

Collins, J. (2004) *Occupied By Memory: The Intifada Generation and the Palestinian State of Emergency*, New York: NYU Press.

Dauite, C. et al. (eds) (2006) *International Perspectives on Youth Conflict and Development*, New York: Oxford University Press.

De Felice, C. and Wisler, A. (2007) 'The Unexplored Power and Potential of Youth as Peace-builders', *Journal of Peace Conflict & Development* 11: 1–29. Online. Available HTTP: <http://www.peacestudiesjournal.org.uk/> (accessed 3 January 2012).

Dhillon, N. and Yousef, T. (eds) (2009) *Generation in Waiting. The Unfulfilled Promise of Young People in the Middle East*, Washington DC: Brookings Institution Press.

Galtung, J. (2006) 'The Theoretical Challenges of Peacebuilding With and For Youth', in McEvoy-Levy, S. (ed.) *Troublemakers or Peacemakers: Youth and Post-Accord Peacebuilding*, Notre Dame, Indiana: University of Notre Dame Press, 259–279.

Goldstone, J.A. (1998) *Encyclopedia of Political Revolution*, Chicago: Fitzroy Dearborn.

Hammack, P.L. (2010) *Narrative and the Politics of Identity. The Cultural Psychology of Israeli and Palestinian Youth*, London: Oxford University Press.

Hart, J. (2006) 'The Politics of "Child Soldiers"', *Brown Journal of World Affairs*, Fall/Winter Volume XIII: 1: 217–26.

Hendrixson, A. (2004) *Angry Young Men, Veiled Young Women: Constructing a New Population Threat,* Corner House Briefing 34. Online. Available HTTP: <http://www.thecornerhouse.org.uk/ item.shtml?x=85999 > (accessed 3 January 2012).

Jeffrey, C. and Dyson, J. (2008) *Telling Young Lives: Portraits of Global Youth,* Philadelphia: Temple University Press.

Kemper, Y. (2005) *Youth in War to Peace Transitions. Approaches of International Organizations,* Berghof Report Nr. 10, Berlin, Germany: Berghof Research Center for Constructive Conflict Management.

Kent, G. (1995) *Children in the International Political Economy,* Palgrave Macmillan.

Kurtenbach, S. (2008) 'Youth in conflict and peace-building – between protection and neglect', conference paper, International Studies Association, San Francisco 26–29 March. Online. Available HTTP: <http://www.humansecuritygateway.com/documents/ISA_youth inconflictpeacebuilding.pdf > (accessed 21 January 2012).

Making Cents International (2008) *Youth Microenterprise and Livelihoods: State of the Field. Lessons from the 2007 Global Youth Microenterprise Conference.* Online. Available HTTP: < http://www. imaginenations.org/documents/MakingCentsInternationalYouthEnterpriseLivelihoods021108. pdf > (accessed 21 January 2012).

McEvoy-Levy, S. (2001) 'Youth as Social and Political Agents: Issues in Post-Settlement Peace Building', Kroc Institute Occasional Paper #21: 2: 1–41, December, Notre Dame, IN: Joan B. Kroc Institute for International Peacebuilding.

McEvoy-Levy, S. (2006) *Troublemakers or Peacemakers: Youth and Post-Accord Peacebuilding,* Notre Dame, IN: University of Notre Dame Press.

McEvoy-Levy, S. (2011a) 'Children, Youth, and Peacebuilding', in Byrne, S., Maytok, T. and Senehi, J. (eds) *Critical Issues in Peace and Conflict Studies: Theory, Practice, and Pedagogy,* New York: Lexington Books/Rowman & Littlefield, pp. 159–76.

McEvoy-Levy, S. (2011b) 'Playing "catch with a hatchet": Integrating Children's Knowledge into Post-War Peacebuilding', in Cook, D.T. and Wall, J. (eds) *Children and Armed Conflict: Cross-Disciplinary Investigations,* Houndmills: Palgrave.

McLean Hilker, L. and Fraser, E. (2009) *Youth Exclusion, Violent Conflict and Fragile States,* Report Prepared for DFID's Equity and Rights Team, London: Social Development Direct.

Newman, E., Paris, R., and Richmond, O.P. (2009) *New Perspectives on Liberal Peacebuilding,* Toyko: United Nations University Press.

Paris, R. (2004) *At War's End. Building Peace After Civil Conflict,* Cambridge: Cambridge University Press.

Peters, K., Richards, P., and Vlassenroot, K. (2003) *What Happens to Youth During and After Wars? A Preliminary Review of Literature on Africa and Assessment on the Debate.* ROWOO Working Paper. Online. Available HTTP: < http://igitur-archive.library.uu.nl/CERES/2005-0523-200444/ youthreport.pdf > (accessed 3 January 2012).

Pruitt, L. (2008) 'They Drop Beats, Not Bombs. Music and Dance in Youth Peacebuilding', *Australian Journal of Peace Studies,* 3: 14–32.

Richards, P. (1996) *Fighting for the Rainforest: War, Youth, and Resources in Sierra Leone,* London: Heinemann.

Rosen, D. (2005) *Armies of the Young: Child Soldiers in War and Terrorism,* New Brunswick: Rutgers University Press.

Salehi-Isfahani, D. and N. Dhillon (2008) *Stalled Youth Transitions in the Middle East: a Framework for Policy Reform,* The Middle East Youth Initiative Working Paper Number 8, Wolfensohn School of Government / Dubai School of Government. Available HTTP: < http://www. shababinclusion.org/content/document/detail/1166/> (accessed 3 January 2012).

Schirch, L. (2004) *Strategic Peacebuilding.* Little Books of Justice and Peacebuilding, Intercourse/ Good Books.

Schwartz, S. (2010) *Youth and Post-Conflict Reconstruction. Agents of Change,* Washington DC: United States Institute of Peace Press.

Setrakian, L. (2007) 'Young and Out of Work in the Middle East', ABC News. December, 23. Online. Available HTTP : < http://abcnews.go.com/International/story?id=4044047&page=1> (accessed 21 January 2012).

Shepler, S. (2005) 'The Rites of the Child. Global Discourses of Youth and Reintegrating Child Soldiers in Sierra Leone', *Journal of Human Rights,* 4: 197–211.

Singer, P.W. (2006) *Children at War,* Berkeley: University of California Press.

Sommers, M. (2006a) *Fearing Africa's Young Men: the case of Rwanda,* Social Development Papers Conflict Prevention and Reconstruction, Paper No. 32, Washington DC: World Bank. Online. Available HTTP: < http://www.eldis.org/vfile/upload/1/document/0708/DOC21389.pdf > (accessed 3 January 2012).

Sommers, M. (2006b) *Youth and Conflict: a Brief Review of Available Literature,* Washington DC: EQUIP 3/USAID. Online. Available HTTP: < http://www.equip123.net/docs/e3-YouthandConflictLitReview.pdf > (accessed 3 January 2012).

Theissen, C. (2011) 'Emancipatory Peacebuilding. Critical Responses to (Neo)Liberal Trends', in Byrne, S., Maytok, T., and Senehi, J. (eds) *Critical Issues in Peace and Conflict Studies: Theory, Practice, and Pedagogy,* New York: Lexington Books/Rowman & Littlefield, pp. 115–40.

UNDP (2006) *Youth and Violent Conflict. Society and Development in Crisis?,* New York: United Nations Development Program. Online. Available HTTP: < http://www.undp.org/cpr/whats_new/UNDP Youth_PN.pdf > (accessed 3 January 2012).

Urdal, H. (2004) 'The Devil in the Demographics: The Effect of Youth Bulges on Domestic Armed Conflict, 1950–2000', *Social Development Papers.* Washington DC: Conflict Prevention and Reconstruction Unit, World Bank. Online. Available HTTP: < http://www.prio.no/Research-and-Publications/Publication/?oid=57846 > (accessed 3 January 2012).

USAID (2008) Anonymous interview.

USAID (2010) Technical Brief, *Youth Bulges and Conflict,* Winter.

Venhaus, J.M. (2010) 'Why Youth Join al-Qaeda', United States Institute of Peace Special Report, May, Washington DC: United States Institute of Peace.

Walzer, M. (1999) 'Intellectuals, Social Classes and Revolutions', in Skocpol, T. (ed.) *Democracy, Revolution and History,* Ithaca: Cornell University Press, pp. 127–42.

Watson, A.M.S. (2006) 'Children in International Relations: A new site of knowledge', *Review of International Studies* 32: 237–50.

Watson, A.M.S. (2009) *The Child in International Political Economy: A Place at the Table,* London: Routledge.

Wessells, M.G. (2009) *Child Soldiers: From Violence to Protection,* Cambridge, MA: Harvard University Press.

Wright, R. (2011) *Rock the Casbah: Rage and Rebellion Across the Islamic World,* New York: Simon & Schuster.

PART VI

The infrastructure of peacebuilding

24

THE INTERNATIONAL ARCHITECTURE OF PEACEBUILDING

Edward Newman

International peacebuilding in conflict-prone and post-conflict societies – aimed at preventing the resumption of armed conflict and promoting the consolidation of peace – has developed rapidly in recent years in terms of the scope and types of activities conducted, and the number of operations deployed. It is widely accepted that preventing the resumption of violent conflict and establishing a durable and self-sustaining peace requires a range of activities which engage with social, political and economic sectors as well as shoring up stability and security. In line with the multifaceted nature of peacebuilding the number and variety of international actors involved in these missions has increased significantly, and so has debate regarding the role of these actors and the fundamental nature of peacebuilding. However, it is far from certain whether the different actors operate in a coordinated, complementary manner around a coherent vision of what peacebuilding should involve and what it should seek to achieve.

This chapter will survey the broad range of actors and policies relevant to international peacebuilding and consider if, and to what extent, it is possible to identify an international architecture of peacebuilding based upon a coherent peacebuilding doctrine. This is defined as a network of international actors with a shared vision of the objectives of peacebuilding and their role in it, and a system which coordinates their interests and activities. A number of questions will be addressed. Do the different actors directly or indirectly involved in peacebuilding – such as the United Nations political organs, local stakeholders, UN development and humanitarian agencies, national development agencies, international financial institutions, regional organizations, and international non-governmental organizations – share a vision of what peacebuilding involves and how it is measured? How can the relationship between international peacebuilding agencies and local actors within conflict-prone and post-conflict societies be defined? When do the different interests and priorities held by actors involved in peacebuilding conflict, and with what effect? In particular, are there tensions between 'liberal institutionalist' models of peacebuilding and those premised upon ideas of social justice and the resolution of the underlying sources of conflict in the context of local institutions? If there is no consensus on the scope and fundamental nature of peacebuilding, and the actors involved have different interests and priorities, and sometimes do not wish to be 'coordinated', is an architecture of peacebuilding based upon a coherent peacebuilding doctrine possible in theory or in practice?

The actors of international peacebuilding

Almost all post-Cold War peacekeeping and peacebuilding operations have been carried out in – or subsequent to – situations of civil conflict and have involved tasks related to promoting security, development, humanitarian assistance and strengthening governance and the rule of law. Such activities have included supporting ceasefires and peace processes; demobilization and disarmament of former combatants and reintegrating them into society; stabilizing the economy; employment creation and economic development; repatriation (or resettlement) of refugees and internally displaced persons; responding to food insecurity; responding to acute health concerns; strengthening law and order; promoting and facilitating democratic practices; strengthening institutions of justice and legislation; resuming and strengthening public service delivery; promoting human rights and reconciliation; addressing land reform claims; and sometimes constitutional drafting or amendments. Most peacebuilding operations also reflect the liberal peacebuilding model: the top-down promotion of democracy, market-based economic reforms and a range of other institutions associated with 'modern' states as a driving force for building peace.

Major international peacebuilding operations – under UN auspices – have been conducted in Cambodia, Angola, Burundi, Liberia, Mozambique, Sierra Leone, Sudan, Côte d'Ivoire, Democratic Republic of the Congo (DRC), Somalia, Kosovo, Afghanistan, El Salvador, Guatemala, Haiti, East Timor, and Bosnia and Herzegovina (Ramsbotham, Woodhouse and Miall 2011). In addition to these major high-profile UN operations, a much larger number of cases exist in which international and national development agencies support and undertake a range of similar activities. The key actors involved are the following.

United Nations organs and agencies are widely associated with international peacebuilding because UN peacebuilding is the most visible and politically high profile type of this activity. Large UN missions have attracted the greatest amount of academic interest, even though a far broader range of peacebuilding work goes on beyond this in many more countries. The UN Security Council issues the mandate, legal authorization and resources for the deployment of major peacebuilding missions, both for civilian activities and military peacekeeping forces. The UN Secretary-General provides overall political authority, and his Special Representatives, under an integrated country peacebuilding system, provide operational authority and direction to the missions. The UN Peacebuilding Commission brings together the relevant international actors, generates resources, provides analysis and policy support for post-conflict peacebuilding and recovery, and gives attention to specific peacebuilding cases. Various UN secretariat units – such as the Electoral Assistance Division of the Department of Political Affairs – provide specialist assistance in specific parts of the peacebuilding agenda. UN specialized agencies and programmes – such as the UN Development Programme, the UN High Commissioner for Refugees, the Office of the UN High Commissioner for Human Rights, the Food and Agriculture Organization, the World Food Programme, the World

Health Organization, the UN Children's Fund, and the UN Volunteers – formulate and implement aspects of the broader peacebuilding agenda on the ground.

Within the broader UN family, international financial institutions – such as the World Bank Group and the International Monetary Fund – provide assistance and policy advice for economic development and reform. Indeed, the World Bank is very active in conflict analysis and peacebuilding, and this is an illustration of how wide the peacebuilding agenda has become (World Bank 2011). Under UN auspices and the lead agency principle a unified and integrated mission brings together all of the various actors in order – in theory – to promote cohesion and coordination.

National development agencies are also very active in international peacebuilding, although their work is not always defined as such and they are engaged in a far wider range of countries in the developing world than those specifically defined as 'post-conflict'. In particular, the UK Department for International Development, the US Agency for International Development, the Canadian International Development Agency, the German Corporation for International Development Cooperation, the Japan International Cooperation Agency and the Swedish International Development Cooperation Agency are very significant both as financial donors and as field agencies, implementing programmes through country offices in cooperation with local stakeholders. These programmes are generally in the area of development, humanitarian assistance and strengthening governance and the rule of law. Naturally, their programmatic approaches, and the countries in which they are engaged for peacebuilding work, are a reflection not only of multilateral peacebuilding and aid priorities but also national interests and a broader politicization of aid (Lancaster 2006; Easterly 2007). For example, there is a fairly clear correlation between the presence of national peacebuilding and overseas aid and economic and strategic interests. It will also be interesting to see how national peacebuilding priorities are reflected in the rise on the international stage of countries such as Brazil, India, China and South Africa, and – if these rising powers play a significant role in peacebuilding – if broader changes in international order have an impact upon approaches to peacebuilding at the international level.

Regional organizations also play a significant and growing role in international peacebuilding, in line with Chapter 8 of the UN Charter which encourages the settlement of conflict by regional arrangements (Bellamy and Williams 2005). Direct involvement by regional organizations is generally undertaken with the support of the UN Security Council, and sometimes in operational cooperation with the UN on the ground. Moreover, many of the missions undertaken by regional organizations have been significantly narrower than larger UN missions, and they contribute specific activities such as observing elections or supporting power-sharing. The African Union has undertaken peace activities in Somalia, Burundi, Angola, Comoros, DRC, Sudan, and Liberia. The Commonwealth of Independent States has undertaken operations in Georgia and Tajikistan. The Commonwealth Secretariat has deployed observer missions to South Africa and Zimbabwe. The Economic and Monetary Community of Central African States has been involved in the Central African Republic. The Economic Community of West African States has deployed to Liberia, Ivory Coast, Guinea Bissau, and Sierra Leone. EU observer missions have served in South Africa, Zimbabwe, DRC and Zambia, and post-conflict reconstruction and policing units in Croatia, Bosnia, Serbia, and Kosovo. In addition, the Humanitarian Aid and Civil Protection department of the European Commission (ECHO) channels development assistance and implements projects throughout the developing world, including in post-conflict societies. NATO has deployed enforcement missions to the former Yugoslavia and post-conflict stability missions to the former Yugoslavia and Afghanistan, amongst others. The Organization for Security and Cooperation in Europe (OSCE) has been involved in conflict resolution activities in Georgia, Azerbaijan, and Moldova, and verification or policing missions in Kosovo, Macedonia, Estonia, Latvia, Bosnia and Eastern Slavonia. The Organization of American States has been active in electoral assistance, often in the context of a broader UN peacebuilding mission, in Haiti, Nicaragua, Paraguay, Dominican Republic, Guatemala, Costa Rica, and Panama. The Southern African Development Community has deployed diplomatic missions to the DRC, Zimbabwe and Angola, and has been involved in peacekeeping in Lesotho and DRC. The role of regional organizations is important; they are generally considered to have greater legitimacy and are familiar with the protagonists. However, there are sometimes concerns about the role of local hegemons in the context of regional arrangements using peace operations to promote their own agenda.

International non-governmental organizations have been involved in peacebuilding in a range of capacities, and in particular CARE International, Safer World, International Alert, Berghof Conflict Research, International Crisis Group, the International Committee of the Red Cross, the International Rescue Committee, Swisspeace Center for Peacebuilding, World Vision International, Search for Common Ground, Médecins Sans Frontières, Oxfam, Save the Children, and many others. These NGOs are engaged in a very wide range of activities, often in cooperation with national and international organizations, but especially in providing medical and humanitarian assistance, assisting displaced and vulnerable communities, facilitating community peacebuilding and reconciliation, assisting in local infrastructural reconstruction and supporting the development of local civil society, amongst other things. Some of the large international NGOs receive funding from national donor agencies and the UN and they implement major projects and services on behalf of these organizations, often in the context of peacebuilding missions. Others work on a smaller scale and independently, often at the grassroots level, and often eschewing official contact with UN and national donor agencies (Pouligny 2005; Hemmer et al. 2006).

National actors within the target country play an important – but sometimes under-utilized and occasionally marginalized – role in international peacebuilding missions. In theory peacebuilding activities by almost all actors are undertaken in cooperation with national actors – government agencies and ministries, politicians, local civil society organizations. This is important so that local capacity is developed and so that local stakeholders have a sense of ownership over the pace and content of peacebuilding activities. The effectiveness and legitimacy of international peacebuilding activities rely, to some extent, on them being embedded in local institutions and local needs. As a result some peacebuilding actors – and especially the UN – attempt to work hand in hand with national actors and to employ local staff for project work as far as possible. The relationship between international and local actors is, however, one of the most challenging aspects of contemporary peacebuilding and a significant source of controversy (see below).

Clearly, these different types of actors and activities illustrate that peacebuilding activities are not entirely undertaken by a single organization – such as the United

Nations – even when the UN has a leadership role. Large peacebuilding cases over the last twenty years – such as Cambodia, DRC, Bosnia, Kosovo, Liberia, East Timor, Afghanistan – reflect a multitude of different actors within the same peacebuilding space. In theory, at least, there is increasing coordination amongst these different actors which points towards the idea of a coherent architecture and doctrine of peacebuilding. In major peacebuilding missions, and especially those under the auspices of the UN, there are mechanisms for coordinating activities, sharing information, and exchanging ideas. This often results in the acceptance of a formal or informal hierarchy of authority within a peacebuilding country, with the UN Secretary-General's Special Representative having a senior position.

The coordination challenge

Coordination challenges are inherent in all complex activities which involve different actors, especially at the international level involving multifaceted operations. Different ways of working amongst different actors, exclusive institutional jurisdictions, and different priorities and ideas of sequencing all present significant coordination challenges in peacebuilding operations. One of the biggest challenges to the idea of an 'architecture of peacebuilding' is therefore the multiple and often disparate actors and interests involved.

The perennial 'coordination challenge' has received significant attention amongst policy analysts and in policy circles, and to some extent within academic debates (de Coning 2007). In terms of policy actors this challenge has moved to the forefront of the debate, apparently as the key to successful peacebuilding. In line with this, a number of policy developments have occurred. There is now, in large peacebuilding missions, an emphasis upon 'integrated missions' under a lead agency in order to facilitate clear lines of communication amongst the different actors involved, avoid duplication of activities and, in theory, bring coherence across the different activities. This coordination extends across the broader UN family and sometimes beyond; periodic meetings in large peacebuilding missions will see representatives from across the specialized programmes and agencies around a table chaired by the UN Secretary-General's Special Representative – a reflection of the broader commitment to delivery as 'One UN' at the country level – and sometimes also key national donor agencies and NGOs.

The establishment of the UN Peacebuilding Commission also represents a step forward both in the coordination of peacebuilding activities and actors, and in the formulation of an international architecture of peacebuilding. The Peacebuilding Commission was established in 2005 to 'bring together all relevant actors to marshal resources and to advise on and propose integrated strategies for post-conflict peacebuilding and recovery; To focus attention on the reconstruction and institution-building efforts necessary for recovery from conflict and to support the development of integrated strategies in order to lay the foundation for sustainable development; To provide recommendations and information to improve the coordination of all relevant actors within and outside the United Nations, to develop best practices, to help to ensure predictable financing for early recovery activities and to extend the period of attention given by the international community to post-conflict recovery' (General Assembly Resolution 60/180, 30 December 2005). This intergovernmental organ focuses on thematic challenges and specific countries, which are currently Burundi, Sierra Leone, Guinea, Guinea-Bissau, Liberia, and Central African Republic.

The Commission represents a milestone in UN institutional mechanisms for supporting peace and security, focusing significant diplomatic attention on certain cases, generating additional resources, and generating knowledge about peacebuilding challenges in general. However, the rather limited remit given to the new organ is a reflection of the inherent caution of an intergovernmental approach. The background to the establishment of the Commission gives an illustration of this. The Report of the High Level Panel (2004: 83), endorsed by the UN Secretary-General, suggested that the core functions of the Peacebuilding Commission should include identifying 'countries which are under stress and risk sliding towards State collapse' and organizing, in partnership with the national government, 'proactive assistance in preventing that process from developing further'. It therefore envisaged a clear conflict-prevention function. However, the 2005 UN World Summit Outcome Final Document (UN 2005: paragraph 98) prescribed more modest – and less proactive – ambitions for the new Peacebuilding Commission. The main purposes of the new Commission are 'to bring together all the relevant actors to marshal resources and to advise on and propose integrated strategies for post-conflict peacebuilding and recovery'. Nevertheless, the Commission is at the heart of the evolving peacebuilding architecture and – despite the political idiosyncrasies and constraints of the intergovernmental context – it has generated new thinking on peacebuilding doctrine. Indeed, the small but dynamic Peacebuilding Support Office, established to support the Commission, is staffed by UN secretariat members with experience of the wide range of challenges related to peacebuilding in post-conflict societies. This office has facilitated policy analysis on the record and effectiveness of peace operations and has also been open to interaction with external analysts and academics, supporting a number of debates on challenges related to coordination, local ownership of peacebuilding activities, capacity development, etc.

From this reading the challenge of coordination – at the heart of the architecture of peacebuilding – is one of 'problem solving'. The overall assumptions and objectives are seen to reflect broad consensus amongst the different actors involved in terms of what peacebuilding should achieve and involve. The liberal approach to peacebuilding and development in fragile states, around which these actors work, is driven by the belief that the principal 'problem' with conflict-prone and post-conflict states is the absence of 'effective' state institutions. With this rationale (re)building viable institutions becomes a priority. The institutionalist view assumes that state institutions and the right market conditions will drive the material goals of peacebuilding, and it concentrates on institutional benchmarks and peacebuilding targets relating to sequences. According to this, certain institutions are believed to be universally viable – secular citizenship, electoral democracy, free market economics, a centralized state, civil and political human rights – so once these are achieved, political and economic development will move forward and serve peace, in a mutually supportive process.

Within this model, the roles of different actors are thought to be clear, and they share a broad support for the liberal peacebuilding project. The challenge is therefore to optimize communication between the different actors, to agree upon priorities and coordinate activities in a complementary manner, to identify and implement the correct sequence of programmes, and to bring the necessary resources to bear upon the peacebuilding mission (Paris and Sisk 2009). In many peacebuilding missions this takes the form of a division of labour: different actors, including states, are responsible for specific policy areas and objectives. Clearly, the different actors described above contribute on the basis of their organizational mandate: UNDP takes the lead with governance and development issues, the UN Electoral Assistance Division assists with elections, the World Bank assists with economic policy, the UN specialized agencies assist in their areas of expertise, and national agencies generally take the lead with security sector reform. As far as there are reflective debates within these circles – and the Peacebuilding Commission Support Office has certainly encouraged and facilitated these – they largely fall within, and do not challenge, the prevailing liberal peacebuilding consensus.

The peacebuilding architecture and doctrine: Is the challenge deeper than that of coordination?

Within peacebuilding policy circles, problem-solving challenges relate to how to make the liberal peacebuilding project 'work': to build or rebuild state institutions and good governance, including democracy, develop a responsible civil society, and promote a liberal market. The challenge is to find the right fit at the local level and the right sequence of activities. Whilst every case is different, the actors and activities which constitute the international peacebuilding architecture rest upon this consensus.

However, a fundamentally different reading of international peacebuilding exists, and this challenges the idea that a peacebuilding architecture can emerge on the basis of a universal vision of peace and development. Some tensions within the peacebuilding project, and between international peacebuilding actors and local stakeholders in post-conflict societies, go far deeper than mere problems of 'coordination', and point to differences in ideological approach and to serious internal inconsistencies in the peacebuilding consensus. According to this, the challenge of coherence is not a simple function of better coordination, because the problems of peacebuilding – related to its record, effectiveness and legitimacy – are a result of its fundamental inconsistencies and internal tensions. These tensions can be illustrated in a number of ways.

There are a range of controversies related to the prevailing liberal peacebuilding model. Critical challenges are increasingly voiced by scholars and stakeholders who argue that there is a need for a greater emphasis in peacebuilding upon human security, local solutions, social justice and the resolution of the underlying causes of conflict (Newman, Paris and Richmond 2009; Mac Ginty 2011; Richmond 2009; Campbell, Chandler and Sabaratnam 2011; Jacoby 2007; Tadjbakhsh 2011). The liberal approach has tended to stress the top-down building or rebuilding of institutions as a priority, the promotion of liberal democracy, and free-market led development. This can result in a lack of sensitivity towards local needs and desires, and programmes which are not regarded locally as effective or legitimate. Externally led state building based on institutionalist models may undermine traditional indigenous authority structures, raising questions of legitimacy in addition to effectiveness. Self-sustaining public institutions often fail to take root; a phenomenon that has been observed in Sierra Leone (Taylor 2009). When economic growth is insufficiently regulated and concentrated among the elite, large sections of the population depend upon the informal economic sector to survive – and in turn fail to pay taxes and shun public institutions. Where institutions are not organic and thus not durable in the absence of external support, local ownership is jeopardized. In these circumstances, combined with poverty and an apparent lack of opportunities, citizens continue to support sectarian political forces which prolong the polarization of society and in the worst cases threaten violence and insecurity. The efforts – and resources – of donor agencies do not fully achieve their goals, aid is wasted and society is prone to the danger of falling again into cycles of conflict (Newman 2011).

The promotion of market reform has been controversial. There are claims that this approach can result in inequality, unemployment and social problems, resulting in perceived injustice and social grievances. It can hamper the development of public services at a time when they are most needed. It may even contribute to the underlying sources of conflict, while perpetuating problems such as the reliance of people upon the informal economy. Of course, progress in public service delivery and welfare requires economic growth, and this can only come from a free market and a climate conducive to investment. However, ill-timed or premature economic liberalization – including privatization and public spending cuts – in volatile societies can result in growing inequalities and alienation, which threaten broader peacebuilding goals.

The liberal peacebuilding agenda encourages, as a long-term goal, constrained public expenditure, deregulation and privatization. There is thus an internal paradox: peacebuilding implies the strengthening (or (re)construction) of the state, yet the liberal economic and social policies that are promoted threaten to undermine the state, along with public service delivery. Privatization in Iraq during the conflict period after 2003 is illustrative of this. There is ample evidence that rapid marketization is unhelpful in volatile conflict-prone societies which have been characterized by inequality and social grievances. Contrary to a liberal economic approach, the evidence suggests that the emphasis – at least in the short term – should be upon poverty alleviation and employment generation, on the basis of local provision. While some agencies – notably the Department for International Development (DFID) – apparently take this seriously, broader international peacebuilding remains embedded in the prevailing development assistance mind-set that has been widely challenged.

Liberal institutionalist approaches aimed at containing instability and building generic state institutions based upon external models have arguably neglected the welfare needs of local populations at the street level, and have failed to engage with indigenous traditional institutions. Indeed, these approaches are not grounded in the everyday politics, experiences and needs of individuals and communities.

Faith in electoral democracy in post-conflict settings has also been questioned (Paris 2004). Consolidated democracies tend to be peaceful but democratizing, transitional societies – especially in conjunction with factors which make them fragile – can be highly volatile. In fact, a significant amount of research suggests that transitional societies – when moving towards democracy – may be more likely to experience civil conflict, especially in poor and divided societies (Goldstone et al. 2010; Collier 2009). The promotion of democracy can therefore be destabilizing in conflict-prone and divided societies since it may exacerbate political conflict and sectarian divisions, especially in conjunction with vulnerability factors: ethnic heterogeneity and domination, social inequality, identity politics, and weak state capacity. Democratization in such situations encourages politicians to campaign on sectarian grounds, including ethnicity, tribal affiliation and religion. In volatile or post-conflict societies elections can exacerbate societal differences, and when a victorious political group is dominated by members of an exclusive identity group, this can create insecurities among communities on the outside of this group. There is ample experience to support this view: Angola in 1992, Burundi in the first half of the 1990s, Bosnia in the 1990s, and Côte d'Ivoire in 2010, among others. The central role of early elections as a part of peacebuilding doctrine is therefore questionable.

There is also often a tension or disconnect between international and local actors and activities in large peacebuilding missions, underpinned by the perception of an absence of local ownership of the peacebuilding agenda. This is heightened both by a lack of consultation between peacebuilders and local stakeholders, and the feeling that international peacebuilding activities are not appropriate for the local context. There can also be a disconnect between the formal lead agency and formal lines of command, and the reality of where influence lies.

Many of the problems and controversies discussed above are manifested in a lack of coherence – and sometimes conflicts – within international peacebuilding circles, and this challenges the idea of a 'peacebuilding community' or a coherent peacebuilding architecture or doctrine. The role of international financial institutions involves the promotion of free market economics in post-conflict settings – including deregulation and privatization – as a means of promoting economic growth, but this is potentially in tension with those organizations which promote social welfare and poverty alleviation as a key component of peacebuilding. Large international peacebuilding operations involve the brokering of power-sharing bargaining amongst local elites – including those which may have played a role in the preceding conflict – and this is at odds with those actors, such as civil society organizations, which seek to give a voice to grassroots peacebuilding groups and promote social justice and emancipation as peacebuilding goals. In a number of peace operations there is a tension between the coercion of enforcement actions and the work of humanitarian actors so that in cases such as Iraq and Afghanistan all peacebuilding actors are seen by local insurgents as legitimate targets of violence.

Building peace or international security?

Some of these tensions and controversies derive from fundamentally different interpretations about what international peacebuilding should seek to achieve (Newman 2010). Some analysts view peacebuilding as a project which should, in theory at least, be directed above all towards local, grassroots peace, oriented around human security and social justice – or even emancipation (Conteh-Morgan 2005; Begby and Burgess 2009; Richmond 2006; Newman 2011). However, in practice, in policy circles, peacebuilding has become directly or indirectly merged with the international security agenda. There is wide – though not uncontested – agreement that unstable and conflict-prone societies pose a threat to international security and stability. Many analysts, especially after 9/11, now consider these situations as the primary security challenge of the contemporary era. Theories of conflict and instability increasingly point to the weakness of the state as a key factor in the onset of violent conflict, and a merging of the security and development agendas. Among foreign policy elites this is a paradigm shift in security thinking: existential challenges to security no longer come from rival global powers but from failing or weak states. According to Fukuyama (2004: 92) 'weak and failing states have arguably become the single most important problem for international order'.

This thinking has been internalized across foreign policy elites, and with it the idea that in the contemporary world poverty, inequality and poor governance are key drivers of global insecurity (Cabinet Office 2008; HM Government 2010; United Nations Secretary-General 2005; US Department of Defense 2008; Straw 2002; OECD 2008; Krasner and Pascual 2005). It is debatable whether this view reflects 'reality' or is rather a political construction (Newman 2009). Nevertheless, greater efforts and resources have been forthcoming from powerful states to contain, resolve and to some extent prevent civil war. In recent years international peacebuilding activities in conflict-prone and post-conflict countries have increased in number and in complexity in line with this evolving security discourse. These activities have also become an exercise in state building, based upon the assumption that effective (preferably liberal) states form the greatest prospect for a stable international order. Peacebuilding is therefore a part of the security agenda insofar as the pathologies of conflict-prone and underdeveloped states have been constructed as international threats. Viewing conflict, weak statehood and underdevelopment as a threat to international security has brought much-needed resources, aid and capacity building to conflict-prone countries in the form of international assistance. This has arguably contributed to a reduction in the absolute numbers of civil wars and the consolidation of peace in many countries (HSRP 2010).

However, 'peacebuilding as security' has also generated a number of critical challenges. This approach translates into peacebuilding policies which often ignore the underlying sources of conflict because the emphasis is upon stability and containment, rather than conflict resolution. It also results in conditional and coercive forms of peacebuilding assistance – most obviously for example in Bosnia and East Timor but more subtly in many other contexts. When international stability becomes the priority, rather than addressing local conflict or demands for justice, international peacebuilding tends to rely on top-down mediation among power brokers and on building state institutions, rather than on bottom-up, community-driven peacebuilding or the resolution of the underlying sources of conflict. Instead of promoting a sense of social justice and reconciliation, this can perpetuate the influence of sectarian leaders because international peacebuilding actors believe that the latter must be engaged with as the key to local control – a part of the 'facts on the ground'. This excludes or obstructs the emergence of alternative – potentially more conciliatory and cosmopolitan – leaders and civil society, and thus alternative visions of peace.

The peacebuilding agenda itself often becomes an externally (often donor) driven exercise, because it is ultimately oriented towards the promotion of stability, often without a genuine understanding of local political culture, desires or needs. As a result, this approach can be insensitive towards – and exclude from the peacebuilding agenda – local traditions and institutions. Indeed, there are numerous reports of local opposition and civil society initiatives being discouraged by international peacebuilding agents because they apparently do not fit the 'agenda' (Hughes 2009). There is also evidence of peacebuilding actors – especially major UN operations – failing to recognize traditional social and political institutions in the countries in which they are working (Hohe 2003). Peacebuilding is often reduced to a technical exercise, the implication being that peacebuilding assistance is essentially value-free and that it does not represent important choices and interests. Yet the apolitical model of peacebuilding can miss the reality on the ground and fail to create conditions conducive to durable stability. Moreover, in this context there is a danger that state building may undermine traditional indigenous authority structures (Chesterman 2007; Lemay-Hebert 2009). This may be morally questionable and illegitimate, but also, if the new centralized agendas fail to take root, instability and conflict can ensue (as in East Timor in 2006). This raises the question: is the liberal peace being promoted in societies, such as Sierra Leone, East Timor and Côte d'Ivoire, in which it may, for social or cultural reasons, be fundamentally inappropriate?

The mixed record of peacebuilding is therefore hostage to its prevailing rationale to promote strong states and contain conflict as a matter of international security, rather than to resolve conflict or address its underlying sources. Of course, stability and 'negative' peace are important values: the ending of violence and establishing stability is a great achievement, and clearly the prerequisite to any further peacebuilding and reconstruction objectives. Many policy analysts would argue that the promotion of stability in conflict-prone societies is the realistic extent of what international peacebuilding can achieve. However, there is ample evidence that a negative peace can be a fragile peace; research shows that conflict is often recurrent in societies that have experienced conflict in the past, and this remains the case, despite the apparent downtrend in armed conflict (Mason 2009; Walter 2011). The tendency for international peacebuilding to emphasize stability through brokering elite bargaining has meant that the sources of conflict – and the overall atmosphere of sectarianism in public life – have often been perpetuated, which in the worst cases can make 'peace' fragile. Although international peacebuilding is often described as 'liberal', this may be a misnomer. Is international peacebuilding truly 'liberal' when (in terms of conflict resolution) it tends to mediate – from the top down – between local power brokers, who are often politically extremist or exclusionary, and does not – despite the civil society empowerment programmes that are invariably a part of peacebuilding activities – sufficiently engage with grassroots community actors who are potentially more inclusive and moderate? Thus, the essential mechanism of a liberal social contract is generally absent in post-conflict states, which instead are held together by external actors. This obstructs more progressive bottom-up forms of peacebuilding that cultivate alternative approaches to peace and address underlying sources of conflict. It also suggests that the international community is far from having a coherent and universally shared understanding of what peacebuilding is.

Conclusion

Clearly many of the tensions, controversies and internal inconsistencies of the 'peacebuilding consensus' go far beyond mere problems of coordination or different priorities amongst the different actors involved. In particular, the effectiveness and appropriateness of promoting liberal democracy and market economics in volatile conflict-prone societies are contested. The tenets of liberal peacebuilding – liberal democracy, liberal human rights, market values, the integration of societies into globalization and the centralized secular state – are not necessarily universal (or universally applicable) values. The perceived absence of 'local ownership', and insufficient consultation with local stakeholders, have led some observers to question the legitimacy of peacebuilding operations. The apparent emphasis in international peacebuilding on top-down mediation among power brokers and building state institutions – in contrast to more bottom-up, community driven peacebuilding – has raised concerns about the sustainability of peacebuilding projects. The attention to reconstruction and stability and the neglect of the underlying sources of conflict suggest, to some, that the nature of the 'peace' that is being built is not entirely inclusive. The seeming paradox of combining reconstruction with coercion – most obviously in Afghanistan and Iraq, but also more subtly in Bosnia and elsewhere – and the manner in which other components of the peacebuilding agenda also appear to be in tension with each other suggest that there are deep and unresolved internal contradictions in the peacebuilding project.

The liberal peace and its neoliberal economic dimensions are not necessarily appropriate for conflicted or divided societies (Parekh 1993). Indeed, democracy and the market are arguably adversarial or even conflictual forces – taken for granted in stable Western democracies but not necessarily suitable for volatile societies that do not enjoy stable institutions. Peacebuilding activities are thus not neutral in their normative orientation or impact. There is real concern that post-conflict peacebuilding programmes may therefore sow the seeds of their own failure by exacerbating the social tensions that resulted in violent conflict in the first place, or by failing to create the domestic foundations for democratizing and marketizing reforms. As a result, different components of the liberal reform agenda may be in tension with each other in ways that cast doubt on the viability of the larger liberal peacebuilding project.

These issues point to fundamental divergences between different actors based upon different, and possibly incompatible, worldviews about the nature of conflict-prone societies, and a wide gap between the policies and assumptions of international peacebuilding actors and the perceptions and aspirations of local stakeholders. Above all, this suggests that the liberal institutionalist model of international peacebuilding does not rest upon universal consensus, and is certainly not supported unreservedly in post-conflict settings. All of this raises questions about the extent to which there is truly an international architecture of peacebuilding with a coherent doctrine.

References

Begby, E. and Burgess, J.P. (2009) 'Human Security and Liberal Peace', *Public Reason*, 1(1): 91–104.
Bellamy, A.J. and Williams, P. (2005) 'Who's Keeping the Peace? Regionalization and Contemporary Peace Operations', *International Security*, 29(4): 157–95.
Cabinet Office (2008) *The National Security Strategy of the United Kingdom: Security in an interdependent world*, Norwich: Cabinet Office.
Campbell, S., Chandler, D., and Sabaratnam, M. (eds) (2011) *A Liberal Peace?: The Problems and Practices of Peacebuilding*, London, Zed Books.
Chesterman, S. (2007) 'Ownership in theory and in practice: transfer of authority in UN statebuilding operations', *Journal of Intervention and Statebuilding*, 1(1): 3–26.
Collier, P. (2009) *Wars, Guns & Votes: Democracy in Dangerous Places*, The Bodley Head.
de Coning, C. (2007) *Coherence and Coordination in United Nations Peacebuilding and Integrated Missions – A Norwegian Perspective*, Oslo: NUPI.

Conteh-Morgan, E. (2005) 'Peacebuilding and Human Security: A Constructivist Perspective', *International Journal of Peace Studies*, 10(1): 70–86.

Easterly, W. (2007) *The White Man's Burden: Why the West's Efforts to Aid the Rest Have Done So Much Ill And So Little Good*, Oxford: Oxford University Press.

Fukuyama, F. (2004) *State-Building: Governance and World Order in the 21st Century*, Ithaca, NY: Cornell University Press.

Goldstone, J.A., Bates, R.H., Epstein, D.L., Gurr, T.R., Lustik, M.B., Marshall, M., Ulfelder, J., and Woodward, M. (2010) 'A Global Model for Forecasting Political Instability', *American Journal of Political Science*, 54(1): 190–208.

Hemmer, B., Garb, P., Phillips, M., and Graham, J.L. (2006) 'Putting the "Up" in Bottom-up Peacebuilding: Broadening the Concept of Peace Negotiations', *International Negotiation*, 11(1): 129–64.

High Level Panel (2004) *A more secure world: Our shared responsibility Report of the High-level Panel on Threats, Challenges and Change*, New York: United Nations.

HM Government (2010) *UK Strategic Defence and Security Review: Securing Britain in an age of uncertainty*, London: HM Government.

Hohe, T. (2003) 'The Clash of Paradigms: International Administration and Local Political Legitimacy in East Timor', *Contemporary Southeast Asia: A Journal of International and Strategic Affairs*, 24(3): 569–89.

Hughes, C. (2009) '"We just take what they offer": Community empowerment in post-war Timor-Leste', in Newman, E., Richmond, O.P., and Paris, R. (eds) *New Perspectives on Liberal Peacebuilding*, Tokyo: United Nations University Press.

Human Security Report Project (HSRP) (2010) *Human Security Report 2009/2010: The Causes of Peace and the Shrinking Costs of War*, Vancouver: HSRP.

Jacoby, T. (2007) 'Hegemony, modernisation and post-war reconstruction', *Global Society*, 21(4): 521–37.

Krasner, S.D. and Pascual, C. (2005) 'Addressing state failure', *Foreign Affairs*, 84(4): 153–63.

Lancaster, C. (2006) *Foreign Aid: Diplomacy, Development, Domestic Policies*, Chicago: University of Chicago Press.

Lemay-Hebert, N. (2009), 'Statebuilding Without Nation-Building? Legitimacy, State Failure and the Limits of the Institutionalist Approach', *Journal of Intervention and Statebuilding*, 3(1): 21–45.

Mac Ginty, R. (2011) *International Peacebuilding and Local Resistance: Hybrid Forms of Peace*, Basingstoke: Palgrave.

Mason, T.D. (2009) 'The evolution of theory on civil war and revolution', in Midlarsky, M.I. (ed.) *Handbook of War Studies III: The Intrastate Dimension*, Ann Arbor, MI: University of Michigan Press.

Newman, E. (2009) 'Conflict research and the "decline" of civil war', *Civil Wars*, 11(3): 255–278.

Newman, E. (2010) 'Critical human security studies', *Review of International Studies*, 36(1): 77–94.

Newman, E. (2011) 'A Human Security Peacebuilding Agenda', *Third World Quarterly*, 32(10): 1737–56.

Newman, E., Paris, R., and Richmond, O. (eds) (2009) *New Perspectives on Liberal Peacebuilding* Tokyo: United Nations University Press.

OECD (2008) *Annual Report 2008*, Paris: OECD.

Parekh, B. (1993) 'The Cultural Particularity of Liberal Democracy', in Held, D. (ed.) *Prospects for Democracy: North, South, East, West*, Oxford: Polity Press.

Paris, R. (2004) *At War's End: Building peace after civil conflict*, Cambridge: Cambridge University Press.

Paris, R. and Sisk, T.D. (2009) *The Dilemmas Of Statebuilding: Confronting the Contradictions of Postwar Peace Operations*, Abingdon: Routledge.

Pouligny, B. (2005) 'Civil Society and Post-Conflict Peacebuilding', *Security Dialogue*, 36(4): 495–510.

Ramsbotham, O., Woodhouse, T., and Miall, H. (2011) *Contemporary Conflict Resolution*, Oxford: Polity Press.

Richmond, O.P. (2006) 'Human security and the liberal peace', *Whitehead Journal of Diplomacy and International Relations*, 7(1): 75–87.

Richmond, O.P. (2009) 'A post-liberal peace: Eirenism and the everyday', *Review of International Studies*, 35(3): 557–80.

Straw, J. (2002) 'Order out of chaos: the challenge of failed states', in Leonard, M. (ed.) *Reordering the World: The Long-term Implications of September 11*, London: Foreign Policy Research Centre.

Tadjbakhsh, S. (ed.) (2011) *Rethinking the Liberal Peace: External Models and Local Alternatives*, London: Routledge.

Taylor, I. (2009) 'Earth Calling the Liberals: Locating the Political Culture of Sierra Leone as the Terrain for "Reform"', in Newman, E., Paris, R., and Richmond, O.P. (eds) *New Perspectives on Liberal Peacebuilding*, Tokyo: United Nations University Press.

United Nations (2005) World Summit Outcome, General Assembly Resolution A/RES/60/1.

United Nations Secretary-General (2005) 'In larger freedom: towards development, security and human rights for all', Report of the Secretary-General, New York: United Nations.

US Department of Defense (2008) *National Defense Strategy*, Washington: US Government.

Walter, B. (2011) 'Conflict Relapse and the Sustainability of Post-Conflict Peace', input paper for the *World Development Report 2011: Conflict, Security, and Development*, Washington DC: World Bank Publications.

World Bank (2011) *World Development Report 2011: Conflict, Security, and Development*, Washington DC: World Bank Publications.

25

THE POLITICAL ECONOMY OF PEACEBUILDING AND INTERNATIONAL AID[1]

Susan L. Woodward

Introduction

No peacebuilding operation can begin without commitments from those who will provide the financial and material resources necessary. One influential strand of the peacebuilding literature even argues that success is best explained by the amount of resources provided (in relation to the complexity of the case). The more resources, the more likely efforts at peace are to be effective.[2] The design of United Nations missions and their mandates, including the frequency of decisions on their renewal, is shaped by negotiations with countries willing to commit troops and the budgetary politics of the UN system. The evolution of the international peace architecture itself since the era of activism began in the early 1990s has been characterized as a drive to expand in every way possible the resources, tools, and leverage at its disposal, above all, the financing.[3]

The availability of funds not only shapes what the mission can do, but also which components of any peace agreement can be implemented. What countries emerging from war are able to accomplish depends not only on leaders' political will, as outsiders argue, but even more on what resources flow in from outside, from whom, and with what constraints. The donors and banks providing this assistance, in turn, see it not only as funds for projects and activities, including the early 'peace dividend' to the local population that the policy literature since 1995 declares essential to get the peace process going and keep on track, but also as economic incentives to leaders – selective rewards and punishments of external aid – to induce cooperation.

The key debates in the literature on international assistance focus on less than half the total, however: the 30–40 per cent, at most, for all humanitarian, economic, and political goals. Why the far more costly component, between 60 and 70 per cent for the military, gets little or no attention or critical research is not debated, although the increasing militarization of aid decisions and delivery since the mid-1990s and especially since 2001 has provoked concern from the humanitarian community and should be the subject of critical analysis in the peacebuilding and development communities.

This chapter first traces the evolution of economic assistance to peacebuilding since the early 1990s, and then turns to the main subject of debates, the research findings on the effects of aid on peace. Three main debates are then outlined. It concludes by proposing that both the debates and the aid policies themselves assume a world that does not exist. If the goal is to explain and improve outcomes, we need a political economic understanding of aid, its providers, and the peace process itself.

Evolution of the aid for peace regime

Aid for peacebuilding has evolved over the past two decades in three phases, with a fourth now on the horizon. As with peacekeeping in general, the first phase reflected the profound change in the strategic environment with the end of the Cold War. Not only was the UN Security Council freed to mandate an ever-larger number of peacemaking and peacekeeping operations, but aid donors could also begin to address the needs of the populations themselves, independently of strategic interests and calculation. While the United Nations Development Programme (UNDP) and middle powers such as Norway and Japan attempted to shift attention away from state security and military budgets to human development and human security, aid focused on human rights (soon to be called 'rule-of-law' assistance) and humanitarian relief.

The mounting experience of this period of unplanned activism provoked a new phase beginning in the mid-1990s of a more conscious articulation of goals, policy frameworks, and bureaucratic specialization, what we might call the institutionalization of an aid regime. The now classic article by the head of the UN mission in El Salvador, Alvaro de Soto, and its chief economic advisor, Graciana del Castillo, appeared in 1994, and its analysis of the tensions and even contradictions between the peacebuilding mandate and its necessary political objectives, on the one hand, and the orthodox economic policies of the Bretton Woods institutions (the World Bank and International Monetary Fund (IMF)), on the other, set the main lines of the aid debate even today. At the same time, however, the World Bank was defining the concepts and policy framework that would guide their aid and that of most development donors ever since. A 1995 task force to identify what might distinguish war-torn countries from other kinds of emergency decided it was being 'failed states', that the primary problem they posed for the Bank, that 'the majority of countries in arrears to the Bank are countries in conflict' (World Bank 1998: 8), required an explicit recognition of the link between security and development and a new aid framework for 'post-conflict reconstruction'. The new framework was not driven, as de Soto and del Castillo proposed, by special economic policies attuned to peacebuilding, but the operational difficulties of working in these conditions. The technology of aid delivery deemed appropriate to the first years after war, they concluded, was greater speed, flexibility, transparency, aid coordination among donors, and more targeted conditionality.

It was growing Bank assertiveness in particular cases, however, that most influenced the emerging aid-for-peace regime. Already during the Bosnian war, Bank staff began planning a multi-year postwar reconstruction strategy and aid program for Bosnia-Herzegovina and within a month of the signing ceremony for the 1995 peace agreement, organized the first of four annual donors' aid pledging conferences and a now universal practice. To influence fiscally responsible political decisions (especially governmental design), the Bank also began to participate in peace talks starting with Bosnia and Guatemala. The Bank also assumed management of the 1994 multi-donor Johan

Jørgen Holst Fund for Start-up and Recurrent Costs to finance the new Palestinian authorities after the Oslo Accord, the first of the now hundreds of specialized trust funds for countries donors do not trust, above all, beginning in Kosovo in 1999 for general budgetary support (such as civil servant salaries, including police and teachers). In-country assessment missions prior to planning a country's postwar reconstruction strategy soon followed, eventually including others such as UNDP, and thus called joint assessment missions (JAMs).

This influential role of the World Bank meant, necessarily, a growing role for the IMF because the Bank cannot lend to a country that is not first a member of the IMF and such membership requires negotiation of a prior IMF agreement for payment of the country's foreign debt. An early macroeconomic stabilization program to repay debt is thus an inevitable component of the aid-for-peace regime, and although bilateral development donors have their own funding interests and mandates, in practice, they do not challenge, but work within, the terms of aid and conditionality set by that IMF agreement. As a result of the compromise between the International Financial Institutions (IFIs) and the Jubilee 2000 debt relief campaigners, since 1999 post-conflict countries – which are all Highly Indebted Poor Countries (HIPC) – must also first write a Poverty Reduction Strategy Paper (PRSP) to access IMF and World Bank credits and loans. Although done under strict and voluminous World Bank guidelines and subject to veto by either, this PRSP is considered the postwar government's national development strategy and the basis on which donors from the OECD Development Assistance Committee (DAC) commit to align their aid under their 2005 Paris Declaration on aid effectiveness.

This phase of operational and bureaucratic expansion was taking place, however, at the time when these rich donor countries were in the throes of political debate about aid ineffectiveness in general. The growing sense of overload, donor fatigue, and recognition that external assistance could as likely be 'redundant, harmful, or squandered' (Forman and Patrick 2000: 30) as palliative was matched in the humanitarian community with a crisis over the appearance of Mary Anderson's critique of the way that aid could promote more violence. Her call for *Do No Harm* led donors to begin developing conflict impact assessments of their aid and aid planning, while the UN High Commissioner for Refugees, Sadako Ogata, in January 1999, convened a Brookings forum to address the 'gap' between relief and development, that is, the absence of financing mechanisms and operational mandates for the transition between relief and the more stable conditions suited to development, a period now called 'early recovery'. This second phase culminated in the admonition in the Brahimi Report of 2000 of the Panel on UN Peace Operations that the Security Council and Secretary-General match mandates and resources, even to the point of saying 'no' to a request for peacekeeping if member states did not provide the resources necessary to implement it effectively.

What should have been a new era of reform following this Report was pre-empted, however, by another change in the strategic environment after September 11, 2001. During the decade that followed, up to 90 per cent of the aid monies for peace from the OECD DAC donors, at least, was redirected to Iraq and Afghanistan.[4] Use of peacekeeping troops to deliver aid in the first years after war, a technique pioneered in Bosnia-Herzegovina and then Kosovo in 1996–99, metamorphosed to ever greater militarization of humanitarian and development assistance, including for parallel counterinsurgency operations. Aid instruments to protect donors' 'fiduciary risk' were now compounded by concern for 'risk protection' of their staff. At the same time, the IFIs became ever more intrusive in drafting laws, designing government ministries and procedures, and administering aid as a component of the peacebuilding process, bordering as Boon says on the 'legislative' (Boon 2007: 515).

A fourth phase is possibly beginning. Reacting against donors' calls for country 'ownership' (government responsibility) to make their aid more effective, recipient countries have begun to join their forces to negotiate with donors over their common complaints about the lack of genuine ownership in the design of aid, the excessive fragmentation and volatility of aid to post-conflict countries, and the administrative burden of hundreds of distinct aid missions and their conditions.[5] An 'International Dialogue on Peacebuilding and Statebuilding', a standing forum of donors and recipients, and the g7+, a coalition of seven, now 19, post-conflict countries led by Timor-Leste emerged from the Third High-Level Forum on Aid Effectiveness at Accra in 2008.[6] Arguing 'Work with us, not against us' (Crook 2010), the expanded g7+ proposed at the Fourth High-Level Forum in Busan, South Korea, in late 2011, a 'New Deal for Engagement in Fragile States'. A 'New Global Partnership for Effective Development Cooperation' also formed among 'emerging donors',[7] the many countries which choose not to join the DAC because they have different agendas, interests, and aid modalities and whose percentage of total aid is rising. Although it is too soon to say how they and the increasing number of private donors will change the aid regime for peacebuilding or its outcomes, the g7+ have succeeded at least in changing the rhetoric from aid to development and cooperation (with increased emphasis on South–South cooperation and its premise of horizontal rather than hierarchical relationships).

Outcomes

Before discussing the debates around international aid to peacebuilding, a caveat is in order. These debates focus almost entirely on current outcomes and proposals for changes in policy and practice. Yet our knowledge about the effects of aid is severely constrained by donor practices and the characteristics of aid: the woeful lack of transparency, particularly by the IMF and World Bank; the absence of baseline statistics in war-torn countries; the allergy to bad news that limits evaluations, if they are done at all, to financial accounts and positive reports; and the predominance of individual and sectoral projects that do not combine to an overall effect that could be studied. Although four multilateral banks, three global funds, four UN agencies, the European Commission, and 14 bilateral donors have signed the International Aid Transparency Initiative (IATI) formed in 2006, Publish What You Fund documented in late 2011 a decline in transparency (Beattie 2011). Data, whether they ever existed, were destroyed by war, or statistical agencies were closed by IFI structural adjustment policies in the 1980s. Donors could have placed a priority on creating necessary baseline data with early funding, but they do not.

What we do know comes from country and project case studies. A consistent theme is the stark contrast between what is needed in the first years after war and what is actually funded and done. The reasons are many. Aid is supply-driven according to a range of organizational, political, and strategic interests of the donor's home country or organization. It has a short time horizon and impatience for 'results' that can be reported, ignoring the requirements of sustainability or the long time necessary to accomplish those results (Pritchett and de Weijer 2010). However worthy the goals, such as minority and women's rights, anti-corruption, or capital infrastructure, their linkage with the goal of peace is rarely articulated explicitly.

Instead, the goal they all share is statebuilding because without a state as sovereign partner, institutional capacity to 'absorb' (use) aid, and a reform-oriented (market-friendly and democratically accountable) political leadership, aid cannot be given. The alternative, which characterizes most international aid practices to peacebuilding countries, is to do it themselves, that is, to bypass governmental authorities, create parallel budgets, administrations, and implementing agencies (a situation of 'dual legitimacy' [Rubin citing Ghassan Salamé 2005: 97; also Goodhand and Sedra 2010]), and use international non-governmental agencies and externally convened community participation forums (as opposed to local governments) to make decisions on aid and deliver it. Between 40 and 70 per cent of all aid to post-conflict countries goes to salaries for foreign consultants (Kahler 2008: 15). Only 10 per cent of the budget of a UN peacekeeping operation is spent locally (Carnahan et al. 2006). The result is what the literature now calls the 'aid-institutions paradox' (Pettersson et al. 2006) whereby aid actually undermines the capacity and quality of government institutions. A downward spiral of lack of trust, ever smaller lack of capacity, and ever less trust then ensues. As Francis Fukuyama (2004: 40) writes, 'outside donors want both to increase the local government's capacity to provide a particular service … *and* to actually provide those services to the end users. The latter objective almost always wins out because of the incentives facing the donors themselves'. The one exception, documented by the OECD-DAC country surveys after 2005, is public financial management – not, one might suggest, what the literature on peacebuilding would consider a priority.

Additional ways that aid can work at cross purposes to peace appear to be common across nearly all cases. Aid concentrates in the capital city where the peacekeeping mission and donors reside, creating new inequalities between city and country, center and regions even if they were initial causes of the conflict. The 'economic impact of peacekeeping operations' (Carnahan et al. 2006) is hugely distorting of local markets, production, and salary scales with which the government and local businesses cannot compete. The focus on political elites, the executive branch, and closed-door negotiations, distancing the very civil society participants that donors rhetorically value and excluding parliamentarians, political parties, trade unions, women, and marginalized groups from participation in key decisions about the economic (and thus social and political) direction of their country, has a conservative effect, reinforcing the power of those who first emerge dominant from the war and the existing structure of political and economic power in localities (often in reaction to external efforts to upset those local structures). Economically for post-conflict countries, of truly worrisome proportions is the growing aid dependency over time; very high unemployment and rising inequality (across individuals, groups, and regions); and worsening material conditions for the population in contrast to the promised peace dividend. Despite the new forms of civil and criminal violence provoked by this inequality, joblessness, and growing poverty that led the Brahimi Panel to call for a new doctrine of peacebuilding focused on civilian security, funds for police reform and training and judicial institutions remain proportionally very small, perhaps because neither the World Bank by mandate nor the US by Congressional decision can work in this sector, leaving it to the UN and an alarming proliferation of bilateral donors, each seeking to reproduce its own institutions in one segment of what should be an integrated whole.

Debates

Debates in the literature on international assistance to peacebuilding all share the judgment first identified by de Soto and del Castillo. The debates are about the explanation: why is aid so antagonistic to the goal of a sustainable peace? Three reasons dominate: institutions, statebuilding, and economic development strategy.

The first camp argues that current policies are destabilizing because they create new conflicts when conflict reduction and management are needed. For Roland Paris (2004), the priority on building liberal democracy and market economies ignores the fact that both presume and reinforce competition and conflict whereas peacebuilding requires the reverse. Institutions must be built first. Charles Call (2008: 374–7), however, argues that outsiders do focus on institutions, but their design is the source of conflict. The outsiders' constitutional design of the state generates resistance and new violence while the meritocratic principle, in particular, may well be in conflict with the confidence-building goals of conflict transformation. Studies of community driven development (CDD) programs based on local councils of externally created participation so popular among donors and the World Bank document in detail the intense local struggles they generate over power, bases of authority, and resources (e.g., Hohe 2005). Outsiders' institutional templates, argue Dani Rodrik (2007) and Lant Pritchett (Pritchett and de Weijer 2010), actually defy the economic literature proving that economic outcomes, at least, can be achieved equally well by a variety of institutional forms; in addition, imposing one set ignores that institutions are socially embedded and require local legitimacy to work. Thomas Carothers argues the same in regard to rule-of-law programs, said to be so necessary to both economic development and democracy. 'Operating from a disturbingly thin base of knowledge', the empirical evidence suggests that the causal relationship may well be in the opposite direction. They conceive of the rule of law in institutional terms whereas 'law is a normative system': 'simply rewriting another country's laws on the basis of Western models … achieves very little' (Carothers 2006: 18–19). In sum, what it means to 'build institutions' becomes very unclear, as does an accompanying debate on sequencing, that building these institutions should precede, by a decade or more, the democratic reforms, including elections, that currently come very early (Paris 2004; Collier et al. 2003; World Bank 2011).

The second debate emerges from a separate debate over whether statebuilding is destabilizing and undermines peace. Regardless of its effect on peace, is a strategy of statebuilding even possible? For Fukuyama (2004), failure is inevitable if a country's cultural norms and specific history, the little, if any knowledge on statebuilding that is transferable, and the necessity for success of domestically generated demand are not recognized. He is joined by a series of papers commissioned by the OECD Fragile States Group which emphasize that resilience against conflict depends on local legitimacy. No matter what model outsiders consider most effective and legitimate, their intervention will have a 'negative impact' if 'the content of a state's policies is heavily influenced by external actors' and does not respond to citizens' expectations of their government

(Bellina et al. 2009: 4). Ashraf Ghani and Clare Lockhart (2008) disagree, arguing that the problem is not theory or imposition, but disagreements among external actors on what statebuilding entails. This can easily be resolved by forging an international consensus among these actors on their strategic framework of ten core state functions and an organizational structure necessary for their performance.

The Ghani–Lockhart framework belies a far deeper debate from the field of economic development, however. As Tony Addison and Tilman Brück (2009) remind us, the process of economic development necessarily generates conflict and social turmoil, creating a blatant tension with peacebuilding. But if peace requires economic growth, what is the appropriate economic role of the state and postwar economic policy? This debate pits the World Bank orthodoxy of neoclassical growth theory and 'good governance' as measured by its Country Policy and Institutional Assessment (CPIA) against heterodox economists to be found in universities, such as Mushtaq Khan (2010) and Ha-Joon Chang (2002) or in UN agencies such as the Department for Economic and Social Affairs or the UN Conference on Trade and Development, who argue that the Bank's 'market fundamentalism' (Kozul-Wright and Rayment 2007) and campaign against rent-seeking (Khan 2010) run directly counter to the policies used successfully by currently wealthy, developed countries – and even the lessons of effective postwar reconstruction in Europe under the Marshall Plan.

All of these debates on the appropriate strategy for economic development are beside the point, argues del Castillo (2008), because they are debates from the literature on 'development as usual'. The far larger problem is the absence of debate about the appropriate economic strategy for post-conflict conditions and the needs of building a sustainable peace. The 'decisive importance' of political factors in a peacebuilding process must drive decisions on economic assistance and policy. In place of the organizational separation of decisions on strategy and aid between peacebuilding and economic development, the development institutions such as the World Bank, IMF, and UNDP must take a supporting, not leading (let alone confounding) role, to the political objective.

In this light one can also see why there is also no debate over proposals for peace conditionality, conditioning aid on implementation of the peace agreement, and on odious debt, that countries emerging from war must first pay the debts of the prewar regime before any aid can flow. Both silences reflect the resistance and power of the IFIs. The motives and interests of bilateral donors may, in turn, explain the apparent lack of concern about the very high levels of aid dependency, over long periods, of postwar countries when the goal of aid should be to become superfluous. Local pleas for space to focus first on nation-building and reconciliation before governments embark on debt negotiations, formulating a national development strategy, and building market-based financial institutions also fall on deaf ears.

Political economy

The literature on international assistance to peacebuilding contains a puzzle. The funding actors, especially the IFIs and many bilateral donors, are engaged in notable, ongoing efforts to improve the effect of their aid, often in response to their critics, yet evidence about outcomes reveals little or no change at all. The criticisms and lines of debate also have changed little since 1994. How can we explain this puzzle? To do so, I propose that we need a political economic analysis of peacebuilding assistance. The image of neutral actors external to a conflict providing assistance does not fit reality, nor does that of passive recipients in dire need of aid. As Hanafi and Tabar write, 'aid is not a single transaction, but a complex relationship embedded in and shaped by multiple, overlapping interests, agendas, and practical considerations' (2004: 218). All relevant actors, both external and domestic, are political animals with economic and strategic interests. All are interacting, and the aid relationship is replete with competition among donors, implementing agents, and recipients for money, leadership, and policy preferences. Calls for aid coordination and coherence on strategy ignore this competition while the process of implementing a peace agreement is a contest among parties to the agreement and among donors to shape the postwar state and the economic and political interests it institutionalizes as much toward their own economic and political benefit as possible.

The premise of critics, debaters, and aid reforms is that the goal of such aid is peace, but that might not be the case. We should ask what the goals of those who provide financial resources are first. This provides a very different perspective on the general debate in the literature on peacebuilding between an orthodox, problem-solving approach and a critical, conflict transformation one.

Behind each ostensibly technocratic project is a political choice, even if the organizational and budgetary politics are hidden from view. For example, why do the IFIs and some bilateral donors such as USAID focus so much attention on institutions for public financial management or early privatization including of land? Why are resources for creating a new or reformed army so disproportionate in relation to the stark underinvestment in community police and the judicial system? Why do donors neglect aid to parliaments, political parties, local governments, and, more generally, what citizens say they actually want in public opinion surveys? Why does competition appear especially intense in rule-of-law or telecommunications sectors? If employment is so critical to peace and the dominant aid powers insist that job creation is the responsibility of the private sector, particularly small and medium enterprises, why do they neglect domestic (private) entrepreneurs and even insist on policies that demonstrably lead to their destruction? The studies we do have show that donor countries' strategic and foreign policy interests always trump aid effectiveness and peacebuilding principles (Suhrke and Buckmaster 2005: 744; National Academy of Public Administration 2006: 3–5, 15, 29; Goodhand and Sedra 2010; Bradbury and Kleinman 2010; Hanafi and Tabar 2004: 222–3).

Donors and especially the IFIs also have a transformation agenda, but it is in competition with the critical, conflict transformation approach to peacebuilding and its reform. This well-resourced agenda views the 'post-conflict' period as a rare, golden opportunity to be seized, not to build peace but to achieve the fundamental economic and political transformation that is far more difficult to achieve politically in more stable conditions – to build market economies and market-friendly states through domestic laws and procedural rules, technical assistance, and identification of and support for 'reform leaders'. Yet its purpose, as Ngaire Woods (2006) demonstrates persuasively, is to protect the stability of the international monetary and financial system and ensure the very survival of the IMF and World Bank as financial institutions. This agenda is conflict-transforming but rarely peace-promoting, as the literature demonstrates fully.

Notes

1 For further elaboration of the discussion in this chapter, see Woodward (2002; 2010; 2011; 2012).
2 Doyle and Sambanis (2006) and the many RAND publications on nation-building by James Dobbins are most associated with this argument, but it is also the core theme of all United Nations documents on peacebuilding, from Secretary-General Boutros-Ghali's *Agenda for Peace* (1992) and the Brahimi Panel Report on UN Peacekeeping (2000) to the creation of a Peacebuilding Commission and a Peacebuilding Fund by the 2005 World Summit Outcome Document and resolutions of the General Assembly and Security Council.
3 Andrew Mack has made this point in every Human Security Report and Brief since the first in 2005.
4 An Oxfam briefing paper of 10 February 2011 states: 'Since 2002 one-third of all development aid to the 48 states labeled "fragile" by the OECD has gone to just three countries: Iraq, Afghanistan and Pakistan. During this period aid to Iraq and Afghanistan alone has accounted for over two-fifths of the entire $178bn global increase in aid provided by wealthy countries' (p. 2). Separating out post-conflict countries from these categories brings the proportion by general estimates to 90 per cent.
5 In Cambodia alone, there were 400 donor missions, reviews, and studies per year (Ek and Sok 2008: 2).
6 The seven founding members were Afghanistan, Central African Republic, Democratic Republic of Congo (DRC), Liberia, Sierra Leone, South Sudan, and Timor-Leste; attending their Dili meeting in April 2010 were Burundi, Chad, DRC, Nepal, the Solomon Islands, Sierra Leone, southern Sudan, and Timor-Leste.
7 This current label is a misnomer because most have been aid donors as long or longer than the OECD-DAC donors, but their importance is now being recognized and thus, their aid analyzed.

References

Addison, T. and T. Brück (eds) (2009) *Making Peace Work: The Challenges of Social and Economic Reconstruction*, Basingstoke: Palgrave Macmillan.
Beattie, A. (2011) 'Donors Backtrack on Aid Transparency', *Financial Times*, November 15.
Bellina, S., Darbon, D., Eriksen, S.S., and Sending, O.J. (2009) *The Legitimacy of the State in Fragile Situations*, A Report for OECD DAC, Fragile States Group, Paris.
Boon, K.E. (2007) '"Open for Business": International Financial Institutions, Post-Conflict Economic Reform, and the Rule of Law', *International Law and Politics*, 39: 513–581.
Bradbury, M. and Kleinman, M. (2010) *Winning Hearts and Minds? Examining the Relationship Between Aid and Security in Kenya*, Tufts University, Medford: Feinstein International Center.
Brahimi, L. (2000) *Report of the Panel of Experts on United Nations Peace Keeping Operations* A/55/305-S/2000/809. New York: United Nations. Online. Available www.un.org/peace/reports/peace_operations/. Last accessed June 27, 2012.
Call, C.T. with V. Wyeth (eds) (2008) *Building States to Build Peace*, Boulder and London: Lynne Rienner.
Carnahan, M., Durch, W., and Gilmore, S. (2006) *Economic Impact of Peacekeeping: Final Report*, Ottawa and New York: Peace Dividend Trust.
Carothers, T. (2006) *Promoting the Rule of Law Abroad: In Search of Knowledge*, Washington DC: Carnegie Endowment for International Peace.
Chang, H.-J. (2002) *Kicking Away the Ladder: Development Strategy in Historical Perspective*, London: Anthem Press.
Collier, P. et al. (2003) *Breaking the Conflict Trap: Civil War and Development Policy*, New York and Washington DC: Oxford University Press and the World Bank.
Crook, M. (2010) 'Listen to Us, Fragile States Tell Donors', IPS-Interpress Service, July 19, 2011.
Del Castillo, G. (2008) *Rebuilding War-Torn States: The Challenge of Post-Conflict Economic Reconstruction*, Oxford and New York: Oxford University Press.

De Soto, A. and del Castillo, G. (1994) 'Obstacles to Peacebuilding', *Foreign Policy*, 94 (September): 69–83.

Doyle, M. and Sambanis, N. (2006) *Making War and Building Peace: United Nations Peace Operations*, Princeton, NJ: Princeton University Press.

Ek, C. and Sok, H. (2008) 'Aid Effectiveness in Cambodia', *Wolfensohn Center for Development Working Papers No. 7*, Washington DC: The Brookings Institution.

Forman, S. and Patrick, S. (eds) (2000) *Good Intentions: Pledges of Aid for Post-Conflict Recovery*, Boulder and London: Lynne Rienner.

Fukuyama, F. (2004) *State-Building: Governance and World Order in the 21st Century*, Ithaca and London: Cornell University Press.

Ghani, A. and Lockhart, C. (2008) *Fixing Failed States: A Framework for Rebuilding a Fractured World*, Oxford and New York: Oxford University Press.

Goodhand, J. and Sedra, M. (2010) 'Who owns the peace? Aid, reconstruction, and peacebuilding in Afghanistan', *Disasters*, 34: Issue Supplement s1, S78-S102 (January; online publication March 2009).

Hanafi, S. and Tabar, L. (2004) 'Donor assistance, rent-seeking and elite formation', in M.H. Khan et al. (eds) *State Formation in Palestine: Viability and governance during a social transformation*, London: Routledge Curzon, 215–238.

Hohe, T. (2005) 'Developing Local Governance', in G. Junne and W. Verkoren (eds) *Postconflict Development Meeting New Challenges*, Boulder and London: Lynne Rienner, 59–72.

Kahler, M. (2008) 'Aid and State-Building', paper presented to the workshop on economic aid policy and statebuilding, the Graduate Center, CUNY, 3–4 April.

Khan, M.H. (2010) *Political Settlements and the Governance of Growth-Enhancing Institutions*. Online. Available at www.mercury.soas.ac.uk/mk17 (accessed 15 June 2010).

Kozul-Wright, R. and Rayment, P. (2007) *The Resistible Rise of Market Fundamentalism: Rethinking Development Policy in an Unbalanced World*, London and New York: Zed Books.

National Academy of Public Administration (2006) 'Why Foreign Aid to Haiti Failed' (February), Washington DC: Academy International Affairs Working Paper Series. Online. Available www.napawash.org

Oxfam (2011) *Whose Aid is it Anyway? Politicizing aid in conflict and crises*, 145 Oxfam Briefing Paper, Oxford: Oxfam International February. Online. Available at www.oxfam.org. Last accessed June 27, 2012.

Paris, R. (2004) *At War's End: Building Peace After Civil Conflict*, Cambridge: Cambridge University Press.

Pettersson, G., Moss, T., and van de Walle, N. (2006) 'An Aid-Institutions Paradox? A Review Essay on Aid Dependency and State Building in Sub-Saharan Africa', Working Paper 74, Washington DC: Center for Global Development.

Pritchett, L. and de Weijer, F. (2010) 'Fragile States: Stuck in a Capability Trap?' Background paper for the World Development Report 2011.

Rodrik, D. (2007) *One Economics – Many Recipes: Globalization, Institutions, and Economic Growth*, Princeton, NJ: Princeton University Press.

Rubin, B.R. (2005) 'Constructing Sovereignty for Security', *Survival*, 47: 4 (Winter): 93–106.

Suhrke, A. and Buckmaster, J. (2005) 'Post-War Aid: Patterns and Purposes', *Development in Practice*, 15: 6 (November): 737–746.

Woods, N. (2006) *The Globalizers: The IMF, the World Bank, and Their Borrowers*, Ithaca and New York: Cornell University Press.

Woodward, S.L. (2002) 'Economic Priorities for Successful Peace Implementation', in S.J. Stedman, D. Rothchild, and E.M. Cousens (eds) *Ending Civil Wars: The Implementation of Peace Agreements*, Boulder and London: Lynne Rienner: 183–214.

Woodward, S.L. (2010) 'Soft Intervention and the Puzzling Neglect of Economic Actors', in M. Hoddie and C.A. Hartzell (eds) *Strengthening Peace in Post-Civil War States: Transforming Spoilers into Stakeholders*, Chicago: University of Chicago Press, ch. 9 (pp. 189–218).

Woodward, S.L. (2011) 'State-Building for Peace-Building: What Theory and Whose Role?', in R. Kozul-Wright and P. Fortunato (eds) *Securing Peace: State-Building and Economic Development in Post-Conflict Countries,* London and New York: Bloomsbury Academic, in association with the United Nations, 87–112.

Woodward, S.L. (2012) 'The IFIs and Post-Conflict Political Economy', in M. Berdal and D. Zaum (eds) *The Political Economy of Post-conflict Statebuilding: Power After Peace,* Abingdon: Routledge.

World Bank (1998) *The World Bank's Experience with Post-Conflict Reconstruction,* Washington DC: World Bank Operations Evaluation Department.

World Bank (2011) *World Development Report 2011: Conflict, Security and Development,* Washington DC: World Bank.

26

STATEBUILDING

Susanna Campbell and Jenny H. Peterson

International statebuilding aims to build states that will sustain domestic and international peace. Western governments and international organizations have come to see statebuilding as the antidote to 'weak', 'failing' or 'failed' states, which they blame for many of today's most intractable security threats. International peacebuilding, on the other hand, aims to build peace, *in part* by building peaceful and just states. Because peacebuilding and statebuilding try to achieve similar results in countries affected by violence, they are often conflated by both scholars and practitioners, masking important differences and potential contradictions.

The merging of statebuilding and peacebuilding has pushed peacebuilding to the background, stifling local and international efforts to reinvigorate informal institutions that may be critical for sustained peace. In fact, the current predominance of top-down statebuilding may be as likely to cause violent conflict as it is to cause peace. This chapter explains this disconnect. It unpacks the conceptual distinction between peacebuilding and statebuilding and examines the reasons for statebuilding's general failure to achieve its aims in conflict-affected countries.

Linking statebuilding and peacebuilding

Statebuilding aims to ensure that the government is representative of the population, can deliver services to the population, and is responsive to the needs and demands of its citizens (OECD 2011). To achieve these qualities, international actors promote a model of the state that they believe will sustain peace: one grounded in democracy, rule of law, and a market-oriented economy. Although recent statebuilding policies have focused on the importance of supporting locally-led institutional change, in practice statebuilding programming focuses on the physical creation of institutions, not on supporting endogenous processes that may allow peaceful institutions to emerge (OECD 2011).

Similar to statebuilding, peacebuilding seeks to strengthen systems, structures, and behaviours that will enable a war-torn country to sustain peace. In the *Agenda for Peace* (UN 1992: para 21), UN Secretary-General Boutros Boutros-Ghali defined peacebuilding as 'action to identify and support structures which will tend to strengthen and solidify peace in order to avoid a relapse into conflict'. It aims to transform the causes of conflict into the foundations for sustainable peace. Institutions that promoted inequality and exclusion should become inclusive and protect minority rights. People who abused power should be held accountable for their crimes and systems should be set up to ensure that those in power are not able to abuse it. Individuals who used violence to resolve conflict and gain economic advantage should be given peaceful means of resolving conflict and making a living. Former enemies should work together to construct a new society that guarantees respect for all people's rights.

Initially, peacebuilding was largely the work of a few small non-governmental organizations. But peacebuilding is no longer 'localized' and small-scale. The original peacebuilding NGOs view peacebuilding as a 'long-term project of building peaceful, stable communities and societies' (Lederach 1997). These see peacebuilding as a process that aims gradually to 'strengthen and restore relationships and transform unjust institutions and systems' (Lederach 1997). They tend to try and support individual and intergroup change, using tools of conflict resolution, dialogue, and training. To achieve these aims, they seek to work with influential individuals, both within and outside of the state (Lederach 1997). For most of these actors, peacebuilding does not necessarily privilege state powers and institutions. Although there may be a degree of focus on altering citizens' relationship with the state, there is simultaneously an emphasis on human security and local or informal relationships. These actors aim to liberate, or emancipate, the citizens from an oppressive state and society (Booth 2005; Jones 2005; Richmond 2007a, 2007b). Under these models, peace is not defined as stability (or the absence of physical violence) but as the absence of social, economic and political inequality that may paradoxically be caused by a strong state.

In the 1990s and 2000s, the number of international actors engaged in peacebuilding grew exponentially. Peacebuilding was no longer the purview of only a few process-focused NGOs, but was now the business of International Organizations (IOs) and bilateral donors who worked directly with war-torn states. As these bigger actors have become involved in peacebuilding, the policies of many IOs and bilateral donors have focused on the statebuilding aspect of peacebuilding (OECD 2011). This has sidelined the more process-focused approach of many INGOs for a focus on constructing the type of state that international actors believe will sustain peace. Consequently, peacebuilding became largely focused on statebuilding.

For many of the IOs and bilateral donors engaged in peacebuilding today, statebuilding has become the primary means by which they aim to attain peace (Barnett and Zürcher 2008: 26). For these actors, developed states in the global north are the model for what a state 'should' look like. By assisting conflict-affected states in building state institutions that operate effectively and fairly, statebuilders believe that they can help countries attain and sustain peace. They want to help states form in the 'right way'—in other words be democratic, accountable, provide security and basic welfare services for their populations through formal state institutions. This is in contrast to the original idea of peacebuilding: to support institutions and mechanisms that will sustain a just peace in a much broader sense, beyond just building effective state institutions. Statebuilding is one of the approaches used by these peacebuilders, but not the only one. Many critical scholars and practitioners object to the increasing focus on statebuilding because of its emphasis on the state and formal politics. For critical scholars, statebuilding is just one facet of peacebuilding. Peacebuilding is seen as a much wider and diversified phenomenon, focused on formal politics (at international, national, regional and local levels), informal politics and inter-personal relationships and non-political issues, including cultural, economic and social justice.

There are divergent motivations for the increasing focus on statebuilding. From a realist point of view, helping to build strong states abroad is a way of furthering the goals of national security against transnational threats such as crime, terrorism and disease (see Egnell and Haldén 2010; Fukuyama 2004). Strong states are also seen as essential for a functioning and stable global market place. In this sense, the 'statebuilding as peacebuilding' agenda can be used by powerful international actors to justify interventions into the core functions of other states in order to create strong states that reduce threats to other states and the international community more generally. From this point of view, statebuilding contributes to the more self-interested political agenda of other states and global institutions, especially when such interventions take the form of bilateral support, assistance in the security sector or sponsoring modes of economic development that in turn benefit the intervening party.

In most of the peacebuilding literature, however, the motivation for an increased focus on statebuilding stems more from idealistic *cum* liberal motivations with liberal goals and rhetoric now underpinning much of the statebuilding and peacebuilding agendas. The aim is to create human security—protecting persons of all nationalities, not simply states. This more liberal approach has been critiqued by some who argue that the focus on peacebuilding has actually pushed the building of strong governmental institutions to the background, and therefore fails to strengthen institutions that could sustain peace (Paris and Sisk 2008). Paris' (2004) earlier work, for example, argues that for peace to be created, there must be a stronger focus on institutionalization (statebuilding) before the more liberal and relational reforms (peacebuilding) can begin.

In practice, however, international statebuilding and peacebuilding are pursued through the same relatively standard set of activities (Smith 2004: 28). In the security arena, these projects and programmes try to create security through disarmament, demobilization, and reintegration (DDR) of ex-combatants, reforming security-sector institutions so that they are both more efficient and accountable to political and judicial institutions, and the removal of arms from the population. In the governance sector, they aim to establish a political framework that can sustain peace by promoting democratization, accountable institutions of government, and respect for human rights. In the rule of law sector, we see a focus on the reforming of formal judicial institutions, often accompanied by programmes seeking to contribute to reconciliation via dialogue among leaders and grassroots communities, truth and reconciliation commissions, and 'other bridge-building activities' (Smith 2004: 28). They also aim to establish the socio-economic foundations for peace through reconstruction of physical infrastructure (building schools, health centres, roads and communication technologies) whilst also helping to establish economic policies that will encourage an open market, and socio-economic programming that specifically targets services to support the integration of returning refugees, internally displaced people, and demobilized combatants (Smith 2004: 28).

By attempting to accomplish peacebuilding and statebuilding through the same set of activities, international interveners have ignored important differences between the two approaches. At a theoretical level, statebuilding on its own could potentially lead to a limited but sustainable form of peace. It could help to build institutions that ensure that all groups are proportionally, or even disproportionally if this is seen as a way of promoting peace, represented in government. It could help to provide individuals and groups with an equal opportunity for prosperity – reducing intergroup competition and increasing economic growth – by opening up markets and encouraging the free and transparent flow of goods. It could increase the avenues for the peaceful resolution of conflict by strengthening formal institutions that guarantee the rule of law: police, courts, and legislature. However, statebuilding on its own does not necessarily address intercommunal or interpersonal violence which is, in theory, necessary for the broader, more emancipatory mode of peace pursued and discussed by others.

Further, in reality, not only have current practices of statebuilding failed to create peace in a range of cases (Call 2003; Egnell 2010; Goetze and Guzina 2008; Jones 2010), but the policies and practices employed in the name of statebuilding are seen at times to be conflict inducing as opposed to peace building (Angstrom 2008; Call 2008; Goetze and Guzina 2008; Lidén 2009; Menkhaus 2009; Robinson 2007); the increased theoretical and operational focus on statebuilding may actually work *against* the goals of peace and stability (Lake 2010). This may occur for several reasons. The injection of large amounts of statebuilding money into conflict-affected countries creates new incentives and thus potentially new arenas for conflict. In particular, democratization programmes and post-conflict elections, cornerstones of both state- and peacebuilding agendas, can create significant violent conflict by inciting new or deepening old divisions as people fight for power in the new system (Mulaj 2011; Mansfield and Snyder 2007; Paris 2004). In these instances, as opposed to viewing statebuilding as central to solving the peacebuilding puzzle, statebuilding is itself part of the problem. Processes of statebuilding, therefore, do not necessarily have the *peacebuilding effect* that is theoretically assumed. The remainder of this chapter will explore the potential reasons for the failure of statebuilding to promote peace and the ways in which the increasing focus on statebuilding may actually limit the scope for building long-term and sustainable peace.

Statebuilding is ahistorical and apolitical

Statebuilding aims to create formal state institutions that are in many cases poorly matched to the state formation process in war-torn countries (Englebert and Tull 2008; Richmond 2011). It aims to build the components of liberal democratic institutions, but fails to take into account the state formation process that may lead to the long-term and sustainable development of these types of institutions. Historically, in Western Europe, liberal democratic states were formed through violent, tumultuous processes that gradually created a social contract between the state and society over several centuries. Statebuilding aims to create the same type of liberal democratic institutions that emerged from this chaotic decades-long process, but it aims to do so over less than a decade and without a clear idea of the incremental steps or process through which these state institutions could form.

Traditional theories of state formation in Western Europe describe it as a violent process where individuals and communities were coerced into accepting the power and rules of the new state through war or violence (Tilly 1985; Mann 1993). In return for allegiance to these new formal institutions, people received protection from the state. The military capacity necessary to ensure protection required continuous financing through taxation. This further strengthened these new states by giving them resources to wage war and gain new territories and, in turn, provide protection to and collect taxes from more people. Other theorists focus on the more banal administrative processes that transformed neo-patrimonial states into those grounded in formal, rational institutions that solidified the relationship between the state (the rulers) and the citizenry (the ruled) (Weber 1947; Rueschemeyer 2005). The major changes that have occurred in the international system since the Peace of Westphalia in 1648 prevent the same type of state formation processes from occurring today (Ayoob 2007; Eriksen 2005, 2010; Hagmann and Péclard 2010; Hallenberg, Holm and Johansson 2008; Kostovicova 2008; Vu 2010).

Today, state formation is expected to take place with as little violence as possible and not impact territories and people outside its own borders. In other words, the expansionary elements of traditional state formation processes are no longer seen as acceptable. The move towards statebuilding in the international arena as a path to peace was arguably consolidated in the post-Cold War era where the artificial stability provided by the bi-polar power struggle was removed and states' weaknesses were laid bare (Robinson 2007). There was a recognition that states needed a deliberate hand in becoming strong and functional political entities (via statebuilding) as opposed to allowing them to continue down a more 'organic' path (via state formation) which is seen as inherently violent and thus unacceptable to the wider international community.

Regardless of the mode of state formation one considers, the scholarship points to long, fraught and often violent processes through which peaceful relationships are negotiated. Coercion, competition for legitimacy, power, resources, disagreements over institutional form, and a constant renegotiation of the roles and rights of an ever-growing number of actors, have all shaped the ways in which the form and function of the state is negotiated in both stable and conflict-affected states alike. Peace, when it has been sustained, results from this messy process. Current statebuilding efforts fail to take this into account. They take an ahistoric and apolitical view regarding how 'zones of peace' have been created and seek to impose a static set of institutions on dynamic state formation processes.

Just and sustainable peace may fail to take hold as these new or transformed institutions, built via processes of externally led statebuilding projects, are implanted rather than negotiated. Even if international statebuilders succeed in helping to create state institutions that are well financed, abide by democratic standards, and have well-trained staff, they often lack the legitimacy or authority necessary to contribute to peace. For example, newly trained security services in places such as Kosovo and Afghanistan have had the benefit of years of specialist training, including access to the latest policing technologies, but have often failed to provide the expected levels of security. This is due in part to these forces not being seen as legitimate by some sectors of society (for example sectors of the Serb community do not view the institutions of an independent Kosovan state as legitimate) or as independent and working in the best interests of citizens (as in the case of Afghanistan, where segments of the population view the security services as beholden to NATO as opposed to Afghan interests). Modern international statebuilding, in both its theoretical and practised forms, fail to account for these long-term and intensely political internal dynamics and as such, fail to create the modes of peace that is planned for and desired.

Statebuilding is bureaucratic, fragmented, and projectized

Although recent definitions of statebuilding emphasize the importance of supporting 'an endogenous process to enhance capacity, institutions, and legitimacy of the state driven by state–society relations' (OECD 2011), the practice of statebuilding has not caught up. Most IOs, bilateral donors, and NGOs engaged in statebuilding programming use a relatively standard template of short-term projects and programmes that generally fail to support a state formation process or improve state–society relations. The grand state formation idea has been broken down into small projects and programmes. Even projects that do last for several years often lack continuity because of high staff turnover and the absence of funding for the duration of the project. These interventions are often designed and implemented by international staff who have limited knowledge of the national institutions that they aim to change. They are constrained by one- to two-year funding cycles that limit the scope and nature of the change that they can create.

In other words, statebuilding is bureaucratized, projectized, and fragmented. The parts do not add up to a cohesive whole nor do they support a coherent state formation process. These projects and programmes do not directly engage with or allow for how state–society relations may actually be built. The bureaucratic structure of the IOs, bilateral donors, and many of the INGOs doing statebuilding programming partly explains the current approach. Instead of responding to the needs of the post-conflict state and society, international bureaucracies are likely to recreate institutions and programmes in their own image. 'The result is that what began as a relatively narrow technical intervention (training police) expands into a package of reforms aimed at transforming non-Western societies (where most peacebuilding takes place) into Western societies' (Barnett and Finnemore 2004: 34). Rather than catalysing a change process, bureaucracies are likely to try to do much of the work themselves in a manner that fits with their standards and approach (Barnett and Finnemore 2004: 34). This tendency to resort to bureaucratic, state-centred solutions is common throughout the development industry, leading it to prioritize interventions that are 'technically correct' but whose top-down nature is not responsive to citizens (Pritchett and Woolcock 2004: 207).

Where statebuilders desire a technocratic, predictable, and linear path to peace, the reality of how peace is made is necessarily complex, fraught, and even violent. The negotiations between peoples and their state cannot be managed by external actors in the orderly way that a bureaucratic mind-set requires. This often frustrates both external peacebuilders and internal populations who have been promised that cooperation with international interveners will bring a promised peace that rarely, if ever, materializes. In places like the Democratic Republic of the Congo this has created disillusionment and violent reactions against state- and peacebuilding actors. The liberal democratic system that statebuilders put so much faith into will not exist in their desired form for many years (if ever). The liberal democratic models that they promote demand a degree of social, political, economic, and even cultural negotiation that requires long-term, or even perpetual, negotiation. In its current form, statebuilding practice does not allow for long-term change and ignores the many stages that exist in between weak states submerged in war and strong states capable of supporting peace. The reality of incremental movements towards peace, which may result in a range of trajectories and institutional forms (just as the historical modes of state formation also led to different forms of the modern state) is neither accounted for nor encouraged in the current approach to statebuilding.

Statebuilding is too state centric

Alongside its focus on short-term technical projects, statebuilding suffers from the continued predominance of the state in international relations theory and interventions in practice. IOs, made up of member states, are most accountable to the host state which can revoke their permission to operate in the country. They work directly with the central government and rarely openly question or condemn the government. Bilateral donors are, of course, states and therefore primarily interact with and support the central government. Their aid instruments privilege aid that goes directly to the state budget, losing all control over its expenditure. In the absence of willingness by the state or individual ministries to be more responsive and accountable to the population, bilateral donors can do little to improve state–society relations or create liberal institutions. Some INGOs may go around the state and work directly with society, but they rarely work directly with local administrations or reinforce state–society relations from the bottom up, particularly where these relationships do not already exist.

IOs, INGOs, and bilateral donors are therefore often beholden to the state in one way or another. They either work through the state or around it, but rarely reinforce accountability between state and society. Once these newly built or reformed institutions are captured by the state, they are often unable to build peace, which requires that they question the often unequal distribution of resources perpetuated by the state. It is cyclical: IOs are beholden to the state, bilateral donors want to work directly through the state, and INGOs often substitute for the state, but none of these actors can easily help a state to build peace if it is against its interest to do so.

International statebuilding is focused on building the central state at the expense of the provincial administrations and the society. Such asymmetric statebuilding leads to situations where islands of stability and relative peace (usually urban areas) become detached from the rest of the country (usually rural areas or borderlands). Not only does this fail to create peace, but it may actually be conflict inducing as divisions between communities and regions are widened. Again, Afghanistan provides a clear example of the impact of such asymmetric statebuilding. Major centres such as Kabul and Kandahar, whilst continuing to suffer from violent attacks, have become fortressed cities. In these centres, citizens have access to a range of institutions and economic opportunities unlike their counterparts in rural and border regions. Such divisions are made more obvious by external processes of statebuilding, which are then manipulated by insurgent groups and other non-state actors to entrench themselves militarily, economically and politically in these neglected communities, making the reality of peace within and between communities a less likely outcome. In some cases, such as Kosovo, the strategy of political decentralization has been used as an attempt to alleviate this problem. In such cases some political power and decision making is moved to the provincial or municipal levels with the aim of ensuring decisions are made based on local needs and with the goal of making local government stronger and more accountable to their constituents. However, these programmes suffer from the same issues discussed above related to legitimacy and projectization and are by no means an easy solution to expanding governing authority or rebuilding the social contract outside of the centre.

Further, the way that statebuilding projects and programmes are implemented assumes a degree of legitimacy of the state that does not often exist in countries emerging from civil war and large-scale violent conflict. Changes to the international system have meant that the state no longer has monopoly over powers of coercion and citizens now have multiple actors to whom they can grant their legitimacy. As a result, many states that are strong and capable of governing no longer command the legitimacy required for top-down statebuilding to act as a successful path to peace. Other actors now stand out as more legitimate negotiators and builders of peace. Current statebuilding models and practice do not account for the reality that actors and institutions outside of the state (be they international NGOs, or informal/parallel governance structures) might make alternative and more convincing claims to the legitimacy bestowed by citizens, or offer alternative visions of peace that the state cannot or will not provide. When there is a clash between a strong central state's peacebuilding priority and local or non-state focused priorities, more conflict and violence can result.

Looking at governance of the border area in the north of Kosovo provides a useful example. Despite difficult beginnings, the UN-run Customs Service gained a degree of legitimacy for monitoring and securing the border (though this first required dismantling a parallel ethnic Albanian structure who were seen by some as the rightful and legitimate monitors of various border crossings). With the declaration of independence and the creation of a Kosovan state-led border service (again dominated by ethnic Albanians) the Serbian community continued to believe that a UN service would be a better protector of the border than the state apparatus. The international community was seen as the legitimate peacebuilder in this instance, not the formal state apparatus. Whilst of course statebuilding must focus on the building of the state, the utility of these processes in building peace must be seen in terms of both synergies and potential conflicts with other actors engaged in peacebuilding efforts. The role of the state must also be more carefully considered vis-à-vis its relationship with other actors whom they may need to share with or hand over to the power or right to engage in particular modes of peacebuilding. More consideration of the role of local, informal or parallel mechanisms in relation to more conventional processes of statebuilding is needed. In some cases there may be scope for a shared division of labour, in other cases statebuilding may come into direct conflict with these alternative modes of peacebuilding.

Conclusion

International statebuilding threatens to eclipse efforts to build peace. In practice, statebuilding and peacebuilding have been merged into a technocratic set of projects and programmes that tend to strengthen the capacity of the central government, not state–society relations, responsiveness or accountability (Campbell 2012). These efforts often fail to build either an effective state or sustainable peace.

Some scholars have called for institutionalization (Paris 2004) to occur before any other vast changes to social, political and economic systems so that there are bodies in place to manage the conflict and upheaval that such systemic changes entail. In practice, this top-down approach to statebuilding wrongly grants a pacifying role to formal state institutions and assumes that they will be viewed as legitimate by local actors. The focus on state institutions, at the expense of state–society relationships and informal institutions, threatens to side-line processes and capacities that are necessary for the domestic legitimacy and effectiveness of state institutions. It also ignores the fact that other institutions beyond formal state structures may have greater legitimacy to build peace. For statebuilding to promote peace, as it may have the potential to do, it should pay more attention to the processes through which institutions become legitimate agents for peace.

To improve the odds that international statebuilding and peacebuilding efforts will help war-torn societies develop capacities to sustain peace, innovations are needed in scholarship and in practice. New research is needed to identify the multiple paths of contemporary state formation and how this can contribute to just and sustainable modes of peace. How do different formal and informal institutions combine along a country's contemporary war-to-peace (and possibly back again) transition? How do these institutions balance and counterbalance one another, leading to critical junctures that alter the country's path? How do international actors intentionally or unintentionally influence the direction? Are there common trends among different states' war-to-peace trajectories, or is each one fundamentally unique with no observable patterns? How do these modern state formation processes compare with historical state formation processes and current models influencing statebuilding? By identifying the incremental processes by which state formation actually takes place, new models of statebuilding that more accurately reflect the reality of conflict-torn countries can be developed. This would help to provide practitioners and policy-makers with more realistic aims, should they choose to adopt them, for both statebuilding and peacebuilding, and help to clarify important distinctions between the two.

References

Angstrom, J. (2008) 'Inviting the Leviathan: external forces, war, and statebuilding in Afghanistan', *Small Wars and Insurgencies* 19(3): 374–396.

Ayoob, M. (2007) 'State Making, State Breaking, and State Failure' in C.A. Crocker, F.O. Hampson, and P. Aall, eds., *Leashing the Dogs of War: Conflict Management in a Divided World*, Washington DC: United States Institute of Peace, pp. 95–114.

Barnett, M. and M. Finnemore (2004) *Rules for the World: International Organizations in Global Politics*, Ithaca: Cornell University Press.

Barnett, M. and C. Zürcher (2008) 'The peacebuilder's contract: How external statebuilding reinforces weak statehood' in R. Paris and T. Sisk eds., *The Dilemmas of Statebuilding: Confronting the Contradictions of Postwar Peace Operations*.London: Routledge, pp. 23–52. Accessed online 15 March 2012.

Booth, K. (2005)'Introduction to Part 3: Emancipation' in K. Booth ed., *Critical Security Studies and World Politics*, London: Lynne Rienner, pp. 181–188.

Call, C.T. (2003) 'Democratisation, War and State-Building: Constructing Rule of Law in El Salvador', *Journal of Latin American Studies* 35(4): 827–862.

Call, C.T. (2008) 'Building States to Build Peace? A Critical Analysis', *Journal of Peacebuilding and Development* 4(2): 60–74.

Campbell, S.P. (2012) 'Organizational Barriers to Peace: Agency and Structure in International Peacebuilding'. PhD Dissertation. Medford: Tufts University.

Egnell, R. (2010) 'The organised hypocrisy of international state-building', *Conflict, Security & Development* 10(4): 465–491.

Egnell, R. and P. Haldén (2010) 'Contextualizing international state-building', *Conflict, Security & Development* 10(4): 431–441.

Englebert, P. and D.M. Tull (2008) 'Post Conflict Reconstruction in Africa: Flawed Ideas about Failed States', *International Security* 32(4): 106–139.

Eriksen, S.S. (2005) 'The Politics of State Formation: Contradictions and Conditions of Possibility', *European Journal of Development Research* 17(3): 396–410.

Eriksen, S.S. (2010) 'State Formation and the Politics of Regime Survival: Zimbabwe in Theoretical Perspective', *Journal of Historical Sociology* 23(2): 316–340.

Fukuyama, F. (2004) *State-building: Governance and World Order in the 21st Century*, Ithaca: Cornell University Press.

Goetze, C. and D. Guzina (2008) 'Peacebuilding, Statebuilding, Nationbuilding: Turtles All the Way Down?', *Civil Wars* 10(4): 319–347.

Hagmann, T. and T. Péclard (2010) 'Negotiating Statehood: Dynamics of Power and Domination in Africa', *Development and Change* 41(4): 539–562.

Hallenberg, M., J. Holm and D. Johansson (2008) 'Organization, Legitimation, Participation: State formation as a dynamic process – the Swedish Example, c1523–1680'. *Scandinavian Journal of History* 33(3): 247–268.

Jones, L. (2010) '(Post-)Colonial state-building and state failure in East Timor: bringing social conflict back in', *Conflict, Security & Development* 10(4); 547–575.

Jones, R.W. (2005) 'On Emancipation: Necessity, Capacity and Concrete Utopias' in K. Booth ed., *Critical Security Studies and World Politics*, London: Lynne Rienner, pp. 215–236.

Kostovicova, D. (2008) 'Legitimacy and International Administration: The Ahtisaari Settlement or Kosovo from a Human Security Perspective', *International Peacekeeping* 15(5): 631–647.

Lake, D. (2010) 'The Practice and Theory of US Statebuilding', *Journal of Intervention and Statebuilding* 4(3): 257–284.

Lederach, J.P. (1997) *Building Peace: Sustainable Reconciliation in Divided Societies*, Washington DC: United States Institute of Peace Press.

Lidén, K. (2009) 'Building Peace between Global and Local Politics: The Cosmopolitical Ethics of Liberal Peacebuilding', *International Peacekeeping* 16(5): 616–634.

Mansfield, E.D. and J.L. Snyder (2007) 'The sequencing "fallacy"', *Journal of Democracy* 18(3): 5–10.

Mann, M. (1993) *The Sources of Social Power. Volume II: The Rise of Classes and Nation-States, 1760–1914*, Cambridge: Cambridge University Press.

Menkhaus, K. (2009) 'Somalia: "They Created a Desert and Called it Peace(building)"', *Review of African Political Economy* 36(120): 223–233.

Mulaj, K. (2011) 'The problematic legitimacy of international-led statebuilding: Challenges of uniting international and local interests in post-conflict Kosovo', *Contemporary Politics* 17(3): 241–256.

OECD (2011) *Supporting Statebuilding in Situations of Conflict and Fragility: Policy Brief*. DAC Guidelines and Reference Series. Paris: Organization for Economic Cooperation and Development.

Paris, R. (2004) *At War's End: Building Peace After Civil Conflict*, Cambridge: Cambridge University Press.

Paris, R. and T. Sisk (2008) 'Introduction: Understanding the Contradictions of Postwar Statebuilding' in R. Paris and T. Sisk eds., *The Dilemmas of Statebuilding: Confronting the Contradictions of Postwar Peace Operations*, London: Routledge, pp. 1–20: Accessed online [March 15, 2012].

Pritchett, L. and M. Woolcock (2004) 'Solutions When *the* Solution is the Problem: Arraying the Disarray in Development', *World Development* 32(2): 191–212.

Richmond, O. (2007a) 'Emancipatory forms of Human Security and Liberal Peacebuilding', *International Journal* 62: 459–477.

Richmond, O. (2007b) *The Transformation of Peace*, New York: Palgrave Macmillan.

Richmond, O. (2011) 'Failed Statebuilding Versus Peace Formation', Paper presented at University of Gothenberg, November, 2011. Taken from forthcoming book (Yale University Press, 2013).

Robinson, N. (2007) 'State-building and international politics: The emergence of a "new" problem and agenda' in A. Hehir and N. Robinson eds., *State-Building: Theory and Practice*, London: Routledge, pp. 1–28.

Rueschemeyer, D. (2005) 'Building States – Inherently a Long-Term Process? An Argument from Theory' in M. Lange and D. Rueschemeyer eds., *States and Development: Historical Antecedents of Stagnation and Advance,* New York: Palgrave Macmillan, pp. 143–164.

Smith, D. (2004) *Towards a Strategic Framework for Peacebuilding: Getting Their Act Together.* Overview Report of the Joint Utstein Study of Peacebuilding. Oslo: Royal Norwegian Ministry of Foreign Affairs.

Tilly, C. (1985) 'War Making and State Making as Organized Crime' in P. Evans, D. Rueschemeyer and T. Skocpol eds., *Bringing the State Back In*, Cambridge: Cambridge University Press, pp. 169–191.

United Nations (1992) *An Agenda for Peace: Preventive Diplomacy, Peacemaking, and Peace-keeping.* New York: United Nations.

Vu, T. (2010) 'Studying the State Through State Formation', *World Politics* 62(1): 148–175.

Weber, M. (1947) *The Theory of Social and Economic Organization*, New York: Free Press.

27

CIVIL SOCIETY

Thania Paffenholz

Introduction

Although civil society is a widely used concept, 'the big idea on everyone's lips' (Edwards 2004: 2), there is no commonly agreed upon understanding of the term. Consequently, it means 'all things to all people' (Glasius 2004: 3). In fact, this fuzziness (Spurk 2010: 3) may itself be further adding to the concept's popularity.

Though the origins of the concept are found in Western political philosophy (Spurk 2010: 3–6), civil society has since become a central part of the general peacebuilding discourse (Paffenholz 2010: 43–64). Policy and practitioner circles overwhelmingly present civil society as an important contributor to promoting and sustaining peace.[1] In consequence, we have seen a tremendous rise in civil society peacebuilding initiatives over the last two decades. In parallel, the funding to civil society now also comes with a number of expectations about what civil society can, and should, achieve in peacebuilding.

Looking into the research results, we find both supportive as well as very critical findings. On the one hand, civil society gives voice to the unheard (Pearce 1998; Fetherston 2000; Richmond 2005; Paffenholz 2010) and can have an important influence on political change (Kasfir 1998: 143; Ikelegbe 2001: 20). On the other hand, civil society can be 'uncivil' (Orjuela 2004: 210; Spurk 2010: 18–19) as exclusivist, sectarian and occasionally even xenophobic and militant groups (Belloni 2001; Ikelegbe 2001; Orjuela 2003; Paffenholz, Spurk, Belloni, Kurtenbach and Orjuela 2010: 414–420) work alongside inclusive, civic, bridging and pro-peace organizations.

Any comprehensive attempt to understand civil society and its relevance for peacebuilding therefore needs to address the heterogeneous notion of the concept as well as its respective realities in different historical and geographical contexts.

This chapter has two objectives. Firstly, it aims to give a comprehensive overview of the concept of civil society in peacebuilding as presented in theory and case study research. Second, it strives to provide a critical assessment in analyzing the external (mainly Western) expectations of what civil society should contribute to peacebuilding.

To this end, it deconstructs the existing discourses within different peacebuilding paradigms and contrasts them with reality as assessed from available case study evidence.[2]

The remainder of this chapter is divided into four parts. The first analyzes the construction of the concept of 'civil society' in different peacebuilding discourses – liberal, sustainable and critical. The second part deconstructs the nature of civil society as presented in the literature. The third assesses what civil society can and cannot contribute to peacebuilding. The concluding part summarizes the findings, allowing for a comprehensive and evidence-based understanding of what civil society can and cannot contribute to peacebuilding.

Throughout the chapter, the focus lies mainly on local and national civil society groups that aim to contribute to promoting and sustaining peace in their contexts, both at the local as well as the national level.

The construction of civil society in peacebuilding: Expectations and myths

In order to get a better understanding of why the international policy community often expects civil society to provide answers to complex peacebuilding problems it is crucial to take a look at the construction of the concept of civil society within the different peacebuilding discourses. The following provides an overview of the concept of civil society as understood within liberal peacebuilding, sustainable peacebuilding as well as critical peacebuilding discourses.

Liberal peacebuilding and civil society

Although the term *peacebuilding* was first introduced by Johan Galtung (1975: 282–304), its main proliferation began with its use in the 1992 UN Secretary-General report *An Agenda for Peace* (United Nations Secretary-General 1992). In Galtung's understanding, peacebuilding achieves positive peace by creating structures and institutions of peace based on justice, equity and cooperation (Galtung 1975: 297–304). In comparison, the evolving understanding of *liberal peacebuilding* starting with *An Agenda for Peace* focuses mainly on the democratic (re-)building of states after armed conflict. The practice of equaling peacebuilding and statebuilding thus presents a much more narrow focus when compared with Galtung's original definition. An additional component is that the creation of democratic liberal market economies is seen as a guarantor for peace. This assumption is confirmed by an impressive body of academic work dating back to Kant (1795), where he argued that the democratic constitution of states correlates with their relatively peaceful behavior vis-à-vis other states. Confirming Kant's arguments, a mountain of quantitative research makes a clear positive causal linkage between democracy and peace (Chan 1997; Ray 1998; Russett and Starr 2000). Democracies do not only have the lowest level of internal armed conflict (Rummel 1997) but they also do not fight each other (Small and Singer 1976; Doyle 1983a, 1983b) because democracies' shared norms of compromise and cooperation prevent conflicts of interests from escalating into violence.

In this understanding, civil society has an important role to play in support of building peaceful democratic states. It can foster the principles of good governance, ensure the respect for human rights and the rule of law, as well as promote peaceful resolution of conflicts within societies.

The main problem with the liberal understanding of peacebuilding is the orientation of its state and civil society model based on already established functioning liberal democracies. Yet, all the countries that have come out of armed violence and were subject to democratic peace and statebuilding are decades away from functioning democracies. Consequently, the focus should shift to the question of what could be the possible approach during these transition phases. In general, transitions occur over long periods of time, have different phases, may be violence prone or be subject to long-term instabilities and regression. However, liberal peace- and statebuilders pay little attention to the needs of countries and people within these transitions and continue to apply standard liberal democratic recipes regardless of the specific context. The same is true for civil society support even though it remains unclear whether civil society can actually contribute to peace and statebuilding in the way constructed in the liberal peacebuilding discourse.

Sustainable peacebuilding and civil society

The discourse on sustainable peacebuilding dates back to the emergence of the conflict-resolution school (Kelman 1992; Fisher 1997) and it was further developed and conceptualized by John Paul Lederach's conflict-transformation school (Lederach 1997). Both schools aim at addressing the underlying causes of conflict and rebuilding the destroyed relationships between parties and society, thereby supporting sustainable reconciliation. As understood by Lederach (1997), peacebuilding can be achieved through the establishment of structures, processes and training of people within a generation-long time frame.

Civil society is the key actor within the concept of sustainable peacebuilding. Early on, peacebuilders were mainly Western academic institutions carrying out conflict-resolution workshops with unofficial actors close to the conflict parties. As the approach evolved, the scope of actors was broadened. An elite-based civil society approach gave way to a general civil society and grassroots approach including a wide range of actors – from individuals and communities to organized civil society groups. The main activities carried out by the civil society actors are dialogue projects between groups or communities, peace education, conflict-resolution training to enhance peacebuilding capacity of actors from one or different groups, and conflict-resolution workshops. The main suppliers of these initiatives are international NGOs, often working in cooperation with local and national NGOs.

The biggest contribution of the conflict-resolution school is its perspective on peacebuilding as identifying human needs and listening to the previously unheard voices of the ordinary people (Richmond 2005: 100). Similarly, the conflict-transformation school's shift in focus from international to local actors puts even more emphasis on civil society and ordinary people than does the resolution school. The role of outsiders therein is limited to supporting local peace constituencies rather than playing a key intervening role. However, with the development of second-generation conflict-resolution approaches starting in the mid-1990s, the difference between the two schools has become marginal (Paffenholz 2010: 54) and over time, the conflict-transformation school has become the leading school for scholar-practitioners and the international peacebuilding NGO community.

Yet the concept of sustainable peacebuilding is not without problems. Scholars see its core weaknesses in the limited role of outsiders and the failure of addressing the power dimension in the process. Outsiders should not only support insiders directly but also consider the wider peacebuilding arena and engage in political action (Paffenholz 1998: 213–215; 2010: 54–55). There is also a lack of a power analysis in Lederach's approach (Fetherston 2000: 207), which is also true of his understanding of traditional values and local voices in peace processes. These have often been transformed by modern developments, potentially weakening their conflict-resolution authority (Paffenholz 1998: 76; 2010: 54–55). Other critiques have elaborated on some of the negative consequences of the practical application of the approach by international NGOs (Richmond 2005: 103–104; Paffenholz and Spurk 2006: 23–26) such as the NGOization of previously voluntary peace work (Orjuela 2004). Consequently, more evidence is needed on the functioning of civil society support as seen through the lens of sustainable peacebuilding.

Critical peacebuilding approaches and civil society

Increasingly, there is an emerging literature analyzing peacebuilding through the lens of discourse analysis and advocating for an alternative approach to peacebuilding (Fetherston 2000; Richmond 2005; Mac Ginty 2006; Heathershaw 2008). These authors claim that liberal peacebuilding has become a self-referential system that has long lost its connection to the real world and the needs of the people. The critical-discourse school does not present a meta-alternative but instead points to the need to refocus on the everyday peace of ordinary people (Fetherston 2000; Bendaña 2003; Richmond 2005; Mac Ginty 2006: 33–57).

Within the critical-discourse school, Fetherston and Bendaña deliver the most radical interpretations. With a power analysis based on Foucault, Fetherston considers the peacebuilding schools as 'part of an apparatus of power which attempts to discipline and normalize' (Fetherston 2000: 200). Sustainable peacebuilding is, hence, criticized as being blind to power hierarchies. On the basis of an analysis of Southern voices, Bendaña (2003) comes to similar conclusions, emphasizing that peacebuilding becomes an inherently conservative undertaking which seeks managerial solutions to fundamental conflicts over resources and power (Bendaña 2003: 5). The alternative approach suggested here is thus a transformative peacebuilding project that leads to a post-hegemonic society (Fetherston 2000: 213–214) in which oppressed voices are respected and listened to. It implies structural changes and the acknowledgment that peacebuilding is mainly a Western enterprise that needs to engage in a serious South–North dialogue.

The biggest contribution of the critical-discourse peacebuilding school is its focus on ordinary people, oppressed voices, analysis of power structures and assessment based on realities rather than normative assumptions (Paffenholz 2010: 55–58). However, even though the main focus of this discourse is on the local civil society and ordinary people, most authors do not actually analyze these alternative voices. This stands in direct contradiction to the very alternative discourse for which these authors advocate. Instead, the main focus of these studies is the liberal peace and actors of the international community therein, such as the Western governments and NGOs or the UN (Paffenholz 2010: 55–56).

Having looked at the different understandings of civil society within the three dominant peacebuilding discourses – liberal, sustainable and critical – we now look at the concept of civil society itself.

Who and what is civil society: Deconstructing a fuzzy concept

Civil society is generally understood as the arena of voluntary collective actions of an institutional nature, taking place around shared interests, purposes and values that are distinct from those of the state, family and market (Merkel and Lauth 1998: 7). It consists of a large and diverse set of organizations that are not purely driven by private or economic interests, are autonomously organized, show civil virtue, and interact within the public sphere. While civil society is independent from the state, it is both oriented towards it and interacts closely with it (Kjellman and Harpviken 2010: 29–42; Spurk 2010: 6–9).

To define civil society more precisely, many authors describe it as a sector existing alongside the state, business and family. While many see the four sectors as separate, some authors argue that family is not a separate sector but belongs to civil society, while others consider business as part of civil society rather than being a sector on its own. Additionally, Merkel and Lauth (1998: 7) see civil society as the space where the three other spheres (state, business, family) overlap. This approach seems closer to reality as actors within each of the specific sectors can also be active in civil society. For instance, entrepreneurs, who are usually part of the business sector, act as civil society when demanding tax exemptions through their business association. Another example is the media. Although they are part of the business sector, journalists can act as civil society with their associations when they demand, for example, freedom of expression. This understanding also helps to identify other actors who have a role in civil society, such as traditional groups in Africa.

This is particularly important because, historically, the notion of civil society has been an almost purely Western concept, tied to the political emancipation of European citizens from former feudalistic ties, monarchy and the state during the 18th and 19th centuries. As a result, there has always been a debate as to whether the concept of civil society is transferable to non-Western contexts (Lewis 2002; Harneit-Sievers 2005: 1). In this respect, we can observe a number of context-specific discourses.

In Latin America, the concept of civil society gained importance in the fight against military dictatorships at the end of the 1960s. Social movements contributed to the resistance to authoritarian regimes but failed to develop a major role once democracy had been restored (Pinkney 2003: 102–103).

With regard to the main question of whether the concept of civil society is applicable in Africa, we find a number of different viewpoints in the literature. Lewis (2002: 567–577), for example, states that due to the historical developments caused by colonial rule (fostering a small urban elite in cities while oppressing a large majority of the population in rural areas), Africa knows only traditional associations and has no space for a civil society. Schmidt (2000: 301) further argues that the weak development of civil society is partly due to the generally low level of development that hinders societies to further differentiate. Bayart (1986: 111), Kasfir (1998) and Appiagyei-Atua (2002), however, see little problem in applying the concept of civil society to Africa. Instead, they opt for a wider understanding of civil society in the African context as including traditional associations, voluntary organizations, youth groups, elders and chiefs.

In Eastern Europe, as well as in Central Asia and the Caucasus, most countries faced a threefold transition: (1) the political transformation from dictatorship to democracy; (2) the economic transformation from a state to a market economy; and, in some cases, (3) the state transformation due to the disintegration of the Soviet Union (Merkel 1999: 377). The emergence of civil society therefore became linked to the empowerment of dissident opposition movements to counter suppressive regimes (Babajanian et al. 2005: 212). Later on, some of the opposition movements even assumed a political role (Ruffin and Waugh 1999: 27–31). At the same time, civil society organizations based on the communal concept of informal ties (clan, family, or neighborhood) or neopatrimonial structures persisted. In the case of Georgia and Armenia, the church continues to play an important role in helping nurture those ties (Babajanian et al. 2005: 214). A common strand among countries in Asia is that civil society is still not protected, as the state continues to be the central, and often the most repressive, actor in the region.[3]

In light of the above understanding of civil society, the following groups of civil society actors can be identified:

a   Special interest groups (for example trade unions; professional associations for teachers, farmers or journalists; minority or women's organizations; settlers or veteran associations);
b   Faith-based organizations (for example churches and Islamic associations);
c   Traditional and community groups (for example youth groups; councils of elders; women's and mothers' groups; radio listeners' clubs or user groups);
d   Researchers and research institutions (for example local or international think tanks, universities and individual researchers);
e   Service delivery organizations often registered as non-governmental organizations, both local and international (for example human rights, relief, development or conflict-resolution/peacebuilding non-governmental organizations [NGOs] or international non-governmental organizations [INGOs]);
f   Social and political movements which can take the form of broad-based public movements around a common cause (such as the Arab Spring) or longer-term movements (like the environmental, women's or peace movements in Europe or the United States in the last century);
g   Business associations (for example entrepreneur or journalist associations, not to be confused with their profit-making sides of business);
h   Networks which generally represent a larger number of organizations from one of the other categories of actors above (for example a network of religious councils).

What civil society can and cannot contribute to peacebuilding: A reality check

In this part of the chapter, we will look at the evidence regarding civil society's peacebuilding roles as found in case study research. The main results can be summed up as follows. Firstly, most studies found that civil society is a necessary actor in peacebuilding. Secondly, some studies demonstrate that civil society can also be the 'bad society'. Thirdly, many case studies found that international donor support contributes to the 'NGOization' of peace work. Fourthly, only a few studies assessed the relevance and effectiveness of civil society functions and actors. Lastly, research also found that certain contextual factors support or hinder the effectiveness of civil society's peacebuilding role. In what follows, each of these five major findings is developed in greater detail.

Civil society as the 'good society'

Civil society is seen as a necessary actor for peacebuilding. It gives voice to the unheard (Pearce 1998; Fetherston 2000; Richmond 2005) and can have an important influence on political change (Kasfir 1998: 143; Ikelegbe 2001: 20). A number of studies (Aall 2001; Barnes 2005; van Tongeren et al. 2005; Richmond and Carey 2006) illustrate this point with positive examples of NGOs' contribution to peacebuilding. Additionally, Paris (2004) opts for promoting 'good civil society' alongside state-building and Paffenholz and Spurk (2006; 2010: 65–76) offer seven civil society peacebuilding functions for a constructive contribution to peacebuilding (protection, monitoring, advocacy, socialization, social cohesion, facilitation and service delivery).

Civil society as the 'bad society'

However, civil society is not only the 'good society' that contributes to dialogue and democratization (Orjuela 2004: 210). Research found that inclusive, civic, bridging and pro-peace organizations work alongside exclusivist, sectarian and occasionally even xenophobic and militant groups (Belloni 2001; Ikelegbe 2001; Orjuela 2003; Paffenholz et al. 2010: 414–420). This debate is also known under the term 'uncivil society' (Spurk 2010: 18–19).

International donor support triggers 'NGOization'

Many studies found that local civil societies are often products of international donor-driven engagement. This leads to the sidelining of local efforts and actors (Kasfir 1998; Pouligny 2005). Additionally, it has been pointed out that donor-driven NGO civil society initiatives have limited the capacity to create domestic social capital and ownership of the peace process (Belloni 2001, 2008; Paffenholz 2010: 425–430). This 'NGOization' of social protest (Orjuela 2003: 255) leads to the 'taming' of social movements (Kaldor 2003: 79) and, hence, shifts the focus away from peace movements and grassroots civic engagement towards creating NGOs as service deliverers (Pearce 1998; Paffenholz 2010: 428). The exclusive focus on NGOs by Western donors then leads to situations where the disempowered are rarely empowered, as local NGOs have little power to break nationalist power hierarchies and other structural factors (Pearce 1998, 2007; Belloni 2001; Orjuela 2003; Paffenholz 2010: 428–430). As a consequence, civil society has by and large lost its ability to advocate for radical social change (Fetherston 2000; Bendaña 2003; Richmond 2005; Heathershaw 2008).

Relevance of civil society initiatives and effectiveness of civil society actors

Only a few studies explicitly assess the effectiveness of civil society initiatives. Until recently, most studies only assessed the social cohesion projects that are seen to be of key importance in the conflict-resolution school. Here, some studies found positive results of social-cohesion workshops (Malhotra and Liyanage 2005; Ohanyan and Lewis 2005; Çuhadar 2009) but most found that a change of individual attitudes does not have a significant effect on the wider societal change since the effect of these workshops is not sustained over a long period (Atieh et al. 2005; Ohanyan and Lewis 2005; Çuhadar 2009). Other research suggests that these initiatives are often top-down, making real bridging in deeply divided societies difficult given that civil society organizations are often mono-ethnic and radical (Belloni 2001; Ikelegbe 2001; Orjuela 2003). Instead, Varshney (2002), Ohanyan and Lewis (2005) and Çuhadar (2009) found that work-related initiatives focusing on a concrete outcome are more effective.

A four-year research project on the relevance and effectiveness of civil society peacebuilding for the first time assessed all types of civil society initiatives during four phases of conflict/peacebuilding in 13 case studies (Paffenholz 2010). Applying a functional approach, the study was able to capture a wide range of activities and actors including those that are not necessarily claiming to do peacebuilding, but who actually contribute to this agenda in one way or another with their initiatives. The study produced very distinctive results distinguished according to the phase of conflict/peacebuilding and civil society's roles (understood as the seven peacebuilding functions identified above). It was found that, in many instances, the functions that were relevant in a particular phase of peacebuilding (i.e. protection during violent phases) were not necessarily performed by civil society. This is mainly because those activities supported from the outside, and consequently often implemented, are mostly driven by liberal and sustainable peacebuilding discourses rather than by the actual needs of the people and the peace process. Hence, the overwhelmingly performed activities include training in conflict resolution and transformation, dialogue and peace education initiatives (Paffenholz 2010: 381–404). While these activities are relevant in the phase after large-scale violence comes to an end, they are performed during all phases of peacebuilding, creating a disconnect between supply and demand in peacebuilding. In addition to identifying the functions and their relevance in each conflict phase, the study also proposed a set of effectiveness criteria for each function (Paffenholz 2010: 381–404).

The same study also analyzed the effectiveness of key civil society actors (Paffenholz 2010: 425–430). It found that civil society was not comprised only of NGOs as implied in many outside-driven discourses. While the research confirmed earlier critique of the NGOization of peace work, it also found that NGOs can be effective in providing protection and in conducting targeted advocacy campaigns. Moreover, the study found that mass-based organizations and schools have far greater potential to promote socialization and social cohesion than NGOs – even though their peacebuilding performance was rather low and often even counterproductive. Additionally, traditional and local entities (like elders or spiritual leaders) were found to be effective in facilitation and protection and eminent civil society leaders could be effective in preparing the ground for national facilitation and in helping parties break out of a stalemate in negotiations. Women's groups performed well in support of gender, women's and minority issues and could be effective in bridging existing divides. Yet it also became clear that broader change required the uniting of all available change-oriented mass movements. Aid organizations – if they are aware of their peacebuilding potential and make systematic use of it – could further support protection, monitoring and social cohesion.

Supporting/hindering context factors for civil society's peacebuilding effectiveness

The context surrounding each case strongly influences the space for civil society to act and thus strengthens or limits its effectiveness. The main context factors identified in the same study (Paffenholz et al. 2010: 405–424) were: (a) the level of violence; (b) the behavior of the state; (c) the performance of the media; (d) the behavior and composition of civil society itself (including Diaspora organizations); and (e) the influence of external political actors and donors. The impact of these contextual factors could be summarized as follows. The higher the level of violence, the more reduced the space for civil society to act. The more repressive the state is towards civil society actors, the more it limits the space for action and the more democratic the form of governance, the broader the space for civil society to act. Moreover, the more state institutions fulfill traditional functions like protection and service delivery, the more civil society can concentrate on other functions. In general, mass media are among the key opinion leaders in society. Hence, they can tremendously strengthen or limit civil society's peacebuilding roles in different ways. While the media can support civil society in their endeavors, they can also play a destructive role due to their biased reporting. In response, donors often choose to support peace media that may have only limited effect since such outlets usually do not enjoy a broad audience. Additionally, external powers – especially those from the region – can create both enabling and disenabling political environments. The composition and characteristics of civil society also influence its effectiveness. This means that the more civil society is polarized and dominated by radical tendencies, the more difficult it becomes for it to act towards a common cause for peacebuilding. The former also includes diaspora organizations that can often be very influential. Overall, the study also found that men from dominant groups in society (ethnic, religious, castes, etc.) hold most of the leading positions in civil society organizations.

Conclusions

Civil society is seen as a key actor in the dominant liberal and sustainable peacebuilding discourses. As a result, a large number of expectations are placed on civil society to promote and sustain peace and/or statebuilding. However, looking into the evidence from case study research, it becomes clear that civil society cannot meet these expectations. This is mainly due to the fact that supported activities are mostly driven by assumptions constructed within liberal and sustainable peacebuilding discourses and not necessarily by the actual needs of people and the peace process. While outside peacebuilders identify mainly service delivery NGOs (such as aid or conflict-resolution organizations) as key civil society actors, evidence from the available case study research identifies a broad variety of actors from political and social movements, to professional associations, spiritual and traditional leaders or diaspora groups as providing important contributions to peacebuilding. Critical peacebuilding scholars therefore rightly put emphasis on ordinary people and local voices for peace.

Overall, the case study evidence shows many impressive local and national initiatives working towards change without any outside support. However, a critical analysis should also apply here as evidence demonstrates that local civil society does not consist only of the 'good society' but, rather, reflects the society as a whole, acting as a mirror. Hence, polarized hardliner groups advocating against reconciliation and peace processes can, and often do, work alongside moderate pro-peace groups. How effective the pro-peace groups and individuals contributing to peacebuilding are depends on the particular context, the types of initiatives chosen during different phases of peacebuilding, as well as the way in which these initiatives are implemented. Yet, outside support can be important as it is crucial for creating a suitable environment for civil society peacebuilding and there is evidence of many successful protection and advocacy initiatives. Last but not least, rather than acting as a substitution, civil society support needs to go hand in hand with political action.

Notes

1 This is exemplified in numerous policy documents such as United Nations Secretary-General (2005, 2009), World Bank (2005), Forster and Mattner (2006), Organisation for Economic Co-operation and Development (2007, 2011) and Baine and Trolliet (2009).
2 The evidence presented in this chapter is based on a comparative research conducted from 2006 to 2009 in 13 case studies under the project 'Civil Society and Peacebuilding' (Paffenholz 2010).
3 For more information on civil society in different geographical and historical contexts refer to Spurk (2010: 9–17).

References

Aall, P. (2001) 'What do NGOs Bring to Peacemaking?', in C. Crocker, F.O. Hampson and P. Aall (eds) *Turbulent Peace*, Washington DC: United States Institute of Peace Press.

Appiagyei-Atua, K. (2002) 'Civil Society, Human Rights and Development in Africa: A Critical Analysis', *Peace, Conflict and Development*. Online. Available HTTP: <www.peacestudiesjournal.org.uk/dl/Civil.pdf> (accessed 9 March 2012).

Atieh, A., Ben-Nun, G., El-Shahed, G., Taha, R. and Tulliu, S. (2005) *Peace in the Middle East: P2P and the Israeli–Palestinian conflict*, Geneva: United Nations Publications (UNIDIR).

Babajanian, B., Freizer, S. and Stevens, D. (2005) 'Civil Society in Central Asia and the Caucasus', *Central Asian Survey*, 24(3): 209–224.

Baine, S. and Trolliet, P. (2009) 'Stocktaking and scoping of the Peacebuilding Partnership', Study for the European Commission – DG RELEX A/2. Online. Available HTTP: <http://eeas.europa.eu/ifs/pbp/docs/study_en.pdf> (accessed 9 March 2012).

Barnes, C. (2005) 'Weaving the Web: Civil-Society Roles in Working with Conflict and Building Peace', in P. van Tongeren (ed.) *People Building Peace II: Successful Stories of Civil Society*, Boulder, CO: Lynne Rienner.

Bayart, J.F. (1986) 'Civil Society in Africa', in P. Chabal (ed.) *Political Domination in Africa: Reflections on the Limits of Power*, Cambridge, UK: Cambridge University Press.

Belloni, R. (2001) 'Civil Society and Peacebuilding in Bosnia and Herzegovina', *Journal of Peace Research*, 38(2): 163–180.

Belloni, R. (2008) 'Civil Society in War-to-Democracy Transitions', in A. Jarstad and T. Sisk (eds) *War-to-Democracy Transitions: Dilemmas of Democratization and Peace-building in War-Torn Societies*, Cambridge, UK: Cambridge University Press.

Bendaña, A. (2003) 'What Kind of Peace is Being Built? Critical Assessment from the South', Paper prepared for the International Development Research Council (IDRC) on the 10th anniversary of An Agenda for Peace, Ottawa, Canada.

Chan, S. (1997) 'In Search of Democratic Peace: Problems and Promise', *Mershon International Studies Review*, 41: 59–91.

Çuhadar, E. (2009) 'Assessing Transfer from Track Two Diplomacy: The Cases of Water and Jerusalem', *Journal of Peace Research*, 46(5): 641–658.

Doyle, M.W. (1983a) 'Kant, Liberal Legacies, and Foreign Affairs', *Philosophy and Public Affairs*, 12(3): 205–235.

Doyle, M.W. (1983b) 'Kant, Liberal Legacies, and Foreign Affairs Part 2', *Philosophy and Public Affairs*, 12(4): 323–353.

Edwards, M. (2004) *Civil Society*, Cambridge, UK: Polity.

Fetherston, A.B. (2000) 'Peacekeeping, Conflict Resolution and Peacebuilding: A Reconsideration of Theoretical Frameworks', *International Peacekeeping*, 7(1): 190–218.

Fisher, R. (1997) 'Interactive Conflict Resolution', in I.W. Zartman (ed.) *Peacemaking in International Conflict: Methods and Techniques*, Washington DC: United States Institute of Peace Press.

Forster, R. and Mattner, M. (2006) 'Civil Society and Peacebuilding: Potential, Limitations and Critical Factors', *Social Development*, no. 36445: 52. Online. Available HTTP <http://siteresources.worldbank.org/EXTSOCIALDEVELOPMENT/Resources/244362-1164107274725/3182370-1164110717447/Civil_Society_and_Peacebuilding.pdf>> (accessed 9 March 2012).

Galtung, J. (1975) 'Three Approaches to Peace: Peacekeeping, Peacemaking, and Peacebuilding', in J. Galtung (ed.) *Peace, War and Defense – Essays in Peace Research*, Copenhagen: Christian Ejlers.

Glasius, M. (2004) *Civil Society*. Online. Available HTTP <http://www.fathom.com/feature/122536/> (accessed 9 March 2012).

Harneit-Sievers, A. (2005) '"Zivilgesellschaft" in Afrika: Anmerkungen aus historischer Perspektive', Lecture Manuscript, Berlin: Humboldt-Universität.

Heathershaw, J. (2008) 'Unpacking the Liberal Peace: The Dividing and Merging of Peacebuilding Discourses', *Millennium: Journal of International Studies*, 36(3): 597–621.

Ikelegbe, A. (2001) 'The Perverse Manifestation of Civil Society: Evidence from Nigeria', *Journal of Modern African Studies*, 39(1): 1–24.

Kaldor, M. (2003) *Global Civil Society: An Answer to War*, Cambridge, UK: Polity Press.

Kant, I. (1795) *Perpetual Peace: A Philosophical Essay*, translated with Introduction and Notes by M. Campbell Smith, with a Preface by L. Latta (1917), London: George Allen and Unwin.

Kasfir, N. (1998) 'Civil Society, the State, and Democracy in Africa', *Commonwealth and Comparative Politics*, 36(2): 123–149.

Kelman, H. (1992) 'Informal Mediation by the Scholar/Practitioner', in J. Bercovitch and J. Rubin (eds) *Mediation in International Relations: Multiple Approaches to Conflict Management*, London: Macmillan.

Kjellman, K.E. and Harpviken, K.B. (2010) 'Civil Society and the State', in T. Paffenholz (ed.) *Civil Society and Peacebuilding: A Critical Assessment*, Boulder, CO: Lynne Rienner.

Lederach, J.P. (1997) *Building Peace: Sustainable Reconciliation in Divided Societies*, Washington DC: United States Institute of Peace Press.

Lewis, D. (2002) 'Civil Society in African Contexts. Reflections on the Usefulness of a Concept', *Development and Change*, 33(4): 569–586.

Mac Ginty, R. (2006) *No War, No Peace: The Rejuvenation of Stalled Peace Processes and Peace Accords*, Basingstoke, UK: Palgrave.

Malhotra, D. and Liyanage, S. (2005) 'Long-Term Effects of Peace Workshops in Protracted Conflicts', *Journal of Conflict Resolution*, 49(6): 908–924.

Merkel, W. (1999) *Systemtransformation. Eine Einführung in die Theorie und Empirie der Transformationsforschung*, Opladen: Leske and Budrich.

Merkel, W. and Lauth, H. (1998) 'Systemwechsel und Zivilgesellschaft. Welche Zivilgesellschaft braucht die Demokratie?', *Aus Politik und Zeitgeschichte*, 6 (7): 3–12.

Ohanyan, A. and Lewis, J. (2005) 'Politics of Peacebuilding: Critical Evaluation of Interethnic Contact and Peace Education in Georgia-Abkhaz Peace Camp, 1998–2002', *Peace and Change*, 30(1): 57–84.

Organisation for Economic Co-operation and Development (2007) *Principles for Good International Engagement in Fragile States*. Online. Available HTTP: <http://www.oecd.org/dataoecd/28/5/43463433.pdf> (accessed 9 March 2012).

Organisation for Economic Co-operation and Development (2011) 'Busan Partnership for Effective Development Co-Operation', Outcome Document of the Fourth High Level Forum on Aid Effectiveness, Busan, Republic of Korea. Online. Available HTTP: <http://www.aideffec tiveness.org/busanhlf4/images/stories/hlf4/OUTCOME_DOCUMENT_-_FIN AL_EN.pdf> (accessed 9 March 2012).

Orjuela, C. (2003) 'Building Peace in Sri Lanka: A Role for Civil Society', *Journal of Peace Research*, 40: 195–212.

Orjuela, C. (2004) 'Civil Society in Civil War, Peace Work and Identity Politics in Sri Lanka', PhD Dissertation, Department of Peace and Development Research, University Göteborg.

Paffenholz, T. (1998) *Konflikttransformation durch Vermittlung. Theoretische und praktische Erkenntnisse aus dem Friedensprozess in Mosambik (1995–1996)*, Main: Grunewald.

Paffenholz, T. (2010) *Civil Society and Peacebuilding: A Critical Assessment*, Boulder, CO: Lynne Rienner.

Paffenholz, T. and Spurk, C. (2006) 'Civil Society, Civic Engagement and Peacebuilding', *Social Development Papers,* Conflict Prevention and Reconstruction paper no. 36, Washington DC: World Bank.

Paffenholz, T. and Spurk, C. (2010) 'A Comprehensive Analytical Framework', in T. Paffenholz (ed.) *Civil Society and Peacebuilding: A Critical Assessment*, Boulder, CO: Lynne Rienner.

Paffenholz, T., Spurk, C., Belloni, R., Kurtenbach, S. and Orjuela, C. (2010) 'Enabling and Disenabling Factors for Civil Society Peacebuilding' in T. Paffenholz (ed.) *Civil Society and Peacebuilding: A Critical Assessment*, Boulder, CO: Lynne Rienner.

Paris, R. (2004) *At War's End. Building Peace After Civil Conflict*, Cambridge: Cambridge University Press.

Pearce, J. (1998) 'From Civil War to "Civil Society": Has the End of the Cold War Brought Peace to Central America?', *International Affairs*, 74(3): 587–615.

Pearce, J. (2007) *Violence, power and participation: building citizenship in contexts of chronic violence*, Working paper no. 274, Brighton: Institute of Development Studies, University of Sussex.

Pinkney, R. (2003) *Democracy in the Third World*, Boulder, CO: Lynne Rienner.

Pouligny, B. (2005) 'Civil Society and Post-Conflict Peacebuilding: Ambiguities of International Programmes Aimed at Building "New" Societies', *Security Dialogue*, 36(4): 495–510.

Ray, J. (1998) 'Does Democracy Cause Peace?', *Annual Review of Political Science*, 1: 27–46.

Richmond, O.P. (2005) *The transformation of Peace*, London: Palgrave Macmillan.

Richmond, O.P. and Carey, H. (2006) *Subcontracting Peace. NGOs and Peacebuilding in a Dangerous World*, Aldershot, UK: Ashgate.

Ruffin, M.H. and Waugh, D.C. (1999) *Civil Society in Central Asia*, Baltimore: Johns Hopkins University Press.

Rummel, R. (1997) *Power Kills: Democracy as a Method of Nonviolence*, New Brunswick, NJ: Transaction Publishers.

Russett, B. and Starr, H. (2000) 'From Democratic Peace to Kantian Peace: Democracy and Conflict in the International System', in M. Mildarsky (ed.) *Handbook of War Studies*, Ann Arbor: University of Michigan Press.

Schmidt, S. (2000) 'Die Rolle von Zivilgesellschaften in afrikanischen Systemwechseln', in W. Merkel (ed.) *Systemwechsel 5. Zivilgesellschaft und Transformation*, Opladen: Leske and Budrich.

Small, M. and Singer, J. (1976) 'The War Proneness of Democratic Regimes, 1816–1965', *Jerusalem Journal of International Relations*, 1: 50–69.

Spurk, C. (2010) 'Understanding Civil Society', in T. Paffenholz (ed.) *Civil Society and Peacebuilding: A Critical Assessment*, Boulder, CO: Lynne Rienner.

United Nations Secretary-General (Boutrus Boutrus-Ghali) (1992) *An Agenda for Peace: Preventive Diplomacy, Peacemaking and Peace-keeping*, New York: United Nations.

United Nations Secretary-General (Kofi Annan) (2005) *In Larger Freedom: Towards Development, Freedom and Human Rights for All*, New York: United Nations.

United Nations Secretary-General (Ban Ki-Moon) (2009) *Peacebuilding in the Immediate Aftermath of Conflict*, New York: United Nations. Online. Available HTTP: <http://reliefweb.int/sites/reliefweb.int/files/resourc es/EB32DC62E195DB24852575E6006DF2EA-Full_Report.pdf> (accessed 9 March 2012).

van Tongeren, P., Verhoeven, J. and Wake, J (2005) 'People Building Peace: Key Messages and Essential Findings', in P. van Tongeren, M. Brenk, M. Hellema and J. Verhoeven (eds) *People Building Peace II: Successful Stories of Civil Society*, Boulder, CO: Lynne Rienner.

Varshney, A. (2002) *Ethnic Conflict and Civic Life: Hindus and Moslems in India*, New Haven: Yale University Press.

World Bank (2005) *Engaging Civil Society Organizations on Conflict-Affected and Fragile States: Three African Country Case Studies*, Washington DC: World Bank.

28

INDIGENOUS PEACEBUILDING

Anthony Wanis-St. John

...today's conflicts elude traditional management methods...at the same time, the persistence of violent conflict...indicates that modern international methods are defective in facing the challenge.

I.W. Zartman (2000)

If victims' agency is a crucial value, does it not follow that victims should be able to opt out of these international norms, if, say, in their culture and immediate circumstances they would prefer to reintegrate rebels who have committed atrocities into their community through a traditional ceremony of reconciliation than to prosecute them?

D. Orentlicher (2007)

Introduction

Localized, indigenous reconciliation and peacemaking practices resolve local conflicts and manage the webs of social relationships in indigenous communities in culturally relevant ways. But these communities have often been deeply impacted by modern forms of warfare, with the resulting loss of practitioners and distortion of practices of these rituals. In post-conflict peacebuilding contexts, several countries have tried to 'scale-up' indigenous practices to address crimes against humanity, as a form of transitional justice, alongside or in place of *ad hoc* or top-down transitional justice. This chapter looks at the complementarities and tensions between the retributive orientation of international transitional justice and the restorative potential of indigenous practices. Tentative insights into how indigenous and international practices can be harmonized are offered.

Building peace, after violent conflict has begun to subside, is just as much a process as the negotiation of that peace. Rather than a single, time-limited event, there are myriad components in the building and re-building of peace. Peacebuilding and the many activities that fall under this concept are often the result of a peace process – negotiations among armed and unarmed actors to create peace and end political violence. Peace processes may last for years as warring parties and civil society seek negotiated agreements on vexing issues such as distribution of power in a new government, the post-war economic order, security reform and accountability for the crimes of the past. In the building of peace, there will inevitably be some tensions between the preferences of impacted communities at the local level, national authorities and the international community.

One of the activities of peacebuilding that manifests tensions between local and external preferences is *transitional justice*. International transitional justice – one of the components of the liberal peace paradigm – seeks to create robust, global accountability for wartime atrocities, but may fail to embed either peace or justice in the society or region impacted by political violence.

Local cultures, norms and practices may themselves give rise to conflict dynamics (Galtung 1990), but local culture can also embody norms and practices that promote reconciliation (Mac Ginty 2008). Indigenous peacebuilding is increasingly presented as the culturally relevant alternative to externally imposed and retributive international transitional justice.

In practice, indigenous and international-liberal approaches can converge and 'hybridize' through a process that includes international coercion, local resistance and adaptation (Mac Ginty 2010: 403, 404). Thus, there are complementarities and tensions between the retributive practices of international tribunals and the restorative potential of indigenous practices.

Indigenous people themselves face existential dangers and have long found themselves in 'conflict with the dominant society, mostly relating to the loss of their lands, territories and resources or to the deprivation of their civil, political, cultural, social and economic rights' (United Nations 2010). They are at a disadvantage when seeking remedies for social injustice, displacement or genocidal violence through the courts and institutions of the states in which these acts occur. Moreover, governments and international organizations do not accord indigenous peoples the same status as states, so they cannot avail themselves of institutions such as the International Criminal Court or the UN Security Council. Thus even 'liberal' institutions and norms serve to 'validate…the organized plunder' of indigenous people (United Nations 2010: 223, citing Martinez 1999).

Increasingly, indigenous people themselves advocate for 'new systems and institutions of peacemaking that are sourced in indigenous values and that co-exist with existing bodies such as the International Court of Justice' to peacefully resolve disputes (Manila Declaration 2000).

This chapter explores some of the tensions and compatibilities between local, indigenous reconciliation and international transitional justice. This work stems from an ongoing interest in the impact of inclusion and exclusion of civil society and non-elites on peace process negotiations (Wanis-St. John & Kew 2008). Here I delve more deeply into the post-conflict/implementation phases of peace processes in which transitional justice is typically located; examining the main components of transitional justice, their antecedents, and the tensions.

Transitional justice definition and dynamics

Peace process negotiations, especially those addressing civil wars, regional conflicts and insurgencies, must grapple with the consequences of violence that directly impact civilian populations. Post-conflict justice includes the need to hold accountable perpetrators of crimes committed during the conflict. Rehabilitative or restorative aspects of transitional justice include processes for addressing the needs of victims of violence, including opportunities for social forgiveness and for reversing the denial of victims' narratives. The terms of transitional justice are often negotiated during the peace process, but must then be implemented as peace takes hold. Success and failures in the implementation of transitional justice have some correlation with the viability of peace, and are thus a critical component of peacebuilding.

Accountability issues often manifest themselves in peace processes in two ways at the negotiation table. Belligerents seek *impunity for themselves* at the negotiating table, in exchange for laying down of arms or other concessions. Conversely, belligerents threaten to indict or otherwise *hold adversaries responsible* for *their* atrocities. Both tactics are mirror images of one another, and both seek to exploit the adversary and increase negotiation leverage. Sometimes the tactic is based on principle, but it can also be a ploy used to obtain concessions on other issues, i.e., one side might give up its demands for the other side to submit to prosecution in exchange for the latter's concessions on power-sharing.

Transitional justice has been defined broadly in the 2004 *Report of the Secretary General on Rule of Law and Transitional Justice in Conflict and Post-Conflict Societies.* It refers to:

> …the full range of processes and mechanisms associated with a society's attempts to come to terms with a legacy of large-scale past abuses, in order to ensure accountability, serve justice and achieve reconciliation. These may include both judicial and non-judicial mechanisms, with differing levels of international involvement (or none at all) and individual prosecutions, reparations, truth-seeking, institutional reform, vetting and dismissals, or a combination thereof.
> (Report of the Secretary General 2004)

There are key contextual dimensions missing from this text, including the existence of a state of armed conflict or emergence from such conflict; the commission of large-scale violations of human rights; the incapacity or non-existence of national or regional laws and institutions to address such violations; and inadequacies of political will (and possibly of local societal norms) to address such violations. In short, transitional justice is meant to address an *extraordinary* circumstance (the end of violent conflict) for which standard methods (rule of law) are inadequate or non-existent. As implied in the name, it should indeed be transitional: a *temporary measure* that brings the parties closer to nonviolent politics (to contend for power), rule of law (to resolve new disputes) and energized civil society (to assert cultural norms and limit the hegemony of the state). Seen as a factor in facilitating these three conditions, transitional justice has a heavy burden.

International or local?

The internationalization of post-conflict transitional justice serves a number of purposes. It serves as a reminder that human rights norms and customs emerge and can challenge the hegemony of state sovereignty. As any other system of criminal prosecution, international transitional justice serves as a deterrent against future transgressions by showing that powerful actors such as states, as well as their non-state rivals, are not immune to prosecution. For the country or conflict in question, it serves as a mechanism for holding individual violators accountable. This is especially important when the institutions of justice of a given country are weak, corrupt or simply lacking in the capacity to address the diverse sequelae of violent conflict, including prosecuting high-ranking civilian or military officials, opening inquiries about controversial historical events, conducting forensic studies, or simply enforcing the rule of law.

But there are dissenting voices as well. Internationalization, for all its merits, has been criticized as victor's justice. More recently, it is criticized as 'Western' or foreign justice. It relieves national authorities of their responsibility to hold perpetrators accountable and strengthen their own institutions. It is far removed from the victims of violence, who are often no more than witnesses for the prosecutorial phase. While it may serve to help victims feel that some 'justice' was done, it does little to heal fragile and broken societies coping with the effects of violence.

Recent thinking about peacebuilding proposes the concept of hybridity between what are essentially externally imposed, top-down peacebuilding practices emerging from the liberal political philosophies and bottom-up, locally rooted communal practices – which may or may not be 'indigenous', depending on how the term is used (Mac Ginty 2011). The concept of hybridity can be directly extended to transitional justice. Local communities and indigenous populations who pass through transitional justice processes can resist, challenge and transform those practices, rather than passively accept them.

Two ironies need to be considered here before proceeding. First, there may be few untouched and pure indigenous practices that have not been impacted by colonial or other influences. Where they exist as a separate component of justice – customary practices and norms – they may have become devoid of their prior ability to generate forgiveness and reconciliation. They may in fact perpetuate repressive social orders of their own. Second, perpetrators and victims are not always dichotomous, mutually exclusive categories in contemporary conflicts. In Uganda, Rwanda and Sierra Leone, victims of violence were frequently recruited and coerced into becoming perpetrators. In some conflicts such as the inter-communal violence in Iraq during the US occupation of the country, 'civil' society could easily shift and become uncivil, taking up arms, spontaneously and perhaps temporarily allowing itself to become mobilized by conflict entrepreneurs while being simultaneously victimized by them (West 2005). Such considerations muddy the waters and prevent easy categorizations that worked in the past such as military/civilian, perpetrator/victim, and state/non-state.

Diverse processes of transitional justice

In opposition to impunity, vengeance, or forgetting, there are diverse processes that address the needs for accountability, transparency, an end to cycles of violence and forgiveness. Among these are criminal prosecutions, truth commissions and local rituals, each of which is briefly considered in this section. Warring parties and countries in transition also seek out and enact amnesties for selected categories of belligerents. With the passage of time and the strengthening of rule of law institutions, amnesties can be reversed, as the cases of Argentina and Chile have demonstrated. Amnesties directly perpetuate impunity, and are thus a highly problematic manifestation of transitional justice.

International retributive accountability

In the absence of an accepted international entity, and considering the numerous problems of the impunity resulting from reliance on national courts to enforce international laws, the United Nations Security Council established *ad hoc* tribunals in response to the Yugoslav conflict (the International Criminal Tribunal for the Former Yugoslavia) in 1993 and the Rwandan genocide (the International Criminal Tribunal for Rwanda) in 1994. Each was established under Chapter VII of the UN Charter. These have been followed by other internationalized criminal courts, such as those for Sierra Leone, East Timor, Lebanon, Kosovo, Cambodia and elsewhere (Romano et al. 2004).

The permanent institution designed to address such crimes came into being with the Rome Statute of July 17, 1998, which started the process of creating the International Criminal Court (ICC). The ICC faces several operational hurdles, including the 'no' vote of the United States and several other countries, as well as a lack of capacity for apprehension of indictees. The ICC is nevertheless *the* permanent, international forum for pursuing prosecutions against those accused of 'a) the crime of genocide, b) crimes against humanity, c) war crimes and d) crimes of aggression' (Rome Statute, Art. 5). Belligerents no longer have any doubt about whether or not an *ad hoc* tribunal might be created as a result of their violations of human rights – a highly politicized process that relies on deliberations, votes and negotiations in the UN Security Council. The forum to prosecute them already exists and is operational. But the ICC is not the sole forum for accountability. It has become increasingly possible for perpetrators of serious crimes to face prosecution by third party national courts (Minow 2002: 22).

Truth-telling

Truth-telling mechanisms, sometimes constructed as 'truth commissions', are typically a non-judicial process whose purpose is to make transparent the experiences of victims and create new historical narratives of a shared traumatic history. The process may be more or less compulsory for perpetrators but should be and frequently is voluntary for victims. It is sometimes a stand-alone process not tied to criminal prosecution. Alternatively it can be combined with an amnesty, a broad purge (lustration) of former officials accused of wrongdoing, or more selective prosecutions of perpetrators. Truth commissions have often been 'official', state-sanctioned processes, with different degrees of involvement of civil society, religious leaders and institutions or international organizations.

The vast asymmetry of power between states and civil society or other non-state actors, as well as between those who commit violations of rights and those who suffer them, has often had two consequences with regard to the narrative of what transpired. The first is denial or distortion of history, as well as biased, controlled histories replete with blame and enemy images – i.e. histories and rhetoric that portray one side as 'protectors of order and values' against 'subversives', 'terrorists', 'criminals' or other such labels. Limitations on freedom of expression and speech and other coercive measures, including violence, are employed to make sure that the cost of advancing an alternative narrative is very high. The second consequence is at the level of the individual and the community, where non-recognition of lived experience is the main result. This consequence is an internal one for individuals and communities: unresolved trauma, individual or collective denial, isolation, social death or physical violence can result. The antidote to the denial of experience or domination of narrative is composed of systematic attempts to get the narratives of truth out (in the case of hegemonic denial) or to create new, shared histories (in the case of multiple, contested narratives).

As a remedy to denial, truth-telling mechanisms are thought to be an opportunity to experience personal or collective catharsis – a step in social and psychological healing for those who have experienced war, violence, depredations and victimization. However, this is not straightforward. Not every individual or culture places a value on open, transparent exploration or ventilation of traumatic events, experiences and memories. Some feel that they are re-traumatized and re-victimized by the process. The truth-telling itself can be a contest in which prior structural violence and social orders reassert themselves. Getting the story out may not be a safe activity as perpetrators may wish to silence witnesses or otherwise use truth-telling as a way to crowd out alternative narratives and deflect blame. Reconciliation as a component of peacebuilding is by no means simple, straightforward or easy. The deconstruction of enemy images is tied to socially relevant conceptions of accountability and forgiveness, as well as highly variable preferences for silence or expression. Reconciliation is very hard to measure, let alone to do: it 'implies a muddying of the waters and a fundamental change in perceptions of the other' (Hamber & Kelly 2009: 290).

Ritual and reconciliation

The capacity to resolve conflict, reconcile disputing parties, and balance accountability with forgiveness is not a 'Western' capacity. It is a human capacity. Human history is replete with stories of conflict and war, but those same stories are also full of stories of mediating, forgiving and forging new social or even interpersonal relationships out of conflictive ones. Our oldest mythologies, writings and religious traditions provide evidence of what must be a long human familiarity with making peace (Wanis-St. John 2012). Rituals have long accompanied words, and symbolic representations of the ending of conflict help us to commemorate, give witness, close, and celebrate such events.

The ancient human innovations of peacemaking continue in the traditions and practices of indigenous communities around the world, some of whom can be termed 'non-warring societies' (Ury 1995; Fry 2007). Indigenous populations continue to exist, sometimes in relative isolation, but also in some coexistence and intermixing with newer populations through emigration or colonization. Indigenous people currently are thought to comprise 370 million people living in 90 countries (United Nations 2010). In numerous societies, indigenous forms of conflict resolution can be characterized as victim-centered, participatory, egalitarian, consensual, and restorative of communal harmony. They regulate retaliation. They are also affordable and accessible, compared with 'formal' retributive justice. They are recognized as authentic, time-honored and acceptable venues in which to address conflicts. They often culminate in a ritual practice that can – depending on the society – support those who seek forgiveness, enable those who wish to forgive, 'erase' social memory of wrongdoing, re-establish communal interdependence and symbolically purify participants.

That said, the impact of colonialism on indigenous populations has in practice resulted in a 'haphazard hybrid' (Gang 2012: 23) that sometimes provides neither 'impartial' retributive justice through formal court-based systems, nor the social reconciliation and forgiveness previously accorded by indigenous processes before their encounter with colonialism. Deliberate attempts to revive or resuscitate indigenous practices of reconciliation have resulted in interesting experiments in 'scaling-up'. The Rwandan post-genocide use of the *gacaca* process is frequently cited as an example. *Gacaca* was immediately and spontaneously employed by local communities in the aftermath of the genocide (Ingelaere 2008: 35). It soon was supported or appropriated – depending on the interpretation – by the state and scaled-up into 'Gacaca Courts'. However, it was never meant to address crimes such as genocide, and the state's appropriation of it has proven to be both innovative and problematic. Given the sheer numbers of perpetrators Rwanda 'processed' (more than 800,000, as of 2006 (Ingelaere 2008: 42)), perhaps there were few alternatives. Some believe the scaling-up stripped *gacaca* of its conciliatory character and introduced coercion and fear in what had been a consensual process, with the result of enabling impunity and re-victimization (Ingelaere 2008; Gourevitch 2009).

In the transitional justice context, the observer finds indigenous practices proposed within communities who have been participants, victims (or both) of armed conflict. Those practices and practitioners may have suffered delegitimization as traditional authorities get overwhelmed, co-opted or killed in contemporary armed conflict. Indigenous practices have nevertheless resurged in importance as the local consequences of global and regional violence are considered.

Antecedents

The internationalization of transitional and post-conflict justice is often traced to the conclusion of the Second World War with the establishment of the Tokyo and Nuremburg Trials. There had been unsuccessful attempts by the League of Nations to create international criminal tribunals in the wake of the First World War (International Law Commission 1949). Efforts to establish an international criminal court within the UN system also began soon after the Second World War, but fell victim to Cold War politics and outright resistance by member states throughout four decades (Lillich & Hannum 1995). The Tokyo and Nuremberg criminal tribunals set the stage for later practice in international criminal prosecution for those accused of human rights violations, crimes against humanity, genocide and violations of the laws of war. Nevertheless, there was no international organization to manage such enforcement duties in armed conflicts. The Geneva Conventions that codify some of this international law in treaty form leave enforcement to the states signatories, even when violations are the product of a civil war involving internal insurgents, making enforcement at the very least difficult, and frequently unlikely.

In the post-Cold War era of civil wars and democratic transitions, there were renewed calls to end impunity. As part of an ongoing trend in the weakening of state sovereignty and in particular the domestic jurisdiction concept enshrined in the UN Charter (Art. 2(7)),[1] states and non-state actors that commit crimes against humanity and other human rights violations found themselves increasingly confronting mechanisms of international criminal prosecution, ranging from *ad hoc* tribunals set up by the UN Security Council to indictments by the International Criminal Court.

Such mechanisms are structured on several presumptions. The first is that accountability is obtained by punishment. A second is that local norms and institutions of justice – whether formal or informal – are inadequate or non-existent and result in impunity. The logic of international justice seems in part to be predicated on the minimization of the impunity so frequently sought by perpetrators. Where local norms and institutions do exist, the presumption is that cultural factors and power asymmetries will delay justice or impede local prosecution, thereby foreclosing opportunities to deter future crimes at local and global levels. There is therefore an implicit tension between the local and the international processes of justice.

An echo of the tension between indigenous reconciliation and internationalized transitional justice can be found in the political transitions of the 1990s, particularly in Latin America, Central and Eastern Europe. One of the central dilemmas of those transitions involved whether or not (and if so, to what extent) the human rights crimes of prior regimes should be punished. Nascent democracies with weak justice institutions often grappled with demands for impunity by the perpetrators, particularly when former military governments were making space for new, democratically elected ones. Attempts at prosecution were often met with threats against the individuals and organs of the justice system.

Another echo of the tension between international criminal prosecution and local preferences held that local preferences should prevail over international obligations and that 'truth-telling' (official or unofficial investigation and revelation of the erstwhile hidden or denied narratives of abuse) might accompany or even partially offset imperfect prosecution. Another strand held that as long as they fulfilled their international legal obligations, new democracies could choose the extent to which they pursued prosecution, according to their institutional capacity to do so, supplemented by alternative modes of justice more appropriate to the transitional period's constraints (Zalaquett 1999).

More recently, in the context of extremely violent internal wars, regional wars and genocides (rather than transitions away from authoritarianism) a parallel dilemma has been articulated: 'A key question facing democracies emerging from civil conflict is how best to deal with the painful legacy of past…violence, while at the same time maintaining the fragile social harmony that often characterizes post-conflict societies. Should priority be given to bringing the perpetrators of past human rights violations to justice, thereby combating the culture of impunity…? Or is it more important to start by focusing on measures designed to ensure…peace and stability?' (Huyse & Salter 2008).

The emergent nature of transitional justice and the hybridization that occurs in practice may help to reduce the apparent duality of such dilemmas. It may be possible to minimize or at least modify and reduce the impunity of perpetrators while affirming lived experiences of victims and giving wide latitude to local norms and rituals of reconciliation that combine elements of accountability, by prioritizing the preferences of local communities (whether indigenous or not), ritualizing forgiveness and enabling social reintegration.

Uganda, Peru and Burundi

In this section I seek to illustrate some of the tension and complementarity by examining how transitional justice concerns manifested themselves in Uganda, with brief explorations of transitional justice in Peru and Burundi.

In Uganda armed conflict, peace negotiations and transitional justice all occurred simultaneously. There was no neat sequencing from one to the other. The history of failed attempts to end the war between the government and the Lord's Resistance Army by military means is punctuated with negotiation, mediation and various incentives to the LRA to end its insurgency. At the behest of Acholi civil society in northern Uganda, in 2000, the government offered an amnesty program to LRA and other insurgents designed to shrink their ranks while recognizing that many LRA fighters were themselves abductees. Over 20,000 people are believed to have availed themselves of the amnesty, but the conflict continued. In 2003 the government made a formal referral to the ICC, which in turn issued its first, historic indictments against the LRA commanders in 2005. In July 2006 the Ugandan government and the LRA sat down to talks mediated by the leadership of South Sudan.

The intersection of the ICC's indictments and the fragile peace process between the government and the Lord's Resistance Army had the effect of first prodding the LRA to the negotiation table, but then providing the LRA with a new condition for continuing talks and implementing the agreements already reached. The LRA began demanding the lifting of the indictments as a precondition to continuing negotiations in pursuit of a comprehensive agreement. The government, in turn, had held to the position that the ICC would not act upon the indictments as long as the LRA disarmed and fighters at the lower levels took advantage of modified transitional justice mechanisms based on longstanding Acholi traditional rituals. Ugandans began in fact to practice these modified rituals based on Acholi traditions with the support of an emergent pro-peace civil society, itself supported by the international community (Latigo 2008: 105). Nevertheless, the peace process stalled and the military dimension continues as of this writing, albeit at lower levels and in surrounding countries.

Whether or not the ICC indictments were a real cause of the LRA's intransigence or merely a convenient cover for a more strategic return to violence by the LRA, Ugandan civil society raised concerns about whether or not national peace should be sacrificed to international justice. Ugandans from the war-affected areas clearly articulated a desire for a localized approach that included integration of former LRA fighters using Acholi-based rituals, and reliance on local civil society leaders to use informal contacts with the LRA to re-open political dialogue (Conciliation Resources 2011).

The 2007 Agreement on Accountability and Reconciliation signed by the government and the LRA explicitly incorporated this civil society desideratum. Ugandans persevere despite ongoing challenges including the delegitimization of the Acholi rituals, the alienation of some Acholis from these practices, and government arrests of some who availed themselves of these mechanisms.

The Ugandan case demonstrates that both bottom-up and top-down initiatives can meet in a messy, opaque but less violent middle. Governments can more or less successfully reintegrate some former insurgents by co-opting indigenous rituals of reconciliation and incorporating them into formal peace negotiations even as they rely on international retributive justice to act as a deterrent. Acholi civil society, on the other hand, manifested a priority for ending violence early and relying on traditional practices of reconciliation, instead of waiting for internationalized transitional justice or military means to end the suffering. Perpetrators and victims in Uganda are sometimes the very same individuals, and in any case, perpetrators and victims will live in the same communities again. Removal and incarceration of perpetrators would succeed only in punishment but not accomplish any of the other goals of transitional justice.

In Peru, several armed movements arose to challenge the hegemony of the state. The two principal movements were the mainstream Marxist group Movimiento Revolucionario Tupac Amaru, while the more radical armed Maoist group was called Sendero Luminoso, or Shining Path. Sendero did not spare either progressive individuals or entities of the state in its radical project to destroy the state, nor did it hesitate to use violence to coerce the Peruvian peasant population into submission. Sendero did tap into enormous indigenous discontent with the marginalization and social injustice of the Peruvian state and society. Sendero posed a formidable threat to the Peruvian government in the 1990s. Counterinsurgency and hardline state repression were the main methods used by the Peruvian state to combat Sendero.

Thiedon (2010) has observed the truth commission established in the absence of a negotiated peace process, after Sendero had essentially been defeated in military terms. The politics of victimhood in Peru permitted only non-supporters of Sendero to be considered 'true' victims. This sidestepped the underlying and historic marginalization of indigenous communities in Peru, which had helped generate popular support for the insurgents. The truth commission obligated the population to either adopt a 'resentful silence' or seek to adopt an 'untainted victimhood' in order to participate in the truth-telling (Thiedon 2010: 104, 110) and other compensatory mechanisms.

The top-down co-optation of the truth-telling mechanism in Peru would appear to be in some sense a continuation of colonial repression by other means. The underlying ethnic identity divide that demarcates the lines of marginalization in Peru was not in any way addressed by – much less addressed by – the conflict's termination, nor by the terms of the peace.

The indigenous people and traditions of the Andes have found little resonance in the 'victim-centered' truth-telling approach used in Peru. Rather, on their own, at the local, provincial level, communities turned toward ex-Senderistas and engaged them in both retributive and restorative justice with some degree of spontaneity. The state and Sendero brought the war to the provinces and enmeshed rural people in it. But local communities created their own norms for determining culpability of the returned fighters, turning some over to the Peruvian army, but also accepting others. Some communities redistributed land and otherwise re-humanized and rehabilitated selected ex-Senderistas in the most conflict-affected parts of Peru – in the absence of a national policy or program to do so (Thiedon 2006). To the extent there is overlap between indigenous Andean traditions of reconciliation and the village levels of governance (there has indeed been hybridization), this successful reintegration of ex-Senderistas represents an example of an indigenous, communal agency little affected by the state-dominated truth-telling efforts.

Burundi experienced twelve years of genocidal violence and civil war along the same constructed ethnic identities that impacted its neighbor Rwanda. Burundian indigenous peacemakers, the *Bashingantahe*, who used to confer legitimacy on traditional rulers and act as local peacebuilders in Burundian society, were themselves delegitimized during the years of violence and have played little or no role in reintegrating or reconciling Tutsis and Hutus (McClintock 2008). The Arusha Accords, which began the process of ending the war in 2000, called for an 'international judicial commission of inquiry on genocide, war crimes and other crimes against humanity', to be followed by an international criminal tribunal set up by the UN Security Council. Additionally, a 'National Truth and Reconciliation Commission' was to 'make recommendations to promote reconciliation and forgiveness' and to clarify the troubled history of Burundi. As a result of the peace negotiations, transitional justice in Burundi was designed to encompass international, retributive mechanisms, as well as national truth-telling mechanisms. However, 'progress on implementation of these measures has been close to non-existent' and there have not been any national-level convictions for the war in Burundi, nor have there been any indigenous, ritualized reconciliation activities.

Field-based investigations in Burundi found evidence of widespread lack of enthusiasm for two of the pillars of transitional justice: truth-telling and prosecution; a widespread 'normative preference in favor of silence' among their informants was found. At the level of individuals and communities, they found ample reason why the local, culturally relevant preferences have tended toward forgetting. In desiring to 'surmount ethnicity' – the ostensible cause of identity-based conflict – Burundians mostly seem to reject transitional justice as a divisive reminder of a negative past. In Burundi, as in other parts of the world, the struggle for survival requires carefully balanced social cooperation. When this balance is lost, violence is inevitable and escalatory, but when it is restored, transitional justice is perceived to pose a kind of threat to the fragile peace by re-entrenching divisiveness.

The *Bashingantahe* of Burundi are still existent, and continue to symbolically represent values that many Burundians wish to espouse: honorable, wise, socially-esteemed and able to resolve conflicts peacefully despite having no formal role in the peacebuilding there. A National Council of Bashingantahe, formed in 2005, may present a potential mechanism to advance community dialogues and address social concerns and could function as a kind of resuscitated bottom-up mechanism. But the people of Burundi themselves appear to have distanced both the indigenous and the international mechanisms of transitional justice, favoring peace and survival over justice and possible divisiveness. This too, I would argue, may be an expression of an 'indigenous' norm – at the very least a local preference that defies international, liberal and even national-elite preferences.

While by no means an exhaustive review of cases, these three differing conflicts each have indigenous populations and local and indigenous mechanisms in varying states of vigor and have suffered extremely violent internal armed conflict. None have simply accommodated the liberal preferences for transitional justice, accepting and modifying some, distorting others, while proposing and implementing local preferences with little or no external framework of support. In an imperfect world, these give us glimpses of how conflict-affected societies engage with emerging international norms and practices, how national governments co-opt, distort and employ both international and indigenous norms, and how local communities persevere and engage with both of these dynamics.

Harmonization of the indigenous and international

Avoiding strong linkages to impunity

Diane Orentlicher (2007: 21) argued that local cultural preferences for reconciliation and integration might be more meaningful to communities of victims of violence, but implied that local culture should not be used to justify and extend a 'culture of impunity conducive to violence', in other words, peace and justice need not be construed as contradictory, mutually exclusive goals. Orentlicher seems to be arguing for doing both locally informed/indigenous reconciliation as well as international criminal prosecution, but only to the extent that the possibilities of prosecution are not used as an excuse to prolong war or excuse the perpetrators of crimes against humanity. As seen from the cases briefly considered above, these are hard priorities to balance and sometimes, local, indigenous preferences exclude and oppose the priorities of internationalized accountability.

The implication for international mediators as well as national and local peacemakers is that, when embracing an indigenous conflict resolution method for reconciliation at the negotiation table, they need not trade amnesty in exchange for it. It may be possible and preferable to de-couple these. In other words, if a belligerent party wants to avail itself of a relevant, locally preferred cultural norm of reconciliation, this should not automatically erase other obligations under national or international law. Pending prosecutions, whether national or international, should go on. Just as importantly, negotiators should not bargain away the future by promising impunity, as the institutional capacities, cultural norms and local preferences will change over time. Certainly rule of law can be strengthened with time. Where feasible however, preferences of local communities to forego prosecution and deal with repentant perpetrators at lower levels of authority can be embraced.

It is probably impossible to entirely eliminate the inherent tension between local practices and accountability. The legitimacy of any measure implying amnesty, or indeed of measures according 'forgiveness', may be strengthened by reserving them for only certain classes of former fighters, as well as requiring some public accountability (confessions) from those availing themselves of local mechanisms. Low-ranking fighters who have accepted to be demobilized and disarmed, and against whom no judicial process is contemplated, and who have admitted their actions, for example, might be considered eligible for such measures.

Sequencing according to need and institutional capacity

Another way of harmonizing comes through the dimension of time. The diverse remedies available to build peace after war each have different dynamics, resource demands and timelines. There is no reason why they must follow a preconceived order. I would nevertheless argue here that remedies that directly impact the local community level should take first priority, followed by international criminal prosecutions, and finally by national level measures, such as truth-telling. This stems from my prioritization of victims and the need for supporting relevant and culturally appropriate individual and collective healing after traumatic conflict. But it also stems from the idea that the national institutions of justice typically gain the capacity to prosecute serious crimes only over extended periods of time. That, coupled with the political risks of attempting to prosecute armed groups whose collaboration is most needed at the peace table and the undesirability of offering amnesties, points toward this ordering. Naturally, this is only one of many configurations that take advantage of the different risks, time demands and other dynamics of diverse remedies.

Specialization

Local, indigenous practices are often best suited to repairing the tapestry of community by compelling accountability before the community and providing ritualized avenues for forgiveness. At the same time, local indigenous practices sometimes replicate social injustices and are least suited to use as a deterrent to future serious crimes that rise to the level of genocide, crimes against humanity and other atrocities. Where prosecution is required, it must be left to the institutions most likely to render it as quickly, fairly, transparently and visibly as possible. National and international courts and tribunals are more apt to successfully prosecute and punish. Even when international (or even foreign) courts do not succeed in taking custody of an indicted criminal, their efforts may help to empower and inspire the national institutions to take action.

The tasks of truth-telling, reparation, acknowledgement and reconciliation, though sometimes grouped together as non-judicial remedies, are really very different activities. Truth-telling may be led by either international, national or hybrid institutions and should probably be official efforts to make visible the hidden and denied histories of the victims – to the extent there is socially safe space to do so, and to the extent that victims are not re-victimized when they tell their truth. However, in the absence of official action, there may be good reasons to permit civil society actors – religious institutions, coalitions or other civic groups that cross ethnic, sectarian and political divides – to be the leaders and facilitators of truth-telling efforts.

On the other hand the 'officialization' of a truth-telling process may be more able to compel the participation of official or former official actors, especially if the truth-telling mechanism is part of a peace agreement, legislation or other legal or policy instrument.

Reparation may be thought of as a restorative, compensatory program of action that provides material relief to victims and survivors. Since it is typically mediated by either the state or an international mechanism, it does little to promote reconciliation and must be thought of as an interim and incomplete measure that sometimes causes harm when it is distributed in a bureaucratic fashion. The distribution of especially money awards can sometimes generate perceptions of favoritism and relative gains and ultimately become a new driver of conflict. Communal, collective relief, such as community rebuilding or infrastructure may partly offset this to the extent that beneficiaries perceive mutual gains.

Acknowledgements, through gestures, cultural landmarks, works of art, official apologies or other public demonstrations, are symbolic but also relevant elements of transitioning away from violence. But their power can cut both ways. If they are detached from real accountability, they may be interpreted as cheap attempts to gain impunity, and further, will become reminders of humiliation and suffering. If however they are accompanied by real and visible actions to promote justice and reconciliation, they may address the core individual and collective needs human beings have for validation of their experiences.

While it is clear that war and violence are not redressed by inaction and indifference, it is also clear that there are tensions and complementarities among the preferences of the international community, national-level elites and belligerents, and local or indigenous communities impacted by violence. Harmonization among these overlapping levels requires continuous reflection, critique and innovation.

Note

1 UN Charter (1945), Article 2(7): "Nothing in the present Charter shall authorize the United Nations to intervene in matters which are essentially within the domestic jurisdiction of any state or shall require members to submit such matters to settlement under the present Charter; but this principle shall not prejudice the application of enforcement measures under Chapter VII."

References

Conciliation Resources (2011) 'The Lord's Resistance Army', *People's Peacemaking Perspectives*. October. Accessed at http://www.c-r.org/sites/www.c-r.org/files/TheLordsResistanceArmy_201110_ENG_0.pdf. Last accessed 16 June 2012.

Fry, D. (2007) *Beyond War: The Human Potential for Peace*. Oxford: Oxford University Press.

Galtung, J. (1990) 'Cultural Violence', *Journal of Peace Research*, 27(3): 291–305.

Gang, M. (2012) 'Culture, Conflict and the Legacy of Colonialism', Paper presented at the Conference on Indigenous Conflict Management, Kennesaw State University. Kennesaw, Georgia. April 20.

Gourevitch, P. (2009) 'The Life After', *New Yorker*, May 4.

Hamber, B. and G. Kelly (2009) 'Too Deep, Too Threatening: Understandings of Reconciliation in Northern Ireland'. In Hugo Van Der Merwe et al., eds. *Assessing the Impact of Transitional Justice*. Washington DC: United States Institute of Peace Press.

Huyse, L. and M. Salter, eds. (2008) *Traditional Justice and Reconciliation After Violent Conflict: Learning From African Experiences*. International Institute for Democracy and Electoral Assistance.

Ingelaere, B. (2008) 'The Gacaca Courts in Rwanda'. In L. Huyse and M. Salter, eds. *Traditional Justice and Reconciliation After Violent Conflict: Learning From African Experiences*. International Institute for Democracy and Electoral Assistance.

International Law Commission (1949) *Historical Survey of the Question of International Criminal Jurisdiction*. UN Document: A/CN.4/7/Rev.1. New York.

Latigo, J.O. (2008) 'Northern Uganda: tradition based practices in the Acholi region'. In L. Huyse and M. Salter, eds. *Traditional Justice and Reconciliation After Violent Conflict: Learning From African Experiences*. International Institute for Democracy and Electoral Assistance.

Lillich, R. and H. Hannum (1995) *International Human Rights*. 3rd edn. Little, Brown.

Mac Ginty, R. (2008) 'Indigenous Peacemaking Versus the Liberal Peace', *Cooperation and Conflict*, 43(2): 139–163.

Mac Ginty, R. (2010) 'Hybrid Peace: the Interaction Between Top-Down and Bottom-Up Peace', *Security Dialogue*, 41: 391–412.

Mac Ginty, R. (2011) *International Peacebuilding and Local Resistance*. London: Palgrave Macmillan.

Manila Declaration (2000) The International Conference On Conflict Resolution, Peace Building, Sustainable Development And Indigenous Peoples, convened by Tebtebba Foundation (Indigenous Peoples' International Centre For Policy Research and Education), Manila, Philippines on December 6–8. Accessed at http://www.twnside.org.sg/title/manila.htm June 12, 2012.

Martinez, M.A. (1999) 'Study on Treaties, Agreements and other Constructive Arrangements Between States and Indigenous Populations'. Final Report by Miguel Alfonso Martinez, Special Rapporteur UN Doc. E. CN.4/Sub.2/1999/20.

McClintock, E. (2008) 'Managing the Tension Between Exclusionary and Inclusionary Processes: Building Peace in Burundi' *International Negotiation*, 13(1): 73–91.

Minow, M. ed. (2002) *Breaking the Cycles of Hatred.* Princeton: Princeton University Press.

Orentlicher, D. (2007) 'Settling Accounts Revisited: Reconciling Global Norms with Local Agency', *International Journal of Transitional Justice*, 1: 10–22.

Report of the Secretary General to the UN Security Council (2004) 'The Rule of Law and Transitional Justice in Conflict and Post-Conflict Societies', August 23, S/2004/616.

Romano, C., A. Nollkaemper and J. Kleffner, eds. (2004) *Internationalized Criminal Courts and Tribunals: Sierra Leone, East Timor, Kosovo and Cambodia.* Oxford: Oxford University Press.

Thiedon, K. (2006) 'Justice in Transition: The Micropolitics of Reconciliation in Postwar Peru', *Journal of Conflict Resolution*, 50(3): 433–456.

Thiedon, K. (2010) 'Histories of Innocence: Postwar Stories of Peru'. In Rosalind Shaw and Pierre Hazan, eds. *Localizing Transitional Justice.* Stanford: Stanford University Press.

United Nations (2010) *State of the World's Indigenous Peoples.* UN Permanent Forum on Indigenous Peoples. Accessed at http://social.un.org/index/IndigenousPeoples/Library/StateoftheWorldsIndigenousPeoples.aspx. Last accessed 12 June 2012.

United Nations Charter (1945) United Nations Treaty Series. http://www.un.org/en/documents/charter/. Last accessed 12 June 2012.

Ury, W. (1995) 'Conflict Resolution Among the Bushmen: Lessons in Dispute System Design', *Negotiation Journal,* 11(4): 379–389.

Wanis-St. John, A. (2012) 'Ancient Peacemakers: Exemplars of Humanity', in Susan Allen Nan, Zachariah Cherian Mampilly, Andrea Bartoli, eds. *Peacemaking: From Practice to Theory* vol. 2. Praeger.

Wanis-St. John, A. and D. Kew (2008) 'Civil Society and Peace Negotiations: Confronting Exclusion', *International Negotiation*, 13(1): 11–36.

West, B. (2005) *No True Glory: A Frontline Account of the Battle for Fallujah.* New York: Bantam.

Zalaquett D. (1999) 'La Reconstrucción de la Unidad Nacional y el Legado de Violaciones de Los Derechos Humanos', *Perspectivas* vol. 2. http://www.cdh.uchile.cl/articulos/Zalaquett/Reconstr_Unidad_Nacional_Perspectivas_.pdf

Zartman, I.W. (2000) 'Introduction'. In I.W. Zartman, ed. *Traditional Cures for Modern Conflicts: African Conflict Medicine.* Boulder, CO: Lynne Rienner.

29

URBAN PLANNING
AND POLICY

Scott A. Bollens

Planning interventions and policies in cities can play supportive and even catalytic roles in regional and national peacebuilding. There exist several types of practical policy approaches able to move cities of deep ethnic and nationalistic conflict toward greater normalization of daily and political life. This discussion synthesizes findings from 17 years of research involving over 240 interviews with political leaders, planners, architects, community representatives, and academics in the politically contested cities of Jerusalem, Beirut, Belfast, Johannesburg, Nicosia, Sarajevo, Mostar, Bilbao, and Barcelona (Bollens 2012). These cities are 'polarized' where two or more ethnically-conscious groups—divided by religion, language, and/or culture and perceived history—have been or currently are in deep and intractable conflict. Ethnic identity and nationalism combine to create pressures for group rights, autonomy, or even territorial separation.

Cities matter amid nationalistic and ethnic inter-group conflict. Many immediate and existential foundations of inter-group conflict frequently lie in daily urban life and across local ethnic divides and, importantly, it is at this micro level that antagonisms can be most directly influenced by government interventions aimed at their amelioration. After overt conflict and war, debates over urban space and its remaking can become potent proxies for addressing unresolved and inflamed socio-political issues that are too difficult to directly confront after societal breakage (Rowe and Sarkis 1998). The city is important in peacebuilding because it is in the streets and neighborhoods of urban agglomerations that there is the negotiation over, and clarification of, abstract concepts such as democracy, fairness, and tolerance. Debates over proposed projects and discussion of physical place provide opportunities to anchor and negotiate dissonant meanings in a post-conflict society; indeed, there are few opportunities other than debates about urban life where these antagonistic impulses take such concrete forms in need of pragmatic negotiation. The city, asserts Berman (1988), offers perhaps the only kind of environment in which modern values such as tolerance and freedom can be realized. Peacebuilding in cities seeks not the well-publicized handshakes of national political elites, but rather the more mundane, yet ultimately more meaningful, nods of respect and recognition of ethnically diverse urban neighbors as they confront each other in their daily interactions.

Lefebvre (1996) views cities as the territorial locations most likely to generate democratic institutions and practices. The importance of the local place is brought out by Harvey (2009), who argues that globalization should be rooted in human experience and specific places rather than linked to illusory, universal ideals that cause more harm than good on the ground. He contends that processes aimed at justice and liberation 'can never take place outside of space and time, outside of place making...' (p. 260). Polese and Stren (2000) identify several domains of local policy—including governance, social welfare, public services, housing, transport, employment, and building of inclusive public spaces—that can be implemented in ways to increase institutional and territorial inclusion and help build durable urban bridges.

It is in a city where urban practitioners and leaders must do the hard work of creating the practical elements of a multinational democracy, one that avoids the extremes of an engineered and subordinating assimilation, on the one hand, and an unbounded and fracture-prone multinationalism, on the other. Such a balancing act takes place most fundamentally in decision-making forums and lived experiences grounded in the city. Through our shaping of the city, we construct the contours of multinational democracy.

> But you cannot show me—even supposing democracy is possible between victors and the people they have captured—what a democratic space looks like. What effect can the mere shape of a wall, the curve of a street, lights and plants, have in weakening the grip of power or shaping the desire for justice?
>
> Anwar Nusseibeh, in Sennett (1999: 274)

> The politics of conflict is hard to relate to urban design.
>
> Richard Sennett (1999: 274)

Planning practitioners intervening in ethnically volatile cities operate in a political labyrinth, confronting the 'contradictory, idiosyncratic, and microscale territorial conflicts' that characterize divided cities and rival groups (Calame and Charlesworth 2009: 172). They are faced with a challenging dilemma—to respond to group wishes and sharpen territorial identity or to focus on the commonalities of the city and lessen divisions. For some urban scholars, the key is for practitioners to become more attuned to group identity as a criterion within planning processes and decisions (Neill 2004; Amin 2002; Umemoto 2001; Burayidi 2000; Sandercock 1998). This implies an 'expanded view' of planning practice wherein planning plays a more deliberative role in improving inter-group relations (Umemoto 2003). For others, the critical objective is for planners to recognize but also help transcend such urban and societal divisions (Marcuse and van Kempen 2002; Baum 2000). Borja and Castells (1997) assert that city residents' ability to maintain distinct cultural identities stimulates a sense of belonging that is needed amidst globalization; at the same, communication between cultures must be present to counter cultural fragmentation and local tribalism.

> Cities, by definition, are about conflict and contested space. It's how you manage conflict that is the issue.
>
> Paul Sweeney (1995)

A common reaction by planners and policymakers in politically contested cities has been to create urban spaces that are anonymous or neutral in character, assuming that if space belongs to no one in particular that it can be used by everyone. Yet, Sennett (1993) cautions against such an approach, asserting that character-less neutrality actually helps us learn how to hide from difference. The open consideration of violence, of the 'other', in the making of urban form has been repressed and not openly acknowledged (Sennett 1993). Is there a way, alternatively, for policymakers to more openly acknowledge group-based differences and their important influences on urban life and function, and to build an urban policy framework for understanding and dealing with such differences in constructive ways? Can practitioners in urban polarized places go beyond the 'mantra of neutrality' and engage more explicitly with the challenge of multiple and contesting publics (Calame and Charlesworth 2009: 171)? It is to this possibility that I now turn.

I examine interventions and strategic approaches that employ urban planning and policy to advance urban peace and co-existence. Many of these strategies seek to enhance urban stability and mutual co-existence through manipulation of the built environment. Such modification of the built environment amid conflict and contestation is certainly not an end-all. Practitioners must not fall into an environmental determinist frame, believing that changes in the physical environment shape social behavior so extensively that urban peace will result. Planning actions will not turn around a society that is politically splintered or unraveled; they cannot create peace where it does not exist in people's hearts and souls. What urban policies can do, however, and it is significant, is to create physical and psychological spaces that can co-contribute to, and actualize, political stability and co-existence in cities. Deeply entrenched problems of nationalistic conflict are certainly not amenable to simple, one-dimensional solutions. Thus, urban planning interventions need to be part of a broader and multi-faceted approach addressing root issues of political grievance related to political disempowerment and institutional bias.

In the face of conflict and violence, the challenge is not whether public authorities should or should not take action amidst an unstable city. In almost all cities, governments take action when the personal safety of their middle and upper classes is threatened. Rather, the question becomes what types of governmental actions will be undertaken and how these can contribute to urban peace, stability, and mutual co-existence. A common response by politicians and developers in the midst of such crises is to build walls and dividers, increase police and military presence, and build gated communities that seal the middle class, elites and members of an advantaged in-group away from problems. Yet, actions that create physical segregation of groups or facilitate psychological separation may purchase short-term relief at the cost of long-term societal instability. An exclusionary, unequal metropolis does not enhance urban stability and co-existence. Rather, it is the increased interaction of diverse groups and individuals in the workplace and neighborhood and the normalization of urban fabric, *in combination with* a frontal assault upon the root issues of political grievance, that are critical elements in the strengthening of urban co-existence in politically contested cities.

Urban policymakers and practitioners in the fields of planning, urban design, and engineering have within their power the capacity to foster an 'unconventional' sense of urban stability, one built on sustainable co-existence rather than constructed through the more conventional means of police and military might and walled and divided districts.

Intervention strategies and tactics

I advance for consideration by local government administrators and nongovernmental organizations a set of city-building and urban design principles that aim to mitigate socio-economic and political tensions in situations of inter-group conflict.

Engage in equity planning that addresses underlying root issues

Material improvement in urban life is essential to enhancing human well-being for those least well off or historically disadvantaged, but is not sufficient in cities of nationalistic conflict if processes of political inclusion, acknowledgement and reconciliation are absent. It is crucial that policymaking aimed at alleviating the urban symptoms of poverty and inequality be linked with policies that directly confront the structural inequalities and power imbalances that are at the root of inter-group conflict and violence. Development interventions should not only address physical urban inequalities, but also seek to counter individual and group-based feelings of historic grievance, marginality, disempowerment, and discrimination. In post-conflict situations, reconstruction must not solely be physical but also address the social and psychological scars that remain after the active conflict period ends. The psychological and political insecurities that led to inter-group violence and physical division, if left unaddressed after active conflict, will obstruct spatial and political normalization over time.

Planning practitioners and policymakers should be cognizant of, and seek to counter, the structural causes of people's grievances—those pervasive factors that have become built into the policies, structures and fabric of a society and which create the pre-conditions for violent conflict (Africa Peace Forum et al. 2004). Urban strategies and interventions should be targeted in ways that address the local manifestations of long-term structural causes of conflict and tension. Development and planning priorities involving the allocation of basic infrastructure, services, and employment assistance should be used to counter individual and group-based feelings of marginality, disempowerment, and discrimination; in addition, they should address the meeting of basic human needs—public services, human rights, employment opportunities, food and shelter, and participation in decision-making. Several types of governance programs can compensate for past marginalization—employment equity initiatives, political inclusiveness mechanisms, municipal assistance to community organizations, increased access and equity in service delivery, anti-racism initiatives, and use of inclusive municipal images such as symbols and language (Good 2009). Building capacity for a historically disadvantaged group in the city may require some autonomy in city governance, sufficient and contiguous land available for development, mobility and permeability of city boundaries, and security.

The use of planning and policymaking to advance redistribution and reconciliation borrows from the 'equity planning' approach developed by American urban scholars Davidoff (1965) and Krumholz and Forester (1990), a strategy based on social justice goals that employs progressive planning actions to lessen urban inequalities.[1] Such an approach has been used in the conflict- and violence-prone Colombian cities of Medellin and Bogota, where there has been the purposeful and progressive use of public investment (in particular, parks, open space, and transit access) to enhance poorer areas and lessen crime rates (Romero 2007; Kraul 2006). Under former Mayor Enrique Penalosa, Bogota positioned the re-direction of urban priorities and policies as key in promoting social equity and instituted a policymaking model based on equal rights of all people to transportation, education, and open space.

Use planning process and deliberations to empower marginalized groups

Urbanists and planners have power emanating from the fact that they engage at the interface between the built environment and political processes. Urbanists have the ability to connect the local/urban level to the national/political level, to link everyday problems faced by city residents to unjust political structures that underlie and produce these urban symptoms. In three of the cases I have studied, urbanists used neighborhood-based planning deliberations to empower marginalized groups and to connect to broader political opposition to existing regimes. In Johannesburg during the last years of the South African apartheid regime, protests over local payments for rent and city services in Greater Soweto were connected by local activists to more fundamental challenges of the apartheid state, in particular the need to restructure local government along non-racial lines. In Belfast, working-class neighborhood planning efforts countering plans for demolition and population displacement existed alongside the Catholic republican insurrection against the state and British direct rule (Shirlow and Murtagh 2006). And, in Barcelona, urbanists during the Franco regime helped local neighborhood groups connect local place-based problems to larger political ailments (Bollens 2007).

The process of planning and policymaking is itself important and should be used in a deliberate fashion to empower excluded groups and build civil society. Project design and interventions should empower those groups in the city working toward peaceful solutions and co-existence, and the process of project design should be structured to increase communication across different urban groups. In cities of competing nationalistic group identities, public participation from the start is vital in urbanism processes. Beyond the project benefits, this participation in deliberations is of vital significance in reconstructing a politically contested and fragmented city because it demonstrates how democratic deliberation works. The process of planning and urban development should be organized in ways that engage city residents across ethnic backgrounds in projects having common and shared benefits.

Inclusive processes can generate new relationships and new knowledge about how to cope with, and address, inter-group conflict. Concrete, tangible city building issues provide a laboratory and incubator for cross-ethnic inter-group dialogue, negotiations, and joint production of outcomes. In contrast to the common win–lose psychological dynamic associated with ideology, identity, and nationalism, negotiations over tangible urban projects and issues often allow for win–win situations. These inclusive processes should not be viewed as a one-time, project-based endeavor, but rather as sustained over time and ongoing. Such processes allow participants to get to know each other as pragmatic partners, even if nationalistic differences remain. The planning process should be positioned not as a technical exercise, but as a social, political, and organizational mechanism that can increase feelings of inclusion, recognition, and group self-worth.

Create flexibility and porosity of urban built form

Urban planning and policy interventions should seek as much flexibility of urban built form as possible, choosing spatial development paths that maximize future options. Except in conditions where extreme need dictates their use, walls, urban buffers, and other urban forms that delineate physical segregation of groups or facilitate psychological separation should not be built. This strategy allows for greater mixing and freedom of choice of populations in the future, if and when inter-group conflict abates and there can be some normalization of urban living. This does not constitute an integration or coercive assimilation strategy, but rather seeks to create an urban porosity that allows normal, healthier urban processes to occur when individuals and governments are ready.

The design of spaces to encourage interaction and positive behaviors should be prioritized ahead of design approaches that discourage unwanted behavior and commonly separate and contain antagonistic groups. In spaces constructed to encourage interaction, there should be an absence of undesirable, intimidating, and single group identifying artifacts. Instead, there should be functional and aesthetic equal treatment of different ethnic users of such facilities as multicultural community centers. Facilities and activity zones should be built that attract desired clientele who can crowd out undesirables. In terms of specific project or building design, there should be dual entry/exit ways for antagonistic communities so that a facility is perceived by all as located in shared space but is nonetheless functionally connected to ethnic space on either side. Uses that promote interaction are distinctly different from designs such as target hardening, access control, fences and physical boundaries, natural territorial enforcement, and natural surveillance that retard interaction.

A strategic intervention approach to increasing flexibility and porosity of urban form places premiums on actions at borders and interfaces that exist between different ethnic neighborhoods. It is at these places where different parts or layers of the city meet that hybridization can increase, connecting people and activities at 'points of intensity' and along 'thresholds' (Ellin 2006). Creation of urban porosity must take place, however, simultaneously with or after the addressing of core issues of political inequality, disempowerment, and group identity that ignites nationalistic conflict. Absent such engagement with root causes of conflict, interventions such as the building of streets in a way that encourages travel across different parts of the urban fabric or the creation of ethnically mixed housing complexes may actually stimulate violence and conflict (UNHSP 2007). It is critically important to address core issues prior to, or concurrent with, manipulation of urban built form. With core issues included as part of the strategy, urban interventions can increasingly knit different parts of the city together and have an increased chance to enhance mutual co-existence in residential and non-residential environments.

Creating flexibility and porosity of urban form should not be confused with integration of individuals and groups. Indeed, inter-group segregation is an important means for stability in the short term. Amid nationalistic conflict and material imbalances, the mixing of population is not possible in the short term and there often is the need to maintain group identity boundaries. Peace processes can make identity boundaries uncertain and permeable. Thus, in the short term, such boundaries should be respected so that feelings of fear and threat do not retard progress in peacebuilding. Usually interaction between urban ethnic groups would lessen conflict, but positive evolution in inter-group relations that is natural in other cities is not possible in polarized cities if political root issues and grievances are unaddressed. Efforts to bring peoples together prematurely will increase—not attenuate—conflict, at least in the short term. At the same time, public interventions should not foreclose through the physical hardening of divisions the *option* of ethnic integration for those people and groups who are ready for such a move in the future if and when the city normalizes.

Intervene in city landscape with sensitivity to differences across sectarian geographies

When contemplating interventions into the polarized city, planners should be cognizant of differences between urban ethnic homelands and frontiers and between 'hard' and 'soft' interfaces. In cities where ethnic and religious identity are primary drivers of political action, local authorities should, through their regulatory powers, locate sensitive land uses having cultural and historic salience (churches, mosques, private schools, monocultural community centers) within urban ethnic homeland neighborhoods identified with specific cultural groups. At the same time, they should encourage in interface, or frontier, areas between cultural neighborhoods those types of land uses that encourage mixing of different groups in a supportive environment. Joint and mixed land uses (public space, residential, commercial) can be intentionally placed at interface areas between competing (potentially conflicting) groups of an ethnic or other identifiable nature. In this strategy, there is the creation of 'everyman's land' of mutual use and benefit where each side can use or pass through to the other side without being cut off; continuity replaces cut-offs and enclaves; porosity replaces borders.

In order to combat hardened enclaving and partitioning created during conflict periods, policymakers should establish a clear spatial-tactical programming orientation to future urban interventions that includes prioritization and sequencing components. In some urban districts, connectivity across the ethnic divide is a suitable goal; in others, consolidation of ethnic neighborhoods should be pre-eminent. Where there exist 'soft', ambiguously delineated interfaces, the enhancement of permeability of spatial divisions through joint use and mixed activities should be a first priority. Interventions should seek connectivity and linkages building outward from middle class or ethnically mixed areas. In contrast, consolidation of ethnic territoriality and identity should be the guiding criterion where there exist 'hard' interfaces of strict definition, lingering violence, and the presence of ethnic militia guardians.

This interface strategy uses the 'soft' edges of sectarian territories to create common ground and cross-cultural meeting places (Khalaf 1998). There is the creation of 'weak borders rather than strong walls' and the enabling of uses and activities in certain neutral areas that will not give the impression that a particular community's territory is being invaded (Khalaf 1998: 142). Illustrative of this thinking, Israeli planner A. Mazor (1994) uses the metaphor of a river whose banks are in separate sovereignties. Rather than being seen as a dividing line, the river can be viewed as providing mutual benefit, wherein 'both sides can row together in the river without being regarded as crossing the border.' Spaces are constructed malleably enough to permit constant alterations and shifts; porous and malleable demarcations are established rather than confining and exclusionary boundaries.[2]

In cities such as Belfast where there are efforts to advance national political progress through local actions, planners in housing and development agencies are debating the tactics and timing of interventions aimed at normalizing the hardened sectarian geographies of that city. The Northgate development strategy of the mid-1990s in volatile North Belfast illustrates how there could be the tactical introduction of a new development project to justify physical alterations to a potentially inflammatory interface area. It also shows how a public agency is capable of analyzing the potential social, spatial, political and psychological impacts of their actions on ethnic community identity. The analysis takes stock of each of the major participant groups in the urban sub-system and how negative public reaction may be mitigated within a contested, sectarianized environment.

The local problems in the planning area—Duncairn Gardens—were multiple and intense (DOENI 1990). A permanent peacewall was constructed during the sectarian 'Troubles' that divided the Catholic New Lodge neighborhood from the Protestant Tiger's Bay neighborhood. Catholic housing stock, insufficient to meet demand, was endangered further by violence. Much of the Catholic housing fronting the peacewall had front sides grated to prevent damage from petrol bombs, and back doors were used instead for access. Tiger's Bay was fast becoming a ghost town due to Protestant out-migration with major dereliction of building stock. The remaining Protestant population felt frightened, embattled, and insecure (Murtagh 1995). Into this volatile ethnic environment, public authorities proposed an economic development district on the Protestant side that aspired to create neutral and mutually beneficial territory. There would also be redevelopment and consolidation of housing in Tiger's Bay. The strategy overall was intended to soften the rigidity of this line of confrontation; as one government participant stated (identity withheld upon request), this represented a 'novel approach for effectively fudging the line of division.'

The Northgate strategy employed a finely tuned sensitivity to sectarianism and its social, spatial and psychological correlates.[3] Sectarian geography is mapped in detail, documenting potentially inflammatory Catholic residential incursion into formerly 'mixed' areas. The report states that 'there is a collective perception in the Protestant Tiger's Bay community of being gradually outflanked by Catholic territory.' Most revealing of government's awareness is the section examining the possible community responses—from local residents, local politicians, local church authorities, and local commercial interests—to DOENI's economic and housing actions. The area is characterized as one of mutual suspicion, home to strong paramilitary organizations on both sides, and where Protestants are afraid of the Catholic spread into Tiger's Bay. The major problem, cites the DOENI report, is that the project 'might be opposed on sectarian grounds, as taking away too much of the former Tiger's Bay area.' The working group worries that 'major irrational opposition could create significant obstacles; and that many of the local residents could be easily persuaded by individual politicians or others claiming to represent the community.' To diffuse possible negative reaction, the report suggests that an existing Tiger's Bay community group with views sympathetic to the project's overall goals be nurtured and supported. In this way, local politicians and extremist residents may be effectively countered.

In order to guide public interventions in contested urban settings toward more ethnically sensitive outcomes, planners should develop new methodologies that will evaluate in systematic ways the effects on urban ethnic groups of proposed land uses of certain types (those having cultural importance) and in certain spatial areas (areas of interface and mixing). Ethnic impact assessments can explicitly account for potential social-psychological impacts of the proposed land use on the respective cultural communities of the city, and should be used in the decision-making process regarding development proposals. Planners should seek to understand the 'micro' structure of the city in terms of identity and people's perceptions of places and spaces. Special focus should be on 'spaces of risk' in the urban landscape—lived spaces that have low levels of trust and where people feel vulnerable and defenseless against conflict (Jabareen 2006). In such volatile areas, an ill-conceived project can activate latent urban tension to a more intense level.

Ethnic impact analysis at the urban level may borrow some of the nascent methodologies being developed by international and nongovernmental organizations. An example of conflict-sensitive analysis pertaining to public intervention is United Nations Development Programme (2003), which advocates for a better understanding of the linkages between development and conflict. It proposes a methodology, 'conflict-related development analysis', which focuses attention on the structural, underlying issues that lay the foundation for conflict and upon which more visible and immediate causes take place. The Federation of Canadian Municipalities has proposed that a systematic 'peace and conflict impact assessment' (PCIA) be included in the design, implementation, and evaluation of all municipal activities in conflict-prone areas (Bush 2004). Meanwhile, a group of nongovernmental organizations recognizes that development can help prevent violent conflict, yet sometimes also inadvertently exacerbate it, and calls for greater 'conflict sensitivity' in humanitarian interventions and development project planning (Africa Peace Forum et al. 2004).

Protect and promote the collective public sphere

In order for the seed of urban stability and co-existence to grow, the public sphere should be developed physically. Planners should revitalize and redevelop public spaces, historic areas, and other urban public assets as places of interaction and neutrality that promote healthy inter-group and interpersonal life. Instead of focusing on the inflammatory choice between segregation versus integration of residential areas, concentration on improving public spaces offers a third approach that is less politically difficult. Here, there is the push for mixed public spaces rather than mixed neighborhoods. The goal is to enable increased cross-ethnic mingling in non-hostile, non-polarizing public environments rather than try the more contentious approach of having different ethnicities co-habitate residentially.

The physical creation of public spaces, as part of a comprehensive set of interventions that address root issues of conflict, can encourage activities that are the grounds for remaking an urban cross-ethnic citizenship. In Barcelona, in the early democratic years after Franco, architects and designers employed small-scale and context-sensitive improvements in numerous public spaces throughout working-class neighborhoods as a way to illuminate the benefits of the new democracy (Bollens 2007). Public areas can facilitate mix and contact among a heretofore fragmented populous, facilitate and provide avenues for collective expression, and can contribute to cohesion and social equality.

Emphasize short-term tactical physical interventions while articulating a peace-promoting long-range strategic vision

Planning and development agencies should balance emphasis on creating a peace-promoting long-range vision or plan with short-term physical interventions that create and reinforce urban peacebuilding principles. Long-range visions should clearly demarcate a break from the past and articulate a shared city of co-existence. At the same time, for actions in the short term, development agencies should concentrate on specific interventions in the urban fabric that have palpable impacts on people's daily lives and illuminate principles of inter-group mutual co-existence and tolerance. These improvements should have explicit and noticeable equalization objectives and be focused in poorer areas and in areas where aggrieved groups live.

A strategy of 'urban acupuncture' consists of 'catalytic small scale interventions with potentially wide-ranging impacts' which are realizable in a relatively short time (Frampton 2000). Acupuncture interventions in polarized cities should occur at strategic points in the urban fabric—points of rupture, stagnation, trauma, and dysfunction. These interventions contribute to activating places by making connections and caring for neglected or abandoned 'in between' spaces or 'no-man's lands' (Ellin 2006). Because urban acupuncture can be more responsive to site-specific social tensions, it is commonly more suited to politically contested cities than is long-range, comprehensive master planning with its efforts at control and order at a larger scale.

Small-scale tactical interventions should seek to modify or soften the rigidities of conflict-period community dynamics in a local area. Wood and Landry (2008) suggest that particular attention be paid to 'zones of encounter'—housing and neighborhoods, education, workplace, marketplace, sports, arts, and the public domain (both public space and public institutions). The making of intercultural spaces should focus on these domains of day-to-day exchange rather than try to create highly designed and engineered spaces that lack salience to everyday life.

Public interventions in the physical landscape should have a spatial–tactical orientation that both repairs past damage and disparities and sets the foundation for more organic integration of divided districts. Post-conflict urbanists will need to address city spaces of overt conflict and war that have robust psychological and symbolic meanings—places of loss, fear, resistance, and martyrdom that often contain different and opposing interpretations (Purbrick, Aulich, and Dawson 2007). In its most blatant forms, the legacies of conflict consist of sites of domination and control that embed historical differences and create physical legacies of inequality and denial. In addressing reconciliation through urban interventions, there should be the acknowledgement of the co-existence of multiple groups and narratives rather than the inscription and imposition of only the victor's narrative in the built landscape.

In the end, politically contested cities challenge us to confront whether we are hopeful or pessimistic about our ability to get along together. A puzzle faced by policymakers in multicultural cities—whether Beirut or Los Angeles, Sarajevo or New York, Jerusalem or Amsterdam, Johannesburg or Paris—is a basic one that forces us to confront our own beliefs and predilections. In an urban situation where there are antagonistic, or potentially antagonistic, ethnic or racial groups, do we as city-builders create opportunities for these groups to mix and interact or do we accommodate and reinforce the development of ethnically pure neighborhoods and districts? Decisions such as these will send emotive symbols to future generations about what we either aspire to in hope or accept in resignation.

Notes

1 The United Nations uses the label "pro-poor" to describe such redistributive urban policy. Another example of the equity approach is the "inclusive city" strategy (UNHSP 2003).
2 Planners and policymakers should also seek to proactively counter development patterns that are potential precursors to physical partitioning in contested urban settings—biased urban service distribution, residential group clustering, growing symbolism of local residential territoriality, and emergence of informal ethnic demarcations in residential space (Calame and Charlesworth 2009).
3 This report by DOENI, *Northgate Enterprise Park: Interim Report*, was never published. This confidentiality is indicative of the perceived sensitivity of dealing with sectarianism in a candid way. The project itself never broke ground.

References

Africa Peace Forum et al. (2004) 'Conflict-Sensitive Approaches to Development, Humanitarian Assistance and Peacebuilding—Tools for Peace and Conflict Impact Assessment', Resource Pack. Available at http://www.amaniafrika.org/resources/conflict-sensitive-approaches-to-development-humanitarian-assistance-and-peacebuilding

Amin, A. (2002) 'Ethnicity and the Multicultural City: Living with Diversity', *Environment and Planning A*, 34(6): 959–980.

Baum, H.S. (2000) 'Culture Matters—But It Shouldn't Matter Too Much', in Burayidi, M.A. (ed.) *Urban Planning in a Multicultural Society*, Westport, CT: Praeger, pp. 115–136.

Berman, M. (1988) *All that is Solid Melts into the Air: The Experience of Modernity*, London: Penguin Press.

Bollens, S.A. (2007) *Cities, Nationalism, and Democratization*, London and New York: Routledge.

Bollens, S.A. (2012) *City and Soul in Divided Societies,* London and New York: Routledge.

Borja, J. and Castells, M. (1997) *Local and Global: The Management of Cities in the Information Age,* London: Earthscan.

Burayidi, M.A. (2000) 'Urban Planning as a Multicultural Canon', in Burayidi, M.A. (ed.) *Urban Planning in a Multicultural Society*, Westport, CT: Praeger, pp. 1–14.

Bush, K. (2004) *Building Capacity for Peace and Unity: The Role of Local Government in Peacebuilding*, Ottawa: Federation of Canadian Municipalities.

Calame, J. and Charlesworth, E. (2009) *Divided Cities: Belfast, Beirut, Jerusalem, Mostar, and Nicosia*, Philadelphia: University of Pennsylvania Press.

Davidoff, P. (1965) 'Advocacy and Pluralism in Planning', *Journal of the American Institute of Planners*, 31: 596–615.

DOENI (1990) *Northgate Enterprise Park: Interim Report*. Unpublished. Belfast: Department of the Environment for Northern Ireland.

Ellin, N. (2006) *Integral Urbanism*, New York: Routledge.

Frampton, K. (2000) 'Seven Points for the Millennium: An Untimely Manifesto', *Journal of Architecture* 5(1): 21–33.

Good, K.R. (2009) *Municipalities and Multiculturalism: The Politics of Immigration in Toronto and Vancouver*, Toronto: University of Toronto Press.

Harvey, D. (2009) *Cosmopolitanism and the Geographies of Freedom*, New York: Columbia University.

Jabareen, Y. (2006) 'Space of Risk: The Contribution of Planning Policies to Conflict in Cities, Lessons from Nazareth', *Planning Theory and Practice*, 7(3): 305–323.

Khalaf, S. (1998) 'Contested Space and the Forging of New Cultural Identities', in Rowe, P.G. and Sarkis, H. (eds) *Projecting Beirut: Episodes in the Construction and Reconstruction of a Modern City*, Munich: Prestel.

Kraul, C. (2006) 'Columbia City Makes a U-turn' *Los Angeles Times*. page A11. October 28.

Krumholz, N. and Forester, J. (1990) *Making Equity Planning Work: Leadership in the Public Sector*, Philadelphia: Temple University Press.

Lefebvre, H. (1996) 'Rhythmanalysis of Mediterranean Cities', in Lefebvre, H. *Writing on Cities*, Oxford: Blackwell.

Marcuse, P. and van Kempen, R. (eds) (2002) *Of States and Cities: The Partitioning of Urban Space*, Oxford: Oxford University Press.

Mazor, A. (1994) Interview with Author. Co-author of Metropolitan Jerusalem Master and Development Plan. Professor of Urban Planning at Technion Institute. Principal, Urban Institute Ltd. (Tel Aviv). December 19.

Murtagh, B. (1995) Interview with Author. University of Ulster, Magee College. London/Derry, Northern Ireland. February 7.

Neill, W. (2004) *Urban Planning and Cultural Identity*, London: Routledge.

Polese, M. and Stren, R. (eds) (2000) *The Social Sustainability of Cities: Diversity and the Management of Change*, Toronto: University of Toronto Press.

Purbrick, L., Aulich, J. and Dawson, G. (2007) *Contested Spaces: Sites, Representations and Histories of Conflict*, New York: Palgrave MacMillan.

Romero, S. (2007) 'Medellin's Nonconformist Mayor Turns Blight to Beauty' *New York Times*, July 15.

Rowe, P.G. and Sarkis, H. (eds) (1998) *Projecting Beirut: Episodes in the Construction and Reconstruction of a Modern City*, Munich: Prestel.

Sandercock, L. (1998) *Towards Cosmopolis: Planning for Multicultural Cities*, Chichester: John Wiley & Sons.

Sennett, R. (1993) 'Introduction', in Khalaf, S. and Khoury, P. (eds) *Recovering Beirut: Urban Design and Post-War Reconstruction*, Leiden: E.J. Brill, pp. 1–10.

Sennett, R. (1999) 'The spaces of democracy', in Beauregard, R. and Body-Gendrot, S. (eds) *The Urban Moment: Cosmopolitan Essays on the Late 20th-century City*, Urban Affairs Annual Reviews, 49, Thousand Oaks, CA: Sage, pp. 273–285.

Shirlow, P. and Murtagh, B. (2006) *Belfast: Segregation, Violence and the City*, London: Pluto Press.

Sweeney, P. (1995) Interview with Author. Advisor, Department of the Environment for Northern Ireland. February 15.

Umemoto, K. (2001) 'Walking in Another's Shoes: Epistemological Challenges in Participatory Planning', *Journal of Planning Education and Research*, 21: 17–31.

Umemoto, K. (2003) Best Award Commentary related to 'Walking in Another's Shoes: Epistemological Challenges in Participatory Planning', *Journal of Planning Education and Research*, 22: 308–309.

United Nations Development Programme (UNDP) (2003) 'Conflict-related Development Analysis', Bureau for Crisis Prevention and Recovery, October, New York: UNDP.

United Nations Human Settlements Programme (UNHSP) (2003) *The Challenge of Slums: Global Report on Human Settlements 2003*, London: Earthscan.

United Nations Human Settlements Programme (UNHSP) (2007) *Enhancing Urban Safety and Security: Global Report on Human Settlements 2007*, London: Earthscan.

Wood, P. and Landry, C. (2008) *The Intercultural City: Planning for Diversity Advantage*, London: Earthscan.

CONCLUSION

Roger Mac Ginty

Peacebuilding is no longer a young field of study or practice. Substantial scholarship and practical experience exists. Yet, Gerald Steinberg (Chapter 3) is correct to urge caution: what works in one scenario may not necessarily work in another. Moreover, peacebuilding 'successes' seem sparse when measured against other conflict-reducing measures such as suppression or the exhaustion of combatants.

We should not be too negative, however. Just as human history is packed with war, violence and the ensuing social and economic costs, it is also packed with considerable tolerance, coexistence, and social progress. Individuals and communities are adept at developing systems to regulate conflict and minimise disruption. This 'everyday conflict resolution' or everyday diplomacy is often overlooked in the academic and policy literature. Instead, emphasis is placed on conflict resolution 'experts' and 'professionals' who usually come from outside of the conflict-affected society and, through peacebuilding initiatives, projects and programmes, are expected to bring peace. This top-down or outside-in model is often unrealistic, yet it prevails in the thinking and action of many international organisations and INGOs. The danger is that the everyday conflict-avoidance skills of so-called 'ordinary' people are ignored or downgraded in importance. Rather than benefit from peacebuilding projects and programmes, the vast majority of individuals and communities in the aftermath of violent conflict have just had to 'get on with things'. They have not benefited from specialist support. They have had to get on with the daily humdrum of survival, rearing children and making a living. In contexts where members of opposing groups have had to share the same territory, this has meant the peace of what John Darby called 'the weak smile and the hard swallow'. This 'grin and bear it' peace has involved conflict-avoidance techniques such as not raising contentious issues in discussion with out-group members or using self-restraint in the face of provocation for fear of losing employment. The peace described here is a 'negative peace', although sometimes only a negative peace is possible.

But how can a negative peace turn into a positive peace? This requires adopting a holistic approach to peace that goes beyond stopping violence and engages with the range of social and economic factors that often underpin conflict. Clearly this is easier said than done, but this book does contain numerous examples of peacebuilding that go beyond the bare minimum. Whether it is educational initiatives, urban planning or indigenous approaches to peace, there is a rich repertoire of attempts to move peace from a cessation of hostilities towards a more all-embracing approach. In the best possible scenario, peacebuilding becomes embodied in the way of life for individuals, communities and institutions and is manifest in mutual respect and tolerance. This is probably too much to ask in many instances and what we see is a variable geometry of peace in societies emerging from violent conflict: more progress on some issues and in some localities than in others.

There are encouraging signs of change on the peacebuilding landscape. Firstly, there is some evidence that increasing numbers of international organisations, bilateral donors, INGOs and NGOs are moving beyond sloganising about 'local' and 'sustainable' peace towards concrete action in these areas. Certainly more sophisticated understandings of conflict have been developed in recent decades, especially with regard to the links between conflict and development. From these clearer understandings of the dynamics of conflict comes a recognition that peacebuilding efforts have to be long term, locally grounded and culturally sensitive. Of course, the international peacebuilding infrastructure is something of a supertanker and it takes a long time to turn around. But the 2011 'New Deal for Engagement with Fragile States' does show a greater awareness among international peacebuilding actors of the folly of short-termism and top-down peacebuilding. It also recognises the dangers of an addiction to overly technocratic interventions.

A second sign of change on the peacebuilding landscape is a greater prominence of actors from the global south – that is, countries that have first-hand experience of contemporary violent conflict. One remarkable trend in recent years has been the almost complete withdrawal of major western states from United Nations Peacekeeping. The overwhelming majority of UN Peacekeepers come from developing world states. The African Union has adopted a more prominent role in peace-support operations, and there is evidence of 'south–south transfer' in the form of groups such as Viva Rio, a Brazilian NGO that is working to calm gang violence in Haiti. China is becoming more assertive in international fora, and it seems unlikely that the United Nations Permanent Five can perpetuate the fiction that we're in 1945 for ever. Slowly, over the coming decades, we should be able to see the practical experience of peacebuilding actors from the global south shape the language and policies of peacebuilding. Up until this point, actors from the global north have been in the driving seat.

Linked to this rebalancing of the peacebuilding landscape is a third factor: the punctured hubris of a number of states from the global north who had taken a lead in developing peacebuilding policy over the past two decades. This particularly applies to the United States (somewhat chastened after the disastrous entanglements in Iraq and Afghanistan), but also a number of financially embarrassed European states. The confidence of the liberal internationalism of the late 1990s and early 2000s has been replaced by a less confident attitude towards intervention. The 'Arab Spring', or the series of popular uprisings in the Middle East and North Africa, owed very little to leading states in the global north who have been lecturing about 'peace' and 'democracy' for decades. Indeed, these revolutions revealed the irrelevance of leading states in the global north as moral guides and exemplars. The damaged confidence among the self-appointed international 'peacebuilders' may free up space for other actors, particularly from the global south, to make their mark on peacebuilding.

A major theme in this book has been how to 'read' peacebuilding. The book began with a chapter that posited how much of the literature on peacebuilding – especially from the policy sphere – is in the problem-solving paradigm. That is, it focuses on immediate policy issues without much of an awareness of wider structural issues that often underpin conflict. The past decade has seen an upsurge in critical scholarship that has critiqued the limitations of the problem-solving paradigm. To some extent, these criticisms have reached the policy sphere and there are signs (alluded to above) of greater reflexivity in peacebuilding policy. The task for future scholars is to take the critical scholarship to the next level: how can it maintain its critical stance yet offer relevant assistance to societies seeking to lower the costs of violence? How can it have policy relevance without being part of a conflict-reinforcing system? The 'critique without co-option' stance is a difficult one to maintain, yet a careful reading of UN and other documents over the past few years does reveal how the world's premier peace-interested body is increasingly aware of the failings of earlier peacebuilding efforts.

It is important that peacebuilding is not something that we think of as happening 'over there', in a faraway country in the global south. Certainly these contexts are most likely to experience civil war and to require immediate peacebuilding. Yet many of the roots of violent conflict and the means to turn the tide against conflict reside in the global north. Citizens in the global north could take four steps that would have a practical impact on conflict and peacebuilding in the global south. Firstly, they could pressurise their governments to sponsor serious national and international legislation on the arms trade, particularly the transfer of small arms and ammunition. Twelve billion bullets are produced annually, enough to kill everyone on the planet – twice (Hopkins 2012). The international trade in ammunition is virtually unregulated. The arms trade is big business and much employment in the global north rests upon it. The ethics of this industry are too often conveniently parked. Just as citizen campaigns stopped slavery in the global north, there is room for citizens to take action against the export of the means of death. Secondly, states in the global north could take the United Nations more seriously. It is easy to criticise the UN, yet it is merely the sum of its parts (the collective will of states, particularly the five permanent members). The United States in particular has downgraded the importance of the UN, preferring unilateral action and 'coalitions of the willing'. Whether one likes it or not, the UN is the planet's premier conflict management body and, to be more effective, it requires a reinvestment of faith. Its greatest weapon is moral power, but if leading states undermine its status then dictators can ignore it. Again citizen action in the global north can seek to award the UN and the International Criminal Court greater prominence in daily political discourse.

A third way in which citizens in the global north can positively contribute to changing peacebuilding is to hold the international financial institutions to account. The International Monetary Fund, World Bank and others wield immense power particularly in societies emerging from violent conflict. It is these unelected institutions that often set the economic parameters in which peace is built. The international financial institutions often engage in intrusive and restrictive economic interventions that perpetuate uneven trading regimes, the debts of former dictators, and – crucially – limit the ability of post-conflict societies to engage in welfare activities. If post-conflict governments are unable to look after the most vulnerable in their societies, often because of tight financial targets, then there is a real danger of a population becoming alienated from the state and lacking faith in political processes. In a large number of post-conflict states, for example El Salvador, Kosovo, and Mozambique, electoral participation rates have declined precipitously. In part, this is because citizens see no link between democratic participation and an improvement in their material circumstances or everyday security. Part of the problem is that post-conflict governments are unable to finance social provision because of restrictions by international financial institutions. There are signs that the World Bank is changing, but it remains a rather remote institution, insulated from popular opinion. This is something that citizens in the global north could address.

A fourth activity that citizens in the global north can engage in is to pressurise their governments to adopt a more consistently ethical stance on foreign policy. Some states that prey on their citizens have become the target of international pressure, often in the form of sanctions or International Criminal Court indictments. But other states enjoy protected status. Bahrain's regime has engaged in systematic exclusion of its Shia population. As home to the United States Fifth Fleet its ruling dynasty has escaped much international pressure. Saudi Arabia and Israel have similarly privileged positions despite shocking human rights records. International citizen pressure in the late 1980s made it clear that South African apartheid was unacceptable and, if sufficiently mobilised, can do so again in relation to many other states that maintain iniquitous regimes.

A final point to make is that peacebuilding requires bravery, particularly in societies emerging from violent conflict in which enmity still remains. It may require individuals and groups to put their heads above the parapet and to act in ways that are socially unacceptable to their own group. It is understandable that many people find it easier to follow group conventions. Yet there have been startling instances of individuals and groups who have gone against the grain, often at personal risk. This book began with an example from Northern Ireland so it seems appropriate to end with one. In 2005, sectarian graffiti was daubed on a Catholic Church in Northern Ireland. Early the next morning, a Protestant pastor organised his own congregation to go to the Catholic Church to help with the clean-up (BBC 2005). Such an act required courage and humility. It set the Protestants up for criticism from within their own community. But it is acts like this that make a difference and can puncture the cynicism and lack of knowledge upon which many conflicts rest.

References

BBC (2005) '"Solidarity" over church clean up', BBC News Website. Accessed at http://news.bbc.co.uk/1/hi/northern_ireland/4144372.stm. Last accessed 19 June 2012.

Hopkins, N. (2012) 'Arms trade treaty must include global sale of ammunition, urges Oxfam', *Guardian*, 30 May.

INDEX

9/11 64, 107, 110, 151, 198, 201, 228, 245, 300, 319, 327

Aceh 239–40
Afghanistan 6, 27, 60, 64, 191, 198, 202, 203, 211, 215, 221, 223, 227, 228, 229, 341, 342
Africa Union 6, 252, 313, 388
agriculture 19, 231, 240, 264, 266–8, 270
Al Qaeda 202
American Civil War 92, 178
amnesty 171, 184, 233, 256, 363, 368
Amnesty International 253
An Agenda for Peace 26, 27, 28, 29, 348
Annan, Kofi 113, 205
anthropology 93, 132–43
Arab 'Spring' 76, 78, 302–3, 352, 388
Arafat, Yassir 42–3
Australia 300

Basque country 167
bin Laden, Osama 203
Boulding, Kenneth 149, 152–3, 154
Bosnia and Herzegovina 15, 19, 180, 200, 229, 238, 326
bottom-up approaches 7, 18, 43–5, 134, 197, 222, 238–9, 242–3, 245, 246, 258, 272–86, 287, 290, 297, 299, 304, 319, 321, 368–70
Burundi 31, 369–70
Bush, George W. 27, 178

Cambodia 143, 232
Catholic Church 71, 77, 243, 282, 390
ceasefire, 48, 49, 62, 154, 166–7, 253, 254, 312

Central African Republic 29
children 1, 60, 63, 74, 99, 238, 264, 267–8, 270, 282, 290, 293 child soldiers 127, 225, 230
China 32, 388
Christianity 71
civil society 28, 31, 33, 69, 160, 162, 166, 213, 216, 253, 314, 317, 319, 320, 329, 347–59, 361, 363, 368, 372
Cold War 26, 37, 39, 117, 149, 151, 178, 198, 199, 206, 215, 217
Collier, Paul 227, 287
Colombia 45, 238, 242–6, 378
colonialism and empire 37, 109, 137, 140–2, 163, 167, 365
commemoration 162
compensation 179
conflict management 137, 172, 174, 183, 243, 293, 304, 330
conflict prevention 199, 202, 316
conflict resolution 142, 162, 237–8, 256, 272, 290–1, 297, 349, 354
conflict transformation 349, 354
contact theory 37, 38–9, 41, 44–5, 46, 48, 118, 121–4, 298
corruption 5, 13, 19, 30, 220, 329, 363
Council of Europe 252
counterinsurgency 203–4, 327, 369
Cox, Robert 12, 21, 22
crime 168, 171, 207, 227, 233, 245, 289, 338
critical paradigm 3, 4, 7, 11–24, 109, 110, 332, 338, 389
culture 136–40
customary see indigenous

Dayton Accord 135
DDR (disarmament, demobilization and
    reintegration) 30, 112, 185, 186, 222,
    225–36, 241, 255, 312, 338
democracy and democratisation 27, 28, 30,
    81, 109, 113, 139, 288, 290, 301, 303,
    312, 318–19, 330, 353, 376, 388
democratic peace 153, 191
development 30, 197, 199, 203, 205–6, 212,
    213–14, 225, 238, 240, 245–6, 269, 300,
    312, 315, 330
DFID 213, 301, 313, 318
displacement 263–9, 272
donors 69, 73, 113, 199, 206, 213–16, 218,
    221, 222, 243, 314, 318, 325, 327–32,
    337, 353, 355, 388

East Timor 43, 139–40, 240, 328
economics 147–58, 160, 279, 312, 330
education 1, 18, 118, 123, 125–6, 128,
    171–2, 177–80, 227, 239, 243, 246, 265,
    267–70, 280, 287–95, 297, 298, 349, 354,
    374, 384
Egypt 69, 78
elections 28, 113, 258, 313, 318
El Salvador 240, 241, 245, 253
emotion 2, 33, 59, 81–8, 92, 159, 172
employment 14, 16, 18, 19, 20, 230–1, 233,
    263–75, 288, 312, 318, 329, 332, 376
environment 18
epistemology 58
ETA 142
European Union 6, 12, 16, 32, 37, 43, 48,
    149, 179, 214, 244
everyday 58, 61, 65, 96, 136, 243, 287, 290,
    293, 350, 379, 387, 390

First World War 12, 91, 100, 134, 148, 178,
    366
former combatants 162–4, 185, 225–36, 241,
    272, 290
France 93, 99
free market 109, 312, 316, 317–18, 321, 329,
    330, 332

game theory 153, 278
Gaza *see* Palestine
gender 2, 7, 32, 57–65, 75–6, 83, 137, 167,
    225, 230, 264, 267–70, 288, 289, 290,
    293, 296, 329, 354
gender-based violence 62
Geneva Conventions 181, 251, 366

genocide 118, 127, 159, 177, 184, 230, 297,
    361, 364, 366, 369, 372
Georgia 352
Germany 99, 106, 118, 147, 179
governance 5, 143, 164, 212, 213, 219, 270,
    320, 376 good governance 5, 16, 21, 108,
    161, 222, 290, 330, 343, 348
grassroots *see* bottom-up
Guatemala 254, 326
Guinea-Bissau 29

Hamas 69, 180
health 18, 232, 265, 269, 297
history 92, 94, 167, 171–82, 290,
HIV/AIDS 127, 282
Hobbes, Thomas 37–8, 40, 46, 48, 140, 141
Holocaust 176
human rights 15, 27, 30, 62, 106, 108, 110,
    162, 164, 167, 201, 203, 218, 220–1, 249–
    60, 288, 297, 299, 312, 316, 321, 367, 378
human security 198, 212, 218, 288, 290, 337
humanitarian aid 60, 199, 269, 276, 312, 314,
    325–35
Hungary 280–4
hybridity and hybrid political orders 111, 114,
    140, 212, 217, 219–23, 259, 279, 361, 363,
    365–7, 372, 380

identity 87, 94, 97, 121–2, 174, 177, 287
ideology 2, 17, 36, 118, 288, 298
IFOR 200
indigenous approaches (including customary
    and traditional) 5, 216, 220, 290, 298,
    320–1, 360–74
infrastructure 270, 329, 338, 378
INGOs 199
International Committee of the Red Cross
    252
International Criminal Court 255, 257, 361,
    364, 366, 368, 389
International Criminal Tribunal for the
    former Yugoslavia 176–80, 364
international law 250–1, 366
International Monetary Fund 16, 31, 151, 155,
    313, 328, 331, 332, 389
international relations 58–9, 105–14, 160, 162,
    299
internet 180
Iraq 20, 27, 64, 69, 73, 109, 191, 198, 203, 223,
    227, 228, 318, 363
Ireland 95
Irish Republican Army 48

Islam 69, 75–6, 78
Israel 42, 78, 99, 125, 173, 179
Israel/Palestine 28, 40, 42, 43, 49, 69, 70, 71, 73, 75, 77, 98, 125, 126, 297, 298, 303, 390

justice 138–9, 164–5, 207, 213, 219, 233, 372

Kant, Immanuel 37–8, 40
Karzai, Hamid 211
Kelman, Herbert 40, 41, 42–3, 48, 98, 126
Keynes, J.M. and Keynesianism 13, 147–9
Kosovo 20, 172, 173, 176, 200–1, 343

language 126, 280
League of Nations 37, 149, 366
Lederach, John Paul 160, 349–50
liberal peace 3, 14, 19, 27, 57, 62, 65, 105, 107–11, 134–6, 142, 198–200, 202, 212, 222–3, 225, 257–8, 297, 311, 316–17, 318, 320, 321, 322, 338, 341–2, 348–50, 355, 361, 388
liberalism 3, 17, 21, 32–3, 36, 62, 113, 138, 212, 216, 218, 278
Liberia 29, 228, 233
livelihood 14, 148, 152, 231, 233, 263–75
local ownership 11, 15, 215, 290, 319, 322

Marshall Plan 331
media 76, 95, 118, 127, 172–3, 174, 178, 180–1, 214, 351, 355
mediation 252, 253, 293, 320
memory 91–100, 160, 162, 164, 173, 177, 365
microfinance 16
militarism 63
Millennium Development Goals 151, 207
Mindanao 71, 75, 243
monitoring and evaluation 72, 74
Moon, Ban-Ki 14
mutually hurting stalemate 41, 253

NATO 15, 200–2, 214, 314, 341
natural resources 14, 98, 246
needs theory 40
negotiations 62, 161, 162, 184, 253, 257, 362, 368, 370
neoliberalism 11, 13, 14, 16, 16, 20, 21, 22, 31, 297, 322
Nepal 253
neutrality 2, 239, 244, 246, 249, 251, 296, 322, 332, 377, 382
new wars 134
non-violence 62, 71, 78, 112, 305

Northern Ireland 1, 38, 46, 48–9, 93, 122, 123, 124, 126, 128, 162–3, 167, 179, 240, 242, 243, 245, 254, 300, 379, 382–3
Norway 43–4, 326

OECD 199, 204, 206, 207, 213, 215, 327, 330

Palestine 20, 36, 49, 99, 173–4, 181, 303
participation 18, 21, 28, 96, 97, 112, 139, 222, 237, 242, 289, 296, 302, 329, 379, 390
peace accord 161, 253, 254, 257, 259, 267, 287, 325, 372
peace processes 30, 33, 43, 57, 63, 159, 160–9, 183, 228, 229, 241, 251–3, 256, 257, 269, 300, 312, 353, 360, 361, 380
Peacebuilding Commission 15, 16, 31, 312, 315–16
Peacebuilding Fund 31
peacekeeping 21, 26, 32, 33, 111, 112, 199, 201, 202, 227, 263, 312, 326, 329
Peru 369
Philippines 77, 237, 238, 243
policing 249, 254, 255, 293, 314
poverty 212, 264, 266, 290, 318–19, 320, 329, 378
Poverty Reduction Strategy Papers 16, 215
private security companies 214, 216, 220, 256
privatization 16, 19
problem-solving approach 3, 4, 7, 11–24, 40, 126, 316, 332, 389
post-war reconstruction 152, 202, 232, 266, 269, 287, 315, 322, 326
psychology 83, 117–28

quantitative methodology 2, 4, 183–93, 348

race 39, 60, 63, 123, 124, 125, 140–1, 166, 175, 301, 378
Reagan, Ronald, 189
reconciliation 28, 33, 37, 45–9, 62, 81–8, 97, 126, 159–61, 178–9, 203, 232, 241, 287, 320, 331, 338, 361, 363, 365–8, 371, 372, 378
reconstruction *see* post-war reconstruction
refugees 28, 61, 201, 254, 312, 327
relative deprivation theory 119
religion 1, 36, 69–80, 124, 160, 352, 365
remembrance *see* commemoration
reparations 255, 372
resistance 15, 23, 58, 65, 111, 244, 249, 258, 330, 361, 383
Richmond, Oliver 134

ripeness 42
Romania 276–7, 280–4
rule of law 108, 138, 167, 218, 249, 255, 312, 326, 330, 349, 362, 363
Russia 32
Rwanda 6, 19, 31, 43, 45, 127, 230, 267, 366

Second World War 25, 26, 37, 95, 117, 134, 148–9, 172, 178
securitisation 110, 197–207, 218, 302
security 5, 6, 20, 22, 27, 46, 82
security dilemma 106, 111–12, 276, 277
security sector reform (SSR) 207, 211–24, 225, 338, 361
Serbia 297
SFOR 200
Sierra Leone 31, 228, 288, 290, 317
social capital 161, 265, 269, 287, 353
social identity theory 120, 125
sociology 83, 93, 159–70, 279, 303
Somalia 204
South Africa 43, 45, 46, 83, 100, 122, 124, 125, 166, 214, 254, 379, 390
sovereignty 108, 109, 243, 329, 366
Soviet Union 40, 150, 199, 352
spoilers 43, 164, 265, 268, 272
Sri Lanka 69, 71, 163, 258
stabilization 107, 197, 202–3, 204–7, 211, 219
statebuilding 4, 6, 16, 17, 105, 107, 109, 132, 143, 160, 164, 198, 204–8, 219, 223, 321, 329, 330, 336–46, 355
Stiglitz, Joseph 216
structural adjustment policies 16, 18
study of peace and conflict 3, 72, 74, 105, 183, 304, 350
Sudan 241, 369
symbolism 99

Tajikistan 29
Taliban 6, 202
technocracy and technocratic 6, 135, 136, 211, 216, 218, 341, 388
'terrorism' 82, 151, 205, 207, 297, 299, 302, 338
third party 42, 43, 112, 199, 204, 228
top-down approaches 43, 122, 123, 128, 134, 135, 218, 239, 287, 312, 317, 321, 322, 336, 341, 343–4, 354, 387–8
track-two 38, 42

transitional justice 57, 139, 160, 163, 360–2, 370
trust 46, 98, 112, 133, 228, 232, 289, 329
truth commissions 45, 83, 125, 171, 254, 257, 258, 289
truth recovery and truth telling 81, 160, 163, 165, 364–5, 369

Uganda 233, 255–6, 367–9
unemployment *see* employment
United Kingdom 13, 15, 213, 243–4
United Nations 6, 7, 14, 17, 18, 26, 27, 29, 32, 37, 57, 64, 75, 113, 128, 133, 134, 185, 200, 204, 213, 238, 241, 252, 256, 290, 296, 311–24, 325, 343, 351, 388, 389
United Nations Development Programme 12, 14, 16, 19, 207, 301–2, 317, 326, 331, 383
United Nations Interim Administration Mission in Kosovo (UNMIK) 15
United Nations Protection Force (UNPROFOR) 200
United States 3, 6, 32–3, 39, 40, 71, 75, 76, 78, 92, 100, 124, 148–9, 150, 202, 205, 221, 223, 241–2, 301, 329, 352, 364, 388, 389, 390
USAID 300, 301, 313
universalism 137–8, 141, 321, 322
urban planning 375–86

Vietnam 92, 178

War on Terror 202, 257, 299
welfare 18, 22, 263–75, 288, 337, 389
West Bank *see* Palestine
women *see* gender
World Bank 6, 7, 13, 16, 19, 31, 151, 207, 245, 268, 269, 296, 313, 316, 326–7, 328, 330, 331–2, 389–90
World Trade Organisation 16
World War I *see* First World War
World War II *see* Second World War
youth 28, 127, 267, 270, 287, 288, 296–307

Yugoslavia (including former Yugoslavia) 172, 173, 177, 200, 204

Zartman, William 42
zones of peace 237–248, 340